RECEIVED

MAY 27 2017

SOUTHWEST BRANCH

NO LONGER PROPERTY OF
SEATTLE PUBLIC LIBRARY

GOETHE:

LIFE AS A WORK OF ART

BOOKS BY
RÜDIGER SAFRANSKI

Romanticism: A German Affair

How Much Globalization Can We Bear?

Nietzsche: A Philosophical Biography

Martin Heidegger: Between Good and Evil

Schopenhauer and the Wild Years of Philosophy

GOETHE

LIFE AS A WORK OF ART

RÜDIGER SAFRANSKI

TRANSLATED BY DAVID DOLLENMAYER

LIVERIGHT PUBLISHING CORPORATION

A Division of W. W. Norton & Company

INDEPENDENT PUBLISHERS SINCE 1923

New York London

The translation of this work was funded by Geisteswissenschaften
International–Translation Funding for Work in the Humanities and
Social Sciences from Germany, a joint initiative of the Fritz Thyssen Foundation,
the German Federal Foreign Office, the collecting society VG WORT, and
the Börsenverein des Deutschen Buchhandels
(German Publishers & Booksellers Association).

Copyright © 2013 by Carl Hanser Verlag Müchen
Translation copyright © 2017 by David Dollenmayer

Originally published in German as *Goethe: Kunstwerk des Lebens: Biographie*

All rights reserved
Printed in the United States of America

For information about permission to reproduce selections from this book,
write to Permissions, Liveright Publishing Corporation,
a division of W. W. Norton & Company, Inc.,
500 Fifth Avenue, New York, NY 10110

For information about special discounts for bulk purchases, please contact
W. W. Norton Special Sales at specialsales@wwnorton.com or 800-233-4830

Manufacturing by Quad Graphics, Fairfield, VA
Book design by Barbara M. Bachman
Production manager: Anna Oler

LIBRARY OF CONGRESS CATALOGING-IN-PUBLICATION DATA

Names: Safranski, Rüdiger, author. | Dollenmayer, David B., translator.
Title: Goethe : life as a work of art / Rudiger Safranski ; translated by
David Dollenmayer.
Other titles: Goethe: Kunstwerk des Lebens. English
Description: New York : Liveright Publishing Corporation, 2017. | Includes
bibliographical references and index.
Identifiers: LCCN 2017008798 | ISBN 9780871404909 (hardcover)
Subjects: LCSH: Goethe, Johann Wolfgang von, 1749–1832. | Authors,
German—18th century—Biography. | Authors, German—19th
century—Biography.
Classification: LCC PT2051 .S2413 2017 | DDC 831/.6 [B]—dc23
LC record available at https://lccn.loc.gov/2017008798

Liveright Publishing Corporation
500 Fifth Avenue, New York, N.Y. 10110
www.wwnorton.com

W. W. Norton & Company Ltd.
15 Carlisle Street, London W1D 3BS

1 2 3 4 5 6 7 8 9 0

As always,
for Gisela Maria

CONTENTS

CHAPTER 34 • *543*

Eckermann and Goethe's Other Assistants · The Definitive
Edition · Enforcing the Copyright · Schiller Again ·
Zelter: Short History of a Long Friendship ·
Leave-Takings: Frau von Stein, Karl August, Goethe's Son ·
Last Outing to Ilmenau · *"Peace lies over all the peaks"* ·
Against time's *flotsam and jetsam* · Death

FINAL REFLECTION: BECOMING WHO YOU ARE *561*

TRANSLATOR'S NOTE

‖N ORDER TO GIVE A UNIFIED VOICE TO QUOTATIONS FROM GOETHE'S works and letters, I have chosen to translate them myself rather than use previous translations. Goethe employed an astonishingly wide range of verse forms and styles in the course of his long life. Some forms will be familiar to anglophone readers, from the French-influenced rhymed alexandrines of the early verse comedy *The Lover's Spleen* to the doggerel-like *Knittelvers* of the early parts of *Faust*, to the stately iambic pentameter of *Iphigenia in Tauris* and *Torquato Tasso*. Other forms will be less familiar, especially those—so popular among German poets of the late eighteenth century—that imitate the verse of classical antiquity, such as the dactylic hexameter of the bourgeois epic *Herrmann und Dorothea* or the distichs of *The Roman Elegies*.

The lyric poetry that flowed so effortlessly from Goethe's pen poses particular challenges, especially when it is rhymed. I have striven to preserve the sense and meters of the original and gratefully snatched a rhyme when I could. When I couldn't, I had to settle for assonance, consonance, near rhyme, or no rhyme at all, and infelicities are entirely mine.

———

This desire to raise up as high as possible the pyramid of my existence—whose basis and foundation were given to me—outweighs everything else and can hardly be forgotten even for a moment. I dare not tarry. I am already at an advanced age, and perhaps fate will break me in the middle of life and the Tower of Babel will remain an incomplete stump. At least they should be able to say it was a daring attempt.

—GOETHE TO LAVATER
CA. SEPTEMBER 20, 1780

GOETHE WAS A REMARKABLE EVENT IN GERMAN INTEL-
lectual history—but an event without consequences, according to
Nietzsche. Goethe was not inconsequential, however. While it is true
that he was not able to change the course of German history, he was
outstandingly successful in another respect: as the exemplar of a life
combining intellectual riches, creative power, and worldly wisdom.
It was a life begun under auspicious circumstances and full of passion,
but it also required struggle and was threatened by challenges and
dangers from within and without. It is the individual shape of this life
that is endlessly fascinating. By no means was its course a foregone
conclusion.

Our times do not favor the creation of individuality. The price
we pay for our universal interconnectedness is increased conformity.
Although Goethe was intimately connected to the social and cultural
life of his time, he also knew how to maintain his individuality. His
principle was to take in only as much of the world as he could process.
Whatever he could not respond to in a productive way he chose to disregard. In other words, he was an expert at ignoring things. Of course,
he was also compelled to take an interest in much he would have preferred to be spared. But as far as possible, he was bent on determining
the scope and direction of his own life.

Today we have a clear grasp of human metabolism; from Goethe,
we can learn how a healthy intellect and spirit function: how they

complement the body. We can begin to understand what to take in and what not to take in. Goethe knew, and that was part of his worldly wisdom.

And so we are inspired not just by Goethe's work but by the exemplary life he led. Taken together, his life and work serve as an inexhaustible source of inspiration. He had an inkling of his legacy, even though in one of his last letters to his friend Karl Friedrich Zelter he wrote that he was entwined with an epoch that was ending. And yet Goethe seems alive and present, at times more so than many of our contemporaries.

Every generation has the chance to understand its own time better through the mirror of Goethe. By describing the life and work of a great genius and at the same time using his example to explore the opportunities and limits of the art of life, this book will attempt to hold up that mirror.

A young man from a prominent family in Frankfurt am Main studies at the universities of Leipzig and Strasbourg without completing a degree and finally becomes a lawyer. He is constantly falling in love, and both girls and grown women swoon over him. His play *Götz von Berlichingen* makes him famous in Germany, and the novel *The Sorrows of Young Werther* makes him the talk of all literary Europe. Napoleon will later claim to have read the novel seven times. Waves of visitors come to Frankfurt to see and hear the handsome, eloquent young genius. A generation before Lord Byron, he feels himself to be the darling of the gods, and like Byron, he also has poetic dealings with the devil. While still living in Frankfurt he begins work on *Faust*, the canonical modern drama, a task it will take a lifetime to complete. After being celebrated as a genius in Frankfurt, Goethe grows weary of literary life and in 1775 makes a radical and risky break by moving to the small duchy of Saxony-Weimar, where he befriends the young duke and rises to a ministerial post. He dabbles in scientific research, takes off for Italy, and on his return enters into a common-law marriage. And all the while he is writing novels, plays, and unforgettable love poems, engaging in a competition of sorts with his friend and fellow writer Friedrich Schiller. He is politically active and in contact with prominent artists and scientists. Even while still alive, Goethe becomes an institution.

He sees himself historically and writes *Poetry and Truth*, arguably the most important European autobiography since the *Confessions* of Saint Augustine and of Jean-Jacques Rousseau. But stiff and dignified as he could sometimes be, in the works of his old age he shows himself to be a daring and sardonic Mephisto, ignoring all convention.

Yet he was always aware that literary works were one thing and life another. He was determined to give his life the character of a work as well. What is a work? Something that rises out of the flow of time, has a beginning and an end and, between them, a clear form: an island of significance in the sea of inchoate contingency that Goethe dreaded. For him, everything needed a form, and he either discovered it or created it—in everyday affairs, in intimate friendships, in letters and conversations. He was a man of rituals, symbols, and allegories, a friend of intimation and allusion, and yet he always wanted to achieve a result, create a form, complete a work. That was especially true in his duties as an official. The roads should be improved, the peasants freed of unnecessary burdens. The hardworking poor should receive wages and bread. The duchy's mines should generate revenue and its theater audiences have something to laugh or cry about every evening, if possible.

One side of him comprises the works that give shape to life, the other is his attentiveness, the supreme compliment one can pay to life itself—one's own and others'. Goethe felt that nature deserved to be observed with the same loving attention. He was convinced that one need only look carefully for the most important truths to reveal themselves. It was as simple as that and involved no secrets. He practiced a kind of science that did not go beyond what one could observe with the senses. He was delighted by most of what he discovered. He was pleased by what he succeeded at. And if others weren't pleased, in the end it didn't matter to him. His allotted time was too precious to waste on critics. *Adversaries are to be disregarded*, he once said.

Goethe was a collector, not only of objects but of impressions. And he approached personal encounters in the same spirit. He always asked himself whether and how they *furthered* him—his favorite way of putting it. Goethe loved what was alive, and he wanted to capture and give form to as much of it as possible. A moment given form is a moment preserved. Six months before he died, he made his last climb up the Kickelhahn, a small mountain near Ilmenau, to read once more the verse he had scratched on the wall of a hunter's hut long ago: *Über allen Gipfeln ist Ruh—Peace lies over all the peaks.*

There is no other modern author for whom the biographical source material is so rich, but also no author so encumbered by opinions, conjectures, and interpretations. This book approaches perhaps the last universal genius through primary sources alone—his literary works, letters, diaries, and conversations, as well as the accounts of his contemporaries. Thus Goethe comes alive again, as if for the first time.

And with his life, his times also come alive. This is a man who lived through several historical turning points and cataclysms. He was raised in an era of playful rococo style and formal, old-fashioned urban culture; he was challenged by the French Revolution and worried about its intellectual consequences; he experienced the reordering of Europe under Napoleon, the fall of the emperor, the end of the Holy Roman Empire, and a French restoration that could not turn back the clock and restore the ancien régime. He recorded the beginnings of modernism more sensitively and thoughtfully than anyone else, and the span of his life also encompassed the dispassion and speed of the age of railroads and the early dreams of socialism. He was a man whose name would later be used to characterize a period of enormous upheaval: *die Goethezeit,* the Age of Goethe.

GOETHE:

LIFE AS A WORK OF ART

CHAPTER 1

A Difficult Birth with Fortunate Consequences. Family Ties.

Between a Pedant and a Cheerful Nature. Goethe's Sister.

The Child of a Free Imperial City. Practice in Writing.

The Rhymester and the First Gretchen Affair.

Self-Confidence Shaken. An Emergency Postponed.

Finding Poetry in the Everyday.

....

A T THE BEGINNING OF HIS AUTOBIOGRAPHY, *POETRY AND Truth*, Johann Wolfgang von Goethe describes his difficult birth in 1749 but, perhaps ironically, also mentions its fortunate consequences for the town at large.

Through the midwife's carelessness, the newborn infant was almost strangled by the umbilical cord. His face had already turned blue and he was presumed dead. Those in attendance shook him, thumped him, and he started to breathe. Goethe's grandfather Mayor Johann Wolfgang Textor was prompted by this near-fatal delivery to overhaul the practice of obstetrics in Frankfurt. A course of instruction for midwives was introduced, *which may have benefited many of those born after me.* The autobiographer delivers his first tongue-in-cheek punch line.

Grandfather Textor, after whom the newborn was named, had once refused to have a noble title conferred on him—because it would have prevented him from making socially acceptable matches for his daughters. One of them, Katharina Elisabeth, would become Goethe's mother. Textor was not rich enough for the nobility, and as a nobleman would have been too grand for the bourgeoisie. And so he chose to remain what he was: a distinguished citizen who, as mayor, was influential enough to help bring about advances in midwifery.

In the imperial city of Frankfurt, the mayor, or *Schultheiss*, was not only the highest-ranking administrative official but also served as the emperor's representative, for Frankfurt had the privilege of being the location for the election and coronation of each new emperor. As mayor, Textor was one of those permitted to hold the baldachin, or ceremonial canopy, over the emperor. Young Wolfgang basked in his reflected glory, to the annoyance of his playmates. Through him, however, the young boys gained access to the Kaisersaal, the emperor's hall in the Römer, Frankfurt's town hall, where they could play at reenacting the great events that took place there. Goethe remembered his grandfather Textor with great affection. He depicts him tending the flowers and fruit trees in his garden, picking roses while wearing a *dressing gown like a cassock* and a *baggy cap of black velvet*, thereby imparting to his grandson *the feeling of inviolable peace and unending continuity*.

The image is probably a touch idyllic. According to a contemporary account, a rumor circulated in Frankfurt that at a family gathering in late 1759, when the French were garrisoned in the town during the Seven Years' War, Goethe's father reproached his father-in-law the mayor for allowing foreign troops into the city in exchange for money, whereupon Textor threw a knife at his son-in-law, who then drew his dagger. This scene is not reflected in *Poetry and Truth*. Instead, Goethe writes that his grandfather *never showed a trace of violence; I cannot remember ever seeing him angry*.

Goethe's paternal grandfather was a tailor who had moved to Frankfurt, worked his way up to become the leading couturier for the local aristocracy, and married the wealthy widow of the proprietor of an inn called the Weidenhof. So the tailor became a successful innkeeper and wine merchant, eventually leaving his heirs two houses, other real estate, and 100,000 taler in cash.

He wanted something even better for his son Johann Caspar, and since he could afford it, he sent him to the expensive and highly regarded gymnasium in Coburg, then to the universities of Leipzig and Giessen. After a practicum at the Imperial High Court in Wetzlar, Johann Caspar graduated from Giessen as a doctor of law. It was expected that he would spend his career in Frankfurt's municipal government, but he was in no hurry. He wanted to see the world first and set off on a grand tour that lasted a year. He traveled via Regensburg and Vienna to Italy, stopping in Paris and Amsterdam on his way back.

He later wrote, in Italian, a description of his visit to Venice, Milan, and Rome; this travelogue became his primary preoccupation for a decade. He had plenty of leisure time, as he was unable to secure a government position upon his return in 1740.

According to Goethe's autobiography, his father sought appointment to one of the subaltern offices *ohne Ballotage*—that is, without competition and therefore without remuneration either. Denied the position, his vanity was wounded and he swore never again to seek or accept office. Nevertheless, he seized the opportunity to purchase from the Court Council of the Empire, in residence in Frankfurt during the reign of Emperor Charles VII (1741–44), the title of imperial councilor, an honorific usually reserved for the mayor and oldest lay judges. *Thereby*, Goethe writes, *he had made himself the equal of the loftiest and could no longer begin from the bottom.* Not that he wanted to. Thus in 1742 Johann Caspar Goethe was named councilor by the emperor at about the same time that Katharina Elisabeth Textor, his future wife, developed an adolescent crush on the same monarch.

Katharina Elisabeth was the eldest of Textor's daughters. They called her the Princess because she disliked housework, preferring to stretch out on the sofa and read novels. And as she later told the writer Bettine von Arnim, the coronation of Charles VII, which she had witnessed as a young girl in 1742, seemed to her like a scene from a novel. The post horns heralding the emperor's approach had been unforgettable. She had followed Charles into the church and watched the handsome youth with the melancholy gaze praying and batting his long black eyelashes. The emperor had even nodded to her from his horse, and she felt herself to be one of the elect. And so, six years later, when the eighteen-year-old married the thirty-nine-year-old Johann Caspar Goethe, it didn't seem such a momentous occasion to her. She married him "with no particular inclination," although she did allow that he was a "handsome man."

The marriage was a further impediment to Johann Caspar's admission to the town council since the city had strict injunctions against nepotism. And so he remained a *Partikulier*, a private individual, spending his time managing his fortune, writing his travelogue, collecting books and pictures, raising silkworms, and educating his children, especially his promising son Johann Wolfgang.

Whether the career of the imperial councilor really was as Goethe describes it, we don't know. Did Johann Caspar lack ambition or business acumen? Was his knowledge of the law too academic and not practical enough? Were there reservations about him because he was the son of an innkeeper with perhaps too haughty a public manner? Did his allegiance to the Wittelsbach emperor Charles VII disadvantage him with Charles's Habsburg successors? Perhaps all these factors combined to thwart him in his professional career. In any case, if one can believe Goethe's depiction of his father, he was quite satisfied with his lot. *My father considered his life up to that point close to all he could have wished for.*

But there probably were some problems—problems *Poetry and Truth* hints at, although it is usually anxious to smooth out and harmonize things. For example, it relates how as a boy Goethe had to listen to his playmates casting aspersions on his ancestry. They said his father had not had an honorable birth and as an infant had been foisted upon the proprietor of the Weidenhof by a nobleman who had persuaded the innkeeper *to publicly declare himself the father* of Johann Caspar. Instead of pulling the hair of these slanderers or feeling humiliated, however, Goethe writes that he felt flattered by these rumors. *I was not at all displeased to be the grandson of some aristocrat.* From then on, the boy looked for similarities between himself and portraits of high-born men and imagined an entire novel built around his noble descent. Goethe writes that he was infected with *a kind of moral illness* and closes this passage with the self-critical reflection: *How true it is that everything that reinforces a person's inner conceit and flatters his secret vanity is so highly prized that he never wonders whether it otherwise honors or disgraces him.* The imperturbable self-confidence of the boy is remarkable. He was just seven years old when he wrote, *I cannot reconcile myself to what is satisfactory for other people.*

The episode not only reveals the boy's vanity but also suggests that his father's social position was less than secure. And Johann Caspar did not enhance his reputation by living with his young family in the home of his mother, the former proprietress of the Weidenhof. Until the death of this grandmother, whom Goethe remembers as a *lovely, gaunt woman, always neatly dressed in white,* his father was not the master of the house on the Hirschgraben (the "stag pit," a street that followed the course of a filled-in moat that had surrounded the medieval town). Johann Caspar had to wait to realize his ambitious plans for this property. He would have found no difficulty in that, however, since his habit was always to proceed slowly and deliberately.

The house was renovated in 1755. The building next door was demolished, and the first thing to be installed on the cleared lot was a large wine cellar to hold the stock left over from the Weidenhof, which included rare and prized vintages. Much later, Goethe had the remaining bottles shipped to Weimar, where his plucky common-law wife, Christiane Vulpius, defended them from French marauders in 1806.

The simplest thing would have been to tear down the main house too, but a new structure would have had to conform to the strict municipal building code. The existing overhang of the upper stories, for example, would have been forbidden, significantly decreasing the building's floor space. And so at considerable expense and risk, the upper stories were propped up in order to construct a new ground floor. Except for a few weeks, the family remained in the house despite the noise and dirt of construction. All this made a deep impression on the six-year-old Goethe. It is the topic of one of his earliest texts, a dialogue between father and son. The father says, *Add to that all the danger to the workers, especially in building the main staircase, as you can see here, since almost the entire vaulted ceiling had to be held up by countless supports.* The son replies, *And despite all that danger, we have continued to live here. It is good that one doesn't know everything. I would certainly not have slept as soundly as I did.*

The entire renovation—and especially the roomy stairwell—was his father's pride, the work of a man who otherwise had few accomplishments to show. Goethe touched on this sore point during an argument with his father at the end of 1768, when he returned home from the University of Leipzig. Johann Caspar expressed dissatisfaction with his son's academic performance, and Goethe retorted by criticizing his father's plans for the renovation. The expansion of the stairwell, he said, had wasted space that could have been put to better use by enlarging the rooms. He maliciously reminded his father of a quarrel Johann Caspar had had with Count Thoranc, the military governor of Frankfurt during the French occupation of 1759–61, in that very stairwell, the implication being that something about the structure seemed to invite unwelcome encounters. Having learned of the French victory over the Prussians. Goethe's father, who supported Frederick the Great, had refused to congratulate Count Thoranc as he passed him on the stairs. Instead, he growled fiercely, *I wish they had sent you to the devil.* The remark had come close to landing him in prison.

Goethe reports this incident with understanding for his father but, even more, with sympathy for Thoranc, whom he depicts as noble, polite, considerate, and, above all, a connoisseur of the arts. Thoranc set up a French theater in Frankfurt and made sure that the boy was always admitted free of charge. The count also supported the visual arts and employed local painters who came and went in the house on the Hirschgraben. The boy was permitted to watch them at work and was soon dispensing unsolicited advice. Thoranc was quite fond of the cheeky, precocious lad. Goethe's father, however, his authority already undermined by the billeting, was displeased that his son had taken Thoranc's part in the quarrel.

Though there were tensions in Goethe's relations with his father, Johann Caspar spared neither money nor attention in advancing his talented child. He hired private tutors who were expected not only to inculcate his son with the conventional curriculum—Latin, Bible study, etc.—but to promote the aesthetic disciplines as well: drawing, writing poems, making music. He also instructed the child himself, especially in the history of Frankfurt, the law, and geography. *My father*, wrote Goethe, *was by nature a teacher, and since he was removed from doing business, he was eager to pass on to others what he knew and was able to do.* He read his son the Italian travelogue he had written and introduced him to his collection of books and engravings. Delighted to observe his son's literary progress, he conscientiously archived the pieces he considered especially successful, and continued to do so for years. It was not by chance that Johann Caspar had chosen for his newly drafted family coat of arms the lyre, the symbol of the Muses and fine arts.

Of course, his wish was that his son become a lawyer like himself and perhaps even choose the same universities—Leipzig, Wetzlar, and Regensburg—for his training, but not at the expense of an appreciation for the arts. In the brief period during which Goethe practiced law, Johann Caspar paid for him to have a scribe so that he was free to continue to devote himself to literature. He greeted his son's first literary successes with the greatest pleasure and wanted him to travel to Italy in his footsteps. *I was supposed to follow the same path*, writes Goethe, *but farther and in more comfort. He valued my native talents all the more since he lacked them. For he had acquired everything only by ineffable diligence, tenacity, and repetition. Sooner or later, seriously or facetiously, he would often assure me that he would have behaved very differently with my aptitudes and not spent them so profligately.*

When Goethe shared a law office with his father in 1773, the usual hierarchy was turned on its head. It was his father who, *slow to make plans and carry them out*, acted as a sort of *private articled clerk*, presenting drafts to his son, who was as brilliantly quick-witted in legal matters as in his poems. Goethe writes, *I completed the drawing-up so easily that it caused him the greatest possible paternal joy, and once he even went so far as to say that if I were a stranger to him, he would be envious of me.*

Of course, the father commanded the boy's respect, but he was not the kind of authority figure against whom the young Goethe had to strenuously defend himself. No symbolic patricide was necessary. The anti-tyrannical pathos of the Sturm und Drang authors is not to be found in Goethe. His later, Promethean rebellion has other sources and is directed at other targets.

Thus the son had no need to emancipate himself from his father, and in many respects he even adopted his father's idiosyncrasies. Johann Caspar's pedantry and caution, which his son at first felt to be rather tedious, later became evident in Goethe himself. He explicitly praises his father's stubbornness and persistence—characteristics he did not initially claim as his own. And yet Goethe came to embrace both persistence and seriousness by way of the idea of *Spiel*, play. Even Johann Caspar's persistence had something playful about it because in his case, too, it was not imposed by a *profession*. It was his hobbies that he pursued with complete earnestness and pedantic persistence. The same was true of his son, who was led by desire and whim to begin many things and then leave them unfinished, but in most cases completed them later, even if it took a lifetime, as it did with *Faust*.

Father gave me my physique / and an earnest education. / From Mother comes my cheerfulness / and love of fabrication. Goethe's mother was young—closer in age to him and his sister Cornelia than she was to her husband. During home tutoring sessions, she sat with them in the children's corner. She still had a lot to learn herself. She had never learned how to spell correctly. Later, she joked about it and urged her son not to torture his own son: "don't plague the boy about his spelling—Maybe he inherited his spelling habits from his Grandmother." She always wrote just as she talked, and spelled phonetically, the way she heard speech. "Napoleon has even deklared us noocheral," she wrote in a letter of 1806. But she was also aware when she struck the right tone; and she had a talent for vivid description. "The gift God gave me is a lively depiction of everything I know about, great things and small, truth and ferry tails etc. as soon as I join a circul everything turns cheerful and happy because I'm telling stories."

And so she did. She told the children fairy tales. On beautiful summer days, Wolfgang would carry her armchair, which they called the fairy-tale chair, into the courtyard, and decorate it with garlands. It gave his mother pleasure to immerse herself in the children's world, because she had preserved a bit of the child in herself. Hence her talent for storytelling, her *love of fabrication*. She was "extremely eager" to continue spinning out a story, every evening if possible, while Wolfgang sat at her feet, devouring her with his "great black eyes." If he didn't like the way a story was going, the veins in his forehead would swell in anger. The next day he would tell his grandmother how the story should have gone, and she would relay that information to his mother, who would continue the story that evening as the little boy wished. Then he was happy and "with shining eyes awaited the fulfillment of his daring plots."

His mother introduced fairy-tale magic into the house and made peace when necessary. When the Thoranc affair led to serious tension, she calmed the waters. She always tried to mediate in conflicts between father and son. She loved jolly company, and when her son's early fame in the Sturm und Drang period brought many of his friends into her home—Friedrich Klinger, J. M. R. Lenz, Heinrich Wagner—she called them her "sons" and relished their nickname for her, Mother Aja, after the mother in the chapbook *The Four Sons of Aymon*. When Klinger was studying in Giessen and complained about how boring the town was, she offered sage advice: "I always thought it was child's play for you poets to idealize all locations, even the bad ones. If you can make something from nothing, then unless the devil had a hand in it you ought to be able to make Giessen into a fairyland. At least, that's my great strength." Goethe appreciated his mother's talent for poeticizing real life. Her example helped to keep him from any urge he may have had to turn poetry into reality through misguided earnestness. In *Poetry and Truth* he writes, *But whereas I felt relieved and enlightened by having transformed reality into poetry, my friends were confounded by believing they had to transform poetry into reality.*

His mother's realism, tempered by a sense of the poetic, was generously open to surprises (which she loved) and she seized every opportunity for mirth. She kept an open mind and did not allow her worries to embitter her. She once wrote to Anna Amalia, the mother of the Duke of Weimar, Goethe's patron, that she had "sworn a sacred oath to always have one day say to the next, snatch all the small pleasures but don't anatomize them—in a word, enter more and more into a childlike spirit every day." She freely partook of the pleasures that raise one's spirits. Although she would later send the best bottles from her cellar to her son in Weimar, she said she would "drink the less good wines . . . to the last drop to save the cost of transport." And while she had been warned off snuff, she continued to use it into old age, explaining to her daughter-in-law that "without a pinch of tobacco my letters were like straw—like waybills—but Now! they almost write themselves."

She didn't begrudge others their pleasures either. In her letters to her son, she called Christiane Vulpius his "bedmate" and wrote to Christiane herself in 1803, "I hear you've put on weight, gotten nice and Corpulent, I'm glad because it's a sign of good health—and it's the usual thing in our family." She talked about the body without embarrassment—in matters of art as well, irreverently referring to the ancient sculptures in her son's collection as "bare bottoms."

She was proud of and even a bit coquettish about her own artless nature. She once wrote to the actor G. F. W. Grossmann, "But since God has so favored me that, from youth on, my soul has never been laced into a corset but could grow and prosper to my heart's content, spread wide its branches, etc. and has not been pruned and maimed into a fan shape like those trees in boring ornamental gardens; I can thus feel everything that is true and good and honest." She loved the theater and its milieu because there things were less constrained. When the house on the Hirschgraben started to empty out with Goethe's move to Weimar and the death of his father, she invited theater people to fill it. She became good friends with some and exchanged letters, but not regularly or for long. People came and went; out of sight, out of mind. She lived for the moment and let herself be carried along by the changing times, passing on to her son this will to live in the present. It later cost Goethe considerable effort to acquire a sense of responsibility and to think about the future. For that his father was the model.

As spontaneous and devoted to the moment as his mother was, she never neglected or forgot her son, but she also avoided becoming a burden to him. She would have liked to visit him often in Weimar, but Goethe invited her only once, during the wars that followed the French Revolution, when he believed that it would have been dangerous for her to remain in Frankfurt. Although he began making preparations for her visit, in the end she held out at home. She had had French soldiers quartered in the house on the Hirschgraben a few times before. She was used to such tribulations and could accommodate herself to them very well.

Goethe never said directly why he didn't want his mother living near him. Perhaps he feared that her free and easy ways would rub people the wrong way in the rarefied and formal world of Weimar. And he may have wished to spare them both the vexation. On the other hand, he was also aware that she was well liked by those in his social circle. With Anna Amalia, for example, she maintained a cordial, spirited correspondence.

Whatever the reason, after he left his parents' house, he did not want his mother nearby. He no longer wanted to be her *Hätschelhans*— her nickname for her "pampered pet." From 1775 until 1808, the year of her death, he visited her only four times. She did not complain to him, but she confided her disappointment to friends. For her, the days he was with her were cause for celebration. The banker Abraham Mendelssohn, the father of the composer Felix Mendelssohn, encountered the two of them in 1797 outside the theater. "He was accompanying his mother—an old, powdered, pretentious woman—to the comedy."

Her son was her favorite and remained so. His birth was followed, in quick succession, by those of five siblings. Only his sister Cornelia, a year and a half younger than Goethe, survived into adulthood. She and Wolfgang were the closest of companions; it was a fragile relationship that would have long-lasting effects on Goethe. As a child, he experienced the deaths of four other siblings, one after the other. When the seven-year-old Hermann Jakob died, Goethe's mother was surprised—as she later told Bettine von Arnim—that Wolfgang "shed not a tear" but instead displayed a sort of annoyance. Asked whether he hadn't loved his brother, he ran into his room and pulled a pile of papers from under his bed. They were covered with lessons he had written down, and he explained "that he had done all this to teach it to his brother."

He could no longer teach anything to Hermann Jakob, but he could give lessons to his six-year-old sister, Cornelia. Whatever he had learned, read, or picked up along the way had to be passed on immediately. Learning by teaching would remain with him. Cornelia worshipped her brother and was an eager pupil. She also took part in the little plays Wolfgang staged with neighbor children. Whatever there was to be experienced, *the siblings shared and mastered hand in hand*, as Goethe writes in *Poetry and Truth*.

There he also tells a story that would later be applied to the relationship between the siblings—not by Goethe himself but by later interpreters, especially Sigmund Freud. The boy had been playing with the kitchen crockery at a window that gave onto the street. He began to throw dishes out the window and clap his hands at the lovely noise they made. Neighbor boys urged him on, and he collected all the crockery he could get his hands on and threw one piece after another into the street until his parents, returning home, put an end to the game. *The disaster had happened*, Goethe writes, *and at least one had an amusing story for so much broken pottery*.

His parents didn't find the story so amusing and neither did Sigmund Freud, who discovered in it the subconscious aggression of a child who didn't want to share his mother's attention with any siblings. He interprets the smashing of porcelain as an *Ersatzhandlung*, a redirection activity, the expression of a murderous fantasy. The bothersome competitors for his mother's attention should disappear. Hence Wolfgang's lack of sorrow at the death of his younger brother. According to Freud, Goethe tells the tale of the broken crockery in order to unconsciously savor once again the triumph of remaining his mother's only darling. "If one has been the undisputed favorite of the mother, one possesses for the rest of one's life that triumphant feeling, that confidence of success, which not infrequently brings actual success in its wake."*

That Goethe was indeed his mother's favorite was clear; and he developed a strong sense of himself. But that is obviously not what concerns Goethe in this story. He explicitly places it in a different context. He depicts how children lived who didn't grow up locked inside the house but in a myriad of ways came *directly into contact with the street and the open air*. In the summer, the kitchen was separated only by a screen from the life of the street. *One felt free by being accustomed to what was public.* The little story of the smashed crockery was meant to illustrate what that lovely freedom could lead to. The main actors are perhaps actually the neighbor children, the public for whose sake the little boy throws the dishes into the street. Later, Goethe would again and again warn against letting oneself be distracted or controlled by the interests of the audience. The public sphere makes one free and provides stimulation, but it also constrains. With this as background, the anecdote can also be understood as a sort of primal scene in Goethe's lifelong ambivalence toward the public—he needed his audience but also needed to protect himself from them.

Wolfgang grew up a city child. His formative impressions were not of rural solitude and the quiet life of nature, but of crowds of people. It could not have been otherwise in an important commercial hub like Frankfurt, with its thirty thousand inhabitants and three thousand houses, its narrow, meandering lanes, its squares, churches, docks, bridges, and city gates. Goethe gives vivid descriptions of his walks through this labyrinthine world: the smells of spices, leather, and fish from the shops; the sounds of artisans at work, the weavers and blacksmiths, the cries of the tradesmen; the meat on display and swarming with flies in front of the butcher shops. It was a chaos in which everything seemed to be produced by *chance and caprice, not by any directing spirit.* And yet it somehow all seemed to fit together. Over all this present ferment loomed the past, awe-inspiring and mysterious: the churches and monasteries, the town hall, the towers, walls, and moats.

* Sigmund Freud, "Eine Kindheitserinnerung aus *Dichtung und Wahrheit*," in *Gesammelte Werke*, vol. 10 (Frankfurt a. M.: S. Fischer, 1969), 266.

The boy loved to accompany his father when he browsed the bookstalls for old volumes and prints. There the children could find dog-eared copies of their favorite chapbooks, *The Four Sons of Aymon*, *Till Eulen-spiegel*, *The Beautiful Magelone*, *Melusine*, and the *History of Doctor Faustus*. *The lad developed a certain penchant for old-fashioned things*, writes Goethe. He goes through the old chronicles with his father and is especially fascinated by the depiction of the coronation of the emperor right there in Frankfurt. Soon he is so familiar with the origins and significance of the old customs and ceremonies that he takes pride in explaining them to his playmates.

The city spoke of the past: bewilderingly present, loud, mysteriously still there. Goethe was surrounded by people and their work; nature was something separate, where one went on excursions. The city child had to make a point of seeking it out or gazing longingly into the distance—from the third floor of his house, for instance, where Wolfgang learned his lessons at the window, looking out across the rooftops, gardens, and the town walls *to a lovely, fruitful plain; the one that stretches toward Höchst*, some five miles off. When the sun was setting, he could not get enough of the view.

He was a highly gifted boy but not a child prodigy like Mozart, whom he once heard give a virtuoso performance. Wolfgang was a quick study. Languages came naturally to him. While still a boy he had a fair command of Italian, French, English, Latin, and Greek and could even read some Hebrew. With Cornelia, who was similarly talented, he concocted a childhood plan to write a novel in six languages. They never carried it out, but in the letters they wrote to each other while he was a student in Leipzig they both switched easily into French or English. The Bible was read in Latin and Greek, and the boy was most fascinated by the stories of the patriarchs from the Old Testament. In *Poetry and Truth* he retells the story of Joseph as he remembered writing it down in his youth; the act of doing so, he says, brought him inner composure and peace, *even when what was happening outside was so wild and strange*.

He was constantly filling up notebooks, with the advantage that he could dictate to Dr. Clauer, a destitute, emotionally disturbed man whom Goethe's father had taken in as his ward. Clauer liked to take dictation and copy things out; the activity helped calm him. On bad days he could be heard ranting and raving in his room; madness was housed right next door.

The young Goethe devoured all the literature he could get his hands on, from the legal tomes he found in his father's library to Friedrich Gottlieb Klopstock's biblical epic *Messias*, Johann Gottfried Schnabel's enormously long utopian novel *Felsenburg Island*, and the sometimes melodramatic, sometimes salacious French plays by the likes of Racine and Voltaire. And again and again he read the Bible, for him a book full of delightful stories—like the *Thousand and One Nights* he would discover later. In his reading he was always eager to *process, repeat, reproduce* what he had absorbed, which led to countless little plays, poems, fragmentary epics—everything quickly scribbled down in remarkably deft imitations of conventional forms and themes. With apparent ease he could feel his way into various levels of style—at sixteen, for example, he conjures orthodox Protestant emotion in "Poetic Thoughts on Christ's Descent into Hell," offering up the *hellish slough* in gruesome images and reveling in fantasies of punishment. In the end, Christ mounts to heaven triumphant:

> *The lightning blazes*
> *And thunder strikes the violators,*
> *And hurls them into the abyss*
>
> *The God-Man shuts the Gates of Doom,*
> *And soaring up from realms of gloom,*
> *To his splendor is restored.*

A year later, at university in Leipzig, he found this poem embarrassing and regretted not having destroyed it as he did many other juvenilia.

Most of his early efforts at writing are those of a model pupil, but occasionally they are also cocky, like the dialogue with a playmate by the name of Maximilian, originally written in Latin and translated, by Goethe, into German. How shall we pass the time until our schoolmaster arrives? asks Maximilian. With grammar, Wolfgang replies. That's too boring for Maximilian, and he suggests banging their heads together to see who can hold out the longest. *God forbid,* answers Wolfgang, *mine at least is not made for such a thing . . . we'll leave that game to the goats.* But at least you acquire a hard head from the exercise, Maximilian counters. To which Wolfgang replies, *There'd be no honor in that. I'd rather keep mine soft.*

Dialogues of this sort belonged to the art of rhetoric, which schoolboys were required to practice. Composing verses was also part of the curriculum, and that too proved easy for the young Goethe. He soon became convinced that he wrote the best poems. He liked to recite them for his family and friends. There was a regular get-together on Sundays where everyone recited poetry, and the boy was surprised to discover that the others, *who produced very feeble things,* apparently thought that they were very good and took pride in their work even when their tutors had written the poems for them. His comrades' obviously foolish self-assessment unnerved him. Was his opinion of his own verses equally unjustified? Was he himself really as good as he thought? This uncertainty, he writes, *deeply troubled me—and for a long time, for it was quite impossible for me to find some external indicator of the truth. Indeed, I even hesitated in my productions, until at last my frivolousness and sense of self . . . reassured me.* Once again: his extraordinarily sturdy sense of self.

The boy's skill at writing verses, however, eventually entangled him in shady goings-on that included the first model for the Gretchen affair at the core of his great play *Faust.* It is doubtful that things happened just as he presents them in *Poetry and Truth,* but we have no other sources for the incident. In any case, it is a beautiful story about the power of words.

A group of young people who have heard about Goethe's talent as a versifier approach him and ask him for an example of his skill, a *well-turned love letter in verse,* composed as though written by a shy maiden to a young man. He produces one in the blink of an eye. They continue to give him assignments, and he remains oblivious to the uses to which his words are being put. *And so I fooled myself into thinking that I was pulling someone's leg, and the result was some delight and some trouble for me.* Members of the group had persuaded the mayor's grandson to somehow ensnare his grandfather in a complicated scheme of which they would be the beneficiaries. In the end, the talented versifier found himself an unwitting accomplice in a tangled web of corruption, forgery, and fraud. Goethe remarks somewhat portentously that this was his first opportunity to gaze into the social abyss.

The initially pleasurable aspect of the affair was the acquaintance of a pretty, somewhat older girl, probably a waitress, whom he calls Gretchen. He fell in love with her. The fifth chapter of *Poetry and Truth*, a high point of the autobiography, depicts two artfully interwoven stories: the shady machinations he had been drawn into as well as an account of the splendid celebrations surrounding the coronation of a new Holy Roman Emperor, which the young man attended hand in hand with Gretchen, as if the events had been specially arranged for the two lovers.

In the wake of the discovery of the shady affair, Gretchen had to leave Frankfurt, supposedly after testifying, *I cannot deny that I liked seeing him and saw him often, but I always thought of him as a child and my affection for him was truly that of a sister.* The infatuated boy was so insulted that he fell ill. He could hardly swallow and worked himself up into a fit of *weeping and raving.* At the same time, it was degrading *that I had sacrificed my sleep and health and peace of mind for the sake of a girl, a girl whom it pleased to regard me as an infant and, much like a wet nurse, think herself wise compared with me.*

He sought to free himself from these feelings. One of his tutors recommended philosophy. But there he found things presented in such a way that he could not get the ideas into his head. He preferred secrecy and mystification and for that, religion and poetry were more suitable than philosophy, which annoyed him with its persistent explanations. At best, he proved to himself that he was *capable of penetrating* such philosophical works. But what he needed now was self-affirmation.

The Gretchen affair had drawn him out of his self-absorption; it meant the end of his half-childish, naïve self-confidence. He had been made painfully aware of others' opinions. He now saw himself from the outside. It seemed to him that once, even in the *greatest crowd*, he had not needed *to think of others observing him*, but now he was tormented by a *hypochondriacal notion* that all *eyes were trained on my being in order to hold it fast, examine, and censure it.*

In the context of this loss of immediacy and the oppressive experience of being observed, not only by others but by himself, a second incident occurred, one not related in *Poetry and Truth* but preserved in letters.

When he was not quite fifteen, Goethe wrote to the chairman of the League of the Virtuous, asking to be admitted to this secret club, founded by some young people from prominent families. His missive to the seventeen-year-old Ludwig Ysenburg von Buri is the earliest letter by Goethe that has come down to us. In it he admits his faults. He knows that self-examination is part of the ritual. He names three flaws. First, his *choleric temperament*: he is quick to anger but does not bear grudges; second, he likes to give orders, *but where I have nothing to say, I can also refrain from doing so*; third is his immodesty—even to strangers he talks as if he had known them *for a hundred years.*

His application was unsuccessful. They didn't want this young man who pressed his suit so self-confidently. A few letters that circulated among the members of the league have been preserved. "For heaven's sake do not attach yourself to him," writes one, and another: "I learned that he is very devoted to dissipation and many other unpleasant faults I have no desire to enumerate." And a third remarks, "For the rest, he is more a blabbermouth than a steady, thorough character."

The fifteen-year-old Goethe had sought to join the League of the Virtuous because he was attracted to older and presumably more mature contemporaries. He felt superior to and quickly bored by those his own age. He did have some friends: Ludwig Moors, the son of a lay judge and burgomaster; Adam Horn, whose father was a minor municipal official; and Johann Jakob Riese, also from a good family. The four friends made excursions into the surrounding countryside, read to one another, and debated together. Goethe was their undisputed leader. "We were always the lackeys," Moors later recalled, and Horn, who followed Goethe to Leipzig, reported from there in a letter to Moors that one still couldn't get the better of their friend: "no matter which side he takes, he always wins, for you know what force he can give even to specious arguments." It is clear that the young Goethe inspired admiration but also resentment. It's easy to imagine that a boy might not be universally popular who required his mother to lay out three outfits for him every morning: one for at home, one for ordinary sorties and visits, and one with a bagwig, silk stockings, and ornamental sword for ceremonial occasions.

All the same, he was always the center of his circle, with more ideas for games and activities than anyone else had. One of the few that was probably not his idea was the "marriage game." To avoid having spontaneously paired couples become too attached to each other, partners were chosen by lot for a set length of time. It provided practice in being together but wasn't to be taken too seriously. It was congenial to Goethe's spirit of playful curiosity. After the unpleasant Gretchen affair, it allowed him to flirt for a while, practice, and put off not only serious love affairs but other relationships too. He called it *taking pleasure in the poetic side of ordinary things.*

CHAPTER 2

Living Large in Leipzig. The Great Men of Yesterday.

The Kätchen Affair. Preliminary Studies for

an Epistolary Novel.

Behrisch. Therapy for Jealousy: *The Lover's Spleen.*

Practical Exercises in Art.

Dresden. Disappearing in the Image. Breakdown.

. . . .

FTER THE EMBARRASSING GRETCHEN AFFAIR AND HIS rejection by the League of the Virtuous, the sixteen-year-old came to dislike his native Frankfurt. His *rambles through the streets* no longer gave him the pleasure they once had. The ancient walls and towers put him off, as did the people, especially those who knew of his misadventure. Suddenly everything and everyone was cast in a gloomy light, including his father: *And in the end, after all his studies, efforts, journeys, and diverse pursuits, did I not behold him leading a lonely life between his four walls, such as I could not wish for myself?* He longed to leave, to go to a university. His father was also of the opinion that his talented son, who already had effortlessly acquired so much knowledge, should now begin his studies in earnest. Goethe was attracted to the University of Göttingen, where the outstanding classicists Christian Gottlob Heyne and Johann David Michaelis taught. He hoped that a thorough study of the ancients would give his facile poetry more weight and substance and that he could acquire the discipline and rigor needed for an academic career in belles-lettres. But his father urged him to study jurisprudence in Leipzig, where he himself had studied and still had contacts he could mobilize to help his son. Johann Caspar talked endlessly about his student days. His son let him talk but had *no scruples* about holding to his plan to study literature and philology. In retrospect he called his behavior *impious*.

In the fall of 1765 he bid farewell to the friends of his youth. None of them had been permitted to study where they'd hoped. Johann Jakob Riese was sent to Marburg, Ludwig Moors to Göttingen. Johann Adam Horn had to stay in Frankfurt for another half year before he could begin his studies in Leipzig. That's why Hörnchen (Hornlet, as they dubbed him) had to throw the farewell party for his departing friends. He too was a rhymester, and since he knew that Goethe had plans other than to study law, he sent him off with the following doggerel:

> It's off to jolly Saxony where you have longed to live,
> The country where the poets their loveliest verses give.
> . . .
> From childhood on you've striven to master poesy,
> Now show us it's a poet, not a lawyer, you shall be.
> . . .
> The Muse still smiles upon you. Surely you must know it.
> And so in Leipzig too you'll always be a poet.

Goethe depicts his boyhood self riding to Leipzig in a book dealer's coach, packed in coats and blankets and carrying a lot of luggage. The new university student was bringing along his favorite books, his manuscripts, and an extensive wardrobe. He was on the road for six days. Near Auerstedt the coach got stuck in the mud. *I did not fail to eagerly exert myself and must have overstrained the ligaments in my chest in doing so, for soon thereafter I felt a pain that came and went and did not leave me completely until many years later.*

At the time Leipzig was roughly the size of Frankfurt, with about thirty thousand inhabitants. It was not full of ancient winding streets like Frankfurt, however, but had broad avenues, uniform façades, and residential neighborhoods laid out on a grid. It was known for its inner courtyards that functioned like town squares where an active business and social life took place. Goethe's living quarters were in one of these courtyards. He had two bright, comfortable rooms located only a few steps from Auerbach's Cellar, where he was soon a frequent guest. Leipzig, like Frankfurt, had a trade fair that attracted people from all over Europe. There one could see all manner of dress—from quaint to flamboyant—and hear an international babel of languages. Goethe wrote with some pride to Cornelia that everything was much louder and more colorful and diverse than in Frankfurt. He was especially charmed by the Greeks, descendants of the ancient people he knew only from books. When there were great crowds at fair time, students—including Goethe—were expected to turn their rooms and apartments over to the merchants. For a while he had to make do with a tiny attic room in a commercial building on the edge of town. In Leipzig one was less protected from the wind than in the old lanes of Frankfurt, and Goethe was plagued by constant colds. His friends made fun of his red nose.

The medieval town walls had been torn down at the beginning of the eighteenth century and linden trees planted in their place. The populace came to promenade among them, to see and be seen. The fashion of the day was galant, and even the students, known elsewhere in Germany for rowdy behavior, strolled—to the extent they could afford it—in silk stockings and powdered hair, each with a hat under his arm and a diminutive sword at his side. The local poet Just Friedrich Zachariä, whom Goethe knew, celebrated Leipzig for its elegance:

> If you're to live in Leipzig, cast off those awful clothes
> Or else the men will mock you and girls turn up their nose.
> A black bagwig is needed. That pigtail's got to go,
> And no more hats to hide the bagwig's gallant show.
>
> Procure a smaller sword and a ribbon round it wind,
> And that will be an emblem of belonging to our kind.
> Stop brawling. You don't need to rise to every challenger.
> Speak with graceful gallantry; your odor should be lavender.

The young Goethe was well equipped to live in grand style. His father provided him with a monthly allowance of a hundred gulden (the annual income of a hardworking artisan). He ate at a well-stocked table. In a letter of October 1765 to his friend Riese, he boasts of consuming *chickens, geese, turkeys, ducks, partridges, snipe, trout, hares, venison, pike, pheasants, oysters, etc. These appear every day.* The theater was expensive—if one wanted good seats and, like Goethe, invited friends along. He was always generous, giving picnics in the surrounding countryside and paying for tavern visits. Excellent fabrics had been purchased for his wardrobe, but his father had saved money by assigning the needlework to one of his household staff. The results, unstylish, stiff, and clumsily showy, made a ridiculous impression, and so Wolfgang exchanged every last suit, dress coat, shirt, vest, and neckcloth for the latest Leipzig fashions. When Horn saw his friend again he hardly recognized him. In August 1766 he wrote to their mutual friend Moors, "If you could only see him, you would have to either fly into a rage or burst out laughing. . . . In his pride he is also a fop, and all his clothes, beautiful as they are, are of such a mad goût that it distinguishes him from the entire academy." Goethe himself had written to Riese, the fourth member of their group, *I'm cutting a great figure here,* and added, *But as yet I'm no fop.* But apparently he had become one after all, at least to the bedazzled eyes of Hörnchen. He valued his appearance and strove to make an impression because as a stranger in sophisticated Leipzig, he felt easily intimidated. Wherever he went, people made him feel that he was lacking in elegance, the social graces, and the art of conversation. The Saxons took exception to his Hessian vernacular; grotesquely enough, they considered their own dialect to be the epitome of beauty. And since he found card games distasteful, people thought he was a bore, and an annoying one to boot. *I have a bit more taste and knowledge of beauty than our galants, and at large gatherings I often could not help demonstrating to them the poverty of their opinions,* he writes his sister Cornelia. After a few initial successes, he was less often invited to respectable houses. Among his fellow students, however, he was considered an intellectual prodigy, and with his still somewhat awkward charm he was in great demand among both younger and more mature women. The former wanted to flirt, the latter to mother him.

The wife of Privy Councilor Böhme, a professor of history and constitutional law to whom Goethe had a recommendation from Frankfurt, took him under wing, advising him on his clothing and deportment and seeking to soften his manner. He read his poems to her, and she cautiously critiqued them. In her gentle way, she suggested what he had heard more directly from some of his professors—namely, that he should be more modest and devote himself to his studies. But they bored him. *Roman civil law has plagued my memory for the last half year and truly, I haven't retained much*, he writes to Cornelia. Legal history would probably have interested him more if the professor hadn't gotten bogged down in the Second Punic War. There was no comprehensive knowledge to be had here. *I'm going to hang myself I know nothing.* All the same, he never blames himself when he fails to get on with his studies. Rather, he criticizes his father for forcing him to study in Leipzig.

Despite his anxiety and alienation, however, there were moments of high spirits and merriment even in his first weeks in Leipzig. In a letter to Riese, Goethe encloses one of the poems he composed with such ease. Written as a sideline and with no obvious ambition, some of them are particularly good:

> *Just like a bird that perches on a branch*
> *Within a lovely wood, inhaling freedom,*
> *Enjoying the gentle air all undisturbed.*
> *On outspread wings and singing then he glides*
> *Onward from tree to tree, from bush to bush.*

Half a year later he complains of his sorrow to the same friend. He is *Alone, alone, quite alone.* And again a little poem depicts his emotional state: *My only pleasure it would seem / Is lying, from all men removed, / Among the bushes, by a stream, / And thinking of the ones I love.* Back in prose, he spells out what it is that oppresses him and drives him into solitude, and after a few sentences he slips back into verse:

> *You know how great my love for poetry*
> *How great the hate was, beating in my breast*
> *Gainst those whose only thoughts were wholly given*
> *To the law and to its sacred shrines.*
> *. . .*
> *How firmly I believed (yet wrongly, too)*
> *The Muse would love me, give me oft a song.*
> *. . . Yet barely was I here, when the thick fog*
> *Was lifted from my eyes and I could see*
> *The fame of those great men, could hear at last*
> *How much there is required to earn such fame.*
> *At last I saw that what I thought to be*

My lofty flight was nothing but a dream,
And I a worm that, crawling in the dust,
Looks up and yearns to be the eagle mounting
To the sun. . . .

Before the complaint becomes monotonous, a witty turn of phrase fortunately occurs to the author. The worm enviously watching the eagle's flight is suddenly lifted up by a whirlwind and carried with the dust up into the air, where it also can feel lofty for a little while, until the wind inhales: *The dust settles down, / and with it the worm that now creeps as before.*

To be sure, the young poet acts more apologetic than he really is, for he blithely continues to versify. They are poems in which he is at odds with his poetic calling, poems that bring out his self-doubt. He writes to his sister in September 1766 that for the time being, he intends to use his poems only as a decorative addition to his letters.

He is still intimidated by the *great men* of literature who set the tone in Leipzig. He dares not show his face to the greatest of them, Gotthold Ephraim Lessing. There would have been an opportunity to do so when Lessing visited Leipzig for a performance of his play *Minna von Barnhelm.*

The local luminary was Professor Gellert. Through his fables, comedies, and the novel *The Life of the Swedish Countess von G.*, Christian Fürchtegott Gellert was at the time probably the most famous and widely read author in Germany. People revered Klopstock, but they read Gellert. In his works, Enlightenment thought was presented sentimentally and therefore pleasurably, its pedagogical purpose wrapped in a chatty style. Gellert made things easy for his readers. He avoided extremes and was pious in a rational way, as when he begins a celebration of the creation: "Who opens up the womb of Earth / To bless us with Her goods?" His poems were suitable for inclusion in hymnals and his fables for grade-school primers, and he did not shy from offering moral instruction or practical advice. His recommendation to writers was, "Your wit would fain delight the world, / So sing while fiery spirit lasts."

His own wit had burned itself out by the time Goethe attended his lectures, a few years before Gellert's death. Mounted on a white horse given him by the prince-elector, he arrived for his talks at a leisurely trot. The sickly, modest man delivered them in a thin voice and with circumspect gestures, his theme all of morality. He still enjoyed some popularity with the reading public and was accorded great respect. The students were permitted to submit their literary endeavors for his inspection. He took them home and corrected them in red ink, then discussed selected passages in his next lecture. Believing that the young men should first of all learn to express themselves clearly in prose, he was reluctant to accept anything in verse. In *Poetry and Truth*, one can still feel the young Goethe's sense of slight that Gellert took so little notice of his submission of a wedding poem, written for the nuptials of his uncle Johann Jost Textor. Gellert passed it to his deputy and successor Christian August Clodius, who used copious amounts of red ink because Goethe had summoned half the Olympic pantheon in his poem, if with humorous intent that Clodius failed to recognize.

Gellert's star was in decline. That was even more true of Johann Christoph Gottsched, a physically huge man whom Prussian recruiters would have been eager to secure for the *Lange Kerls* of the Infantry Regiment No. 6, composed of taller-than-average soldiers. Between 1730 and 1750, Gottsched had established himself as the arbiter of literary taste. He had driven the stock character of Hanswurst (Punch) from the stage and was at pains to housebreak and domesticate German literature by imitating French models. He demanded that literature pledge itself to uplifting imitation, moral utility, and verisimilitude. Homer, he declared, in having us believe that "two valiant peoples would butt heads for ten long years for the sake of a beautiful woman," violated reality in the *Iliad* to such an extent that he could "in no way be salvaged." Such theories could not but alienate the young Goethe, who read Homer with great enthusiasm. It was clear to him that verisimilitude and closeness to nature must not be defined in a way that resulted in such banalities. To him, Gottsched had quite simply failed to keep up with the times. In *Poetry and Truth*, he depicts an encounter with him as a scene from a comedy. Goethe is ushered into a reception room. At the same moment, Gottsched enters the room, gigantic, in green, wearing a dressing gown lined in red, and bareheaded. A servant bursts in through a side door and hastily hands him an enormous full-bottomed wig. With one hand Gottsched puts it on his head and

with the other he boxes the servant's ears for being late. The latter stag-
gers out the door, *whereupon the sizable old patriarch gravely bade us sit down
and held a fairly long discourse with great decorum.*

By this time the literary lions of Leipzig no longer seemed as *great* as
they had in his apologetic poem to Riese. But that itself could become
a problem. *And so little by little,* he wrote in *Poetry and Truth, the moment
approached when all authority would vanish and I myself began to doubt, indeed
to despair of, the greatest individuals I had known or thought of.*

In the fall of 1767 Goethe ceremoniously consigned the greater part
of his juvenilia to the stove, throwing his landlady into a panic with
all the smoke. No longer discouraged by the *great men,* he was instead
guided by his own high standards, which he had so far failed to meet.
The key words he noted down for a planned autobiography in 1767
were *Self-development through the transformation of experience into an image.*
These few words adumbrated his poetics of the time. It was not enough
to be in conformity with everyday reality, nor to simply express one's
inner life. Experience should be *transformed into an image.* Experience is
fleeting, and artistic creation preserves a lasting trace, an *image:* experience given a form. The young Goethe was already well versed in the
manipulation of forms, but he had since learned that one must fill them
with their own life. He called it working *according to nature,* which also
meant leaving himself free so that something could grow and flourish. He knew he possessed *characteristics . . . necessary for a poet.* He just
needed to be left alone, not distracted by premature criticism. Only
then would he be able to show his true nature. *Let them leave me be. If I
possess genius, I shall become a poet even if no one corrects me. If I possess none,
no critiques will help.*

The young Goethe, who here explicitly claims the right to undisturbed self-expression, had also discovered letters as his preferred training ground for subjective writing. One can feel how much he enjoys
using language to make his new reality vividly present when writing
to his sister. *I open my eyes and look here!—Here stands my bed! There my
books! There a table decorated as your dressing table never can be. . . . But I am
forgetting that you others, you little girls, cannot see as far as we poets can.* But
powerful descriptive language is not enough. What must be added is
the stuff of experience—experience that challenges the art of linguistic
representation.

The great experience that provided the material for a flood of letters was Goethe's love affair with Anna Katharina Schönkopf, three
years his elder. It began in the spring of 1766. Ännchen or Annette, as
Goethe called her (to everyone else she was Kätchen), was the daughter of a wine merchant and innkeeper. The lawyer Johann Georg
Schlosser, Goethe's future brother-in-law, stayed in Schönkopf's inn
for the Easter fair, as did Goethe's friend Horn, who was now beginning his own studies in Leipzig. Goethe came to lunch with them
at the inn, made the acquaintance of the innkeeper's daughter, and
in just a few days, he was head over heels in love. Contemporary
witnesses are unanimous in their description of Kätchen as a pretty,
smart, and somewhat flirtatious young woman, free and easy while
still maintaining her distance. At first Goethe concealed his inclinations. He pretended that he had been drawn in by someone else,
an aristocratic young woman, and even Horn believed him. When
Goethe finally revealed the truth to him six months later, Horn was
very enthusiastic. "If Goethe weren't my friend," he wrote to Moors,
"I would fall in love with her myself." Horn also reports that Goethe
loves the innkeeper's daughter "very tenderly," but "with the completely honest intentions of a virtuous person, although he knows
that she can never become his wife." Indeed, Goethe emphasizes in
a letter to Moors that he has won the favor of the young woman not
with gifts or by displaying his social superiority. *I have gained her only
through my heart*, he writes with pride; the young woman's *virtuous
heart* is for him a *guarantee that she will never leave me except when duty
and necessity bid us part.*

It sounds all too rational, not like a love that will assert itself against
all restrictions, like that of Werther, the hero of his first novel, but
rather a precocious variety of the deliberateness of Albert, Werther's
rival for Lotte's love, who does not come off well in the novel. Goethe
knew that his father would not accept this affair with an innkeeper's
daughter becoming permanent and so never wrote him of it. His sister was in on the secret, but even then he mentioned it only inciden-
tally, downplaying its importance. The little Schönkopf girl, he wrote
to Cornelia in French, did not deserve to go unmentioned among his
acquaintances. She was a housekeeper who looked after the laundry
and clothing. She was very good at it and derived pleasure from help-

ing him in these matters, and he loved her for it. He didn't want to make his sister jealous, and so invented this version.

How different this love appears in his letters to Ernst Wolfgang Behrisch, his closest friend during his Leipzig years! It was also in Schönkopf's inn, at the same time he met Kätchen, that Goethe met Behrisch. Eleven years his senior, he became his spiritual guide. In the years that followed, the young Goethe, who usually felt superior to those of his own age, would continue to seek out older friends more advanced in experience and prudence. He looked to them to help him plumb the depths of his unsettled inner life. Johann Daniel Salzmann and Johann Heinrich Merck would fill this role in Strasbourg and Darmstadt, respectively.

Behrisch had come to Leipzig as the private tutor of the twelve-year-old Count von Lindenau and had taken up residence with his pupil in Auerbach's courtyard, a few steps from Goethe's own rooms. He was an odd fellow, of striking appearance: tall and gaunt, with a long, sharp nose. He affected the grand manner and could have been a model rococo galant, were it not for his aversion to bright colors. He dressed in various shades of gray—bluish gray, greenish gray, plain gray. He assumed a certain ceremonious decorum that contrasted with his waggish nature. He enjoyed disagreeing with the usual way of doing things. He had contempt for poets who had their works printed and thought that the best verses should circulate only in manuscript. He therefore copied out Goethe's poems, which he liked, bound them together under the title *Annette*, and gave them to his young friend with the advice to always publish his work that way. His primary rule was never to cheapen yourself, either toward those above or below you. He mocked empty and stilted behavior and writing. People feared his wit. He combined a refined appearance with a sense for what was natural, but without letting it degenerate into the coarseness that would later characterize the writers of the Sturm und Drang movement. He accompanied Goethe to the pleasure gardens outside the city walls and consorted with girls who, as Goethe would write apologetically in *Poetry and Truth*, were better than their reputation. Behrisch occasionally brought his tutee along on these outings, and that cost him his job as tutor in October 1767. His reputation, however, was undamaged, and afterward he was summoned as tutor to the court of Dessau. It was a severe loss for Goethe, and in an ode to Behrisch he gave vent to his anger:

Honest man,
Flee this land.

Dead swamps,
vaporous October fogs,
Weave their effluence
inseparably here.

Birthplace
of insect pests,
murderous husk
of their evil.

From the beginning, Goethe confided his relationship with Kätchen to Behrisch. Initially, he reported his triumphs. He had conquered the heart of the much-courted girl. He initially writes to Behrisch in French; later, as his passion and jealousy grow, he uses German. He says what a pleasure it is to watch another man striving to please Kätchen while he sits, seemingly unmoved, in a corner, utters no gallant remark, doesn't flirt, so that the other thinks he's a fool lacking savoir faire—and in the end this fool gains rewards for which the other would have made a pilgrimage to Rome.

This self-confidence did not last, however. Kätchen's job at the inn put her in constant contact with young men. In October 1767, a student from the Baltic coast by the name of Ryden took up residence. He was a handsome and self-confident Russian of German extraction, a ladies' man. Goethe grew suspicious, and Kätchen, already familiar with such behavior, sought to reassure him. *With the most ardent caresses she begged me not to plague her with jealousy. She swore she would always be mine. And what won't one believe when one is in love. But what can she swear? Can she swear never to look different than now? Can she swear that her heart should cease to beat? But I will believe that she can.*

Goethe describes to his friend a scene that drives him mad. Ryden enters the room and asks Kätchen's mother for the tarot cards. Kätchen is present. She wipes her eyes as if something had gotten into them. Goethe is familiar with this gesture and thinks he knows what it means. She does it to conceal embarrassment or a blush. Why is she embarrassed, why blushing? The answer is clear to him. There's something going on between her and Ryden. *Enamored eyes see more sharply,* he writes Behrisch, *but often too sharply. Advise me . . . and comfort me . . . . But don't make fun of me, even if I deserve it.*

We don't know what advice Behrisch gave him; his letters have not survived. He could not have been very alarmed—reading, in the very next letter, that the jealous lover at least maintained enough composure to pen a "Marriage Song," in which the possession of a woman is depicted with relish: *In the bedroom, far from feasting, / Sits Amor faithful at the head. / His eye is peeled for wantons seeking / To steal a march on your marriage bed.*

In October, Behrisch left for Dessau, and a veritable flood of letters began. Goethe gives minutely detailed descriptions of the ups and downs of the state of his soul, his bouts of jealousy, his moments of feeling reassured. The letters become noticeably and self-consciously literary, as if Goethe were becoming a figure in an epistolary novel. For pages on end he complains about the pangs of love, describes incidents that arouse his jealousy, moments of reconciliation and devotion, then more disturbances. He sighs and moans, regains his distance, and writes wise reflections as if watching himself from the wings: *Love is misery, but every misery becomes lust when by lamenting we salve the constricting, stabbing sensation that alarms our heart and transform it into a gentle titillation.* The writer of these excited and, at the same time, calculated letters is taking pleasure in these descriptions. Actually, the letters should be saved for later use in a novel, he thinks: *I can't help it; I have many good ideas and can't use them except to write to you. If I were an author I would be more frugal in order to waste them on the public someday.*

The letter-writing lover is genuinely overwhelmed by his feelings, but he's both a participant and a recorder. It is not that he seeks out experiences and gets involved in situations in order to express them in words; he's not indulging in romantic feelings so that he can write about them, but they do acquire an additional *titillation* when he does. He puts his romantic troubles to work, orchestrates, prolongs, and intensifies them, creating an imaginary stage as he writes. The letters are addressed not just to Behrisch but also to himself, the future author. He himself sits in the audience and watches the performance of what he's writing. It's a complicated process in which he is living through an experience that inherently becomes completely real only in the excited language of the letters.

The series of diary-like reports to Behrisch that begins on November 2, 1767, and continues till the end of that month is almost a novel in letters like *Werther*. Goethe's ambition was to write so that two gaps would disappear simultaneously: the gap between him and his love affair and the gap between him and his friend. *This hand that now touches the paper to write to you, this happy hand pressed her to my bosom.* The caressing hand is also the writing hand. He transfers touching his beloved to touching his friend, who is reading what he's writing. The act of writing establishes an intimate connection. At seven o'clock on the evening of November 10, he writes—almost cries out—*Ah Behrisch, this is one of those moments! You are gone, and the paper is cold comfort compared with your arms.* And now we can watch the letter writer (who also is watching himself) as he kindles a fire with words and sentences: *My blood runs more quietly, I shall be able to speak to you more calmly. But reasonably? God only knows. No, not reasonably.* He keeps interrupting himself, hesitating, starting anew: *I've cut myself a new quill to pull myself together. Let's see if we can proceed. . . . Annette is—no not that. Quiet, quiet, I'll try to tell you the whole thing in order.* One of the jealous scenes follows.

Kätchen had gone to the theater without him. He had followed her there. *I found her box. She sat in the corner . . . . Behind her chair Herr Ryden, in a very intimate position. Ha! Think of me! Think of me! in the gallery! with a spyglass—watching them! Curses! Oh, Behrisch, I thought my head would explode with fury. They were playing Miss Sara.** . . . *my eyes were in the box, and my heart was dancing. Now he leaned forward . . . . Now he stepped back, now he leaned over her chair and said something to her, I ground my teeth and watched. Tears sprang to my eyes, but they were from looking so keenly, I haven't been able to weep yet this entire evening.* His first thought is to rush home and describe the experience to his friend. But then he tarries another moment, in doubt as to whether he is really seeing what he sees, or only what he thinks he sees: *I saw how coldly she responded to him, how*

---

* *Miss Sara Sampson*, by Gotthold Ephraim Lessing.

she turned away from him, how she barely answered him. . . . Ah, my spyglass did not flatter me as my soul did, I wished to see it! He storms home with his doubts and sits down at the table to write. *Yet another quill. Again a few moments of peace. Oh, my friend. The third page already. I could write you a thousand and never tire.* But then he tires after all, falls asleep in his chair, wakes up again, and pulls himself together: *But I must fill up the page this evening. I still have a lot to say.* But the incident has already been made the most of.

The power of imagination he had praised to the skies a few days earlier must come to his aid: *It pleases the imagination to wander about in the vast, mysterious field of images, looking there for expressions when truth is not permitted to take the nearest path.* Because his experiences have been exhausted, he gives himself over to his imagination, which conjures up the coming days for him. *What shall I do tomorrow? I know. I shall be calm until I enter the house. And then my heart will begin to beat, and when I hear her steps or her voice, it will beat faster, and after the meal I will leave. If I happen to see her, tears will spring to my eyes and I'll think, God forgive you as I forgive you, and may he give you all the years you have stolen from my life; that's what I will think. I'll look at her, be grateful that I can half believe that she loves me, and leave again. That's how it will be tomorrow, the day after, and forever more.*

He continues in this vein for a little while, then finally goes to bed. The next day he reads the letter through once more and is satisfied with it. *By this impetuous desire and this equally impetuous abhorrence, this raving and this lust you will recognize the youth and will pity him.* A sentence follows that will recur in *The Sorrows of Young Werther* and become proverbial: *What made the world a hell for me yesterday makes it heaven today.* Here we witness a process whereby a brilliant sentence, pregnant with significance, emerges from the uninhibited flow of writing, to be stored away in his inner archive for future literary use. Two days later, having still not mailed the gigantic letter, he notes after rereading it: *My letter has a nice predisposition to become a little work.*

Following the initial storm of jealousy that sweeps through this *little work*, his thoughts cool. As his jealousy subsides, he relaxes, but he also notes with concern what that means: *the violence of love had much decreased from its usual strength.* Jealousy is obviously necessary for passion to reach the proper operating temperature. He also registers the fact that Kätchen seems to enjoy holding sway over him. *It pleases her to see a proud person like me chained to her footstool. She pays him no heed as long as he lies still, but if he tries to pull free, then she notices him again, and her love reawakens with her attention.* So the best thing for him to do is to make Kätchen jealous in his turn. He finds the opportunity to do so among the Obermanns and the Breitkopfs, families in whose houses he was a welcome guest and who had pretty daughters to flirt with. And indeed, Kätchen became jealous and made scenes.

Things went back and forth in this way until the spring of 1768, when the breakup occurred—amicably, Goethe claimed in a letter to Behrisch: *We began with love and are ending in friendship.*

In the same letter he sends his friend the comedy *The Lover's Spleen.* Even before leaving Frankfurt he had drafted it as a conventional rococo pastoral, then revised it several times, bringing it closer and closer to his own amorous troubles until it became a comedy of jealousy. It pleased him so much that it survived the autos-da-fé of the following years. He told his sister it was a *good little piece . . . since it has been carefully copied from nature.*

The lives of two couples are interwoven but also contrasted. Lamon and Egle pursue their games of love in a dallying, charming, and frivolous way.

> LAMON: *Can there be any harm in finding others pretty?*
> *I don't complain if you say, "There's a handsome man.*
> *So charming and so witty." Agreed, and here's my hand,*
> *As pledge I won't be angry.*
> EGLE: *Don't be. I'll promise you*
> *Not to be angry either, for it's my weakness too.*
> *With friendly smiles I listen while men chat in my ear.*
> *. . .*
> *Jealousy becomes me even less than you.*

Eridon and Amine, on the other hand, have problems because Eridon wants complete control of his lover and watches over her suspiciously, his jealousy lying in wait for anything or anyone approaching her. Egle to Amine on her lover's jealousy: *No wonder it upsets him when you go to a dance. / He is even jealous of the grass you tread by chance. / And hates as a rival the little bird you love.* Amine is tormented by Eridon's jealousy, but she is honest enough to admit that it also flatters her pride: *His jealousy's a sign of his great adoration / And compensates my pride for all my tribulation.* Her friend thinks she's deluding herself: *Dear child, I pity you and fear no hope remains, / Since you love misery. You rattle with your chains / And tell yourself it's music.*

Goethe mirrors his own jealousy in Eridon. All the more remarkable, then, how unsympathetic this figure is and how much he gets on the others' nerves, especially those of his beloved. Amine complains about this domineering, hypochondriacal, and frequently bad-tempered fellow:

> *If he tortures me with a silly accusation*
> *It only takes one word, a soft recrimination,*
> *And he's a different man, his sour mood subsiding,*
> *And often he will cry when he sees me crying,*
> *Fall sweetly to his knees to beg me for forgiveness.*

Amine's more experienced friend Egle gives her the paradoxical advice that she should counter Eridon's jealousy not by protesting her innocence but instead by acting ambiguously. Eridon gets himself all worked up precisely because he has so little cause to be jealous. *Without a cause for woe, he fain will make one up.* So he needs to be treated with doses of his own medicine to effect a cure. Eridon is simply too confident of her love and needs to have his confidence shaken: *Let him think without him you'd get along just fine. / He'll rant a little while—sit tight and bide your time. / Then a mere look from you will do more than a kiss. / Teach him fear of losing you and then he'll be in bliss.*

As Egle finally realizes, it's too subtle a strategy for Amine, so she chooses another therapy. She deploys her own seductive charms against Eridon. When he finally embraces and kisses her, she at first lets it happen and then shames him with the question, *You say you love Amine? . . . Yet just now you kissed me. / You'll repent this falsehood, just you wait and see.* She forces him to realize that the two things are not incompatible— being in love yet stealing a kiss from another from time to time, or in Eridon's own words: *A little pleasure will not steal my heart from you.*

The whole affair, however, is not quite so harmless. A motif emerges that will gain great significance in Goethe's later works—above all in his novel *Elective Affinities*: imagined infidelity, embracing one woman while thinking of another. Which one is really intended? The anonymity of desire is unfathomable. Individuals seem interchangeable, the objects of desire obscure. Such aspects are almost too weighty for a rococo comedy. Goethe himself alludes to this in his autobiography by referring to the *insulting and humiliating experiences* that were the source for his insubstantial playlet: *I never tired of pondering volatility, inclinations, the mutability of the human condition, ethical sensuality, and all the heights and depths whose conjunction in our nature can be regarded as the riddle of human life.*

The play about curing jealousy has a happy end. Less happy was the end of the affair with Kätchen, although in the letter to Behrisch Goethe writes, *we have parted; we're happy.* After his apparently calm assertion that they *began with love and are ending in friendship*, he abruptly changes his tone. *But not I*, he continues, *I still love her, so much, my God, so much.* Goethe is by no means done with her. He does not want to leave her but can't make her any promises. He feels guilty and hopes, for the sake of his own exoneration, that she will find an *upright man*; how *happy* he would then be! He promises not to inflict pain on her by taking up with another woman. He will wait until he sees her in the arms of another man and only then feel himself free to love again.

One gets the impression from the letters to Behrisch that in the end, it was the young Goethe who initiated the separation. However, if one follows the later depiction in *Poetry and Truth*, another image emerges. There Goethe presents his younger self as a pest of Eridon's ilk, *infected with the obsession that leads us to make an entertainment out of torturing the beloved and dominating a girl's devotion with gratuitous and tyrannical moods.* For example, he says that he took out on her his *bad mood* about some unsuccessful poems because he felt all too sure of her. This *bad mood* wrapped itself in *absurd bouts of jealousy* that she endured for a while with *incredible patience.* But then he could not help noticing that to protect herself, she was inwardly withdrawing from him. And only then did she give him real cause for the jealousy that was until then unfounded. It led to *terrible scenes*, and from then on he really had to court her and fight for her. But it was too late. He had already lost her.

At the time, however, he didn't see things so sharply, or at least didn't depict them that way to Behrisch. As we have seen, he chose a more flattering version, in which it was he who brought about the separation.

In search of a counterbalance during the turbulent weeks of this love affair, Goethe devoted himself to artistic endeavors: drawing and painting with Adam Friedrich Oeser at the art academy and engraving and etching with Johann Michael Stock. He had met Oeser in his third semester and admired him. He was the director of the newly founded Leipzig Academy in the Pleissenburg castle, well versed in theory, and a versatile painter, His gregarious and humorous personality made him popular with students and clients. He was flooded with commissions. He painted altarpieces and theater backdrops, produced book illustrations and miniatures, and advised princes and aristocrats on the decor of their palaces and the design of their gardens. In Dresden, where Oeser had previously worked, he had been a close friend of the archaeologist and art theorist Johann Joachim Winckelmann and had shared a house with him. In the summer of 1768, he was looking forward to Winckelmann's return from Italy, and Goethe was eager to see the famous man in person. Oeser had given Goethe Winckelmann's writings, for which he expressed the greatest admiration, and Goethe had read them with a good deal of reverence. But then news arrived that Winckelmann had been murdered in Trieste. Oeser was incommunicado for several days, and Goethe regretted that in addition to Lessing, whom he had avoided out of shyness, he had now also missed the chance to meet this other intellectual hero.

Even before Winckelmann, Oeser had begun to favor an idealized version of classical antiquity—later captured by Winckelmann in the phrase "noble simplicity and quiet grandeur"—over the baroque style. But unlike Winckelmann, Oeser had nothing of the missionary in him, no passion for the absolute. Instead, he pursued his art more playfully, cared nothing for the judgment of posterity, and served his clients by giving them no more than what they wanted. Oeser's free and easy lack of affectation and intellectually original manner were good for the young Goethe. Oeser encouraged his attempts at painting and inspired him to think about art. After his return to Frankfurt Goethe wrote him a long letter of thanks, saying that he had learned more from him than in all his years at the university. *My taste for beauty, my knowledge, my insights—did they not all come from you? How certain, how brilliantly true I now find the strange and almost incomprehensible sentence that the workshop of a great artist does more to develop the budding philosopher, the budding poet, than the lecture hall of a world-renowned scholar and critic.*

Gellert, Clodius, and others had found fault with his literary attempts, while Oeser had obviously found a way to be a positive influence. *Whether complete censure or complete praise: nothing is so destructive to one's capabilities. Encouragement after censure is sun after rain, fruitful and productive. Indeed, Herr Professor, if you had not encouraged my love of the Muses I would have despaired.* In *Poetry and Truth*, however, Goethe expresses a less positive opinion of him: *His teaching influenced our thinking and our taste, but his own drawing was too indistinct to guide me—only half conscious as I was of the objects of art and nature—toward rigorous and clear artistic practice.*

Especially during the complicated affair with Kätchen, Goethe had found a peaceful focal point in Oeser. It was also Oeser who gave him the idea of undertaking a trip to nearby Dresden to visit its painting collection. In late February 1768, as he was breaking up with Kätchen, Goethe set off for the Saxon capital. He found lodging with an educated, whimsical shoemaker who appears in *Poetry and Truth* as a combination of Hans Sachs and Jacob Böhme. He spent days looking at the paintings. As yet he had no eye for the Italians, not even for Raphael's *Sistine Madonna*, and was more attracted by the genre scenes of the Netherlandish masters. Suddenly, the shoemaker reminded him of a figure in a painting by Ostade. In *Poetry and Truth* he writes, *It was the first time that I became so acutely aware of a gift that I later made more conscious use of, namely, to see nature with the eyes of this or that artist whose works I had just been looking at with particular attention.*

The trip to Dresden was a pilgrimage to art that gave him the curious feeling of having lived with the shoemaker as if in a painting. He kept the visit a secret; he was consumed by a feeling that he had disappeared into the pictures and was now stepping out of them and back into reality, his friends and acquaintances in Leipzig staring at him as if he had returned from the dead. The distance he felt from them may have softened his separation from Kätchen a bit. And yet that separation was still so difficult and painful that in *Poetry and Truth* he traces the serious illness he would soon undergo back to pangs of love: *I had really lost her, and the madness with which I avenged my mistakes on myself, by assaulting my physical self in several senseless ways in order to punish my moral self, contributed very much to the bodily ills under which I lost some of the best years of my life.*

There were other contributing factors. Goethe had been in Leipzig for three years without completing his studies. For now, the student of jurisprudence had to regard himself as a failure. Even though he talked about it in a jocular tone, it oppressed him. He revealed his anguish to Behrisch: *And I'm going ever more downhill by the day. 3 months, Behrisch, and then it's the end.*

He was weakened physically. The heavy Merseburg beer dispensed in Leipzig and the coffee offered on every possible occasion caused him digestive problems. He had inhaled poisonous fumes at the workshop of Stock the engraver. He didn't know whether the pains in his chest came from that or were caused by the pulled muscle he had suffered three years earlier during the coach accident on the way to Leipzig.

One night in late July 1768 he was awakened by a severe hemorrhage. The doctor who was called diagnosed a life-threatening pulmonary illness. A swelling had appeared on the left side of his neck. For a few days he was near death. The young man had won the affection of several families during his years in Leipzig, and he received devoted care from the Breitkopfs, Obermanns, Stocks, Schönkopfs, and Oesers, and of course from little Horn and his other dining companions. Especially active was Ernst Theodor Langer, Behrisch's successor as private tutor to the young count Lindenau. Langer was a pious man devoted to mystical speculation, though too self-willed to join one of the Pietistic or Herrnhuter circles. He was often in attendance in Goethe's sickroom. He was no zealot and had no desire to proselytize, but he was anxious to win for Jesus the heart of this young patient who was perhaps near death. In *Poetry and Truth*, Goethe speaks with great affection of the companionship Langer provided during these difficult days. *What he had to say with pleasant consistency easily found the ear of a young person detached from the things of this earth by a troublesome illness, who found it highly desirable to turn the activity of his intellect toward the things of heaven.* Goethe's contact and subsequent correspondence with Langer would later influence his experiments with Pietism.

His condition improved. In August 1768 he ventured outside again at last, haggard, emaciated, and pale as a ghost. He describes himself in that way in a letter to Friederike Oeser, the painter's daughter, a few weeks after his departure. She had vigorously tried to help the patient sit up. *She greeted me with a great whoop and laughed herself silly at the comical idea that a man in his twentieth year could think of dying of consumption!*

On August 28, 1768, his nineteenth birthday, Goethe left Leipzig. He stood in front of Kätchen's house but didn't enter or say goodbye. Still sick and weak, provided with a bit of heavenly consolation from Langer, he left Leipzig as a pitiful dropout with no degree.

CHAPTER 3

The Aftermath of Leipzig. *Partners in Guilt*. Illness.

Approaches to Religion. Attempt at Piety.

Two Mentors: Langer and Susanna von Klettenberg.

No Consciousness of Sin. The Pious Magician.

The Sickroom as Laboratory.

The Search for Chemical Revelation.

. . . .

N A NOTE OF 1810 THAT DID NOT FIND ITS WAY INTO HIS AUTOBIO-
graphy, the sixty-year-old Goethe reflects on the disparity between the
ease with which, as a young man, he was able to absorb the rules and
conventions of poetry, drama, and rhetoric, and the difficulties he had
in giving satisfactory form to his life. In that attempt he *lacked the compass needle I would have needed, all the more so since, at every halfway favorable
wind, I always hoisted all my sail and thus was at every moment in danger of
running aground.* Although fate had provided him with *excellent mentors,*
they had unfortunately sent him in different directions. *For one, the primary maxim of life was good nature and tenderness, for another it was a certain
agility, for a third indifference and levity, for a fourth piety, for a fifth diligence
and doing one's duty, for the next imperturbable cheerfulness, and so forth, so
that before my twentieth year I had run through the schools of almost all moral
philosophers.*

These teachings were necessarily contradictory, and he was unsure
how to balance them, especially when each in turn was raised to a primary principle. He writes that in his youth he always threw himself
completely into things, *cheerful, free, and lively.* Moderation and clarity
had not been his cup of tea so far. That would come later.

The year 1769 was a kind of interlude for the young Goethe. As
we shall see, his mentors that year were religious ones. His life was on

hold. It was uncertain whether he would ever really get back on his feet. From time to time he felt himself a doomed man. It may well be, he wrote to Kätchen Schönkopf in late 1768, that he would be dead *before Easter*. They should bury him in Leipzig, and on his name day Kätchen should visit the deceased *Johannismännchen*.* If he should survive, he didn't know how he was going to proceed. He would like to go to Paris to see *how life is lived in France*. He barely mentions continuing his legal studies, although his father insisted on it and could not conceal his disappointment at *finding, instead of a sturdy, active son who will graduate and follow his preordained path through life, a sickling*.

He was as dissatisfied with himself as his father was. He read through the letters he had sent home from Leipzig (carefully filed away by his father) and discovered a *certain smug arrogance* in them, the *aping* of a genteel tone. The poems he had frequently appended to the letters now seemed *all too superficial*. He was looking for his own voice, for himself.

Emaciated and weak, lying in bed or sitting wrapped in blankets, he polished the poems he'd brought home. Some had been included in Behrisch's calligraphic collection; he'd given others to Friederike Oeser as a farewell present. In 1769 he put together a collection for which Theodor Breitkopf, a friend from Leipzig, composed melodies. It appeared under the title *New Songs, Set to Music by Bernhard Theodor Breitkopf* and was Goethe's first publication, although it did not name him as author.

In his sickroom, Goethe worked on the play *Partners in Guilt*. The idea originated in Leipzig. He revised what had started as a one-act farce into a three-act comedy, and it pleased him so much he included it in later editions of his works. In *Poetry and Truth* he calls the play a cheerful burlesque with a *gloomy family background*. A well-to-do traveler named Alcest is robbed while staying at an inn. Söller, a good-for-nothing spendthrift living there at the expense of his father-in-law the innkeeper, commits the theft and then witnesses his wife, Sophie, the innkeeper's daughter, going to an assignation with Alcest. The innkeeper also sneaks in, intending to rifle through the traveler's bag-

---

* A play on Goethe's first name. The "Manikin Johann" was a wooden statue of John the Baptist set up in front of St. John's Church in Leipzig on the saint's feast day, June 24.

gage, so all three—Söller, the innkeeper, and Sophie—encounter one another in Alcest's room, where each accuses the others of being the thief. In the end, when Söller is revealed as the perpetrator, the others feel guilty as well. Order is only apparently restored. *For the time being it's over,* says the relieved thief. It's better to be made a *cuckold* than *hanged* as a thief. According to Goethe's later self-commentary, the piece *expresses playfully, in somewhat rough and crude terms, the highly Christian saying: He that is without sin, let him cast the first stone.*

This set of moral instructions for how to read the little play illuminates the change taking place in the young Goethe. In his search for direction, he was seeing whether piety suited him. To be sure, this was not the first time his thoughts had turned to *heavenly* things. In the autobiography he writes how much the Old Testament enchanted him. As a boy he had tried, with the help of a tutor, to read the Pentateuch in Hebrew. For him, these were simply wonderful stories of the suffering and joy of *religious heroes* who lived in the unshakable conviction that *a God stood at their side, paid them visits, took an interest in, led, and saved them.* In these stories God is superhuman, yet very human in his anger and jealousy, someone with whom the *religious heroes* can commune. In reading about them, you became as familiar with God as they were. God lived in these stories like a figure in a novel, and when you read them, you believed in this God of the desert dwellers in the same way you believed in the pirate Störtebecker, the sons of Aymon, Til Eulenspiegel, or Clever Hans. They were lovely stories that Goethe took refuge in as a boy, finding himself *both in the greatest solitude and the greatest company there among the widely scattered pastoral tribes.*

He was devoted to that fairy-tale world. The *general, natural religion* he learned from other teachers, which was probably also his father's religion, was another matter. It consisted of the conviction that *behind nature was concealed, as it were, a great, productive, ordering, and directing being,* and he adds the comment, *such a conviction is obvious to everyone.* He does not say here whether he thinks this conviction is justified; the phrase *behind nature,* however, is an unusual one for Goethe. He usually stressed that one should not look for God behind but rather within nature. But it was also clear to him that a naïve, childish imagination pictures nature as a product, constructed and controlled by a master craftsman. This *natural religion,* as he calls it, is part of the curriculum one could and should learn as a child. The stories from the days of the patriarchs, on the other hand, were poetry.

The boy had made an attempt to lend the rather dry *natural religion* a personal and ceremonially poetic aspect. In *Poetry and Truth*, Goethe recounts how he piled fruit, leaves, and flowers onto his father's cylindrical music stand (which was painted red and decorated with golden flowers) as an offering to what he could only imagine to be the God of nature. And since he was unable to give him any *form*, he would honor him with his *works*: *Natural products were to be a simile for the world, and above them would burn a flame symbolizing the spirit of man, yearning upwards toward its maker*. At sunrise, incense sticks were to be ignited by means of a magnifying glass. At first, the altar was a success and heady aromas began to spread, but then the candles burned down into the red paint, it began to stink, and his father's beautiful music stand was damaged in the effort to give expression to *the spirit of man yearning upwards*. He closes his depiction of his childhood sacrificial ritual: *One is tempted to regard this accident as a warning sign of how dangerous is any desire to approach God in such a way.*

Yet this approach was not completely wrong. He had observed the taboo against making a graven image and had honored the invisible God through his works. For him God stood *in direct connection* to nature: a God of burgeoning growth, a God of the rising sun. Gratitude for light, the cult of the sun that the boy staged in his earnestly playful way, remained the *most religious of all functions* for all of Goethe's life. As an old man writing "Notes and Essays toward a Better Understanding of the West-Eastern Divan," he uses the example of ancient Persian religion to characterize the sun cult: *Praying to the Creator, they turned toward the rising sun as the most strikingly magnificent phenomenon. . . . Everyone, even the most humble, could realize the glory of this heartwarming ritual every day.* Those who can accept prayer as a daily gift seemed to him *people favored by God*, those who have not yet had their lofty feelings deadened by *pious boredom*.

The boy's worship was directed against just such *pious boredom*, against the Protestant religious education that taught only *a kind of dry morality*, a lesson that could *appeal to neither soul nor heart*. Which is precisely why the lad invented his own personal worship, turning not to the God of morality but to the God of creative nature, in reverence to both God and himself.

Goethe's next significant contact with religion came the year before he moved to Leipzig, when he saw himself enmeshed in the dubious affair of trading in offices and fraud and, as a result, had to part with "Gretchen." The young man felt that he was being regarded skeptically by his fellow citizens: *I had lost the unconscious bliss of walking around unknown and unblemished.* The eyes of society were upon him, and he fled into a protected realm of *beautiful, leafy groves.* Only later does he realize that in so doing, he had chosen a sacred place, so naturally secluded *that a poor wounded heart can hide itself there.*

This sacred space was supposed to protect him from entanglement in a malevolent society. He thought that its anathema could not reach him there. It is thus a sanctuary, an aspect of religion that is explicitly directed against society and promises exoneration. He justifies his behavior to a friend who tries to draw him back into social intercourse: why shouldn't he be allowed to build a fence around this place in order *to sanctify and seclude himself from the world! Surely there is no more beautiful way to worship God than that which arises in our breast in simple conversation with nature and requires no images!*

But this is ultimately a defensive attempt to carve out a sacred space, separate from ordinary life, in order to protect transcendence from the leveling effects of society. The momentary bliss he feels is restricted, for his gaze remains fixed on the limits of space and time. It resembles what happens in prayer. In the "Notes and Essays toward a Better Understanding of the West-Eastern Divan," he writes that in most cases, prayer does not pervade life. Usually an *effulgent sense of momentary bliss* is followed by disenchantment, and the *unsatisfied . . . person, returned to himself, falls back into the most unending boredom,* the boredom of mundane life.

How, then, can strong feeling be stabilized and the magic of the sacred place come to pervade the secular? The boy probably did not ask himself the question in quite that way. But the author of the autobiography asks it—and gives a double answer.

It is art that extracts some lasting divinity from the mundane, and it is the church that transports divinity into everyday life with its liturgical order.

It is the beauty of art, in analogy to the divine, that can celebrate and give permanence to a place or a moment in time by giving it form in visual images or words. In *Poetry and Truth*, Goethe declares that we are unable to perceive what is sacred *when it is not fortunate enough to flee to beauty and enter into a profound unity with it, whereby both become equally immortal and indestructible.* Following this passage, the autobiography relates how, after seeking refuge in the sacred grove, the boy begins to paint in pictures and in words. Precisely because divinity is experienced as something so ephemeral, the boy feels the *urge* to capture something *similar* in word and image. Thus he began to develop an aesthetic religion of vivid clarity. *The eye was the primary organ with which I apprehended the world.*

As a student in Leipzig, Goethe set off on what he describes as *image hunts.* But since on his solitary walks *the observer encountered few objects that were either beautiful or sublime,* and he was moreover plagued by insects, he began to pay attention to the *small lives of nature* and became accustomed to see in them *significance . . . that tended sometimes toward allegory, sometimes toward symbolism, according to whether observation, emotion, or reflection predominated.* The search for meaning in the observation of nature as a continuation of religion by aesthetic means—the artistic cultivation of the sacred—would continue throughout Goethe's life. The epiphany of the natural world takes place in its artistic depiction, which is also a kind of revelation.

The other form in which the sacred is stabilized is in the liturgy and sacraments of the church, especially the Catholic Church. The sympathetic and even celebratory passages about the church in *Poetry and Truth* were a surprise to Goethe's readers. Until the publication, in 1812, of the second volume of the autobiography, readers had known Goethe as a bitter critic of Catholicism, one who had rejected its dogmas—from the concept of original sin to belief in the devil—as the worst superstition. He described the fate of the Catholic Calderón, for instance, as the *saddest case* of an author of genius *forced to idolize what is absurd,* and he considered it Shakespeare's good fortune to be spared the *bigoted delusions* of Catholicism.

The passages in the autobiography about the rich liturgical and sacramental life of the Catholic Church, which stands in contrast to the impoverished rituals of Protestantism, are embedded in the depiction of his years in Leipzig. During those student days, Goethe would hardly have thought as deeply about the essence of Catholicism as he does in the autobiography. But early on he was repelled by the austere moralism of the Protestant Church. It was not a religion to his taste, lacking as it did a *fullness* of imagery and pageantry. Orthodox Protestantism was not a real religion for him, only a moral code.

In retrospect, Goethe remarks that, in the end, his childhood sacrificial ceremony, his worship of nature and the establishment of a sacred grove, his hunt for images of divinity in nature, and the cult of beauty were religious gestures intended to compensate for the lack of a life ordered by ritual. He describes in the seventh book of *Poetry and Truth* how such a life might appear. The churchgoing religious man, he writes, *must be accustomed to regarding the inner religion of the heart and the outer religion of the church as one and the same, as that great, general sacrament that divides into so many other sacraments and communicates its sanctity, indestructibility, and eternity to them all.* He continues, *And so through a shining round of uniformly sacred acts . . . the cradle and the grave, however far apart they happen to lie, are bound together in a constant circle.*

He could well imagine such a life, but it was not the life he led. He writes that he had begun quite early to develop his *own religion*, far from the church and its life of sacramental order. However, he would give a quasi-sacramental order to his own life. He made rituals of the activities of daily life and recognized the value in official acts and ceremonious behavior. Ludwig Wittgenstein once called culture a kind of "monastic rule." That was certainly the case for Goethe, and it became more so with advancing age.

Goethe had not found a spiritual home in Protestantism. In retrospect, he says that his elders tried to instill in him the fear of sin, and it worked for a while. He was tortured by *gloomy scruples*. In Leipzig he tore himself free from them. In *lighthearted hours* he was even ashamed to have ever been beset by such scruples, so foreign did they seem to him by then. He had left behind his *strange bad conscience along with the church and the altar.*

His attempts at piety, in fact, had little to do with church and altar. It was a feeling of love and not contrition that attracted him for a while to the spiritual world of the Herrnhuters and Pietists.

For a short time, his mentor during this phase of his life was Ernst Theodor Langer, who had become his friend during his last months in Leipzig. Langer, although not a Herrnhuter himself, had friends from the sect who lived in Frankfurt, and they tried to draw the young Goethe into their fraternal community. During their long walks together, Langer himself had expounded the Gospel to Goethe with such enthusiasm that the young man was willing to sacrifice many hours to this activity, hours he had meant to spend with his beloved. *I returned his affection most thankfully*, writes Goethe, confessing that under Langer's influence, he at last found himself ready *to say that what I had until then valued as human, I would now declare to be divine.* This remark refers to the image of Christ in the Gospels. Until then, Jesus had been for him a teacher of wisdom. Now he is trying to accept him as God become man, the embodiment of a revelation that, as was usual with the Pietists, was supposed to speak directly to the heart and thus be more felt emotionally than grasped intellectually.

For a while, Goethe was attracted to the social sphere of such heartfelt piety. Because at that time his mother was also drawing closer to the Herrnhuters, gatherings were held, at her instigation and with his father's reluctant approval, in the house on the Hirschgraben. In his letters to Langer, Goethe is relieved to report that the local Herrnhuters were not so strict in *the matter of clothing*, and he is *going to meetings and really finding them to my taste.* It is not lost on him, however, that they accept him only warily, like the fallen angel Abaddon. And they're right not to trust him, for although he is making an honest effort to encounter religion with *love*, the Gospel with *friendship*, and the sacred word with *veneration*, he is still *no Christian*, but perhaps will become one yet.

In another letter to Langer, Goethe analyzes the obstacles from a Pietistic point of view. Pietistic instruction asks that one become free of self-love, for it impedes God's influence on the soul. But he writes that this *love of self* is precisely his problem; it is still too *powerful* within him. He cannot forgo it, because it is part of his actual passion, which is directed more toward authorship than toward God. The decisive sentence in this self-analysis is *My fiery head, my wit, my efforts at and fairly well-founded hope of becoming a good author in time are—now that I'm speaking honestly—the most important obstacles to a complete change of heart.* His gift of lively perception and love of invention make him, in the eyes of the pious, a person who is *still too flustered by his devotion to worldly things.*

But he has no wish to shed this *devotion to worldly things*. He knows that it is what makes him the kind of poet he wants to be. He loves the light, while the Pietists prefer the twilight. During a gathering in his father's house, he interrupts the service. *What's the point of this darkness! I said, and lit a chandelier that hung above us. It brightened things up nicely.*

Goethe's interest in Pietism led to skeptical self-examination. It was the practice of the Pietists to scrutinize the subtle impulses in the soul's relation to God. They developed their own terminology, which the young Goethe adopted and employed with such assurance that he was soon using it as a flexible tool for expressing the stirrings of his soul, even without pious intention. For example, he speaks of *Offenherzigkeit—openheartedness—*not only in the Pietistic sense of the soul's openness to God but also for cordial openness between people. And in his letters to Langer, he describes romantic *matters of the heart—* the aftereffects of his separation from Kätchen—in a play on the Pietistic love for the Sacred Heart. He feels as *cold and calm* as if he had completely forgotten her; his soul is *still, without desire*. This was how the Pietists usually described the soul's obduracy toward Jesus, but Goethe uses these words to describe the extinguishing of his love for Kätchen. Goethe calls the confessions in his letters to his friend *the history of my heart*. In this discourse on love he sometimes means only Kätchen, sometimes Jesus as well. He has lost Kätchen but perhaps gained Jesus. Word of success comes in early 1769: *You see, dear Langer . . . the Savior has caught me at last. I ran too far and too fast for him, but he's caught me by the hair.* He's still unsure, however. In the same paragraph he sighs, *But worries! worries! Always weakness in faith.*

A genuine experience of conversion in the Pietistic sense probably did not occur. But how lovely it would be to have such an experience. He was able to portray it without actually having it. He empathizes with and can tune his language to the Sacred Heart tone. Then there is no need to speak of Jesus himself, only of his own heart. All his attention was focused on it or, as he would soon write in *The Sorrows of Young Werther, And I hold my little heart like a sick child, granting it its own way in everything.*

In Goethe's experiments with piety, Langer was his long-distance spiritual guide. Susanna von Klettenberg, a friend and relative of his mother's, was his local mentor. She was in her midforties and lived in her family's stately town house, unmarried, looked after by servants, and courted by the Herrnhuters. She accepted their attentions but still preferred a pious life according to her own taste. She had once been engaged to the municipal assessor Ohlenschlager, but they had broken off the engagement because she was too spiritual and he too worldly. She took Jesus as her inner bridegroom, enveloped him in a cult of love, and maintained only sisterly—or, in the case of the young Goethe, maternal—relations with the men close to her. He writes in *Poetry and Truth* that *her favorite—indeed perhaps her only—topic of conversation was the moral lessons a person can draw from self-observation; they were then joined by her religious sentiments, which in a very charming, even inspired way she considered to be both natural and supernatural.*

In a section entitled "Confessions of a Beautiful Soul" in book 6 of his novel *Wilhelm Meister's Apprenticeship*, Goethe would draw a portrait of this woman, making use of her notebooks and letters and giving the whole thing the form of an autobiographical report. From this text, we can sense the quality of the piety that the young Goethe found so attractive.

Susanna von Klettenberg had not sought and found her Savior out of a bad conscience, nor did theological subtleties play a role. She was quite interested in natural science and theoretical speculation, but did not find it necessary to seek a rationale for God. For her, God was simply self-evident, a feeling of happiness, a revelation of the heart. Jesus lived within her as an inner *friend* to whom she was attached by an erotically tinged love. *I can hardly recall a commandment*, we read in the "Confessions of a Beautiful Soul." *Nothing appears to me in the form of a law. It is an instinct that directs and always leads me aright; I follow my sentiments in freedom and know as little of restriction as of repentance.*

In Susanna von Klettenberg, Goethe found an attractive piety without sanctimony, living freely by its own resources, with no oppressive dualism between feeling and moral reason, direct experience and dogmatic principle. She did not believe in an external divine reality. Instead, she believed in her own self, which became better in union with Jesus—raised to a higher level and thereby gaining spontaneity, lust for life, and expressive capability. Her soul is beautiful because it is not compelled by anything and also has no need to compel itself. In her, morality is lovely.

What Nietzsche would later call "cross, death, and grave" was central for the Herrnhuters, but it played only a minor role for her. That is why she calls herself *a Herrnhuter sister in my own way.* She certainly believed in Christ's sacrificial death on the cross, but she asks, *What is belief, anyway?* She answers, *To consider the narrative of an event true—how does that help me? I must be able to take possession of its effects, its consequences.* She speaks of the *pull* by which her soul *is led to a distant beloved.* She has a distinctly physical feeling of liberation, and that becomes a truth that only later can be cast as articles of faith. If one has felt nothing, however, then one should not argue about the truth of sentences, even if they are the sacred sentences of the Gospels. In such dogmatic quarrels, even believers can lapse into *injustice* and, *in order to defend an outward form, almost destroy its inner essence.*

Susanna von Klettenberg speaks almost too frequently of the *serenity* with which, despite illness, she leads her life and lives her faith. In *Wilhelm Meister's Apprenticeship*, it is Wilhelm who sees this serenity, coupled with the *purity* of her existence. *What shone out from these writings most was what I would call the purity of existence, not just her own, but of everything that surrounded her. The independence of her nature and the impossibility that she would take up anything not in harmony with her noble, loving spirit.*

In retrospect, Goethe wonders what Susanna von Klettenberg, for her part, found so attractive about him. *She took pleasure in what nature had given me as well as in much that I had acquired.* His restlessness, impatience, his striving and searching, did not repel her, for she interpreted them as expressions of the fact that he still lacked a *reconciled God.* He simply hadn't found Him yet. What was important for her was that one remain true to oneself. She definitely did not want anyone to do anything simply for her sake. What she sensed and appreciated about the young Goethe was his spirited willfulness. She had no desire to convert him. Faith should come from within. If he occasionally behaved *like a heathen* toward her, she preferred that to the way he was *earlier, when I made use of Christian terminology but never really succeeded at it.*

Goethe lacked any consciousness of sinfulness or a need for contrition, and that kept him at a distance—not from Susanna von Klettenberg but from the Herrnhuters. He declared his allegiance to *Pelagianism*, which in the history of Christian dogma represents a benevolent assessment of human nature. This was in contradistinction to the idea of regarding people as essentially corrupt and sinful. The former was more to Goethe's taste; for him, both external and internal nature in its *grandeur* is a delight, not a burden. He once said to Susanna von Klettenberg that he didn't know what he needed to ask God's forgiveness for. He was not conscious of having intentionally incurred any guilt and did not feel responsible for anything that was not volitional.

Goethe was able to take quite a few liberties with her, and she still took him under her wing. She understood something of his illness, for she herself had suffered from tubercular pulmonary hemorrhage. She owed her temporary recovery to the skill of Doctor Johann Friedrich Metz, a strictly observant Herrnhuter, an *inexplicable man with a sly glance, amiable conversation, and for the rest, abstruse.* There was something mysterious about him, and he was said to possess almost magical powers. He was a pious man who experimented in the borderland between natural science and magic.

In early 1769, when Goethe was suffering from a worrisome and rapidly growing scrofulous swelling on his neck, Metz attended him at night with his miraculous medicine, a jar containing a dry, crystallized salt that tasted alkaline and was instantly effective. The swelling subsided, and Goethe became engrossed in *mystical chemical-alchemical books* that Metz recommended to him—Welling, Paracelsus, Basilius Valentinus, Athanasius Kircher, Helmont, and Starkey. Not only did they introduce him to the almost forgotten universe of apocryphal wisdom and Neoplatonic and Kabbalistic lore, but they contained chemical formulas and alchemical recipes. Metz suggested that it was possible, through study, for his patient to learn how to prepare the healing *treasure* himself. These sources would remain important to Goethe his entire life; in them he found *nature presented in a beautiful conjunction, even if perhaps in a fanciful way.* It appealed to his theoretical curiosity beyond the immediate healing of his illness. The marvelous dream of making gold also attracted him. All of it would soon flow into the first drafts of *Faust.*

While he had edifying conversations with Susanna von Klettenberg, Metz helped him set up a small laboratory in his sickroom for the production of marvelous and curious essences. The pious Klettenberg contributed an assay kiln, flasks and retorts, and a small supply of supposedly efficacious minerals. Things went along *quite cheerfully, since we . . . took more delight in these mysteries than their revelation could have provided.*

As was to be expected, the experiments themselves failed. They heated up white gravel from the Main River, hoping that the liquefied stones mixed with certain salts would become the sought-after rare substance—that the transition from mineral to organic form would be effected. But gravel dust was all that was precipitated, and nothing *productive* appeared *from which one could hope to see this virginal earth transition into the maternal condition.* What they had hoped to produce was what later would be called "Earth Spirit" in *Faust.*

Despite these disappointments, however, the sick young man was quite pleased with his forays into religion and chemistry and alchemy. New worlds had opened up to him. He discovered piety in a beautiful soul and natural history tinged with mysticism in his experiments.

Goethe would remain loyal to the study of natural history, but piety in the form of acceptance of Christian dogma went no further than his experiments of 1769.

CHAPTER 4

Piety and Kätchen Recede. Strasbourg. Exhilaration.
The Spirit of the Place. Strasbourg Cathedral as a Test of
Courage. "On German Architecture."
Salzmann. Lersé. The Influential Encounter with Herder.
New Values: Life, Creative Power, Individuality, Expression.
Playing Cards with Herder.

. . . .

I N September 1769, Goethe attended a synod of Herrn-huter congregations in Marienborn, near Frankfurt. The meeting was a disappointment, and he was repelled by the sectarian spirit of the "quiet in the land," as the Herrnhuters called themselves, borrowing a phrase from Psalm 35. Even a year later, he could still write to Susanna von Klettenberg of his annoyance that anyone could confuse *his own whimsies and God's purpose.* He realized that he didn't belong and didn't want to belong. He confessed to his spiritual mentor that these pious folk were *so sincerely boring* that his own *vivacity couldn't put up with it.* Moreover, as has already been said, he lacked any consciousness of sinfulness. And so he once again directed the fervor of his feelings toward worldly things. The theme of emulating Christ disappears even from his letters to the pious Langer.

But Kätchen Schönkopf also began to fade from Goethe's thoughts. In a letter of late 1769, he tells her he is writing only because he dreamed of her the night before. He asks her not to send him an answer and says he has only faint memories of her, *with as little feeling as if I were recalling a stranger.* That his memories were fading can probably be partly attributed to the fact that Kätchen had become engaged. Her fiancé was a law student, Christian Karl Kanne, to whom Goethe himself had introduced the Schönkopfs. Goethe also intimates in his letter that he will soon be moving.

A month later, the decision to move to Strasbourg was definite. It was his father's wish; he had studied there himself. Not only will he go to Strasbourg, he tells Kätchen, to whom he had intended not to write anymore, but from there, he says, he will continue on to the wider world—to Paris. And if he should find a woman to marry, he would set up house at his parents' residence: *I'll get 10 rooms, all well and beautifully furnished in the Frankfurt style . . . I'll have a house; I'll have money. My heart, what more could you want? A wife!*

Exhilarated and with his health on the mend, Goethe arrived in Strasbourg in early April of 1770 and took rooms, first in the inn Zum Geist and then on the Old Fish Market square. Councilor Johann Friedrich Moritz, a Herrnhuter intimate of his mother's, had given him a manual of devotion as a going-away present, and Goethe opened it on the day of his arrival. He found Bible verses that spoke so strongly to him that he immediately told his mother about them. Thirty years later she could still recall them: "Enlarge the place of thy tent, and let them stretch forth the curtains of thine habitations: spare not, lengthen thy cords, and strengthen thy stakes; For thou shalt break forth on the right hand and on the left."*

Goethe interpreted these words as confirmation of his premonition of power and success. He too would break forth and overflow. He felt expansive, whereas in Leipzig he had been fairly intimidated at first. To Johann Christian Limprecht, a friend from his Leipzig days who was a student of theology, poor as a church mouse, and half blind from all his reading, Goethe sent a louis d'or with a note saying that at present he had *an abundance of cheerfulness* and would like to give some away.

His letters written during this period contain long sentences that anticipate the style of *Werther* and attempt to capture his surroundings. In a letter to Katharina Fabricius, a friend of his sister's, he describes his impressions during a hike in the countryside outside Strasbourg: *As I looked out over the green valley on my right and the river flowed so grayish and quiet in the twilight, and on my left the heavy darkness of the beech trees on the mountain hung over me, as the bright little birds moved quietly and mysteriously*

* Isaiah 54:2–3.

through the bushes around the dark rocks, my heart grew still. In *Werther*, he would write, *When the dear valley steams around me* . . . . *When I feel the scurry of the little world among the blades of grass . . . nearer to my heart . . . then when twilight falls on my eyes and the world around me and the sky rest completely in my soul. . . .*

Unlike Werther, the letter writer is, at present, not yet in love. His heart is *quiet*, he writes, because it is still free: *What happiness it is to have a light, free heart!* When one falls in love, however, one is shackled with *chains of flowers*, and, for fear of breaking them, one dare not move. He compares love to a rocking horse, *always moving, always working, but never budging from the spot.* Yet he wants to make progress—for now, in the study of law.

He had left Leipzig without a degree and intended to make up for that in Strasbourg. He would take his exams and graduate. He attended bar reviews that drilled topics for the exam. He did not find them difficult, especially since he had already learned much of the material from his father when he was still a boy. He wrote to Langer, *What am I studying? Above all else, the distinctions and subtleties by which they have made right and wrong fairly similar. That is, I'm studying to be a doctor of canon and civil law.*

On September 27, 1770, Goethe passed the qualifying examination, the first academic test he had successfully completed. He was now a candidate for the degree and absolved from attending lectures. The next step was the composition of a dissertation. Again, he gave himself plenty of time. There were more important things he wanted to do and things of more significance that now rained in upon him.

He was not particularly impressed with the town itself at first. Strasbourg was about the size of Frankfurt—with comparably ancient, winding streets—and completely different from the recently built, elegant neighborhoods of Leipzig. The city had belonged to France for almost a century. Goethe became aware of that immediately upon arrival, when he witnessed Marie Antoinette and her entourage being received into the city, on her way to Paris as the fiancée of the French king. There was a popular celebration. On the meadows beside the Rhine, tents had been pitched that contained exhibits, including a copy of Raphael's *School of Athens* from the Sistine Chapel. *There's nothing one can say about it*, he writes to Langer, *but I know this much: that I will reckon a new epoch in my perception from the moment I saw it for the first time.*

There is a profundity of art in such a work. The festive mood, the hubbub, the surging crowds in the streets and on the squares, the flags and colorful banners in the windows—it all reminded Goethe of the imperial coronation he had witnessed in Frankfurt a few years earlier, but here it was no sentimental reminiscence of former glory but a brilliant self-representation of the French monarchy, a modern political power. His pleasure was not unalloyed, however. He felt *snatched away and whirled around by delight and nonsense* and struggled to retain his sense of self. *Only now do I begin to think that I too exist.* The relation to power was the same as to love: you were enchanted and lost your head and no longer knew who you were: *When we are touched, our pride is ineffectual. That's what our princes and our girls know, and do with us what they will.*

The officers and troops stationed here were French, as were the higher royal officials. The great majority of the population, however, spoke German, although their dialect was difficult for him to understand. It was "the most miserable German one can hear, in the coarsest, most disgusting, hideous pronunciation," according to Friedrich Christian Laukhard, a writer who sojourned in Strasbourg a few years after Goethe. But the latter found the dialect pleasant and later, in the mouth of Friederike Brion, even *supremely lovely.* The city swarmed with transient visitors. Everyone traveling from southern or central Germany to Paris made a stop here, on the border between two cultures to get a taste of either French or northern German manners. Eager to get to Paris, Goethe considered Strasbourg a way station. But it wasn't long before he came to appreciate the city and its relaxed and merry way of life. Since there was dancing everywhere—on the squares, at the inns, and in the gardens of restaurants outside the town—he took dancing lessons. He also became fond of horseback riding. He had the money to rent a horse, and on it he roamed the surroundings. Later, the animal would carry him to his beloved.

The first thing he visited was the cathedral, already regarded in those days as an attraction to be seen. But in the beginning, it was only the steeple that interested him—as a challenge. He climbed the 330 steps to reach the top and triumph over his acrophobia, just as he stood near the drums during evening tattoo to overcome his sensitivity to noise. *All by myself I climbed to the very top of the cathedral steeple and sat in the so-called Neck (beneath the Knob or Crown, as they call it) for probably a quarter of an hour, until I dared step back out into the open air, where you stand on a platform hardly a cubit square, and with no particularly good handholds, and have before you the endless countryside, while things in the immediate vicinity and the decorations hide the church and everything on which and above which you stand. It's exactly as if one saw oneself lifted into the air by a Montgolfier balloon. I often repeated this fear and torture until I became indifferent to it.*

Physical training, tests of courage, conquering his fears—these things would play a role again later during hikes in the Alps and while Goethe clambered over the ruins of Rome, where he had to walk across planks without railings to get a closer look at some of the artwork. Thus even before he realized the artistic significance of the Strasbourg cathedral, it was an athletic challenge that he also mentions in "On German Architecture," his essay on Erwin von Steinbach, the legendary architect of the great church. Goethe wrote it shortly after his residency in Strasbourg, and Johann Gottfried Herder made the text famous when he included it in his own monograph *On German Character and Art.*

Kant had declared that in the presence of the sublime, man becomes aware of his insignificance and learns humility. But only a small shift is necessary to reveal that the individual himself is also great—for example, when one realizes that human creativity was necessary to construct such greatness. The young Goethe—and with him the entire era—used the term *genius* to refer to human greatness as a creative force. In genius, which included a measure of defiance and also of presumptuousness, humanity reached its true height. *It was given to few to beget the idea of Babel in their soul* is how Goethe puts it in his essay on the Strasbourg cathedral and its architect. The cathedral is just such an *idea of Babel,* realized in stone, whose challenge you really meet only if you climb it. Then you no longer belong among the *ants crawling around it,* or to the *weakling aesthetes.* They *will always get dizzy from your colossus.* A genius must have a head for heights, as must anyone who approaches those who possess genius.

For the rest, Goethe was determined to enjoy the *free, convivial, animated way of life* offered by Strasbourg. He had a new circle of friends, his fellow boarders at Mlle Lauth's near the Fish Market. As in the Schönkopfs' house in Leipzig, both students and more mature gentlemen, mostly bachelors, gathered there. They would prolong their lunch into the afternoon and discuss matters academic and amorous and, often, political. It struck the young Goethe as the French way of life, but he had as little taste for political discussion as he did for the dry Alsatian wine that flowed like a river here. The authority figure in this circle was the forty-eight-year-old Johann Daniel Salzmann, head clerk in the office of the surrogate's court and a journalist of Enlightenment inclinations. He was worldly wise, amiable, and well-connected to the intellectual life of Strasbourg. Through him, Goethe was able to establish contacts, and the two men carried on intense discussions of philosophy and religion. Goethe has Salzmann in mind when he paints for Susanna von Klettenberg the portrait of a levelheaded antitype to the Pietists: *a man of much good sense and extensive experience who has always viewed the world with sangfroid and believes he has discovered that we have been put upon this earth especially to be useful to it, and that we can make ourselves capable of that, to which end religion is of some help.*

Like Behrisch and Langer in Leipzig, Salzmann was Goethe's mentor in Strasbourg. Goethe tells Salzmann that he considers himself a person of genius, but one in need of judicious direction from an older friend. He calls himself a *weather vane.* He will write to Salzmann from Sesenheim* about his love for Friederike Brion, and those letters are the few pieces of direct evidence we have of the affair. After his time in Strasbourg, Goethe maintained contact with Salzmann for a while. In the end, it was the older man who allowed the connection to peter out. His younger friend's pursuit of genius was probably too far removed from the reality of surrogate's court, where Salzmann spent his days protecting widows and orphans. *Write to me soon and don't consider it a sin to write more often,* Goethe urges in his last letter to Salzmann.

Goethe made another friend at Mlle Lauth's table, a theology student his age named Franz Lersé. He would later borrow his name for the *doughty Lerse* in *Götz von Berlichingen.* In the play, Lerse is the steadfast friend, the paragon of loyalty and upright sentiments, and that is how the real Lersé is described in *Poetry and Truth.* (He wrote and pronounced his name with the accent, which makes it sound less than *doughty.*) In Goethe's autobiography, Lersé appears as someone

---

* Goethe's spelling of the Alsatian village Sessenheim has become so entrenched in the history of German literature that I have preserved it here.—Trans.

who *always knew how to remind us in his dry, humorous way what we owed to ourselves and others and how we should behave in order to live in peace with our fellow man as long as possible.* Goethe needed to be reminded, since *a certain irritability remained* from the illness he had survived. Lersé helped him regain his *balance.* A talented fencer, Lersé was good at refereeing physical and mental contests. He remained neutral and intervened only if someone behaved unfairly. Artful and quick-witted, he was feared as a debater and liked to experiment and play with theses and arguments. Although not a law student, he declared himself willing to play the role of opponent when Goethe was preparing to defend his dissertation, and Lersé was able to argue his friend into a corner.

An encounter with especially far-reaching consequences was with Johann Gottfried Herder. Only five years older than Goethe, Herder was already a famous man and liked to parade his superiority by playing the grand seigneur. Like his other friends, the young Goethe at first did not challenge Herder's authority. He called his acquaintance (he avoids the word "friendship") with Herder *the most significant event* of his time in Strasbourg. In book 10 of *Poetry and Truth* he especially recalls their first meeting, when at the entrance to the Zum Geist inn he caught sight of a man about to climb the stairs. He vividly remembers the way the fellow had casually stuffed the long tails of his black silk coat into his pants pocket. He was so elegantly dressed that one might have mistaken him for an aristocratic abbé. Herder was friendly, but Goethe soon found himself cast in the role of a pupil being reprimanded, a role he could not shake during the months he spent in Strasbourg. It was a new experience for him; up to then, the older and more mature people he had attached himself to had *gently sought to mold* him, and perhaps he had even been *spoiled* by their *indulgence.* Things were different with Herder, however. From him *one could never expect approval, no matter how one behaved.* Goethe put up with it because Herder filled his head with new ideas.

The older man had come to Strasbourg to undergo a painful operation on his lacrimal sacs by the famous surgeon Johann Friedrich Lobstein. The bottom of the sac had to be cut open and a hole bored into the bone behind it. A horse hair would then be inserted into the hole to keep it from growing closed so that a new tear duct could form. Goethe forced himself to attend this horrific operation and was able *to be of service and help to such a worthy man in several ways.* Herder, who bore the torture with fortitude, was forgiven his often moody and critical episodes.

Famous and frequently attacked for his writings on literary history, philosophy, and theology, Herder had given up his position as cathedral preacher in Riga in 1769 and had gone to sea aboard a merchant ship to escape the aggravations of his office and of the literary scene. While storms raged around the ship, he noted down that he had been living with "crippled senses" and that the time had finally come for a great exercise in loosening things up. Pregnant with projects and plans, Herder disembarked in France and continued on to Paris, where he met the skeptic Diderot. He was treated with respect in the salons, but people found his ideas exaggerated and unclear. Back in Germany, he was offered a position as tutor and travel companion for the depressive son of the prince-bishop of Lübeck on a tour through Europe. Although far below the level of his ambition, the assignment was well paid, and so he accepted it with some misgiving. It was in this state of mind, dissatisfied and bursting with ideas, that he encountered the young Goethe.

Herder was certainly susceptible to the beguiling charms of the younger man's personality—Goethe's candor, eagerness to learn, self-confidence, unself-consciousness, inventiveness, talent for improvisation, and playful and carefree nature. And yet, a great reservation remained. Herder wrote to his fiancée, Karoline Flachsland, in Darmstadt, "Goethe is really a good person, but extremely light—much too light and sparrow-like."

As Goethe's first major works, especially *Götz* and *Werther,* began to appear one after the other, Herder usually had a critical and disparaging reaction ready for Goethe, or was at best patronizing. To others, however, he expressed respect and even admiration. Again and again, Goethe surprised Herder with his published works, about which he would remain mum while writing them. He explains why in *Poetry and Truth.* Whenever he was attracted to certain themes and objects, he did not want to be influenced by Herder's impulse to criticize, *for no inclination . . . is so strong that it could maintain itself in the long run against the negative comments of outstanding men whom one trusts.* Goethe here refers to *Götz* and especially to *Faust,* a story that by the end of his time in Strasbourg was already *ringing and humming in multiple tones* in his head.

While Herder lay in bed recovering from his operation, Goethe visited him twice every day, in the morning and in the evening. If Herder was in a state of inner discord—attracted by Goethe's brash genius yet also critical—it was no different with Goethe. On the one hand he felt *great affection and veneration* for Herder, but on the other also *discontent* with the patronizing and critical way he treated him. Nevertheless, he spent entire days with him and gradually got used to his *chiding and reproving* as he *came to appreciate more each day the breadth of his knowledge and depth of his insights.*

What were those insights? They were what gave birth to a new way of thinking in the last third of the eighteenth century.

The Enlightenment had developed its image of man from the starting point of human reason, as if it were the strongest, most decisive faculty. As a result, society and morality were intellectualized and viewed with an eye to their utility. Like a German Rousseau, Herder rebelled against this line of thought. He aimed to loosen sclerotic systems, dismantle their conceptual structures, and take hold of life, understood as the unity of intellect and nature, reason and feeling, rational norm and creative freedom. Reason, Herder once wrote, is always a "later reason." It operates with concepts of causality and is thus incapable of grasping the creative process, which does not proceed causally. Herder is searching for a language that clings to the mysterious emotion and ambiguity of life, a language that often makes use of metaphors instead of concepts, seeks empathy rather than structure. Much remains vague, suggestive, intuitive. The floating, rambling nature of Herder's thought and language offended rigorously conceptual contemporary thinkers like Kant. But not Goethe. And ultimately, Herder's philosophy of life inspired the cult of genius in the Sturm und Drang movement.

In the idea of the genius, a newly awakened and self-confident generation found a way to challenge the hierarchical, rigid, circumscribed world of bourgeois and courtly decorum. *O my friends!* writes Werther, *why does the river of genius so seldom break forth, the flood tide so seldom rush in.* Petit bourgeois obsequiousness, breadwinning, the entire machinery of society in which one feels like a tiny cog or screw, and added to that, a dry rationalism with no respect for secrets—the younger generation was disgusted by it all. They were devoted to intellectual freedom and, above all, the spirit of beauty, but were forced to face mundane daily life. Goethe declared that Shakespeare, to whose work Herder had introduced him, had overcome artistic paralysis by daring to chase *all noble souls* from the *Elysium of so-called good taste*, where *in tedious twilight* they *drift and yawn through a shadow life*.

In the German Sturm und Drang, only the artist was classified as a genius, whereas in England and France, politicians, scientists, and men of fashion could also count as geniuses. Herder's idea of the artist as the epitome of genius has had a long-lasting effect, right down to the present.

When irrational creative power was ascendant, it followed that art need not imitate a prescribed, universally valid reality. Art became an expression of individuality. From that point on, art would not just imitate life but be itself the expression of an individual life. Instead of mimesis, *poiesis* now reigned, and that involved a normative shift. It was no longer a question of conforming to prescribed, eternally valid patterns and conventions. Originality was what was wanted now. It was a point of pride to be an original genius, or at least be regarded as one.

And so an enormous artistic self-confidence took hold, a confidence that found bold expression in Goethe's poem "Prometheus": *I sit here, forming men / In my own image.* An exaggerated individualism, a powerful sense of self, is at work here. And yet Herder had also turned his philosophy of life toward the collective. The single person, shaping himself into an individual, is and remains the center of significance. But the life the individual feels is also alive in a community, which Herder imagines as a sort of larger individual. For Herder, life is ordered in concentric circles, from the family to the clan, the people, the nation, to all of humankind. He speaks of the peoples of the earth as the "folk spirits" that thrive in peaceful proximity like various plants in the garden of humanity, contributing to the richness of human diversity. The point of unity of a so-called folk spirit lies not in its intellect but deeper, in its emotions. What applies to an individual also applies to the culture of an entire people: its cultural expression is an end in itself, the awakening to a higher, enhanced life. There is no reason, Herder declares, to look down on a nation's folk poetry. Original geniuses should learn from the folk, listen to songs and folktales. And so they listened, collected, and sometimes put into circulation ancient folklore that wasn't actually genuine. The epic poetry of "Ossian," which had great currency among the Sturm und Drang writers, was attributed to an ancient Scottish bard but was actually written by their contemporary James Macpherson. Herder himself published Goethe's poem "Little Heath Rose" in one of his collections of folk songs. Goethe had no objection, for he had developed a taste for such things and collected folk songs in Alsace that he passed on to Herder.

Herder gave Goethe a wealth of ideas and suggestions. In retrospect, however, Goethe emphasizes that in many cases the groundwork had already been laid, the ideas were already fermenting within him. In any event, he now was in a *happy position . . . to complete everything I had thought, learned, acquired, and attach it to something more lofty.* Thus Goethe describes the process by which his intuitions and obsessions come into their own in the larger intellectual sphere. The time was ripe for what he desired and what he was capable of doing.

His relationship to Herder would later be weighed down by heavy conflicts and end with a complete rift shortly before Herder's death. Goethe's look back on this friend is thus not completely sunny, and he admits that sometimes the only way he could put up with Herder was to restrict contact to playing cards with him.

CHAPTER 5

Jung-Stilling. The Aperçu, or Sudden Inspiration.

The Psychology of Awakening and Creativity.

Friederike and the Romance Novel in Sesenheim.

Not On to Paris.

The Shakespeare Speech. The Diminished Doctorate.

Leaving Strasbourg.

. . . .

A LTHOUGH A THEOLOGIAN BY TRAINING, HERDER OPENED up a world to the young Goethe in which religion proper played almost no role. For Herder, man was a being animated by spirit, a spirit he considered to be both man's inner nature and the living principle of all nature. This was more congenial to Goethe than the Pietists' conception of man as the child of God or the Herrnhuters' devotion to Jesus. Such piety no longer spoke to him, but he continued to be impressed by men who were guided by powerful religious experience: converts with no burning need to convert others to confirm their belief, pious men with no missionary zeal or dogmatic assertiveness. He admired inspired individualism in matters of belief and found sympathy with men *who sought their salvation on their own.*

Just such a man turned up in the Strasbourg circle in the summer of 1770. Nine years older than Goethe, Johann Heinrich Jung was a former tailor and schoolteacher who had come to Strasbourg to study medicine, with the goal of perfecting his skill at removing cataracts, a procedure he had already been practicing. Goethe felt immediately drawn to this gentle yet energetic man. He had asked him to relate his life story and found it so riveting that he encouraged Jung to write it down. The resulting autobiography appeared in several volumes between 1777 and 1817; the author added "Stilling" to his name to suggest that, though he kept his distance from Pietistic and Herrnhuter circles, he counted himself among the "quiet in the land" (*die Stillen im Lande*). An autodidact who had worked his way up from the humblest of circumstances (his father was a charcoal burner, village schoolmaster, and tailor in Westphalia), Jung-Stilling lacked money or long-term patrons, but was inwardly buttressed by an almost childlike trust in God. He reminded Goethe of his mentor Susanna von Klettenberg, although that well-to-do aristocrat was not as dependent on God's help. Jung-Stilling's trust in God helped him in ways that were sometimes so miraculous Goethe was still impressed when writing about him decades later: *The elemental part of his energy was an indestructible belief in God and the unmediated help that flowed from Him, which was evidently confirmed by uninterrupted provision against and unfailing rescue from all want and every evil.*

For Goethe, Jung-Stilling demonstrated that trust in God could mobilize one's own powers. In that sense, trust in God represented a kind of higher trust in oneself, one that involved not only the empirical self but also an elevated, enhanced self that felt secure in God. Jung-Stilling was an active, hands-on person but still resembled a *sleepwalker*, as Goethe writes, *whom one must not call out to*, lest he plunge down from the heights of belief that give his life security.

For his part, Jung-Stilling depicts how Goethe made certain that the company at table would not make fun of him and his piety, although Goethe belonged to the "savages" and insouciantly lived out his "free existence." Jung-Stilling similarly kept himself in check, avoided becoming an annoyance, and was left in peace "except that Goethe occasionally would roll his eyes toward me." He exercised undisputed "reign over the table without seeking it."

What was it about Jung-Stilling that so fascinated Goethe? It was not his confidence that everything in his life, both good and bad, was portioned out by God. Such *divine pedagogy* seemed *presumptuous* to Goethe, who by this time no longer believed in a God who took a personal interest in directing and overseeing one's life. Such a conviction, he writes, was *neither pleasant nor beneficial* for him. It must have been something else that attracted him. He found in Jung-Stilling an intellectual experience, elevated to the realm of religion, that he calls an aperçu; a weighty concept in Goethe's late philosophy, he defines it, in *Poetry and Truth*, in connection with Jung-Stilling's character: *to become aware of a great axiom, which is always the operation of an intellect imbued with genius.* He continues, *Such an aperçu gives its discoverer the greatest joy because it prefigures the eternal in an original way. It needs no period of time to be convincing, but springs complete and perfect from the moment.*

When a flash of insight, an idea, or a sudden intuition illuminates some relation until then obscure and puzzling, making it instantly clear and evident, that is what Goethe calls an aperçu. At first he uses it primarily for insights about the natural world. *In science, everything depends on what we call an aperçu, becoming aware of what actually underlies appearances,* he writes in the *History of the Theory of Color.*

To Goethe, there are three major aspects of the aperçu as an extraordinary perceptual event.

Its true object is not some random or inconsequential phenomenon but one that grants insight into an entire complex, into *the eternal.* Though the object may be individual and concrete, its symbolic transparency also allows a glimpse of the *eternal harmony of existence.* Goethe, for example, will interpret the discovery of the intermaxillary bone in humans (which he also describes as a sudden insight) as a glimpse into the total interconnectedness of nature, since this bone, which had been discovered in animals but not yet in man, served as proof of a continuous transition between man and animal, proof that nature makes no sudden leaps. Thus the intermaxillary bone becomes the object of an aperçu: a totality suddenly revealed in a single thing.

Vis-à-vis the subject, the aperçu leaves the person feeling transformed, as if liberated from his isolation and elevated into an awareness of a totality. It is a perception that allows *a presentiment of his similarity to God.* He has been touched by a *revelation,* not of a transcendent God, as in the Christian religion, but rather owing its existence to the inspired perception of nature. Its effect is nonetheless similar to the way one can be reoriented and transformed by a relationship to God.

The third aspect relates to the sudden, instantaneous nature of the entire process. All at once one sees things anew, looks at the world with new eyes and experiences a turning point in one's life. From then on, everything is transformed. Life has been interrupted and there is a dramatic sense of before and after. While an aperçu is conventionally understood as nothing more than a trenchant turn of phrase, for Goethe it implies an existential shift in the wake of an inspiration.

Goethe calls an aperçu with these three aspects—experience of a totality, transformation of the subject, and suddenness—an *operation of cognitive genius.*

If Goethe was fascinated by Jung-Stilling—though he did not share his childlike relationship to God, his *divine pedagogy*—it was because he sensed the *operation of cognitive genius* in this pious man. Jung-Stilling had experienced a wholeness—namely, the God of the Bible: his inner man had been completely transformed. And it all happened suddenly, as in an aperçu.

The young Goethe, who, as we have seen, senses something of genius in himself and soon will live through his own epoch of the cult of genius, sees in Jung-Stilling a type of religious genius. Jung-Stilling also draws life from an aperçu, which, however, has been transported from the cognitive to the religious realm. What the pious call awakening, conversion, or rebirth fascinates Goethe not because he himself is still pious but because it helps him understand the psychology of genius, to grasp what it is that also drives him, this sudden inspiration that shines a whole new light on life and transforms the inner man.

Jung-Stilling lived among his friends and acquaintances in Strasbourg as such a person, one who has experienced a transformational aperçu. He was open and talkative whenever he encountered sympathy and understanding, but withdrawn when unappreciated. If others teased him, Goethe would leap to his defense. Goethe visited him, writes Jung-Stilling (who tells his life story in the third person), "grew fond of him, became his brother and friend, and under all circumstances endeavored to show his affection to Stilling." Turning to those who would not have expected Goethe to have such a friend, Jung-Stilling adds, "It is a shame that so few are acquainted with the heart of this excellent man!"

Goethe was generally helpful to his friend in practical matters, and when Jung-Stilling left Strasbourg suddenly in the summer of 1770 to hurry to his deathly ill fiancée in Westphalia, Goethe lent him money. When he returned, his first thought was to visit Goethe, who greeted him cordially and renewed the introduction to his circle of friends. Since the summer of 1771, in addition to Lersé and Salzmann, it now also included Jakob Michael Reinhold Lenz. Jung-Stilling's autobiography goes on to say that "Stilling's enthusiasm for religion did not keep him from also feeling cordial affection for men [such as Goethe] who were more freethinking than he, as long as they were not scoffers."

Johann Konrad Engelbach and Friedrich Leopold Weyland too belonged to the company around Mlle Lauth's table, and Goethe went on horseback rides with them into the surrounding countryside. Engelbach, a few years older than Goethe, had also come to Strasbourg to finish his uncompleted bar examination as quickly as possible. Unlike Goethe, he had done so in only five weeks, by June 1770, and turned over his lecture notes to his fellow student to use in preparation for the exam. Goethe and Weyland escorted Engelbach on his journey home to Saarbrücken, a trip that led Goethe to Sesenheim, where his love affair with the pastor's daughter Friederike Brion would begin. Weyland was a distant relative of the Brion family and introduced Goethe to them. He was a medical student and later had a practice in Frankfurt. He never forgave Goethe for his behavior to Friederike and avoided any further contact with him.

Goethe narrates the Sesenheim idyll in *Poetry and Truth* as a self-contained novella, with the hint that it wasn't so idyllic after all, because of its dissonant ending. The lover leaves his beloved, and the farewell was perhaps different from that in the poem from the spring of 1771: *You left, and I stood looking down, / And watched you go with tear-blurred eye.* Or the other way around, as in a later version: *I left, and you stood looking down / And watched me go with tear-blurred eye.* About the end of the idyll, *Poetry and Truth* notes laconically, *Those were painful days whose recollection did not remain with me.*

It is not necessary to retell in detail the pretty story Goethe relates in *Poetry and Truth*, but a few aspects of it are noteworthy. Goethe and Weyland arrived in Sesenheim on a beautiful summer day, the former pretending to be a poor student of theology. He loved such masquerades, traveling incognito, playing hide-and-seek, and continued to do so later, during his trips to the Harz Mountains and Italy.

At the Brion home he even appeared in two different disguises. At first, he was a poor theology student. When he realized he was falling for Friederike after their first walk together in the moonlight, he fled the house the next morning and in the neighboring village disguised himself as a village lad named Georg, which caused even more confusion. The romantic affair with Friederike was soon in full swing: games of forfeits, cheerful socializing, walks, languid summer days, and starry nights all played a part. Her parents noticed something was afoot and were willing to let the couple *continue along for a while in such an indeterminate state.* Pastor Brion discussed his plans for the renovation of the parsonage with his guest. It reminded Goethe of his own father's passion for remodeling. The days passed. On Friederike's first appearance: *At that moment she really appeared at the door; and truly the dearest star rose into this rural heaven.* The lover on Friederike: *Her nature, her form never appeared as lovely as when she was walking along a raised footpath; the grace of her demeanor seemed to compete with the flowers of the field and the irrepressible cheerfulness of her face with the blue of the sky.* There is a presentiment of the end: *Such a youthful inclination, conceived by chance, can be compared to a cannonball fired at night. It climbs in a gentle, shining line, mixes with the stars, even seems to pause among them a moment, whereupon, however, it describes the same trajectory, only reversed, downward, at last bringing ruin where its path ends.*

Why this ending? Why doesn't the lover keep the promise he appears to have made, if not explicitly, then certainly by his behavior? *The reasons a young woman pulls back always seem valid, but never those of a man,* according to *Poetry and Truth.*

Goethe presents the story in retrospect as if it had been clear to him from the start that *premature inclinations cannot promise lasting success.* Isn't this a projection of adult sangfroid back into the beginnings of youthful love? But let us recall what the young Goethe wrote to his schoolmate Moors about his love for Kätchen Schönkopf: *The virtuous heart of my S. is my guarantee that she will never leave me except when duty and necessity bid us part.* Even then, love's tempest of emotion was undercut by a sober, realistic awareness: what I am getting myself into and experiencing at this moment will not stand the test of reality. The usual course of things will part us, and perhaps that is for the best. . . . The young man seems to be aware that he does not yet want to commit himself to a lasting relationship. So it was with Kätchen, and so it obviously was in his relationship with Friederike.

We have only a few remnants of their romance. The draft of a letter from Goethe to Friederike has been preserved, as well as a few letters to Salzmann from the early summer of 1771, written during his several weeks at the parsonage in Sesenheim. Those and the poems he sent to Friederike are all there is.

These documents reveal the lover's dramatic mood swings. In one he compares himself to a *weather vane* turned by every shift in the wind. The world is *more beautiful . . . than I have seen in a long time.* Then an abrupt shift. He senses *that one is not a whit happier when he gets what he wished for.* He has conquered Friederike, but that no longer satisfies him. Perhaps Friederike has noticed, for *the dear child continues to be sick with sadness and that gives the whole affair a skewed appearance.* This is followed by the revealing comment, *Not even taking into account conscia mens, unfortunately not rec-ti,* that accompanies me,* a reference to the passage in Virgil's *Aeneid* that depicts how, with the help of Juno and Venus, Aeneas makes Dido fall in love with him while knowing he will leave her. He therefore cannot have a clear conscience. Obviously, at this point Goethe knew he would leave Friederike, though she didn't know it yet. Two years later, Goethe would send his *Götz* to Salzmann and ask him to forward it to Friederike, remarking that it would be a consolation to her that Weisling's betrayal of Maria in the play is avenged.

In his disguise, Goethe showed his skill at playing a *double role . . . one real and one ideal.* He wished to lead a life like literature, which can be more incisive and meaningful than life itself. This making life into literature, *the youthful urge to compare oneself to figures in novels,* was one of his *most venial attempts to acquire something higher.* In *Poetry and Truth* he confesses not only that he is modeling his presentation of the entire Sesenheim episode on Oliver Goldsmith's *The Vicar of Wakefield,* but also that he had lived out many of the situations in that novel, from which Herder had been giving him and his friends enchanting readings at about the same time. When he was introduced to Sesenheim and the pastor's family, it seemed that he had been *transported from this fictitious world into a similar, real one.* The family, their heartfelt intimacy, and especially the mother and daughters seemed to him just as honest, cheerful, unpretentious, and wise as in the novel, if fortunately not as tested by suffering. There is a masquerade in the novel as well. The family's benefactor, the uncle of their villainous landlord Mr. Thornhill, conceals himself behind the figure of the quirky Mr. Burchell—

---

* A conscience (which is) unfortunately not right.

quite possibly what gave Goethe the idea for his own disguise. He would also have liked to see himself as the benefactor of this family, though after he left Friederike, that was certainly not what he was. Only the quiet beauty of his poems remains, poems faithfully preserved by Friederike.

These verses represent the real birth of Goethe as a lyric poet, free of the rococo and anacreontic elements of his Leipzig years: no more conventional dalliance, pretentious maxims, or pedagogical posturing, no stereotyped languishing or flirting. One detects the influence of Herder: naturalness, powerfully subjective expressiveness, insouciant delight in singing out his song, reflectiveness without over-intellectualizing, simplicity, and unaffected symbolism. In his Sesenheim songs, some of which were first published in Johann Georg Jacobi's journal *Iris* in 1775, Goethe appears even younger than in the early poetry from his Leipzig days. They are definitely occasional poems, originally addressed to Friederike and sent to her from Strasbourg. Some he may also have written down in Sesenheim, improvising with a light touch, as was his habit. Some were intended to be sung on the spot, "May Day," for example:

> *How brightly nature*
> *Shines for me!*
> *Now beams the sun!*
> *Now smiles the lea!*
>
> . . .
>
> *You bless with beauty*
> *The dewy field,*
> *In a haze of blossoms*
> *The burgeoning world!*
>
> *O maiden, maiden,*
> *How I love thee!*
> *Your eyes are flashing!*
> *How you love me!*

They were separated during the winter of 1770–71. The lover looks back on their first meeting and their first game of forfeits:

I love the angel, she feels the same,
I won her heart in a parlor game
And she is mine now, heart and soul.
Fate, you turned to joy my sorrow.
Now let today be like tomorrow
And teach me to deserve her love.

He had promised another visit in the spring of 1771, and Friederike must have sent him frequent reminders:

You golden children, I'll be there soon.
In vain the winter seeks to lock us
Up within our heated room.
We'll sit ourselves down by the fire,
Regale ourselves a thousandfold
And love each other like the angels.
There we shall weave us little wreaths,
And make each other small bouquets
And be like little children.

As spring approached, he sent her a painted ribbon and enclosed a poem that again sounds somewhat anacreontic:

Little leaves and little blossoms
Strewn for me with gentle hand
By good and youthful gods of springtime
Dallying on this airy band

Zephyr, take it on your pinions
Wrap it round my dear one's dress.

It is unfortunate that we don't know exactly when he wrote the famous poem that in the later versions of 1789 and 1810 bears the title "Welcome and Farewell," for it connects meeting and parting so intimately:

My heart was beating—quick, to horse,
Like a hero setting off to fight!

Already evening cradled earth,
And on the mountains hung the night.
The mist already clothed the oak tree,
So like a giant looming there,
Where darkness peered out of the bushes,
Its hundred eyes were one black stare.

The moon upon its hill of clouds
Shone through the haze, so dismal, drear;
The quiet wings of wind were beating
Ghastly whispers in my ear;
The dark night spawned a thousand monsters—
Yet courage grew two thousand ways;
My spirit—a consuming fire,
My heart—dissolving in the blaze.

I saw you, and the gentle joy
Flowed from your sweet gaze to me.
My heart—completely at your side,
And every breath I drew for thee.
Fair weather, rosy-pink with spring
Lay upon your lovely face,
And tenderness for me—ye gods!
I, undeserving, hoped to gain.

The farewell, how distressed and gloomy!
From your glances spoke your heart.
What love there was in your sweet kisses,
What joy there was, and oh, what hurt!
You left, and I stood looking down,
And watched you go with tear-blurred eye;
And yet, what joy! to have been loved,
And loving, oh God, what a joy.

Almost nine years later, during his second journey to Switzerland, in late September 1779, Goethe again visited the Brion family in Sesenheim. He saw the coach that he had not very successfully painted a decade earlier. He found copies of the songs he had *contributed*. The neighbors were summoned to see him, including the barber who had always shaved him. As he writes with some satisfaction, they all had vivid *recollections* of him. After this second visit, he left Sesenheim with the feeling that now he again *can return in thought to that little corner of the world with contentment and live in peace with the reconciled spirits of these people within him*. Whether that was really the case is anyone's guess. Friederike never married, and after her death her sister, with whom she had spent the last years of her life, burned Goethe's letters to her.

As in Leipzig, Goethe made no plans to complete his studies swiftly. He was happy in Strasbourg. It was not only the affair in Sesenheim and Herder that kept him there, but also the beautiful countryside and the pleasant way of life. Originally he had thought of using Strasbourg only as a jumping-off place for Paris, the world capital of culture. He had probably said nothing to his parents about that, and in the end he gave up the plan precisely because of his experiences in the borderland between the two cultures. In *Poetry and Truth* one can feel his suppressed annoyance and sense of insult at what he felt to be arrogant rejection and snubs by some Frenchmen. Goethe read French and spoke it fluently, even if, as he himself admits, his facility was *much more motley than that of any other foreigner*, patched together from scraps of reading and idioms overheard from theater people, domestics, and officials. He thought he was completely at home in the language but was forced to realize that at every turn, he was being corrected. The Frenchmen in Strasbourg, at least the officers and higher officials, treated him courteously at first. But when they noticed that he was not satisfied with the role of guest in a foreign culture, they started to correct and improve his French. He felt *humiliated*. When he was in conversation and had something interesting to say, he wanted people to respond, not make petty corrections. He became convinced that, at best, one might be tolerated by the French but would *never be accepted into the bosom of the church of the one true language*. His injured pride made him critical. Wasn't French culture perhaps overvalued, had it not become old and sclerotic, its formal traditions ossified? Herder encouraged him in this view, one that had already been expressed a decade earlier by Lessing in a critique of the French theater. In *Poetry and Truth* Goethe writes, *We thus found ourselves on the border of France, suddenly entirely free and devoid of French character. We found their way of life too set and too genteel, their literature cold, their criticism destructive, their philosophy abstruse and yet inadequate, so that we had reached the point of devoting ourselves at least experimentally to raw nature.*

In his Sesenheim songs, Goethe had hit this natural tone exceptionally well. Encouraged by Herder, he began to collect folk songs in the Alsatian countryside. He sent them to Herder with a note saying, *Until now, however, I've carried them next to my heart like a treasure; any girls who want to find favor in my eyes must learn to sing them.*

Lest nature in their poetry became too *raw*, they took Shakespeare—whose star was just beginning to rise in Germany—as their model. Goethe had first read him in Leipzig in Christoph Martin Wieland's prose translation. Under Herder's tutelage in Strasbourg, Goethe and his friends began to make a cult of him.

While still there, Goethe got the idea of celebrating the revered dramatist on his name day, following the example of the English actor David Garrick, who had initiated the first such festival in Stratford-upon-Avon in 1769. Goethe drafted a celebratory speech, but he was back in Frankfurt on October 14, 1771, the appointed day, so he summoned a few friends (whom his father had to feed) and read his encomium of Shakespeare to them.

Precisely because it has hardly anything informative to say about Shakespeare or his work, this speech provides insight into Goethe's enthusiasm for the English playwright. For him, Shakespeare was a symbol of a new kind of writing and thinking. He saw in him a reflection of his own ambitions. *We have within ourselves the germ of merits we can appreciate.*

In constantly varied turns of phrase sprinkled with exclamation points, the speech evokes the pleasure of life and criticizes judicious folk who burden life with trouble for themselves and others. Shakespeare is mobilized against them as someone who with *gigantic strides* takes the measure of life's enormous riches. Whoever follows this *great wayfarer* will know the world, and himself, in an enhanced form: *I vividly felt my existence expanded by an eternity.*

Goethe was referring both to life and to art: to the fact that Shakespeare was said, for instance, to have swept aside the rule of the three unities promulgated by the French theater. The unity of place—*imprisoning timidity*. The unities of action and time—*onerous shackles on our imagination*. The liberation from such rules will find a mighty reverberation in *Götz von Berlichingen*, which Goethe was already contemplating while writing this speech. It is there in the play's saber-rattling diction. He is in a *feud* with traditional theater, he declares, and fulminates against French adaptations of Greek antiquity: *What are you doing with that Greek armor, little Frenchman? It's too big for you and too heavy*. Against the artificiality of French figures he invokes Shakespeare's vigorous characters: *And I cry nature! Nature! Nothing as natural as Shakespeare's men and women*. Goethe's tutelary spirit Prometheus is already mentioned in this speech. Shakespeare *vied with Prometheus, copied his humans feature by feature, but in colossal size*.

He praises and polemicizes in powerful, wild, and vague words. One passage characterizes Shakespeare's dramatic art so succinctly and aptly, however, that Goethe often returned to it later: *Shakespeare's theater is a beautiful cabinet of curiosities in which the history of the world flows past our eyes along the unseen thread of time. . . . His plays all revolve around that hidden point (which no philosopher has ever seen or determined) where the uniqueness of our self, our supposed free will, collides with the necessary course of the world*. Hegel could not have said it better half a century later.

With this speech, Goethe wanted above all to rouse himself to creativity. It was more difficult for him to pull himself together for the examination for doctor of law that he still had not taken. *I lacked real knowledge and no internal direction urged me to that subject matter*.

If he lacked internal direction, it would have to come from without: his father was pressing him. In the early summer of 1771, Goethe finally wrote his dissertation. As his topic he chose the relationship between state and church. He intended to resolve the question of whether the state was permitted to determine the religion of its subjects. Since the dissertation itself has not survived, we can only extrapolate from *Poetry and Truth*, where Goethe gives a twofold answer. He argues that the state may establish the mandatory public rituals of the religious communities for their respective clergy and laity but that it ought not attempt to control *what each individual thinks, feels, or meditates in private*. He thus grants the state dominion over external, but not internal, religious life. Subjective religiosity should remain free. He owed that much to Susanna von Klettenberg, Langer, and Jung-

Stilling. He also of course claimed freedom for his own recent experiment with piety, but without letting the least trace of it appear in his dissertation. Although he defends a protected space for the affairs of a *domestic, heartfelt, homey* religion, he seems to have adopted so little of the *heartfelt* and *homey* aspects of the Christian religion that the dissertation was regarded as a scandal by the Strasbourg theological faculty. A professor named Elias Stöber wrote to a friend, "Herr Goethe has played a role here that has made him an excessively witty half-scholar, and not just suspected of being, but well-known to be, a demented despiser of religion. It is almost universally believed that in his upper story he must have a screw either loose or already missing." Another professor suspected that the young man had puffed himself up with "some of Herr von Voltaire's spiteful opinions," having claimed that "Jesus Christ was not the founder of our religion" but rather "scholars using his name" in order to facilitate a "sound politics."

The dean of the faculty asked Goethe either to withdraw his dissertation or publish it without the university's blessing. The university simply would not accept the responsibility for printing it. In *Poetry and Truth* Goethe claims not to have cared; that he was still reluctant to make anything of his publicly available. He sent the dissertation to his father, who prepared a copy and carefully filed it away. It was eventually lost. His father was obviously disappointed by the course of events. It could not have pleased him that, after the failure of the dissertation, his son was satisfied with a licentiate's degree. For this less prestigious degree Goethe needed only to propose and defend a few simple theses—child's play for him. He could have purchased a doctorate, but he declined to do so. The licentiate was generally regarded as the equivalent of a doctorate, though not by the lawyers in Frankfurt, who insisted on the distinction. For that reason, Goethe was later unable to use the title in business dealings in that city. Everywhere else he was referred to as "Dr. Goethe."

In August of 1771 the newly minted "doctor" left Strasbourg to return to his father's house in Frankfurt. There is no evidence that he paid another visit to Friederike to say a final farewell.

CHAPTER 6

The Lawyer. Litigation as an Exercise and Prelude to
Götz von Berlichingen. Götz as a Wild West Hero.
The "Law of the Fist." The Sovereign Individual versus
Modernity. Sticking to It, Thanks to His Sister.
The Author Helps Himself. First Reactions.

. . . .

I N AUGUST 1771, GOETHE APPLIED TO BE ADMITTED TO THE
bar before the court of lay judges, employing the deferential officialese
of the day: *Thus for me at present, nothing can be the object of more interest
and ambition than to place the science and knowledge I have by now acquired in
the service of my fatherland, namely, initially as a lawyer . . . in order thereby
to prepare myself for any more important tasks which it might be the pleasure of
the excellent and venerable authorities to entrust to me.* His father regarded
admission to the bar as a path to higher office, and to that end Goethe
hinted, in his application, at larger ambitions. Johann Caspar wanted
his son to be a mayor like his grandfather Textor, who held that highest civic office in the free imperial city until 1770 and died shortly
before Goethe's return from Strasbourg. Goethe was admitted to the
bar on September 3, 1771. He would continue to practice law—at first
seriously, later almost entirely pro forma—until the fall of 1775, taking
frequent time off for travel and writing. From 1771 through 1775, he
conducted twenty-eight trials.

It was not difficult for him to find work as a lawyer. His prominent
family and good contacts were helpful. There was a glut of lawyers
in Frankfurt, but friends and acquaintances with successful practices,
such as the Schlosser brothers, passed litigation and trial work on to
him. His father helped, too, not entirely selflessly—for Johann Caspar,

it was an opportunity to be more than a man of independent means and to step back into the practice of law.

In a town like Frankfurt, infamous for its legal squabbles, lawyers did not enjoy the best reputation. Goethe alludes to the fact in *Götz*, where a doctor of canon and civil law by the name of Olearius says of Frankfurt, *The rabble almost stoned me when they heard I was a lawyer.* Though someone of Goethe's pedigree was spared the fate of a hack lawyer, like other beginners he still had to seek out his first clients among small tradesmen, artisans, and Jews from the ghetto. Almost all his cases were civil.

The practice of law in Frankfurt did not usually involve oral arguments. Cases were negotiated in writing between litigants. In Goethe's first trial, a curious situation arose. The opposing lawyer was his school chum Moors, who had begun practicing in Frankfurt half a year earlier. The two friends began—no doubt with some amusement—to inflate the case. Instead of merely representing their clients, they began to "play" them, exchanging insults under their names. The briefs were so devoid of official restraint that the court issued a reprimand to both lawyers for their "indecent style, which serves only to exacerbate the litigants' existing feelings of anger and bitterness." Johann Georg Schlosser had warned him: Goethe had read one of his briefs to Schlosser and proudly declared that the client had been very satisfied with it, and his friend had responded, "In this case you have proved yourself more a writer than a lawyer; you must never ask how such a document pleases your client, but how it will please the court." The court was not pleased, and though his client won the case (which involved a complicated inheritance), it was only because the court was equally dissatisfied with Moors, and for the same reason.

Of interest here is Goethe's style. He characterizes Moors as *a furious termagant . . . whose overheated brain, incapable of arguing with reason and cause, exhausts itself in abusive language. . . . After his deeply concealed legal erudition has long writhed in labor pains, out pop one or two laughable, mousy, digest definitions that bear witness to their mother. Let them run!* Moors very likely answered with coarse language of his own. In his second brief, Goethe writes, *The same register of insults that characterize the previous brief is again on parade in this one. . . . Impertinence and vileness sound from every*

*part of this document. . . . What can one expect from such an opponent? To con-
vince him? It is my good fortune that the matter does not depend on that. It would
take superhuman powers to help the congenitally blind to see, and restraining
madmen is a matter for the police.*

For Goethe, this juridical role playing was a warm-up for literary
role playing; in November and December 1771, he was simultaneously working on the first version of the historical drama *The History
of Gottfried von Berlichingen with the Iron Hand.* Published a year and a
half later, the play would at one stroke make him famous throughout
Germany. In the trial, he played a single role, that of his client. In the
drama, there were various roles into which he had to think his way and
among which he could distribute himself. Each would have something
of him, but he was especially close to Götz.

In Strasbourg, Goethe had envisaged a play about the historical figure
after reading his autobiography. Götz (circa 1480–1562) was a knight who
lived during the Reformation and the Peasants' War and was constantly
entangled in feuds. By the early sixteenth century, the era of wild, free
robber barons was coming to an end, a development in which the historical Götz played no prominent part. But Goethe gave him one, realizing
he could make him the embodiment of an entire vanishing world. It was
the same spiritual world of the fifteenth century that Goethe had become
acquainted with in his alchemical and Kabbalistic explorations during
his year of illness in 1769. Herder, too, had expressed enthusiasm for this
era of towering figures such as Luther, Ulrich von Hutten, and Dürer.
For Goethe, the legendary figure of Faust also belonged to this circle of
great men who had appeared as the old empire was breaking apart and
its intellectual unity splintering, thus reopening a space for powerful,
original, highly individual figures. Götz was such a figure to him, an
example, as he later wrote, *of a rough-hewn, well-meaning, and self-sufficient
individual in a wild, anarchic time.*

What fascinated Goethe about Götz was precisely what fascinates
us in westerns today: a romantic look at a bygone world in which the
individual still counts. The man who looks out for himself and never
cedes his independence to social institutions. For although one gains in
security thereby, one is also diminished in stature. Goethe created Götz
as a counterimage to a modernity that Schiller so tellingly described as
making man smaller in order to do something great with him. The

species gains while the individual loses. Götz is the great individual whose downfall is preordained.

In *Patriotic Fantasies*, by the jurist and social theorist Justus Möser, Goethe had already discovered a defense of the old *Faustrecht*—under baronial law, the right to pursue justice for oneself: the "law of the fist." Its promised liberation from the legal thicket that so vexed the student of jurisprudence drew Goethe to Götz, and to his refusal to be diminished. Instead, as he says in the play, he is *subject to no one except the emperor*. What is vexing but also inevitable is that society intervenes between the highest authorities—God, the emperor—and oneself. This complicates and confuses matters. Götz despises this state of affairs and will founder on it, yet even in defeat still feel independent. Society can destroy but not change him. He remains true to himself. That is how Goethe sees his Knight with the Iron Fist and perhaps how he wanted to see himself.

As his Shakespeare speech shows, Goethe's reading of the great English dramatist provoked his sympathy for loners of *colossal stature*, doomed heroes of independence. With *Götz* he wanted, like Shakespeare, to discover the *hidden point . . . where the uniqueness of our self, our supposed free will, collides with the necessary course of the world.*

Götz is not the sort of champion of freedom who would later appear on stage in figures like the Marquis Posa in Schiller's *Don Carlos*. He does not demand political freedom, but demonstrates how to live freely. In Götz, freedom is not primarily a matter of consciousness but of being.

The young author wanted to take part in this free existence by writing about it. *We have within us the germ of achievements we can admire.* In writing, a world unfolds and he is caught in its spell. He lets his alter ego operate in an imaginary space and feels an incomparable expansion: *I feel with incredible vividness how my existence is infinitely extended.* How could it be otherwise when even the counterworld that will bring Götz down originates in the absolute authority of the playwright? Adelbert von Weislingen, for example, belongs to that counterworld. He switches sides and abandons Maria, Götz's sister. He, too, has something of the author who abandoned Friederike. As for the seductive Adelhaid, who intrigues against Götz, Goethe confessed that had positively *fallen in love* with her. Thus if his *existence is infinitely extended,* that extension assuredly also includes the social reality hostile to Götz. The author's imagination lives in Götz and at the same time transcends the limits imposed on him. As the author of a little *theatrum mundi*, he also commands the *necessary course of the world* to which Götz succumbs. The example of Shakespeare had taught Goethe what characterizes a great dramatist: he doesn't identify only with his hero, but grants all his figures the right to life. Götz's adversaries are not there merely for contrast. Only in this way can theater become that *cabinet of curiosities in which the history of the world flows past our eyes along the unseen thread of time.*

It was ambitious to try to follow in Shakespeare's footsteps, but the young Goethe had self-confidence to spare. He writes to Salzmann in Strasbourg that he is throwing his *genius* into the work on this play so that his *productive power* will not *have to hum to itself.* In the process, he is able to enjoy *all the power I feel within myself.* He is through with the *distracted life in Strasbourg.*

He set resolutely to work even before he had completely worked out the plot. During these weeks, his sister was very important to him. He had already told her so much about his plan that Cornelia began to lose patience and urged him *not to always just indulge in windy talk, but finally set down on paper what is so vividly alive in me.* And so he plunged in and wrote swiftly. In the evening he would read to her what he had written during the day. She applauded his effort but also expressed some doubt about her brother's perseverance. Would he really finish the play? Her doubts were an additional challenge. He had to prove something to her—and to himself—by pressing ahead. *And so I kept ceaselessly at work, following straight along, looking neither backwards nor to the right or left, and in about six weeks I had the pleasure of seeing the bound manuscript.*

That he looked neither *backwards nor to the right or left* suggests diligence. But he also ignored conventional aesthetic rules governing the unity of time, place, and action. In a series of colorful scenes with an epic narrative feel, one location gives way to the next: an inn, the forest, Götz's castle, the bishop's palace in Bamberg, the soldiers' camp, the town hall in Heilbronn, the Reichstag in Augsburg, a Gypsy encampment, the courtroom. Time is discontinuous, sometimes compressed and at others drawn out, with frequent jumps. The events of the play took place over several decades in the life of the historical Götz. One can gauge this in the figure of Georg; in the course of the play he grows from a boy to a young man and becomes Götz's squire. The main action, the dispute between Götz and Weislingen, is interwoven with numerous secondary plots, some of which are acted out while others are only narrated. Goethe was giving free rein to his *imagination*, which blossomed into particular situations and characters without heed to the unity of the whole. Thus the plot has several focal points, but no single climactic scene.

Even between Götz and Weislingen there is not just one turning point but three. At the beginning of the play, Adelbert von Weislingen, the friend of Götz's youth who has become his adversary at the court of the bishop of Bamberg, is captured by Götz's men. Götz treats him as a friend and successfully woos him back to his side. Weislingen becomes attached to Maria, Götz's sister. That is the first turning point. When Weislingen returns to Bamberg, he succumbs to the seductive Adelhaid—the second turning point. When Götz joins forces with the rebellious peasants, Weislingen is the enforcer who is supposed to carry out the death sentence against his former friend, but after a parley with Maria, he withdraws the sentence. That is the third turning point, but it comes too late for him. Adelhaid, who in the meantime has her eye on the successor to the throne, has him poisoned. Her verdict on him is, *You always were one of those miserable creatures without the power to do evil or good.*

That is decidedly not true of Adelhaid. She lives through the magic of her erotic attraction, which she has no hesitation in deploying to further her political and economic interests. The beautiful widow collects men—first Weislingen, then his manservant Franz. Even Sickingen, one of Götz's comrades, falls under her spell, at least for one night, *An error that made me into a god.* In the end she is hauled before a secret tribunal, and the executioner stabs her with the words, *God, you made her so beautiful, and couldn't you make her good?*

It gradually becomes clear that it is these shifting pairings that actually drive the play's plot. Weislingen is brought back to Götz's side by Maria. But his attachment to her dissolves when he succumbs to Adelhaid's more potent charms. Maria, abandoned, attracts Sickingen, but not for long, since he in turn falls under Adelhaid's spell after she rejects Weislingen. In this game of musical chairs, Maria is the loser. She is unable to hold on to either Weislingen or Sickingen, losing them both to Adelhaid.

It is probably not insignificant that Goethe chose to make Götz's sister Maria the erotic loser, for his own sister, who had helped him so much with the play, was in his eyes also a loser in love.

He would intimate as much in his autobiography, where he speculates about why Cornelia had so little physical attraction for men. He mentions *that her skin was seldom clear,* that her strongly rounded forehead *made an unpleasant impression,* and that her person possessed *not the least bit of sensuality.* Thus she failed to form close attachments to the young men she found attractive. That was her misfortune, he wrote, which she felt all the more strongly because she was perfectly conscious of her own worth. "But how can I aspire to bliss when I have no charms that elicit tenderness?" she wrote in a secret diary she kept at the time. Her brother, however, felt drawn to her as if *by a magnet.* The siblings were intimately connected. She was his confidante during the development of his *physical and moral powers.* It is natural that many have suspected Goethe of incestuous inclinations toward this sister, who was only a year younger, because he hinted at it himself: *The inquisitiveness of youth, the astonishment at the awakening of sensual urges . . . many wayward stirrings and confusions arising from them were shared and overcome by the siblings hand in hand, and they were all the less enlightened about their strange condition since the more they drew near to each other, the more powerfully the sacred reserve of their close relation kept them apart.* Against this backdrop, it is not surprising that Goethe would present his sister as an asexual being. *I must honestly admit,* he writes, *that sometimes when I fantasized about her fate, it pleased me to think of her not as a housewife but as an abbess, the leader of a community for noblewomen.*

It is exactly because his sister had no success in love that he sees her as having a beneficial effect. It is the same with Götz's sister Maria. In the long run she is unable to preserve her relationship with either Weislingen or Sickingen, but her moral influence is strong enough to persuade Weislingen to take back the death sentence against Götz.

The play opens up a field of erotic tensions where people struggle for victory and suffer defeat. Adelhaid is the actual victor. Goethe, who fell in love with his own figure, had to force himself to prevent her from enjoying her triumph. In the end she gets punished; it was necessary to have that much sympathy for the losing sister. Maria (and with her, Cornelia) had to obtain satisfaction.

Weislingen's servant Franz is buffeted by the lovers' quarrels, a helpless victim of his desire. He, too, is in love with Adelhaid, but he loses any will of his own. In his servile devotion, he abases himself and secretly poisons his master at Adelhaid's behest. He embodies a perverted kind of love that Goethe warned against in a letter written in Strasbourg: *They say it* [love] *gives you courage. Not at all. As soon as our heart is soft, it's weak.* Franz is the lovesick weakling gone berserk.

All around Götz conditions are changing: intrigue, shifting coalitions, betrayal. The whole world conspires against him. He alone remains unchanged. His attachment to his wife, Elisabeth, is indissoluble; they are a couple whom only death can separate.

But even in Goethe's version, Götz is not a knight in shining armor. The quarrels he picks are quite dubious. For instance, when a tailor from Heilbronn wins a prize at a shooting match in Cologne, the local merchants' guild illegally refuses to award it to him. Götz has taken up his cause, rides to Cologne, and—as Elisabeth tells it—*bullies* the gentlemen there until the prize is given. Maria, however, reminds her that to settle such a trifling matter, a number of innocent people were *slaughtered* and asks, *When we try to replace one misery with another, isn't the general evil increased thereby?* Elisabeth, otherwise a warmhearted woman, is suddenly transformed into a subtly arguing jurist, and one gets the impression that here Goethe, the freshly minted lawyer and licentiate of canon and civil law, is taking the floor: *Whoever mistreats the citizens of another city neglects his duty to his own subjects, for he exposes them to the right of retaliation.* Goethe realized that such a speech did not fit Elisabeth's character, and he deleted it from the second version of *Götz*.

Other fights that Götz starts are similarly hard to justify. When the bishop of Bamberg detains one of his men, Götz ambushes a transport of goods on its way to the bishop. This was one of the raids that the historical Götz boasted of in his autobiography. Whenever the real-life story of the Knight with the Iron Hand enters the play, there is always—even in the view of Goethe's contemporaries—a lack of justification. The only mitigating fact is the knight's loyalty to the empire. The princes and rulers of provinces pursue their territorial interests, and only Götz is loyal and brave and declares himself prepared to defend the imperial border against the Turks for the emperor. Neither the historical Götz nor Goethe's hero actually does so, but his declarations of intent are enough to gain the favor of the emperor. That is why the monarch, on the occasion of the imperial decree of execution against Götz (and Selbiz), does not want *any harm to come to them.*

When Goethe describes Götz as one of the *noblest Germans* in a letter to Salzmann, he doesn't mean the historical ruffian, but his own cleaned-up image of him. He is the model of a powerful, successful man less in his behavior than in the judgment of posterity.

For Elisabeth, Götz is a benevolent man, but not out of weakness or conciliation. *Charity is a noble virtue, but it is the prerogative of strong souls alone. Men who are always benevolent out of softness are no better than people who can't hold their urine.* A man like Götz wants to live well himself, but he lives and lets live and is without resentment. Envy is also foreign to his nature. He is able to act out his anger and doesn't let it eat at him. In an altercation with one of the leaders of the rebellious peasants, he expresses his disdain toward the *coward whose bile eats away at his insides like a malignant tumor because his nature doesn't have enough strength to spurn it once and for all.* He is the guarantor of his own honor. He can defend himself and doesn't have to go running to a lawyer. He loathes complicated social arrangements, institutional interventions, and the machinations of diplomats. The same is true in matters of faith. Götz has no need of intercession by priests. He approaches his God directly, preferably when he is feeling strong. *God reflects on a prayer only when we put all our strength into it.* From the perspective of Brother Martin, distantly reminiscent of Martin Luther, Götz seems to represent unspoiled nature. The monk laments three things that cripple human nature: *poverty, chastity, and obedience,* and Götz is for him the diametric opposite. He lives well, loves well, and is his own master. Because he can fight, he has no need to grovel. At the sight of Götz, Martin cries, *It's a pleasure to behold a great man.*

In sum, Götz is the embodiment of freedom. He doesn't demand it and doesn't take it, he simply lives it. Adelbert to Götz: *You alone are free, you whose great soul is sufficient unto itself and has no need either to obey or to rule in order to be something.* It's precisely that greatness that envious natures like Adelbert's find hard to take in the long run. Götz's freedom reminds him of his own inner lack of freedom. He cannot bear *to see a powerful rival flourish,* and so *all feeling of greatness* in another *becomes a torment.* That is another reason he betrays his former friend.

Before Götz is driven from his besieged castle by imperial troops, he has visions that are too softhearted for his nature. He dreams of rulers who will *feel boundless joy to be fortunate in their subjects.* These visions must be chalked up to an author who indulges in softhearted moods as well as blood and thunder. The great hour of reconciliation draws near. Götz, the tough guy from the era of the Peasants' War slips into the sentimental literary German of 1770: *When their well-cultivated, blessed land seems to them a Paradise compared with their prim, constrained, solitary gardens . . . then neighbor will grant peace to neighbor because he himself is happy. Then no one will seek to extend his borders. He will rather remain the sun in his circuit than be a comet running its terrible, erratic course through many others.*

Such views are too idyllic for Georg, Götz's squire. He asks anxiously whether he'll still be allowed to *ride.* Götz reassures him that there will still be plenty of opportunity to ride and hunt. *We'll clear the mountains of wolves, fetch a side of meat from the forest for our neighbor peacefully tilling his field and then sit down to supper with him.* What's more, there were still the Turks and the French, who'd need their heads knocked together to protect the empire. *What a life that would be, Georg, to risk one's skin for the general good.*

This vision of an orderly world in which the knights are no longer ruffians but the defenders of the fatherland was retained in the second version of the play, but to keep it from seeming too unrealistic, its connection to reality is reinforced. Götz exclaims, *Have I not known excellent men among the princes, and will their kind have died out?* And he tells how the Landgrave of Hanau gave a hunting party, and how they ate *in the open air and the country folk all came running to see them . . . nothing but cheerful faces, and how they took part in the glory of their lord, who feasted among them there on God's good earth.*

Goethe has Götz dream of a better future, thereby not entirely neglecting the Enlightenment doctrine, promoted by Gottsched and Lessing, that the public be morally instructed and improved. Yet in the end, Götz declares what the reader has long since guessed: that his time has passed. Great characters no longer had a chance in a bourgeois world of petty regulation. Götz's melodramatic forecast shortly before he dies promises nothing good for the future: *The time of deception is approaching. . . . The weak will reign with cunning and the brave man will fall into the nets that cowardice stretches across his path.*

Goethe finished the play in December 1771. For the time being, he was satisfied at having proved to himself and his sister that he could persevere until he finished something. He had gotten down on paper what he had been carrying around in his head for a while. Copies of the play circulated among his friends and acquaintances. He didn't yet know whether he would have the play printed; he hadn't even thought about the possibility of having it performed. Whether it was suited for the stage was not a factor he had considered, since it was meant for the inner stage of his imagination. Yet like every author, he imagined the reactions of the public and the critics. What would they think of it? Would they raise a clamor because it violated the rules not just of the theater but of convention and propriety?

He sent the play to Johann Heinrich Merck, the military paymaster of the Landgrave of Darmstadt and eight years Goethe's senior, along with an accompanying poem. Its mocking, sarcastic tone mirrors that of this new friend, who was a great connoisseur of literature. It's not always new cider that bursts old wineskins, he writes. Sometimes the opposite occurs, and it is content from olden times that sends up a feeble present.

> *To all the fools in powdered wigs*
> *And all the literary prigs*
> *Councilors, scribblers, maidens, brats*
> *All sinners against poetic arts—*
> *Contempt and scorn now be their fate.*
> *They all deserve undying hate.*
> *And so if critics and their kind*
> *Or philistines with narrow mind*
> *Chance before our house to pass,*
> *To them we'll show our naked ass.*

Herder was also sent a copy of the play, with a note from Goethe saying he wouldn't undertake any more revisions *until you have voiced an opinion; for I know that then a radical rebirth must occur if it is to enter into life.* Herder let him cool his heels for six months before he sent his assessment. In the meantime, there were new projects. Goethe planned to write a play about Caesar and another about Socrates. He was already beginning to collect material and make notes. He was sticking with great figures. At last Herder's verdict on *Götz* arrived. His letter has not survived, but we can gather from Goethe's answer that Herder played the schoolmaster. But as he had not done in Strasbourg, Goethe now protested the criticism. Herder had belittled Götz, and Goethe answered, *I belittle him even more than you do.* He trumps the criticism with self-criticism, even though he doesn't go into details. Herder had written that the play was too contrived. Goethe responded, *That's annoying enough.* He pointed to Lessing's tragedy *Emilia Galotti*, one of Herder's favorite plays; wasn't it just as contrived? To other people, Herder expressed a much more positive opinion of the play. He told his fiancée, Karoline Flachsland, that she would enjoy "some hours of heavenly bliss" when she read *Götz.* "There's an uncommon amount of German strength, depth, and truth to it, although now and then only the thought is there." That's always how Herder was. He was incapable of freely praising and admiring anything. He always had to mix in a little poison.

While copies of the play were still circulating among his friends, Goethe was already polishing it and making improvements. For Merck, who had immediately liked the play, the revisions were going on too long. He pushed Goethe to publish it. Revisions only made a thing different, but seldom better. "Hang the diapers on the fence and they'll dry soon enough!" he said.

In *Poetry and Truth* Goethe claims to have revised *Götz* so often that *a completely new play lay before me.* He could say so only because at that point, his first draft hadn't been published yet. If you compare it to the second version, you can see that it was essentially still the same play. The language had merely been smoothed out and tightened up and a few scenes rearranged or deleted, especially in the last act, where in the first version the action around Adelhaid and the Gypsies had gotten too long.

The play finally appeared in the spring of 1773; Goethe published it himself. The response was tremendous. Overnight, Goethe had made a conquest of the German reading public. The author had created a work, and then another story began about how the published work changed the author.

CHAPTER 7

Goethe's Busy Idleness. Poetry without a Profession.

Johann Georg Schlosser. The Infanticide Trial and the

Gretchen Tragedy in *Faust*. Johann Heinrich Merck.

Among the Darmstadt Sentimentalists. The Wayfarer.

The Reviewer. Goethe's Early Aesthetics.

A Summer Love in Wetzlar.

. . . .

GOETHE HAD NO PARTICULAR AMBITIONS AS A LAWYER.
But even in the painting, drawing, and writing to which he was
entirely devoted, he still saw himself as far from mastery. In a letter to
Herder written in the summer of 1772, he is highly self-critical. He has
only *strolled around* and nowhere really *taken hold* of anything, *the essence
of any mastery*. In his own judgment, what he lacks is stamina and thoroughness. What he is doing doesn't feel like work; everything simply
comes too easily to him. It's as if his poems were carried to him on the
wind. Sometimes he writes them down so quickly he doesn't even take
the time to fold the paper neatly and place it on his desk before beginning. At parties and in company he can take requests and improvise
poems on the spot. It's a game, and one with occasional amorous over-
tones. He doesn't give a thought to having his work published. *Götz*
was also drafted in a single burst of inspiration, quickly written down
and circulated among Goethe's friends with no clear plan to publish.

Known as a writer mainly to his circle of friends, he as yet didn't feel
like a writer himself. He had a sense of his own capabilities, but he knew
he still lacked discipline. In another letter to Herder, he for the first time
invokes the image of a charioteer he'd found in Pindar: *When you stand
boldly in your chariot with four fresh horses rearing wildly against your reins, and*

you discipline their power, whipping the errant ones into line and the rearing ones down to earth, and you drive and steer them, turning, whipping, stopping, and driving forward again, until all sixteen hooves carry you to the finish in a single rhythm—that is mastery. It was an image he would use again—and with special intensity in *Egmont* and at the end of *Poetry and Truth.*

In Frankfurt there was some surprise that this highly talented young man hadn't yet settled down to pursue his legal career. And yet he circulated, proud to display his elegant clothes. He was always the center of attention wherever he went. People sought him out, and he sought out convivial companions. His circle of friends grew, and what he wrote was at first meant only for them, as a favor and sign of affection.

He didn't need to worry about earning a living, and his artistic output had nothing to do with money. Financially, it was only a supplement. And that seemed only right to him, since writing and making poems arose from an abundance of inner riches. Was it also superfluous? At times he suggested it was. As Götz says, *Writing is busy idleness. It's sour work for me. While writing down what I've done, I get annoyed about wasting time in which I could be doing something.* In a letter to Betty Jacobi, Goethe writes: *Although the Bible says Ye shall know them by their fruits, are the things we scrawl onto paper, whether written or printed, our fruits?*

Expressions like these betray self-doubt on the part of a so-called man of action. But he rarely articulated such doubts; certainly they did not preoccupy him. More often than not, he was moved by his own artistry. As he wrote in his essay on the Strasbourg cathedral, *there is a forming nature in man that becomes immediately active once his existence is assured. As soon as he has nothing to worry about and nothing to fear, the demigod, active in his tranquillity, reaches out for material into which to breathe his spirit.*

This hints at the figure of Prometheus whom Goethe had chosen as the patron saint of artistic omnipotence. In letters from the period, Goethe frequently invokes creative *genius* and speaks disparagingly of his father's attempts to tie him down to a bourgeois existence. He puts up with them, he writes to a friend, because he is confident of his own *power: One tug and all the sevenfold raffia ropes are severed!* People sensed his power, but not all were persuaded by it or by him. For some, the talented young man was too much of a lightweight. Others were enchanted. Women were especially drawn to him, among them Herder's fiancée, Karoline Flachsland; her friends the Darmstadt ladies-in-waiting Henriette von Roussillon and Luise von Ziegler; and Sophie von La Roche and her daughter Maximiliane. They all gushed about this brilliant young man who showered them with poems. Men of all ages felt attracted to him. Quite simply, he impressed people with a promise of great things to come. Johann Georg Schlosser, who had known Goethe since childhood and would remain his friend until his marriage to Goethe's sister, Cornelia, ended their relationship, wrote to Johann Kaspar Lavater, a Swiss pastor, poet, and physiognomist who also cultivated Goethe's friendship, "If he ever finds happiness in the world, he will make thousands happy, and if he never does, he will always be a meteor that our contemporaries will never tire of gaping at . . . it takes a certain strength of soul to remain his friend."

Like Goethe, Schlosser was from a respectable family of lawyers in Frankfurt. His father had been a member of the city council and a lay judge. Schlosser was already an experienced and successful lawyer when Goethe, ten years younger, began dabbling in the profession in the fall of 1771. Schlosser was conscientious and competent, but the work left him feeling unfulfilled and ambivalent. He wasn't devoted heart and soul to his practice. The love of truth was his supreme ideal, and he therefore sometimes felt uncomfortable as a lawyer: "Here by secret means, a sly scoundrel is making my innocent tongue into the tool of hidden injustice."

Schlosser was a highly literate connoisseur of English, French, and Italian literature, which he also translated. He wrote English verse in the style of Pope, French epigrams on the model of Voltaire, and Italian arias in the manner of Metastasio. He was also working on a German translation of the *Iliad*. An aesthete and a moralist who was also deeply pragmatic, his *Catechism of Moral Doctrine for the Rural Populace*, which offered suggestions for the improvement of rural living conditions, earned him recognition in political circles. He proposed that the clergy teach and do humanitarian work, thereby freeing themselves from pedantry and doctrine.

Goethe admired this work—it inspired his 1773 "Letter of the Pastor in ✳✳✳ to the New Pastor in ✳✳✳"—but he was blindsided by Schlosser's marriage to his sister. Schlosser seemed to Goethe to be too incommunicative, cool, and sober to be anything like the right match for Cornelia. On the other hand, in religious matters he was too effusive. Above all, as Goethe admits in *Poetry and Truth*, he was also simply *jealous* of Schlosser.

Schlosser had passed several legal cases on to the neophyte Goethe. But more important was the insight he gave Goethe into the prosecution of Susanna Margaretha Brandt, an infanticide who was publicly executed by the sword on January 14, 1772. The event stirred up the entire town; executions had by then become rare.

It was an experience that Goethe would use in the tragic story of Gretchen in *Faust*, which he had begun to work on in the early 1770s. He had a close connection to the events, since he had several relatives and acquaintances who were directly involved in the trial, as the scholar Ernst Beutler* has discovered. Besides Schlosser, who participated as a lawyer, there was also Goethe's uncle Johann Jost Textor, who as a member of the court had the official duty of asking the executioner whether he thought himself capable of decapitating the condemned woman with a single blow of his sword. And it was Schlosser who, on behalf of the executioner, petitioned the court to allow the latter's son to carry out the execution. The town clerk who prepared the arrest warrant had served as private tutor to both Goethe and his sister. The doctor who attended the condemned woman before her execution was Johann Friedrich Metz, the family friend who had treated Goethe in 1769 and encouraged him to carry out his experiments in alchemy. Goethe knew the head judge who found the woman guilty and solemnly pronounced the death sentence; he had been involved in the Gretchen affair when Goethe's first love and her dubious friends were being investigated by the court.

Partial copies of the transcript of the trial have been discovered among Goethe's possessions, and he was familiar with the details of the woman's confession, which are reflected in the Gretchen tragedy in *Faust*. Susanna Margaretha Brandt named a journeyman goldsmith as the father of the dead child. He had moved on to Russia. *For a jaunty lad / Good air is elsewhere to be had. And he is gone*, as the early version of *Faust* has it. Brandt stated that the man had used a magic potion to take

---

* Ernst Beutler, *Essays um Goethe* (Frankfurt a. M. and Leipzig: Insel, 1995).

advantage of her. Poison is also at play when Faust seduces Gretchen. The infanticide declared that she was acting under the compulsion of the devil. In Goethe's play, it is Mephisto.

Scholars have long tried to determine which scenes of *Faust* were written first. Perhaps Ernst Beutler is correct in surmising that, following the trial and execution of Brandt, Goethe penned the prison scenes. The prison where Brandt awaited her death, the tower of the old Katharine Gate, was a mere two hundred yards from Goethe's house on the Hirschgraben.

Goethe was present at the elaborately ceremonious execution. The head judge, clad in a red cloak and accompanied by the headsman and his assistants, came to lead the condemned woman to her death. She was brought into the "Poor Sinners' Chamber" as the tower bells tolled. The last meal was served, and the judges, the headsman and his assistants, the watch, and the clergy ate their fill while Susanna Brandt took only a swallow of water. She was then led in procession through the city by soldiers and clergymen who sang and prayed. At the place of execution, she was bound, her neck was exposed, and "amid unceasing cries of the gentlemen of the clergy" her "head was successfully taken off in one stroke." Almost the entire population attended the spectacle. The corresponding scene in *Faust: Just listen to the townsfolk shuffling through the streets! Do you hear? Not a loud word. The bell is calling!—The death sentence is pronounced!—Every neck twitches at the edge that's twitching for mine.—Hark, the bell.*

Half a year earlier, in his licentiate examination in Strasbourg, Goethe had defended the death penalty in his fifty-third thesis, as was customary. In the fifty-fifth thesis, however, he had deflected the question *whether a woman who kills her newborn child should be subject to the death penalty* by simply pointing out that this was a *matter of dispute among doctors of law.* Which side Goethe took during his oral defense we do not know. But in the Gretchen tragedy, Faust would like to free his lover from the punitive hands of the law. Faust scolds Mephisto, the evil spirit, whom he blames entirely. *That lovely, innocent creature locked up in prison as a malefactor and subject to horrible torments! . . . And meanwhile, you lull me in insipid pleasures, conceal her growing misery from me, and let her perish helplessly.* Mephisto answers, *She's not the first!* And Faust: *. . . Not the first!—Misery! Misery! . . . I am pierced to the marrow by the affliction of this* *one woman alone and you calmly grin at the fate of thousands.* But Faust isn't concerned with the *fate of thousands* either; he wants to rescue from punishment *this one woman alone,* for whose fall he is responsible. Gretchen prefers to be saved by means of her punishment. *God's judgment come upon me, I am yours! Save me,* and turning to Faust she implores, *You holy angels save my soul—you terrify me, Heinrich.* Even though her punishment itself is not questioned and is sealed by Mephisto's *She has been put to death!* it is still remarkable that the author looks at the lover, who escapes scot-free, from the perspective of the condemned Gretchen. He cries out, *I won't abandon you!* But he is immediately dragged off by Mephisto—whether to new adventures or to his ruin remains ambiguous in the early version. He rages on without a backward glance. Goethe was just as driven. As he wrote to Salzmann, *My friends must forgive me. My nisus* forward is so powerful that I seldom can force myself to take a breath and look back.*

The trial and execution of Susanna Brandt seem to have turned Goethe from the law. He refused an offer from the faculty in Strasbourg to award him, for a fee, a doctorate in jurisprudence. As he wrote to Salzmann, he had lost his desire *to be a doctor.* He was *so sick of the business that, at the most, I do my duty only for the sake of appearances.*

In late December 1771, Georg Schlosser had introduced Goethe to Johann Heinrich Merck, a court official in Darmstadt. In *Poetry and Truth* Goethe calls him a *singular man* who had *the greatest influence* on his life. Like Schlosser, Merck was both a professional bureaucrat and a man of letters. He had sought to make Goethe's acquaintance because he hoped to win him as an author for the *Frankfurter Gelehrte Anzeigen* (*Frankfurt Literary Advertiser*), a review whose editorship he assumed in 1772. The periodical appeared three times a week and was a continuation of the old *Frankfurter Gelehrte Zeitung,* a once important academic journal that had lost its relevance owing to its dry, academic style. Merck was determined to shake things up, engage new reviewers, and speak to a broader readership with literary interests. He exploited his good contacts in the literary world and succeeded in acquiring prominent contributors such as Herder. But he was also on the lookout for new talent, and through Schlosser he became aware of Goethe.

* Latin: effort; pressure.

Goethe wrote to Herder about the first evening he spent with Merck in December 1771, *I was as pleased as I could be to find another person in whose company feelings develop and thoughts are clarified.* Merck was no less pleased: "He's a man after my own heart, one of the very few I have found." He was beginning to "fall in love" with him, he wrote to his wife.

Goethe left the recently completed manuscript of *Götz* with his new friend at their first meeting. Merck had asked to see it; Goethe's "enthusiasm and genius" made him curious to read the work.

Merck was eight years older than Goethe. Born in Darmstadt, he had remained there, and was highly regarded at the little court of the Landgrave of Hesse-Darmstadt. He served officially as military paymaster, but in reality he was a kind of finance minister for the ministate and exercised influence on its affairs. He advised the court on the purchase of artworks and was presumed to have made some money for himself from such transactions. With his learning and personal connections, he was the center of educated society in the town. He was esteemed but also feared, for this tall, gaunt, sharp-nosed man was notorious for an equally sharp tongue and for dispensing ridicule, sarcasm, and harsh opinions. Goethe thought his glance had *something of a tiger,* and in retrospect he speaks of an incongruity in Merck's character: *by nature an upright, noble, reliable man, he had become embittered against the world and allowed this unhealthy, mercurial aspect such free rein within himself that he felt an irresistible urge to deliberately play the joker and even the rogue.*

Goethe had great respect for Merck's opinions because he realized that they were free of flattery. In fact, one had to be prepared for some maliciousness. He often went about things *in a negative and destructive way.* But once you'd gotten used to that, there was much to be gleaned from his opinions and advice. A few years later, Goethe wrote in his diary that Merck was a *wonderful mirror,* the only person *who completely understands what I am doing and how I do it, and yet sees it differently than I do, from another vantage point, and that produces a beautiful certainty.*

Goethe was willing to take advice from Merck. As we have already seen, it was the latter who urged Goethe to publish Götz, with the adage "Hang the diapers on the fence and they'll dry soon enough!" Merck was mercilessly critical of other works by Goethe. The play *Clavigo,* for example, he declared to be at best conventional, and he advised his friend to restrict himself to things that others weren't capable of. Goethe accommodated Merck and accepted his criticism without resentment. In retrospect, however, he suggests that in the end the friend he valued so much did himself no favors with his basically *negative* attitude. And in fact, Merck's story took a sad turn. Eventually he quarreled with most of his old friends and acquaintances, making few new ones. His relationship with Goethe grew distant. Finally, he lost all interest in literature and art. He attempted to become an entrepreneur, but with little success. A cotton spinning mill he founded went bankrupt. Worn down by serious illness, he put an end to his life on June 27, 1791.

When their friendship began, Merck was an all-around talent who painted, wrote poetry, translated, was well informed about science, and had a knack for technical things. And for all that, he had a cool intellect. It is all the more surprising that in addition to writing literary criticism, he belonged to the circle of so-called Sentimentalists. Goethe met this group on his first visit to Darmstadt in March 1772.

Members included a man named von Hesse, who served as privy councilor, and his wife and her sister Karoline Flachsland, who since 1770 had been secretly engaged to Herder. She was waiting impatiently to marry him; he was in Bückeburg working as court chaplain. Others in the circle were Henriette von Roussillon, who served as a lady-in-waiting to the court. Despite her youth, she was plagued by the illness that would claim her life, and she had ceased to seek a lasting relationship. When not lying sick in a darkened room, she by turns entertained brilliantly and was steeped in a melancholy that she directed into an obsession with poetry. Her friend and fellow lady-in-waiting Luise von Ziegler was healthy, pretty, and just as mad about poetry. She had a hut built in a park where she passed pleasant summer days with a white lamb, which she led across the meadows on a red leash.

The three young women had made a pact of friendship and given one another nicknames. Henriette von Roussillon became "Urania," Luise von Ziegler "Lila," and Karoline Flachsland "Psyche." Since the two ladies-in-waiting were often traveling with the court, there were frequent farewells, which afforded wonderful opportunities for tears. There was much weeping in general, and appropriate poems were read. Klopstock was high on the list of favorites, but they also read Gellert and Johann Wilhelm Ludwig Gleim as well as the

"Night Thoughts" of Edward Young, the sentimental novels of Samuel Richardson, and, of course, Rousseau. There was no holding back—voluptuous emotion, lachrymose inwardness, and a playfully rococo cult of friendship prevailed. The apostle of this sentimental circle was Franz Michael Leuchsenring, a soft, affectionate man who was a tutor at the Darmstadt court. He was deeply devout, but for most members of the circle, the cult of feeling was more aesthetic than religious. The important thing was one's feelings and feeling one's feelings, sensing sentimentality—an intensification by reduplication. The Sentimentalists were sophisticated, not naïve. Much attention was paid to verbal expression and the staging of their meetings. The whole thing was a parlor game, with nonstop embraces, caresses, and tears.

It is astonishing that the sarcastic Merck belonged, and that he thoroughly enjoyed participating. Perhaps it was exactly because the playful aspect of the group's emotional intensity was so obvious. It was something that could please even as cool a head as his. The poet Gleim, one of their idols, once paid a visit—another opportunity for a sentimental scene. Karoline Flachsland wrote to Herder, "Merck, Leuchsenring, and I surrounded dear old gentle, sprightly, honest Father Gleim in a corner and surrendered ourselves to the full sentiments of most tender friendship. He wept a tear of joy and I, I lay with my head on Merck's breast. He was extraordinarily moved, wept with me, and—I don't know what all I did."

It was into this circle that Goethe strayed on his visit in the spring of 1772. Numerous arms reached out to embrace him, for they all realized that a true poet had arrived. "Goethe is full of songs," the enraptured Karoline writes Herder, who was not exactly pleased by his fiancée's enthusiasm.

For his part, Goethe enjoyed his new friends much more than he did the company of lawyers in their stuffy chambers. He spent many lovely spring days with Karoline and the others. Goethe saw himself as a wayfarer, stopping here and there to sample and flirt, and he was familiar with their notion of the reduplication of feeling. He, too, knew what it meant to be in love with being in love, and what's more, he could make poetry out of it. Lila, Urania, and Psyche—these three Graces are immediately commemorated, in an encounter edged with lyric gold.

When for the first time you
approached the stranger
in loving anticipation,
stretched out your hand to him,
he felt in advance
all the bliss
stirring toward him.

The gods gave us
Elysium here on earth.

That was for Urania, and a few strophes later, it was Lila's turn:

I cast a hopeful glance
at Lila; she comes toward me.
Heavenly lips!
And I stagger toward her,
look and sigh and stagger—
What bliss! What bliss!
The feeling of a kiss!

Psyche, a.k.a. Karoline Flachsland, got a poem of her own that would cause a good deal of trouble in days to come.

The Sentimentalists went on group rambles in the pretty country around Darmstadt, dedicating hills and rocks to one another. Each had at least one little rise that bore his or her name. Goethe chose for himself a rock that was somewhat higher than the others', scaling it to scratch his name onto it. In a little ceremony, he consecrated the rock with a poem dedicated to Psyche. It depicts a scene in which Karoline leans against the stone, her head cushioned by the moss, and thinks of the *absent one*, meaning Herder. The poet wishes, however, that she also think of the

bewildered wayfarer: and a tear wells up
at the thought of past joys,
then you lift to heaven
your pleading eye,

see above you
there, my name.

Herder was not amused by the poem and was very put out when he heard that, after Goethe's departure, Karoline actually made a pilgrimage back to the rock in question. He composed a parody of Goethe's consecration of the rock and wrote to Karoline in a fit of pique, "In more ways than one you cut a very sorry figure" in Goethe's poem. Goethe sent Herder an angry reply: *So I also want to tell you that I was recently infuriated by your answer to the "Consecration of the Rock" and called you an intolerant cleric. . . . As far as that point is concerned, from now on your right to cause your girl melancholy hours will not be interfered with.* The relationship between the two men took a cooler turn and didn't warm up again for two years.

The Sentimentalists liked to call Goethe the "Wanderer," and he indeed often walked from Frankfurt to Darmstadt, even in wind and rain. On one of these hikes he conceived the hymn "Wanderer's Storm Song," a daring, formally experimental poem. *When I was met on the way by a terrible storm that I had to brave, I passionately sang this half-nonsensical stuff out loud.*

If we compare the Sentimentalists' flirtatious lyrics with this poem, which Goethe circulated among his friends but didn't publish until much later, in 1815, we can measure how far he was from their delicately amorous rococo style. "Wanderer's Storm Song" is a skillful expression of wild, chaotic feeling. The poem, with its energetic defiance, strikes a Promethean tone:

> *Genius, he whom you do not forsake*
> *Not the rain or the gale*
> *Breathes a chill on his heart*
> *Genius, he whom you do not forsake,*
> *Will sing against the rain cloud*
> *Against the hail storm*
> *Sing against them like the*
> *Lark, you up there*
> *Genius, he whom you do not forsake.*

That incantatory repetition, *Genius, he whom you do not forsake*, is a declaration, a plea, a wish, a demand. Who is this *Genius*? The pantheon of Greek gods is mobilized: Phoebus Apollo, the god of the sun, warmth, and song; then Father Bromius, a pseudonym for Dionysus, the god of wine, fertility, and ecstasy; and finally Jupiter—Zeus, ruler of the gods. It was from Pindar that Goethe learned to weave these appeals and demands into his poem. Herder had introduced him to the Greek poet, and he was attempting to translate him. *I live in Pindar now*, he wrote to Herder in July 1772. *To be sure, when he shoots his arrows one after another toward his target in the clouds, I still stand and gape*. Now he *gapes* no more but, instead, shoots his own arrows into the clouds at the gods. But the gods of Pindar can help him only if he helps himself and has confidence in himself. The *Genius* to whom he appeals is in the last analysis his own. Whatever the gods have ordained for him, he will not be distracted from his goal:

> *There on the hill—*
> *Heavenly might—*
> *Only enough glow—*
> *There is my hut—*
> *To wade that far.*

Those are the closing lines. In contrast to the broad opening verses, one hears panting. Someone has actually run out of breath here. We must not forget—if we can believe Goethe—that the poem was actually composed during his hike. The *wade* at the end sounds quite unheroic and casts an ironical light on the emotional gestures of the beginning. Exhaustion after great effort makes itself felt: it is the exhaustion of the path Goethe has traveled. He is daring himself to measure up against Pindar. The poem's rhythms imitate the bursts of exertion needed to fight against wind and rain. Anacreon, who makes an appearance *with the pair of doves / In his tender arm*, is mentioned almost contemptuously, for this wanderer has contended with more powerful forces—namely, with the *Gale-breathing godhead*.

So this is how Goethe may sometimes have arrived in Darmstadt to visit the Sentimentalists, having trekked from Frankfurt on foot.

Wind-blown and rain-soaked, he made his way to them and then returned to Frankfurt, staying in one of the inns in the Fahrgasse.

Goethe the Wanderer had in the meantime become a reviewer in Frankfurt. The man who would later write, *Strike him dead, the dog. He's a reviewer* was one himself. Merck, having utterly transformed the *Frankfurter Gelehrte Anzeigen*, had finally persuaded him to write for it. Its pages were stripped of didactic philosophizing and boring moral commentary and filled with gripping, irreverent criticism. In accordance with the changing spirit of the times, expressions of opinion had a personal edge.

Wit instead of pedantry—this was to Goethe's liking. His very first piece, a scathing review of a German imitation of Laurence Sterne's *Sentimental Journey*, strikes a tone unusual even for the latest reviews under Merck: *As police officers of the literary court . . . we will allow the preceptor* [that is, the author] *to continue living for a time. However, he must be sent to the new workhouse where all useless, prattling writers grate Oriental roots, sort variants, scrape documents, cut up indexes, and perform other similar manual tasks.* He dismisses a tragedy by a certain Pfeufer in a single sentence: *Herr Benignus Pfeufer may be an upright man in other respects, but with this wretched play he has prostituted his name once and for all.* A thick tome on *Moral Beauty and Philosophy of Life* bores the reviewer, who calls it *pathetic twaddle.*

One can tell that he wrote the reviews quickly and offhandedly, sometimes without even having read the book: a glance at the introduction was enough. But sometimes he feels challenged to provide a more thorough discussion—for instance, of Johann Georg Sulzer's influential *The Arts in Their Origin, Their True Nature, and Best Application.* In his review, Goethe attempts to clarify his own aesthetic principles.

He writes that it is still too early for an authoritative theory of the arts. Everything is still in ferment, and the artist and lover of the arts should remember that *with any theory, he blocks the path to true enjoyment.* Above all, the reviewer challenges the commonly held principle, elaborated by Sulzer, that art is an *imitation of nature.*

Goethe confidently declares that with its forms, art creates a new nature: an artificial, incomparable, original, and surprising nature. It has no need to measure itself against what already exists, but should be judged according to its own inner truth. Thus Goethe opposes the principle of imitation of nature with the principle of creative expression.

But since the principle of imitation applies not just to concrete natural objects but also to the traditional forms of representation that one should emulate as well, the critique of imitation has a double significance: art needs to be liberated both from conventional forms and from dull realism. With his *Götz* as well as his nature and love poetry, Goethe was attempting exactly that.

Whoever ties art to the imitation of nature assumes the goodness and beauty of nature, Goethe claims, and quotes Sulzer, who says of nature that it touches us "through pleasant impressions." Goethe answers, *Are not raging storms, floods, rains of fire, subterranean infernos, and death in all the elements just as true testimonies to its eternal life as glorious sunrises over ripening vineyards and perfumed orange groves?*

Goethe denies that beauty in nature only needs to be imitated, and in the fervor of his polemical dismissal adopts the extreme counterposition: beauty must be forcibly wrested from a cruel nature. Far from following the *example of nature*, art must resist it. He advances an entirely novel thought: *art is precisely the counterforce, it arises from the individual's struggle to maintain himself against the destructive force of the whole.*

From this vantage point, he ventures a daring look at the culture of the future. Humanity, he writes, is in the act of closing itself off in a cultural *palace* behind *walls of glass*. A century later, Dostoevsky would define modernism in exactly the same way.[*] The young Goethe anticipates him en passant and also suggests Dostoevsky's conclusion that the glass palace, the artificial world that has been wrested from nature, becomes a site of complacency. The powerful assertion of self against nature morphs into luxurious relaxation. Decadence threatens. Man, Goethe writes, gradually becomes *softer and softer*. How was such decadence to be avoided? The reviewer can answer even that. Since art and culture owe their existence to the resistance to nature, one should ally oneself with this resistive power and not simply take it for granted. One should pay attention to the difficulties artists have to overcome and the power that allows them to do so. That is how the creative impulse is fortified—nature pays it *tribute*.

---

[*] See Fyodor Dostoevsky, *Notes from the Underground*, pt. 1, chap. 7.

Yet the artistic power of anti-nature that is here invoked is, in the final analysis, itself nature, and the young Goethe knows that too. What else could it be? There is a kind of natural impulse to oppose what seems complete and finished in nature. Or, according to the traditional formulation, "natura naturans," creative nature, opposes "natura naturata," incarnate nature. In another review, Goethe defines this power of natural anti-nature as genius. *It is our firm belief that genius does not imitate nature, but rather itself creates, like nature.* His early aesthetic is concentrated in this sentence.

There is one more review that deserves to be quoted at length. Goethe wrote it after he had already moved to Wetzlar. He used a review of a trivial, conventional love story to describe a pair of lovers who would truly deserve to be depicted:

O Genius of our Fatherland, let a young man flourish soon who, full of youthful strength and high spirits, would be first the best companion for his circle of friends, choose the best games, sing the happiest little songs . . . to whom the best dancer would joyfully give her hand . . . let him find a girl worthy of him!

When more sacred feelings lead him from the bustle of society into solitude, let him discover a girl on his pilgrimage whose soul is all goodness and whose form all gracefulness, who has had the good fortune to develop in a quiet family circle of active, domestic love. Who is the favorite, friend, and support of her mother and the second mother of her home, whose always affectionate soul irresistibly wins every heart for her, from whom poets and wise men would willingly learn and take delight in her native virtue, prosperity, and grace.—And if she feels in hours of solitary peace that with all the love she broadcasts she is still missing something, a heart that is as young and warm as she and would yearn with her for more distant, more hidden joys. Firmly yoked to his invigorating company, she would strive toward all the golden prospects, eternal togetherness, lasting union, eternally entwining love.

Let the two of them find each other. At the first approach they will sense, darkly and powerfully, what an epitome of bliss each is taking hold of in the other. They will never leave each other. . . . Truth will be in his songs and living beauty, not colorful soap-bubble ideals like those floating about in hundreds of German songs.

But do such girls exist? Can there be such youths?

The reviewer has good reason to think that such a girl and boy really do exist, for he himself is the boy and the girl is Lotte Buff, and what happens between them takes place half in Wetzlar and half in a dream.

Goethe arrived in Wetzlar in the middle of May 1772 to register as a trainee at the Reichskammergericht, the Imperial Chamber Court. Like his father before him, he was there to gain further professional experience, especially in the area of constitutional and administrative law. The Imperial Supreme Court was the highest court for all civil disputes among the imperial estates, as well as between subjects and the authorities. Criminal cases were not tried there. The court had been in existence since 1495, first in Speyer and, since the end of the seventeenth century, in Wetzlar. The little town of about five thousand inhabitants was swarming with judges, procurators, lawyers, diplomats, and their subordinate officials, legation councilors, and officers of the court, all pursuing their abstruse and never-ending cases. Some had already lasted over a hundred years. They concerned sinecures, taxes, debts, border disputes, and tenancy arrangements. The litigants spent money attempting to speed up or slow down their cases. Corruption was widespread, and to put a stop to it an inquiry had been ordered five years before Goethe's arrival, thanks to which the army of officials had grown even larger. In the summer of 1772, its investigations were still in progress.

There was no specific program for trainees. One could poke around in the piles of documents and had an enormous number to choose from: sixteen thousand unresolved cases were stacked up in the offices—the dense juridical underbrush of the venerable Holy Roman Empire of the German Nation. The scene in *Faust* in which Mephistopheles introduces a newly arrived student to the various fields of study summarizes Goethe's experiences in Wetzlar: *Laws and rights are handed down / Passed on like some eternal plague / From generation unto generation, / They shamble on from place to place.*

Goethe devoted hardly any time to such things. He attended very few trials, which consisted of the public reading of long, learned writs. Goethe had barely arrived in Wetzlar when people started making jokes about the slim doctor of law with the large eyes who was studying every possible subject except law. He was reputed to be an aesthete and a philosopher, and it soon got around that he also wrote reviews. The legation secretary Wilhelm Jerusalem, whose suicide would make him famous not long afterward, knew Goethe from his days in Leipzig and referred to him disparagingly as a "Frankfurt newspaper writer." *Götz* had not yet been published but was already being talked about, and a group who dined together and, like the Sentimentalists, made a game of giving one another nicknames dubbed Goethe "Götz the Upright." Here too, Goethe made an impression and people sought his friendship. He could discourse beautifully on Homer, Pindar, Ossian, and Shakespeare and read from their works in his sonorous voice. Goethe socialized with young lawyers and legation secretaries. He was not attracted to the circles of higher officials, who were often aristocrats. Wherever he went, he immediately became the center of attention. The Hanoverian legation councilor Johann Christian Kestner, Charlotte Buff's fiancé, describes how he met Goethe that summer. He was out in the neighboring village of Garbenheim, a popular destination for excursions. "There," writes Kestner, "I found him lying on his back in the grass under a tree while conversing with those standing around him—an Epicurean philosopher (von Goué, the great genius), a Stoic philosopher (von Kielmannsegg), and a middle thing between those two (Dr. König)—and quite at his ease."

He lies nonchalantly in the grass while the others stand around and listen to his words. Kestner depicts the scene with some irony. This man in the grass is certainly impressive, but how seriously can one take him? Is that any way to talk to people if you have any self-respect? Or doesn't he have any? Kestner had joined them and noticed that "interesting things" were being discussed, and the most interesting things were being said by this Goethe fellow. "You know that I don't make snap judgments," Kestner writes. "I did find that he has genius and a lively imagination, but that wasn't enough for me to esteem him highly." He got to know him better at the home of his fiancée, Lotte Buff. There Goethe had been introduced pretty much as he would later describe Werther's introduction in the novel: Goethe had taken part in an excursion to the hunting lodge in Volpertshausen, where the party had also planned to organize a dance. Twelve gentlemen and thirteen young women of impeccable reputation had been invited. The nineteen-year-old Charlotte Buff was riding in the same coach as Goethe. He falls in love with the dainty young woman with sky-blue eyes and curly blond hair. Dancing went on for half the night. According to Kestner's testimony, Goethe did not yet know on that first night that Lotte "was no longer free." And since the engagement was not yet official, when Kestner later joined the party, he acted as if he and Lotte were only good friends.

The next day Goethe paid Lotte a visit in the so-called Deutsches Haus, the seat of the Order of Teutonic Knights, where her father was the bailiff of the order's holdings. His wife had died some time ago, and as his oldest daughter, Lotte took care of her younger siblings. On this first visit, Goethe came upon a scene he would later depict in *Werther*: Lotte, surrounded by the crowd of her little brothers and sisters, cuts slices of bread for them, wipes their noses, settles their arguments, and scolds or praises them as needed.

In *Poetry and Truth* Goethe stresses that it was precisely the fact that Lotte was already engaged that made him *carefree*. It took him by surprise to suddenly find himself so passionately *entangled and enraptured that he no longer knew himself.* All the more so because Lotte was the kind of woman who finds *general favor* but does not *excite intense passion.* That was, by the way, also the opinion of Merck (as ruthless as *Mephistopheles*) when he paid a visit to Wetzlar. He told his friend he would do better to seek out a more attractive lady friend instead of wasting his time on a hopeless *romance.*

Lotte had set clear limits on Goethe's romancing, but with the approval of her fiancé wanted to continue the friendship. Kestner also found Goethe attractive and didn't want to do without him. And so after the misunderstanding had been cleared up, Goethe remained a friend of the engaged couple. *Thus they continued to live through the splendid summer in a genuine German idyll, to which the countryside lent the prose and a pure affection the poetry.* They walked through the fields of grain, listened to the song of the lark, groaned under the heat, got drenched by thunderstorms, and sat around the kitchen table shelling peas. It could have continued like that for quite a while, but according to Kestner, Goethe had "qualities that can make him dangerous for a young woman, especially one who is sensitive and has taste." Although Kestner had confidence in his beloved, he doubted whether he was capable "of making Lottchen as happy as he could," as he wrote to a friend. He wanted to lose neither Goethe nor Lotte. Thus it was a great relief for him when Goethe finally realized "that he would have to use force to obtain his peace of mind." Force in this case meant the decision to depart Wetzlar in secret.

Goethe left Wetzlar early on September 10, 1772, without announcing his departure. The three had spent the previous evening together. Kestner wrote in his diary, "He, Lottchen, and I had a curious conversation about conditions after this life, about going away and coming back, etc., a conversation initiated by Lottchen, not by him. We agreed that whichever of us died first should, if he could, give those still alive news of the conditions of that life. Goethe became quite despondent." The next morning, Goethe left behind two letters of farewell, one for Kestner and, enclosed in it, one for Lotte. To Kestner he wrote, *If I had stayed a single moment longer with you, I wouldn't have been able to control myself.* And to Lotte: *Now I am alone and can weep. I leave you two happy and shall not go out of your hearts.*

Lotte cried when she read his letters. Despite the relief she felt, some sadness was inevitable. "But she was happy that he was gone," Kestner notes in his diary, "since she couldn't give him what he wanted. For he was very much in love with her—to the point of mania. But she always distanced herself from such things and never granted him anything but friendship, which she formally declared. We spoke only of him."

They would speak of him many more times, at first in a friendly and affectionate way, but for a while, after the publication of *Werther*, with bitterness and resentment. But that too would pass.

CHAPTER 8

A Portrait of the Young Goethe. Correspondence
with the Kestners. Jerusalem's Suicide.
Götz Is Published. Becoming a Star.
Exhilaration. *Prometheus*. Poet or Prophet? Muhammad.
Satirical Campaigns against False Prophets.

....

BEFORE FOLLOWING GOETHE ON HIS PATH, LET'S PAUSE
for a moment to consider how he must have appeared to those around
him: to a sober, insightful observer such as Kestner, for instance, who,
despite great respect for Goethe, had grounds to regard him skeptically. A surviving draft of one of Kestner's letters contains perhaps the
most powerful and vivid portrait we have of the young Goethe.

"[Goethe] has what one calls genius and an extraordinarily lively
imagination. He is intensely emotional. He has a noble way of thinking. He is a man of character. He loves children and can become very
involved with them. He is bizarre, and there are various things about
his behavior and appearance that could make him unpleasant. But
nevertheless, he is in the good books of children, women, and many
others.—He does whatever occurs to him without worrying whether
it pleases others, is fashionable, or permitted by good breeding. He
hates all constraints.—He holds the female sex in high regard.—*In
principiis* he is not yet settled and is still searching for a certain system. . . . *He is not what one would call orthodox, however not from pride or
caprice or to make a show.* He . . . doesn't like to disturb others in their settled opinions. . . . He does not go to church, not even to Communion,
and seldom prays. For, as he says, 'I'm not enough of a liar for that.' . . .
He has great respect for the Christian religion, but not in the form in
which our theologians would present it. . . . He strives for truth but has

more regard for feeling it than for demonstrating it. . . . He has made belles-lettres and the arts his principal study—or rather, all branches of knowledge except those by which one earns one's bread. . . . He is, in a word, a very remarkable person."

The wealth of ingenious ideas, the strong emotional presence, the disregard of convention and fashion, and the spontaneity—these are the characteristics that make an immediate impression. More subtle are the seriousness and conscientiousness, especially evident in religious matters. He has respect for religion but not for its claims to temporal power or its dogma. This "remarkable person" follows his own path in everything and has boundless curiosity about the world, which he satisfies in his own way. He is far removed from the branches of knowledge "by which one earns one's bread" and so also from the exclusive focus on getting ahead in his profession. Of course, he can also afford to be that way. Kestner, very much a sober man who had to earn his bread, records this characteristic of Goethe's without contempt or enthusiastic admiration; he is simply amazed at so much free-and-easy self-assurance.

Goethe left Kestner in Wetzlar with this image of himself as he set off on foot down the Lahn Valley toward Frankfurt. On the way he paid a visit to the celebrated author Sophie von La Roche, who lived with her husband and children in a stately residence in Ehrenbreitstein. Her husband was an enlightened diplomat, worldly-wise, tolerant, and somewhat patronizing toward the aesthetes his wife attracted to their house. Sophie, a cousin of Wieland's and at one time engaged to him, gained fame with her epistolary novel *The History of Fräulein von Sternheim.* People mistook the novel's sensitive, virtuous heroine for the author and were disappointed with von La Roche the cool society woman. That had also been Goethe's first impression when he met her through Merck in the Darmstadt circle in early 1772. Now she opened up to him, however, and though an innate reserve would always remain, the two developed an intimate, trusting relationship, Goethe occasionally calling her *Mama* in his letters. He was the witty conver-

* Two modern translations are *The History of Lady Sophia Sternheim*, trans. Christa Baguss Britt (Albany: State University of New York Press, 1991), and *The History of Lady Sophie Sternheim*, ed. James Lynn, trans. Joseph Collyer (Worcester: Billing & Sons, 1991).

sationalist, entertaining but careful to keep his mercurial temperament in check. He would remain in contact with von La Roche over three generations: through her daughter Maximiliane von Brentano, whose black eyes he borrowed for Werther's Lotte, and her granddaughter Bettine von Arnim.

Back in Frankfurt, his father's reproaches awaited. Goethe's sojourn in Wetzlar had been expensive, but what had it added to his professional development? The father kept track, but the son didn't and simply let his father pay. In a letter to Kestner, he complains, *Dear God, when I grow old, will I be like that? Will my soul no longer cling to what is amiable and good? Strange that one should believe that the older a person becomes, the freer he should be from everything mundane and petty. He becomes more and more mundane and petty.*

Goethe found the atmosphere at home oppressive. There was also trouble with the *Frankfurter Gelehrte Anzeigen*. Some of the senior clergy had taken offense at the cheeky tone of the reviews, and the periodical had been sued. The publisher also complained that some things were too difficult for readers to understand. Goethe decided to give up his work as a reviewer, and wrote an ironic "Epilogue" as a farewell to his audience at the end of 1772. He says he has learned *what it means to want to communicate with the public, to be misunderstood, and so on and so forth.*

In October 1772, news arrived from Kestner that an acquaintance in Wetzlar, the former legation secretary Siegfried von Goué, who had devoted himself to drinking and writing tragedies, had taken his own life. *I honor such a deed,* writes Goethe, *and bemoan humanity and leave all the shitty philistines to such tobacco-smoked reflections as "I told you so." I hope to never burden my friends with such news.*

It proved an unfounded rumor. Goué was alive and well and had in the meantime moved to Göttingen. Two weeks later, however, a real suicide occurred in Wetzlar. Wilhelm Jerusalem shot himself. Everyone was talking about it, because Jerusalem's name was familiar to many. He was the son of a well-known religious writer who was a close friend of Lessing's. There was much speculation about what could have driven the young man to take his own life. Was it *an anxious striving for truth and moral goodness*, as Goethe wrote to Sophie von La Roche? Had Jerusalem perished from his lofty moral aspiration? Kestner wrote that an unhappy love affair with a married woman was said to have played a part. *This news was terrible and unexpected,* answered Goethe, immediately blaming Jerusalem's father, who had raised his son to be overly pious: *If that damned cleric his father isn't to blame, may God forgive me for hoping he breaks his neck.*

Goethe asked Kestner for details of the suicide. Kestner wrote an extensive, detailed report, itself almost a literary masterpiece, on which Goethe would draw a year later for *Werther,* not just its concrete details but also a number of felicitous phrases. The famous last sentence of the novel—*No clergyman accompanied him*—is straight from Kestner's report.

In *Poetry and Truth* Goethe describes the composition of *Werther* as though the news of Jerusalem's suicide was the initial spark for the literary reworking of his summer romance in Wetzlar. In fact, an entire year went by before Goethe began writing the novel. And several other things had happened in the meantime.

Goethe was in a gloomy but frivolous mood. He had an active correspondence with Kestner and flirted with the role of a romantically frustrated family friend. As if wanting to torture himself, he demanded that he be allowed to procure the wedding rings for the couple. He sent the rings on April 7, 1773, with the message that, from then on, he would no longer be *eager* to see the two of them. Nor would he attend the wedding. He had taken Lotte's silhouette down from where it hung above his bed. Only when he heard the news that she was *lying in* would *a new era begin and I will love her children instead of her.* And then once again, in a letter to Kestner, he turns over the question whether it was right for him to leave Wetzlar so hastily. Was he too cold or too hot? *It cost me little, and yet I cannot understand how it was possible.* It's as if he must defend himself against the charge of having been too cool a lover—an absurd thing to say to Kestner, who had been happy to have Goethe out of the running. But Goethe acts as if he had thereby cut a sorry figure in Kestner's eyes. Should he have fought more for Lotte? Is he not really a ladies' man? *And between you and me, without boasting, I know something about girls.* He writes that he is not jealous of Kestner and hints at his own intention to get married. There is mention of a possible candidate—he probably had Anna Sibylla Münch in mind, having drawn her name in a marriage-lottery parlor game. He writes that he has dreamed about Lotte: he was walking through an allée with her on his arm and people were stopping to stare at them. *And so I dream,* he continues, *and dawdle through life, conduct nasty trials, write dramas and novels and so on, sketch and flirt and keep it up as fast as I can go.* At times he acts relieved to be out of the affair, at others he complains that he can't get Lotte off his mind. In any case, he feels very strange. *I don't know why I'm writing so much. I'm such a fool.*

He also strikes gloomy notes. *I'm wandering through the desert,* or *My poor existence is congealing into barren rock.* He hints that he is sometimes in a *shooting* mood. In *Poetry and Truth* he talks of a dagger that he kept for a while on his nightstand, with which he often experimented to see whether he *could succeed in sinking the sharp point a few inches into my breast.* He couldn't, and so in the end *laughed at myself, threw off all hypochondriacal fancies, and resolved to live.*

Then came the success of *Götz.* The play appeared in June 1773, anonymously and without place of publication, paid for by Merck and Goethe. And since the experienced businessman Merck had left for Russia in the entourage of a Darmstadt princess, Goethe also had the expense of marketing and distribution. It was a huge best-seller, for its time, making it impossible for the author to remain anonymous. Nor did Goethe want to. A half year later, there was a second authorized printing, to forestall pirated editions, which it did not succeed in doing. Despite Goethe's opinion that the play was a closet drama because of its shifting locations and lack of unified plot, it was almost immediately staged, first in Berlin (with the addition of a Gypsy ballet) and then in Hamburg, Breslau, Leipzig, and Mannheim. The newspapers introduced the young author to a wider public. With *Götz*—and a year later to an even greater extent with *Werther*—Goethe had conquered a new reading and theatergoing audience. A reading public, until then quite sedate, discovered a sudden taste for sensationalism. Everyone who was anyone had to know the play and its author, or at least to have heard of him, and the new star in the literary firmament brightened the correspondence of his contemporaries, especially women. Somewhat later hubbub about the play even reached the ears of Frederick the Great, and the king of Prussia was not amused. He called *Götz* a "vile imitation of those bad English plays," by which he meant the works of Shakespeare. Without mention of his name, the author was berated as the destroyer of literary taste. But the public was proud of him on patriotic as well as literary grounds. People were no longer content to be lectured on literary matters by the king. A national literary self-confidence had grown, owing in large part to the success of *Götz*.

Most reviews ranged from approval to euphoria. In Christoph Martin Wieland's monthly *Der Teutsche Merkur* (*The German Mercury*) the play was "the most beautiful and interesting monster" that deserved the "liveliest thanks of all German patriots." Wieland himself maintained a cautious distance from such praise, but also admitted that an author had emerged who raised the greatest hopes. Of course, Goethe's former house organ, the *Frankfurter Gelehrte Anzeigen*, also praised the play: "We could tell from the very first pages that things would get pretty boisterous, but we forgot our Aristotle and reveled in it."

Numerous imitations appeared. The theme of knights became fashionable. Heroes alone against the world, with or without hands of iron, capable matrons looking after the castle, lovely maidens, evil schemers in armor, and beautiful, wicked women now peopled the stages. Since Götz was a historical person and there were descendants who could now bask in their ancestor's reflected glory, other bearers of famous names got the idea to have themselves portrayed in plays. A Baron von Riedesel of Eisenach announced a prize of twenty ducats for a play about one of his ancestors. He even had Lessing in mind as the judge, but nothing came of the scheme.

Overnight, Goethe's name became so famous all over literary Germany that people even attributed to him J. M. R. Lenz's *Der Hofmeister* (*The Tutor*), published anonymously shortly after *Götz*. Goethe's name stood for the new, earthy, powerfully visceral tone, for theatrical picture books, liberation from the conventional rules, lack of didacticism, and verbal originality. Not long thereafter, however, Goethe had no trouble returning to traditional forms with the play *Clavigo*, as if to prove that he could do both the one thing and its opposite.

He had an overwhelming sense of omnipotence. Not only did he want to do what he was capable of, but he also felt capable of doing whatever he wanted. On September 15, 1773, he tells Kestner what he's working on: *And a drama for performance so those fellows see that if I choose to, I can observe the rules and depict morality and sensitivity. Adieu. One more word in confidence as a writer: my ideals of beauty and greatness are developing more each day, and if my vitality and my love don't desert me, there is still much to come for the people I love and the public can have its share too.*

In his euphoria, Goethe sketched out the play *Prometheus*. In mid-July 1773 he writes Kestner, *The gods have sent me a sculptor, and if he finds work here as we hope, I can forget many things. . . . I'm adapting my own situation as a play in defiance of God and man.*

He found material on Prometheus from Aeschylus, Lucian, and Ovid in Benjamin Hederich's *Basic Lexicon of Mythology*. Two fragmentary acts were as far as he got. They do not contain much action, but instead a series of great verbal gestures, the theme being defiance of the gods. Prometheus is cast as a rebel, no longer a willing subject of the gods. In the background, one sees the Caucasus. Those who know their mythology know that there the gods chained Prometheus to a rock as punishment for bringing fire to men. But the play chooses a different episode from the story of Prometheus. To sideline him, the gods offer Prometheus a comfortable place in Olympus. But he would be dependent on them still, a sort of *castellan*, as Prometheus says mockingly in a *Götz*-like tone. His brother Epimetheus recommends he accept their offer. Prometheus replies, *They want to share with me, and I maintain / That I have nothing I need share with them. / What I have they cannot snatch away. . . . The circle my activity completes.*

For Goethe, this *activity* (the German *Wirksamkeit* also means "effectiveness") is above all his literary output and the power of the word, and so he brings in Minerva as the goddess of inspired speech. Prometheus sees himself in league with her and depicts the wonderful effect the goddess has on him. These lines are about the peculiar process of inspiration. Goethe knew what it felt like to suddenly experience yourself as a medium for the thoughts and ideas flooding through you; to have your normal consciousness creatively expand; to become a different person and yet stay the same. Prometheus to Minerva:

> *And you are to my spirit*
> *What it is to itself*
>
> . . .
>
> *Always as if my soul were speaking to itself*
>
> . . .
>
> *So was I not myself,*
> *It was a god who spoke*
> *When I thought I was speaking,*

And when I thought a god was speaking,
I spoke myself.
And thus with you and me
So indivisible.

In the second act, Prometheus gives a sample of his *activity*. He does what authors also enjoy doing—forms men in his own image, though with clay rather than words:

Look down, Zeus
Upon my world: it lives.
A world that I have formed in my own image
A race of men who are my equal.
To suffer, weep, enjoy, and to be happy
And to ignore you, as do I.

The story continues a little further. Men learn to assert themselves against one another, to defend their freedom and the property they have acquired through their work. Then they are initiated into the mysteries of the unity of love and death. It all happens hurriedly, in quick succession. But what one recalls above all is Prometheus's defiant rebellion against Zeus: *And to ignore you.*

These rebellious lines recur in the famous ode, also entitled "Prometheus": *Cover your heaven, Zeus.* It was probably meant to open the third act, but was published as a stand-alone poem in 1785, without Goethe's permission, in his friend Friedrich Heinrich Jacobi's *On the Teachings of Spinoza in Letters to Herr Moses Mendelssohn*, as an alleged example of daring atheism in the style of Spinoza. There will be more to say about this later.

The tone struck in this first-person poem attacking the Olympian gods is even more aggressive and self-assertive than that in the play. Though it ends, as in the play, with *Here I sit, forming men*, the powerlessness of the gods is pilloried even more sharply:

I know nothing so pitiful
Under the sun as you gods.
Your majesty kept alive

By offerings and whispered prayers
And you would wither if not for
Children and beggars,
Those hopeful fools.

Why should that be true only of the Greek gods and not of the Christian God as well? *Who aided me against / The malice of the Titans / . . . Did not you, my sacred, glowing heart / Do everything yourself?* A heart that dares such things doesn't need the Christian God either. Whoever was so disposed could hear something blasphemous in the poem, doubtless why Jacobi published it and why it caused a scandal. In *Poetry and Truth*, Goethe tries to blunt the explosive critique of religion. *Even though one can and did engage in philosophical and even religious reflections about this work, it properly belongs completely to poetry.*

Goethe's Promethean self-confidence is based on the *most secure foundation* of his life at the time, namely, his poetical *productive talent*. Something always occurred to him. He was full of ideas and wrote before he got out of bed in the morning, at night, during the day, in company, alone, and with or without wine. You could request whatever you wanted from him, *I was ready to deliver*. Since his *natural gift* at this point in life was available whenever and wherever he needed it, *in my thoughts it pleased me to make it the foundation of my entire existence. This idea was transformed into an image: the old mythological figure of Prometheus occurred to me. . . . The story of Prometheus came alive within me. I altered the old robe of the Titans to fit my size.*

There was something cocky and insouciant about Goethe. He tried everything: poems in the folk-song manner, odes in Pindar's style, theater in imitation of Shakespeare, county fair–style slapstick, and doggerel like Hans Sachs's all flowed easily from his pen. He was a quick-change artist able to change others as well.

And that was the impression he made on people around him: that he was a magician. Bolstered by the success of *Götz*, he was surrounded by an aura of the unprecedented. People called him a "genius," sought him out, and hung on his every word. Some called him "possessed" (Jacobi) and others a "genius from head to toe" (the writer and art critic Wilhelm Heinse). The Swiss writer Johann Jakob Bodmer feared that "his fire will consume him." People regarded him as a miracle of nature.

He attracted people who honored him with almost religious fervor. An acquaintance from his Strasbourg years wrote, "This Goethe, the only one I must . . . stammer and sing and wax dithyrambic about . . . this Goethe has all but taken wing and risen above all my ideals. . . . I would never have been so able to experience the feeling of the disciples at Emmaus in the Gospel, when they said, 'Did not our heart burn within us, while he talked with us?' Let us make him our Lord Jesus forever and let me be the last of his disciples!" At times people gathered around him as around a prophet. Ludwig Julius Friedrich Höpfner, a former colleague at the *Frankfurter Gelehrte Anzeigen*, reported on a visit Goethe paid to Giessen: "some sitting, some standing—a few of the learned gentlemen were even standing on chairs and looking over the heads of their colleagues into the assembled circle from whose center the full voice of a man emerged, a man who was enchanting his listeners with his spirited talk." People compared him to Jesus and felt incapable of "writing anything comprehensible about this extraordinary creature of God." When Goethe set off from Frankfurt on one of his hikes, he sometimes had a train of young girls and children following him. And in Darmstadt, where he stayed with Merck, the curious gathered in front of the house. Merck made jokes about it and urged his friend to go out and bless the crowd. At times the whole business became creepy for Goethe, especially because people even beset him in his own house. He had to give regular audiences, four times a week, but agreed to see people only in the morning. The room was always full.

It was never Goethe's aim to force or exploit the impression he made. Instead, he was aware of the problems it caused. Was he still a poet or already a prophet? That was the question.

In the euphoria of his poetic inspiration, he felt enough the prophet to be able to empathize with figures like Muhammad or Abraham when God manifested fully in them. In his fragmentary drama *Mahomet*, the prophet says, *Dost thou not see him? At every quiet spring, under every blooming tree I encounter him in the warmth of his love. How I thank him; he opened my breast, took away the hard hull of my heart, that I might feel his approach.*

Goethe the poet had clearly experienced things that led him to think about the descent of the Holy Spirit in the miracle of Pentecost: *The fullness of the holiest, deepest feeling pushed man for one moment into a supernatural existence. He spoke the language of the spirits and from the depths of the godhead his tongue blazed life and light.* Thus he describes it in a short essay entitled "What Does It Mean to Speak in Tongues?"

He felt a similar spirit in himself. It did not reveal the hereafter, however, but made his own inner life and the temporal world gleam with beauty and gave him the feeling of participating in the creative power that animates the universe. This spirit spurred him on so that at times his writing hand could hardly keep up.

Prophet or poet? In the end, Goethe opted for poetry. The true poet is inspired like a prophet, but without missionary zeal or the claim to be a mouthpiece for God. And yet: *As a temporal gospel, true poetry announces itself by knowing how to liberate us, through internal serenity and external pleasure, from the earthly burdens that weigh us down. Like a balloon, it lifts us and the ballast that we carry into higher regions, leaving earth's tangled paths lying spread out before us in a bird's-eye view.*

Both prophet and poet are overwhelmed, enraptured by their inspiration, and feel themselves to be a medium—that is their similarity. But Goethe is looking for the difference. Poetic inspiration and a prophet's divine afflatus may flow from the same source, but unlike the poet, the prophet *also wants to spread abroad the divinity that is within him.* The prophet seeks to attract followers. He must put himself on the level of the *coarse world* that he wants to influence. And so he becomes calculating and alienates himself from his original inspiration—even to the point of becoming violent.

It was the prophet's fate that the young Goethe intended to portray in the play *Mahomet*. At the same time, he was also using satire to skewer suspect "prophets," some of them made-up, like the forest devil *Satyros*, and some drawn from life, like the *false prophet* Pater Brey.

He had planned a lofty ending for *Mahomet*. Muhammad was to be cleansed and purified. With the satires of prophets, however, Goethe sought to immunize himself against the corresponding dangers. Poetry is prophecy in homeopathic doses. When Goethe writes in *Poetry and Truth* that he *altered the old robe of the Titans to fit my size,* he did it also with the intention of playing at something without having to become it.

He intended to present Mahomet (the eighteenth-century spelling of Muhammad) as a religious genius whom divine inspiration transforms into a new man. He exudes such power that his surroundings are also transformed. The people he touches are drawn into his orbit. In an antiphonal passage between Mahomet's daughter Fatima and his son-in-law Ali, the inspiration is expressed in the image of a river that absorbs all tributaries and, swollen to a mighty stream, finally reaches the sea. But it was to be more than just the epiphany of the inspired founder of a religion. By getting involved in the earthly—ordinary humanity and everyday power relationships—he loses his purity. *The things of this world grow and proliferate,* Goethe writes of his plan for the play; *the things of the next withdraw and are obscured.* Religion becomes a pretext for power and conquest. Atrocities are committed and Mahomet orders people to be killed. He loses himself. In the last, unwritten act there was to be a purification, and Mahomet would return to the sources of his inspiration. Goethe gives a succinct summary of the play's intention: *Everything that Genius is able to do with people by force of character and spirit would be depicted, and what it thereby gains and loses.*

At the same time, as we have said, Goethe treated this theme in two farces, the *Shrovetide Play of Pater Brey* and *Satyros, or The Wood-Devil Deified.* Here the effects of supposed geniuses and false prophets are presented from their comical side.

The Shrovetide play is a ribald farce. A *priestling* has wormed his way into a community as a prophet. He plans to convert people, but is really just out for himself, and is a skirt chaser to boot. Leonore has almost fallen for him, but fortunately her betrothed, a robust captain, returns just in time. The priest has caused much furor and set people against one another, but the captain restores order and chases the nasty charismatic priest off to a pigsty. In a final witty monologue, the captain settles scores with this pious swine, but in it one can still detect the author's serious critique of religion. He is concerned with the unholy alliance between supposedly divine inspiration and a lust for power, including sexual conquest, and the dangerous temptation to want to heal a muddled world with a single idea:

> He thinks the world would end today
> If he weren't here to make it stay.
> He claims that he is heaven-blessed
> And serves us up the queerest jests.
> Says he's here to save the world,

To make our earthly bliss assured.
Yet all of us are living still
As best we can, for good or ill.
He says it all depends on him,
The whole world's weight upon him lies.
But meanwhile, let him catch our flies!

The satire *Satyros, or The Wood-Devil Deified* is also about a false prophet. In *Poetry and Truth* Goethe suggests that he had in mind not just a type but a specific person, and there has been much speculation about who it could be. Suggestions range from Lavater, Heinse, Leuchsenring, and Goué to the educational reformer Johann Bernhard Basedow and even Herder.

Herder was certainly charismatic and attracted loyal adherents. He also was mocked for his fondness for Rousseau, and even occasionally called "Pan" or "Satyros." Moreover, the satire was written in the summer of 1773, when relations between the two men were strained. Even so, Goethe had so much admiration for Herder that it's unlikely his barbs were aimed directly at his friend. However, one must also bear in mind that Goethe showed no mercy even to people for whom he felt great esteem—for instance, in his farce *Gods, Heroes, and Wieland*. He always insisted that his figures had characteristics that, if they were not invented, were drawn from several different persons. That was likely true for *Satyros* as well. There is probably something of Herder in the ludicrous wood-devil who talks like a satirical version of Herder the natural philosopher:

Hearken how confusion reigned,
In monstrous unbeing, unrestrained.
. . .
How primeval order then unfurled,
The power of light in a night-black world
Pervaded being's deepest mire,
Provoked the onrush of desire
And all the elements, set free,
Are hungry intertwined to be,
All penetrating, penetrated.

The Pan-footed satyr berates his benefactor the hermit while the latter feeds him, then puffs himself up: *There's nothing in the world as good as me / For God is God but I am me.* He not only promulgates the *onrush of desire* as a universal principle, but also practices it by ensnaring a tender maiden who answers to the name Psyche (which is the main reason people connect the satire to Herder, whose fiancée went by that name among the Sentimentalists of Darmstadt). When he makes seductive speeches clad in his loincloth, he succeeds for a while in casting a spell on people. And indeed, he speaks with such passion that it sounds as if he really has been filled with a higher spirit. He gushes about a *burgeoning nature* that one can feel both in the universe and in oneself. People should divest themselves of their *foreign adornments* and *enjoy the earth* at last. Goethe could have put this speech into the mouth of Prometheus or some other true prophet. The satyr, however, is soon unmasked and chased away, but the impression remains that religious enthusiasm lies very close to religious delusion. In these matters, original and forgery are difficult to distinguish. The satire leads the audience out of the labyrinth of deceit. As rarely happens in real life, everything is cleared up in the end. Here is the deceiver and there the deceived.

Goethe described these explorations of enthusiasm and seduction— some impassioned and some satirical—as altering *the old robe of the Titans to fit my size.* A true prophet has self-confident access to a higher world. He brings mankind teachings that give life a direction. The prophet can say, You must change your life! But not the poet. He gives only himself. That too, however, can be a tremendous gift that lives on in the memory of mankind.

CHAPTER 9

Making *poetic use* of One's Own Life. Paths to *Werther*.

Personal matters. The Weariness of Living.

Werther's Love and the Fate of Imagination.

What Is Missing When We Are Absent from Ourselves.

Werther's Impact.

. . . .

I N FEBRUARY 1774, WITHOUT AN OUTLINE OR A FIRST DRAFT, Goethe began to write *The Sorrows of Young Werther*. He wrote it in one burst; the whole novel was apparently worked out and ready in his head. Three months later, it was finished.

This was the period of his life when, as he says in *Poetry and Truth*, *My passion to create was boundless*. New ideas and motifs were constantly occurring to him. Poems, satires, and comic tales seemed to pour out of him: *Lumberville Fair*, *A Shrovetide Play of Pater Brey*, *Satyros, or The Wood-Devil Deified*. He didn't seem to consider these works to be of special or lasting significance, *but in convivial company I and others recalled them with pleasure, and then the urge to write more returned*. The fact that *Götz* had become known beyond his narrow circle of friends, causing a great public stir that made Goethe suddenly an important literary figure, had no effect on his method of production. His spontaneous *passion to create* was unchanged. He turned to ambitious plans and worked simultaneously on his plays about Muhammad, Prometheus, and Faust. Yet as he wrote in late 1773, shortly before beginning *Werther*, he felt that his works were not yet close enough to his own life to be regarded as the actual *fruits* of his experience. It was in *Werther* that he would make *poetic use* of his *recent life* for the first time.

The affair with Lotte in Wetzlar was now a year and a half in the past, and its acute pain had subsided. Melancholy still obtruded from time to time, but otherwise his recollection of the experience was calmer. His letters to the Kestners no longer have the sound that will characterize Werther's letters in the novel. Goethe writes mostly to Kestner, but includes Lotte in his news. The affectionate words he uses to explicitly address her remain within the bounds of propriety. One can sense the delight he takes in expressive formulations and witty turns of phrase. He also likes to tease, wondering for instance whether Lotte still owns her *blue striped bed jacket*. He would be very put out if she did not, for he *loved it almost more than he loved her*. If he was worried about nothing more than Lotte's bed jacket, she and Kestner really didn't need to be concerned about him.

The Lotte affair had receded in his mind; things had happened to him in the meantime.

Poetry and Truth calls *Werther* a *general confession*. Goethe adds, *through this composition more than any other, I had rescued myself from a stormy element*.

On his return journey from Wetzlar to Frankfurt in the fall of 1772, Goethe had paid a visit to Sophie von La Roche in Ehrenbreitstein and met her daughter Maximiliane, to whom he felt an attraction. The eighteen-year-old was engaged to the widower Pietro Antonio Brentano, a well-to-do Frankfurt merchant twenty years her senior. They were married a few weeks before the composition of *Werther* began. Goethe quickly fell in love with "Max." He came and went at the Brentanos', again acting the part of a loving family friend whose intention was to support the young wife. Maximiliane was overwhelmed by her new status: suddenly she found herself in the role of stepmother to the children of Brentano's first marriage, who were about her age. It was too much for her. The resourceful Goethe consoled her, played music with her, brought her books, and read to her from his own manuscripts. Merck made the wicked comment that Goethe also consoled Max for the smell of oil and cheese that clung to her husband, and for his coarse manners. The husband became jealous, and there were scenes. It's unclear whether Goethe was banished from the house or avoided it on his own. He wrote to Sophie von La Roche, *If you knew what went on inside me before I left the house, you would not think of luring me back, dear Mama. I suffered enough for all eternity in those terrible moments*.

The goings-on in the Brentano house became a scandal in Frankfurt. For a while, Goethe and Maximiliane met in secret. Goethe began to write *Werther* while still in turmoil over the situation. Thus the *stormy element* that gave birth to the novel is more likely to be found here than in the affair with Lotte, by now a mellow memory. Yet the novel's fluctuations between tempestuousness and depression likely have yet other sources, to be found not in external situations but in internal agitation.

As we have seen, Goethe surrendered himself to *whims concerning suicide* and kept a dagger on his nightstand; but he banished such *hypochondriacal fancies and resolved to live.* In retrospect, Goethe insists that he had freed himself from thoughts of suicide before he began to write his novel about a suicide. So the crisis had been overcome. Why write about it then? The answer: so that instead of simply continuing to live, he could do so with *cheerfulness.* Writing was an exercise in cheering himself up, despite—or even because of—the fact that his subject matter had little in the way of cheer. Jerusalem's suicide and Kestner's description of it supplied him with a story around which he could assemble his thoughts and the moods he had experienced and suffered through. He would take a *bird's-eye view. From all sides, the whole thing coalesced and became one solid mass.*

In his retrospective depiction, it is not the pain of love but rather *Lebensekel*—revulsion at or weariness of living—that is at the center of the novel. But what is so important about this revulsion? How serious an existential threat was it to Goethe himself? At first, he distances himself from it in *Poetry and Truth* and refers to the historical background, the mood of the time. He mentions an English melancholy then in fashion—the cult of Hamlet, the worship of Ossian. He credits English depression for being grounded not in petty circumstances, as in Germany. Instead, he sees it as the shadow cast by the possibility in England for great deeds and significant action, as melancholy writ large: world-class depression. Such melancholy could definitely be *impressive.* The *gloomy aversion to life* of young people in Germany was something else altogether. *Here we have to do with people for whom life is actually spoiled by a lack of things to do, under the most peaceful conditions in the world, by their exaggerated demands on themselves.* People allowed themselves to be tortured by experiences drawn not from active life but from literature, which is why German melancholy was nothing more than a literary fashion.

Was that also the source of Goethe's own depression? Much later, in conversation with Johann Peter Eckermann, he would deny it: *What's more, I hardly needed to derive my own youthful melancholy from the general influences of my times or the reading of particular English authors. On the contrary, it was individual, personal matters by which I was so beset.*

What personal matters? It was no longer his relationship with Lotte or Maximiliane, nor the complications in the Brentano house, by which he *was so beset.* Those were only the external catalysts.

He was, rather, possessed by *Lebensekel, taedium vitae,* as he wrote four decades later to Karl Friedrich Zelter after the latter's son had committed suicide. Those who suffered from it were to be pitied, not berated. *Werther will leave no one in doubt that all the symptoms of that strange illness, as natural as it is unnatural, once coursed through my innermost being.*

So it was an illness, not a fashion.

Nor was it a metaphysical destiny, as Friedrich Gundolf claimed in 1916. For him, Werther is a "titan of sentiment" caught in a "conflict between the cosmically expansive fullness of life and the restrictions of the moment."[*]

In Goethe's retrospective self-analysis, the *taedium vitae* is presented prosaically and almost clinically: the defect lies in the individual, not in the world. Understood as an illness, weariness of living says nothing about the worth of life, but only about a dissonance in the sufferer, an inability to find an adequate access to life. Defined as an illness, *taedium vitae* cannot be promoted to the status of an instrument of insight. According to a gloomy philosophy and aesthetic, *taedium vitae* provides knowledge of the supposedly true nature of life, namely, that it is worthless. In other words, weariness of living is the correct attitude. And that is precisely a position Goethe would refuse to accept in his later years. Anything but a condemnation of life! And that is why in retrospect he calls his bouts of *taedium vitae* an illness.

According to *Poetry and Truth,* contentment is found in the customary and dependable *recurrence of external things,* the succession of day and night and the seasons, the round of activities and people, familiar

---

[*] Friedrich Gundolf, *Goethe* (Berlin: G. Bondi, 1916), 169 and 163.

behaviors and routines. All these things make relation to the world possible. But this very repetition can also become a torment. What ought to provide support in external life becomes instead repellent. One is inwardly unable to *take part* in it, unreceptive to *such lovely offerings* and rhythms. Goethe writes that there are people who hang themselves out of disgust that every day the sun rises and sets and they must put on their clothes and then take them off again.

Love, which at first seems unique and unforeseeable, also suffers from regular recurrence. By the second or third time, it has lost its significance. *What actually uplifts and supports love, the notion of something eternal and never-ending, is destroyed. It appears transitory, like everything that returns.* Love is not infinitely rich, but a restricted repertoire. The love that at first makes everything new becomes, in the end, a loving habit. The person who finds that repellent refuses life's offerings and shrinks into himself. Everything becomes a burden. One must dare to leap outside the self and find a foothold in life as it is. Thus the only antidote to *taedium vitae* is openness to life.

But how does one open up? The Goethe of *Poetry and Truth* has two answers. We should step outside ourselves and act according to what the circumstances of the world demand by fulfilling the duties of the day. If we make exaggerated demands on ourselves, we are merely preparing for constant defeat and depriving ourselves of life's pleasures.

In his later reflections on *taedium vitae* as an illness, Goethe places the destroyed relationship to the world at its center. The individual, for all his feelings, no longer sees real life and shuts himself off from the tasks and opportunities of the day. The only defense against life-weariness is active participation in life. For the late Goethe, *taking part* is key to self-therapy. It means an approach to the world that strives to be objective; that is the only way to gain vital strength from outside the self: *To rejoice in your own worth / You must grant worth to life on earth.* In 1814, this was the maxim he wrote in the album of the young Arthur Schopenhauer. It was advice Schopenhauer desperately needed.

Werther addresses *taedium vitae* in a different way. It doesn't speak of it but rather from within it. In his later meditations, Goethe introduces a concept that leads us into the intellectual center of life-weariness, the concept of *paralyzing imagination*.

Like his author, Werther is a young man whom children and women

find attractive. Like Goethe, he is eloquent and capable of sophisti-
cally making a weak cause sound strong. He has a lot of free time and
no strong connection to bourgeois professional life. He indulges his
feelings—"sentimentally," as Schiller would later say—and not only
falls in love but falls in love with love. He takes pleasure in pleasure
and is sensible of sensibility. He is a virtuoso at such doublings. With
all that, he is a man of imagination. Werther's story, told as a monologue in letters to a friend (and to Lotte and Albert), is a love story
and, at the same time, a depiction of what his imagination makes of
circumstances and people.

In early spring, Werther arrives in a small town where, at the behest
of his family, the well-to-do young man is supposed to straighten out
some matters of an inheritance. He is also fleeing a complicated love
affair. *I intend to enjoy the present and let the past be past*, he writes in his
first letter. The main theme of *taedium vitae* is already touched upon,
for in the same letter he also cautions himself to keep his *imagination*
in check. He must not dwell on the past and give himself a bad conscience but, instead, turn to the present. And at first he does. He takes
delight in everything: the surrounding countryside and its little villages, the blossoming trees and children at play. He also reads Homer,
which lends a golden nimbus to the scenes he witnesses at the village
well. He tries his hand at drawing and remarks that unadorned nature
itself is more beautiful than its likeness could ever be. At a dance party
in the country he meets Lotte, whom he knows to be *as good as engaged*.
A sudden spring downpour reminds the two of a poem by Klopstock,
which unites their hearts—for a moment in Lotte's case, more lastingly
for Werther. Later he observes Lotte slicing bread for the younger siblings crowding around her, an unforgettable image for Werther. He
meets her fiancé, Albert, and becomes his friend. They argue about
infanticide, madness, art, and suicide. Albert defends rules and reason;
Werther is on the side of strong feelings and individual cases. But inevitably, his rival slowly begins to rankle him: *when she speaks of her fiancé
with all that warmth, all that love, then I'm like someone who has been stripped
of all his honor and dignity and must surrender his sword.*

Werther's mood becomes gloomy, and finally he tears himself away,
quits the field, and accepts a diplomatic post in another town. Although
there he is liked by his superiors and also attractive to women, he is

dissatisfied. For the talented and spoiled young man, the thought of suicide is nearly constant. He feels it as he carries out his dry official duties and again when he suffers an insulting slight in a gathering of narrow-minded aristocrats. Later, it is no surprise that Werther really does commit suicide, since the wish to kill himself is always at hand, looking for an occasion. After wandering a bit from place to place, he returns to the little town where Lotte and Albert have since become husband and wife. *A shudder passes through my whole body . . . when Albert puts his arm around her slim waist*, he writes, and yet he still sits around in the couple's house, cleaning vegetables and shelling peas. Gradually, he becomes a burden to them, and Lotte says to him, *I fear, I fear it is only the impossibility of possessing me that makes that wish so attractive.*

Werther cannot have Lotte. But much worse is that now he is tortured not by excessive passion, as one might imagine, but by the fear that his imagination will become blunted, the imagination that has up to now served him so well in his relationship with Lotte. He is terrified by the return to *cold dull consciousness.* To be sure, Lotte draws back from him, but it is worse that his imagination is drying up, that he is alienated from himself. *I have no power of imagination, no feeling for nature, and all books nauseate me. When we're absent from ourselves, we lack everything.* That is of supreme significance. It is not the beloved woman he lacks, but himself. What is missing when one is absent from oneself? The *sacred, animating power with which I created worlds around me* is lacking, and therefore he will choose suicide.

The final events are reported by an anonymous editor. Before doing the deed, Werther summons up strong emotions one last time. He shoots himself with pistols he has borrowed from Albert. His burial is a hushed and private affair.

Of course *Werther* is, among other things, a novel about doomed love, and that is how it was read by most contemporaries. But it also tells of the power and fate of the imagination, which Werther calls his *heart, which on its own is the source of everything—all power, all bliss, and all misery.*

Goethe wrote to Lavater about the novel, *And now I have lent my feelings to his story, and it makes a wonderful whole.* Obviously, the author is not identical with Werther, although he is close to him by virtue of the letters in which he writes not about him but from within him. If

Goethe had adhered directly to the form of the epistolary novel, hugely popular since Rousseau's *Julie, or The New Heloise*, he would have presented a correspondence that showed the letter writers' influence on one another, thereby objectifying the action. But except for the final passage reported by the fictitious editor, *Werther* consists exclusively of letters written by the eponymous central character to a friend named Wilhelm, who does not appear in the novel, and a few to Lotte and Albert. The reader feels directly spoken to and drawn willy-nilly into Werther's inner life.

Goethe explains in *Poetry and Truth* that he chose this monologic epistolary form because he liked to conduct conversations with himself as a *dialogue*. A dialogue? But there is no real interlocutor, so there must be an imagined one. It isn't Goethe's way to turn inward and brood. Things that pertain to him must be discussed, become the topic of a conversation. To put something into words means discovering oneself. In language and then in writing, he produces himself, presents himself to others, and to himself as well. He will know who he is only when he has said or written it. We recall the extravagantly expressive letters that Goethe wrote to Behrens during his time in Leipzig. Back then, he was experimenting with writing as a power that could generate reality and create the self. Those were real letters, but also already literature. In Leipzig, he wrote to a real person, his friend Behrens, about what he was experiencing. Werther's letters are addressed to an imaginary correspondent—and to the public at large.

The author creates a figure who reveals himself in what he writes. The author writes and has his figure write. He hovers both above and within his figure. Goethe is and isn't Werther, for he always transcends him. At times, that leads to paradoxical situations. He has Werther complain that when looking at nature, he *can no longer pump a single drop of bliss into my brain*, yet he has just expressed his impressions of nature in words. Werther is left high and dry, but not the author, who makes Werther write what he actually cannot write because of his paralysis: *When I look out my window at the distant hill and see the morning sun breaking through the mist above it and illuminating the silent bottomland, and the gentle river meanders toward me between leafless willows—oh, when this glorious nature stands so numbly before me.*

Such contradictions usually go unnoticed, but they point to an important problem. An emotive description can actually express the corresponding feeling, but it can also simply represent the feeling without its being there. That is the case in the passage quoted above. Werther sketches the image of the silent bottomland as if to say, "Just look how much one could feel at this sight, but how sad it is that I now feel absolutely nothing." The author has Werther describe experiences that he has and also those he would like to have but cannot because he is absent from himself. In *Werther*, Goethe speaks of *creation bereft of itself*. What is missing when one is absent from oneself has already been named: it is simply the animating principle, the imagination.

The imagination is powerful but not omnipotent. It requires external reality. Things cannot go well in the long run when someone like Werther *paints the walls that imprison him with colorful figures and bright prospects*. Werther paints his walls not just according to his own ideas but also according to patterns from literary tradition. He is a person with a rich interior life, but he has also read a lot; lived experience and the fruits of his reading intermingle, and what he thinks and feels and what he imagines comes not only from himself but also from literature. The images of the simple life are seen through the lens of Homer, the idyll in the house of Lotte's father through the lens of Goldsmith, and the spring storm through Klopstock. At his last meeting with Lotte, they read Ossian together. In this instance, it becomes especially clear that literature must come to his aid when he is threatened by inner emptiness—literature as an antidote to *horror vacui*. When he is at risk of being *brought back again to dull, cold consciousness*, it's best to reach for a book.

Werther has something of *Don Quixote*, the classic novel about the power of literature. True, Werther doesn't tilt at windmills, but armed with his powerful impressions from literature, he does struggle against the impossibility of his love. The novel is realistic because of its precise description not just of a character but also of the cultural and literary circumstances that have shaped him. Werther is a literary figure in two senses. First, he is a figure in a novel, and second, he is a character who has been shaped by literature. Werther is what he has read, a sentimentalist from the school of an ink-stained epoch, as Schiller would call it in *The Robbers*. It is a novel about the power of literary fashion, and it became in its turn a fashion that intervened in the lives of contemporaries, who in their thoughts and feelings began to imitate those they found in *Werther*. It was, however, only a rumor that there were copycat suicides, a rumor that persists to this day. As we have seen, Goethe referred to it in his autobiography vis-à-vis his Sturm und Drang friends: *But whereas I felt relieved and enlightened by having transformed reality into poetry, my friends were confounded by believing they had to transform poetry into reality, reenact the novel, and if necessary shoot oneself.* The philosopher Christian Garve had already said all that was necessary about such rumors in 1775: "One hardly gets seduced into suicide."

Even without copycat suicides, *Werther* was an overwhelming success with the public, reaching essentially every contemporary reader in Germany. It was immediately translated from one end of Europe to the other. In the first year alone, there were seven printings in Germany, not including countless pirated editions. There was a hail of rebuttals and parodies. The novel was read by some as a defense of suicide, which called forth the churches and other official defenders of morality. In Leipzig, the theological faculty of the university caused the sale of the book to be banned, which only excited more curiosity about it.

The leading literary authorities such as Klopstock, Wieland, and Lessing, who had been rather restrained in their reception of *Götz*, were now full of praise, even when they had some reservations. Lessing, for example, expressed his "pleasure" in the book but criticized the character of Werther as too soft—poetical, but without moral beauty.

The novel marked a new epoch like no other literary work before it. It introduced a new tone into the world, and a new will for subjectivity. *I turn back into myself and find a world*, writes Werther, and many imitated him. Not everyone, however, found a world that was worth telling about. Goethe had gotten something off his chest and, in so doing, revolutionized literature. Previously, declarations about the state of one's heart had been regulated by the churches and public morality. Now there began a deregulation of talk about the workings of the psyche. There was a desire to speak freely and originally about everything, like Werther: about love, marriage, and child-rearing; religion, art, and the state; about social conventions and madness. People thought they should be able to talk about whatever was on their mind. One's inner nature, feelings, and individuality should be given a hearing. People switched from reason in general to individual reason. Werther declares that the individual is the seat of truth and continues, *no argument in the world upsets me as much as when someone comes up with a platitude when I'm speaking from the fullness of my heart.*

When reason is emancipated from its common form and becomes an individual matter, it plunges into the living element of existence, into the unconscious, the irrational, spontaneous—in other words, into the mystery of freedom. Why mystery? Because freedom cannot be explained but only experienced. Any attempt at explanation, and freedom disappears. What remains is causality, sufficient grounds. That was already true in the enlightened thought of Goethe's time and is still true today. Freedom has to be experienced. Figures like Werther set an example of freedom, and after the novel appeared, people considered the author Goethe himself to be a genius of freedom. They thought he did as he pleased. He provided an example of an independence that seemed worth imitating. We have seen that there wasn't much to his independence. Werther is dependent on his reading. That's why it is, among other things, an expression of independence when he writes in one of his first letters, *You ask whether you should send me my books? Dear friend, for God's sake please keep them off my back. I don't want to be led, encouraged, spurred on anymore, for this heart is already humming enough on its own.* No books. But in this lengthy sentence he then describes how he reaches for Homer. The will to be obstinate is there, and the public took it as encouragement.

A taste for obstinacy was awakened. People discovered that things and individuals had their own rights. It had to be gratifying for those who no longer wanted to be just cogs and screws in a great machine, but yearned to express their own ideas. Each person, Werther declares, has genius within himself. Genius is not just the great individual, but the greatness in every individual. However, it is suppressed by society's rules. *O my friends!* Werther cries, *why does the flood of genius break forth so seldom, its great waves so seldom rush in to unsettle your astonished souls.* Genius is life, powerful enough not to allow itself to be kept from growing, streaming out, being expressed. For Werther, everyone has genius, at least at the moment of love.

In Sturm und Drang, the intellectual and literary movement Goethe set in motion with *Götz* and *Werther,* the cult of genius was so widespread that the epoch has even been dubbed the *Geniezeit*, the Age of Genius. Later, Goethe would look back on it fairly skeptically: *This mutual agitation and ferment that came close to debauchery was a welcome influence on each one in his own way, and out of this whirl of activity, this live-and-let-live, this give-and-take that so many youths ruthlessly pursued with an open heart and no theoretical lodestar at all . . . there sprang up that celebrated, famous, and infamous literary epoch in which a mass of young men of genius, with much bravery and presumption . . . broke forth and by the use of their powers produced some joy, some good, and by their misuse some vexation and some evil.*

Little remains of the works of this *mass of young men of genius*. The only ones still known are those who had ties to the young Goethe, especially Klinger, Wagner, and Lenz. But the total effect was profound and made a change in the literature that followed. Herder and Johann Georg Hamann provided the *theoretical lodestar* that had been missing, and a few years later the young Schiller would continue the rebellious outbreak in his own way with his play *The Robbers*. A generation later in the same tradition, the Romantics would search for a new way to push the boundaries.

When genius became a synonym for the creative person or for human creativity, it was inevitable that not only the work of art but, through and beyond the work, the person who created it would become interesting. The cult of the star author began with Goethe. The author outshone his work, and the life of the artist was now considered a kind of artwork. Although this idea was encouraged by Goethe's charisma, it also proceeded from the characteristic idea of the Sturm und Drang movement that creative potential is superior to the forms in which it is realized. How magnificent the possibilities remain when they don't need to be put through the needle's eye of reality! In the case of the artist, this idea could be interpreted to mean that the personality as the epitome of potential was to be regarded as even more important than the work. The moment of the promising artist was at hand, as was the rise of the cult of personality, whose vigor was compromised only by the fact that there were too many who considered themselves geniuses.

Goethe, however, was a real genius, and no one could deny it, although he was often envied. In communication with foreigners, people were even proud of him. "Everything I have read of yours," Christian Friedrich Daniel Schubart wrote to Goethe, "delights me, swells my heart with noble pride that we can show other countries a man whom they don't have, and, addicted as they are to fossilizing their greatest writers, will never have."

Goethe was unsettled by his fame and found it uncanny that a novel written in a state of internal agitation should agitate so many others. Inevitably, from the time of its publication to the end of his long life, the general public thought of him only as the author of *Werther*. Napoleon spoke to him about the novel when they met in Erfurt in 1808, claiming to have read it seven times. In Goethe's poem "To Werther" (1824), there is a glint of unintended irony in the line *Predestined, I to stay and you to go*, for Werther simply would not leave him. Goethe could never get rid of his early stroke of genius.

He was also bedeviled by the countless curiosity seekers who read *Werther* as a roman à clef. They found out who his models were, made pilgrimages to Jerusalem's grave, pestered the Kestners, and blamed Goethe for still being alive. Goethe had foreseen that people would pounce upon what they recognized from the novel. He both approved and disapproved. In a letter to Charlotte that announced the book's publication, he wrote, *Very soon I will send you a friend very much like me and hope you will receive him well*. On the other hand, he warned Kestner, probably also intending to reassure him, that he would find familiar people in the novel, but they had been *patched together with passions foreign to them*.

When the Kestners read the novel that fall, they were horrified and outraged. There was *too much* in it that could *not but point strongly to them*, and therefore the invented parts were also attributed to them. Lotte was scandalized that in the novel she is presented as returning Werther's love, and Kestner felt insulted by Albert's depiction as a narrow-minded, petty philistine.

Goethe responded with guilt and contrition: *The thing is done, it's published. Forgive me if you can*. That letter was written at the end of October 1774, when the book had just been shipped. In November, when there were signs that it would be a huge success, he again wrote to Kestner: *If you could feel a thousandth part of what Werther means to a thousand hearts, you would not count what the book has cost you!*

No more contrition from Goethe, no more sense of guilt. On the contrary, there is now an implicit criticism of Kestner for being self-centered; he's ignoring how the story enriches the lives of others. *Werther must—must be!—You don't feel him. You only feel me and yourselves.* In this way, he makes clear to him that in the meantime Werther has become a public soul, and both he himself and the Kestners have simply lost their proprietary rights to the parts of his psychology they contributed. In a late edition of the novel, however, Goethe did undertake a few touch-ups and changes to satisfy the Kestners' objections.

Werther had a huge effect on the public and enormous repercussions for the author. The novel and its reception would steer Goethe's life into new channels.

CHAPTER 10

Cornelia's Misfortune. *Clavigo*, the Faithless One. Lavater and
Basedow. *Prophets right and prophets left, the World's child
in between.* A Summer Cruise down the Rhine.
Celebration of Friendship. Friedrich Heinrich Jacobi.
An Invitation to Weimar. Lili and Auguste, an Amorous House
of Mirrors. Two Different Speeds. Journey to Switzerland.
Weimar, an Escape of Sorts.

. . . .

IN *WERTHER* GOETHE WAS PROCESSING NOT JUST THE ROMANCE
in Wetzlar and the unpleasantness concerning Maximiliane Brentano;
he was also in turmoil about parting with his sister Cornelia. In late
1773 she married Georg Schlosser and moved to Emmendingen, in
southern Baden.

The relationship between Schlosser and Cornelia had its beginnings
in the summer of 1772, while Goethe was still in Wetzlar. He had not
been aware of what was afoot and was completely surprised when confronted with it on his return. He said nothing against it but thought to
himself *that if her brother hadn't been absent, things could not have gone so far
with his friend.*

After an almost euphoric beginning, the story of Cornelia and
Schlosser would take an unhappy turn. Before the wedding in 1773,
Cornelia had written in her diary, "Although I have long rejected
romantic notions about marriage, I was never able to extinguish an
exalted idea of wedded love, the only love that in my judgment can
make a union happy."

She does not say clearly what kind of marriage would have been her
ideal, but the relationship with her brother was doubtless her touch-

stone. She had taken an active and intimate interest in Goethe's life and career, and he had discussed his literary plans with her, taken her seriously as a critic, and valued her taste. She had a decisive influence on the evolution of *Götz*, and Goethe confided in her about his other literary projects as well. He wanted to share with her the *new world* that revealed itself to him *in the field of imagination*. Their intimacy also transcended literature. In *Poetry and Truth* Goethe circumspectly suggests incestuous desire, and though what he says applies to their early childhood, there remained an erotic edge to their relationship, and she encouraged Goethe to plan a novel about this kind of sibling love.

For Cornelia, the role of trusted adviser in literary matters was not just a token of love. It also raised her self-esteem. However, that was the case only in matters of art and literature, since she had little knowledge of anything else. That turned out to be a calamity. The eighteen-year-old Goethe had earnestly and somewhat precociously written to her from Leipzig, urging her to acquire housekeeping skills for her future role as a wife and mother. She, however, wanted to be acknowledged as an intelligent woman with literary judgment and artistic talent. Nothing else interested her. Later, as a married woman, she had to manage a large house and care for two children, and she broke down under the burden.

Schlosser, who had known Goethe well since boyhood, had set out to find a wife with his usual thoroughness, but at first without success. He would have become a confirmed bachelor had not it occurred to him to seek out Cornelia, whom he'd known for a long time. He courted her, and Cornelia accepted him as a suitor, probably in part because he was her brother's friend.

The wedding took place on November 1, 1773. Schlosser had postponed it until his appointment to the post of district president in Emmendingen by the Grand Duke of Baden in Karlsruhe. As the duke's official representative, he had authority over the entire administrative district of twenty thousand inhabitants. It was the highest-paid official post in all of Baden.

In *Poetry and Truth* Goethe admits to some jealousy, for Cornelia's departure in late 1773 was a painful loss. His sister, however, was close to losing herself. Goethe foresaw that. In the second version of *Werther*, revised after Cornelia's death, he mirrors his sister's drama in Lotte's feelings for Werther: [Lotte] *was used to sharing everything interesting she felt or thought with him, and his departure threatened to tear a hole in her entire existence that could not be filled in again. Oh, if only she could have turned him into a brother at that moment!*

Cornelia never got over the separation from her brother. Schlosser was not the man to make up for the loss of Goethe. In a letter to the naturalist and revolutionary Georg Forster, Schlosser once complained about his own "bashfulness and physical clumsiness" and "porcupine's skin," enough to scare off any woman. He had made attempts to be more attractive and act jolly for his fiancée, and perhaps actually did succeed in loosening up. He was once seen wandering like a ghost through the vineyards at harvest time, wearing wax candles on his hat. No one had never known "Doctor and Privy Councilor Schlosser" to behave like that, as Goethe's mother wrote Anna Amalia in October 1778, probably referring to an isolated incident from the time of the engagement.

The wedding took place in Frankfurt, and Cornelia asked Goethe to accompany her and Schlosser as far as Karlsruhe to ease the pain of parting. But he declined and holed up at home, nursing his own pain at their departure.

In Emmendingen, the Schlossers moved into the stately, roomy official residence. There was much to be done, but Cornelia, who was pregnant, withdrew and took no part in the renovation and furnishing of the house. Schlosser complained about her in a letter to Lavater, saying that she had not been correctly educated. "Every wind, every drop of rain shuts her into her room, and she is still too intimidated by the cellar and the kitchen." She passed her days in apathy and depression while the levelheaded Schlosser rolled up his sleeves and devoted himself to his duties. He saw to the improvement of agriculture, public education, and transportation, concerned himself with skilled trades and crafts, and founded public lending libraries. All of it, however, passed Cornelia by. She stayed in darkened rooms, paralyzed by inactivity, and rarely left her bed. The capable and always obliging Schlosser was unable to help her.

In the summer of 1774 came the difficult birth of her first child, from which Cornelia took weeks to recover. Schlosser had settled into his job and was running things as though he were the grand duke himself. He had hoped for support from his wife, but there was no chance of that. Cornelia withdrew more and more. "My love disgusts her," he complained to his brother Hieronymus. Goethe must have known about it, for he would later tell Eckermann, *The thought of giving herself to a man was repulsive, and one can imagine that in their marriage, this peculiarity caused many an unpleasant hour.* Cornelia was withering away at the side of the hardworking Schlosser. That's how Goethe found her when he visited Emmendingen for the first and only time, in May 1775. She did not recover from the birth of her second daughter and died on June 8, 1777.

The year 1774 was Goethe's first in the house on the Hirschgraben without Cornelia and the daily conversation that meant so much to him. Three years earlier, he had described the situation that had now come to pass in a defiantly self-confident letter to Kätchen Schönkopf: *We have an entire house, and if my sister gets married, she must leave. I won't put up with a brother-in-law. And if I get married, we'll share the house, I and my parents, and I'll get 10 rooms.*

Cornelia was gone, there was no brother-in-law to contend with, and he could spread out, if not into all ten rooms. However, there was no bride in sight either: Kätchen Schönkopf was married by now, the abandoned Friederike was mourning in Sesenheim, the sentimental ladies in Darmstadt idolized him but were already promised to others or out of reach by virtue of their social status, and Lotte in Wetzlar was also married and had given birth to her first child. He had no real prospects. But Goethe was not even on the lookout for anyone as seriously as his parents might have wished. He continued to be satisfied with the marriage game cultivated by his friends in Frankfurt. He had drawn the name of Anna Sibylla Münch as the partner with whom he was to play at being married. Goethe's father would have considered her quite a suitable match.

For Goethe, she was at least the occasion for his next play, *Clavigo.* In the spring of 1774, after finishing *Werther,* he had read her an episode from the memoirs of Pierre Augustin Caron de Beaumarchais in which he writes about Clavigo, the faithless lover of Beaumarchais's sister, and Anna Sibylla asked Goethe, somewhat flirtatiously, to make this faithless lover the central character of a play. For Goethe it was a challenge to his skill as a writer. He wanted to prove that besides writing plays in the "wild style" of *Götz,* he could also produce ones in the traditional "controlled manner" and in record time to boot. He promised to finish it in a week and indeed came calling with it soon thereafter. Anna Sibylla liked it very much, but the more demanding Merck dismissed it with the words *you don't need to write such rot anymore as far as I'm concerned; others can do it just as well.*

Goethe himself didn't think the play was rot, or he wouldn't have published it under his own name in the summer of 1774, almost simultaneously with *Werther*. It was, in fact, the very first work to appear under his name. It gave him *joy* and there was *romantic, youthful power* in it, he wrote to Jacobi shortly after it appeared. In another letter, he explained what particularly pleased him about it: he had succeeded in depicting a mixed character, *an indeterminate, half-great and half-petty person*, a character like Weislingen in *Götz*, a man who is not strong and steady enough for love. Clavigo is talented and brilliant but inconstant, a ladies' man on his way to becoming a cynical courtier. The death of his beloved, however, returns him to himself. This chamber drama of a faithless lover who in the end contritely realizes his wrong, returns to his betrothed, and then dies at the sword of his outraged brother-in-law found little approbation. As for Anna Sibylla Münch, however, *it was as if through an intellectual offspring, our relationship was drawn closer and strengthened by this production.*

As has been said, his father was pleased, for he considered Anna Sibylla a socially appropriate match. He longed for his son's *indecisive roaming* to come to an end. All the hubbub about genius, the unending stream of friends and acquaintances, the *literary garrisoning*, the ready generosity and *loan guarantees*—Goethe was supporting several friends such as Lenz, Klinger, and Wagner—began to be a financial burden, especially since neither Goethe's work as a lawyer nor his literary publications brought in much money.

But his parents had to be patient. The relationship with Anna Sibylla Münch did not turn serious, and the so-called genius cult still continued for some time and even heated up, since the young author's fame was growing. Nor did the stream of visitors show any sign of letting up. Among them was one guest who was to play a significant role in Goethe's life.

On June 23, 1774, Johann Kaspar Lavater, on his way from Zurich to the spa in Bad Ems, stopped in Frankfurt to pay Goethe a visit and stayed for a week. Lavater, a pastor in Zurich and eight years older than Goethe, was already famous. Well-known not just in religious circles, he excited public notice everywhere he went. He was a talented preacher with social skills and called himself a "fisher of men." He traveled frequently and made contacts wherever he went. He knew how to win people over to his many projects, be they anthologies, serial publications, or edifying pamphlets. Today we would call him a networker. People gathered around him, and there was even a rumor that he possessed the power to heal. He spoke softly and intensely and exuded an intense friendliness. People liked to accompany him on his travels and to have him visit. Newspapers reported his doings, including his first visit to Goethe. *"Bischt's?"* was supposedly the first thing he uttered—"Is that you?" in broad Swiss dialect—followed immediately by an embrace.

Lavater had first made a political splash in 1762, when he and the painter Johann Heinrich Füssli (who later settled in England and changed his name to Henry Fuseli) mounted a public campaign against an unjust governor of Zurich and forced his dismissal. The two men had simply refused to back down. What was of greater importance to Lavater, however, was religious expression in a contemplative and soulful key. In 1768 he published *Prospects of Eternity*, reveries on life after death. Written in a spirit of sentimentalism, the work became hugely popular in Germany. Goethe had praised the book in the *Frankfurter Gelehrte Anzeigen* in 1772, but at the same time distanced himself from it. Lavater's discussion of *forgiveness of sins*, he wrote, *might reassure some people about this matter*, but the reviewer was not among them. After all, if one is not worried, one doesn't need reassurance. Goethe had already annoyed some of his acquaintances among the Herrnhuters with similar remarks, and he raised the same argument against Lavater— namely, that a sense of sin was foreign to him. He made positive mention of the book's engaging style, however. It was clearly not meant for the *brooding* segment of Christianity, but rather for those who found enjoyment in beauty, for Lavater *conjures . . . before our eyes a marvelous world*, whereas usually one just becomes entangled *in gloom and confusion*. In conclusion, the reviewer had recommended that the author forgo theological speculation altogether and concentrate on observation, a somewhat perplexing piece of advice, for what was there to observe in "prospects of eternity"?

For his part, Lavater first became aware of Goethe in early 1773, through his fictitious "Letter of the Pastor in ★★★ to the New Pastor in ★★★." Lavater was quite taken by its advocacy of simple, heartfelt piety and opposition to dogmatic theological quibbles. After reading *Götz*, he wrote to Herder, "I know no greater genius among all the writers." In August 1773, he initiated an enthusiastic correspondence with Goethe. Goethe's first letters in reply have not been preserved, but despite his exuberance, he seems to have also expressed what separated the two of them. *I am not a Christian*, Lavater quotes from a lost letter of Goethe's, a frank admission that Lavater struggled with, but in the end overlooked out of love and admiration for the writer. It was Lavater's firm belief that he understood Goethe better than the younger man did himself. Like many others, when Lavater saw genius in Goethe, he saw nothing but God working within him without his knowing it. Lavater did not expect to find traditional piety in Goethe, nor did he wish to convert him, to "harass" him or "play the partisan." He would take his chances with a noble battle of intellects: "You shall become *one* [i.e., a Christian], or I will become what you are." The spirit bloweth where it listeth.

Lavater also wanted to win Goethe as a contributor to his new project, a great work on physiognomy. He was collecting prints, silhouettes, and portrait drawings of both well-known and unknown persons who would provide material for physiognomic interpretation, partly by himself and partly by friends and acquaintances he recruited. The *Physiognomic Fragments for the Promotion of Knowledge and Love of Mankind*, the title of the work in progress, was really intended as a group project. Lavater laid no claim to special interpretive competence, but he prided himself on drawing general attention to the physiognomic aspect of anthropology.

The basic idea was simple enough: it assumed a connection between outward appearance and the formation of character. As was later true of psychoanalysis, physiognomy was a mixture of serious scientific inquiry and parlor game. It soon became fashionable to "physiognomize," which both flattered and annoyed Lavater, since it endangered the reputation of the entire undertaking. He wrote to Goethe in November 1773, "By means of many complete, robust observations, will you help me to confirm or disprove a great, enormously important conjecture gathered from half, quarter, and one-eighth observations?" Goethe was ready to help, especially since the basic approach made sense to him: conclusions about the interior can be drawn from the exterior, not just vice versa. The path from sensory perception to inner spirit was one he had already trod.

In the first years, Goethe contributed frequent portraits and descriptions for Lavater's work in progress—of Klopstock, for instance: *This gently descending forehead indicates pure human intellect; its height above the eyes, singularity and delicacy; it is the nose of someone who notices.* Beneath the silhouette of Charlotte von Stein, whom he had yet to meet, he noted in the summer of 1775, *It would be a wonderful spectacle to see how the world is reflected in this soul. She sees the world as it is, and yet through the medium of love. Thus gentleness is the general impression.*

Lavater's ideas were too rhapsodic and enthusiastic to be effectively defended against his critics and skeptics. He therefore turned to Goethe, his newly won-over physiognomic adept, for some fundamental remarks on the subject, which Goethe willingly provided, since they offered an opportunity to clarify his own thinking. Goethe wrote that in interpersonal relationships, the web of effect and countereffect remains mostly unconscious. Without being aware of it, we are constantly reading the face of our interlocutor and accommodating to it. Everyone *feels where he should approach or withdraw, or rather, something attracts or repels him, and so there is no need for investigation or explanation.* We should not disturb this unconscious or only half-conscious process. As a rule, it facilitates social intercourse. In particular situations, however, physiognomic observation can be helpful—when you want to know what exactly is attracting or repelling you, what you expect of another person or what you have to expect from him. You may want to understand the web into which you are woven. The art of reading another person can be taught and learned.

Goethe accepted Lavater as his teacher, at least in this area. He treated him with respect when Lavater arrived in Frankfurt on June 23, 1774. They addressed each other as "brother," and Goethe's mother called her guest "dear son." Lavater immediately began to make physiognomic observations. Goethe, he wrote in his diary, said surprising and wonderful things "with the expression of a genius who feels himself." The Swiss pastor paid a visit to Susanna von Klettenberg, and they talked about the Lord Jesus and Goethe in turn. Lavater waxed ecstatic about his friend: "I have never found such harmonious sensitivity to nature." Lavater remained in the house on the Hirschgraben for a week and gave audiences to the streams of people who came to see him. At the end of June, he left for Bad Ems, the goal of his journey, where he hoped to cure his rheumatism and Goethe accompanied him. For the time being, the two were inseparable.

Lavater noted in his diary that Goethe had recited to him some things from an epic poem about the legend of the Wandering Jew that he was working on. Therein were described the peregrinations of Ahasver in eighteenth-century Germany. As Goethe imagines him, Ahasver has witnessed the primitive Christian community. For him, present-day ecclesiastical Christianity is an aberration by contrast. The risen Christ also appears in the poem and is described thus: *In a land to which He came / He was there—on a church's weather vane, / Aside from that (it was quite odd) / There was very little sign of God.* The message is that, whereas Ahasver once failed to recognize Jesus, now it is the churches, priests, and theologians who sin against Christ. "The Wandering Jew" was probably the fruit of the same mood we find in a letter Goethe wrote to Herder, in which institutionalized ecclesiastical Christianity is called either a *Scheinding* (an illusory thing) or a *Scheissding* (a shitty thing)—depending on how one reads his handwriting.

The pious Lavater did not note down whether he liked the poem or not. He was, after all, a man of the (reformed) church and would have heard the satire of contemporary Christianity with mixed feelings, even if his own belief in Christ was very personal, inward, and nondogmatic.

Goethe was scarcely returned from Bad Ems when he had another visitor to welcome: Johann Bernhard Basedow. A clergyman determined to reform the school system, Basedow was traveling to recruit financial backers for his projects. He had also founded the so-called Philanthropinum in Dessau with support from the local prince. Basedow attacked pedantry and rhetorical windiness. He said that instruction should be made graphic and vivid, with examples from real life. Pupils should learn the right way to learn, and doing so should be fun. These were very sensible ideas, but Goethe found it hard to be in Basedow's company for any period of time. He was a fairly coarse fellow who smoked cheap tobacco and drank. Goethe could only stand to be with him outdoors.

Basedow was also on his way to Bad Ems, and Goethe, who seized every opportunity to travel, accompanied him, although he had just come from there. Basedow sat in the coach puffing on his pipe, while Goethe sat on the coach box. Lavater and Basedow got on famously together, and both were jawboning Goethe. The three friends continued by boat down the Lahn and Rhine rivers as far as Koblenz, Goethe writing, *As if to Emmaus we bumped along / With stormy, fiery speed. / Prophets right and prophets left / The World's child in between.* From Koblenz, now minus Basedow and his cheap tobacco, Goethe went on to Düsseldorf. In the nearby town of Elberfeld, he had his first encounter with Friedrich Heinrich Jacobi and his brother Johann Georg. On the basis of nothing but rumors that the Jacobi brothers were sensitive pansies, Goethe had earlier composed satires about them. But having met them in person, he was charmed, and in those bright, sunny summer days he began a friendship with Friedrich that was to last a lifetime. The younger of the two, he was six years Goethe's senior. Goethe called him Fritz.

Friedrich Heinrich Jacobi had taken over his father's trading house in Düsseldorf and was also a financial and customs official. A handsome man with an elegant, winning demeanor, a competent and very well-to-do businessman with a keen love of philosophy, he knew everyone and corresponded with anyone who had made a name for himself—Lessing, Wieland, Klopstock, Hamann, and Kant. Goethe was very impressed, and they were soon on an intimate footing. For his part, Jacobi wrote Goethe what amounted to love letters after their first meeting: "Walked up and down all morning; my whole soul is yours alone, to do with as you please. How powerfully you work within me!—You have probably never experienced such a thing. Continue to do good and great things for me, on your own account as well."

A trip via Bensberg to Cologne, an overnight in the inn Zum Geist, a conversation about Spinoza, Goethe's reciting in the moonlit night— it all made an overwhelming impression on Jacobi, an impression he would recall later when their friendship was in one of its periodic crises: "I hope that in this epoch you don't forget . . . the arbor where you spoke so unforgettably to me of Spinoza; the room in the inn Zum

Geist where we watched the moon rise over the hills of the Siebenge-birge, where you sat on the table in the twilight and recited the ballad 'There was a beau, a cheeky lad' and others . . . What hours! What days!—At midnight you sought me out in the darkness—I felt like a new soul. From that moment on I could never leave you."

When they parted, Jacobi promised to visit Goethe in Frankfurt. On December 12, 1774, Goethe was working on a painting in a darkened room when he saw the outline of a tall, slim man approaching. He thought it was Fritz Jacobi and rushed forward to embrace him—but it was Knebel.

That was the moment when Goethe's Weimar story began. Karl Ludwig von Knebel, a Prussian officer and lover of art and literature, had recently been appointed military adviser to the court of Weimar. Knebel and Johann Eustachius Graf von Görtz, tutor to Karl August, heir to the duchy of Weimar, were accompanying the seventeen-year-old prince and his younger brother on a trip to Mainz, where Karl August's engagement to the Hessian princess Luise was to be negotiated. After that, they planned to continue on to Paris.

The literature fan Knebel had intended to visit Goethe out of purely personal interest, but he soon realized that he should also introduce this man to the future duke. In a letter to Friedrich Justin Bertuch he called him "one of the most extraordinary phenomena" of his life. That same day, Goethe met Karl August for the first time in the Rotes Haus inn. They talked about *Werther* and Justus Möser's *Patriotic Fantasies*, which Goethe had just reread. Goethe apparently repeated with great sympathy that book's defense of the traditions and political effectiveness of small states that had to fend off the aggrandizing desires of larger states. It must have been music to the ears of the future ruler of a small duchy. Görtz was the only one present who did not at all like the much-admired genius: "This Goethe is a vulgar fellow. . . . That's for sure; Goethe and I will never find ourselves in the same room."

The meeting happened at a time when Goethe was again embroiled in romantic complications, this time with the seventeen-year-old Elisabeth Schönemann, known as Lili. The Schönemanns were a well-to-do family who owned one of the largest banks in Frankfurt. After the death of her father, Lili's energetic mother ran the business from their town house on the Kornmarkt. The family had many close relatives and cultivated an elegant social life. They belonged to the reformed community in which people were fairly aloof, maintaining large households yet remaining quite private. Their love of privacy would play a role in the affair between Goethe and Lili.

He fell in love with the young woman at some point in January 1775, during a soirée where she had played some pieces on the piano. The carnival season, with its parties, dances, and masquerade balls, was just getting under way, and the couple met often and danced the night away. We know much about Goethe's state of mind at the time, since he had chosen another woman to whom he could write and bare his soul. Countess Auguste zu Stolberg was the sister of Christian and Count Friedrich Leopold zu Stolberg, with whom Goethe would take his first trip to Switzerland, in the summer of 1775. The twenty-two-year-old Countess Stolberg, who belonged to the circle around Klopstock, was so enraptured by *Werther* that she wrote an anonymous letter to the author in early 1775. Goethe, in turn, was so charmed by the letter that he fell a little in love with the writer, who at first remained only a phantom. He sent her a silhouette of himself. In the meantime, he had learned her name, and a lively correspondence began. He was soon calling her *Gustchen* (an affectionate diminutive of Auguste) and overwhelming her with endearments, once even begging her to *save me from myself.*

She had asked him whether he was happy, and in his first letter, he answered, *Yes, dearest friend, I am, and if I am not, at least all the deep feelings of joy and sorrow dwell within me.* That was at the end of January 1775, when his romance with Lili was beginning. He wrote nothing of the affair in that first letter, but he did in his next. There he depicts the *carnival Goethe* cavorting at balls, his identity concealed behind a mask, being gallant to the ladies, and especially *courting a dainty little blonde* (Lili) and *being captivated at the gaming table by a pair of lovely eyes* (Lili again, or perhaps another girl). This *carnival Goethe* deems himself *insufferable* in the eyes of Gustchen. He commends the other Goethe to her, that is, the one *who, always living, striving, and working within himself, attempts in his own way to express the innocent feelings of youth in little poems, the powerful spice of life in various dramas, the shapes of his friends and his surroundings and his beloved household effects.* Goethe uses Gustchen in order to look through her eyes at Lili, that is, to peer from one romantic relationship at another. He writes as if the real Goethe was with Gustchen and Lili's lover is the *carnival Goethe*. As his passion for Lili increases, the tone of the letters to Gustchen becomes more passionate too: *o dear friend, how shall we find expressions for what it is we feel!*

The correspondence with Gustchen lasted longer than his relationship with Lili, and did not cease until he was living in Weimar. Almost four decades later, in 1822, Gustchen, who in the meantime had married Count Bernstorff and been widowed, contacted Goethe again, concerned about his eternal soul. In his answer, Goethe bid this lover of his youthful self farewell; the two never met in person.

In this phase, as Goethe divided his inner self between Gustchen and Lili and sought emotional relief from the one for his entanglement with the other, he wrote the play *Stella* in just a few weeks. About the love of a man for two women, it ends with a three-way wedding, and caused a predictable public scandal. He prepared Gustchen for that eventuality with the remark that he didn't ask *what people will think of what he was writing.*

The play would not have found an enthusiastic audience in the Schönemann house either. Goethe was unable to make up his mind about Lili. Ought he to marry into the financial aristocracy of Frankfurt? The Schönemanns (mother, brothers, and other relatives) expected Goethe to get serious about a professional career, either as a lawyer or in the bank. But such a prospect filled him with horror: *to float around in this pond in a gondola and go hunting spiders and frogs with great affability.* Faced with having to decide on that path, he recognizes what he would later describe in a letter to his mother as the difference between two speeds: *The disproportion between the narrow and slowly moving bourgeois circle and the breadth and speed of my nature would have driven me mad.* It is a topic to which we will return.

While Goethe pondered whether to acquiesce to a high-class marriage, he composed a farce entitled *Hanswurst's Wedding, or The Way of the World* as a bawdy antipode to the civilized behavior of respectable people. A tutor named Brustfleck ("Breaststain") is the advocate of social propriety. He introduces what he considers his well-brought-up pupil Hanswurst ("Hans Sausage," the German equivalent of Punch), who is to be married. Preparations for the celebration are under way. Brustfleck says, *The greatest names in Germany, / Believe me, are now on their way / To your house, from north and west and east / To celebrate the wed-ding feast.* But everything takes too long for Hanswurst, who gets impa-tient: *With these boors I'll have no truck / They want to gorge; I want to fuck.* (Obviously the poet of *Werther* can play different tunes.) Hanswurst is utterly shameless and gets right to the point with no detour through civilized behavior. Although the tutor Brustfleck boasts of his success, he has to admit, *His lessons are not quite complete. / He still likes shitting in the street.* Goethe never published this unfinished farce, and it's unlikely he showed it to Lili, but the *carnival Goethe* must have gotten a kick out of writing it.

Lili was a young lady of feeling, very pretty, with natural grace but also coquettishness. She was smart, and courted by many men—all in all a very good catch. When she appeared with Goethe—himself a handsome and popular young man, after all—it was talked about in the great houses of Frankfurt. And there was a lot of talk, so much in fact, that the pressure on him grew greater and greater. We do not know the details of what went on between them, but it was probably the wax and wane of emotions that Goethe described in his letters to Gustchen. Soon the Schönemanns were no longer so pleased to see Lili and Goethe together, since he still had not declared his intentions. That is why the couple began to meet at the country estate of Lili's uncle in nearby Offenbach. A friend of Goethe's, the composer Johann André, also lived in Offenbach, and there they spent cheerful, at times even carefree summer days. A poem composed in Offenbach depicts Lili feeding animals in the park and leading by a silk ribbon a bear that is devoted to her—the lover she has *tamed. / Up to a certain point, of course!*

But the vexatious question still remained: was all this going to result in marriage? A poem dedicated to Lili's uncle says, *I've no use for tolling bells in the steeple / and rattling coaches and chattering people. / And I don't take the church's advice / For I've already been in Paradise.* Goethe was still wary of a long-term commitment, but he didn't want to lose Lili either. Lili was endearingly, urgently real, unlike Gustchen, who existed only in her letters and in his imagination. Of course, his imag-ination was also at play in the relationship with Lili. There is some evidence that the two were hatching romantic plans to elope: a coach waiting in the predawn twilight, and off they would go, perhaps even to America. Goethe suggests such a thing in *Poetry and Truth*, and late in her long life Lili, by then Frau von Türckheim, told an acquaintance that Goethe was the "creator of her moral existence" because he did not take advantage of her willingness to sacrifice her "duty and feeling of virtue" to him.

It came as a relief that Gustchen's brothers, Friedrich Leopold and Christian zu Stolberg, invited Goethe to join them on a trip to Switzerland. The two youthful counts belonged to the circle around Klopstock and to a literary group known as the Göttingen Grove, which lived by the principles of sentimentalism. Fritz zu Stolberg was an especially handsome youth with a self-assured manner. He was always the center of attention, idolized by both men and women. Goethe allowed himself to be persuaded to go, not only to get away from romantic complications but because the trip could be combined with a visit to his sister in Emmendingen. His parents had been urging him for a while to finally visit Cornelia, about whom they were receiving sad reports, especially since she had given birth to her first daughter. Goethe felt it to be his duty, although he would have preferred to avoid his sister's emotional troubles.

In mid-May 1775, the traveling companions set off. In Strasbourg, Goethe paid a visit to Salzmann and met with Lenz, who had been longing to see him. Since they had last seen each other, Lenz had begun a relationship of his own with Friederike Brion and also with Cornelia. Thus he was following in Goethe's footsteps. He accompanied him from Strasbourg to Emmendingen, where they spent some happy days, bringing some measure of cheer to Goethe's sister. They took long walks and stayed up till all hours; Cornelia, who had hardly left her bed for months, seemed briefly transformed. Goethe's enjoyment was overshadowed by his sister's obvious unhappiness, and he left Emmendingen with a heavy heart. He was dismayed to hear Cornelia speak dismissively of Lili, but this was familiar territory for them, for Goethe had also been jealous of Schlosser. He wrote laconically in *Poetry and Truth* that he intended to give the reader only an *inkling of his serious feelings* during the visit to his sister.

The trip to Switzerland took them first to Zurich, where Goethe was Lavater's guest for a while, met his circle of friends, and began a lifelong friendship with Barbara Schulthess, his *most loyal reader*, as he once called her. From Zurich they continued to Lake Lucerne—Wilhelm Tell territory—and from there to the Gotthard Pass in the high Alps. At the top of the pass he felt tempted, as he would on later visits, to simply keep on going, down into Italy. But in the end, they turned around. On the return trip, he again tarried awhile with Lavater and his other new friends and acquaintances in Zurich. At Lake Zurich they got into trouble with residents who objected to the young men's swimming naked and threw stones at them. It was a different story in Zurich and Basel; there people were eager to meet the author of *Werther*. Some were disappointed by Goethe's reserve. Some found him arrogant, vain, and in love with paradoxes. "I admire the genius of this man in the highest degree—although I do not at all love the use he puts it to," noted the Basel town clerk Isaak Iselin.

After two months, they started home. Again, they traveled via Strasbourg, where Goethe spent time with Lenz, as he had on the way to Switzerland. "I have enjoyed divine days with Goethe," Lenz wrote. Together they visited friends and taverns from Goethe's Strasbourg days. Again they climbed the cathedral steeple and made excursions to their favorite places in the countryside. But Goethe did not ride over to Sesenheim to see Friederike; nor did he pay a second visit to Cornelia in Emmendingen.

At the end of July, Goethe returned to Frankfurt. The first letter after his arrival went to Auguste zu Stolberg: *Whenever I'm feeling really low, I turn to the north. . . . Last night, my angel, I longed so much to lie at your feet, to hold your hands . . . I have so often betrayed the female sex—Oh Gustchen, if I could only look into your eyes!*

His relationship to Lili was still unresolved. The trip had had no effect on matters. Goethe sought her company and, at the same time, shied away from commitment. Once, in Lili's absence, he sat down at her desk and got his troubles off his chest—with a letter to Auguste: *Here in the room of the girl who is making me unhappy through no fault of her own, with the soul of an angel, whose happy days I—I!—darken.* Lili returns, is surprised to find him in her room sitting at her desk. She asks whom he is writing to, and he tells her. Goethe depicts all that in minute detail, but says nothing about Lili's reaction. At the same time, he wrote to Merck: *I'm stranded again on a shitty sandbar and feel like giving myself a thousand slaps for not going to the devil when I was afloat.* Lili and Goethe agreed not to see each other for a while. But it didn't help. Goethe wrote to Gustchen, *Unfortunately, her distance from me only makes stronger the enchanted bond that ties me to her.*

We have a contemporary account in which it was Lili's mother who finally put an end to the indecision. A certain Herr von Bretschneider, no friend of Goethe's, reported the events—or were they only rumors?—in a letter to the writer and publisher Christoph Friedrich Nicolai. Goethe had finally asked for Lili's hand, but "her mother asked for time to think about it, after a few weeks invited Goethe to dinner, and in the presence of a large company, answered Goethe's offer by declaring that the marriage was not proper because of the difference in religion. Of course, Goethe had to have taken this rudeness quite badly, because she could have told him the same thing in private, but the woman says she wanted to put an end to the matter once and for all and knew no better means, and had feared an argument from him if they had a tête-à-tête." This last remark is so characteristic that one is inclined to believe the rest as well.

In September 1775, Karl August, who had reached his majority and was now a duke, traveled to Karlsruhe to marry Princess Luise. On the way, he stopped in Frankfurt and invited Goethe to travel to Weimar with his chamberlain, Johann August Alexander von Kalb, who was to arrive with a coach in Frankfurt in mid-October.

Since the spring of 1775, when a visit to Weimar was first broached, Goethe had had some time to think about the invitation and had been toying with the possibility. But now he had to decide. About the same time he began to think seriously about it, he wrote to Auguste, *Will my heart finally feel something in true, poignant pleasure and suffering . . . and not always be driven up to heaven and down to hell . . . on the waves of imagination?* What one's imagination projects is one thing, but deciding on a particular reality is something else again. Forced through the needle's eye of decision, his many possibilities became a single reality; early in October he decided to go to Weimar.

In *Poetry and Truth* Goethe says that a decisive motive was needed to *flee from Lili*, but that was not quite all. At the time, he declared to

Fritz zu Stolberg that he was going to Weimar *not for the sake of anyone, for I'm piqued by the whole world*. It was not just Lili. It was the entire situation—*the whole world*—that he wanted to escape. It is important to note that there was nothing he found overpoweringly attractive about Weimar. A much stronger motivation was the desire to just get out of Frankfurt! Besides, he didn't yet know what would only slowly emerge: that going to Weimar was a life-changing decision.

For now, it was merely a more extended journey, a provisional sojourn at a court. Why shouldn't he try that out, too? He borrowed money from Merck, for as yet there had been no talk of an appointment to a post or an income. His father had to contribute money as well—grudgingly, since he did not like to see his son going to a court, especially such a small one. Weimar did not yet have the reputation it would acquire once Goethe got there. Wieland was there of course, and the duke's mother supported a *Musenhof*, a "Court of the Muses," that had achieved some fame, but that was about all. The palace had just burned down. It was yet to be proven how effective the eighteen-year-old duke would be. As far as population was concerned, compared with Frankfurt, Weimar was a small, provincial backwater with a ducal residence. So Goethe was also traveling from a metropolis to a provincial town, although one with ambitions. In Weimar's favor, it was far enough away to promise a life that would be somehow different. It would remain to be seen whether this was only a moratorium or a new beginning. While waiting for the arrival of the duke's coach, Goethe wrote to the author Gottfried August Bürger, *The first moments of composure . . . the first since the most distracted, confused, completest, fullest, emptiest, most powerful, and most foolish three-quarters of a year I have ever had in my life.*

But the coach did not arrive. He waited more than a week, with no coach and no news. He had told all his acquaintances in Frankfurt that he was leaving. He was considered as good as gone, and thus it was embarrassing to show himself. So he stayed home. He sat in his room and worked on the play *Egmont*.

Finally, he lost patience. What now? He had decided to leave Frankfurt, and he was not about to change his mind. As his anger at having to wait grew, he made a snap decision to change plans. He decided to make up for what he deprived himself of in Switzerland by going to

Italy. On October 30, he set off and wrote in his travel diary, *I packed for the north and am heading south. I acquiesced and will not come. I declined and I come!* The first stop was Heidelberg.

There a courier arrived with the message that Kalb had finally reached Frankfurt with the coach and was waiting to carry Goethe to Weimar. Goethe could have continued on to Italy, but he turned back instead.

INTERMEDIATE REFLECTION

———

Unbearable Lightness

WHEN WE LOOK AT THE WAY GOETHE DESCRIBES HIMSELF IN *Poetry and Truth* and at the early biographical evidence, we see a child who was expected and wished for. From the very beginning, he received recognition and encouragement, stimulation and approval. He was the family darling, a boy who had no problem with his own identity and could devote his energy entirely to discovering the world. He had an enormous thirst for knowledge and was quick to grasp how things were done and then to imitate them: foreign languages, rhythms and rhymes, pictures, puppet plays, fairy tales, solemn religious services, and biblical stories. Hugely self-confident, he was loved and at peace with himself. He thought of himself as a fairy-tale prince, someone who could make a present of himself to others. He explored his surroundings without misgivings or fear. Then he fell in love for the first time—with a girl named Gretchen—and he and she attended the coronation of the new emperor hand in hand.

His life was bathed in the warm glow of friendliness and enticing mystery, until this first shadow fell across it. Partly through the girl, the boy gets involved with bad company. An alien side of life is revealed to the sheltered son, who is also alienated from himself for the first time. He loses some of his directness and lack of self-consciousness. He goes to study in Leipzig, and the young man—still a boy in some ways—is strong enough to recover his natural spontaneity. But from then on, a certain amount of calculation is always in play. No longer so insouciantly full of himself, he now wants to do something unheard-of, to outdo himself. He plans to be a poet, and in his letters he practices creating a reality on the page through which he can intervene in and change the rest of reality. But this can lead to confusion. Life becomes mysterious when the imagination gets involved, but it also becomes labyrinthian. It's not always easy to separate actual and imagined experience. And his new friend Behrisch, that brilliantly odd fellow, contributes to the confusion.

The student Goethe made a somewhat blithe conquest of Leipzig and even began a promising love affair, but it soon ran into trouble. After his first success, the young man began to meet with obstacles, as he had at the end of his childhood in Frankfurt. There was an inner dissonance before Leipzig and again after Leipzig.

He falls seriously ill and experiments with religion among the Herrnhuters, but without success, for he lacks the necessary consciousness of his own sinfulness. Feelings of guilt are foreign to his nature, and he has no need of a heavenly savior. When the poetic urge is upon him he feels completely unconstrained. A new, unheard-of lyrical language takes possession of him; he is overpowered by it. In Strasbourg he becomes the whiz kid later referred to reverentially as "the young Goethe." Overflowing with ideas he cannot write down fast enough, he can seem possessed at times. Verses come wherever he happens to be—during long country rambles, under sunny skies, in rain and snow. He claims to have composed some of the early, defiant hymns while battling wind and rain.

He not only lived poetry, he poeticized life. In hindsight, his affair with Friederike seems like an idyllic novel. But the enchantment is not merely retrospective. The young man himself could enchant friends with poetry, had read Goldsmith's *Vicar of Wakefield* and replayed the novel. Life springs from literature before literature can be reborn from life.

As for fame as a writer, Goethe had achieved everything possible before he left for Weimar. Practically overnight, *Götz* and *Werther* had made him the voice of his generation. As a rule, turning points in intellectual history are seen only in hindsight, but in the case of *Götz* and *Werther*, it was already clear that a new era had begun. Goethe became an instant cult author (as he would be called today): admired and envied, he was also respected, if at times reluctantly, by older authority figures. He clearly recognized his own importance. He had not sought such notoriety; it simply came to him, but not, he thought, undeservedly. Talented people hit the bull's-eye even when they aren't aiming for it.

Because others were astonished, he ended up being astonished himself at the playful ease—as if it were a matter of course—with which he produced new works. He called his lyrics occasional poems, and the best do seem inspirations of the moment, poems developed on their own rather than made. And it is true that the young Goethe did not labor over his works. Either he succeeded on the first try, or he abandoned the effort until a more propitious moment. Some things were never completed; others were, even if they took a lifetime, as would be the case with *Faust*. If he ran out of steam, he started something new. In general, he was fond of beginnings—a notorious beginner.

Goethe was bursting with ideas. He could not make something out of all of them, because there were simply too many. That is why it was easy for him to destroy earlier attempts. He could be certain that something new would follow. He could burn his bridges behind him because he was always moving blithely forward. We live looking forward and understand looking back. The time for understanding would come; later, his father's pedantic influence would awaken, and he would begin to collect everything relating to himself.

His early self-confidence was like sleepwalking. He couldn't even imagine himself on the wrong track. He intended to follow the necessity he sensed within himself. Adjusting yourself to your own nature, he called it. He was certainly advantaged by his family's wealth. With that security at his back, he did not have to tailor his life to making money or to a professional career. He devoted himself to education, not just training. He didn't want to become a professional man, and although he did end up practicing law, he did it in his own talented way, with playfulness and imagination—too much imagination, according to his colleagues and clients. He made a brilliant impression, but also an unreliable one. His legal briefs were well written but failed to have the hoped-for effect on the court. He himself, not wanting to do anything as a *profession*, suspected that he lacked the necessary thoroughness in legal matters, but also in general. Hence his strange striving to prove himself a poet who could break the rules but also master

them to the point of perfection and pedantry. His later projects in natural science should be understood as a lifelong attempt to prove his
thoroughness for fear that people would think him incapable of it.

There were moments when the young and still insouciant Goethe
doubted himself. But it was not others who made him uncertain.
Instead, it sometimes happened that this young man with such a rich
imagination was *absent from himself*, as he calls it—given to moments of
depression and emptiness. He called it an illness, and it is what *Werther*
is about. Looked at closely, it is not so much love that makes Werther
unhappy, but the feeling of emptiness that seeps in when his large emotions fade away. That was the real crisis Goethe himself experienced,
as he admits in *Poetry and Truth*. He calls it *taedium vitae*, the weariness
of living. Which arises not from life's burdens, entanglements, or acute
disasters but from monotony and emptiness. What threatens is not
superfluity but nothingness. There is no wildly gesticulating despair,
only paralyzing boredom. Goethe depicts how he escaped such emptiness by working himself up to the melodramatic gesture of keeping
a dagger handy and taking the suicides of great historical figures as his
models: Emperor Otto falling on his sword or Seneca slitting his wrists
in the bathtub—textbook acts of desperation. But they were active
individuals, and he accuses himself of despairing from a dearth of
action. The remedy was to force himself to write the novel *Werther*. By
writing of Werther's *hypochondriacal fancies*, he rid himself of his own
and resolved to live, as he says in *Poetry and Truth*. But perhaps something
of the weariness of living and its emptiness survived in his later unease,
which he combatted with a love of order and a dose of pedantry.

There is actually no need to explain periodically recurring *taedium vitae*, for it is part of being human. It would need explanation if
he had never felt it. But there is another sort of weariness: caused not
by emptiness but by excess—a weariness that everything he puts his
hand to succeeds so effortlessly. It was already true of Goethe as a boy.
He could not hear a story without spinning a continuation and making it into a new story. He wrote his own Bible. He was enchanted by
a puppet show and immediately set out to enchant others. Too impatient for entire systems of thought, he would pick out a few thoughts
from them and make something of his own. He did that, for example, with Spinoza and Kant, whom he never read thoroughly. Even

in philosophy, he had an overpowering urge to play. From that same urge came the pleasure of disguise. He first encountered Friederike in Sesenheim in the disguise of a poor theology student. He played parts not just for others but for himself. If you were playacting, you had no need to deceive yourself; a person at play has gone beyond truth and falsehood.

He didn't feel weary of playing, but sometimes the unbearable lightness of his creative being made him weary. Almost all of his life, all his activities had something playful about them, especially the creative ones. Well into his years in Weimar, he could never regard his writing as work, even when he pursued it with exhaustive devotion. It was simply too easy for him. That's why there was something unresisting at play, even when the theme was psychological stress and strain, as in *Werther.* The urge to play makes even stress and strain into something all too easy.

The impression of ease also came from the way in which everything seemed expressible in words. There was language at hand for everything. The young genius had the feeling he could master anything he encountered. There was something carefree and easygoing about it, something almost childlike. Herder condescendingly called the approach *"spatzenmässig"*—"sparrow-like." And it's true that the young man could bubble over, indulge himself, juggle ideas and inspiration. That's how it was in the first years, the years of genius. But even before Weimar, one occasionally notices his efforts to restrain himself, even an intentional stiffness. He had been touched by an odd weariness brought on by having too much. Whatever is so easy to produce has not yet really been born—born into a world that puts up resistance. That was the world now sought by Goethe, the darling of fortune who succeeded so easily at everything. And that was why he followed the call to Weimar. He wanted at last to have a relationship for which he was *unprepared on every side.*

As he made his way to Weimar, he was already famous throughout Europe. But he felt that, so far, he had done and accomplished nothing.

CHAPTER 11

Complications at Court. The Wieland Affair.

Charlotte von Stein. Wild Antics at First.

Klopstock Rebuffed. Herder Receives the Call.

. . . .

GOETHE REACHED WEIMAR ON NOVEMBER 7, 1775, IN THE
company of the young chamberlain von Kalb, who would soon succeed
his father as Kammerpräsident, the director of the duchy's finances.
They followed part of the same route Goethe had traveled ten years
before on his way to study in Leipzig. Back then, Goethe's mother had
wrapped her son in blankets like a little child. When an axel broke, he
had been eager to lend a hand to get the coach moving again and had
injured a ligament in his chest that continued to plague him for a long
time. That had been his first real acid test.

Ten years earlier he had been at the beginning of a phase in life
during which he came *to regard* [his] *intrinsic poetic talent as completely natural*. He was able to write poetry as easily as *sleepwalking*. But that was
also precisely why he didn't like to take credit for it. For him, it was
part of his vitality seeking expression, but he never thought of it as
work. *Through field and wood I tramped along / Piping out my little song, /
And passed the day away.*

Having given free rein to his imagination, Goethe was now
embarking on a different journey that would possibly test his capacity
for the *business of the world*. *So I encountered . . . the thought: shouldn't I . . .
employ the things that were humane, rational, and sensible about me for the use
and advantage of myself and others?* He did not know exactly what awaited
him in Weimar. The invitation had been urgent but vague, its intended
purpose unstated.

The young duke, who had assumed the reins of government from his mother, Anna Amalia, on September 3, 1775, was in need of a capable administrator and adviser, for the little duchy was again threatened with bankruptcy. The court budget of the ministate, with its eighty thousand inhabitants, was being financed on credit because its revenues were insufficient. Agriculture consisted of small holdings and craft production was only for personal consumption. A textile factory in Apolda was in decline, unable to compete with products from the lower Rhine and England. The grain trade was crippled by the high cost of transport. There were few if any exports, but local production and yields were not enough for self-sufficiency. Even salt had to be imported despite a number of saltworks in the duchy, for they were poorly managed.

And this state with its meager economic power had to support a bloated administrative apparatus and a lavish court, regularly leading to large indebtedness. It tried to cope by counterfeiting coinage, keeping false books, and raising taxes. At the time Goethe arrived, the tax rate was 30 to 35 percent, compared with about 20 percent in Prussia and 12 percent in England.

But as yet, the new arrival had no eye for Weimar's social misery, only for his own shortness of funds. He was not being paid, and it did not look as if he had been invited for an extended stay. And thus he had to ask his father for money. He found it unpleasant to approach him directly, so he chose "Aunty" Johanna Fahlmer, a relative of the Jacobis and a friend of Goethe's mother, as a go-between. He wanted the two women to find out whether Johann Caspar would show his appreciation for *his son's reflected glory* by making a financial contribution.

Reflected glory after only two months? That could only be the effect of his personality, for as yet he had done nothing at court or for the state. His status in Weimar was that of a private person, a visitor and new friend of the young duke's. But he was a brilliant figure and attracted much attention. Goethe was enjoying himself. *My life is going along like a sleigh ride, off with a bound and a jingle and promenading up and down.*

In fact, the first real innovation he introduced was ice-skating. The great Klopstock had celebrated the activity in a poem, and while the duke's courtiers considered it beneath their dignity, now one could see Goethe showing Karl August and his chamberlains Einsiedel and Kalb how to cut figure eights on the frozen water meadows of the Ilm River. The ladies soon followed. Older people sat on benches equipped with runners. The effect of their new visitor lay chiefly in the new amusements he beguiled them with. For reasons of protocol, he was not yet permitted a place at the ducal table, but he held sway over social activities. He told such witty and vivid stories, could improvise poems on the spot, and at every opportunity was asked to read from his works, even—or especially—from ones still in progress: *Faust*, for instance. Whether he took all the parts himself, assigned roles to members of the court, or staged an improvisation, Goethe was always master of ceremonies.

He brought a new dynamic into the tangled web of relationships at court, playing the game and receiving his share of hard knocks. His letters are full of dark hints: *I'm certainly having a pretty wild time here,* he writes to Merck in early 1776. *I hope you'll soon hear that I've been able to stage a tragic something in the theatro mundi and play my fair part in all the tragicomic farces.* Or: *Every day I learn to steer better on the waves of humanity. I'm far out at sea.* Or: *I can't tell you anything about my state of affairs. It's too complicated.*

The situation at court was indeed *complicated*. The young duke was crazy about Goethe. The two were almost always seen together, taking rides in the woods or to the surrounding villages, at evening gatherings, and sometimes even standing in the square and competing to see who was best at cracking a whip. There wasn't much talk yet about the business of governing, although the duke energetically asserted his sovereign authority over his mother, Anna Amalia, who had no intention of retiring completely from public life. So for the time being there were two centers of power at the Weimar court: the youthful duke and the dowager duchess. Caught between the two was the young duchess, feeling neglected by her new spouse and repulsed by the newly lax behavior of his circle. The duke's former tutor Count Görtz, now the duchess's chamberlain, drew back resentfully and cultivated his ties to the Prussian court. He even went to Berlin for a time, where he would later enjoy much success. His wife, who stayed behind in Weimar, kept him abreast of the goings-on at court. Her letters provide a glimpse into the web of intrigue in which Goethe found himself entangled. Both Görtzes disliked him intensely. The countess always calls him "the postscript." She writes that he behaves arrogantly, "but he is coddled and people run after him."

Görtz had accompanied Karl August to Frankfurt and was present at his first meeting with Goethe in December 1774. He considered the poet's paean to small states pure flattery intended for the ears of Karl August, and had harbored a deep distrust of him ever since. He took pride in his nobility and felt superior to the bourgeois man of letters— Goethe was nothing more to him than that—especially with regard to political and diplomatic skill and social polish. Goethe was not really his competitor; Görtz's ambitions exceeded any reward that such a small dukedom could offer. All the same, his dislike soon developed into downright hatred: "This Goethe is a boy, a boy in need of daily improvement with the rod," he wrote in March 1775, a comment triggered by Goethe's behavior toward Wieland, still Weimar's intellectual in chief.

Provoked by Wieland's adaptation of Euripides's *Alcestis*, Goethe had composed the farce *Gods, Heroes, and Wieland* on a single October afternoon back in 1773—with the help of a bottle of burgundy, according to *Poetry and Truth*. Wieland is shown in his nightcap, appearing before Euripides and some mythological heroes from *Alcestis*. He had reinterpreted them as virtuous and sensitive figures and called it an improvement on the Greek original. That is what irritated Goethe. It has also been taken amiss in Hades. Hercules in particular, whom Wieland presents as a paragon of virtue, proves instead to be an antique muscle man who blusters away at the man in the nightcap.

In *Poetry and Truth* Goethe denies having had the text published; he says it was Lenz who did it. Personally, he would not have bothered with this fruit of a momentary whim. But the farce got printed and it caused a great stir. Wieland felt insulted, even though he reviewed it sympathetically in his own journal, *Der Teutsche Merkur,* calling it a "satirical masterpiece," an act of generosity that had the intended effect of shaming Goethe.

The matter was discussed during Goethe's first encounter with Karl August in Frankfurt and a few days later in Mainz. If Wieland was insulted, all Weimar was insulted—at least that's how Görtz saw it. Goethe gave voluble assurances of his great respect for Wieland and wrote him a conciliatory letter on the spot, to which Wieland wrote a friendly reply. These letters have not survived, only Goethe's report of them to Sophie von La Roche. There one finds no trace of contrition, only mild regret at having allowed himself to be persuaded to apologize in the first place. *That's the damn thing about it, that I'm not getting into any more misunderstandings with anyone.* Knebel had recognized this characteristic of Goethe's early on: "He has an intellectual need to make enemies he can quarrel with . . . . He spoke to me about all the people he had attacked with especially deep respect. But the lad is combative. He has the spirit of an athlete."

A few weeks after his conciliatory letter, Goethe's belligerence was reawakened when he read remarks made by Wieland about so-called genius societies and took them as a personal attack. In a March 1775 letter to Johanna Fahlmer, he had given vent to his anger: *Wieland is and will always be a sh——head. May eternal enmity reign between his seed and mine.*

At about the same time, another farce appeared anonymously, entitled *Prometheus, Deucalion, and His Reviewers.* "Prometheus" stood for Goethe and "Deucalion" for his creation Werther. The reviewers were not named, but introduced as physiognomic caricatures. Wieland is again the target of derision. He humbly approaches the great Prometheus: "Since last you made the trip to Mainz / The sun upon our friendship shines. / Am I allowed to kiss your spur?" To be depicted as abasing himself before the great Goethe was even more insulting to Wieland than the first satire.

Goethe was thought to be the author of this farce, too. Someone was even found to testify that Goethe had brought the manuscript to the printer. Goethe denied writing it and distributed a printed declaration that it was his friend Heinrich Leopold Wagner who had written the farce and had it printed *without my knowledge or support.* But he didn't go so far as to completely deny some participation—albeit involuntary—in the undertaking. He admitted that his jokes were being imitated.

It was *Prometheus, Deucalion, and His Reviewers* that raised Görtz's ire and prompted his remark that Goethe was in need of the rod. Karl August himself took the matter less seriously. Perhaps as early as December 1774, but certainly by May 1775 after his return from Paris and before traveling home, he invited Goethe to Weimar for the first time; the official invitation followed in September. It was an invitation to pay him a visit; there was no talk of a permanent move.

During the following months, Countess Görtz kept watch on the doings at court with the eyes of Argus. In a letter of November 1776, she reports a rift between Anna Amalia and the young duchess: "the two women are completely sick of each other." And of the duke she writes, "It is certain that he no longer wants his mother to attend to anything." She describes the depression of the young duchess, who blamed her husband's neglect on Goethe's influence and had insisted that the latter not be permitted a seat at the ducal table. Anna Amalia, however, drew Goethe into her circle, among other things because she hoped to learn from him what was going on with Karl August.

The matter had a political aspect as well, if not in the first months after the duke's accession to power, then later. In the struggle to preserve the duchy's autonomy and independence, Karl August leaned toward Prussia. He had a passion for military life and had assumed the command of a contingent of Prussian troops as a major general. Anna Amalia, although—or perhaps because—she was a niece of Frederick the Great, believed it was instead best to seek protection from the empire, and so was a proponent of closer dependence on the Habsburgs. Goethe's letters from his first years in Weimar make no mention of this political background. When tensions developed between Prussia and the Habsburg Empire a few years later, Goethe, like Anna Amalia, would incline toward the imperial side. In other respects, too, Goethe found himself in a tricky position between the duke and his mother, since instead of playing politics, he wanted to remain open and trusting toward both of them—toward Karl August in any case, but also toward Anna Amalia. He felt genuine affection for her, as she did for him. When he arrived in Weimar, Anna Amalia was still a very pretty woman of thirty-six who liked to dance, paint, compose music, and put on amusing entertainments. She read the newest literature, gathered about her a circle of readers, admired Goethe's *Werther*, and had Wieland teach her about ancient and modern philosophy.

Many at court assumed that she and Goethe had more than a close social relationship. Countess Görtz called Goethe Anna Amalia's "favorite" and kept a log of his calls upon her, indeed of both parties' comings and goings. She also observed—or thought she had—that Goethe once spent an entire evening alone with Anna Amalia. The little town, the ducal seat where nothing stayed hidden, buzzed with rumors, which the Countess Görtz promptly passed on. "Maman [Anna Amalia] is on a better footing with the genius par excellence [Goethe] than ever before, and despite his caution in public, it is being slanderously talked about." She reports that Herder thought that there was something fishy at court: "He is constantly sad and regrets the unfortunate fate of Weimar, the aberrations of the master [Karl August], the situation of his wife. He disdains the mother [Anna Amalia] more than ever and blames the favorite." Countess Görtz wrote this several years later than 1776; matters continued to be murky for some time. Wieland called himself "merely an observer" of the "comedy of state," and the chamberlain Sigmund von Seckendorff professed to be irked by the commotion Goethe had helped to stir up: "The whole court is divided into two parties, of which that of the duke is noisier, the other quieter. In the first one, they run, hunt, shout, lash, and gallop and, strangely enough, think they're doing it with style because of the aesthetes who participate. There is no wantonness they deny themselves. The second party"—presumably young Duchess Luise's circle, which was fairly stiff and very class-conscious—"is usually bored, sees all its plans confounded by the first, and the pleasure they seek usually vanishes."

It was to the second party that Charlotte von Stein belonged. She had been a lady-in-waiting to Anna Amalia and remained loyally devoted to her now that she was a companion to Duchess Luise. Goethe wrote her effusive letters; even as he thus sought her out, she expressed grave concern to her fatherly friend the renowned physician Johann Georg Zimmermann that Goethe was corrupting the morals of the young duke. She said that she avoided contact with Goethe, who deserved a severe reprimand: "There is an astonishing amount on my mind that I need to tell that monster. It is impossible that he will make his way in the world behaving as he does! . . . Why does he always lampoon everyone? . . . And now, his indecent behavior with his swearing and using vulgar, low expressions . . . he ruins others. The duke is astonishingly changed. Yesterday he was with me, asserted that anyone with propriety, with manners, didn't deserve the name of an honest man! . . . That's why he can no longer abide anyone who isn't a bit rough around the edges. That all comes from Goethe. . . . I feel that

Goethe and I will never be friends." Goethe, for his part, thought that he had found a friend in her.

Frau von Stein was thirty-three years old and married to the head equerry, Josias von Stein. The couple had had seven children, of whom three survived. Frau von Stein came from a noble family, the von Schardts, and had been reared in a strict courtly setting. She moved among her peers in perfect form and saw to it that others did the same. She read widely, liked to quote from what she had read, and had strong opinions. Her social equals considered her a scholar. She had a petite, slim figure and despite her numerous pregnancies seemed almost girlish. There was something Mediterranean about her brownish complexion, glossy black hair, and dark eyes. In public she was self-confident but reserved, often serious but sometimes also ironical. And she always kept her distance. Her laconic judgments of others were feared. There was nothing effusive about her. Some thought her melancholy. Without being a great beauty, she was extremely elegant.

After a long conversation by the fireside during his first visit to Grosskochberg, Frau von Stein's country estate, a few hours from Weimar, Goethe scratched his name and the date onto a tabletop: December 6, 1775. In the letter he wrote to her shortly thereafter—the first of what would eventually be fifteen hundred letters to Charlotte, Goethe writes, *And just as I can never tell you my love, I can never tell you my joy.* The tone of the early letters is flirtatious, linguistically playful, even coquettish. There is constant talk of love, but the mood is rococo, touched with irony. *But God only knows where all my foolishness and all my wit have gone to!* he writes in one, and then follows up with a cascade of witticisms. In a letter from late January 1776, he suddenly switches from the formal pronoun *Sie* to intimate second-person forms: *Dear lady, permit me to love thee* [dich] *so much. If I can love anyone more, I shall tell thee* [dir]. Perhaps she forbade him to speak in that way, for the following day he is contrite: *I'm trying to make up my damn mind and heart whether to stay or leave.* He had probably also spoken to her about his unfortunate sister and his own guilty conscience, and had found some sympathy, for he writes, *Oh, if only my sister had a brother the way I have a sister in you.* In one of his first letters, he calls her a *soother.* In her he expects to find not excitement but lovely, soothing peace of mind.

Sometimes, however, he finds that she overdoes the soothing peace of mind, in particular whenever she simply avoids him. With bitter irony he remarks, *You are right to make me into a saint, i.e., to remove me from your heart. . . . And here is an urn, if it should ever come to pass that only relics of the saint remain.* The next day he reverts to the formal second-person *Sie* to add, *But since my love for you* [Sie] *is one continual resignation. . . .* And so it goes, back and forth between agitation, reassurance, and being left alone. His desire is coquettishly expressed; he makes an advance and then retreats. He is voluble, occasionally laconic, sometimes fresh, and now and then he breaks into poetry. In any case, he cannot leave her alone and finds in her an opportunity to pull out all the stops of his expressive capabilities.

He is so preoccupied by the relationship that news from Frankfurt barely affects him. Upon learning from Johanna Fahlmer that Lili has become engaged, he answers, *No more about Lili; she's been written off.* That same day he writes to Auguste zu Stolberg, *My heart, my head—I don't know where to begin, my circumstances are so multitudinous and new, and changing, but good.*

However, his *circumstances* are also such that the feeling of intimacy with Charlotte seems almost spooky. In mid-April 1776, he confides to Wieland, *I cannot account for the importance—the power—that this woman has over me except by way of metempsychosis.—Indeed, we were once man and wife!—Now we know it of ourselves—in a veiled way, in a spectral haze. I have no name for us—the past—the future—the universe.* During the same period, he asks Charlotte to make him a copy of a poem of his that he no longer has: *I'd like it in your hand—and then I won't bother you anymore.* Goethe never published this poem:

> *Fate, why did you grant this deep perception*
> *So that we can see what is to come,*
> *And never, blissful, trust in the deception*
> *Of love and earthly happiness, like some?*
> *Why did you grant us feelings, intuitions,*
> *so that we see into each other's heart,*
> *And through all the strange crush and confusion*
> *Discern the truth we shared in from the start.*

The verses were written at about the same time Charlotte was writing the letter to Zimmermann quoted above. Obviously, Goethe was not yet able *to see into* [her] *heart* the way he wished he could. The poem suggests the feeling of a curious transmigration of souls between the two of them that Goethe had confided to Wieland: *Tell me then, What does fate have in store? / Tell me how it yoked us in this life. / Ah, in times gone by we were together, / And you were my sister or my wife.*

He would continue to cast Charlotte in the role of *soother.*

> *Drop by drop you cooled his heated blood,*
> *Gave direction to his errant ways.*
> *In your angel's arms his ravaged breast*
> *Could at last find peace and healing rest.*
> *With a gentle hand you kept him tethered,*
> *Dandling days away for his delight.*
> *Unparalleled the hours of sunny weather*
> *When, grateful, he would stretch out at your feet.*
> *Feeling his heart swelling next to yours,*
> *Feeling in your eyes that he was good,*
> *He felt the brightening of all his senses*
> *And the calming of his racing blood.*

We don't know whether the role suited her or whether she found his poem indiscreet. There were rebuffs. Again and again, Charlotte had to remind him of the bounds of propriety. Once he writes her after a meeting, *Whenever I want to close my heart toward you, I never feel good about it.*

As a wife, mother, and lady-in-waiting to the strict and proper duchess, Charlotte was very concerned about her reputation. Her city residence was not far from the garden house in a park along the Ilm River that the duke had given to Goethe as a present, but she avoided visiting him there alone. She received him in her house in the presence of her children and other visitors though without her husband, who was rarely home. Often she withdrew for months at a time to her country estate in Grosskochberg. For Countess Görtz, the reason was obvious: "They say that Lotte will spend the entire winter in the country to put a stop to the malicious gossip." But it may have had exactly the opposite effect.

Goethe often combined a visit to Charlotte with one to Anna Amalia, as if trying to maintain a kind of balance. There is some evidence that Charlotte was not pleased about the arrangement. Once when he had been with Anna Amalia at her summer residence in the Ettersburg castle, he wrote to Charlotte, *I see now how my presence bothers you*, and notes in his diary, below the sun symbol that stood for Charlotte, *eclipse*. But he also wrote, of one of his visits to the Ettersburg castle, *Marvelous night*. We do not know (although there were those who thought they did) whether Charlotte had any grounds for jealously; was Goethe maintaining an amorous relationship with Amalia at the same time?

Gossip also swirled around Corona Schröter, the beautiful actress whom Goethe and the duke had persuaded to leave Leipzig for Weimar. She was protective of her reputation and had a chambermaid with her who acted as a kind of duenna. The duke courted her assiduously but had no success as a suitor. Goethe was also attracted to her and later wrote the title role in the play *Iphigenia in Tauris* expressly for her. In it, she could be as he saw her: beautiful and passionate, but also modest and pure. He had difficulty mastering his infatuation with Schröter. His diary records a visit to her on January 2, 1777, and then *a feverish night*. On January 6 after another visit: *Didn't sleep. Pounding heart and hot flushes.* Corona excited him. On May 8, he took advantage of Charlotte's absence and spent an entire day with her in his garden house. Perhaps Charlotte got wind of it; a few days later, she met him there, a very rare occurrence.

While his ties to Charlotte grew gradually stronger despite occasional setbacks, Goethe was also living through the first, passionate phase of his friendship with the duke. Merck, who knew the duke well, wrote about the relationship between the two in a letter to Lavater: "The duke is one of the most remarkable young people I have ever seen. . . . Goethe loves him as he does none of us, perhaps because no one needs him as much as the duke, and so their relationship will last forever—since Goethe cannot leave him, or he would no longer be the person he is, and the duke will no sooner break with him than would one of those who are Goethe's friends."

The duke had been raised and educated in the spirit of the Enlightenment. He loved Voltaire above all other writers and revered his granduncle, the Prussian king Frederick the Great, who had brought the French writer to his court. Like Frederick, Karl August wanted to have a famous intellectual and writer at his side as adviser and companion. But since falling instantly under the spell of Goethe's personality at their first meeting, he also wanted him as his friend. The duke was a decisive, roll-up-your-sleeves young man with an unerring talent for sizing people up. His insight into human nature was said to be his strongest talent. Animated by the new ideas of the Sturm und Drang, he prized candidness, naturalness, and occasionally even crudeness. He considered sentimentalism ridiculous. Religion didn't mean much to him beyond its usefulness in the task of governing. He had a natural sense of sovereignty and had been impatient to reach his majority and take over the reins of government completely from his mother. He intended to rule the duchy rationally, on the model of his granduncle, without yet knowing exactly what that would entail. He loved commanding and leading his soldiers around, riding hell-for-leather in great hunting parties, and making conquests of local girls.

When Merck met the duke, he understood at once why Goethe liked him. "I'll tell you honestly," he wrote to Nicolai, "the duke is one of the shrewdest and most respectable people I ever saw—and just think, he's also a prince and twenty years old to boot." Karl August was mature for his age, but not precocious. He'd retained something of his carefree, rash youth. People worried about his health because he loved to brave wind and weather, ride recklessly through the woods, climb trees, and sleep in hay barns or in the open air. In the first *crazy* weeks, Goethe was with him in almost all his exploits, but not without expressing to his ducal friend his concern about the *all too great heat, with which you are always in danger of doing something if not unjust, then unnecessary—and of straining your own powers and the powers of your nearest and dearest for nothing.* One time, Karl August fell out of a tree. Another time, he dislocated his shoulder while wrestling with a chamberlain. Another, he spent a half-frozen night with peasants, having taken refuge from a blizzard. He longed for adventures and danger and mocked the "artificial gentlemen," as he called some of his over-sensitive courtiers. He gathered around him men who wanted to be part of the action: Einsiedel, Bertuch, Otto Joachim Moritz Wedel, the painter Georg Melchior Kraus, and—above all—Goethe.

The duke would have gladly spent the first Christmas after Goethe's arrival with his friends, but he had been invited to the court of the Duke of Saxony-Gotha, and so his friends trooped to a remote, snowed-in Waldeck forester's lodge near Bürgel without him. The letters Goethe wrote from there to the duke give us a taste of what must have been the usual, carefree tone of this all-male society. Goethe sits in his room after a drinking spree and *scrawls* his letter. *They're still sitting downstairs after supper's been cleared away, smoking and jabbering so I can hear it through the floor.* On their pub crawl they come upon pictures of the duke in the taverns. They pay him their respects, bow and scrape, and realize *how much we love you.* They are snug in the snow-covered, quiet house while outside the wind howls and the stars glitter. Goethe's thoughts stray to the duke, who is constrained to sit through a gala reception in honor of his accession to power:

> *Behave yourself amidst all those sconces*
> *Shining upon you*
> *And all those faces*
> *Swarming around you*
> *And singing your praises.*
> *True joy and peace can only be found*
> *Where trusty, loyal souls abound.*

The duke sends a messenger to say he misses Goethe so much that his friend should come over to Gotha and keep him company, especially since people are curious to see him. Goethe sets off and puts in an appearance at the court of the Duke of Saxony-Gotha, where he makes a strong impression. He makes an even bigger splash a few days later in the house of the von Keller family, to whom Wieland had sung the praises of the new resident of Weimar. Wieland had forgotten all his anger at Goethe's satire and now praised him to the heavens. He wrote to Jacobi that he was "quite in love" with him, and he asks Lavater "to destroy" his last letter, in which he had spoken ill of Goethe. And in a letter to Johann Georg Meusel, he simply declares, "Goethe, whom

we've had here for nine days, is the greatest genius and the best, most
likable person I know."

So now, lured by Wieland, Goethe arrives at the Kellers' in Sted-
ten, near Gotha. Wieland had not promised the assembled company—
especially the daughters of the house—more than he could deliver.
Goethe was in a good mood and in splendid form. He sparkled with
wit, read aloud, told stories, and played pranks. Wieland memorialized
his impressions of the evening in the poem "To Psyche," in which his
irony melts away in the sun of adulation:

> It is a wizard who arrives,
> With a pair of jet-black eyes,
> Eyes divine that cast a spell
> With power to delight or kill.
> He walked among us, a lord sublime,
> Monarch of spirits, in his prime!
> And no one asked, who might he be?
> At once we all felt, It is He!
> That truth invaded all our brains,
> We felt it coursing through our veins.
> Never before on God's green earth
> Had son of man possessed such worth.
> . . .
> All nature encompassed by his might
> So deep he delves in every creature,
> And is alive in every feature!
>
> That's what I call a real magician!
> . . .
> What power he has to move our souls!
> Who blends together joys and woes?
> Who tortures with such gentle art,
> With such sweet music melts our heart?
> Who can awaken from depths so deep
> And with such boisterous delight
> Feelings that without him might
> Stay hidden, lost in darkest sleep?

Karl August, also present on that memorable evening, felt proud of the "magician" who was, after all, his first conquest for Weimar.

Goethe's repertoire extended to dubious pranks. In the summer of 1776 the duke and his friends were in Ilmenau, exploring the possibility of reopening the silver and copper mines there, and made an excursion to the nearby Stützerbach. The mining official F. W. von Trebra was in the party and writes in his memoirs of that "lively circle" in which apparently "everything was permitted." "Here, unobserved, acting boisterous was, if not encouraged, at least not frowned upon, probably even expected." In their cups, they decided to cut off their hair. Goethe advised against it with a play on the two meanings of *machen*: one could do (*machen*) it, but not so easily undo it by "making (*machen*) it grow back."

Trebra wrote his account many years later and was obviously at pains to give the "amicably presiding genius" credit for trying to mitigate their wilder ideas. Frau von Stein, who at first deplored all the genius business, came to terms with Goethe's behavior in the same way: "Goethe is causing a great revolution here; if he is able to restore order, so much the better for his genius! His intentions are certainly good, but too much youth and too little experience—however, let's wait and see!"

Goethe was a bit uncomfortable at the thought that his parents in Frankfurt might hear too much about the goings-on in Weimar. In the spring of 1776, Josias von Stein, Charlotte's husband, was to travel to Frankfurt on business, and while there he planned to pay a call on Goethe's parents. As a precautionary measure, Goethe sent "Aunty" Fahlmer some instructions. They should give the *honest fellow* a warm welcome but be prepared to hear some unpleasant things about the situation in Weimar. It would be best not to make further inquiries but to remain reserved. *You just shouldn't seem too delighted about my status here. Moreover, von Stein, like almost the entire court, is not completely satisfied with the duke because he doesn't dance to their tune, and I am both secretly and openly blamed. If he should let drop something of the sort, you must also ignore it. In general, ask more than you tell, and let him talk more than you do.*

The rumors, however, were reaching not just his parents in Frankfurt but the public at large. Goethe's move to Weimar had attracted attention, and now people were curious to know how it was turning out. His friendship with the duke was frequently compared to the alliance between Voltaire and Frederick the Great; people had anticipated that the intellectual and the prince were joining forces for the sake of the larger good. Yet now they were hearing of a wild "state of affairs in Weimar" and, as the classicist and translator Johann Heinrich Voss reported from hearsay, the duke was traveling through the villages with Goethe like a "wild fellow. He gets drunk and, like a brother, shares the same girls with him." Klopstock had heard the same gossip, and since he considered himself the head of the "republic of letters," he wrote Goethe, whom he had won over with his poem about ice-skating, in a tone of reproach and admonishment: "what will be the unfailing result, if the duke continues? If he continues to drink to the point of illness, instead of—as he says—thereby strengthening his body, he will succumb and not live long. . . . Until now, the Germans have justifiably complained that their princes want nothing to do with their learned men. Currently, people are happy to make an exception of the Duke of Weimar. But what will other princes, continuing in their same old way, not be able to adduce in their defense if that will have happened which I fear will happen?"

Goethe left the letter unanswered for two weeks to allow his outrage to cool, devoting himself instead to his asparagus bed, among other things. Then he wrote a reply: *You can feel yourself that there is no answer I must give. I would either have to intone a pater peccavi,* or make some sophistical excuse, or defend myself like an honest fellow, and in truth, perhaps in the end it would be a mixture of all three, and to what end?—So not another word between the two of us about this affair! Do you think I would have a single moment of existence to myself if I were to answer all such letters, all such admonishments?* Klopstock answered by return mail: "Your misconstruction of what I wrote was as great as my intention that the letter be a token of my friendship . . . and so I hereby declare that you were not worth giving it to." That was the end of their relationship.

The duke was eighteen when he chose Goethe as his friend and exercised all his powers of persuasion to bring him to Weimar. He wanted him nearby, but had no further plan as yet. However, in order to keep him nearby, after three months he held out the prospect of an

---

* Latin: Father, I have sinned.

official position, against the opposition of some courtiers and officials. He also showed Goethe extreme generosity, such as making him a present of the garden house. On March 16, 1776, the duke wrote a will that stipulated a lifetime pension for Goethe, for the time being without offering him an official position. From time to time in the first months, Goethe toyed with the idea of leaving Weimar. It was important to him to know that if he felt like it, he could go at any time. In that way, he remained free. He had also chosen freely to be with the young duke. The next few years would prove the strength of Goethe's attachment to him. He often spoke quite openly about it. In a later letter to Charlotte von Stein, there is a strangely idealized, highly stylized image that encapsulates the significance of the friendship: *Then . . . the duke came, and without being devils or the sons of God, we scaled high mountains and climbed onto the parapet of the temple, there to view the realms of the world and their toils, and the danger of suddenly plunging into the depths . . . and we were enveloped in such an apotheosis that the past and future hardship of life and its difficulties lay at our feet like dross, and we—still in our earthly garb—could already feel through the still dull quills of our wings the lightness of a blissful fledging to come.*

He was quite a bit more succinct in a letter to the duke four months after his arrival in Weimar: *And thus you can never cease to feel that I love you.* At this point, Goethe had decided to stay, at least for the time being. He writes to Merck, *My situation is advantageous enough, and the duchies of Weimar and Eisenach are always a stage where one can see how a world role suits one . . . although more than ever, I'm in a position to recognize the thorough shittiness of this temporal magnificence.*

Even before Goethe himself assumed an official position, he pulled all the strings he could to have Herder appointed to fill the vacant post of *Generalsuperintendent* (church administrator), as his friend no longer felt satisfied in Bückeburg. He won over the duke, but there was resistance from the local clergy and officials. *Dear Brother,* Goethe writes to Herder, *we've always had bad relations with the shitheads, and the shitheads hold all the reins. The duke wants you, wishes to have you, but everyone is against you here.* Herder had a dubious reputation as a freethinker. That didn't frighten the duke, but, on the other hand, he didn't feel like quarreling with the church council. He was going to order an expert assessment by an orthodox theologian, but at Goethe's urging, he forwent it and appointed Herder by fiat. It fell to Goethe to see to the renovation of his friend's office and living quarters.

This affair stiffened the government officials' resistance to Goethe. When he was appointed privy councilor with a salary of 1,200 taler and a seat on the privy council, its chairman, the long-serving Jakob Friedrich Baron von Fritsch, announced his resignation. There were, he wrote, other and more experienced experts whose loyal service qualified them and whom one ought not to pass over. He implied that he considered Goethe's appointment to be a case of favoritism. The duke stuck by his decision and called Fritsch's judgment of Goethe an insult to his friend. He did not want to lose the experienced civil servant, however, and urgently requested him to stay at his post. With help from Anna Amalia, Fritsch finally allowed himself to be persuaded. For his part, Goethe was wise enough to work at getting along with him.

By the summer of 1776, Goethe was well established in Weimar. Something useful had become of the author of *Werther* after all—that was the spirit in which he informed the Kestners of his advancement: *I shall stay here and can enjoy life where I am and, after my own fashion and in many circumstances, be of use and service to one of the noblest of men. The duke, to whose soul I have now, for almost 9 months, felt the most genuine and heartfelt connection, has at last attached me to his government, from our love affair has come a marriage, and may God give it his blessing.*

CHAPTER 12

My writing has become subordinated to life.
Genius Doesn't Protect You from Being a Dilettante.
Against the Literati. The Disastrous Case of Lenz.

. . . .

ROAMING THE DUCHY, SPENDING NIGHTS IN BARNS AND foresters' lodges and then in palaces and castles, camping, ice-skating, flirting with country girls (known as *Miesels* in the local dialect), attending balls at court—such were the diversions Goethe enthusiastically pursued. He enjoyed them not least because the young duke did too. Karl August longed to experience the wild student life, or what passed for it at the time. Goethe encouraged the duke but also served as a moderating influence. Wieland wrote that Goethe had the knack of "trampling on convention yet always being smart and circumspect enough to see *how far* he dared go."

He had mood swings as well. *Of course, I'm leading a pretty wild life here*, he wrote to Merck at the beginning of 1776; a little more than a week later he sent Frau von Stein the poem "Wanderer's Night Song" with the lines *Ah! I am so tired of striving, / Why all this passion and unrest? / Peace, sweet quiet / Come! Come dwell within my breast.* But such weariness was only temporary and soon gave way to restlessness: *I've sampled the court and now I intend to sample the regiment too, and on it goes.* He no longer wanted to be a mere guest, a visitor, the personal companion of the duke. He wanted to take part in the serious business of governing.

Artistic endeavors were put on the back burner for the time being. He painted watercolors and made sketches, but most were hasty experiments given away as presents, mailed to distant friends, or simply tossed out. Goethe kept only a few. He did write poems—indeed, some of his most beautiful ones. They, too, were inspirations of the moment, most coming in letters to Frau von Stein. More ambitious projects under way—works like *Faust* or *Egmont*—remained untouched. During a visit to Leipzig in the spring of 1776, an old acquaintance, the playwright Christian Felix Weisse, asked when they could expect another work from his pen. Goethe's brief answer left no doubt: he would *turn* [his] *literary career over to Lenz, who will soon present us with plenty of tragedies.* When Goethe made this declaration in March 1776, he had no idea that Jakob Michael Reinhold Lenz, his anointed successor, was already on his way to Weimar. Finding him there upon his return from Leipzig, Goethe would give him a warm welcome, but in the long run he found Lenz's visit unpleasant. His fellow writer was a reminder of the problematic aspects of a literary existence—precisely what he had hoped to escape in Weimar.

Goethe had taken a step whose full import he only gradually came to realize: *My writing has become subordinated to life*, is how he would put it later.

That life in his first few months in Weimar was playful and eccentric, guided by whim and fancy. Something of the literary still clung to it, if in a form largely free of serious occupation and responsibility— precisely why it became problematic, as he'd come to Weimar ostensibly to engage with reality in a different way. He hadn't simply been looking for new territory in which to live out his impulses; he was seeking firmer footing. In retrospect, the imaginative excesses, the surrender to every mood, and the lack of attachments came to seem empty and unstable. He referred to his last months in Frankfurt as the *idle life at home, where I can do nothing with the greatest pleasure*. Of course, he had done a great deal of writing. But writing now seemed to him pointless, negligible. He needed the heavy lifting of action, and as he looked back on his life, it seemed to him a wheel that spun faster and faster only because it had lost contact with the ground. The things that set him apart and of which he was still proud—his rich inventiveness and supple empathetic power, his enduring sensitivity, his mood swings, all the fireworks of his soul—were now showing their problematic aspect. He suffered from the two different speeds, his inner life now too fast for external reality.

While Goethe made a proud and self-confident impression and was the instant center of attention whether at court or among bourgeois company, he was inwardly unsure of himself. He was not unaware that there were still many things he needed to know in order to be able to play an effective role in real life. Goethe the quick study, the imaginative genius, now took pleasure in things that were solid and basic. He had a sense of what he was lacking, and that was what he intended to work on. The free flights of fancy would come of their own accord, no need to worry about that. He had to concentrate on how to shape real life. Producing art is easier than making one's life a work of art, and he recognized that he still had much to learn; genius did not protect him from being a dilettante at life. A writer's presumption of moral superiority was particularly suspect to him, Klopstock's behavior being a cautionary example. With no insight into the actual circumstances, Klopstock had assumed the role of moral judge of Goethe and the young duke. The poet of the biblical epic *Messiah* might have some knowledge of conditions in heaven, but he knew nothing of what was going on in Weimar. Treating great themes doesn't automatically make you a great human being. While the literati made literature the measure of man, Goethe had become convinced it should be the other way around, for truth emerges from the practice of life, not from literature. Writerly arrogance toward people with practical skills was out of the question. It's fine to strike poetic sparks from real life, but not to confuse poetry with life. Life has its own purposefulness, as does poetry. Goethe intended to be an expert in both.

His decision to *subordinate* literature to life was also a protest against the overvaluing of literature still in vogue among his Sturm und Drang friends. He would write later that literature had led them to *undermine* themselves through their *exaggerated* demands on social reality, the *unsatisfied passions* to which they gave ever-renewed hypochondriacal expression, and even through *imaginary suffering*. In a fit of this mistrust of literature, he once wrote to Jacobi that he had *always had an uncomfortable feeling when things that preoccupy an individual mind under particular circumstances are distributed to the public.*

Just as Goethe had decided to *subordinate* literature, Jakob Michael Reinhold Lenz came to his doorstep, on April 4, 1776, like an emissary from his own youthful impulses. The young man Goethe had once called the *son whom I love as my soul* now seemed like a messenger from the world of inept and emotionally unstable scribblers. And indeed,

Lenz had arrived in Weimar a broken man, seeking refuge and support at the court and from his friend and *brother*—the two had referred to each other thus in the past and at times still did.

Two years earlier, Lenz had attained some literary fame with his comedy *The Tutor, or Advantages of a Private Education* and his *Observations on the Theater*, an ambitious attempt at a new theory of drama on the Shakespearean model. Both *The Tutor* and *Observations* had appeared anonymously and been attributed to Goethe, an expression of high regard that could have had advantages for Lenz. But the young man, whose behavior veered between bashfulness and bursts of cockiness, seemed almost to attract bad luck. When he identified himself as the author of the two celebrated works, he was promptly dubbed a Goethe imitator.

In *The Tutor*, Lenz depicted the humiliations he himself had suffered as a tutor in noble houses, an unlikely theme for Goethe—all the more reason to be surprised by the misattribution. That probably owed more to the great virtuosity with which Lenz's figures are characterized by the way they speak, as in *Götz*. Lenz was an imaginative and witty author of great talent who could improvise satire, poetry, and puns on the spot. None of that bolstered his self-confidence, however, for he regarded it merely as the expression of his nature and nothing to be proud of. His central problem was that he was plagued by guilt for having torn free of his authoritarian father, a high church official in Livonia (today's Latvia), abandoned a career as a theologian, and embraced the uncertainty of a writer's life, which held little prospect of success at the time. His father refused to support him, and Lenz went into service for miserable wages as the companion to the young barons von Kleist. Accompanying them to Strasbourg, where they joined a French regiment, Lenz lived among them essentially as a well-educated stable boy. It was a humiliating life, which he eventually drew on for his play *The Soldiers*.

Short and of delicate build, Lenz looked almost like a child. Goethe called him *the odd little thing*. Not just physically small, he constantly reduced himself, to the point of self-abasement. "We've spoken enough . . . about my scribblings," he wrote Goethe, "—now let me begin again with the little muck heap of myself and—find you." In a satirical sketch about the literary scene entitled "Pandaemonium Ger-

manicum," Goethe appears—spirited, carefree, and full of energy—
and climbs a steep mountain, leaving everyone else behind, Lenz
following at his heels, tediously "creeping." When they reach the top,
the critics approach, calling out from below, condemning Lenz as an
"imitator" who doesn't really belong up there. Lenz sent the manuscript to Goethe; embarrassed, he advised against publishing it. Lenz
took that as a command, just as he forwent publishing other manuscripts because Goethe recommended against it or simply didn't return
them. Conversely, there had been a near falling-out in 1774, when
Goethe sent Lenz his satire *Gods, Heroes, and Wieland* and Lenz turned
it over to a publisher without Goethe's permission—or so the latter
would later claim.

More often, the two friends exchanged manuscripts in a spirit of
intellectual kinship. For Goethe, Lenz was like a struggling younger
brother who needed to be taken under his wing. For Lenz, Goethe was
a mirror image of himself, but successful, enlarged, and radiant with
everything, an image in which pain and suffering seemed to dissolve
into beauty and grace. Lenz watched the girls and women who treated
him as a plaything—or so he thought—melt with love and devotion
for Goethe. He nonetheless tried to follow in his friend's footsteps in
matters of love. After Goethe left Sesenheim, Lenz courted the abandoned Friedericke and wrote her poems, which she kept with Goethe's.
When the packet of mostly unsigned poems was later discovered, it
was very difficult to tell which were by Goethe and which by Lenz. All
were infused with the same spirit and mood.

Goethe's friendship both inspired and depressed Lenz, for no one
made him feel as small as Goethe did. Those who knew Lenz well and
had sound literary judgment were free with praise and recognition. Lavater, Sophie von La Roche, Fritz zu Stolberg, and Merck all wrote him
letters full of praise. Herder, as a rule sharply critical and disinclined to
enthusiasm, asked him to send a copy of *The Soldiers*: "You are the first
person for whom I write, and you have such wonderful insight, forgiveness, comprehensive understanding, advice. Please send me the play."

In the fall of 1774, Lenz had resigned from the service of the barons
von Kleist and made a second attempt to support himself as an author.
He had written numerous dramas, comedies, and individual scenes in
the two years since, as well as essays on moral philosophy, theology,

dramaturgy, and philology, many of which remained unpublished. He lived for months at a time in a flurry of happy creativity, if also weighed down by financial worries: Lenz, who could not pay the rent on his living quarters in Strasbourg, often didn't know where his next meal was coming from. He borrowed money, paid his debts by borrowing still more, and became involved in an unhappy love affair that cost him dearly: a girl kept him waiting until she got a better offer. You have to fight your way "through excrement," as he wrote to Herder; he was always painfully aware "that we are still animals and only Klopstock's angels and Milton's and Lavater's angels ride on sunbeams."

In the spring of 1776, he decided to seek refuge with his friend in Weimar, hoping Goethe could secure a position for him. He wanted to be of use. In his baggage was a draft plan for reforming military training, the result of reflection on his depressing experience of military life in Strasbourg. In that position paper, he presented his ideas on the humane treatment of soldiers to the duke. "What does our soldier fight for?" he asks. "For the king? For the fatherland? Ha, if he is to fight vigorously for them, he must be able to love them, must have received good things from them . . . *prosperity, self-defense*: there you see the only remaining seeds of the valor that is dying out. If you stifle them, all is lost. The soldier must fight for himself when he fights for his king."

The working and living conditions of the soldiery were as important to him as if his own life were at stake. "I am working on an essay on *married soldiers* that I would like to read to some prince," he'd written Herder as he was leaving Strasbourg, "and after its completion and discussion I—will most probably die." Lenz did not intend to come to Weimar as a supplicant; he wanted to be able to give something back to the powers that be. And although he didn't want to burden Goethe, this undertaking did in fact task his famous friend, to whom Lenz seemed an example of those ivory-tower writers who think they can cure the world with ideas but are incapable of taking care of themselves. *The defects of that profession* [the military] *were described fairly well*, Goethe would write in *Poetry and Truth; the cures, however, were laughable and impractical*. Repelled by the public flogging of soldiers on the Marktplatz, Goethe nonetheless advised Lenz to be cautious in the matter. A few years later, as chairman of the military commission, Goethe had his own struggles with the state of the army; not until 1782, when he was head of the finance commission, was he able to push through a drastic reduction in the size of the little army in order to lessen the state's horrendous deficit. It was an alternative way to realize humane reforms: the need for frugality forced the issue.

Having arrived in Weimer, Lenz sent Goethe a note with the verse "The lame crane has reached the town, looking for a place to lay its head." Goethe, newly returned from Leipzig, had not yet moved into his garden house and was staying near the ducal palace with the court treasurer König. Unable to take Lenz in, he found him another place to stay for the night, introducing him the day after to Frau von Stein and at court. Lenz's reputation as a playwright, however, had already traveled to Anna Amalia's literary circle. Wieland, eager to meet an author who had written satires about him, was immediately fond of the lad, as he wrote after their first meeting, surprised to find such a gentle and bashful person. Lenz was handed around to general approval, though four weeks later some half-annoying and half-ridiculous incident led Goethe to write Charlotte von Stein: *Lenz's asinine behavior last night caused a gale of laughter. I haven't recovered yet.*

Though the exact reference is unclear, it may have been the incident that the writer Johannes Daniel Falk related many years later. According to him, Lenz had arrived at a masked ball at court in a domino costume. He either didn't realize the exclusive nature of the ball or simply refused to be deterred by it. It caused a scandal. Women retreated when he asked for a dance, and the men stood and sat in stony silence. Goethe finally ushered him out.

At first, the trouble caused was soon forgotten, and Lenz continued to be popular at court. "Here I am engulfed by the whirl of the court, which barely allows me to get my thoughts in order," he wrote to Lavater. Courtiers like Kalb and Einsiedel took him along when they went riding and introduced him into the wild gang around the duke and Goethe. Even Frau von Stein took a fancy to him. They called him a "nice boy" and treated him as such, somewhat patronizingly. Sometimes they buffeted him around a bit when they played blindman's buff. They took him seriously as well, allowing him to read from his manuscripts and tutor Anna Amalia in Greek. The duke supported him from his privy purse but could not or would not hold out any hope of a permanent position, and after the initial weeks of euphoria, disappointment set in. Goethe spent a good deal of time with him at first, then gradually pulled back. Lenz, who had begun to feel the center of the social whirl, felt suddenly abandoned. He made an abrupt decision to leave, but remained in the vicinity. He wrote to Goethe, "I'm going to the country since I can do nothing with you."

At roughly this moment, Goethe was appointed to the privy council with the title of Legationsrat against the opposition of long-serving officials who were annoyed that the duke was favoring an "aesthete." This was grounds for Goethe to want to put some distance between himself and the dubious aesthete Lenz, who'd found lodgings in Berka, a little town not far from Weimar. There he wrote "The Forest Brother," a story about a complicated love affair that was a variation on the *Werther* motif and even copied its epistolary form. The central character is a sensitive youth named Herz (heart), whose adversary is the narcissistic but otherwise sober and almost cynical Rothe, a figure clearly modeled on Goethe. One clearly sees Lenz's disappointment, perhaps even a feeling of betrayal, in this story. Rothe is a total "epicurean" whose "narcissism" has left little room for virtue. He is a conformist, seeking to gain an advantage, who never becomes discouraged, never gives of himself or reveals himself, but plays the people around him like marionettes. Disoriented, realizing painfully that he lacks social skills, Herz considers emigrating to America and entering military service, leaving it up to fate whether that will save him or mean throwing himself away. Full of bitterness and revenge, he writes in his last letter, "Rothe is a traitor . . . he will not escape my hands."

Lenz never finished the story. It can no longer be determined whether he entrusted the manuscript to Goethe or it was found among the papers he left behind in Weimar and given to Goethe. In either event, the draft and other manuscripts were in Goethe's possession twenty-one years later, when Schiller asked about them, hoping to publish something by the then long-forgotten author in his journal *Die Horen (The Horae)*. Goethe turned the Lenz manuscripts over to him in 1797, and Schiller wrote to him, "As far as I have been able to see, the Lenziana contain very crazy stuff, but the reappearance of this way of feeling at the present time will surely not be without interest, especially since the unhappy life and death of the author have extinguished all envy, and these fragments must always have a biographical and pathological value." The two friends decided to publish "The Forest Brother"—a great concession for Goethe, who until then had refused to allow any of the manuscripts to be printed. It was even forbidden to mention Lenz's name in his presence. Goethe retained painful memories of Lenz that he did not want to revive. Not until decades later was he able to write in a tranquil tone about this friend of his youth.

When Lenz left Berka and returned to Weimar, there must have been some dramatic incident between him and Goethe. We have no direct evidence about it except for Goethe's diary entry of November 26, 1776—in which the ominous phrase *Lenz's asinine behavior* is used again—but whatever it was, it prompted Goethe to ask the duke to expel Lenz forthwith. The duke hesitated, but then gave the order for Goethe's sake. Through Herder, Lenz requested a one-day reprieve, which was granted, and on the following day, he departed. All the parties involved—Goethe, the duke, Anna Amalia, Frau von Stein, Herder, and Kalb—maintained complete silence with regard to what actually happened. It may have involved a satire, or "pasquinade," containing suggestive material about Goethe and perhaps Frau von Stein or Anna Amalia as well. In a farewell letter to Herder, Lenz writes that he felt himself "expelled from heaven as a vagabond, a rebel, a pasquin. And yet there were two passages in this pasquinade that Goethe would have liked very much. That's why I have sent you a copy." The envelope addressed to Herder that may have contained the pasquinade is preserved in the Goethe and Schiller Archive in Weimar, but it is empty. Lenz's remark in his letter to Herder suggests that Goethe had not seen the fatal satire at the time of Lenz's expulsion. As Lenz writes in the same letter that he hoped Goethe would not misunderstand the "purity" of his intentions, "despite how much I have insulted him," it seems likely there must have been some other insult, of a nature so severe all those involved never spoke of it.

Frau von Stein had invited Lenz to give her English lessons at her country estate in Grosskochberg after his stay in Berka. That went very well, as Lenz wrote to Goethe: "Frau von Stein finds my method better than yours." His visit to Frau von Stein came at a time when there was tension between her and Goethe. In early September 1776 Goethe had written her, *We can be nothing to each other and mean too much to each other . . . I do not want to see you again . . . . Anything I could say is stupid.*

A few days later, when Lenz, coming from Berka, turned up in Weimar again and received the invitation to Grosskochberg from Goethe's hands, Goethe wrote Charlotte a curious letter: *I'm sending you Lenz. I've finally overcome my opposition. Oh, you have a way of torturing me like Fate. . . . He should see you, and in your presence his troubled soul should sip the balsamic drops for which I envy anyone. He should be with you—He was quite affected when I told him of his good fortune: to be in Kochberg with you, walk with you, teach you, draw for you. You will draw for him, be for him. And I—we're not talking about me, however, and why should we?—He was completely in a dream when I told him, asks you only to have patience with him, asks only that you allow him to be the way he is. And I told him it would be so even before he asked. . . . Adieu. You'll hear nothing more from me now. I forbid you to send me any news of yourself or Lenz.* He did nothing with the letter at first, but mailed it two days later with the postscript, *I hesitated to send you the foregoing page, but you should see how things sometimes look in my heart, and how unjust I can be toward you.*

Either Goethe was really jealous or he was playing the jealous admirer. Charlotte's wish to offer Lenz lodging for a while *tortures* him. He torments himself by dwelling on Lenz's *good fortune*, pictures to himself the other two in cozy togetherness, and pictures himself as one no longer worth *talking about*. If that is how things stand, then he doesn't care to hear any more about them, and forbids her to send *any news*. In the postscript, he admits that he may be *unjust* toward her. What did that mean? He knew very well that he had no grounds for jealousy. In this letter, Lenz appears as his creature: *I'm sending you Lenz*, he writes and reports how he told him of his good fortune, waved away his self-doubt, and encouraged him. Encouraged him to do what? Obviously, to grasp the chance presented to him. He practically incites him to it. Charlotte must have felt insulted by the way Goethe acted tortured by jealousy but at the same time played the matchmaker in his letter.

Did Lenz see through this game? After only a few days, he writes Goethe in an ecstasy of happiness and optimism: "I am too happy, dear friend, not to disobey your order forbidding me to tell you anything about myself; . . . I would have to be more of a poet than I am to describe the fairy tale in which I now exist." A "fairy tale" with Charlotte? That made Goethe restless. His remedy was a cold bath.

I got into the water and drowned the Old Adam of my phantasies, he writes to Charlotte.

In November, Lenz returned to Berka. He had bid Charlotte farewell with a poem: "Where into my heart the heavens sank, / From her eyes—how blissful!—and from the glimmer of / Divinity upon her cheek I drank." He was firmly resolved not to let himself be made a fool of or treated like a plaything. In "The Forest Brother" he quotes Rousseau: "Man must not desire what is not within his power, or he remains eternally useless and weak, a half person." Charlotte had held out the prospect of a position with the duchess, possibly as a reader, something he could do.

While Lenz was again living by himself in Berka, making plans, devoting himself to his prospects, and then again falling into despondence and despair, Goethe's mood had brightened. *How much has sprung to life again!* he writes to Charlotte on November 8, 1776. *Ah, those eight weeks buried many things in me, and I still remain a very sensuous person.* Happily devoting himself to the still unfamiliar business of governing, he rode the countryside, made frequent visits to the court, and called regularly on Frau von Stein, the duchess, and Anna Amalia. He worked in his garden, planted linden trees and *all sorts of stuff*, and in his free moments worked on the play *Brother and Sister* for Weimar's amateur theater. Rehearsals began in mid-November.

Amid this activity, the grave incident of November 26, 1776, occurred. Lenz likely came to Weimar, clashed with Goethe, and returned to Berka. According to Goethe's diary, he rode to Berka the following day, probably in an attempt (which proved unsuccessful) to have it out with Lenz. A day later, Goethe requested Lenz's expulsion. This demand must have seemed exaggerated to the court official Einsiedel, for Goethe wrote him brusquely: *Lenz will leave. I have become accustomed to let my actions follow my heart, without considering disapproval or consequences. My existence is as precious to me as anyone else's to them. However, I shall just as little change anything in my behavior in deference to you.*

As we have said, the reason for Goethe's abrupt decision—the actual insult—remains a mystery. In view of Goethe's sour mood during Lenz's time with Frau von Stein, we can conjecture that it had something to do with this triangular relationship. Perhaps she had also complained about Goethe to Lenz, and he had mentioned it to Goethe during their dustup. It must have been a romantic wound, because he says so defiantly that in this matter he can do nothing but *follow my heart*. He writes as if the decision to have Lenz expelled was a question of his very existence: him or me.

Lenz's life was now truly ruined. He was offered financial compensation, but refused it. He wanted not mercy but "justice"; he rejected the suggestion that he "admit to a crime I am not aware of having committed." In great despair, he left Weimar and headed for Strasbourg. But he could not seem to free himself from Goethe. He stopped in Emmendingen and the Schlossers took him in. There were intimate conversations between him and Cornelia. He remained with them for half a year. Later, he wandered restlessly through Switzerland and Alsace, dogged by bouts of madness. In the Alsatian village of Waldersbach, he found refuge with the pastor and philanthropist Johann Friedrich Oberlin, after whom Oberlin College in Ohio is named. Two generations later, Georg Büchner would treat this episode in his famous story "Lenz."

Early in 1778, Lenz returned to Emmendingen, where Cornelia had died in the meantime. For a while, he found help and care there. That ended in the summer of 1779, when his brother Karl came to take him back to Livonia. But he could not bear to stay in Riga with his father, the church official. He went on to Russia and eked out a living as a private tutor and translator, first in St. Petersburg and then in Moscow. There were episodes of insanity. He wrote philosophical essays, sketches for plays, exposés, and proposals for reforms, none published. For the literary world he had long been as good as dead. On April 22, 1792, he was found lying in the snow on a Moscow street, frozen to death.

Goethe knew nothing of all this. Nor did he seek to find out anything. No one mentioned Lenz in his presence. Shortly after Lenz's expulsion, he wrote to Charlotte von Stein, *The whole affair tears me up so much inside that only thereby do I feel again my inner strength and what it can put up with.*

CHAPTER 13

More Sturm und Drang Visitors: Klinger and Kaufmann.
Goethe's Wards. A Lesson in Behavior.
Pegasus and Red Tape. *Wilhelm Meister's Theatrical Mission*:
Dictated, Not *scribbled down*. December 1777:
"Winter Journey in the Harz" and a Trial by Ordeal.

. . . .

GOETHE FELT INSULTED BY LENZ AND REACTED HARSHLY.
When Friedrich Maximilian Klinger, also a friend from former days,
showed up in Weimar in the summer of 1776 hoping that Goethe
would do something for him, he too was sent packing, although he
was not expelled like Lenz. *Klinger with his rough eccentricity is a thorn
in our flesh. He's festering and will fester his way out*, Goethe wrote. In the
same letter, Lenz is described as a *sick child*. But Klinger was a tougher
nut. Physically imposing and extraordinarily self-confident, he was
well liked by women. With a resonant, booming bass voice, he radiated decisiveness and was well mannered without being subservient.
His play *Sturm und Drang* had given a name to the entire movement.
The talented son of a poor widow, he had been a frequent guest in
Goethe's house in Frankfurt. Both Goethe and his mother had supported him financially. He had studied law, was earning his keep as
a private tutor, and gave the strong impression that he could look out
for himself.

Anna Amalia, who had a soft spot for robust, manly beauty, tried
to find Klinger a military post in a country other than Germany, and
in fact he later had a brilliant career as an officer in the tsar's army,
culminating in his position as a highly decorated lieutenant general
and trustee of the University of Tartu (today in Estonia). Ennobled

and rich, he wrote several *Erziehungsromane*—novels of development and education—in which he remained faithful to the ideals of his youth: sincerity, directness, naturalness, and pride. He followed the German literary scene from afar, occasionally making critical remarks about Goethe's works. Goethe remained in touch regardless, sending him cool but respectful letters, and after Klinger's death wrote, *He was a loyal, earthy fellow like no one else. In former years, he also caused me a good deal of trouble because he was one of those geniuses of strength who didn't really know what he wanted.*

Christoph Kaufmann, a peripatetic, charismatic apostle of the Sturm und Drang, arrived in Weimar with Klinger in the summer of 1776. A former apothecary's apprentice, then surgeon, faith healer, and, finally, an itinerant preacher of "natural humanity," Kaufmann attracted the notice of intellectuals like Lavater, Hamann, and Herder. Even the skeptical Wieland was impressed by this odd fellow who traveled around in a green kaftan with a fur collar, his hair flowing and his shirt open at the neck. Rather than a literary *genius of strength*, he was an apostle of strength and a fisher of souls. People in Weimar marveled at this bizarre apparition—for a while, though they were relieved when Kaufmann moved on. Many would later recall with horror the feasts he presided over. Karl August Böttiger—later director of the Weimar gymnasium (high school)—tells of a "genius banquet which began with throwing all the drinking glasses out the window and making a couple of filthy urns that had been taken from an old grave nearby into drinking vessels." Klinger supposedly distinguished himself at this event by eating raw horse meat, while Kaufmann ate flowers from the park. *I praise the gods*, wrote Goethe when the whole appalling episode was over.

If Goethe wanted to rid himself of these friends as soon as possible, it wasn't because he was stingy. He could be very generous indeed, as when he found an orphaned Swiss shepherd boy named Peter im Baumgarten at his door. Baron von Lindau, whose acquaintance Goethe had made in Switzerland, had taken the boy as his godson, but then emigrated to America and left him behind, penniless. Goethe took him in for some time, looked after him, and gave him lessons, but with no success. The lad smoked a pipe all day and chased the girls every chance he got. Goethe then put him into foster care with the head forester in Ilmenau, but Peter didn't prosper there, either, and disappeared a few years later. Goethe had expended much care, energy, and money and, in the end, thought he had achieved nothing.

Another beneficiary of Goethe's generosity and helpfulness was Johann Friedrich Kraft, a name this man of unknown origins had adopted as a pseudonym. He was a failed official in hopeless circumstances who had applied to Goethe for help. The unfortunate man's plea had so impressed Goethe that he supported him for over ten years with an annual stipend of 200 taler, a sixth of his own initial salary. He also gave Kraft small administrative jobs in Ilmenau and Jena (the university town within the duchy of Weimar), which were performed satisfactorily if pedantically. Kraft remained bitter and despairing. Goethe's letters to him show impressively how steadfast and sensitive he was in seeing to the needs of his ward. When he offered him a position in Jena, for example, he wrote, *But act completely according to your heart, and if my reasons do not reach your heart, if along with conviction they do not also hold out the promise of peace and hope in Jena, then remain in your present tranquillity.* He explicitly promised Kraft support even if he turned down the offer. Goethe avoided anything that could be construed as humiliating. He wanted Kraft to feel as little dependent as possible, so he especially thanked him for the services he had rendered—for example, seeing to the education of Peter im Baumgarten, as Goethe had asked. He encouraged him to write down his life story; *it will also be a distraction and I shall enjoy reading it.* Another time, he writes, *I would so much like to be able to brighten up your gloomy condition and keep you in continuous cheerfulness.* When Kraft suffered bouts of melancholy and complained about his "worthlessness," Goethe reassured him: *You have neither sunk in my estimation, nor do I have a worse opinion of you, . . . nor has your way of thinking become blemished in my eyes.*

At the time when Goethe was proving his readiness to help poor Kraft as well as the Swiss boy with his pipe and incomprehensible dialect, he set down in a letter to Charlotte von Stein some maxims he promised to be guided by: *We should do what we can to save individuals from ruin—That is little enough, however, for there are innumerable steps from misery to prosperity.—The good one can do in the world is a minimum, etc.*

There is no good unless one does it, and does it in individual, concrete cases. He rejects the high-flown rhetoric of improving humanity typical of the Sturm und Drang, whose ambassadors now stood on his doorstep. From 1779 on, Goethe carried out the tasks he was assigned: road construction, swamp drainage, tillage of the fields, improving fire prevention and the working conditions in the copper and silver mines of Ilmenau, organization of flood relief. He also attempted to reduce expenses at court in order to provide tax relief, put the brakes on the duke's excessive passion for hunting (which was ruinous to the farmers), decrease the number of soldiers, and insist on their more humane treatment. In all these endeavors, he went beyond individual cases and thought of the larger good. We should do what we can, where we happen to be, and do it without bombast—that was his policy. But he had no illusions. He understood the bounds of his influence—knew, really, how little he could do. All the same, it was better to try than not to act at all.

Goethe certainly did not lack empathy, and it was clear to all that he was eager to help. If he was brusque with Klinger and Lenz, it was in a spirit of the new pragmatism he was learning. He had come to abhor the grandiloquent, rebellious posturing of the literati he had so recently been a part of; anything that reminded him of them was now anathema to him. A few years later, contemplating the consequences of the French Revolution, he would angrily disparage writers who made political pronouncements as the *excitable ones*. Goethe's pragmatism stood in opposition to dilettantish political opinions, a contempt that was not confined to aesthetics. He had nothing against amateurism, but it should be aware of its own limits, in both art and politics. In political matters, too, people should stick to good, solid craftsmanship. He notes in his diary, *Every work of man has what I would call a smell. As, in a rough sense, a rider smells of horse, a bookstore a little of mildew, and a huntsman of dog, it is true in a finer sense as well.* . . . . A master *does not dream in generalities.* . . . *When the time comes for him to act, he takes hold of whatever is needed now.* Thus, the sense for the correct intervention means in the political realm that *all arrogance* must *wither away*. Only then can *beautiful strength* prove its worth.

Friends and acquaintances began to notice a gradual change in

Goethe's behavior. He was becoming more reserved, sometimes mono-syllabic, especially in initial encounters. But then, once the formali-ties were relaxed, he could open up and be as delightfully eloquent, approachable, and devoted as ever. He contained himself and gave of himself at his own speed: *I'm adapting myself to this world without deviating a hair's breadth from the character that preserves me inwardly and makes me happy.* He separates his inner from his outer life more sharply than he used to, but with a sure feeling for his own *character that preserves me inwardly.*

Some were quite offended and disappointed by this new behav-ior. Wieland, for example, who had been so enchanted in the first few months, complains in a letter to Merck, "Now it's as if . . . his genius had deserted him entirely; his imagination seems extinguished; in place of the all-enlivening warmth he used to emanate, he's now encased in political frost." At first, Merck repudiates this point of view. Goethe has "not cast off the least bit . . . of his former poetic individuality, but instead, like a man, he hungers and thirsts to learn more about human nature and worldly transactions, and for the intelligence and wisdom that results." A year later, however, Merck too was vexed by Goethe's behavior. Goethe met him "with such dryness and coldness, as if I had changed from his old friend into a subaltern servant and supplicant."

Merck wrote those words after a visit to Weimar in the summer of 1779. Goethe's experience of the visit was quite different, for he noted in his diary, *Good effect on me of Merck's presence. It didn't shift anything in me, but only sloughed off some withered husks and reinforced me in the old good-ness . . . showed me my actions in a marvelous mirror, since he is the only person who completely understands what I do and how I do it, and yet sees it differently than I do, from another point of view, producing a lovely certainty.*

In the first two years, Goethe did not yet have the *lovely certainty* that his decision to come to Weimar had been the right one. One can see him trying to convince himself. He had something to prove to himself. And he went about it energetically and systematically. Step by step, he assumed responsibilities and got deeper into the business of governing. But he also calls it an experiment to see how a *worldly role* suits him and how it will affect his poetic nature.

One expression of this inner balancing of inclinations—the pull toward poetry and art, on one hand, and the other toward the *affairs of the world*—was *Wilhelm Meister's Theatrical Mission,* his second novel's earliest version, which remained unpublished during his lifetime. He began to dictate it in early 1777 and continued throughout the year, completing the novel's first book. Then he put the manuscript aside and did not take it up again until the early 1780s. The fact that he did not draft the novel in his own hand, as he had done with *Werther*, betrays a certain distance. You write differently when you dictate; you're not alone with what you are writing, and it loses some immediacy— some pure, heartfelt expressiveness—through the intermediacy of the scribe. Thus the text no longer draws the reader into the fictive intimacy of expressively *scribbled-down* letters, as does *Werther*. Instead, the predominant tone is that of an authorial narrator who begins with the childhood of the protagonist. It is the narrative of a passion for the stage that begins with a puppet theater: *With them he was by turns a hunter, a soldier, a horseman, whichever the characteristics of the plays required, but he always had this advantage over the others: that he was able to properly construct the necessary props.*

To slip into a role and display himself in it—for Wilhelm that is a heightened existence. But he is also willing to learn the mechanics of acting. He is enchanted by being onstage but also wants to know his way around backstage. Gripped by the play himself, he enjoys his ability to grip the audience as well. He believes in what he performs for others. His mood depends on the approbation he receives. Soon he realizes that the world of the theater is a fragile construction, kept in balance only by the enthusiasm with which those involved infect each other. A source of disruption is robust realism that doesn't accept make-believe. He feels that such bourgeois sobriety is like *pitch that limed the wings of his spirit*; he sees in it *ropes that tethered the lofty momentum of the soul.*

Wilhelm's first attempts as an artist, as well as his romantic entanglements, are depicted with gentle irony. The narrator always lets the reader know that Wilhelm never really reaches the heights he thinks he does. His poetic and romantic enthusiasms are filtered through the eyes of an external observer. In contrast to *Werther*, the primacy of feeling is disrupted. While the sentimental Werther has adversaries, they have no voice of their own; what we know of them we learn through his letters. In *Wilhelm Meister* there are numerous adversaries, weighty ones with their own specific points of view. It is through them that the novel succeeds in constituting a world. A real world opens up only when things are not delivered in a single voice; when there are shifting perspectives, and when there is opposition.

One adversary is Werner, Wilhelm's friend and future brother-in-law. He is a realist, but quite capable of enthusiasm. Although he is slow to *flare up*, his passions are lasting and consequential: *Werner was proud of apparently getting Wilhelm's excellent, although unfortunately sometimes excessive, talents under bit and bridle.* Werner has nothing against Pegasus, but he wants his friend to be able to ride the horse of poetry without getting thrown. He embodies a reality principle that is not hostile to poetry but accepts it within its own boundaries and tries to give it the necessary grounding.

In the same way, Goethe himself wished to make the tension between his connection to the real world and his poetic nature tolerable. It was not easy for him. How abruptly the draft horse of office routine could turn into Pegasus, and vice versa! In life, it was Charlotte whom he assigned the task of making sure he wasn't thrown. In the novel, it is Werner.

Sometimes Wilhelm lacks the words he needs: *thus speech often stuck in his throat when he wanted to relate his feelings vividly. He could never find enough great words to express what he felt.* As such, he can't tell his story; that is left to the narrator, who occupies a space somewhere between Wilhelm and Werner. The narrator has the required distance, and a sense of reality; and he has enough imagination and sentiment to put into words everything that longs to be expressed. Wilhelm is all life with too little structure; Werner has a lot of structure and too little life. The narrator manages to create a living structure. Significantly, then, the world is unpacked by a narrative voice that is at some remove and not, as in *Werther*, by a person who gets lost in himself and thus lost to the world.

Goethe began *Wilhelm Meister* in January 1777 without knowing what course it would take. In a letter to Knebel on November 21, 1782, he floated the subtitle "Theatrical Mission," which suggests that the story would end not with Wilhelm's departure from the theater—as does the final, published version, *Wilhelm Meister's Apprenticeship*—but with the vision of a firmly established, purified, reputable theater, saturated with both reality and idealism. It would be a theater that spoke from heart to heart, that retained the childlike joy of play, and that was yet adult—without becoming sclerotic. Goethe may have dreamed that the story of the growth and development of his hero would anticipate the development of a thriving theater in Germany. *The German stage,* reflects the narrator, *was at that time in crisis. It had thrown away its baby shoes before they were worn out and in the meantime had to go barefoot.* Out of this could come a theater of which one need not be ashamed when one had advanced from poet to privy councilor. But such perspectives were still only aspirational; for now, Goethe was satisfied to direct and provide inspiration to the amateur theater company in Weimar, which consisted mostly of courtiers. It was not to be expected that a reform of the theater could begin with him or, for that matter, in Weimar. At the end of 1777, he laid the manuscript of the novel aside.

The big event of 1777 was his journey to the Harz Mountains in December and the ascent on horseback of the Brocken, at 3,750 feet the highest peak in the range. It was an event that took on the significance of a private myth and produced the great hymn "Winter Journey in the Harz."

The story of his solitary ride through snow and hail began on June 16, when the news of his sister Cornelia's death reached Goethe in his garden house. *Dark, disrupted day,* he wrote in his diary. Cornelia had never fully recovered from their separation, and Goethe's fear that Schlosser was not the right husband for her seemed to have been borne out. Probably no man would have been, except her brother. She lay down in bed, pulled the curtains shut, and seldom got up again. She became animated only when visitors arrived who were connected to her brother and brought news of him. That's how it was when Lenz appeared in Emmendingen. Three weeks before her death on June 8, she had given birth to a second child, another daughter, and never recovered. Schlosser wrote to Lavater, "I cannot tell you the story of her suffering! It hurts too much!" By the time he wrote to Goethe on June 14, he had recovered his composure: "I will not complain. It is unmanly. . . . This is my first true misfortune, and thank God it struck me when my body and my soul still have some strength. Now nothing else can break me." Thus Schlosser, capable and diligent, closed the chapter and turned toward his future life. Nine months later, he married "Aunty" Johanna Fahlmer.

Goethe hadn't written to Cornelia since the trip to Emmendingen in the summer of 1775. He had found the visit difficult, a *real ordeal*. There was no quarrel. He had seen how miserable she was. By the time he left, he had reached the bitter conviction that she lacked vitality and was beyond help, and he suffered under the knowledge. Because he couldn't help her, he did everything he could to keep Cornelia, and his own pain, at arm's length. The news of her death stunned him, jolting him out of circumstances he frankly described as *happy*. The stark contrast between his happiness in Weimar and her fatal misery in Emmendingen pained him deeply. He would surrender himself to *nature*, he wrote, *which allows us to feel tremendous pain only for a little while, but lets us mourn for a long time*. A month later, his mourning produced a poem he sent to Auguste zu Stolberg: *To their favorites the gods gave everything, / The immortal ones, / All our joys unendingly, / All our pains unendingly—all of them.*

The letters from these weeks speak of his *joys*, but then he is seized by something that throws him off balance. He writes to his mother in mid-November, *Ever since, my heart and mind are used to being a ball for fate to play with. . . . With my sister, such a strong root anchoring me to the earth has been chopped off that the branches above, which were nourished by it, must also die.* To Johanna Fahlmer he writes laconically, *I am very much changed*.

Something had happened to him. Two weeks later, he set off alone on horseback, through wind and snow flurries, toward the northern Harz. He told no one he was leaving, neither the duke nor Charlotte von Stein, for whom he left a note: *My thoughts are in wonderfully dark confusion. Listen to the wind, it will be blowing hard about me.*

Goethe later gave two reasons for what seemed to his friends to be a very abrupt departure. He had made efforts to put the mines in Ilmenau back in operation and wished to gather information about the mines in the Harz. And he wanted to call on a man who had written to him in great distress after reading *Werther*. His name was Victor Leberecht Plessing, and he lived in Wernigerode. Goethe had not replied to Plessing but wrote later that it was *the most wonderful thing in the self-tormenting vein that I had ever laid eyes on*, and that he felt a sense of responsibility. Perhaps Goethe felt guilty about his sister. He had not helped her, and now he had received another cry for help, so he set off.

But there was a third reason, one he talks about in his diary, in letters to Charlotte von Stein, and in "Winter Journey in the Harz."

The entire trip was staged with intentional obfuscation. Goethe left on November 29, under *heavy snow clouds*, in the direction of Sondershausen and Nordhausen. In his letters to Frau von Stein, he avoids mentioning towns or even the area in which he finds himself. He traveled under the name Weber and claimed to be a lawyer or a painter; other times, he gave no name. *It's a curious feeling to travel unknown about the world; I seem to feel a much truer relationship to people and things.* On the day of his departure, he wrote in his diary, *pure peace in my soul.* The snow flurries and hailstorms diminished and toward evening, he got the first *glimpses of sun* over in the direction of the Harz. The following day, almost everything was frozen solid, *the sun rose with the most magnificent colors,* and in the distance he saw the summit of the Brocken. Then the weather darkened again and it began to rain. *Night arrived quietly and sadly.* The inn at Ilfeld was already full, but they offered him a tiny chamber next to the pub room. Through a knothole he watched the convivial wine-drinking company next door—some officials on an inspection trip. He didn't announce his presence but remained in his hiding place. He liked observing without being observed. In retrospect, he paints a cozy scene: *I saw the long and well-lit table from the foot to the head. I surveyed it as one often sees in paintings of the Wedding at Cana . . . in short, it was a jolly, large meal which I was able to observe at leisure in its particulars by the brightest candlelight, just as if the limping devil were standing by my side and favoring me with the direct observation and understanding of a completely foreign state of affairs. . . . Sometimes it seemed to me quite spooky, as if I were watching lighthearted spirits diverting themselves inside a cavern in the mountains.*

He prepared for a visit to the famous Baumann's Cave on the following day. He had guides show him around, lighting the way through the dark cave with torches. He crawled on all fours down the narrower passages. *To be sure, all the fantasy images it pleases a gloomily active imagination to create from formless shapes disappeared before my calm gaze, and in their place, my own, true vision remained, and I felt myself well rewarded.*

Thus rewarded, the man who had just fought his way through wind and weather and darkness made a note in his diary: *Like the vulture.* And with those words begins the poem "Winter Journey in the Harz":

Like the vulture,
Winging on heavy morning clouds
Softly, at ease,
On the lookout for prey,
Let my song float.

For a god has
Ordered for each
His path,
Which the happy man
Swiftly runs to its
Joyful finish.

He had accomplished his first goal: to gather information about the mines. Now he set his sights on the second. The opening passage of "Winter Journey in the Harz" quoted above is followed immediately by a reference to Victor Plessing and the next station of Goethe's journey:

But when misfortune
Has shriveled a heart,
It struggles in vain
Against the restraints
Of adamant thread
That the bitter shears
Cut only once.

Two strophes later, the unhappy person is again recalled:

But off to the side, who is it?
In the bushes his path peters out
Behind him the branches
Spring back together
The grass straightens up,
The wasteland swallows him.

Alas, who can heal the pains
Of him whom balsam has poisoned,

Who drank misanthropy
From the fullness of love?
First despised and now despising,
He consumes in secret
His own merit
In selfish dissatisfaction.

Goethe had to overcome some reserve to initiate this encounter with Plessing. In a letter to Charlotte, he calls it an *adventure* that he has *survived* intact. He describes the details of what happened in the autobiographical work *Campaign in France, 1792.* The proprietor of the inn where he stayed in Wernigerode had shown him the way to Plessing's house. *He was completely like his letter, and like his writing, he aroused my interest without exerting any charm.* Goethe introduced himself as an illustrator from Gotha. Plessing remarked that Gotha was near Weimar and asked whether he knew any of the famous people who lived there. Goethe, maintaining his incognito, reeled off a few names, from Bertuch to the pedagogue and philologist Johann Karl August Musäus. The young man interrupted impatiently: and the great Goethe, surely he'd met him too? Goethe replied that he knew him, and had received some support from him in his painting. The young man now demanded with *some vehemence* that he depict that *curious individual* about whom there was so much talk. And then Goethe described himself. Plessing did not guess that the man he was talking to was Goethe himself. He lacked clear vision, Goethe writes. Plessing's attention was directed wholly inward.

It was an odd encounter. Goethe had to listen to Plessing read the very long letter he already knew so well and hear the young man's complaints that he had not received an answer. Plessing asked him what he guessed Goethe might have thought about the letter, and why he didn't answer it, and what he could have answered. Goethe replied that Goethe would probably have urged him to consider that *one would rescue and free oneself from a painful, self-tormented, gloomy state of the soul only by observing nature and taking heartfelt part in the external world. Even the most general acquaintance with nature, no matter from what angle, an active engagement—whether as a gardener, plowman, hunter, or miner—draws us out of ourselves; the direction of our intellectual and spiritual powers toward real, genuine phenomena will gradually yield the greatest pleasure, clarity, and instruction.*

Plessing was having none of it. He continued to complain of his disappointment with people and places he had expected more of. That was just the problem, replied Goethe. He should allow reality to surprise him and not try to force it to fit his own ideas. But Plessing refused to be dissuaded from defending his *gloomy phantom* against the value of *clear reality*. His suggestions rejected, Goethe felt certain that he had done his duty. He felt, furthermore, *released from any further obligation.*

And not just toward Plessing. It had now been a year since he had spurned Lenz. In visiting Plessing, he was also seeking to salve his conscience vis-à-vis Lenz and Klinger. The remark that introduces his recounting of the Plessing episode is striking: *I was already burdened . . . with a number of young men who, instead of accompanying me on my path toward a purer, higher development, persisted along their own path, were not any better for it, and were hindering me in my progress.* So one reason Goethe had set out for Wernigerode was to confront Plessing and free his conscience of a matter that had begun to weigh on it. Plessing, who realized with whom he had been speaking only after Goethe was gone, stubbornly maintained the connection, even paying Goethe a visit and writing him more letters. Now and then Goethe would reply, noticeably at pains to play down his comfortable circumstances: *I can assure you of this much, that in the midst of happiness I live in persistent austerity.*

In the end, Plessing managed to achieve some professional success. He became a professor in Duisburg, wrote a few books and numerous letters to famous people, ran around in threadbare clothes, and now and then went off into the forest, disappearing for weeks without a trace. *Behind him the branches / Spring back together,* as in "Winter Journey in the Harz."

The third reason for the trip to the Harz was revealed in the poem:

> *And for him the snow-shrouded*
> *Crown of the dreaded peak*
> *Becomes an altar of sweetest thanks,*
> *Which an ancient people's presentiments*
> *Bedecked with hosts of spirits.*

The *altar of sweetest thanks* is the summit of the Brocken. In those days, it was unusual to attempt the climb during a snow and ice storm, but what was important to Goethe was not the mountaineering feat but the *sign of confirmation* that reaching the summit sent. *I want to reveal to you (don't tell anyone else) that my trip was to the Harz,* Goethe wrote Charlotte von Stein, *and that I wanted to climb the Brocken.*

If he succeeded in reaching the summit, he would take it as a sort of trial by ordeal. But confirmation of what? *What is man, that thou art mindful of him?* he wrote in his diary after the climb. This much is clear: it was to be a sign that the gods—fate—continued to wish him well. A confirmation that his decision to go to Weimar was the right path to take? That is Albrecht Schöne's conjecture, and it is likely correct.[*]

Goethe had spent the weeks before his departure for the Harz in the Wartburg, a castle on a hill overlooking Eisenach, while down below the duke and his boisterous retinue were out hunting. He had once again been plagued by doubt, sensing how foreign this society was. There is a noteworthy diary entry: *however, am surrounded by much alienation where I thought there was still a bond.* These people seem very distant from him. But not the duke. He feels connected to him, and that gives him support. The *duke grows closer and closer to me, & rain and raw wind draw the sheep together.* And then, underlined and followed by two exclamation points, *Govern!!* There were also storms raging around the Wartburg; it was again the mood of the "Wanderer's Storm Song," the defiance of wind and weather, the self-confidence of *He whom, Genius, you do not forsake.* Now he foresees defying all adversity and governing with the duke. Yet what did governing mean in this small duchy? Wasn't there more at stake? Wasn't it a decision of even more consequence?

In any event, his decision to remain in Weimar was more lasting than any other. Goethe would spend his entire future life and career there, together with the duke. Weimar was to be and remain his world, one into which he was able to draw many other worlds. After his ascent of the Brocken, he writes proudly, *God deals with me as he did with his old saints.*

As far as the actual climb is concerned, Goethe provided a vivid, almost sacramental description of it in a letter to Charlotte von Stein.

* Albrecht Schöne, *Götterzeichen—Liebeszauber—Satanskult* (Munich: C. H. Beck, 1982), 44.

Early in the morning, he had arrived at the so-called Peat House at the foot of the Brocken, where he found the forester at his *morning sip*. The man assured him that in this snow and fog, climbing the mountain was out of the question. He himself, at any rate, had never tried it, and he knew what he was doing. They looked out the window, but the mountain was invisible in the fog. *I was silent and asked the gods to change this man's mind—and the weather—and was silent. Then he said to me, Now you can see the Brocken. I stepped to the window and it stood before me, as clear as my face in the mirror. Then my heart rose and I cried, And I'm not to get to the top? Don't you have a servant, no one—and he said, I will go with you.—I scratched a sign into the window pane as a testimony to my tears of joy, and I'd think it a sin to write about it if it weren't to you. I didn't really believe it until we were on the highest cliff. All the fog lay below, and on the summit it was marvelously clear.*

The last strophe of "Winter Journey in the Harz" addresses the mountain itself in describing the clear view,

> You stand, with unfathomed breast,
> A mysterious revelation
> Above the astonished world,
> Gazing down from the clouds
> At its realms and their riches,
> Watered by the veins
> Of the brothers surrounding you.

On the one hand, these *veins* signify mineral deposits and are a mining metaphor. On the other, a motif is sounded here that Goethe had already richly elaborated in "Mahomet's Song": the way a spring emerges, swells into a river, irrigates and makes fruitful the surrounding country, absorbs thousands of other streams, and finally empties into the sea. It is an image for the fertility—the *genius*—of the spirit. That too is implied by his experience on the summit: a heightened self-confidence, not just for governing but surely also for poetry.

During the descent from the Brocken, he and his guide witness an unforgettable display of colors. In the caves and mines of the Harz, Goethe discovered the geologist and mineralogist in himself, and now the play of light and shadow awakens his appreciation for the peculiarities of color. In his 1810 *Theory of Color*, he recalls the moment almost as a primordial event: *On a winter journey in the Harz I was descending from the Brocken toward evening. The broad expanses above and below me were covered in snow. . . . If during the day pale violet shadows had already been noticeable against the yellowish tone of the snow, one would now have to call them deep blue, as an intensified yellow was reflected from the sunlit areas. When the sun at last began to set, however, and its beams, very much moderated by the stronger mists, bathed the entire surroundings with the most beautiful purple color, the color of the shadows was transformed into a green which, in its clarity could be compared to a sea green, in its beauty to an emerald green. The spectacle grew more and more vivid. I felt I was in fairyland.*

Three adequate reasons for the winter journey in the Harz: practical on-the-spot observation for the future director of mines, expiation of his guilt feelings through wind and weather, and the oracle on the Brocken: Govern! And then, the magic of evening colors, a gift to the future theoretician of color—all in all, they were enough to create a wonderfully poetic mystification.

CHAPTER 14

A Farce on the Sublime: *The Triumph of Sentimentalism.*
Christel Lassberg's Suicide. A Political Mission.
Weimar's Self-Assertion and the League of Princes. In Berlin.
"Govern!" The Blended and the Pure.
Conscripting Soldiers and *Iphigenia.*
The Temple Precincts of Art.

....

WHAT IS MAN, THAT THOU ART MINDFUL OF HIM? GOETHE
had written this highly emotive sentence—an expression of the
sublime—in his diary on the day he climbed the Brocken. In the wake
of those lofty feelings, he took aim at shallow, sham sentiment. In just
a few weeks back in Weimar, he finished the farcical comedy *The Triumph of Sentimentalism,* first planned as a comic opera but now called a
"dramatic fancy." On January 3, 1778, it was performed by the amateur theater group with Corona Schröter in the leading role of Queen
Mandandane and Goethe himself playing King Andrason.

Goethe had climbed the Brocken to consult the oracle of fate; in the
farce, he makes fun of the court's addiction to oracles. King Andrason
must compete with a traveling prince, a rival for his wife's affections.
Andrason has asked an oracle for help: what should he do? The king
brings back an enigmatic reply no one can understand. Rather than
continue to puzzle over it, he solicits help from the ladies in waiting.
They are to ensnare the prince and keep him from the queen.

The prince is a caricature of sentimentalism. He loves nature, but
not mosquitoes and ants. So he has an artificial nature constructed for
himself, with all the comforts *that steel springs and coils can provide.* He
even brings it along when traveling, packed up in crates and boxes and
with a portable arbor. In the blink of an eye he can set up an appro-

priate natural scene, complete with grassy banks, flowers, and bushes. Clockworks provide birdsong and smoke, and wind machines produce the fragrance of spring. Only the interior of the arbor remains a secret. During the prince's absence—he, too, is here to visit the oracle—the inquisitive ladies open the arbor, where they find a doll stuffed with chaff and fashioned to look like the queen, as well as a sack of books containing the entire sentimentalist canon, from Rousseau's *Nouvelle Héloïse* to *The Sorrows of Young Werther*. Thus it's revealed: the prince's outpourings of feeling are secondhand and addressed to a lifeless dummy. Everything is fake, both nature and the *sentimentalisms*. In the end, they make a fool of the prince: presented with the genuine Mandandane and the dummy, he is so entangled in artificiality that he can't tell them apart.

The play was performed on the duchess's birthday and did not excite universal admiration. Some thought the author of *Werther* not only mocked himself but showed a lack of gratitude to his sentimental readers. The author Emilie von Berlepsch wrote to Herder, "Tell me something about this strange new play Goethe has written! Presumably a satire on the unfortunate girls and young men he used to make dizzy with his writings, and now he's laughing at them. An odd person! . . . I find him quite distasteful with his everlasting vacillation between wit and feeling, weakness and power. And it's proving more and more difficult to get a clear idea of him from the things I happen to know about him."

Goethe's ridicule of Werther-like sentimentalism could surprise only those who hadn't read *Werther* closely. For the novel presents Werther as a young man who has read too much of such literature, and whose feelings come more from books than from life. We hear the rustle of paper not only in the emotional outpourings of the prince in *The Triumph of Sentimentalism* but in those of his predecessor Werther. Enthusiastic fans of *Werther* had simply failed to notice. *The Triumph of Sentimentalism* makes fun of this confusion of literature and life at the very moment when the still active Werther cult had apparently produced another fatal result.

One of the daughters of Colonel von Lassberg took her own life on the evening of January 16, 1778. She was embroiled in an unhappy love affair and had jumped from a pontoon bridge into the icy waters of the Ilm and drowned. It was the bridge Goethe always crossed on his way from the garden house into town. The next day, while Goethe was ice-skating with the duke on Schwansee Pond, the girl's body was discovered and carried to the nearest house. It happened to be Frau von Stein's, and Goethe was immediately summoned. Why him? Was it Frau von Stein who ordered it, or Goethe's servant, one of the party that found the dead girl? Did it have to do with the rumor that immediately circulated, that Christel von Lassberg had jumped into the water with a copy of *Werther* in her coat pocket? In any event, Goethe rushed to the scene and that evening paid a call to the Lassbergs to console and support them. The following day, he met with the palace gardener to plan construction of a small memorial in a quiet spot near the bridge, a grotto in which a bust or urn could be placed. Goethe himself wielded a pickax and shovel. *We worked into the night,* he wrote to Charlotte von Stein, *in the end I continued alone until the hour when she had died; that's the kind of evening it was. Orion stood so beautifully in the sky. . . . There is something dangerously attractive and inviting about this grief, like the water itself, and the reflection of the stars of heaven that shines from both beckons to us.*

Did Goethe take such an active role because he felt a certain share of responsibility? Or was there simply an alluring melancholy emanating from the event, as the letter suggests? It took some time for him to regain his composure. He wrote in his diary, *A few days in quiet mourning, preoccupied with the scene of the death, afterwards forced back to theatrical frivolity.* The next entry refers to the performance of *The Triumph of Sentimentalism.* These were abrupt transitions: from a touch of *Werther* melancholy to satirizing it.

After these mood swings, a curious calm set in, one so remarkable to Goethe that he wrote an extensive diary entry about it, something he rarely did: *This week, often out on the ice, always in the same, almost too pure mood. Beautiful enlightenment about myself and our household, quiet and premonition of wisdom. Always continuous joy in economy, savings, making ends meet. Lovely peace in my domestic affairs compared to last year. More confident feeling of austerity, and thereby genuine expansion.*

This calm he found in the retreat to his garden house was disturbed at the end of February by the visit from Plessing, who had in the meantime discovered the identity of the "Herr Weber" who had sat with him two months earlier in Wernigerode. *I didn't get comfortable with him,* the diary says.

In these weeks, Goethe was again overtaken by the impact of *Werther*, both on Fräulein von Lassberg and then on this unhappy man, he too a desperate reader of the novel who finally showed up on his doorstep. He stayed for two days. Goethe gave him money for his return journey and, considering that an inadequate response, also sent the departed Plessing a letter.

He had been enjoying the feeling of peace, but now his mood darkened again, and he composed rhymed epitaphs, one of which he sent to Auguste zu Stolberg:

> *I was a young lad, warm and good,*
> *And then a youth of flesh and blood,*
> *With promise of a man.*
> *I suffered some and loved some too*
> *And laid me down, my life is through*
> *I've done all that I can.*

Of course, there was still official business, work in his garden in the spring, and early flowers and vegetables for Charlotte von Stein. He sent Gottfried August Bürger fifty-one louis d'or for the continuation of his Homer translation, drafted a few more texts to accompany Lavater's *Physiognomic Fragments*, finished work on the first book of *Wilhelm Meister's Theatrical Mission*, and made a few revisions to a draft of a play about the Count of Egmont. In mid-April, he and the duke paid an official visit to the mines in Ilmenau. In the nearby village of Stützerbach, they suddenly relapsed into their wild behavior of earlier days. They were dining at the house of a well-to-do merchant named Glaser, who was proud of a handsome oil portrait hanging above the dining table in his best room. Goethe cut the face out of the life-size head of the canvas and "through the opening created thereby," as the mining official Trebra later recounted, "stuck his own manly, tanned, intellectual face with its fiery black eyes—now framed on both sides by a heavy powdered wig—sat down in an armchair, placed the painting in its gilt frame on his knees, and concealed his legs under a white cloth." After the meal, they went on to take Glaser's wine barrels out of the cellar and roll them down the hill. *Tom foolery during the day . . . teased Glaser,* Goethe wrote in his diary.

There was a change of mood a month later when, for the first time, Goethe accompanied the duke on a diplomatic mission. They traveled via Leipzig—where they met with the duke's friend Prince Leopold von Anhalt-Dessau—to Berlin and Potsdam. War was looming between Prussia and Austria, and the little duchy of Weimar was at risk of being caught between the fronts.

The prince-elector of Bavaria had died in December 1777 without direct descendants. His successor, Karl Theodor from the Palatinate-Sulzbach line, already possessed the Electoral Palatinate and the duchies of Jülich and Berg and kept residence at Mannheim. He had made a pact with Vienna to trade his Bavarian inheritance for the Habsburg Low Countries (today's Belgium), and Prussia was alarmed. Frederick the Great was not willing to accept a Habsburg expansion into the territory of the Holy Roman Empire. He declared himself the protector of Protestant interests in the empire and sought to win over the small and midsized principalities to his side. It was to be feared that in preparation for possible hostilities, Prussia would conscript soldiers on Weimar's territory with or without consent of the duke, making it difficult for him to stay neutral in the conflict.

Preparations for war were in full swing when the duke and Goethe traveled to Potsdam and Berlin in mid-May 1778. Arriving at the park in Wörlitz, halfway between Leipzig and Berlin, Goethe took pleasure once more in peaceful surroundings. He fully expected that things could soon change and they would arrive *in the clamor of the world arming for war. And I seem to get closer and closer to the goal of dramatic events, since I am more and more involved in how the powerful play with the people, and the gods play with the powerful.*

Goethe's impressions of Berlin were such that he would never go there again, not even later to visit his dear friend Zelter. The life of the city seemed to him like a *clockwork* that Frederick (whom he admired) had constructed to execute his program; it reduced the people to puppets kept in motion by *hidden gears.* He found no self-confident personalities: *No dirty joke or foolishness in a farce is as disgusting as the behavior of the great, the middling, and the little people all together. I have beseeched the gods to let me keep my courage and uprightness to the end and rather make the end sooner than have me crawl the last stretch like a miserable louse.*

Anything but becoming a toady of the powerful—that was his firm resolution. He acted buttoned up and unapproachable. In the long run, it was a strain, because he realized that the *flower of public trust, of devoted love,* was fading away day by day. He felt himself becoming standoffish and thought it was diplomacy. It was difficult terrain in which to operate and prove himself—for example, during a meal with Prince Heinrich, the brother of Frederick the Great (the latter had already left for Bohemia, where the hostilities were expected to begin). Goethe and the duke needed to sound out Prussia's intentions vis-à-vis Weimar and at the same time not reveal their own plans, which were still inchoate. At official occasions, Goethe wrapped himself in an icy silence, which the sleek, experienced diplomats found inappropriate.

Berlin's writers and academics, on the other hand, took it amiss that he paid no attention to them at all. Men like the publisher Nicolai, the poet and philosopher Carl Wilhelm Ramler, the pastor Johann Friedrich Zöllner, the historian Jean Pierre Erman, and the theologian and pedagogue Friedrich Gedike expected at least a courtesy call. Goethe's only visit was to Moses Mendelssohn, the great Enlightenment figure and friend of Lessing, but he arrived so late that Mendelssohn refused to receive him. In these circles, too, Goethe was considered too proud.

At the end of his visit to Berlin, he registered a strange change in himself, and it isn't entirely clear whether he regretted it or considered it an increase in worldly wisdom: *My soul used to be like a city with few walls and a citadel on the hill behind it. I defended the castle and left the city defenseless in peace and war. Now I began to fortify it as well, if for the time being only against lightly armed troops.* If nothing else, his first and only visit to Berlin found him successful in scaring off the *lightly armed troops* of the literary world.

Goethe's increasing involvement in government forced profound changes in attitude regarding both himself and his environment. In late fall 1777, shortly before his journey to the Harz, he had already been aware of what would be expected of him. Just prior to urging himself to *Govern!!* he wrote that he felt himself *destined for much alienation.* His relationship with the duke was all the more important. Goethe could count on him and felt sure of himself in his company. Other than that, however, diplomacy and international politics remained minefields where he didn't know his way around and where events were almost entirely out of his control. He had to act with caution and suspicion rather than intuition and spontaneity. It was amazing how skillfully he ended up going about it.

The quarrel over the Bavarian succession came to a head in the summer of 1778. Prussia declared war on Austria and invaded Bohemia. What they had feared now occurred: Prussia asked the duke to make volunteers available, which meant either sending the troops himself or allowing Prussian recruiters free hand in the duchy. The duke declared himself against Prussian recruiting and tried to string the matter out. He was indeed in a dilemma. If Weimar voluntarily provided troops, it would forfeit its neutrality and be drawn into the Prussian camp against Austria. If it refused Prussia's request, it was in danger of losing its integrity as a sovereign state. In this tense situation, the duke chose to appoint Goethe, of all people, as the director of the military commission in early 1779 and, shortly thereafter, as director of road construction as well; roads were important militarily as well as for civilian use.

As a member of the privy council, Goethe composed a policy brief for the duke on February 9, 1779. He outlined the alternatives for action as well as their possible ramifications and long-term consequences.

If Prussian recruiters were allowed into the duchy and found no enthusiasm among the populace after a certain grace period, they would begin to use force. In that event, they would *settle in and put down roots everywhere*, and the duchy would never get rid of them. It was a threat to the independence of the state.

If the duchy instead decided to carry out conscription for Prussia itself, it would be *an unpleasant, hateful, and shameful business*. Moreover, some of the conscripted men would desert, whereupon Prussian soldiers would enter Weimar territory to catch them or find replacements for them. There would also be no *end of trouble*; Austria would not tolerate a ducal conscription of soldiers for Prussia, and would either undertake its own conscription in the duchy or count it as part of the enemy coalition, with the dire consequence that Weimar would then really be at war. What was to be done?

Goethe encouraged the duke to temporize and recommended using whatever time he gained to come to an understanding with the other small and medium-sized principalities of Hanover, Mainz, and Gotha and establish a *closer bond* with them in order to *protect themselves as much as possible from the hardships of the war next door.* That would be profitable even if Weimar could not fend off the current impositions of Prussia. The overarching recommendation of Goethe's brief was a confederation of the small states lying between the two major powers of Prussia and Austria.

He had thought it out well, with arguments anchored in the possibility of survival for the smaller states. He finds order in a balance of power among multiple political units, rather than in adherence to a hegemonic order. In his inclination for cooperative diversity, he proved himself still a student of Justus Möser.

What he had hoped for and wanted to participate in did not come to pass. It would be another twenty years before the Confederation of the Rhine, a league of small and medium-sized powers, came into being, and then not as a defensive pact against the great powers but rather as the instrument of a single great power: Napoleonic France.

For the moment, however, Goethe's idea gained traction. In its meeting of February 21, 1779, the privy council adopted his argument and decided to seek contact with other courts that wanted to remain neutral and in the meantime to protest the forceful conscription of Weimar inhabitants and strengthen Weimar's military presence.

The duchy was lucky: on May 13, 1779, the War of the Bavarian Succession was ended by the Treaty of Teschen. Throughout a bitterly cold winter, combatants had spied on each other, gone hungry, and scrapped over a few frozen potatoes.

In the early months of the year, however, this happy ending was not yet in sight. As chairman of the military commission, Goethe traveled around the duchy to oversee the precautionary conscription of recruits. During these months, he wrote the first prose version of *Iphigenia in Tauris*, the play that he would later describe to Schiller as *diabolically humane.*

In previous years, the lightweight pieces *Lila* and *The Triumph of Sentimentalism* had been performed on January 30, the birthday of the duchess. This year, the duchess was pregnant and due to go into labor shortly. On February 3, 1770, she gave birth to a daughter. She was expected to recover by March 14 and to attend church. When Goethe began work on the manuscript of *Iphigenia*, the thought was to have the play performed by the amateur theater company on that day or shortly thereafter. This time, given the occasion, the play was to be more serious and edifying, and it was correspondingly planned as an uplifting entertainment that would not cause any excitement. In that sense, it was an occasional work. The performance was well received, partly because Corona Schröter played Iphigenia and Goethe himself played Orestes. Corona's Junoesque figure and her carefully draped silk costume went with the court's taste for classical antiquity, and Goethe showed himself to such advantage that the physician Christoph Wilhelm Hufeland was still reveling in the memory as an old man: "We thought we were seeing an Apollo. I've never seen such a union of physical and intellectual perfection and beauty in a man as I then saw in Goethe."

After two performances, Goethe took the play out of circulation, allowed only a few friends to read it, and made sure no copies were made. He wrote to the Catholic bishop and statesman Karl Theodor von Dalberg that it was *much too carelessly written to leave the amateur theater and venture out into the wider world*. It was performed again, if to less effect, for the duchess's birthday in 1781. Goethe filed away at it, making improvements. The work had a hold on him. He thought he would be able to finish a version in iambic pentameter before he left for Italy in late 1786. It remained incomplete until he was living in Rome and even then its structure and content were little changed. It is possible that Goethe wanted to make something very different out of it, but the power the first draft had over him was too great.

The first version of the play was composed in the six restless weeks he spent traveling the duchy to oversee the conscription of recruits. At first, he tried to get into the necessary mood by having musicians play in the adjoining room while he wrote. *Little by little, through the lovely tones, my soul frees itself from the fetters of reports and documents. A quartet next door in the green room, I sit quietly and call the distant figures to me. One scene ought to be completed today, I think.*

The spiritual territory he opened up with *Iphigenia* lay very far removed from the importunate realities of his immediate present. From Apolda he wrote to Charlotte von Stein, *Here, the drama simply refuses to progress. It is cursed. The king of Tauris is supposed to speak as if there were no starving hosiers in Apolda.* Two days later, he describes to the duke what it's like when the young fellows *get measured and inspected* for conscription. Once that's out of the way, he continues, *I enter my old castle of poesy and cook away at my little daughter* [i.e., Iphigenia]. *On this occasion, I can also see that I treat this good gift of the gods a little too cavalierly, and I once more have time to become a better caretaker of my talent if I ever want to produce anything again.*

Goethe himself is surprised at the progress he is able to make on the play despite the adverse conditions. He feels his genius, his *good gift*, stirring again and resolves to take better care of it in the future. He is obviously able to compartmentalize things: *Now I am living with the people of this world—eating and drinking and even joking with them—but I'm barely aware of them, for my inner life unerringly follows its own path.* Deep within, his thoughts play *a lovely concert.*

And in fact, this muted chamber drama is a beautiful concert—if for some of Goethe's contemporaries, one all too beautiful—with only gentle dissonances and a reconciliation at the end. The world of ancient horror has left only faint traces.

The mythological story of Iphigenia in Tauris as Goethe knew it from Aeschylus and Euripides and in the later adaptations of Ovid and Hyginus is lurid and violent. Orestes avenges his father, Agamemnon, by killing his mother, Clytemnestra, and her lover Aegisthus, who together have murdered the king upon his return from Troy. Now the matricide Orestes is pursued by the Erinyes, the female Furies of vengeance. To free himself from the curse, he visits the oracle at Delphi, where he is directed to steal the sacred image of Artemis from Tauris and return it to Greece. He does not know that the guardian of that image, the priestess of Artemis, is his sister, Iphigenia, brought to Tauris by Artemis herself, before Agamemnon could sacrifice her, his own daughter, to gain favorable winds for the voyage to Troy. So Orestes and his friend Pylades arrive in the land of the Taurians, which we are to imagine as a country of "barbarians" somewhere on the Black Sea, where it is the custom to slaughter strangers landing on the coast. This is to be the fate of Orestes and Pylades as well, with Iphigenia, as priestess, to carry out the sacrifice. Euripides achieves great effect with the scene of the two siblings recognizing each other, in which Iphigenia invents the plot to trick King Thoas and flee with the image of

Artemis. The second half of Euripides's play is almost a comedy, full of scorn and ridicule for the slow-witted barbarians who let themselves be duped. Cruelty at the beginning, mockery at the end, and in between a dramatic high point—that was the style of the ancients.

Goethe made something very different out of the story. Later he realized that while it might conform to Winckelmann's image of classical antiquity's "noble simplicity and quiet greatness," it was otherwise very un-Greek. He told his secretary Friedrich Wilhelm Riemer in 1811, *Inadequacy is productive. I wrote my Iphigenia based on a study of Greek material, but my study was inadequate. If it had been exhaustive, the play would have remained unwritten.* Like his Iphigenia, Goethe had been *seeking with my soul the land of Greece.*

His *Iphigenia* differs most in its presentation of the barbarian king Thoas, whose character and behavior make a completely new play of the traditional material. The moral focus now lies in the relationship between Iphigenia and Thoas, which is where it proves to be *diabolically humane.* Thoas is courting Iphigenia, his noble prisoner. He desires her and, having lost his son in war, wants her to bear him a successor. But he also admires her, or he would not have agreed to her request to do away with the tradition of human sacrifice in the temple of Artemis. Iphigenia gives him much credit for that but is unable to return his love and, without loving Thoas, cannot enter into the marriage he desires. In this respect, Iphigenia is quite modern; she requires that spouses love each other. Anything else goes against her concept of purity. *What? The king would do a thing no noble / Man . . . would ever dare? He thinks by force / To drag me from my altar to his bed?* She turns him down, and to scare him off, recounts her own ominous genealogy, relating the atrocities of her ancestors in the house of Atreus. The story begins with Tantalus, who still eats at the tables of the gods but is damned for his insolence. One of his descendants, Atreus, kills his brother's sons and serves them to him at a banquet. The horrors continue down to her father, Agamemnon. Artemis has rescued her from him, and now she hides behind the goddess. Within the temple precincts, she intends to serve Artemis and remain free of any other ties. Her only desire is to return home. She too is *seeking with my soul the land of Greece.*

Thoas is insulted by the rejection. He does not take her by force, but lets her feel his wrath. He reinstates the cruel tradition Iphigenia has done away with: strangers will again be sacrificed. Iphigenia is to begin the practice with two men who have just been apprehended. Neither Iphigenia nor Thoas knows at this point that they are Orestes and his friend Pylades. If Thoas's order is carried out, Iphigenia will be killing her own brother.

Orestes has come here to absolve himself of guilt. He is at the end of his strength, longs for death, and is even prepared to be sacrificed. But then the siblings recognize each other:

> IPHIGENIA   *Oh hear me! Look at me! My heart is opening*
>   *After all these years of being shut,*
>   *Opening to bliss, that I can kiss the head*
>   *Of the most precious man upon this earth,*
>   *And clasp you in these arms that have stretched out*
>   *To nothing but the empty, soughing winds.*
>   *Oh, let me hold you! . . . Orestes! Dearest brother!*
> ORESTES   *. . . Lovely nymph,*
>   *I cannot trust in you or your cajoling.*

Then Orestes, who includes his sister in his death wish: *. . . and my advice is: do not / Love the sun too much, nor yet the stars; / Come, follow me down into the dark realm! / . . . / Come, childless, without guilt, come down with me!* Madness envelops him, he sinks into a numbed sleep, awakens in Iphigenia's arms, and—is healed.

> *My heart is telling me: the curse is lifted.*
> *The Furies are returning—I can hear them—*
> *To Tartarus, slamming the brazen gates*
> *Like distant, booming thunder, closed behind them.*
> *The earth is steaming with refreshing smells,*
> *Inviting me to roam its lovely surface*
> *In search of the joys of life and noble deeds.*

This scene is not unique in Goethe's oeuvre. Faust falls asleep after Gretchen's death and awakens guilt-free and ready for action. Egmont overcomes his fear of death—while asleep. Schiller, for one, would never have stood for such a device. When Goethe asked him to adapt

Iphigenia for the professional stage in 1802, he took exception to this scene. He did not like people sleeping through crises instead of overcoming them through freely chosen action. But Goethe was in favor of the sleep of forgetfulness, the merciful operation of nature. For Goethe, man is rooted in his past, but still capable of opening himself to the demands and opportunities of the present. When the past possesses too much power, as with the fury of the Erinyes, it can overwhelm and extinguish life in the present. To make conscience the inner representative of the absolute, as does Kant, seemed to Goethe like an excess of Protestantism. Even in old age he praised the art of forgetting, writing to Zelter at eighty, *Just consider that with every breath we draw, an ethereal Lethean stream suffuses our entire being, so that we recall our joys but moderately, our sorrows hardly at all. I have always known how to treasure, use, and augment this great, divine gift.*

So Orestes is healed and the Furies have no more power over him. All that's left is to free Iphigenia from the hands of Thoas. Euripides makes her the inventor of a clever ruse to escape. Goethe has Orestes and Pylades hatch the plan while Iphigenia hesitates. That is the moment that reveals her extraordinary humanity. And even she must struggle to achieve it. Within the temple precincts, her refuge, it would be easy for her to remain *pure* and abstain from devious methods. A beautiful soul loath to demean herself, she fears having to leave this place.

> *Oh my soul, be calm, be calm!*
> *Would you give in to wavering and doubt?*
> *You must abandon now the solid ground*
> *Of solitude and board the rocking ship!*
> *The waves beleaguer you. In gloomy fear*
> *You will misjudge the world, misjudge yourself.*

Orestes and Pylades's plan to trick Thoas calls for Iphigenia to have the image of Artemis taken to the seashore, allegedly to purify it, but in fact to get it aboard a ship waiting to take her and the image to safety. In a dialogue between Iphigenia and Pylades, the idea of purity clashes with the usual way of the world, humanitarian idealism with skeptical realism:

IPHIGENIA   *I call that worry noble when it warns*
                  Me not to deceive the monarch who became
                  My second father, not to betray and rob him.

PYLADES   *You flee a king who'd butcher your own brother.*

IPHIGENIA   *The very man who treated me with kindness.*

PYLADES   *Necessity absolves you of ingratitude.*

IPHIGENIA   *Pardoned by need, it's still ingratitude.*

PYLADES   *Pardoned, surely, before gods and men.*

IPHIGENIA   *Yet my own heart is still dissatisfied.*

PYLADES   *Too strict demands conceal a hidden pride.*

IPHIGENIA   *I do not analyze, I only feel.*

PYLADES   *Feel rightly and you will revere yourself.*

IPHIGENIA   *My heart must feel itself unsullied.*

PYLADES   *Thus you preserved yourself within the temple;*
                  Life teaches us, however, to be less strict
                  With others and ourselves; you'll learn it too.
                  The race of men's so wonderfully constructed,
                  So manifoldly linked and intertwined,
                  That none of us can ever remain pure
                  Within himself and unconfused with others.
                  Nor are we meant to be our own accusers.

The argument advanced by Pylades was one Goethe himself often subscribed to, for example, in the late verses *The days of man are oft congested, / Things of beauty oft contested, / Even the clearest eyes grow dim*, or in the laconic declaration *In our actions we are always without conscience. No one has a conscience except in contemplation.* Societal conflict demands compromise of us and sometimes the use of questionable means—up to and including force—to defend and assert ourselves and protect our loved ones. There are many reasons not to judge too harshly. For a moment, Iphigenia herself is tempted to adopt this point of view. *I am almost convinced that you are right*, she says. But face to face with Thoas, after initial hesitation, her will to purity wins out. She does not want to deceive him. She reveals the cunning plan of escape to him and thereby places herself, Orestes, and Pylades in the greatest peril. She risks much with her appeal to the nobility of the barbarian king, asking that he let them leave. She wants to break through the vicious circle in which mistrust begets mistrust and hostility is answered by hostility, and replace it with the reciprocity of good will. She trusts Thoas and hopes he will reward that trust. She treats him like a human being and seeks to be treated humanely in return. Yet in the reciprocity of good will on which Iphigenia bets, there is a hidden imbalance. Iphigenia and her brother gain freedom and the return to their homeland, but Thoas will suffer a painful loss. Iphigenia argues that the consciousness of having acted well will compensate him for it. She appeals to his self-esteem and, in the end, depicts the situation as if it provided Thoas an opportunity to ennoble himself, a chance he must absolutely not pass up. It is almost a sophism when Iphigenia tells him, *Look at us! It is not often that / You have the chance for such a noble deed.*

In the end Thoas agrees. He feels a challenge to his pride and wants to prove that even a barbarian can hear *the voice of truth and of humanity.* But in the certainty of her triumph, Iphigenia is not satisfied with his command *So leave!* Thoas must not simply grudgingly allow them to leave; she wants his blessing so that, in the future, mutual hospitality, good will, and faithful recollection will reign between her world and his. Thoas struggles to that concession as well, leaving it to her to construe his *Farewell!* as a blessing. Both his final word and the last word of this play, it is consecrated to an elevated ideal of humanity.

The idea of purity dominates the entire work. Iphigenia wants to enjoy an *unsullied* heart, which is why the *pure* temple precincts are so significant for her. Pylades responds that in human affairs no one can remain *pure . . . and unconfused with others.*

The question of purity would continue to evolve in Goethe's thought—particularly its tension with the rich diversity of the world, where variety and conflict are the norm. Actually, nothing is *pure* in the world or in nature. It requires some effort and artificial adjustments to produce purity. What is needed is some method to separate out or at least define what does not belong or is inappropriate, as purity is not self-evident. It is not simply there; instead, one must have decided, a priori, what to regard as the actual element that needs protection or liberation from contamination. Goethe later borrowed from Schelling the term *selfish principle* for this actual element: the power of the individual to preserve his uniqueness even—or especially—when exposed to a multiplicity of influences and complications. Purity thus also means the preservation of uniqueness. Only the individual who preserves and asserts himself as such becomes a self.

That self, however, understood as such, is constantly dependent on contact with the world. Everything therefore hinges on becoming involved with the world without losing oneself to it. The tension between self and world can fail in two ways: by becoming rigid, hard, and narrow; or by dissolving. By becoming a blind egotist or by *frittering oneself away. Pure intermediate effect in accomplishing what is right and good is quite rare; usually we see pedantry, which seeks to retard, or temerity, which seeks to go too fast.* By *pedantry* he means in this context narrow self-referentiality and by *temerity*, a diffuse relation to the world.

If Iphigenia wanted to preserve her purity by staying in the temple precincts, she risked losing connection to the world. This is the danger of a beautiful soul, as powerfully described in Hegel's *Phenomenology of Spirit.* Such a being "lives in fear of staining the glory of its interior life by acting and being; and in order to guard the purity of its heart, it flees contact with reality and remains in stubborn powerlessness . . . its action is yearning, which . . . merely finds itself to be lost; in this transparent purity of its moments, an unfortunate so-called *beautiful soul* flickers out within itself and disappears as a shapeless mist that dissipates in air."

But this is not the case with Iphigenia. She wants to preserve her purity of heart not merely within the enclosed temple precincts but with Thoas as well. She preserves her self-esteem by esteeming Thoas, who is also an adversary she must fear. This epigram from the collection of satirical verses entitled "Tame Xenias" emphatically does not apply to Iphigenia: *In silence maintain your purity, / Let others rant and scream; / The more you feel your humanity / The more godlike you will seem.* She cannot keep herself pure *in silence;* she wants to prove her worth outside, in the bustle of the world, but without deception or deceit. The play would have become a tragedy if the noble candidness with which Iphigenia approaches the king was not rewarded but, instead, punished by the completion of human sacrifice. It is rewarded, because the beauty of her soul is infectious. The abyss of possible horror closes, and the scenery of cruelty turns into a utopian vision of humanity.

Iphigenia leaves the temple precincts, but the entire play was a sort of temple precinct, screened off from the real world of impending war, the conscription of troops, and the starving hosiers of Apolda. That's why Goethe, as we have seen, had music played in the adjoining room while he worked on the play. The temple precincts of pure writing were thus protected, and his inner life could develop unhindered.

Now we can see why Goethe was dissatisfied with the first version in prose and found it *carelessly written*. It was not *pure* enough. The rhythms had not yet been smoothed into blank verse, and he would keep working on it until his departure for Italy in 1786. He did not complete this temple of beauty—*with a rich interior but poor exterior life*—until he was in Rome. In the interior life of the play, one can discern shadowy autobiographical elements. For one, the brother-sister relationship: Orestes finds peace in the arms of Iphigenia. In Goethe's life it was the other way around. There his sister sought peace in her brother's company. For another, Goethe had to struggle like Orestes with guilt—toward his sister and toward Lenz and Klinger, friends he had rebuffed. On the other hand, the loving depiction of the friendship between Orestes and Pylades is colored by Goethe's friendship with the duke. And finally, Iphigenia's enchanting and soothing influence is reminiscent of Charlotte von Stein.

Thus the play, set in a remote time and place, echoes Goethe's life in the present. Yet at times it seemed foreign to him, and he was unable to find in himself the necessary purity. When he accompanied the duke on a military expedition against revolutionary France, they made a stop at the Jacobis' in Pempelfort, and his friends asked him to read from *Iphigenia*. *It wasn't at all to my taste, however*, he writes in the *Campaign in France*, continuing, *I felt alienated from the gentle spirit*. What does he mean by *the gentle spirit*? Probably the feeling of purity, which did not fare well amid the tumult of a military campaign. What he noted about the audience after the first performance applied to him as well: *Performed Iph. to quite good effect, especially on pure persons.*

It was only rarely that he felt close to the play again, however. It was, after all, so *diabolically humane*.

CHAPTER 15

The Idea of Purity. Goethe's Tao. The Crucifixion
of *Woldemar*. Jacobi Insulted. The Second Journey to
Switzerland. Friederike and Lili: Two Wrongs Righted.
The Beautiful Branconi and Confusion: *Peace lies over all
the peaks.* Goethe and Lavater: Religion on Trial.

....

THE *GENTLE SPIRIT* FROM WHICH *IPHIGENIA* WAS BORN—THE IDEA
of purity—had existential importance for Goethe. On August 7, 1779,
shortly before setting off on his second journey to Switzerland, he
reviewed his life in one of the longest passages in his entire diary. He
reveals how much his present life is dominated by the idea: *Straightened up at home, went through my papers and burned all the old husks. New
times, new concerns. Tranquil review of my life, of the muddle, bustle, thirst for
knowledge in my youth, how the young roam everywhere in search of something
satisfactory. How I took special delight in secrets and dark, abstruse relationships.
How I only halfway came to grips with anything scientific and soon let it drop,
how a sort of abject complacency runs through everything I wrote at the time.
How narrow-mindedly I cast about in matters human and divine. How there
was such a dearth of accomplishments and of purposeful thought and writing, how
many days and hours were wasted in sentiment and shadow passion, how little of
that was useful to me, and now that half my life is past, I have covered no ground
along its path, but rather am just standing here like a drowning man who has
pulled himself out of the water and whom the benevolent sun begins to dry off. I
cannot yet venture to survey the time I have spent on the activities of the world
since October '75. May God help me to continue and provide light so that we
don't get in our own way so much. May he allow us to do what is proper from
morning to night and give us a clear idea of the consequences of things. May I not
be like people who use the entire day to complain about a headache and every eve-*

ning drink too much wine. May the idea of a purity that extends even to the bite
I put into my mouth become clearer and clearer within me.

It is a remarkable passage. Before his departure, Goethe takes stock
of his life, surveying what he has done up to his move to Weimar. He
cannot *venture to survey* the most recent years. As far as he can summarize it, his life up to now has not been *pure*. What does that mean?
In order to answer that, let us see how he characterizes the presumed
impurity of his life. It was, he writes, devoted to *muddle, bustle,* and
taking delight in *abstruse relationships,* not to *purposeful thought and writing*
but to time-wasting *sentiment and shadow passion.* Based on this distinction, the purity he has in mind is the ability to turn his actions and
thoughts toward the real world. It is clarity, purposefulness, and a practical sense of reality. Certainly passion is still involved, not for abstruse
shadow beings but for reality, whatever that may mean in practice. He
has rescued himself from the water—where he had no solid ground
beneath his feet—onto dry land, where a benevolent sun is drying him
off. Ungroundedness is impurity, and it is associated with an alcoholic
stupor from which he awakes with a headache.

Is this emphasis on purity an attack on the creative power of the
imagination and the confusions it causes? Does purity mean looking
reality in the eye and satisfying its demands? Does it perhaps come
down to being purified of poetry? That is hardly credible, especially
when one considers that he had just been working on and producing
Iphigenia, a play consecrated to an elevated ideal of humanity.

It is difficult to imagine that it is meant as a general attack on
the productive power of the imagination. Instead, the idea of
purity demands that one make a clear distinction between the two
spheres—reality here, poetry there—and have the prudence not to
confuse the two realms but rather do justice to the claims of each as
separate areas of life. For example, there is one kind of tenacity in
governing and quite a different kind in poetry. The art of such distinctions may be what Goethe meant with the formulation *May he*
allow us to do what is proper from morning to night and give us a clear idea of
the consequences of things.

Such a clear distinction of the spheres to which the idea of purity
applies means that it can reach into any field but has a unique signifi-

cance in each. Behavior and action in the practical sphere should be pure *even to the bite I put into my mouth*—a way of life so prudent it included one's diet: well-regulated and punctual. It means earnestly completing each task, confronting the *day's duties*, and always with emphasis on what one is doing at the moment. It was this attentiveness, this almost Taoist daily discipline, that Herder found so admirable in a letter of 1784: "Recently, he read to us from a new, very beautiful volume of his *Wilhelm Meister*, and another time the beginning of a new, very excellent work [the treatise on the intermaxillary bone]. Such work and the hours he devotes to it are probably the only ones that restore the splendid man to himself, although he also dwells on the minutest and even the most hateful occupations with utter calm, as though that were his only true nature."

This basic discipline was not a given for Goethe, but something he had to make an effort to learn and practice. This is how he expressed it later in *Maxims and Reflections*: *Whoever desires or needs to act must only think about what is proper for the moment, and then he will get through it without circuitousness.* He does not give up the lyrical longing that reaches beyond the moment, but he ties it to the problems of daily life and its demands in such a way that it must make the detour via the activity at hand. In *Wilhelm Meister's Journeyman Years*, Leonardo declares that *yearning vanishes in productive activity*. But it doesn't disappear without a trace; an unsatisfied residuum remains that nourishes new action and liberates fresh imagination. Purity in the realm of action thus means devotion to the tasks of the day. Only thus is practical mastery possible.

Poetry demands a different kind of purity, a different mastery. Though different from the purity of practical affairs, it has similar characteristics—precisely what Goethe is pondering in his diary when he formulates his imperatives of purity. He writes that one must have the confidence to grasp what is appropriate to the matter at hand like the English agronomist George Batty, then traveling the duchy. There is an approach appropriate to every activity, including poetry. That approach will reveal the inner wealth of its object and allow it to emerge. Every theme, every material, every idea has its inner entelechy and requires a certain way of developing. The mature artist senses what is appropriate for that entelechy. He is *pure*, free of personal caprice. He brings work to fruition—serves the work and is essential to its creation. In art, too, there is a craft to master, like the potter at his wheel, *according to whose will there emerges now a jug, and now a bowl*, and yet one has the impression that jug and bowl have achieved visible existence on their own. Goethe also thought about the cabinet maker Johann Martin Mieding, the factotum of the theater in Weimar. With his carpenter's skill, Mieding was able to fashion anything needed to make the stage approximate the world: scenery, costumes, lighting, and mechanical devices to produce the illusion of reality. When Mieding died in 1782, Goethe wrote him a tender epitaph:

> *Whatever touched a lovely, tender soul*
> *He copied faithfully. That was his role:*
> *The green of grass, a cascade's silvery wonder,*
> *The songs of birds or a loud clap of thunder,*
> *A bower's shadows and the moon's pale light—*
> *Not even a monster could put him to flight.*

There is an ironic edge to this praise for the craftsmanship that is the prerequisite of poetic effects, an irony against the pretentions of people who are proud of their inspiration. There is a purity of craft that the poet needs in his own way to prove his worth.

It is against this background that we can best understand the aggressive ridicule Goethe unleashed, shortly before leaving for Switzerland, upon the recently published novel *Woldemar, a Rarity from Natural History*, by his friend Fritz Jacobi. Here too, it was a question of dubious *purity*. In August 1779, at a festivity in the Ettersburg Palace, north of Weimar, people had read from Jacobi's novel. Goethe had recited some parodistic verses, climbed into a tree, and nailed the novel to its trunk to scare off birds and readers. There is no eyewitness report of this incident, but Goethe later confirmed it in a letter to Lavater. An immediate topic of gossip (the "crucifixion of Jacobi"), it caused him to break off his friendship with Goethe.

In his letter to Lavater, Goethe explained what had bothered him about the book. He calls it the *whiff of pretension*. The book was only half successful, it lacked mastery, but it had pretensions to being a masterpiece. Its claim to that status was not supported by any corresponding moral, aesthetic, or psychological substance. In Goethe's vocabulary, this too is *impurity*. Moreover, the novel had a certain moral vanity. The eponymous hero Woldemar is a paragon of virtue and chastity. He lives with Henriette in an unconsummated union. He allows her to marry him off to a friend of hers, upon which the three of them form a league of love and friendship in which there is much apparently disembodied sentiment. They are all noble and good. Goethe found Woldemar's smugness unbearably irritating. You needed only to alter a few lines, he later told Johanna Fahlmer (a relative of Jacobi's), and *it is inevitable and no different than if the devil would have to come fetch him.*

To be sure, there is some reason to doubt that Goethe's outrage at the novel's moral pretentiousness was entirely *pure* itself. A completely different motivation may have been in play. It isn't difficult to read the depiction of an unconsummated union as a reflection of his own relationship to Charlotte von Stein. Perhaps that was another source of anger driving his ridicule.

The resolution to make purity a lifetime goal was made at an important juncture: his impending departure on a lengthy journey. Another act of purification was his destruction of letters and notes on August 7, 1779. Traveling was a risky business in those days, and precautions had to be taken in case one did not return. It was an auto-da-fé in that sense, but also one of the inner changes he usually referred to as *moltings*, when he cast off things he had outgrown. A visit to Lavater in Zurich would also play an important role because, at this point in Goethe's life, Lavater was still a credible and revered apostle of purity.

On September 5, 1779, just a few days before his departure, Goethe was named privy councilor. He writes to Charlotte von Stein, *it seems miraculous to me, like a dream, that at the age of thirty, I have reached the highest honor a bourgeois in Germany can achieve.*

On September 12, a traveling party—the duke, the head forestry official von Wedel, Goethe, and several servants, among them Goethe's manservant Philipp Seidel—set off. Their official destinations were Frankfurt, the Lower Rhine, Cologne, and Düsseldorf, and so people in Weimar were surprised when they learned that the group had headed south toward Switzerland. The duke assured everyone that it was the same for him; he too had been surprised by the change in plans. He wrote to his mother, Anna Amalia, "I am sorry that you don't believe me and think I made a secret of the long journey; so I must repeat, it was only between Friedberg and Frankfurt, just at the halfway point, that it was decided; that's when I and the others learned of it through the inspiration of the angel Gabriel." Which would mean that Goethe had been given the authority to determine their goal. That is hard to believe, since it would not have been permissible for Goethe to act so high-handedly toward his duke. The two probably hatched the scheme together.

Goethe had an educational plan for this journey with regard to the duke, who considered it a sort of belated grand tour. For that reason, they traveled incognito, although their true identities did not remain concealed at the courts they visited along the way. Goethe wanted to draw the duke into his program of self-purification, and that's why he put so much stock in a meeting with Lavater in Zurich. From Emmendingen, he wrote to Charlotte von Stein, *to see Lavater and to know that he is closer to the duke is my greatest hope.* He hoped that Lavater's gentle nature and unbigoted, cordial piety would soothe the duke's impetuous nature and give him a taste for the inner harmony of which the Zurich preacher was such an outstanding exemplar. Lavater did indeed make an impression on the duke, at least for the moment: "There's something uniquely soothing about Lavater's presence," Karl August wrote to his wife, "I make use of it as much as ever I can . . . I cannot better express how he seems to have affected me than with the words 'cleaning up my mind.'"

If the duke found Lavater "soothing," for Goethe he was like *taking the waters.* One felt refreshed *when one sees again such a completely true person.* The attributes of purity pile up in Goethe's description of Lavater: *I am with Lavater here, in the purest mutual enjoyment of life; in the circle of his friends there is an angelic stillness and peace . . . so that everyone . . . has a pure human existence even with just the basic necessities.* Goethe here accentuates the curative effect of the visit, which he hopes it will also have on the duke. *Only here do I clearly realize what a moral death we usually live in together, and where the shriveling and freezing of the heart comes from, the heart that in itself is never arid and never cold. May God grant that, among many other great advantages, this one may also accompany us home, namely, that we keep our own souls open and are also able to open the good souls of others. If I could depict for you how empty the world is, we would hold tight to one another and never let go. However, I am prepared for the sirocco of dissatisfaction, dislike, ingratitude, carelessness, and pretention to blow our way again.*

This sirocco had not yet had the feared effect on the duke or on Goethe, for back in Weimar people thought they could detect a changed attitude in both of them. The duke seemed somehow chastened and ennobled, with "behavior that won one's heart,' and Goethe seemed "good as a child." Since Goethe was regarded as the guiding spirit of the entire enterprise, he was also credited with the success of the trip. This Swiss journey, Wieland said, was "one of Göthe's most masterful dramas."

The journey enabled other settlings of accounts. On their way south, they passed through Strasbourg, and it was probably Goethe's intention from the beginning to visit lovers of former years, lovers he had felt guilty for abandoning. Here too, there were things that needed clearing up.

On September 25, 1779, he rode from Strasbourg over to Sesenheim—a route teeming with memories—and found the parsonage outwardly unchanged and the Brion family still together, as if he had only just parted from them. *Since I am now as pure and calm as the air, the breath of good, quiet people is very welcome.* In a long letter to Charlotte he provides a vivid description of his reunion with Friederike: *In former days, the second daughter of the house had loved me more than I deserved and more than others on whom I expended much passion and devotion. I had to leave her at a moment when it almost cost her life. She passed over that quietly and told me about what still remained of her illness from that time, behaved in the dearest way, with so much friendly cordiality from the moment I appeared unexpectedly on her threshold and we almost bumped noses with each other, that I was quite content. I must also acknowledge that she never undertook by even the slightest suggestion to awaken an old feeling in my soul. She led me to that arbor, and I had to sit there, and I was content.* But a note written twenty years later describes it differently. There he writes that the *largest part of the conversation* with Friederike was about the annoying behavior of Lenz and how he had pestered her and pretended to be in love with her, but only to gain access to Goethe's letters. Goethe presents it not as his conjecture, but as Friederike's judgment of what occurred: *She explains to me that it was his intention to do me harm and destroy me in public opinion and otherwise.* By this account, it wasn't just a tranquil conversation in the arbor. Old wounds were touched upon, but in such a way that Friederike's emotional damage and Goethe's guilty conscience could be transferred onto poor Lenz. The next morning, Goethe was able to ride off in the nostalgic but cheerful certainty *that I can now think about that little corner of the world with satisfaction and live at inner peace with the spirits of these reconciled friends.*

The next settling of accounts came the following day in Strasbourg. He paid a call on Elisabeth (Lili) von Türckheim, née Schönemann. *There too I was met with astonishment and joy.* Lili, the *good creature,* seemed to be happily married. Her husband was a well-to-do man with a beautiful house and *impressive social position.* Lili had *everything she needed.* Goethe hints at Lili's need for luxury and fashion, which could now be adequately satisfied, but would have become a problem if their relationship had continued. Lili had what she needed, and so he didn't have to burden himself with guilt. On this evening, too, the moon was shining as it had at Friederike's house the night before. He found life at the wealthy Türckheims' a bit *prosaic,* but not displeasing. The feeling of having cleared something up, purified it, was far stronger: *and so there is a quite ethereal delight in the feeling of continuous, pure good will, and in the way I have, as it were, recited a rosary of the most staunch, reliable, inextinguishable friendship. Now my relationships with the people who remain can enter my soul unclouded by a limited passion.*

It was important to him then to be unclouded by passion. But that would not prove so easy when he encountered the beautiful Antonia von Branconi in Lausanne. Charlotte von Stein must have taken some offense at the way he wrote of this woman: *She seems so beautiful and pleasant that, in her presence, I have several times asked myself if it's possible she can be so beautiful.* She invited him back. *In the end, one must say of her,* he writes in the letter to Charlotte, *what Ulysses reported about the rocks of Scylla: "Without an injured wing no bird can pass them by."* Frau von Branconi was a celebrated beauty. At Lavater's house, Goethe had seen a silhouette of her that piqued his curiosity, and he paid her a visit in Lausanne. She had been the mistress of the hereditary prince of Braunschweig, which according to the mores of the time did nothing to damage her reputation in society. She lived part of the year in Lausanne and part at her country estate near Halberstadt, where Goethe would later visit her again. He had to work hard to resist falling under her spell. It was a great challenge to his resolve to remain pure, both during this first encounter in Lausanne and during her return visit to Weimar a year later, in 1780. In a letter to Lavater from this time, Goethe writes, *I cannot answer your question about that beauty. I behaved to her as I would to a princess or a saint. And even if it were only an illusion, I would not like to sully such an image by connecting it to a transitory desire. And God save us from a serious attachment, in which she would wrest the soul from my body.*

To Charlotte von Stein, Goethe presents his struggle for purity and freedom from *transitory desire* in a somewhat different light. The thought of her, he wrote on the day Frau von Branconi visited him, protected him from that beauty: *The beautiful lady will take up my whole day today. . . . She is always beautiful, very beautiful, but it is as if you, my beloved, would have to be taken away if another being were to touch me.* But of course, he is touched nevertheless. There must have been some inner turmoil, for he had difficulty maintaining his composure. When the beauty had taken her departure, he sent her some lines that were telling but also left much untold: *Only now do I feel that you were here, the way one feels the wine only a while after drinking it. In your presence one wishes for better eyes, ears, and spirit just to be able to see and find it believable and comprehensible that it has pleased heaven, after so many unsuccessful attempts, to try—and succeed—at making something like you. I would have to continue on and on with this apparent hyperbole . . . and because not even that is, as they say, proper, I must break off and keep the best to myself.*

Soon thereafter, Goethe went to Ilmenau with the duke on mining business. There he climbed the highest peak in the area, the Kickelhahn, and spent the night in a hunter's cabin. From there he writes to Charlotte von Stein, indulges in tender memories of her, and describes how he has *bedded down* in solitude in order *to avoid longing, the incorrigible perplexity of humankind.* He did not mention that a letter from Frau von Branconi also reached him there; he would later write to her, *Your letter could not have reached me at a more beautiful and solemn moment.* It seemed to him like seeing a *comet.*

Perplexity? Perhaps it was the feeling of being pulled back and forth between Charlotte and Frau von Branconi. It was that restless evening on the Kickelhahn that inspired his incredible evocation of the calming effect of nature:

Peace lies over
All the peaks.
In all the trees
You sense
Hardly a breath;
The little forest birds fall silent.
Wait, and soon
You too will rest.

But now let us return to the visit to Switzerland in the preceding year.

The sublime peace above the peaks was also an echo of his mood in the high Alps. He described the sight of the mountains in a letter to Charlotte von Stein: *The sublime gives beautiful peace to the soul, which is completely filled by it and feels itself as great as it is possible to be. The sublime grants pure feeling.* From Basel they traveled southwest via Bern and Lake Geneva into the Savoy Alps and the glacial regions in the canton of Valais, encouraged by a sunny late autumn in November. Several natives of the area had advised against it—as the onset of winter could be expected at any moment—but others, including the famous alpine explorer Professor Horace-Bénédict de Saussure, had urged the band of travelers to continue. They set off along the sometimes difficult high route, west to east, via Chamonix and the Furka to the Gotthard. Goethe, though eager to climb as high as possible, was concerned about the young duke, who tended to be a daredevil. It was his older friend's job to restrain him from time to time. *If I had been alone*, he writes to Charlotte, *I would have gone higher and deeper, but with the duke I have to do what is moderate.* This time Goethe did not feel the lure of the South, as he had on his first trip to Switzerland. Because he felt responsible for the duke, he knew that he needed to turn around. *Even now, Italy doesn't tempt me,* he writes from the top of the Gotthard Pass. *The fact that going to Italy would be of no use to the duke at this time, that it would not be good to stay away from home any longer, that I will see you all again—everything turns my eye away from the Promised Land for the second time—the land I hope to see before I die—and leads my spirit back to my poor roof, where I will have you at my hearth, as jolly as ever, and will serve you up a good roast.*

There would, however, be one more peak experience: a second meeting with Lavater in Zurich. As we have seen, part of Goethe's plans for his journey with the duke was to introduce him to Lavater. Goethe had great expectations of bringing the two together, and they were fulfilled. *Neither in Israel nor among the heathen is there such truth, faith, love, patience, strength, wisdom, goodness, diligence, integrity, diversity, serenity, etc.,* Goethe writes about Lavater, and *he is the flower of mankind, the best of the best.* The two weeks at the end of November 1779 were a high point in their relationship. A high point, but also a turning point, for from then on, a gradual alienation began that would finally end in a rupture.

Even before their reunion in the fall of 1779, Goethe had indicated that he was more interested in Lavater's person than in his religion. The Swiss pastor was truly devout and clung fervently to the word of God, in both the Old and the New Testament. For him, the Bible was literal truth, the revealed word of God, and possessed living, authoritative power. For Goethe, however, it was poetry and, at most, evidence of inspired wisdom. Goethe, too, speaks of *God* when he expresses his joy at the imminent reunion with Lavater: *My God, to whom I have always remained faithful, has secretly given me a rich blessing, for my fate is completely hidden from others. They can neither see nor hear it. I am happy to lay in your heart whatever can be revealed of it.*

What Goethe here calls "God" is the power of fate, which he feels is well disposed toward him. Goethe speaks of God the way Socrates spoke of his *daimon.* This power of fate is something that everyone can experience for himself. It remains hidden from others, although the effect of the life-shaping power of such inner certainty can unquestionably be noticed by others. One cannot proselytize this personal power of fate as God, much less force it on others through preaching, persuasion, or admonishment. Everyone must sense and find their own God, which means nothing more than grasping the guiding principle of their life. Nor can one invoke any supposedly sacred texts to back up the certainty of being led by one's own *daimon.*

However, the inspiration drawn from such experiences of being led by an inner force can flow into texts of one's own. People who believe in the Bible believe in a history of salvation for everyone, but Goethe believed only in his personal history of salvation, which seemed possible (as he wrote to Lavater) only as long as he remained true to himself and thus to his personal God. The same letter to Lavater also contains a hidden warning. Lavater should not hope that they will ever reach agreement on the subject of belief. What Goethe admired in Lavater was something else, namely, his style of life. Goethe calls it the *purest mutual enjoyment of life*. What he meant was a cordial openness that overcame artificial barriers and separations. Precisely because one is firmly anchored elsewhere, one can feel free to enjoy life here. That enables a carefree spontaneity that frees us from narrow, calculating behavior. It was this higher carefreeness, after all, that had led Goethe to perceive Lavater as naïve, undaunted, in harmony with himself, and therefore inwardly free. It was a higher, not a limited naïveté. Goethe was attracted by the pious man's imperturbability even—and especially— in earthly affairs. In general, his friendship with Lavater promised a relaxing and loosening up of his own being, which he saw endangered by *the shriveling and freezing of the heart* at the court in Weimar. What he appreciated about Lavater's religion were not the individual articles of faith but rather its influence on how he shaped his life.

In the world of religious belief, however, Goethe appreciated only what possessed poetic color, imagination, and feeling. He writes to Lavater that what gave him *pleasure* in the pastor's epic poem based on the Book of Revelation and entitled *Jesus the Messiah, or The Future of the Lord* were the passages where the *promise of eternal life* was beautifully illustrated by *sheep grazing under palm trees* or the *triumphant feeling of the angels*. In such *figures and similes*, he writes, *you have done well*, and then continues, *but for me, your monsters dissipate too quickly in allegorical steam*. In other words, Goethe sees the matter aesthetically, not theologically. Thus, he thinks little of the revelation of damnation when it doesn't succeed poetically.

Although flattering to the poet, Goethe's characterization of his friend's commentary on Revelation was actually blasphemous for the believer. The burden of his remarks is that Lavater's poem is no more or less a revelation than the biblical text on which it is based. In the final analysis, both are poetic works, expressions of an excited soul: *for my taste, your portrayal makes the same impression as the original sketch*. It is a poetic advantage when one finds the reflection of a soul in a text, but faith depends on seeing in such texts more than what a soul has put into them. The believer sees in them a higher power, not just the soul of a fellow man. Even before their reunion in the fall of 1779, Goethe had clearly staked out the limits of their agreement; perhaps their personal relationship succeeded so well because they remained conscious of what separated them. Over and above that, they agreed to disagree.

For that, however, physical proximity was indispensable. When they were apart, the power of their differences grew. It didn't take long after they parted before that distance began to exert its alienating influence. Lacking the belief in each other that personal contact fosters, one's other beliefs and thoughts have greater and greater weight. Two friends cease to understand each other aright, and in the end, they no longer want to. That is what happened to Goethe and Lavater.

For a while after Goethe's departure from Zurich, a cordial bond continued, a bond that made Goethe feel called upon to reflect on his own life's plan in contrast to Lavater's. It was as if he needed to prove to this friend, who had placed himself under the guidance of a higher power, that he was sufficiently guided by himself. In his letters to Lavater soon after his visit to Zurich, Goethe expressed the design of his life in memorable images: *The daily work assigned to me, which every day becomes easier and more difficult, demands my presence, waking and dreaming. This duty grows more precious to me every day, and in its performance I would wish to be the equal of the greatest men, and in nothing greater. This desire to raise up as high as possible the pyramid of my existence—whose basis and foundation were given to me—outweighs everything else and can hardly be forgotten even for a moment. I dare not tarry. I am already at an advanced age, and perhaps fate will break me in the middle of life and the Tower of Babel will remain an incomplete stump. At least they should be able to say it was a daring attempt, and if I live, my strength, God willing, should be enough to complete the tower.*

Goethe admits to Lavater, the man of God who presents himself as humble, that he has the presumption to construct his own life like a Tower of Babel—reaching for the stars, but with a firm foundation. It is founded not on the promise of eternal life, as in Lavater's case, but on the belief in his own worth and on the trust in the power of his personal destiny. There are distant echoes of his defiant Promethean tone: *You must leave my earth / Just as it is / And the hut / That I built, not you.*

More and more often in his letters to Lavater, which continued to be full of praise and avowals of cordiality, there were also pointed and even facetious remarks, as when he mentions the masques composed for the New Year's celebration at the Weimar court and then says, *As you beautify the celebrations of godliness, I beautify the parades of foolishness.* Another time he teases Lavater when the pastor intends to "put on Jesus," as the pious were wont to say. Goethe remarks, *every day the scales and fogs are falling from my spirit, so that I think in the end it will stand there, stark naked.*

Goethe grew skeptical about Lavater's faith when it became indistinguishable from banal mysticism. In January 1781, Lavater paid a visit to the adventurer Count Alessandro di Cagliostro (whose real name was Giuseppe Balsamo) in Strasbourg, where he had arrived from Italy. Lavater was taken in by the swindler and wrote to Goethe that Cagliostro was "strength personified." Goethe regarded this as an example of how easily noble willingness to believe could tip over into credulity: *And yet, a fool with strength is so closely related to a rascal. There's nothing I can say.* In fact, he had not only said but written a few things about it—for example, in *A Shrovetide Play of Pater Brey* and in *Satyros, or The Wood-Devil Deified*, where false prophets and their foolish followers are mocked. The fact that Lavater himself was threatening to succumb to a similar swindle provided Goethe an opportunity for a sharp attack on spiritualistic mumbo jumbo. He writes Lavater that he can very well understand how one could feel the need to expand the *narrow limits of the self* into a *Swedenborgian spiritual universe.* For him as a poet, it was in fact a matter of course—but only as a poet. What does the poet do with such a thing? He purifies such upsurges of anything *silly and disgusting* and makes something beautiful of them. Beauty may ensnare and seduce, but there is nothing coercive about it. Beauty proceeds from free play and is addressed to the free person. It requires no subservience, unlike hocus-pocus, which makes people stupid and submissive. Goethe becomes outraged: *What can I say to minds that obey such people, propound such nonsense, and commit such acts?*

He wrote this only a few years before Cagliostro was implicated in the Diamond Necklace Affair, an event which even before the revolution led Goethe to fear the collapse of the ancien régime. Already, he fears the consequences of Cagliostro's meteoric rise. *Believe me,* he writes to Lavater, *our moral and political world is, like a great city, honeycombed with subterranean passages, cellars, and cloaca . . . except that, for the person who has*

*some knowledge of it, it is much more understandable when here the ground col-
lapses, there smoke rises from a crevice, and there strange voices are heard.*

On account of Lavater's credulity, Goethe felt justified in using
heavier artillery against his religious faith. About the pastor's love of
Christ, Goethe wrote how marvelous it was *that an image has remained
to us from ancient times into which you have transported your all and, mirror-
ing yourself in it, can worship yourself.* That was laying it on a bit thick.
Lavater, who acted so humble, was accused of fooling himself. Which
wouldn't be so bad, according to Goethe, if only he would admit it to
himself. Then everyone could revere himself in his own *bird of paradise,*
but he should allow others their birds of paradise and not try to pluck
the most beautiful feathers from them. Everyone can create his own
image of a deified self, and it befits the truly pious to respect creative
freedom in religious matters, too, and acknowledge a whole world of
various birds of paradise. No need for envy.

Goethe thus advocated more tolerance, something Lavater himself
had displayed in abundance. It was not for nothing that Goethe had
repeatedly praised his *liberality.* But it was not the tolerance of others'
beliefs that Goethe increasingly found lacking, for in that regard Lavater was blameless. What annoyed Goethe was a condescending tolerance that sees itself in possession of the truth and others on a false
path. That irritated him to the point that he finally burst out: *Exclusive
intolerance! Forgive me for these harsh words.*

For Goethe, Jesus was an exemplary human being, worthy of love
in the highest degree, a genius of the heart and of devotion, but not
a god—and divine only to the extent that a divine spark exists in
everyone. A human being, nothing more. Goethe did not doubt that
he was a historical figure whose continuing influence arose from his
image in the Gospels. And he attributed their effect not to an act of
revelation but to their power as literature. When Lavater writes so
grippingly about Jesus, that too is only literature and as such—but
only as such—admirable.

But mere literary acknowledgment was not enough for Lavater.
Jesus existed not as a character in a novel. He was not a fictitious carrier
of meaning. Lavater insisted that Jesus did not merely symbolize the
idea of a son of God. He was the son of God, as real, for example, as
the real Goethe in Weimar. But if he was the son of God, then mira-

cles such as walking on water, feeding the five thousand, and the Resurrection were true not merely in a metaphorical sense but factually. For Lavater it all boiled down to the existence of the supernatural as an expression of divine power. Goethe protested. For him, nature was what reveals itself empirically to our five senses; all the rest is speculation and poetry, admirable as an expression of the human spirit, but not part of a realistic image of the world. To regard the supernatural as an actual manifestation of the divine was *a blasphemy against the great God and his revelation in nature.*

Therefore, to the extent that Jesus with all his miracles was supposed to have really existed as the son of God, Goethe declared himself to be *decidedly not a Christian.* That sounds very definitive, and it was meant to. He no longer wished to be importuned by Lavater playing the prophet, and he attempted to lay down the rules for their continued correspondence: *So, let me hear your human voice so that we can stay connected on that side, since it doesn't work from the other side.*

Nevertheless, their conversation about religion continued. Goethe may have been annoyed at Lavater, but their disputes were also important in consolidating his views on religion. Goethe was feeling his way toward an understanding of religion as natural history and cultural anthropology. *Nature also deserves great thanks,* he writes, *for placing so much healing power into the existence of every living being, so that if it be torn at one end or the other, it can patch itself back together again; and what are the thousands of religions but the thousandfold expressions of this healing power. My sticking plaster doesn't work for you, nor yours for me. In our Father's pharmacy are many prescriptions.* Thus religion is a spiritual and at the same time natural means of healing man's inwardly riven nature. That means we have no need of a transcendent God; it is the better nature in us that comes to our aid. This better nature takes on the form of a religion. This is the conclusion that Goethe reached, anticipating a future anthropology that would culminate in the twentieth century in Arnold Gehlen and Helmuth Plessner's thesis that man is a deficient being, by nature dependent on culture. That culture includes what Goethe called *healing power.*

So much for the anthropological line of thought. In the same letter, Goethe develops a psychological perspective as well. Belief—any belief—is in and of itself opaque. Whoever believes doesn't really know what it is within him that believes. In any event, it is something else than what the believer—believes. Especially in questions of belief, man finds himself in his own blind spot. *What man notices and feels about himself seems to me the smallest part of his existence.* Consciousness is not the same as consciously being. It is always lesser than one's own being. It was a brilliant insight, stated here almost offhandedly, but later more emotionally formulated. In the essay *Morphology* he declares, *I hereby confess that the great and so weighty-sounding adage "know thyself" has always seemed suspect to me.* In the letter to Lavater, he was already saying that one *shrivels up* in the attempt to fathom oneself. Why? Because you are more likely to notice what you lack and what causes pain than what you possess and are supported by. It is above all our deficiencies that we are conscious of, not our riches. The ordinary, popular religions are fantastic compensation for the deficiencies we are conscious of, and that is why they are superficial. Religion would reach deeper if it was the expression of the experience of plenitude. If Goethe feels empathy for a religion, it is—as we will later see in the collection of poems *West-Eastern Divan*—a religion of fullness, abundance, and affirmation.

After the long letter of October 4, 1782, the correspondence gradually petered out. The very last letter is again a remarkable one. In December 1783, Goethe wrote to Zurich that his friendship with Herder had been repaired. One amicable bond comes undone and another is stitched back together again. From then on, Goethe discusses religious issues primarily with Herder and Jacobi, with whom he had also been reconciled, while Lavater disappears from his life.

On July 21, 1786, Lavater visited Goethe for the last time in Weimar. They had little left to say to each other. Goethe wrote to Charlotte von Stein, *We exchanged not a single cordial, intimate word, and I am free of hate and love forever. . . . I have also drawn a large line under his existence and now know what remains of him on balance.* Lavater sensed the alienation as well and wrote to an acquaintance, "I found Goethe older, colder, wiser, stiffer, more incommunicative, more practical."

Ten years later, in the fall of 1797, there was a last encounter—which wasn't really an encounter at all. During Goethe's third journey to Switzerland, he saw Lavater approaching down a street in Zurich. Goethe crossed to the other side to avoid a meeting. Lavater passed by without recognizing him. *His gait was like a crane's,* was all Goethe had to say about it.

CHAPTER 16

Peace and Granite. Reconciliation with Jacobi.
Reading Spinoza. Spinoza, Lessing, Jacobi, and the
"Prometheus" poem: *tinder for an explosion.*
Naturalism and Idealism: Opposing or Merging.
Jacobi's Philosophy of Religion and Goethe's Nature Study.
The Intermaxillary Bone. Reconciliation with Herder.

. . . .

BACK FROM SWITZERLAND, GOETHE AGAIN THREW HIMSELF into his official duties. In April 1780, Kalb left the mining commission and, as its chairman, Goethe assumed responsibility for the silver mines in Ilmenau. He began to study minerology to increase his technical expertise—thus at first for purely practical reasons—but he soon fell under the spell of a world that proceeded with steady, slow persistence in contrast to the surging fluidity of inner experience. *Thousands and thousands of thoughts rise and fall within me. My soul is like an everlastingly restless firework,* he wrote to Charlotte von Stein. But in nature, in the world of minerals and especially of granite, he believed he had found peace, even if, as he wrote in the draft essay "Granite I," some poets foolishly claim to see in it *an image of discordantly raging chaos.* When we descend into the self, we lose our grounding. Nothing is stable; everything is moving. The granite we find in the earth, however, provides a reliable base, a *foundation.*

The 1784 text on granite gives ample evidence of the desire that motivated Goethe's nature study: *And thus anyone familiar with the allure that the secrets of nature hold for us humans will not be surprised that I have left the sphere of observation that I formerly inhabited and, with a quite passionate inclination, have turned to this one. I do not fear the reproach that it must be the spirit of contradiction that has led me from the contemplation and depiction of the human heart—the newest, most diverse, mobile, changeable, and fragile part of creation—to the observation of the oldest, firmest, deepest, most immovable son of nature. . . . I, who suffer and have suffered much from the vagaries of human sentiments, their rapid fluctuations within myself and others, I ask for the sublime peace granted by the solitary, mute proximity of great, soft-spoken nature, and let everyone who has an inkling of it join me.*

The *rapid fluctuations* of his mind have been a source of suffering, he writes. But they have also caused suffering in others as did, for example, his public ridicule of Fritz Jacobi's novel *Woldemar* shortly before the journey to Switzerland. Jacobi had written him as soon as he got wind of the "crucifixion of Woldemar" and asked for an explanation, since he didn't want to rely on rumors. Goethe did not answer the letter, although his friend had written that he would have to regard silence as a confirmation of what he had heard. What was Goethe to write? He could not and would not deny what he had done. The novel had displeased him and still did. Would he lose a friend on that account? He found himself in a dilemma that might have been less painful if he had known what Jacobi told "Aunty" Johanna Schlosser. The entire affair, he wrote her, had "made the character of this pompous dandy a good deal more loathsome and contemptable. I shall turn my back on him forever, as almost all upright men of our country have long since done. . . . I thank God that our friendship is at an end." If Goethe had learned of this condemnation, it would likely have caused no dilemma but destroyed his inner tie to Jacobi for good.

As it was, there was no contact between them for the next three years, when Goethe's conscience was awakened by the Schlossers and his mother reminding him that Jacobi had lent him money for the move to Weimar and had never been repaid. Because of this debt, Goethe broke his silence and asked for forgiveness: *When we get older and the world closes in, then of course we sometimes painfully recall the occasions when, to pass the time, we forfeited friendships and in reckless high spirits could not feel the wounds we caused or think of healing them.*

Jacobi's wound was healed the instant he received Goethe's letter. He promptly replied, "I always interpreted to your advantage the fact that you hadn't paid me back yet. What I had recognized in you was

deep and inextinguishable." This ushered in a renewal of their correspondence and their friendship blossomed again, but within limits that
Goethe described in retrospect: *we loved each other without understanding
each other. I could no longer grasp the language of his philosophy.*

At first, after their reconciliation, he grasped it quite well. When
Jacobi visited Weimar for a week in September 1784, they talked
about Spinoza. Jacobi, who was preparing a publication about the
Dutch philosopher that would later cause great public furor and some
private irritation between the two friends, now reawakened Goethe's
old love for Spinoza. They had already spoken about him during
their first lengthy time together, in 1775. Jacobi had never forgotten
Goethe's enthusiastic comments during those discussions, in which
Lavater had participated. Lavater later wrote down Goethe's remarks;
they had less to do with Spinoza's philosophy than with his person.
Goethe called him a *homo temperatissimus,* an *extremely fair, honest, poor
man.* Inspired by Jacobi, Goethe studied Spinoza's *Ethics* with Charlotte von Stein, whom he talked into the difficult undertaking. In the
long evening hours, they read Spinoza together, sentence by sentence.
Whenever Goethe wanted to understand something thoroughly, he
needed to talk about it. Learning by teaching was also his method
in this case; now he felt *very close* to Spinoza, *although his mind is much
deeper and purer than mine.*

Thus it was Jacobi who led Goethe back to Spinoza in the fall of
1784. Less than a year later, Goethe would have to defend the rediscovered Spinoza against Jacobi in the great controversy stirred up by the
latter's publication on the philosopher.

When Goethe first read him in 1773 and 1774, Spinoza was considered an infamous, dangerous atheist, a heretic of the worst kind. People didn't read him; they merely cited him as a cautionary example.
Goethe had not yet read him either when, in 1770, he dismissed his
philosophy as *vile heresy* even though he himself was moving toward a
pantheism that made him almost an unconscious Spinozist.

The seventeenth-century philosopher, a descendant of Jewish merchants in Amsterdam, equated God with nature. For him, revelation
occurred in nature, not in some sacred text. God was not outside the
world, he was in the world—the world's "substance," as Spinoza calls
it. Humans themselves are part of this substance, although they do not

want to acknowledge it. How can one achieve conscious participation? By following the path of rigorous thought and not by a pious acceptance of supernatural inspiration. Thinking "more geometrico"—in a geometric manner—as Spinoza calls it, is an ascetic discipline. Rigorous, free of vanity and showmanship, the thinker merges with the object of his thought in order to do it justice. You must first disregard yourself in order to see things aright, and only then can you return, enriched, to yourself. Without being religious, this ascetic thinking has a religious aspect. It was likely this piety of thought that held such a strong attraction for the young Goethe when he called Spinoza a *homo temperatissimus*. Spinoza himself had clearly enunciated the character of his philosophizing at the beginning of his essay "On the Improvement of the Understanding." Experience had taught him, he wrote, that everything making up the usual contents of life is vain and worthless. Therefore he had decided to investigate whether there was some true good through which a person could experience lasting, complete joy. For him, wealth, honor, and sensual pleasure were not part of this true good, for they are transitory, ephemeral, unstable, and make us dependent. Stability is achieved only by perceiving the unity that joins the mind to all of nature.

It was a daring thought, for the traditional intellectual edifices that Spinoza opposed were not self-supporting structures. If the premises of Christianity or Judaism cease to be felt as reality, everything collapses. In both traditions, belief has universal received truths, which human reason then reproduces. Stability is found in belief, but also in the institutions, traditions, and rituals by which the entire collective history of faith is reinforced. The old belief was an experience of communal, mutual self-reinforcement, not isolated, solitary introspection. Spinoza forwent the support of communal belief and religious community. The Jewish congregation of Amsterdam persecuted him as a heretic and threatened his life. He withdrew and earned his living as a lens grinder.

Is the perception of the unity of mind with all of nature really capable of supporting one's life and lending it peace and even happiness? Goethe asked this question. It can probably be answered only by trying to understand Spinoza's views. For him, thought and perception have the power to free us from fear. In Christian metaphysics, there is no such trust in the redemptive power of thinking. In Christianity, only love can overcome the fear of the world; the Creator's love is the basis for trust in the world. Just as divine love created the world out of nothingness, the experience of being loved and affirmed protects us from nothingness. In comparison with such a belief, trust in thought is secondary. Spinoza, however, puts his complete trust in thought. To be sure, love is also involved. But he does not believe in a transcendent source of love. For him, the perception of the world, the reflection of its entirety in the human mind, is in some sense an act of love. "Divine love," of which Spinoza also speaks, is nothing more than the act of perception. In perception, consciousness merges with being. That is the great confluence in which the essence of "substance" becomes clear: substance comprehends spirit and matter, the two sides of a single nature. Mind does not stand in opposition to nature. One could say it is the other condition of nature; it is that part of nature that is conscious of itself. Except for this substantial nature, which is at the same time extensive and thinking, there is nothing. How could there be? God is not beyond or outside the world. He is all nature. "Deus sive substantia sive natura" in Spinoza's formulation: God or substance or nature.

It all depends on how we regard nature—as a realm of freedom or of necessity. Creationism sees nature as a product of freedom, for God created it voluntarily, not because he had to. And nature is not a self-perpetuating mechanism, but remains dependent on the inflow of God's grace. Man, himself a part of creation, can and must behave accordingly. Human freedom can respond to divine freedom.

But that's not how things work for Spinoza. For him, nature is a universe of necessity. The consciousness of freedom is an illusion. He declares that it is as if a stone would believe it fell to earth of its own free will. Everything happens from causality. Even what happens within and between men is determined by it, without exception. The causal nexus is not based on a goal. There are no final causes, processes that happen because they have a goal in mind. That is why it makes no sense to ask what the purpose of nature is. But it is also misleading to believe that humans act with intention and have a goal in mind. Superficially, it looks as if they do, but in reality, people have intentions because causality is urging them on behind their backs. The thirty-second theorem in part 1 of Spinoza's *Ethics* (probably the only work of Spinoza's that Goethe ever read) states, "Will cannot be called a free cause, but only a necessary cause. . . . therefore . . . no volition can exist, nor be conditioned to act, unless it be conditioned by some cause other than itself, which cause is conditioned by a third cause, and so on to infinity."*

The denial of final causes and the idea of the world as a mechanism would become powerful sources of the nineteenth century's materialistic image of nature. Supplemented by some dynamic components, it has remained the dominant image of the world to the present day, a world that gets along with no God at all. Even the act of cognition is no longer, as it still was for Spinoza, in the service of God, but follows practical considerations of usefulness and domination.

Although it still includes some residual religious warmth, the image of nature into which Spinoza thinks his way functions like an inanimate mechanism. It is a place where we can feel at home, because we are made of nature's material and function in the same way. If we "purify" ourselves, free our consciousness from the illusions of imagination and discipline the emotions that prevent a free overview, then we can act in accord with reality and will not be plagued by superfluous fears and worries.

But before the image of nature as an inanimate mechanism became fully solidified in the nineteenth century, Spinoza's residual religious warmth had inspired a pantheism that arose around 1800. One can see this connection in Herder, Goethe, and Schelling. They were all influenced by Spinoza, but needed to restore to the concept of nature a creative life that Spinoza had taken away even though he himself had spoken of the difference between *natura naturans* and *natura naturata* (approximately, "creative nature" and "incarnate nature"). But for Spinoza, everything is already completed, a compact whole. The pantheistic currents in Herder, Goethe, and Schelling emphasize the aspect of development. For them, being is a constant becoming. For Spinoza, becoming is actually a rounded being, nothing more than the temporal unfolding of what is always already collected in substance.

Let us see what Goethe takes from his reading of Spinoza. During

---

* Benedict de Spinoza, *The Ethics (Ethica Ordine Geometrico Demonstrata)*, trans. R. H. M. Elwes, available at http://www.gutenberg.org/files/3800/3800-h/3800-h.htm.

their joint study of Spinoza's *Ethics* in the late fall of 1784, Goethe dictated some thoughts to Charlotte.

First, he records the idea that eternity does not belong to the sphere of some divine, transcendent paradise. No, it begins with every concrete object and state of affairs: if we become involved in it, we are transported without transition into the eternity and enormity that unfathomably surround and enclose us. Each object and living being, however, has its restricted place therein. That is obvious, of course, yet Goethe emphasizes it, apparently because he is especially eager to assert the existence of limits within infinity. Instead of one great intermingling, everything should retain its own center and particular outline. Everything that exists is, on the one hand, determined from within and, on the other, limitlessly determinable from without. Goethe is interested in the balance between inner formative powers and the susceptibility to formation from without. Spinoza is concerned with universal laws, but Goethe emphasizes the law of the individual. *We cannot think that a limited being exists in and of itself, and yet everything really does exist in and of itself, although its circumstances are so interlinked that one person must develop from others, and thus it seems that one thing is produced by another, which however is not the case, but rather one living being gives another the occasion to be and, in a particular condition, compels it to exist.* Goethe takes up Spinoza's idea of the "deus sive natura" (God or nature) but directs our gaze from the whole back to the individual. The individual being or thing, with its distinctive significance, must not be drowned in the whole. This insistence on the distinctive significance of the individual distinguishes him from Spinoza, of whom he says, *in his view all individual things seem to disappear.*

The second thought that Goethe emphasizes from his reading of Spinoza proceeds from this reflection on the topic of limits in the midst of limitlessness. In his text, he states that there is a danger that someone will close the *circle* around himself and *in defiant modesty* let it be known that *in the truth he has found a security transcending all proof and understanding.* Here Goethe is thinking of the pious who explain the world to themselves from a few articles of faith and think they can dispense with the effort of cognition by claiming that one needs only to become *more and more simple* and *renounce all multifarious, confusing conditions.* One should not withdraw into one's faith when much still remains to be done in order to understand. Such self-restriction is unworthy of a thinking being. In a final ironic remark, however, he notes that perhaps it is a *blessing* that *nature has* made limited people *content with their narrowness.*

Goethe places no special emphasis on the idea of necessity, which governs Spinoza's work. He said all he needed to say on that subject in a letter to Knebel: *Nature's consistency compensates beautifully for man's inconsistency.* He does not get entangled in a tedious discussion of the problem of free will. The stoic composure Spinoza derives from the concept of necessity is enough for Goethe. He admires the calm that comes with it and wishes some would rub off on him. That is why he sometimes reads Spinoza *with the greatest edification as my bedtime prayer.*

As already mentioned, it was Jacobi who put Goethe back onto Spinoza. Goethe knew that his friend was preparing to publish something on the philosopher. What he didn't know was that he himself would make an involuntary contribution to that publication with his previously unpublished ode "Prometheus" (*Cover your heaven, Zeus*). Goethe describes the effect of the Prometheus poem in book 15 of *Poetry and Truth*, where he writes that this innocent poem served *as tinder for an explosion that opened to discussion the most private relations of worthy men, relations they themselves were not conscious of, although they slumbered in an otherwise highly enlightened society. The disruption was so powerful that, because of accidental occurrences, we lost Mendelssohn, one of the worthiest of our men.*

Jacobi's *On the Teachings of Spinoza in Letters to Herr Moses Mendelssohn* appeared in the fall of 1785.

The work had a complicated genesis, but the salient point was that in the summer of 1780, Jacobi had had an extensive conversation with Gotthold Ephraim Lessing shortly before Lessing's death. In it, the playwright had declared himself an adherent of Spinoza. According to Jacobi's report, Lessing had said, "The orthodox concepts of the divinity aren't for me anymore. I cannot enjoy them. *Hen kai pan* [One and All]! That is all I know." Jacobi replied, "Then you would be pretty much in agreement with Spinoza." Lessing: "If I must call myself after someone, I know of no other."

Jacobi had heard that Mendelssohn intended to write a work about the character of his deceased friend Lessing, and sent him an inquiry asking whether he knew that in his final days, Lessing had been "a decided Spinozist." Mendelssohn, himself an avowed deist and strong opponent of pantheism, was extremely upset and asked Jacobi for more information. Jacobi composed a report of his conversation with Lessing and sent it to him. Jacobi then heard from people close to Mendelssohn that it would be better to "conceal" Lessing's Spinozism as far "as the sacredness of truth allows." For Spinoza was still regarded as a dangerous heretic, an atheistic wolf in pantheistic sheep's clothing. Until then, the sole German translation of Spinoza's *Ethics* could appear only disguised as an anti-Spinoza polemic by the philosopher Christian Wolff. And now Lessing was supposed to be a Spinozist! Among the educated public it caused a sensation—even a scandal. Of course, Lessing was known as a free spirit and original thinker with his own understanding of Christianity, but he was assumed to believe in a personal God. At least Mendelssohn assumed it. But whoever declared his allegiance to Spinoza was denying God's existence as man's counterpart, a transcendent, personal power one could pray to and who could be merciful or not. God in the Spinozist sense is nothing more than the epitome of everything that is and works through causality.

Mendelssohn had reacted to Jacobi's letter with hesitation and temporizing. He had promised an extensive answer and clarification of the matter, but failed to deliver. So Jacobi finally published his own work in 1785. Only then did Mendelssohn compose a long response entitled "To Lessing's Friends," in which he defended his deceased friend against what he considered the slanderous accusation of Spinozism—for him the equivalent of atheism. Before the work was published, Mendelssohn died—from anger and distress, it was said. It was also said that Jacobi had him on his conscience. That is what Goethe is alluding to in *Poetry and Truth*. In reality, Mendelssohn had contracted a bad cold when he took his manuscript to the publisher in January 1786, and that was what killed him.

Lessing's profession of Spinozism had been a spontaneous reaction to Goethe's unpublished poem "Prometheus," which Jacobi had shown him. Lessing's declaration that the orthodox concepts of divinity were no longer for him was an expression of agreement with the poem, whose daring self-empowerment is a defiant rejection of the gods in heaven: *You'll have to leave my earth / Alone. . . . / I know nothing so pitiful / Under the sun as you gods.*

Jacobi had published his work on Spinoza, and included the poem without Goethe's permission. It irritated Goethe all the more because the overly cautious Jacobi explicitly mentioned the possibility of censorship and therefore had the poem inserted as a loose, unbound sheet along with a set of instructions: "The poem Prometheus . . . has been printed separately so that anyone who would prefer not to have it in his copy of the book does not need to. . . . It is not entirely impossible that in one place or another, my work will be confiscated on account of Prometheus. I hope that in such places, people will be satisfied to remove only the culpable sheet."

"The culpable sheet"? Goethe was outraged by the phrase even if he understood his friend's tactical calculation. At first, however, he was at pains to look on the lighter side of the affair. *Herder finds it amusing that on this occasion, I'm to sit on the same funeral pyre as Lessing,* he writes to Jacobi.

In his book, Jacobi had not only developed his own religious philosophy but presented Spinoza's philosophy in such a comprehensible way that the reading public was not quite sure that Jacobi wasn't a Spinozist himself. The work not only made the poem "Prometheus" known but also restored Spinoza's philosophy to a wider public. From this point on, it represented the significant intellectual possibility of a spiritualized naturalism, an indispensable source for the creative development of philosophy in the following decades. With the appearance of Jacobi's book on Spinoza, the year 1785 became an important date in the history of German idealism.

On the one hand, there was natural philosophy's way of seeing things. Its starting point was nature, and from there it sought to comprehend the entirety of the perceptible world. Some viewed nature as a blindly functioning mechanism; others like Herder and Goethe saw it as a universally animating principle, a vital, dynamic nature as opposed to a mechanical nature. Common to both views, however, was their point of departure in objective reality, a nature accessible to external observation.

In contrast to these partisans of objectivity were others who sought their starting point in the self-awareness of the subjective mind. The extreme case was Johann Gottlieb Fichte. For him, the model for the inner dynamics of the world and natural processes was the free creative will that revealed itself in self-consciousness. But starting with the subjective mind could also lead in different directions. Jacobi, for example, sees the experience of faith as central, while for Fichte it is thought and reflection on it. Nevertheless, their common starting point is in subjectivity, not in nature.

So that is the great divide. Some begin with nature and, if they escape naturalism, end up at the subjective mind. Others begin with mind and, if they don't get lost in the world of ideas, end up at a nature suffused with mind. Put another way, some fetch the mind into nature, others fetch nature into the mind. But things develop that way only if the two directions do not become rigidly opposed to each other, with the result that some get stuck in a naturalism remote from the spirit and others get stuck in an idealism remote from reality. This definitive opposition, however, is what Jacobi expects: "There are only two philosophies that are essentially different from each other. I will call them Platonism and Spinozism. One can choose between these two, i.e., can be gripped by one or the other, so that one must adhere to it alone, consider it the sole spirit of truth." Fichte formulates the alternatives in a similar way: "These are the only two philosophical systems . . . possible . . . . Neither of these two systems can directly refute its opposite . . . each rejects everything about its opposite, and they have no point in common from which they could agree and unite with each other."

That is not the way it would play out, however. The stimulating intellectual activity of the following decades would be aimed at precisely such a union of nature and spirit. Schelling and Hegel, particularly, would search for syntheses wherein nature could be understood as unconscious mind and mind as conscious nature. Goethe, too, was part of this great movement toward unifying mind and nature.

Jacobi, however, put no stock in such a union. He was convinced that the reckoning, measuring mind, proceeding with strict logic and empiricism, would never cross the boundaries of immanence. He argued for an expanded concept of reason. He asked whether reason was identical to the logical and empirical operations of the mind, and he answered: no. For reason contains a component of being able to hear. Every day—and especially as children—we depend on what we receive and believe on faith. Faith is the main thing. Since we know so little ourselves, we must have faith in the knowledge of others. As a rule, we are believing confidants. We even have to believe in our own knowledge if it is to have the power to determine our lives. Knowledge not connected to the power of belief is pale, disappears quickly, and is forgotten. Faith is fundamentally vital. We cannot dispense with it, even in matters of knowledge, much less in all other areas of life. Jacobi challenges the idea that faith plays a role only in the realm of religion—in our relation to God—as a great misunderstanding. Faith is at work in every personal relationship. Not only does faith connect us to what is utterly other—i.e., God—but only in faith can we adequately encounter what is familiar but other: our fellow human beings. We call it trust. Jacobi's philosophy is an attempt to designate faith as the basis for experience, knowledge, and thought. Spinoza, who represented a completely different type of thought, was for him an opponent of the very first order, which is why Jacobi could follow his thought with such great understanding. He did not want to make it easy for himself. He intended faith to stand its ground against a truly great adversary.

In the battle of faith against the pretentions of knowledge, Jacobi found no ally in Goethe, however. At first, the latter restricted himself to a few trenchant remarks: Spinoza *does not prove God's existence. Existence is God.* And, *Forgive me that I prefer to remain silent when there is talk of a divine being, which I recognize only in rebus singularibus.* But Jacobi pressed him, and so he expressed his opinion at last: *Forgive me for not writing more to you about your little book! I don't mean to seem either lofty or indifferent. You know that in this matter, I am not of your opinion. . . . Nor can I approve of how you use the word "faith." I cannot allow you to get away with this manner; it's only suited to sophists of faith, whose greatest interest must be to obscure and wrap in the clouds of their wobbly, breezy realm all certainty of knowledge, since they are unable to shake the foundations of truth.*

As he wrote this letter to Jacobi, Goethe was discovering *the foundations of truth* in the study of natural history, to which he now diligently devoted himself. In a later conversation reported by Goethe's friend Friedrich von Müller, who became chancellor of the grand duchy in 1815, he described this development: *I came to Weimar quite ignorant of*

---

* Latin: individual things.

all nature study, and only the need to give the duke practical advice in his various undertakings—construction projects, parks—drove me to study nature. Ilmenau cost me much time, trouble, and money, but in exchange I also learned something and acquired a conception of nature that I would not trade at any price.

In the Sturm und Drang period, we recall, the concept of nature was a watchword, a confession of faith. Werther vacillates between fervent immersion in nature and repellent coldness. In the hymn "Ganymede," nature is *Enfolding enfolded*, but the poem "Divinity" declares, *For nature / Is unfeeling*. Now Goethe attempts to overcome this emotional fluctuation and arrive at a sober, objective, and pragmatic attitude. But that does not mean that he keeps nature at arm's length like some foreign object. It is the organs of sensation—the nature of his own body, if one will—that are expected to connect him to external nature. He wants to enter into a living exchange with it. In so doing, he is quite prepared to discipline his use of those organs through empirical research. Observation, perception, is everything, but it must be controlled observation and verified perception. He is suspicious of speculation and abstraction that have become unmoored from a grounding in empirical experience. That is what he meant when he wrote to the duke of Saxony-Gotha in late 1780 that *the observing concept is vastly preferable to the academic one.*

Goethe wrote this letter at the first stage of his nature studies and still drew a stark contrast between the observing and the academic concept. As he worked his way into the individual disciplines, however, he no longer divorced himself so strictly from academics, but advocated a science supported by observation. His ideal was the careful observer. In the same letter he wrote, *May neither legend nor history, neither theory nor opinion keep him from looking.* One should not approach nature with too many preconceptions, or the clear view will get lost. But having no idea doesn't work either, for then one sees nothing at all. For him, the idea of development is a guiding principle—the notion that nature too has a history. At the time, that was by no means self-evident. He is fascinated by the fossils he finds imprinted in rocks. He digs them up and collects them. He investigates geologic layers in the Harz and the nearer surroundings of Weimar, and they tell him the history of the earth. Later he would become an adherent of Neptunism, the theory that rocks were formed gradually by crystallization from the waters of a primeval sea, but now he was quite open to the drama of Plutonism, the theory that rocks such as granite were formed by solidification from the molton state: *Now if one assumes that the volcanoes continue to the right up to Cassel and then farther to the left to Frankfurt and even Andernach, it would then be most interesting to investigate whether and how the enormous volcanic fury of this large stretch of country was broken by the unshakable bedrock of the Thuringian Forest, which resisted it like some enormous dam.* Typical Goethe—his home country around Weimar is presumed to have played the geologic role of finally arresting all that volcanic activity! A very energetic genius loci was obviously at work.

Goethe also pursued studies in the field of comparative anatomy. That was the specialty of the physician Justus Christian Loder, for whom Goethe obtained an appointment to the University of Jena in order to have him nearby. From November 1781 to January 1782, Goethe delivered a series of lectures at the Weimar Academy of Art on human skeletal structure, in which he treated the bones *as a text to which all life and everything human can be attached,* as he wrote to Lavater. Here too, the guiding principle was history, the idea of the great chain of being. More precisely, it was the question of the steps by which man developed out of the animal kingdom. In order to complete the progression of forms, he was still missing the intermaxillary bone found in the apes but apparently not in humans. Goethe surmised that it regressed in the human fetal stage. In March 1784, he was sent the skull of a human embryo, on which he found a barely visible suture that he interpreted as the trace of an intermaxillary bone. *I feel such joy that all my innards are in turmoil,* he writes to Charlotte, and to Herder, *I have found—neither gold nor silver, but something that gives me untold joy—the os intermaxillare in a human! . . . You will be heartily pleased as well, for it is like the capstone to man.* Experts were skeptical at first, although another researcher in France had already postulated the existence of an intermaxillary bone in the human fetus. Only Loder included Goethe's discovery in his *Manual of Anatomy.* Subsequently, Goethe investigated the rhinoceros's horn and even had an elephant skull sent to him. He hid it in his room so the housekeeper didn't think him mad.

If nature had a history, it also meant that nature was by no means complete. History continues, in both nature and mankind. That man can open his eyes and recognize that fact is the latest chapter in human history. Nature has created within us an organ of cognition so that it can see and perceive itself. This act of perception is almost a love affair for Goethe. Hence his insistence on the use of the senses. *I think a scholar by profession is capable of denying his five senses. They are seldom interested in the living idea, but only in what has been said about it,* he writes to Merck.

Knowledge of nature is part of the whole person and therefore remains connected to other inclinations and skills such as drawing and writing poetry. Goethe used his drawing talent to sketch and classify landscape forms, types of minerals and flowers, and anatomical relationships in humans and animals. In his letters from 1782 on, he talks of plans to write a *novel of the universe.* Perhaps the text about granite, quoted above, was to become a chapter of such a *novel.*

For Goethe, poetry and cognition were not as separate as they would become in later academic culture. As both a poet and a naturalist, he strove for truth that was grounded in the evidence of the senses. Later, while working on the *Theory of Color,* in which he quarrels with Newton, he would bluster against apparatuses that refract light: it was necessary to free *phenomena . . . once and for all from the gloomy, empirical-mechanical-dogmatic torture chamber.* And he would write to Zelter in 1808, *Man on his own, to the extent that he makes use of his own healthy senses, is the greatest and most precise physical apparatus there can be.* For the time being, however, he was happy for the support of observational prosthetic devices such as telescopes and microscopes. A microscope enabled him to observe protozoa, which he was at times very keen on. Some people made fun of this new passion, but he gave back as good as he got. *What are you up to, you old metaphysician?* he asks Jacobi, and continues, *If you needed any protozoa I could supply you with a few million.* And another time, he writes him ironically, *However, God has also chastised you with metaphysics like a thorn in the flesh, me on the other hand he has blessed with physics, so that I find comfort in the contemplation of his works.*

As Goethe became more absorbed in the study of natural science, he again drew closer to Herder. He had brought Herder to Weimar in 1776, then became increasingly alienated from him. Although Herder had a well-paid position as the highest ecclesiastical official in the duchy, he was dissatisfied with it. His connections to the court were not as close as Goethe's, nor did he cultivate them, retreating instead into lofty resentment. He was hurt that both the duke and Goethe

hardly ever attended his church services and scarcely concerned themselves with or budgeted enough money for the Weimar schools, which
Herder supervised. For instance, the establishment of an academy
for teacher training had long since been approved, but Herder's frequent reminders to begin the project were to no avail. He felt personally insulted. Moreover, he had expected the position in Weimar to
be more of an honorary sinecure that would leave him ample time for
his writing. Goethe had made him promises to that effect, but things
had not turned out that way. Herder was overwhelmed with official
duties, and his literary production ground to a halt. He was embittered
and feared that his best years were being squandered. He regarded with
envy the career of Goethe, a man whom in the past he had patronized
and treated like his pupil.

For a while, Goethe had accepted that role and allowed Herder to
play the "master." But with the younger man's breakthrough as a writer
in 1774, their positions began to reverse. In Weimar, Goethe was dominant and Herder felt he had been demoted. In 1782, he wrote bitterly of
Goethe to his friend Hamann, "So now he is really a privy councilor,
finance director, chairman of the military commission, supervisor of
construction down to the level of road building, and in addition director of recreations, court poet, the author of pretty festivities, court
operas, ballets, masquerades, inscriptions, works of art, etc., director
of the academy of graphic art where during the winter he delivered
lectures on osteology; is himself everywhere the first actor, dancer—in
short, the factotum of Weimar and, God willing, soon the major domo
of the entire Ernestine branch of the House of Wettin, among whom
he circulates in order to be idolized. He has been made a baron, and
on his birthday . . . his ennoblement will be announced. He has moved
from his garden into the city and maintains a noble household, gives
readings that will soon turn into assemblies, etc. etc. In the face of all
that, official business here has to look after itself. My presence is almost
useless and becomes more irritating to me every day. Whoever knows
of a position elsewhere longs to leave . . ."

Goethe made overtures to Herder in the summer of 1783. As he had
before leaving for Switzerland, he felt the need for purification and clarification of personal relations—as when, a few months earlier, he had
reestablished contact with Jacobi and written to the Kestners after a

long silence, once again apologizing for the trouble he had caused them with *Werther.* Now it was time to renew his friendship with Herder.

Herder was ready for reconciliation. Dissatisfied with himself, he felt his creative powers stagnating, and he was contemplating a large work on cultural anthropology and natural history. It was a great aspiration, for there had been nothing of the kind since Giambattista Vico. He had hesitated, but now felt that he could accomplish such a thing. He had overcome his crisis of confidence and was able to write fluently again, and so could confront his old friend with self-confidence. Goethe, in devoting himself to the study of nature, was interested in the material that also absorbed Herder. He read the great work, *Ideas on the Philosophy of the History of Mankind,* as it was being composed, chapter by chapter, so filled with the work that he shared his enthusiasm with Charlotte von Stein. She in turn told Knebel, "Herder's new book makes it probable that we were first plants, then animals; how nature will mold us in the future will likely remain unknown. Goethe is now ruminating deeply on these things, and everything becomes extremely interesting once it has passed through his imagination. That's how he made me feel about his ugly bones and the dreary world of stones."

Both Goethe and Herder were exhilarated by their renewed friendship. They had much to say to each other and devoted themselves without envy to conversation about works and deeds. Herder wrote to Jacobi, "Goethe visits me often and I find his company a refreshing balm." And Goethe wrote to Lavater, *One of the most outstanding joys of my life is that Herder and I no longer have anything standing between us to divide us. If I weren't so adamantly reticent, it would all have been resolved sooner, but now it will last.*

But it was not to be forever. The friendship lasted ten years, then Goethe met Schiller and another great friendship began.

CHAPTER 17

Should He Stay in Weimar? Difficulties of a Double Existence.
The Origins of *Tasso*. Ineffectual Offices. Crisis.
The Complete Works: A Graveyard of Fragments?
Goethe Wants to Change His Life. The Escape to Italy
as a Test of Self. The Risks. Departure in Secret.

. . . .

IN SEPTEMBER 1780, GOETHE WROTE THAT HE WANTED *TO RAISE
up as high as possible the pyramid* of his existence. Though he was confident he could do that in the service of the duke, complaints about the
latter accumulate over the following year in his letters to Charlotte
von Stein. The duke was a good fellow, he wrote, cordial and open,
but lacked refinement. His interests—hunting, skirt chasing, traips-
ing through the woods, playing at soldiering, giving orders, political
scheming in Berlin—were far from Goethe's own. He remained loyally devoted to the duke because he valued him as a human being who,
in his own way, knew what was right and did it; yet he sometimes
doubted that Weimar was the right place for him. Goethe may have
only wanted to alarm Charlotte and make her beg him to stay. And
perhaps she wrote him such a letter, but since her side of the correspondence was destroyed we shall never know.

Other friends had the impression that life in Weimar didn't particularly suit Goethe anymore. Wieland thought he was losing weight, to
Herder he seemed dissatisfied, and people found him stiff and frosty at
court. Some who thought they had been prevented from advancement
wished him gone.

Merck in Darmstadt, who had last visited Weimar in 1780, was also
convinced that his friend had held out at court long enough. Instead
of confronting him directly, Merck voiced his concerns to Goethe's

mother in Frankfurt, who, greatly worried, wrote her son that Merck had told her to do everything possible "to fetch Him back here, the Infamous climate there is certainly not healthy for Him—He has accomplished the main thing there—the duke is now as He should be, and somebody else can do the rest of the dirty business. Goethe is too good for that etc."

Goethe sometimes called Merck his *Mephistopheles*, and he was quite irritated by his friend's solicitude this time. In July 1781, he wrote to Charlotte, *an evil genius . . . depicts the most troublesome side of my condition and advises me to save myself by fleeing.* Goethe seems to have had no intention of actually leaving and was incensed when others suggested he might. In the same letter, he even told Charlotte that she and he were as good as *married* and how could he think of flight under those circumstances? Five weeks later, he summed up his earlier and current life in a momentous letter to his mother, explaining why he was so determined to remain in Weimar: *I ask you to have no concerns on my account and not let anything mislead you. My health is much better than I previously could think and hope, and since it will be sufficient to do at least the greater part of what weighs upon me, I certainly have reason to be satisfied with it. As far as my situation itself is concerned, despite great difficulties there is also much therein that is desirable to me. The best proof is that I cannot think of another situation to which I would rather go at present. For I don't find it very seemly to yearn with hypochondriacal discomfort to exchange one's skin for another. Merk [sic] and others assess my condition quite wrongly; they see only what I'm sacrificing and not the benefits I'm gaining, and they cannot understand that I am daily enriched by daily giving so much of myself.*

He goes on to elaborate those benefits. He doesn't mean good income or creature comforts. They were a matter of course. The benefits are in the development of his personality. *You recall the last time I spent with you before coming here. If such circumstances had persisted, I would certainly have gone to the dogs. The disparity between the narrow, slow-moving bourgeois circle and the range and speed of my nature would have driven me wild. Despite my vivid imagination and intuition for human things, I would still have been unacquainted with the world and would have remained in an everlasting childhood which—mostly through conceit and all related errors—becomes unbearable to oneself and others.*

Frankfurt, the free imperial city with a robust economic life, the city where the emperor was elected and crowned—Frankfurt was *narrow* compared with Weimar? That was news. What he must have meant was that everything in Frankfurt was too familiar and his path in life predetermined. At any rate, Frankfurt lacked real challenges, and so Goethe's quick and capacious nature was *driven . . . wild.* His imagination displaced his sense of reality. Inwardly rich but *unacquainted with the world,* he ran the danger of *conceit.* The move to Weimar rescued him from all that. *How much more fortunate it was to see myself placed in circumstances for which no part of me was prepared, where frequent errors of comprehension and haste gave me plenty of opportunity to get to know myself and others, and where, left to myself and fate, I went through so many tests that I was sorely in need of for my education, although for hundreds of others they might not be necessary. And even now, given the way I am, how could I wish for a happier situation than one that for me has something unending about it. For even were I to develop new skills every day, . . . I would find opportunities every day to apply all those qualities in ways both large and small.*

He had been able to develop in Weimar because his duties and tasks forced him to take in and process more of the world. That is why he was reconciled with himself and his environment. It would be *irresponsible,* he writes, *at a time when the trees I have planted begin to grow and when, come harvest time, one can hope to separate the wheat from the weeds, if I were to go away out of some sense of discontent and deprive myself of shade, fruit, and harvest.*

That was how he had worked things out, and that was how he tried to reassure his mother about his present condition. All rumors to the contrary, he told her, he was not unhappy, though he saved the decisive reason for the very end of the letter: *Believe me, however, that a great part of the good humor with which I bear up under my work flows from the thought that all these sacrifices are voluntary, and that I would only need to have post-horses harnessed up in order to rediscover in the absolute peace of your house life's necessities and pleasures.*

While he had talked earlier of internal and external growth, now he writes of *sacrifices,* albeit *voluntary* ones. Yet sacrifices they remained. He thus articulated the disparity between his spirit and his official duties, and his confidence in being able to live with the disparity, keeping his duties and his thoughts and writing clear and distinct. *I follow my nature, as you can well imagine,* he wrote to his friend Merck, who had put his mother into such a state, *and gradually reconcile myself more and more to my onerous duties. I buckle on my armor to fit my frame and whet my weapons in my own way. My other hobbies continue on the side, and I always keep them up by paying one fee or another, just as one does not like to shut down a practicable mine as long as there is still some hope of future advantage to it.* The disparity is bearable when everything apart from his official duties is defined as a *hobby,* a word that would take on a negative connotation only much later. *I'm adapting myself to this world without deviating a hair's breadth from the inner essence that sustains me and makes me happy.*

It amounted to a double existence. *Just as in my father's house it never occurred to me to connect the appearances of spirits with my legal practice, I now keep the privy councilor just as separate from my other self, without whom a priv. couns. can get along just fine.* Goethe took pride in his ability to lead this double existence. As he confessed to his friend Knebel, by exaggerating the amount of work he had, he could fend people off and gain time for his own interests. Or he relates how he holds a *big tea* once a week, thereby fulfilling his *duties to society* in one go. And his double existence did not mean the two spheres were entirely separate. *Only in the innermost reaches of my plans and resolutions and undertakings do I remain true to myself in a mysterious way and thus tie my social, political, moral, and poetic life back together again in a hidden knot.*

That *hidden knot* was best found in the creative realm of poetry, so it is not surprising that, at a time when he was acutely conscious of his double existence, he began work on *Torquato Tasso,* a play that divides his inner state between the poet Tasso and a court official (named Antonio in the final version of the work). There is no reconciliation between these two characters. They envy each other; and each rejects and fights within himself what he sees completely realized in the other. Antonio is a realist, a seasoned diplomat. He is well educated and partial to the arts, but appreciates them only as decorative ornaments that do not even remotely approach the more weighty business of life. He is insulted and resentful of the success at court of a man like Tasso, who, after all, is capable only of making beautiful words. When the Duke Alfonso of Ferrara has his sister the princess crown Tasso with a laurel wreath, Antonio's envious commentary is: *I have long known that Duke Alfonso is / Immoderate in rewards.* Tasso seeks Antonio's friendship although he senses the gulf that separates him from this man. Antonio rejects his advances, and Tasso draws his sword. Alfonso intercedes, reprimanding Antonio and confining Tasso to his quarters, a mild and well-intentioned punishment.

That is about as far as the draft had progressed before Goethe's departure for Italy. Reminiscences of Charlotte von Stein can readily be found in the princess's cautious behavior: her precise observation of courtly conventions and repressed, disciplined feelings of love for the master of the word. She says to Tasso,

> *And shall I tell you of another virtue*
> *Your song appropriates, although unnoticed*
> *We listen, and step by step we are beguiled.*
> *We listen, and hearing, think we understand,*
> *And cannot censure what we understand,*
> *And in the end, your song has won our hearts.*

The princess allows herself to be captivated by the magic of the words, and she knows it. Antonio knows it too and disapproves. For his part, he remains immune to such enchantment. And Tasso, in turn, knows he does, which is why he explains in dialogue with the princess,

> *. . . He possesses—*
> *How shall I put it?—everything I lack.*
> *And yet, did every single god contribute*
> *To the heap of gifts beside his cradle?*
> *Ah no, it was the Graces who were absent,*
> *And he who lacks a present from those fair ones,*
> *For all that he possess, all he gives,*
> *You cannot rest your head upon his breast.*

He puts it with much beauty and grace, but to no avail: the princess does not allow herself to be coaxed out of her reserve. She advises Tasso to get on Antonio's good side by maintaining decorum, whereupon Tasso gushes out a utopian fantasy in which all that counts between two people are the pure tones of the heart: *permitted is what pleases.* The princess responds: *permitted is what is proper.*

That principle, Tasso objects, benefits only those who pursue their own advantage behind a veil of decorum, like Antonio. The princess cannot accept that and launches into an extended defense of propriety in which one can almost hear the voice of Charlotte von Stein:

> *Would you know exactly what is proper,*
> *You've but to ask of any noblewoman*
> *Because they have the greatest stake in seeing*
> *That all that happens here is right and proper.*
> *Propriety encircles with a wall*
> *The gentle sex, so easily offended,*
> *and where they reign, propriety holds sway,*
> *If insolence prevails, then they are nothing.*
> *And if you would inquire of both the sexes,*
> *The man seeks freedom, the woman morality.*

Tasso is insulted by Antonio and put in his place by the princess. He is permitted to feel loved, but it is a love that lacks the palpable life Tasso longs for. He remains just as dissatisfied as Goethe was in his relationship with Charlotte von Stein, despite all their intimacy. It was something of which he became fully, sharply aware only in Italy. He writes to her from Rome, employing the familiar second-person *du*: *Ah, dear Lotte, you don't know how much effort it has cost and still costs me to control myself, and that the thought of not possessing you—no matter how I twist and turn it about—basically wears me down and consumes me. I want to give my love for you the forms that I choose, always always—*, and there he breaks off.

He would express himself more clearly only when, upon his return from Italy, he found erotic satisfaction in his relationship with Christiane Vulpius, a relationship he defended to Charlotte with the explanation that she herself had laid no claim to such *feelings*. Charlotte behaved like the princess. When Tasso embraces the princess with the words *You've conquered me entirely and forever, / So take possession of my entire being*, she pushes him away and rushes off.

Humiliated and desperate, facing the abyss, he throws himself into the arms of his opponent Antonio. We must not forget that Antonio represents a fundamental challenge to Tasso's existence. He is the embodiment of the counterprinciple that undermines Tasso's self-confidence. Yet now, in his breakdown, Tasso goes for support straight to Antonio, of all people, as if this opponent represents the other, unrealized side of his being. Another courtier, Countess Leonore Sanvitale, describes the thorny relationship between the two: *I've felt for quite a while: here are two men, / Enemies to each other because nature / Could not make of them a single man.*

When he began to write *Tasso*, Goethe felt he was just such a person, uniting the Tasso and Antonio aspects within himself. His efforts had not resulted in the peaceful coexistence he led his mother and many friends to believe existed; rather, the relationship was as tense and conflicted as that between his two characters. In *Tasso* he attempted to create a counterpart, in the poetic world, to his own existence. But work on the play halted after the first two acts—outwardly because official duties kept him from the right mood, though possibly because he doubted that these contradictions could be balanced. He felt torn between the demands of his literary and official existences.

Though repeatedly assailed by doubts, Goethe had striven to fulfill the role of an Antonio before the journey to Italy. There was discontent and irritation and at times; the burdens of his offices were great. Yet he managed to suppress all his troubles or meet them with good humor. He writes of one inspection tour to the Ilmenau mine, *Today, in the bustle of business, I compared myself to a bird that for some good purpose has plunged into the water, and as he is about to drown, the gods change his wings little by little into feathered fins. The fish who come to his rescue cannot understand why he is not immediately comfortable in their element.* In the same letter, he plays with another metaphor that expresses at least the hope that it is sometimes still possible to live the right life within the wrong one: *I extract as much water as possible from these fountains and cascades* [of poetry] *and divert them to the mills and irrigation canals, but before I know it, an evil genius pulls out the stopper and everything spurts and sprays. And just when I think I'm astride my nag and riding dutifully on business, suddenly the jade beneath me takes on a magnificent shape, sprouts wings, uncontrollably takes to the air and carries me away.*

It was a happy event for Goethe when his *jade* was transformed into a Pegasus. Some at court saw Goethe in a different light and made jokes about him. A courtier named Karl von Lyncker wrote, "Amusingly enough, the court horse on which Goethe . . . rode around had been given the stable name 'Poesy,' and they say that wherever this horse appeared with its brilliant rider, prodigious events took place."

By 1782, Goethe was at the peak of his bureaucratic career. He had accomplished everything a commoner could achieve in Weimar. More Antonio was not possible. His title was Wirklicher Geheimer Rat— "real" or "actual" privy councilor—the highest possible title for a civil servant. He had been ennobled and was thus officially privileged to dine with the court. As a permanent member of the council, he had charge of military affairs and road construction as well as the mine in Ilmenau. After the retirement of the chamberlain von Kalb, he also supervised the duchy's finances. He was the director of the academy of graphic art and—as a sort of master of ceremonies—saw to the decorations for festive events. Since June 1782, he had been renting a large house on the square called the Frauenplan.

There was a limited amount Goethe could accomplish in his official capacity, however. His greatest success came in the area of military affairs. The duke had built his army to more than 500 men by 1778, naming himself supreme commander, and drilling the troops regularly. Early in the 1780s, with the duchy on the verge of bankruptcy, Goethe pushed through a massive reduction of troops to only 136 men, restoring the public purse to health. Having lost his martial toys, the duke turned his attention to foreign policy, energetically pursuing the creation of a league of the princes of small and medium-sized states. Goethe had himself been in favor of such an alliance in 1779, but now drew back from the plan as Prussia came to dominate the alliance and strove to exploit it in its own interests in the struggle against Vienna. Now the duke could indulge his passion for the military in Prussia's wake. Given the rank of major general and permitted to command a contingent of Prussian troops, in 1787 the duke was sent on a political mission to Belgium and Holland, where the citizens had risen against their Habsburg rulers as they had in the days of Egmont. It was exactly at that time that Goethe, in far-off Italy, was completing the play *Egmont*. In Goethe's version of the story, Egmont stirs the hearts of women more than those of his soldiers. That's why the duke, who otherwise was himself devoted to the hearts of women (he contracted gonorrhea on the mission to Holland), was dissatisfied with the play. He wanted his Egmont to be a brave soldier.

Although Goethe succeeded in downsizing Weimar's military, he was less effective in carrying out his other plans. Although Weimar was considered the capital of German culture, it continued to be a backwater as far as the condition of its roads was concerned. Goethe wanted to change that. He ordered plans set in motion to upgrade the roads connecting Erfurt to Weimar and Jena. Beyond that, a new road was to be built from Weimar to Naumburg. The plans were ambitious, with multilayered paving the equal of English standards. But the work did not proceed well. When Goethe left for Italy, after four years of construction, nothing had been completed, but they were so far over budget that, for the time being, further work was out of the question. For the director of road construction, that amounted to a failure.

The Ilmenau mine, whose reopening was dear to Goethe's heart, proved a fiasco. The sinking of a new shaft had begun in February 1784 amid official celebration. Goethe had made a speech that was printed in the literary periodical *Deutsches Museum* that same year. It happened to be the first text of any kind he had published in eight years, which was why the editor noted, "It has been a long time since our readers have had anything new from their favorite author Göthe, but he laid down his pen in order to be active."

Goethe had surely imagined a different return to the reading public, but the occasion did have great significance for him: *And so let us not look upon the humble opening we shall make in the surface of the earth today, with indifference.... This shaft, which we open today, will become the door through which men will descend to the hidden treasures of the earth, through which those deep-lying gifts of nature will be brought into the light of day. We ourselves will yet be able ... to see and examine with the greatest joy that which we can now only imagine in our minds.*

There was a curious interruption during Goethe's speech, an interruption vividly recalled by an eyewitness almost fifty years later. "[Goethe] seemed to have his speech firmly in mind, for he spoke completely fluently for a while, with no stumbles whatever. Suddenly, however, he seemed to take leave of his senses. It was as if his train of thought had been cut off and he seemed to have completely lost the overview of what he had left to say. This would have thrown anyone else into great consternation, but not him, not at all. Instead, for at least ten minutes, he gazed calmly around the circle of his audience, who were as if spellbound by the power of his personality so that during the almost laughably long pause, everyone remained utterly quiet. At last he seemed to regain the mastery of his material, he continued the speech and brought it very handily to a conclusion, without stumbling, and did so with as much ease and cheerfulness as if nothing at all had happened."

This lapse, however, was perhaps a harbinger of misfortune. Even before his departure for Italy, the mine operators needed another injection of capital. Goethe had to mollify the existing investors and gain new ones, which was an additional blow to his optimism. In Italy, he waited in vain for good news from Ilmenau. Not until 1792 did they finally reach the first ore-bearing seam, but it soon proved to be of inferior quality. The opening to a new seam was prevented by a catastrophic influx of water in 1796 in which several miners lost their lives. But they still didn't give up. One shaft remained open until 1812, and only then was the mine finally closed for good. The undertaking had been an economic disaster, consuming enormous amounts of money and producing no results. For Goethe, who had discovered his passion for mineralogy by way of the project, the end of the Ilmenau mine was a personal defeat. In a 1797 "Self Portrait" in the third person, he wrote, *he is useful in business if the business needs a certain outcome and, in the end, a lasting work somehow arises from it.* Goethe had stubbornly pursued the business in Ilmenau, but no *lasting work* had resulted.

In other areas as well, his official activities lacked much success. In his letters, he uses the mythological images of Sisyphus, who rolls his stone up the mountain in vain; of Ixion, who keeps his fiery wheel constantly spinning; and of the Danaides pouring water into a sieve. In one of his letters to Knebel, he writes that he thought he would only have to steer the boat, but now he knows he has to tow it upstream.

He was not even spared small annoyances and needling. Goethe had managed to establish a polite relationship with Baron von Fritsch, the former chairman of the privy council who had initially opposed Goethe's appointment and probably served as a model for the figure of Antonio. But the old animosity kept resurfacing. For example, Fritsch objected when Goethe addressed his colleagues in the chamber of finance as *meine Herrn Cameralen* (my dear councilors). If anything, they were the duke's dear councilors, not Goethe's. In a long and schoolmarmish letter, Goethe defended himself by referring to customary usage: *One uses the word "mein" to indicate a relationship to persons with whom and things with which one is connected by inclination or duty, without thereby arrogating to oneself mastery or possession of them.*

Here he defended normal usage against officialese. On other occasions, however, he stood up for official usage against relaxed colloquialism. The language of bureaucrats was justifiably *pedantic*, he declared, for it forced official business to slow down, which was good, because *Haste is the enemy of order.*

Goethe grappled with such questions and also with more weighty ones—questions of finance, misappropriation of tax monies, the conviction of a woman for infanticide. At the same time, he hoped to find time to write—to finish the chapter in *Wilhelm Meister* in which literature is defended against those who would make of it merely a lovely pastime for *idle hours.* Wilhelm tells his sober, hardworking friend Werner, *How mistaken you are, dear friend, to believe that such work, whose conception fills one's entire soul, could be produced in interrupted, cobbled-together hours. No, the poet must live for himself, completely engrossed in his beloved object. He whom heaven has endowed with the most precious inner life, who has received from nature indestructible wealth, must also live inwardly, with his treasures, in undisturbed bliss.*

He wrote to Charlotte von Stein that he had spent a *good hour* with *Wilhelm Meister. Really, I was born to be a writer.* And shortly thereafter, *I was created to be a genuinely private man and cannot conceive how it has pleased fate to patch me into a government administration and a princely family.*

Goethe held on for a while longer and in his letters repeated formulaic assurances that, on the whole, he was living quite *happily.* But he was plagued by melancholy thoughts. His mother reacted with concern to such letters, and he tried to reassure her: *it is natural that serious things make you serious, especially when one is pensive by nature and wants the world to be just and good.* Then he falls back into a melancholy key: *Enjoy my present existence, even if I should leave the world before you do. I have not disgraced you with my life, I leave behind good friends and a good name, and so your best consolation can be that I shall not die entirely.*

In his official capacity, Goethe had contact with many people, but shut himself off in his personal life. There were periods when he was on intimate terms only with Charlotte. He wrote her (in French) that she had isolated him from society and he had absolutely nothing to say to anyone. The only reason he still talked was so as not to fall silent. And then he became tight-lipped even with her. She complained, and he replied with long, voluble letters in which he assures her of his love. In August 1785, Charlotte's husband was relieved of his duty—or the privilege—of dining, as head equerry, at the ducal table. For the first time, he began to lead a normal domestic life with Charlotte. That had a near-catastrophic effect on her relationship with Goethe, as there were now far fewer opportunities for intimate association. Goethe flooded her with reproaches: *Just now I intended to complain that you can leave me so alone, for with all these people I am alone in the end, and my heart burns with yearning for you.* Less than a year later, while rereading *Werther* in preparation for a new printing, he wrote to her in a similar mood of despair that he always finds *that after finishing his work, the author did badly not to shoot himself.* One gets the distinct impression that Goethe was not exaggerating when later, from Rome, he wrote to the duke that he had been so beset by physical and moral afflictions before leaving for Italy that they had *at last rendered me useless.*

In the summer of 1786, through the mediation of F. J. Bertuch, the publisher Georg Joachim Göschen approached Goethe with a proposal to issue a complete edition of his works. No new work of his had appeared since 1775. Göschen guessed that after such a long time, Goethe would have some completed manuscripts in his drawer and thought there was some profit to be made. Goethe thought it over and then agreed to the plan, if only to have something with which to counter unauthorized reprints and pirated editions.

As he made preparations for the new edition, he realized with a shock that—except for *Iphigenia* and a few playlets and *singspiele*—in the last ten years he had brought nothing to completion. *Faust, Egmont, Wilhelm Meister,* and *Tasso*—all started but still unfinished. He had barely begun work on the long, ambitious nature poem that he called a *novel of the universe.* He would write the duke from Rome, *When I undertook to allow my fragments to be printed, I considered myself dead. How happy I shall be when I can legitimize myself as alive by completing what I began.*

While Goethe felt himself to be a writer when engaged on one of his works, as he surveyed his collected fragments, it seemed to him that he no longer was. In the summer of 1786, he resolved to force a decision. Either the complete edition would be a graveyard of buried projects, or he would complete the works he had begun. He would either become a living privy councilor but a dead author, or he would prove to himself and his public that the artist within him was still alive and perhaps even reborn. He would not be able to carry out this test of himself under ordinary circumstances. He would need an extended leave of absence from his duties.

His determination to reach a decision about being an author merged with his old dream of going to Italy. Beneath the southern sun he intended to bring his works to completion. That being his main goal, his luggage contained, above all, manuscripts on which he worked wherever possible, so intensively he sometimes feared the pleasures of the Italian paradise would elude him. His father had been happy in Italy. Goethe recalled the pictures and other mementoes he had brought back. And so he decided, as he wrote to the duke, *to travel a long, lonely road to seek the objects I was drawn to by an irresistible desire. For in recent years, it became a sort of sickness that only their sight and presence could cure me of. Now I can confess that in the end I was unable to look at any book written in Latin, any drawing of an Italian landscape. My lust to see this land was overripe.*

He was determined to reawaken the poet and artist in himself, finish half-completed works, and free himself up for new things; and he simply yearned to be in Italy. In addition, he desired an interval of distance from the affairs of state. And from—Charlotte: *this separation will give you more than my presence often did*, he writes in his first letter to her from Italy.

The exact date when Goethe set his sights on Italy is uncertain, though he seems to have made up his mind by the time he posted a July 12, 1786, letter to Jacobi in England: *when you return, I shall be removed to another side of the world*. He made his preparations in secret; only his secretary Philipp Seidel even knew the name Goethe intended to travel under: Johann Philipp Möller. It was also the name he used to receive the remittances he had arranged to be sent to him along his route. Why the clandestine preparations, and why travel incognito?

Goethe was running a risk by taking off without requesting a leave of absence from the duke. He was expecting to be gone a few months (and had no idea that would stretch into almost two years). He was reluctant to ask the duke's permission beforehand, as that would have made the trip dependent on the duke's favor. He wanted to decide by himself and for himself, create a fait accompli. He would have to run the risk that the duke would be displeased and perhaps even call him back. By giving no locations in the letters he wrote while en route, he hoped to avoid a recall that could reach him before he was in Rome. Only then would he feel safe because he would be far enough away. Such was his thinking, and he carried out his plan.

A recall to Weimar was not the only risk he ran. The duke could have withdrawn his trust in Goethe altogether and dismissed him. There is no evidence in his letters of the time to friends and acquaintances nor in his later writings that he ever seriously considered that possibility or its disastrous consequences, in particular for his financial situation. That possibility was hinted at only in a letter to the duke three months after his departure, triggered by the latter's silence: *Do not deny me a testimony of your thoughts and your love. Alone and cast adrift in the world, I would be in worse shape than a beginner.* Goethe seems otherwise to have been fairly certain of the duke's trust, esteem, and loyalty, just not certain enough to forgo the almost obsequious tone of his first letters from Italy. One senses his hope to make the duke forget his insubordination.

There was an irrational component to the secrecy, however, as there had been to his journey to the Harz in the winter of 1777. Then too, he told no one about what he had long been planning, his secretiveness tied to an inner perplexity, for climbing the Brocken was a sort of trial by ordeal to induce a decision about staying in Weimar. Secrecy protects the magic circle of higher significance. And so it was with the journey to Italy. Goethe hoped Rome would cure him, body and soul. And he kept superstitious guard for fear that premature discussion would destroy the miraculous power of the place. *At last I can open my mouth and send you joyous greetings,* he writes the duke when he reaches Rome. *Forgive the secrecy and my almost subterranean journey here. I hardly dared admit to myself where I was headed.*

Having made himself independent of the duke until he got to Rome, he placed his fate in the ruler's hands again once there: *The length of my present sojourn,* he writes in his first letter from Rome, *will depend . . . on the signal of your assent.* In constantly varied phrases he stresses that he will return a transformed man; he begs the duke to *preserve* his *love so that returning, I can enjoy with you the new life I have only here learned to treasure.*

Though of course annoyed by Goethe's secretiveness, the duke didn't hold it against him in the long run. Indeed, as Goethe had hoped, the trip built a new basis for their relationship. Charlotte, however, would never forgive him for his escape to Italy and the breach of trust it represented. Her first reaction was to demand that he return her letters.

The practical side of his secrecy included the pains he took to remain incognito. If he didn't travel under his real name, he could not be recalled. In Goethe's secretive schemes, his pseudonyms also always had a deeper meaning. In his first visit to Friederike Brion's house in Sesenheim, he had worn a disguise and introduced himself under an assumed name. And again on his winter journey to the Harz, when he wrote to Charlotte, *It's a curious feeling to travel about the world as a stranger. It's as if I felt a more genuine relationship to people and things.*

As a rule when putting on disguises and assuming false names, Goethe descended the social ladder in hopes of arriving at certain truths: not only would others perhaps be more open and frank in their encounters with him, but he might open up and discover facets of himself that he would not have otherwise been conscious of. In a later letter to Schiller he would speak of the *tic by which I find it comfortable to shift my existence, my actions, and my writings out of people's sight. Thus I shall always like to travel incognito, choose more modest over finer clothes, and—in conversation with strangers or casual acquaintances—prefer unimportant topics or rather, a less weighty way of expressing myself. I act more frivolous than I am and thus occupy a place between myself and my own appearance, so to speak.*

And so he set off for Italy as the painter Johann Philipp Möller. The ennobled privy councilor made himself almost ten years younger, and in Rome he would immerse himself in a community of artists below his station, where he then felt like a fish in water.

His departure had been well planned. He had even circumspectly reshuffled his official responsibilities and done it so unobtrusively and effectively that he could write the duke, *In general, at the moment, I am certainly dispensable, and as for particular tasks that have been assigned to me, I have arranged them so that they can go along for a while without me; in fact, I could die and it wouldn't cause a ripple.*

He left in July 1786, stopping, as he had the year before, at the spa in Carlsbad. The Herders were already taking the waters in Carlsbad, and soon the duke and Charlotte von Stein joined them. To everyone who saw Goethe in the weeks he spent there, he seemed jolly and carefree. The waters were taken in the morning; there were long rambles during the day and soirées in the evening. Goethe read from the manuscript of *Faust* and had long conversations with the duke. One evening, Goethe surprised Karl August—and even himself—by giving the duke a rough account of his life, as if leaving him a bequest. He did not reveal his imminent departure, however.

At three o'clock in the morning on September 3, 1786, he set off. The company he had kept right up to the previous day felt duped. The canoness Amelie von Asseburg wrote to the duke, "Herr Privy Councilor von Goethe is a *deserteur* whom I would like to subject to the full force of martial law. He seized his opportunity without bidding us farewell, without the least hint of his intention. It was really quite nasty! I almost want to call it *à la françoise* [*sic*]. No! we Prussians deceive our enemies but never employ deceit against our friends."

CHAPTER 18

The Italian Journey: No Forwarding Address.
Beginning to Relax. Palladio.
I'm studying more than enjoying myself. Rome.
Iphigenia Completed. Among the Artists. Moritz.
Naples and Sicily. The Enchantment of
the Phaiakians. Second Sojourn in Rome.
Egmont Completed. Faustina. Farewell to Rome.

. . . .

OR THE FIRST PART OF THE TRIP—VIA REGENSBURG, MUNICH, Innsbruck, and Bolzano to Trento—Goethe urged his coachman to hurry. They made fewer stops than usual. In his *Diary of the Italian Journey for Frau von Stein, 1786,* he noted, *What all am I not leaving behind to realize a Single Idea that has grown almost too old in my soul?* That single idea was to get to Rome. And yet, following his plan, he also took time to collect fossils and do some botanizing. Charlotte, who was waiting for an explanation of his secretive departure, had to be satisfied with tedious descriptions of the climate, rocks, and vegetation. The only thing that prevented his tarrying anywhere too long was his *drive and restlessness* to get to Rome.

Goethe had other intentions as well. In fact, everything he did on his journey was very deliberate, as his letters from the road confirm. He writes to his mother, *I shall return as a new person*; to his friends in Weimar, *For a new life . . . is beginning*; and to Herder, *One must be born again, so to speak.*

But is being born again something one can plan, like an assignment? And how would the new Goethe like to be? Of course he didn't know exactly, but he hinted at a few things, for example, in a letter to Herder a week after his arrival in Rome: *But what I can say and what gives me the deepest pleasure is the effect I already feel in my soul: it is an inner solidity with which my spirit is, as it were, stamped; earnestness without dryness and a steady character, and joyful.*

Earnestness and a *steady character*—surely these were qualities already well developed in the privy councilor. No change was necessary in that regard. But he was aiming at *earnestness without dryness*; the stiffness some had complained about was supposed to relax under the southern sun, and his *steady character* to be combined with joy. He wanted to give of himself without compromising himself, to loosen up while remaining securely centered. He calls it *inner solidity,* and with it, he didn't have to feel shy about immersing himself in the picturesque life of the people. *In my dress, which usually includes wearing linen stockings (by which I immediately slip down a few pegs), I stand in the market square, converse about every subject, ask them questions, see how they behave to one another, and I cannot praise enough their naturalness, free spirit, good nature, etc.*

After such immersion in the crowd, he was aware of what was missing in Weimar: *I cannot tell you how much humanity I have already gained in such a short time. But also, how I sense what miserable, lonely people we are forced to be in our little sovereign states, because— especially in my position—there is almost no one you can speak to who doesn't want or wouldn't like to get something from you.*

Sometimes Goethe spontaneously surrendered himself to a situation, pursued some attraction down a byway, or was even led astray. He needed to get used to such freedom again, for he had become more methodical than he used to be. He had armed himself with guidebooks to places and works of art and was determined to work his way through them. Most important for travelers of the day was Johann Jakob Volkmann's *Historical and Critical Notes on Italy.* Later Goethe would pedantically direct Charlotte to please read up on his itinerary in Volkmann, and he assigned himself a minutely detailed sightseeing program. He did not want to be taken for some Englishman on a grand tour, however. In Verona he bought himself some clothes of the kind Italians wore and was also glad he could speak the language, which he had secretly boned up on before leaving Weimar. He mixes with the common folk: *I talk to the people I meet as if we were old acquaintances. It gives me great pleasure.* He likes the colorful life of the streets and piazzas.

The people walking up and down remind you of the loveliest pictures. The braids wound up on the women's heads, the men's bare chests and lightweight jackets, the most splendid oxen they drive home from market, the little donkeys laden with packs. . . . And then when evening falls and in the mild air, a few clouds clinging to the mountains.

By contrast, the region from which he came seemed cold and gloomy, and he himself felt like a *Nordic bear.* On another occasion he writes, *but we Cimmerians scarcely know what day is. In eternal fog and darkness, it is all the same to us whether it's day or night, for how often can we really ramble and regale one another beneath a clear sky?* The thought of the foul weather that awaited him at home among the North Germans would haunt him throughout his entire time in Italy.

Powerful descriptions of the life of the common people fill the early pages of his travel diary, more succinct and inventive than his more verbose depictions of paintings and sculptures. He writes of the ancient amphitheater in Verona, *When you . . . stand up at the top edge, it is a curious sensation to be seeing something grand and yet, really, to be seeing nothing. For it is not made to be seen empty, but filled with people. . . . Because actually, an amphitheater like this is made to impress the people with themselves, to let them make fun of themselves. . . . Since people are otherwise only accustomed to seeing one another running around in a disorderly, undisciplined crowd, the many-headed, many-minded, fluctuating beast now sees itself united into a whole . . . and animated into a form as if by a single mind.*

He tarried a few days in Vicenza, where the buildings of Andrea Palladio kept him. *I simply keep walking around and around, exercising my eye,* he writes. Palladio's Old Town Hall and Olympic Theater, with their free use of antique architectonic elements, are for him majestic examples of the creative expansion of a sublime tradition. One's soul is raised up, he writes, and one is made to feel *the glory of a great, authentic existence.*

Goethe had already acquired and closely studied some copper engravings of Palladio's buildings. Now he could compare them with the originals and was overwhelmed by their reality. It was probably due to this experience of Palladio that Goethe never abandoned classicism as his ideal. The Gothic style that had attracted him in the Strasbourg cathedral now faded into that distant, foggy region, and three decades later, in the final version of the *Italian Journey,* he would dismiss it mercilessly: *Of course,* [classical architecture] *is different from our saints in the Gothic manner, hunkering on their little corbels and stacked on top of one another, different from our tobacco-pipe pillars, sharp little steeples, and spiky flowers. Now, thank goodness, I'm rid of those forever!*

Traveling along the Brenta River, he is again impressed by Palladio's buildings. Then came Venice. He entered the city in a mood of reverent awe and also feeling relieved of a certain pressure of expectation: *And so, thank God, Venice too is no longer simply a word, a name that has so often frightened me, always the mortal enemy of bombast.*

He encountered beauty at every step—in churches, palazzos, paintings, the picturesque street life, the gondolas, and in the singing—and was almost overwhelmed by it. For a change of scene, he paid a visit to the workers in the Arsenal and then made the following surprising entry: *On this journey I hope to calm my mind by way of the arts, to really impress their sacred image into my soul and preserve it for quiet, pleasurable contemplation. But then to turn to the craftsmen, and when I return, study chemistry and mechanics. For the era of beauty is past; our times call only for the urgent necessities.*

Clearly, Goethe had not yet gotten far enough from Weimar, either in distance or time. He was still in thrall to its circle of duties, the *urgent necessities* of his bureaucratic activities still obtruding. Perhaps he was also plagued by a guilty conscience; after all, not only was his salary still being paid, but he had burdened his fellow officials with extra work. Perhaps that's why he was so strict in denying himself the simple enjoyment of the beauty around him. So that even the encounter with beauty should look like work, he repeatedly affirms that he is *studying more than enjoying myself.*

For days, Goethe wandered the labyrinth of streets and canals, observing daily life and work. His respect grew as he came to see that not merely the brilliance of individual artists and architects, rulers and financiers, had built this miraculous city: *It is a grand, admirable work of collective human ability, a splendid monument, not of a single ruler but of a people.* He loved to hear people singing, not only in church but in the streets, and he observed how much the Italians love public life—their understanding of how to be open and expansive coming directly from the fact that so much of their life took place in the streets, including such encounters as this: *Today for the first time, a woman of the streets accosted me in broad daylight in a little alley near the Rialto.* He doesn't record whether she was successful.

Goethe stayed in Venice for seventeen days. *The first phase of my journey is finished. May heaven bless the ones to come.* He continued on through Ferrara and Bologna, his impatience to get to Rome mounting so steadily that he didn't slow down for Florence, speeding through the city in three hours. *I take no pleasure in nothing* [sic] *till that primary need is met.* Far too slowly, the trip wound through the Apennine valleys, their lovely landscapes inviting him to linger. *I will control myself and wait. If I've been patient these thirty years, I can survive another two weeks.*

For many attractions there is only a laconic *We'll take a closer look on the return trip.* He hurries toward Rome and can hardly wait. *I don't even get undressed anymore so I'm all ready to go in the morning. Two more nights! And if the Angel of the Lord doesn't strike us down on the way, we'll be there.* And a day later: *Now good night. Tomorrow evening in Rome. After that, I have nothing more to wish for, except to see you and my nearest and dearest again, and in good health.*

On October 29, 1786, he is there at last. *Now I begin to live for the first time, and I pay homage to my genius.* In the later version of the *Italian Journey*, the arrival is depicted more sedately. The exhilarating breathlessness that characterizes the diary letters is no longer in evidence.

His arrival in Rome followed two false starts. The first was in 1775, when he headed south in irritation that the coach that was to take him to Weimar had not arrived on schedule. They'd caught up with him in Heidelberg and brought him back. In 1779, on the trip to Switzerland, Goethe would have gladly continued on to Rome, but refrained out of consideration for the duke. This time, his success felt like a victory. *I'm counting it as a second birthday, a true rebirth, from the day I set foot in Rome,* he writes Charlotte on December 2; two months later, to the duke, *I'm living a new youth.*

His circumstances in Rome really did have a touch of the student life. Goethe had found lodging with the painter Johann Heinrich Wilhelm Tischbein, whom he had known and encouraged in the past. It was a roomy apartment on the Corso, only a few steps from the Porta del Popolo. The main tenants of the apartment were a former coachman named Collina and his wife, who supported themselves by subletting some of their rooms. In addition to Tischbein, two other young

German painters lived there, Johann Georg Schütz and Friedrich Bury. Tischbein, who already had a reputation as a talented artist, sublet three rooms for himself, and he let Goethe have the smaller guest room. The painters among whom Goethe found himself were all much younger than he and not remotely as famous, circumstances that forced him into a youthful role he was happy to adopt. There is a drawing by Tischbein that shows Goethe sitting at his ease and reading, his chair tipped comfortably back against the wall on its rear legs. Another shows him and another man lounging on a sofa, Goethe on his back, thrashing his legs in the air. They had a good deal of fun together, although his letters reported little of it and the later *Italian Journey* even less. In the latter, Goethe is at pains to be serious, and descriptions of his encounters with works of art verge on the tedious.

He was constantly on the go, looking at what Volkmann's guidebook recommended. *Since I've been in Rome*, he writes to Charlotte, *I have been tirelessly looking at everything worth seeing and have really filled my spirit to the brim with it.* Occasionally, he lets a remark slip suggesting he was finding the pursuit of art tiresome. He confesses to the duchess *that it is, namely, easier and more comfortable to observe and appreciate nature than art. The most insignificant product of nature has the circle of its perfection within itself, and all I need is eyes to see it. . . . An artwork, on the other hand, has its perfection outside itself, the "best" in the artist's conception, which he seldom or never achieves. . . . There is much tradition in works of art; the works of nature are always like a first word uttered by God.*

Making that tradition his own—that is, learning what one ought to know before seeing a work of art—required special effort. It would have been easier if all he had to do was look, and if looking alone was enough. If only one didn't have to talk about art all the time, he sighs in a letter to Karl August. *The longer you look at objects, the less you trust yourself to say something general about them. I would prefer to express the thing itself in all its parts or remain silent.* He kept at it for hours at a stretch, gazing at art and architecture. In one letter he says he feels like Orestes— not pursued by the Furies, but harried through the city by the *Muses and Graces.* He knew pretty much what he wanted to see and what one ought to see, and made no unexpected discoveries. He was impressed by the works that any educated visitor of the time would have named: the façade of the Pantheon, the Belvedere Apollo, Michelangelo's frescoes in the Sistine Chapel, the colossal bust of Juno Ludovisi. He had a huge plaster cast made of the latter and set it up in his room, *his first amour in Rome, and now I possess her.*

He worked on *Iphigenia* whenever he was not walking the city or spending time with his artist friends in the first weeks after his arrival. He was determined to finish the play. He began to feel pressure to free himself of that *sweet burden* so that he could devote himself completely to the marvelous present of the Eternal City. It was done just as the new year of 1787 arrived.

As Roberto Zapperi has discovered, during those weeks of work on the noble, exceedingly pure *Iphigenia*, Goethe was also flirting with Costanza Roesler, the daughter of a Roman innkeeper with family ties to Germany.* A note she wrote (or had written for her) has survived in which she asks for the gift of a fan. Her "dearest friend" should please get one for her "immediately" and thereby prove "that there are other and perhaps even more beautiful fans" than the one she has previously been given. All we know is that there must have been something between the two. There is a drawing by Tischbein, "The Accursed Second Pillow," in which Goethe is apparently hastily removing an extra pillow from his bed. The right half of the picture is taken up by the gigantic bust of Juno, who sternly surveys the scene. It could be Tischbein's joke about a failed attempt at a tryst. To the duke, Goethe wrote, *The zitelle (unmarried girls) are more chaste than elsewhere. . . . For either you should marry them or marry them off, and when they have a husband, that's the end of the story.* Costanza may have been such a case. At first, she was involved with "Filippo Möller," but when no proposal was forthcoming, she drew back or was reined in by her parents. In any event, by the summer of 1787, the pretty Costanza (a picture of whom survives) had been led to the altar by someone else.

It was proving harder than he'd hoped to find girls to flirt with. The duke, to whom he had written of it, must have recommended painters' models; as Goethe answered, *The girls—or rather, young women—who come to model for the painters are sometimes extremely sweet, and willing to let themselves be admired and enjoyed. In this way, it would be a very convenient*

* See Roberto Zapperi, *Das Inkognito: Goethes ganz andere Existenz in Rom* (Munich: C. H. Beck, 1999).

pleasure, if only the French influences didn't make this Paradise unsafe as well.
The fear of contracting syphilis, the "French disease," would later crop
up in his cycle of poems entitled "Roman Elegies."

Goethe made many new friends from the beginning of November
1786 until the end of February 1787. One was the painter Angelika
Kauffmann, a few years older and well-known for her productivity.
Her pictures reflected the reigning taste for classicism and had made
her wealthy. She had been living in Rome for a few years with her
Italian husband, also a painter, and so was able to introduce Goethe to
Italian artists. He spent Sundays with Angelika, they went on excursions into the surrounding country in her coach, he read to her from
his manuscripts, and she gave him drawing lessons. She painted a
portrait of Goethe, but he didn't think it was particularly good: *He's
a handsome fellow all right, but without a trace of me.* When Goethe left
Rome, she wrote, "The day of your departure was one of the saddest
days of my life."

He grew closer to Tischbein, who later accompanied him to Naples.
I've hardly ever seen such a pure, good, and yet wise, educated person, Goethe
writes about him to the duke. When Tischbein later decided to withdraw from a trip to Sicily they had planned together, Goethe was out
of sorts. He was annoyed when people who were important to him
had other commitments. Unlike the well-off Goethe, Tischbein had
commissions to worry about and thus was not always the master of his
own time. Still vexed, Goethe wrote about Tischbein, *It was otherwise
a good life with him, and there was only one tic that caused difficulty in the long
run, namely, he left everything he had to do in a sort of vagueness which, without any bad will on his part, often caused harm or displeasure to others.* Their
friendship had cooled by the time Tischbein finished a large oil portrait, *Goethe in the Campagna.* The portrait pleased Goethe, and he took
it home to Weimar with him.

There was also Karl Philipp Moritz, who had made a name for
himself as the author of the autobiographical novel *Anton Reiser* and as
the publisher of the *Magazin zur Erfahrungsseelenkunde* (*Journal of Expe-
riential Psychology*). He had worked his way up from poverty, fulfilled a
long-cherished dream to travel to Rome on foot, and was delighted to
hear that Goethe had also recently arrived in Rome. He did not dare
look him up, but they met in the circle of German artists in Rome

and developed a cordial relationship. "I feel ennobled by my contact with him. The most beautiful dreams of years long gone are coming true," Moritz wrote to a friend. Since he had just published his *Essay on German Prosody*, he was able to be of immediate service by helping Goethe recast *Iphigenia* in iambic pentameter. In late November 1786, Moritz fell from his horse during a joint excursion and suffered a badly broken arm, which gave Goethe the chance to show his gratitude. He organized the care of the invalid, scheduled his artist friends to provide nighttime care and regular visits, and himself spent many an hour at Moritz's bedside. He wrote to Charlotte von Stein, *Moritz, who is still in bed with his broken arm, told me bits of his life when I was with him, and I was astonished at their similarity to mine. For me, he is like a younger brother, with the same character, except neglected and damaged by fate where I am favored and preferred. It gives me a curious retrospect on myself. Especially at the end, when he confessed that he was causing his heart's beloved distress by being so far from Berlin.*

It was not just Moritz *causing his heart's beloved distress* with his journey to Rome; Goethe had greatly offended his own *heart's beloved* Charlotte. She had had no word from him for three months, and he was taking his sweet time with the travel diary meant for her. She could interpret his secret departure and subsequent long silence only as a rupture in their relationship and in her first letter to him, she was hurt and disappointed and demanded he return all her letters.

At first Goethe was unable to see his behavior as the reason for her harsh and bitter reaction. He even reproached her, writing, *So, that was all you had to say to a friend, a beloved who has yearned so long for a good word from you, who has not passed a single day or hour since he left without thinking of you.* But a few days later he came to his senses: *Your note pained me, but most because I have caused you pain.* Though the relationship seemed somewhat patched up when she received a few packages of his travel diary manuscripts (the greater part of which still lay unopened in his house on the Frauenplan), there was an irreparable breach between them. Charlotte writes him a *bittersweet letter*, which he answers with the wish that their correspondence *will not be interrupted again as long as we live* and that such *faltering times* in their relationship will *never return again*. He has changed, he writes, has become *a good deal freer. Every day I cast off another husk.*

In this letter full of promises and expectations for their future together, he also makes plans for the rest of his journey. If those in Weimar wished it, he would return as early as Easter. *I have looked my way through Rome,* he writes Herder on February 3, 1787, *and it is time for me to take a break.* He had drawn up a catalog of what he had seen in Rome and things he still hoped to see, the latter growing steadily larger. If he really wanted to be back in Germany by Easter, he would have needed to spend the remaining weeks in Rome, but he decided to continue on to Naples. On clear nights, flashes of fire from Vesuvius could be seen from the hills of Rome, an all too tempting sight. Goethe tarried in Rome until carnival was over, then headed south with Tischbein.

Naples was overwhelming in a different way. While it was the art in Rome, it was nature and the picturesque Neapolitan street life that enchanted him. *Just as in Rome everything is serious, here everyone is merry and lighthearted.* That lust for life was infectious. *I forgave all the people who lose their mind in Naples and was moved to recall my father, who had preserved an inextinguishable impression, especially of the things I saw today for the first time:* the view of the bay, the shore, Vesuvius, the gardens, the harbor, the bustling city, the Castel Nuovo, the ridge of Posillipo, and the grottoes. You could never again be completely downcast, he wrote, once you had seen Naples, for you could always think back on it. *I am in my own way quite still now, and when things get too madcap, I just become more and more wide-eyed.* He was constantly on the go, exploring the rich natural environment, hammering on rocks to examine their volcanic origin, and climbing Vesuvius, where he gazed into the bubbling crater and walked across the hot ground, singeing his shoes. In the botanical garden the idea of an *Urpflanze*—a primordial plant—first occurred to him. Although he didn't actually see one, he believed it must be there somewhere in the midst of all that lush vegetation. Along the shore he collected dried sea creatures, shells, and stones.

Whereas in Rome he'd lived in relative seclusion and spent time mainly in the company of German artists, in Naples he let himself be drawn into the best society. He was a frequent visitor to the home of Sir William Hamilton—the English envoy and a famous collector of art and antiquities—especially on account of his beautiful mistress Emma Hart, whom Hamilton would marry in 1791. Emma was famous for arranging *tableaux vivants* in which she herself participated, usually in rather scanty attire. In the decades that followed, the fad for arranging groups of people into live imitations of paintings would sweep Europe.

Goethe frequented other aristocratic houses as well. In Rome, Tischbein had opened doors for him; in Naples, it was the German painter Philipp Hackert, who had made a brilliant career and knew everybody. He worked for the Neapolitan royal house and introduced Goethe to the intellectual and artistic elite of the city. Goethe now rarely bothered with the pretense of an assumed name. By the end of his first period in Rome, he had already stopped using it. Even at the court in Vienna, they had heard of his presence in Rome and suspected he was on some sort of secret diplomatic mission. A spy had even approached Tischbein and tried to sound him out.

Whether under his real name or incognito, Goethe lived free and easy in Naples and enjoyed himself. *Naples is a Paradise. Everyone lives in a kind of drunken abandon. I'm the same way. I hardly know myself. I seem a completely different person. Yesterday I thought: either you used to be mad, or you're mad now.*

Until the last minute, Goethe was undecided whether he should continue by boat from Naples to Sicily. At the time, it was a long voyage and not without perils. *The doubts about whether I should go or stay made part of my sojourn here unsettled. Now that I've decided, things are going better. For my disposition, the journey is salubrious, even necessary. Sicily portends Asia and Africa, and it is no small thing to stand at that wondrous spot where so many radii of world history converge.*

Goethe had followed his father's route as far as Naples. His father had not made it to Sicily. Outdoing him was a powerful motive. Goethe boarded a ship for Palermo with his companion, the painter Christoph Heinrich Kniep, on March 28, 1787, and though seasick during the voyage, he worked on *Tasso* in his cabin. It was the only manuscript he had brought along on this trip. He felt he was in the *belly of a whale.* It was his first long sea voyage. *If you have never found yourself surrounded on every side by the sea, you have no idea of the world and your relationship to it.*

He went for long walks through Palermo and its surroundings, looked at artworks, enjoyed the lively street life, and kept an eye out for the *Urpflanze* in the lush gardens. The news of Goethe's presence got around in the town's better circles. He was invited to visit the viceroy, who asked him how much of his real life was contained in *Werther*. He wrote that such questions made him want to flee to the seaside, listen to the surf, and smell the seaweed. *The blackish waves on the northern horizon, their advance toward the curves of the bay, even the distinctive smell of the misty sea—all that conjured up in my memory the island of the blessed Phaeacians. I hurried off to buy a Homer in order to read that episode with greater edification.*

Goethe was turning over the idea of writing a tragedy about Nausicaa. The daughter of the king of Phaeacia would fall madly for Odysseus and then perish from that hapless love. In retrospect, he would write about the plan, *There was nothing about this composition that I would not have been able to depict naturally, from my own experience. Even as a traveler, even when in danger of arousing affections which, although they do not end tragically, still are sufficiently painful and can become dangerous and destructive—even in the case . . . of being taken for a demigod by the young and for a braggart by more staid persons, of receiving many an undeserved favor, encountering many an unexpected obstacle—all that made me so attached to this plan, this resolution, that I dreamed away my sojourn in Palermo, and in fact the greater part of the rest of my journey to Sicily.*

In four weeks in Sicily, Goethe wrote some text for the plan, the words Nausicaa speaks to Odysseus, for example, revealing feelings she does not yet recognize in herself but that hint at disaster to come:

> *You are not one of those deceiving men,*
> *The strangers who come singing their own praises*
> *And uttering smooth words . . .*
> *You are a man, a man one can rely on.*
> *Your lovely words have sense and context.*
> *To my ear they sound like a poet's song.*
> *They fill my heart and ravish it away.*

The enchanting Mediterranean atmosphere informs the story of Nausicaa: *A radiant whiteness rests on land and sea / And fragrant ether floats in the cloudless sky.* Goethe was never again able to conjure these days flooded with sunlight and shimmering with heat, and the work remained incomplete.

He learned that the confidence man Cagliostro, known through-out Europe and recently involved in the Diamond Necklace Affair in France, was a Palermo native by the name of Giuseppe Balsamo, infa-mous in his hometown *for various nefarious escapades*. Goethe, seeing the Diamond Necklace Affair as a symptom of the disintegration of society, had quarreled with Lavater about Cagliostro a few years ear-lier. Thrilled that the land of Homeric dreams was also the home of an imposter and fraud, he paid a visit to the family of Giuseppe Balsamo with a local lawyer familiar with the town and to his surprise found poor but honest folk. Once back in Weimar, uncomfortable that he had gained admission to their house with a made-up story, he sent the fam-ily a large sum of money to salve his guilty conscience.

Goethe and Kniep crisscrossed the island, visiting Agrigento, Cata-nia, Taormina, and also Messina, which had been destroyed a few years earlier by an earthquake. The *desolate sight* was so depressing that they resolved to seize the next opportunity to return to Naples, and on May 11, 1787, the two friends embarked for the mainland on a French mer-chantman. It was a rough voyage of four days in which they almost ran aground on the rocks near Capri. Goethe relates with some pride how he talked the passengers and crew out of their panic and restored calm and confidence. By quieting the others' fears, he overcame his own.

They landed in Naples on May 14, and Goethe stayed another three weeks. He had seen his fill of artworks and ruins, but not yet of the col-orful bustle of the streets. He was wary of having too romantic notions about it, however, and looked for opportunities to really understand the people and their way of life, so different from his own. *Then one would perhaps note that, on the whole, the so-called lazzarone* [Neapolitan dialect: beggar, loafer] *is not a hair less active than all the other classes. But at the same time, one would perceive that no one works simply to live, but in order to enjoy life—each in his own way—and that they aim to enjoy it even while at work.*

He finds this zest for living every moment to its fullest very sym-pathetic, although he surmises that it is not particularly conducive to economic progress. People are more industrious in the *Nordic lands*, but also slave away at their work. They pursue their business with less cheerfulness, but more effectively. And yet, isn't it better to *make a joke out of business* instead of allowing it to plague you, merely so that, in the end, you can make a profit or secure an advantage? The love of life will not suffer postponement; if you wait until you've reached your goal, you will have lost it along the way.

It was in these weeks that friends reminded him of the still unfinished *Wilhelm Meister* and urged him to resume work on it. After some consideration, it became clear to him that *beneath this sky, it will probably not be possible.* Why? Is it that Wilhelm is a *Meister aus dem Norden*—a master from the north? Doesn't he amble through life like a *lazzarone*, get involved with women and theater troupes when he pleases, and lack any real bourgeois ambition? Isn't Mignon's song *Knowst thou the land where lemons are in bloom* a hymn to the South? All that would argue that the southern sky might actually suit the Wilhelm of the *Theatrical Mission* quite well. But what Goethe had in mind for his hero by that time didn't blend so well with the Italian atmosphere, for he wanted to make him serious and hardworking. Mignon and her entourage would disappear and the enticements of the South be resisted. In Naples he began to have second thoughts about that conception: *perhaps something of this heavenly atmosphere can be imparted to the final books,* he writes in a letter from Naples.

Goethe left Naples for Rome on June 3, 1787. At first, he intended to stay only four more weeks, work through his list of sights still to be seen, and then set off north and return to Weimar by the fall. On May 29, shortly before leaving Naples, he wrote as much to the duke. This letter is especially important, since for the first time Goethe clearly formulates his wishes and plans vis-à-vis his future duties in Weimar. He writes that the court officials Johann Christoph Schmidt and Christian Gottlob Voigt have proved their worth in office and have taken excellent care of Goethe's duties as well as their own, and could continue to do so even after his return, couldn't they? Freed of his previous duties, *without disadvantage* to the running of the duchy, for the duke he could *become more than I often was before, if only you permit me to do what no one but me can do and assign the rest to others.* And he imagines his future life side by side with the duke, what he expects of his sovereign, and what Karl August can expect of him: *I already see how this journey has benefited me, how it has enlightened me and gladdened my existence. As you have supported me up to now, continue to care for me and do more good for me than I can myself, or than I can wish or demand. Give me to myself, to my fatherland, give me back to yourself, so that I can begin a new life with you! I trustingly place my entire fate in your hands. I have seen such a large and beautiful piece of the world, and the result is that I want only to live for you and in you. If I can do it less loaded down with details—for which I wasn't born—I can live to be a joy to you and many others.* Modesty was clearly not Goethe's strong suit. *Only rascals are modest*, he once said. If they permitted him to be what he was, he could become a gift to others—to the duke, the fatherland, and not least, to himself.

Six weeks after this letter, Goethe changes his mind. He asks the duke to let him stay in Rome until Easter of 1788. And he also reimagines his future activity in Weimar. After his return he would like to travel around the duchy like a stranger who needs to get an overview because everything is new to him. His intention is *to qualify myself anew for every kind of service . . . if heaven will second my wishes; then I will devote myself for a time exclusively to the administration of the duchy, as now to the arts. I have long groped and experimented, now it is time to take hold and have an effect.*

Once the duke granted him an extension of his unpaid leave of absence, Goethe never again mentioned this proposal to devote himself completely to administration. He had gotten what he wanted. Instead, he now stresses his intensive pursuit of practical artistic skills: *Art is serious business when you get right down to it. . . . This winter I still have plenty to do, not a day or even an hour to waste.* In fact, his efforts were entirely systematic during this second sojourn in Rome. He engaged a series of artists to teach him perspective, use of color, and composition for his drawings and paintings. He studied anatomy, now considering the human body the greatest work of art. The more he immersed himself in the techniques of visual art, however, the clearer it became that he was not a born painter. He knew his limits in this regard, yet he now also knew that his practical exercises—even if they were only imitative in character—would help him attain a better understanding and a *lively perception* of art. When Goethe writes the duke at the end of his time in Rome that he has *found myself again; but as what?—As an artist!*, he certainly doesn't mean the painter, but the poet.

In Rome in the late summer of 1787, Goethe felt at the pinnacle of his newly revived creative power as a poet. He completed *Egmont* by early September. *It was an unspeakably difficult task that I never would have completed without unlimited freedom of mind and body. Just think what it means to take up a work written twelve years earlier and finish it without revision.*

He had been working on the play in the fall of 1775, in the weeks before moving to Weimar; he closes the final book of *Poetry and Truth*, in which he depicts the end of his years in Frankfurt and his departure for Weimar, with the bold and fateful words of Egmont: *As if lashed by invisible spirits, the solar horses of time bolt off with our fate's flimsy wagon, and there is nothing left for us but to calmly and bravely keep hold of the reins and steer the wheels clear of a stone on the right, a precipice on the left. Where are we going? Who knows? We hardly know whence we've come.*

These words of Egmont's at the end of the autobiography suggest the author's strong identification with his figure. The play had remained a fragment for so long and Goethe had undertaken so many attempts to complete it, not because he had lost emotional touch with it but because he was still too close to it. In one letter to Charlotte, he called it a *wonderful play*. In it he could see himself—almost too clearly—sowing his wild oats. *I only intend to try to delete all that is too much like an unbuttoned, rowdy undergraduate in its manner.*

Egmont is a man of great vitality and lust for life. Spontaneous, passionate, hedonistic, free and easy, reckless, amicable, and energetic, he knows how to live and let live. Goethe writes in *Poetry and Truth* that he gave Egmont *immeasurable love of life, unbounded trust in himself, the gift of winning over everyone (attrattiva) and hence, of gaining the favor of the common folk, the silent affection of a princess, the explicit affection of a child of nature, the sympathy of an able statesman—and even endearing himself to the son of his greatest antagonist.*

Well aware he possessed this *attrattiva* himself, Goethe lent it to his favorite Egmont in such an exaggerated form it bordered on the *daemonic*. The description of Egmont in *Poetry and Truth*, quoted above, is followed immediately by the famous reflection on the *daemonic*. In modern parlance, daemonic means more or less "charismatic." Whichever word one uses, there is always something mysterious about the magnetism of the life force that charismatic people emanate, for good or evil. Goethe writes that they project *an enormous strength, and they exercise unbelievable power over all creatures.*

Egmont has this charisma but is too amiable to use it in a calculated way. He lives and embodies it, and it's not so much what he does but what he is that is attractive and even overwhelming. Egmont is not just the darling of women—especially Klärchen—but of the common people as well. In their struggle for independence from Spain, the Dutch have chosen him as their hero and liberator. In Goethe's drama, he is not really a political figure; he stumbles into politics and in the end pays with his life. The Duke of Alba is advancing. William of Orange, the politician, sees through the Spanish plans to eliminate the untrustworthy Netherlandish nobility. Orange warns Egmont and urges the count to join him in fleeing to safety in order to wait for a more favorable moment to mount a rebellion. But Egmont throws caution to the wind and ignores the warning; he puts his trust in the king, the people, and, above all, in himself. He despises clandestine plans, intrigue, and calculation and is thus caught in the trap Alba has set for him. That happens in act 4, the turning point of the play. Here Alba proves to be another grandiose character: cold, calculating, and rational, the incarnation of the daemonic in politics. He emanates a different kind of power. The source of Egmont's power is his personality, while Alba embodies a system of power—embodies it literally, which means more than just representing it. These are the antipodes of power, personal versus suprapersonal.

Goethe struggled mightily with the contrast between his two figures, getting hung up in the play's fourth act all the years he worked on it. As late as 1781, he wrote to Charlotte, *My Egmont is almost finished, and if it weren't for the exasperating fourth act, which I hate and need to revise, I would finish this play as well, which has dragged on for so long.* On August 1, 1787, the fourth act was completed and the greatest difficulty thereby overcome. But what did that difficulty actually consist of?

Goethe did not want to take the easy way out by reducing Alba to a political villain. On the contrary, Alba was supposed to represent the sphere of state power and policy in a dignified and necessary—though from Egmont's point of view, terrifying—way. On the basis of his own position in Weimar, Goethe felt himself duty-bound to make him so. Although his own official duties were utterly undaemonic and rarely a matter of life and death, Goethe had experienced a logic at work in the realm of public policy that was different from that in the private realm of poetry, a logic that demanded practical actions to get things done. The poetic sensibility, for example, values life in its uniqueness and approaches it on an individual basis; state policy is governed by general rules, where the interest of the individual must defer to the general interest. Poetry is anarchic; it tolerates no domination, even by morality. Politics, on the other hand, means control and the creation of order. Above all, government policy is dominated by a spirit of concern. After all, that's why the state is there: to care for the security and welfare of the body politic in the perilous turmoil of the times. That is why, when Goethe fled to Italy, he hoped he would be happy when finally rid of such concerns for a while. As he wrote to Charlotte, *when I banish from my mind what I for so long regarded as my duty and really persuade myself that man should accept the good that happens to him as lucky booty and concern himself neither with right nor left, much less with the fortune or misfortune of the whole.*

Goethe does not make Egmont an anarchic poet in his great dialogue with Alba, but he does present him as sympathetic, full of insouciant vitality. Since he is self-confident, he has confidence in his fellow man as well and refuses to dominate others. *It is easy for a shepherd to control the movement of an entire flock of sheep*, he tells his antagonist Alba, *the ox pulls his plow without resistance; but if you want to ride a noble horse, you must learn to read his thoughts. You must never ask anything foolish of him.* Alba responds that people do not know what is good for them. They are like children, and that is why it is the king's intention *to restrain them for their own good, to impose well-being upon them if necessary, to sacrifice the pernicious citizens so that the rest can be at peace.* This is the voice of absolutism, and in opposition to it, Goethe has Egmont argue like Justus Möser, the author whose *Patriotic Fantasies* Goethe admired for its defense of the rights and freedoms of the traditional estates. Like Möser, Egmont declares that a citizen wishes *to keep his old constitution, to be ruled by his compatriots, because he knows how he is led, because he can hope from them disinterestedness and a shared destiny.* For Egmont, leadership springs from habits and customs, insinuating itself into life instead of, as Alba would have it, confronting life abstractly and subjugating it. Egmont is arguing politics, but it is also clear that politics is not his real element.

Egmont is not an artist, but he is a master of the art of living, although in the end, he pays for his insouciance with his life. But should he have allowed his life to be spoiled sooner, spoiled by concern? In prison, shortly before his execution, Egmont bequeaths to Alba's son Ferdinand the words *I have lived, and you too should enjoy life. Take pleasure in it and do not dread death.* Egmont does not dread it at this moment, because earlier he has suffered such an agony of fear that the Duke of Alba thought it unbefitting for a nobleman and called it *womanly.*

During a walk in the park of the Villa Borghese, Goethe drafted the closing scene with its dream sequence: *Sweet slumber! You come as purest happiness, most willing when unbidden, unimplored. You loosen the knots of heavy thoughts and blend together all the images of joy and pain. The circle of inner harmonies flows without impediment, and enfolded in accommodating illusion, we sink down and cease to be.* Goethe was relieved when the play was completed and he could allow Egmont to blissfully disappear. He had almost stopped believing it would ever be done. He owed it, he wrote, to the *freedom of mind* he had gained in Italy.

There is some supposition that Goethe had a love affair during his second stay in Rome. If he did, he likely also owed it to that same *freedom of mind.* The name of the beloved in "Roman Elegies" is Faustina, who is not mentioned in the *Italian Journey.* However, when the *Italian Journey* reports on the events of January 1788, a poem from the singspiel *Claudine von Villa Bella* is inserted without transition: *Cupid, wanton and capricious boy, / You asked if I could put you up an hour! / How many days and nights you've hung around, / And now you're lord and master in this house.* In the remarks that immediately follow the poem, Goethe explicitly attempts to quash any suspicion that erotic references are intended, but that attempt only excited more curiosity. The same is true of a remark reported by Eckermann: the king of Bavaria had been pestering Goethe *to tell him how much of the story* [of Faustina] *was factual because it appeared to be so charming in my poems, as if there was really something to it. But it seldom occurs to people that a poet usually knows how to make something good out of minor occasions.*

In a letter to the duke of February 16, 1788, however, there is a striking hint. The duke had told him about a venereal disease from which he had halfway recovered, and Goethe makes a little joke at his expense, writing that at first, he had thought it was hemorrhoids *and of course, I see now that the damage was in the same neighborhood.* The duke had probably described the pretty girls responsible for infecting him, and

Goethe responds that he too could tell *of some charming strolls. This much is certain . . . that such exercise, taken in moderation, refreshes the mind and brings the body into delightful balance. And as I have experienced the same more than once, I have also, on the other hand, felt the inconvenience when I wanted to direct my steps off the broad highway and into the narrow path of abstention and security.* These remarks would seem to support the suggestion of a love affair in the *Italian Journey*'s report on the month of January 1788.

There is other evidence adduced by Roberto Zapperi,* such as a remark in a letter to Herder. The latter had asked for the manuscript of Goethe's travel diary, but he withheld it, citing the *pudenda*† he was reluctant to make public. The bills for food, submitted by Goethe's landlords the Collinas, may also provide some clues. On a number of occasions, they mention an unnamed guest who has had supper with Goethe, and this may have been his lover. A more persuasive clue, however, is a love letter found among Goethe's Italian papers. Poorly spelled and ungrammatical, it says, "I fear you are angry with me, but I hope not. I am all for you. Love me, if you can, as I love you." It may refer to a jealous scene like the one that plays a role in the "Roman Elegies." Discovered among Goethe's papers, the letter, problematically, is addressed to Tischbein. But as Goethe, hoping to maintain his alias, had people write letters to him addressed to Tischbein, this love letter could have been meant for him. Be that as it may, when Karoline Herder told her husband that Goethe had said he had wept "like a child" every day for the two weeks before leaving Rome, it could also have to do with a lover who then is given the name Faustina in the "Roman Elegies."

There had been some acrimony between Goethe and the duke in the fall of 1787, the latter having expressed a wish that Goethe be prepared to act as a sort of tour guide for his mother, Anna Amalia, then planning her own trip to Italy in the near future. The duke had made this request after they had already agreed that Goethe would return by Easter of 1788. Goethe took a dim view of having to leave his circle of artist friends for the courtly sphere while still in Italy, and let the duke know as much. However, he still signaled his willingness to pre-

---

* In *Das Inkognito: Goethes ganz andere Existenz in Rom* (Munich: C. H. Beck, 1999).
† Latin: things of which one ought to be ashamed.

pare for Anna Amalia's visit and, if necessary, to accompany her. He was relieved, however, when the duke canceled the entire undertaking. Goethe wrote him on March 17, 1788, *I answer your friendly, cordial letter with an immediate, joyous "I'm coming!"*

On April 24, Goethe set off from Rome. A few days earlier, on a clear, moonlit night, he had taken leave of the city by walking once more along his often traveled route down the Corso, then up the Capitoline, which *stood there like a fairy palace in the desert*, and from there to the ruins of the Forum Romanum and to the *noble remains* of the Colosseum. *I cannot deny*—he would write in the *Italian Journey*—*that I was overtaken by a shower that hastened my return.*

At the very last, he recalls the elegy Ovid wrote when he was banished from Rome to the distant Black Sea: *Since that night the sorrowful image hovers before me / Which for my soul was its last glimpse of the city of Rome.*

That was how Goethe felt at the moment: like someone going back into exile.

CHAPTER 19

Return to Weimar. Charlotte von Stein and Christiane Vulpius.

Erotica. "Roman Elegies."

Meeting Schiller. Moritz and a New Concept

of Art's Autonomy.

Art and Other Vital Forces. Tasso and Antonio Again.

Familial Bliss in the Hunting Lodge.

....

G OETHE LEFT ROME ON APRIL 24, 1788, ACCOMPANIED
by the composer Philipp Christoph Kayser, whom he had known since his days in Frankfurt. Goethe had encouraged Kayser, made plans to write singspiele with him, and hoped he would compose incidental music for *Egmont.* Nothing much came of all that, but Kayser proved a good traveling companion.

En route, Goethe's letters to the duke—and he wrote mostly to him—no longer have the melodramatic tone of the March 18 letter in which he had expressed his willingness to return: *Lord, here am I. Do with your servant as you will.* Instead, they scarcely concealed a bitterness bordering on cynicism. His irritation also emerged in ill-tempered comments about art and architecture, as if his eager enthusiasm was finally exhausted. He accuses the builders of the Milan cathedral, for example, of forcing *a whole mountain of marble into the most vulgar forms.* He speaks bitterly not only of many works of art but of himself. *For by the way,* he writes to the duke on May 23, *I have gone terribly to seed. To be sure, I never amounted to much my whole life, so my consolation is that you won't find me so very different.*

He doesn't seem particularly bothered that such a remark blatantly contradicts earlier assurances he would return a *changed,* a *transformed,* a *purified* person in order to be able to serve the duke even better than before. Instead, a depressive tone creeps in. *Bidding Rome farewell has cost me more than is right and proper for my years*, he says in the same letter to the duke. He bought himself a hammer for the Alps and wrote to Knebel that he would *tap on the rocks to drive out the bitterness of death.*

As expected, bad weather set in on the other side of the Alps: rain, wind, cold, and low-hanging clouds. He had arrived in the foggy regions and wondered how people could stand living here and why the devil they settled here in the first place. If he had his druthers, he would turn around on the spot and go back. As he rode in a carriage somewhere on the northern edge of the Swabian Alps, between Biberach and Giengen, he wrote down some good resolutions for living in Weimar: he would have to keep his discontent in check.

On June 18, 1788, Goethe arrived home in Weimar. The first thing he did the following morning was to summon his ward Fritz von Stein, and then he called on the duke. The first person he encountered at court was Kornelius Johann Rudolf Ridel, the tutor of the duke's son, who described him thus: "He has gotten leaner and was also very brown from the sun—I didn't even recognize him at first!"

Initially Goethe's good resolutions bore fruit. He was more approachable at court than before. "He proved more talkative than usual, and had really brought back with him encouragement and contentment." But people also noticed that he was holding something back; that he "dwelt on details in order to avoid main points he did not want to hold forth about."

One point he did not want to hold forth about among his acquaintances and at court was his relationship with Charlotte von Stein. He could not talk to others about it, but he couldn't talk to her either. She was unwilling to air her grievances, and he couldn't find the right tone; nor did he know where things stood between them. So they tiptoed around each other and failed to clear the air. Charlotte found fault with the situation and demanded more. Goethe fended her off. *I am happy to listen to everything you have to say to me. I must only ask you not to be too much of a stickler for details about my state of mind, which is so preoccupied—not to say inwardly torn—right now. You are one person I can tell that my inner self is not like my outer self.* It was indeed so, for he was preoccupied with an event he did not want to reveal to Charlotte.

On July 12, 1788, he had been approached by the twenty-three-year-old Christiane Vulpius, seeking help for her brother Christian, who had been unable to find a position after studying law. Goethe and Christiane would always remember this date, for it marked the beginning of their relationship.

Christiane's parents were dead, and she was living with her sister and an aunt in Weimar in impoverished circumstances. Their father, a minor official, had been dismissed because of irregularities in his work. A "girl of the people," in the language of the day, Christiane earned her keep in Bertuch's workshop for artificial flowers, and in Goethe's several drawings of her, she looks self-confident and natural. Her full, wavy hair falls freely to her shoulders. She was not as slim as Charlotte, but more compact and pleasingly plump. Once Goethe's mother had had a look at her, she always called her his "bedmate" and meant it as an affectionate compliment.

They kept their relationship secret the first few months, the only one in Goethe's house in the know being his faithful manservant and secretary Philipp Seidel. Christiane was admitted through the rear entrance. Things became less inconvenient once Knebel moved out of the garden house, which he had occupied during Goethe's absence. As always, the duke was the first person Goethe informed of this "men's business," and the affair was treated as private for the time being. Goethe gives a first hint of it in a little poem he called an *Eroticon* about the *worries of love* that help drive away all other worries, verses that would become part of the "Roman Elegies." He wrote that he wanted to *recommend erotica to tender hearts*, and continued, *I do not deny that in private I am addicted to them.* And then this ambiguous defense: *I haven't done anything I could take pride in, but much I can enjoy.*

By the spring of 1789, half a year later, the affair had become an open secret. Karoline Herder wrote to her husband, who had since embarked on his own Italian journey, "Now I have it from Frau von Stein herself why she is no longer very fond of Goethe. He keeps the young Vulpius woman as his Klärchen [Egmont's lover in Goethe's play], often has her come to his house, etc." Herder answered from Rome, where he had come into contact with Goethe's acquaintances, "What you write about Goethe's Klärchen displeases me more than it surprises me. A poor girl—I wouldn't permit myself such a thing for all the world! However . . . the certain way he lived here among crude—but good—people, could have had no other outcome."

Charlotte must have seen it in something of the same light: Italy had corrupted Goethe. He had become "sensual," she coolly put it once she had gained some perspective, but in the first year after Goethe's return, she lacked the composure for such a characterization. She was scandalized and wounded by his desertion. Almost fifty years old, she had one grown-up son, Karl, and another approaching maturity, Fritz, whom Goethe had as good as adopted. Her husband had suffered a stroke and threatened to be a permanent invalid. She didn't want to lose Goethe, but her pride didn't allow her to compete for his attention. And if she fought, she was at war with herself. Normally poised and *comme il faut*, she lost her balance for a time.

Initially, she tried to avoid being in Weimar whenever possible, instead traveling or staying at her estate Grosskochberg, near Rudolstadt. At the end of May 1789, as she set off on a trip, she left a letter for Goethe that, to judge by his response, must have contained a damning summary of the past few months—a reproachful letter that forced him to defend himself. *I hesitated to answer it*, he writes, *because in such a case, it is hard to be honest and not to cause injury.* But he does become injurious, even as he tries to justify his relationship with Christiane in cautious wording. *What kind of relationship is it? Whom does it injure? Who lays a claim to the feelings I grant to the poor creature? To the hours I spend with her?*

Which can only mean that Charlotte has fended off his physical desires, and so nothing is being withheld from her when he now satisfies them with Christiane. Of course, he doesn't express it quite so harshly, but makes it clear enough. And since he's already letting off steam, he continues, *But I freely admit that I cannot tolerate the way you have treated me up to now. . . . You oversaw my every expression, my gestures; criticized the way I behaved.* He writes himself into a fury and feels so justified that he can slip into completely inappropriate warnings about her coffee consumption: *Unfortunately, you have long scorned my advice concerning coffee and introduced a diet that is highly detrimental to your health.* She ought not to be surprised at her unhappiness, for coffee has reinforced her *hypochondriacal* tendencies. In the next letter, of June 8, 1789, which was to be the last for a long time, Goethe retracts his scolding tone and instead expresses self-pity. He begins with the weather and ends with the miserable condition of humanity. The whole business was insufferable and it took much self-control, he wrote, not *to make a plan that could little by little set one free.* These remarks are in sharp contrast to the cheerful tone that predominates in other letters; things seem to have been going quite well with Christiane. Another indication of his contentment are the erotic poems that originated during this "honeymoon" period with Christiane. For the time being, however, only his closest friends knew about these works—Knebel and the duke, as well as Wieland, who had a lively appreciation for everything gallant, risqué, and erotic. Women were not considered an appropriate audience for erotica.

The secrecy surrounding these poems had a direct effect on the editing of the final volume of his collected works being published by Göschen. Goethe wrote to the publisher on November 6, 1788, *There are reasons why I do not want the last two poems of the first collection—"Pleasure" and "The Visit"—printed.*

Although the poem "Pleasure" was written in 1767 and had already appeared in print, it seemed advisable not to republish it for the time being; it is about *lust* being greater when one doesn't have to pay for it, and he feared people might connect it with Christiane. "The Visit," on the other hand, had really been written in the first weeks of their relationship and depicts the beloved asleep. Her lover lets himself into her chamber, leaves two pomegranates on the night table, and slips out again without waking her. Although it contains nothing more suggestive than that, for Goethe it was apparently enough that people might recognize Christiane in the charming portrait of the beloved, presented as a child of nature. Another *eroticon*, the poem "Morning Complaint," which Goethe sent to Fritz Jacobi on October 31, 1788, slipped past his self-censorship although it alludes more clearly than "The Visit" to his love affair with Christiane. Here, the lover is waiting for an assignation with his mistress. He hears the cat and the mice and the creaking of the floorboards, but unfortunately, the expected beloved never shows up. The rising sun, usually a welcome sight, is now *utterly hateful*, and the only thing left to the frustrated lover is to *mix my hot and yearning / breathing with the cool, sweet air of morning.*

"Morning Complaint" and "The Visit" were the beginnings of an attempt to capture the erotic feelings of these weeks. His pleasure was even greater when he was able to connect his lovemaking with his memories of romance in Rome. Having read Catullus, Tibullus, and Propertius, he realized that he could ennoble the subject by deploying forms and motifs from Roman antiquity. Throughout 1789 his friends received bulletins about *eroticis* or *entertainments in the style of the ancients*.

He continued to work on them until the spring of 1790. On April 3 he wrote to Herder, *I believe my elegies are finished; there is almost no trace of this vein in me anymore.* And no wonder, since at the time he was in Venice, far from Christiane. The "Roman Elegies" were finished, but Goethe had no intention yet of publishing them. Herder advised against it, as did the duke, who was certainly no prude. He feared there would be talk, and it would be better to avoid trouble. Such things were only for the cognoscenti, not the general public. The "Roman Elegies" were not published until four years later, at the urging of Schiller, who was looking for something engaging for his cultural journal *Die Horen*. Goethe sent a version that deleted two of the elegies, and they were finally published in 1796.

The elegies tell the story of a little love affair with a beautiful widow. They begin with Goethe ironically making fun of his own assiduous appetite for cultural enrichment: *Tell me, oh stones, and speak to me, lofty palazzos! / Streets too, utter a word! Genius, not yet astir? / . . . / Certainly you are a world, oh Rome, but unless there be love, / Then were the world not a world, Rome then would not be Rome.* Not until his Roman lover joins him in bed does Rome come alive. First, however, her vigilant mother must be propitiated with generous gifts: *Mother and daughter enjoy their guest from the northern lands / And the barbarian rules Romans, body and soul.* The third elegy is devoted to the theme of the unexpected. It is beautiful when things go quickly—not the lovemaking itself, but the preliminaries: *Do not, Beloved, regret that you surrendered so quickly. / Know that I think nothing low, think nothing mean of you.* Christiane is discernible behind the portrait of the beloved, especially in the description of her hair: *Once she appeared to me, a nut-brown maiden. Her hair / Fell, a cascade rich and dark over her brow and down. / Shorter locks made ringlets round her delicate neck. / Waves of unbraided hair fell from crown to shoulders.* And then the famous fifth elegy. Goethe's contemporaries were surely asking themselves if the subject of the poem was a fictitious Roman lover or the very real Christiane. The question remains unanswered.

All the night long, however, it's Amor who keeps me busy.
     If I only learn half, I am doubly amused and
Do I not learn, after all, by tracing the lovely breasts'
     Forms, by running my hand down the beautiful hips?
Only then do I grasp the marble aright, I think and compare,
     See with a feeling eye, feel with a seeing hand.
If my beloved steals a few hours from my day, she
     Gives me hours of the night—compensation enough!
Kissing is not our sole occupation. We talk and reason,
     And if she falls asleep, I lie awake with my thoughts.
Many's the time I've lain in her arms and made poems,
     Counting hexameter's feet, fingers quietly tapping them
Out on her sleeping back.

Goethe deleted two elegies—originally the second and sixteenth—because they contained, as the duke said, "a few too lusty thoughts." One follows a disrobing scene to its inevitable conclusion: *We delight in the joys of the genuine, naked Amor / And in the rocking bed's charmingly creaky tones.* The other describes at great length the fear of venereal disease.

Though their publication was delayed, the "Roman Elegies" were intended for a broad readership from the first. Some poems were shown only to the duke and a few other intimates. They were *erotica*—"men's business"—commentaries on priapic poems from late antiquity that Goethe wrote in Latin. Their main topic is Priapus, the god of gardens, usually depicted as a short, stocky, bearded man with a huge, erect, openly displayed penis almost as large as himself. Goethe's commentaries ponder jokingly the question of all questions, how *the desired stiffening can always be made to succeed* and whether it could be of possible help *to apply a searing iron to one's pubic hair and curl them with a curling iron.* There is also a spoof of Saint Augustine in this collection of texts written for the duke. In the *City of God*, Augustine criticizes Roman polytheism for "filling the bed chamber, where the bridesmen themselves withdraw, with a swarm of deities." Goethe appends a fictitious continuation he attributes to Augustine in which the responsibilities of individual deities during foreplay and copulation are minutely prescribed. It offered an opportunity to go into salacious detail. The goddess Virginensis, for example, will help *to untie the girl's waistbelt . . . remove uncomfortable clothes, will make you lustful and will spread her thighs when you lie down upon her. And the god Subigus will not be absent at this union . . . while you seek entry, applying your belly tenderly to the body beneath you.* Other gods and goddesses give aid until the seed has been led to the right place and perhaps engenders new life.

Goethe wrote these texts in the weeks he was preparing to become a father himself for the first time. Christiane was pregnant. Goethe acknowledged paternity and was willing to take his lover into the house on the Frauenplan. The duke was of the opinion that they could not expect Weimar society to accept this arrangement and offered to give to his friend and Christiane, whose pregnancy was already far advanced, two hunting lodges outside the city walls as residences. They wouldn't be on public display there. Although the lodges were practical and pleasant places to live, as Goethe assured the duke several times, the move there meant a demotion in social status. His letters do not mention that, but it was obvious how decisively and happily Goethe later seized the opportunity to return to his house on the Frauenplan. For the time being, however, he put the best possible face on things. He sent the duke a witty report on his move: *I'm maneuvering into my new quarters with great care. The heavy artillery is in the vanguard, the troops are moving, and I cover the rear guard. The heavy artillery* must be the pregnant Christiane, *the troops* her entourage of aunt and sister-in-law, and *the rear guard* the house servants.

The baby, a boy they named August, was born on December 25, 1789. Two days later, on the day he was baptized, Goethe wrote to a man named Christian Gottlob Voigt, with whom he worked in court, *A sacred rite, completed this very moment, reminds me again of the kindness with which you promised, six months ago, to assist me in re incerta.** It has been conjectured that this thank-you was for Voigt's willingness to spare him and Christiane the unpleasant bureaucratic aspects of an illegitimate birth. By the laws in force at the time, Christiane ought to have been punished with a fine, a public warning, and public penance. In special cases, fathers were even called to account. So arrangements had to be made in order to avoid a possible scandal.

In the fall of 1788, when Christiane was still visiting the house on

---

* Latin: a doubtful matter.

the Frauenplan in secret, Goethe had acquired a new neighbor who was unaware of all this. Friedrich Schiller had come to Weimar in 1787 to investigate the possibility of moving there. Since the duke had made him an honorary councilor a few years earlier, he had hopes of a paid position, although of course one as lucrative as Goethe's was beyond his expectations. Schiller was ambitious enough to measure himself against Weimar's local "gods and idolaters." After initial meetings with Herder and Wieland, he noted, "I have considered myself too small and the people around me too great." His real yardstick was Goethe, still in Italy at the time. Like others in Weimar, Schiller was now waiting for Goethe's return and had taken rooms not far from the house on the Frauenplan.

Their first encounter took place in the home of the Lengefeld family, in Rudolstadt. Schiller was visiting Charlotte von Lengefeld, his future wife, who orchestrated the meeting of the two writers. She had an almost familial relationship to Goethe, being a goddaughter of Charlotte von Stein. On September 7, 1788, Goethe visited the Lengefelds with Charlotte von Stein, her sister, and Herder's wife. For Schiller, this first encounter with Goethe was a disappointment. "Of course, the party was too large and everyone too eager to talk to him for me to be able to spend much time alone with him or talk about anything other than generalities," he wrote to the dramatist Theodor Körner. Goethe made no note of the meeting. He had preconceived notions about Schiller; as he later confessed, he had been shocked at the great celebrity Schiller enjoyed. He had hated Schiller's first play, *The Robbers*, and Schiller was for him nothing more than its author, *a powerful but immature talent* who had just *poured out over the Fatherland in a full, irresistible gush the ethical and theatrical paradoxes of which I have striven to purify myself.*

Schiller sensed this disapproval at the Lengefelds' and was more hurt than he cared to admit to himself. In the following months, he could not avoid observing how guests came and went at Goethe's house, while he was kept at arm's length. His resentment grew until he finally gave vent to it in a letter to Körner: "It would make me unhappy to be around Goethe very much: even toward his closest friends there is never a moment of heartfelt effusion. There is no way to get a handle on him. In fact, I think he is an egotist to an unusual extent. He has the talent of captivating people . . . but he always knows how to maintain his own independence. He makes himself known as a charitable person, but only like a God, without giving of himself. . . . People should not allow such a being to gain prominence among them. I find him hateful on that account, although I love his spirit with all my heart and think highly of him. I regard him like a proud, prudish woman whom you must get with child to humble in the eyes of the world." Schiller loved Goethe's work but hated what he saw as the privileged circumstances under which it came into being: "This man, this Goethe, stands in my way, and he reminds me so often that fate has treated me cruelly. How easily *his* genius was supported by his destiny, and how I must struggle right down to the present moment!"

Schiller's resentment of Goethe was not softened by the offer of a chair in history at the University of Jena, made at Goethe's initiative. On the contrary, he felt himself "duped" when he learned that it was an unpaid position. Should he consider it an honor or an insult? Körner warned him off it: "I must tell you this much," the playwright wrote, "that the title of professor is not an asset for you; you are an asset for Jena." Körner had hit the nail on the head, for Goethe had indeed written to the privy council that they should appoint Schiller, *especially since this acquisition can be accomplished at no expense.*

Schiller moved to Jena in the summer of 1789. He tried to come to grips with his ambivalent feelings for Goethe—so that envy would not poison him. He had to find a way to overcome it, and that would be possible only if he believed in himself and unswervingly followed his own path. So he put together a strategy: he would remain in Jena, where he came to enjoy an extraordinary reputation as a teacher, and look forward to a time when he and Goethe might collaborate on plays for the same theater. He would avoid expressing his intentions in the latter regard; you hit the mark best when you don't take aim.

Goethe was gradually realizing the extent of the younger man's talents. For example, he was so taken by Schiller's poem "The Gods of Greece" that during a coach ride he recounted it, stanza by stanza, for his female traveling companions, if in a rather pointedly didactic recitation. He praised Schiller's *History of the Succession of the United Netherlands from Spanish Rule* for its powerful historiography and brilliant style. And he wrote to the duke about Schiller's review of *Egmont* (which was positive, although the ending of the play was criticized as a "salto mortale into the realm of opera"): the *moral part of the play was very well analyzed. As far as the poetic part is concerned, the reviewer may have left something for others to do.*

Though Goethe could hardly ignore the outstanding role the younger writer played in literary life, he still kept his distance. Indeed, he kept his distance from people in general, even more than before. It was not what had been expected. His letters from Italy had promised a relaxation in his social interactions. Instead, he was more cautious and reserved than ever. Some part of this was due to his initially clandestine relationship with Christiane, which resulted in a kind of double life. Karoline Herder had the impression that Goethe was "wary of making any remark from which conclusions could be drawn."

There was another contributing factor, again noted by the sharp-eyed Karoline Herder. "It's just a shame that he always has his armor on. Sometimes I see through it anyway!" Somewhat later, she intimated to her husband, still in Italy, what she thought she had discovered: "I've had really a great insight about Goethe. It's that he lives like a poet with the whole world, or the whole world within him. . . . He feels he is a higher being. . . . Since I have discovered what a poet and an artist is, I don't ask for a closer relationship."

She may have been right; in retrospect, Goethe himself connected this *withdrawal into my inner self,* which made him seem brusque, with a mature artistic self-assurance. In the *Campaign in France* he wrote, *In Italy I felt myself torn away little by little from petty thoughts, relieved of false wishes, and my longing for the land of the arts was replaced by a longing for art itself; I had become aware of it, and now I wanted to penetrate it. . . . By filling our inmost being with great objects and sentiments, art supplants all wishes for what is outside ourselves, . . . we feel less and less need to communicate.*

Thus, in retrospect, he asserts that his newly rekindled devotion to art made him withdrawn, unapproachable, and, above all, taciturn in accordance with the maxim *Artist, don't talk! Just create!* In the first months after his return from Italy, it was especially *Tasso* that he wanted to finally finish. The duke had agreed to extend the leave from his official duties until he did so. And a visit from Karl Philipp Moritz for several weeks in the winter of 1788–89 proved to be of great importance. His essay "On the Plastic Imitation of the Beautiful," which

Moritz and Goethe had worked on together in Rome, had just been published. For Goethe, it was so much a part of his inner transformation in Italy that he later even included excerpts of the text in the *Italian Journey*. He called the work *the real result of our association* and stressed *its share in my Tasso*.

In his essay, Moritz developed an incisive and compelling argument for the autonomy of art. His central idea is to apply Spinozism to art. Spinoza had declared that the entire universe is God. Therefore nature—the world as a whole—was not to be reserved for some transcendent purpose. It cannot be of use for anything that lies beyond itself. All significance is contained within it and is not to be found outside of it. That is, Moritz models his concept of art on Spinoza's concept of the world as a whole, as a self-enclosed totality in miniature. Like the world as a whole, art is defined by the fact that it is not subordinate, not useful, not tied to a purpose. It is a rich but self-enclosed nexus of meaning that reveals itself only to the person who—whether as creator or audience—seeks everything that is within it and nothing outside of it. An artist can create only if the focus of his activity lies completely within the work, and if he has no other considerations. If he wants to be accommodating or make money, to satisfy political demands or conventional morality, it will tear him away from the center of his creation and he will lose the source of his creativity. Something analogous happens to the audience—"recipients" of the work. Art will speak to them only if it is the work itself that attracts; if there are no other considerations or interests. Following Moritz, Kant would later call this lofty lack of practical purpose "disinterested pleasure."

The idea of the autonomy of art acquired great significance for Goethe after his return from Italy. Could it be the way to preserve the artistic life of Rome in the midst of prosaic, everyday life? Before Italy, the art of living consisted of his double existence as an artist and a government official, and Goethe recognized how important it was to keep the two separate. While one could strike poetic sparks from life, one could not allow poetry to dominate life.

What was new was that the idea of autonomy establishes from within art itself the reason why it, and by extension the artist, should be allowed to exist unto itself, a "disinterested whole" in its own self-contained world. Previously, the separation of artist and official was imposed by the external circumstances of life. Now it is required by the inner nature of art, and in such a way that art is elevated, with its inner value enhanced, rather than relegated to the status of an attractive side issue. Previously, art had been seen to be a useless undertaking. That charge vanishes in the face of the autonomy of art. Art is a closed circle, meaningful within itself, and for precisely that reason not subservient to any other purpose. All possible purposes are collected within it. Lines of intentional force lead into art, not out of it. Where there had been insult, there would now be pride: art is no one's subject! Knebel, who knew Goethe very well indeed, notes with astonishment, "Art has completely occupied his mind; he sees it as the goal of all human advancement."

For the completion of *Tasso*, the conviction that the artist embodies the higher man and, implicitly, may be useless in the business of life means that both the artist Tasso and the man of the world Antonio can coexist in a way other than as originally imagined by Goethe. Since the artist in his work belongs to a higher, autonomous sphere, he doesn't threaten the rights and wisdom of worldly affairs. They are no longer competing for the same ideal. The artist is simultaneously empowered and disempowered. Antonio says of Tasso,

> *I've known him for years. To know him is so easy*
> *Because he is too proud to dissimulate.*
> *He sinks into himself as if the world*
> *Within his bosom were enough and he*
> *Complete in his own world, and everything*
> *Around him simply vanished. He ignores it,*
> *Or rejects it, lets it go, and is content—*
> *But suddenly, as when some random spark*
> *Ignites a mine—be it joy, or sorrow,*
> *Anger, or a whim—he then bursts out:*
> *And now he wants to grab and hold it all.*
> *Whatever he thinks up has to happen now;*
> *Something that takes years of preparation*
> *Must now be realized this very instant,*
> *And in an instant that must be abolished*
> *Which years of weary work would scarce undo.*

From himself he demands the impossible
So that he can demand the same from others.

In poetry anything is possible, even the impossible; politics and other areas of life, however, deal with the art of the possible. Antonio is shown to be right to the extent that Tasso's incursions from poetry into other areas of reality do not respect the inner logic of those areas. That is true not just for politics but also for love. The princess loves Tasso, but in an incorporeal way. Those are the rules of the game. As long as she is the unspoken heroine of his poems, everything is in order. But once Tasso gives in to his physical desire and actually touches her, it is an invasion from poetry into life in the flesh. It happens in the next-to-last scene. Tasso says to the princess, *I feel myself relieved of all affliction, / Free as a god, and owe it all to you!* He feels empowered by his feelings; he overflows: *My heart drives on, unstoppable, toward you.* He falls into her arms, and she pushes him away. By the final scene, Antonio is quite prepared to acknowledge Tasso's genius. After Tasso's declaration *And if a man's struck dumb by misery, / A god gave me power to say how much I suffer,* Antonio approaches him and gives him his hand. Antonio is given more than just the opportunity to show his magnanimity; he also gets to show that he is the wiser one who can survey both spheres—of poetry and of practicality—unlike Tasso, who is always in danger of becoming obsessively absorbed in poetry. Antonio tells him, *And when you seem to lose yourself entirely, / Compare yourself! Realize what you are!* Tasso is still more than just his poetic existence, as Antonio reminds him: *You're not as miserable as you think. / Pluck up your courage! Don't indulge yourself.* The poet in Tasso is whole and complete, but he is not the whole Tasso. Real life is more comprehensive than the life of poetry. And that is why, in the end, Tasso seeks stability from his opponent with the words (they are his last), *Just so the drowning sailor clasps his arms / Around the rock he thought would be his ruin.*

The autonomy of art that Goethe and Moritz found so useful is a formula for empowerment in the sense that it enhances artistic self-confidence. It is effective as long as the spell of art is unbroken. Then all intention and significance are enclosed within it—Spinoza's All is One. If the spell is broken and the circle opened, however, what made sense and had significance a moment ago may collapse in on itself. And then everything depends on whether one is anything more than just a poet. Then a Tasso needs his Antonio and the poet his privy councilor.

Goethe returned from Italy with heightened self-confidence as an artist, but without Tasso's illusions. He intends to be both things: Tasso, the poetic genius, and Antonio, the wise man of the world. For his erotic life, that no longer means just the disembodied Platonic friendship with Charlotte von Stein, to whom, as he once wrote her, he was reciting his inner novel. Perhaps he would have continued that friendship for a while longer in the same way, but he needed an additional, sensually satisfying partner. Fortunately, he found Christiane. In the end, he writes in the *Campaign in France*, he might have been left alone with his poetic passion *in that strange period, if a happy domestic relationship had not known how to sweetly refresh me.*

In 1790, at the request of the duke, Goethe set out for Venice to accompany Anna Amalia on her return from Italy. Eager to get back to his *domestic relationship*, he found little pleasure in the journey, confessing to the duke, *confidentially, that this journey has dealt a fatal blow to my love for Italy . . . the first bloom of inclination and curiosity has fallen. . . . In addition, there is my proclivity for the erotio I left behind and for the little creature in diapers.*

Without any lengthy journeys in the year 1791, able to devote himself fairly uninterruptedly to his new life, he found contentment with Christiane in the hunting lodge outside the town walls. He wrote to Knebel on March 20, *My life on the whole is pleasant and good. I have every reason to be satisfied with my situation, and I can only wish this state to continue.* Böttiger, just beginning his post as principal of the Weimar gymnasium, left a not terribly flattering portrait of Goethe's circumstances at the time: "Nothing is simpler than his current domesticity. In the evening he sits in an armchair in a well-heated room with a white carter's cap on his head, wearing a flannelette jacket and long fleece pantaloons, in down-at-the-heel slippers and drooping stockings, while he rocks his little boy on his knees . . . on the other side, Donna Vulpia with her darning. This is the family group."

CHAPTER 20

The Revolution, *this most terrible of all events.*
Against Pervasive Politicizing. Goethe's Praise of Restraint.
In the War. Goethe's New Realism. Back in Weimar.
Revolution as Farce: *The Citizen-General* and *The Agitated.*
Atrocities in Mainz and *Reineke the Fox.*

····

OETHE HAD RETURNED FROM ITALY TO VERY ADVAN-
tageous terms. The duke allowed him to continue to enjoy all the privileges of office while releasing him from some of its responsibilities
and even raising his salary. He retained his seat on the privy council,
was free to attend its meetings or not, and for a while continued as pro
forma chairman of other commissions, their day-to-day business conducted by professional bureaucrats. There was no longer much work
for him to do, and he restricted his involvement to occasional inspec-
tions. It was what he found most congenial: getting an overview of a
situation, understanding it, intervening, planning—and then watching things develop and prosper. His one added obligation—as principal
director of the newly founded court theater—didn't feel like a burden.
At first, it was more a hobby than a duty.

Goethe now had more time to devote to science and art, a wish he
had expressed in a letter to the duke from Rome: *Accept me as a guest.*
Let me fill out the entire measure of my existence and enjoy life at your side; thus
will my strength, like a hilltop spring now opened, concentrated, and purified,
be easy to channel in this direction or that, according to your will. Asking the
duke for the security and appropriate elevation for the development of
his powers placed the emphasis on the individual aspect, *the entire mea-*
sure of my existence. He didn't want to slog away at things others could
likely do better—routine administrative tasks, for example. Instead, he

wished for the space to do what he was best at. In filling out his own life, he would at the same time *enhance* the life and environment of the duke—a sort of self-realization as public service.

The societal order that enabled Goethe's individual development in the first place soon found itself in turmoil and under threat, however—if not in Germany, for the time being, then across the border in revolutionary France. Day after day, week after week, this was written about, discussed, and vociferously trumpeted everywhere: the Tennis Court Oath on June 20, 1789, when the deputies of the Third Estate organized themselves as the National Assembly and, in the words of the great Mirabeau, confirmed their intention to remain together until the new constitution was passed; the rumor of counterrevolution and the subsequent storming of the Bastille on July 14; the outbreak of lynch law with the first aristocrats swinging from lampposts; the formation of a National Guard; the king bowing before it and accepting the cockade; Federation Day on the Champ de Mars in 1790 (the largest assemblage of people in history up to that time). And then the revolutionary storm that swept through the country: the revolt of the peasants; the "great fear" that had the country holding its breath; the beginning of aristocratic emigration, with the cream of the ancien régime slogging along muddy roads toward Germany; the king's attempt to flee; his imprisonment, trial, and execution; the Jacobins' Reign of Terror; the military mobilization of the masses; and the wars in which the revolution first defended itself against the allied forces of the old powers, then went on the counteroffensive.

Most of Goethe's contemporaries were immediately convinced that what was happening in France was of world-historical importance and would continue to evoke horror or admiration for generations to come. These events possessed a mythic aura even as they occurred, and were interpreted as the birth of a new age. They moved hearts and minds in Germany—in Weimar, among Goethe's friends and associates, Wieland and Herder were the most sympathetic—until people began to feel their practical consequences. In retrospect, Goethe noted that it had taken him many years *to get a literary grip on this most terrible of all events in its causes and consequences.* He couldn't get free of it, not even when he took refuge in his plants, bones, and color theory. And worse yet, *the preoccupation with this vast subject* had *unnecessarily almost sapped my poetic capabilities.*

Though he found the revolution *terrible*, he empathized with the overwhelming passion driving it. In *Hermann and Dorothea*, his epic poem about the revolution's refugees, he wrote,

> *Who could ever deny it? Our hearts beat higher and stronger,*
> *Beat with a pulse more pure in breasts that breathed more free*
> *Then, when the first bright gleam of a new morning arose,*
> *When first we heard of the Rights of Man, common to all,*
> *Felt the thrill of freedom and sang in praise of equality!*
> *Everyone hoped to live as he chose, and it seemed to us all that*
> *Now the bonds in which many a land was ensnared would loosen,*
> *Bonds that were held in the hands of idleness and self-interest.*
> *In those teeming and urgent days all nations looked toward the*
> *City long since become capital of the world.*
> *Did it not now, more than ever, deserve that glorious name?*

What made the revolution so *terrible* for Goethe? He was well aware of the flagrant injustice and exploitation that surrounded him even in the duchy, for which he bore some responsibility. He wrote to Knebel a few years before the revolution, *But you know that when the aphids sit on the rose boughs and have sucked themselves nice and fat and green, then the ants come along and suck all the filtered juice out of their bodies. And so it goes, and we have come to this pass, that in the upper region, more is eaten in one day than the lower region can gather / organize (ad alia)** in one day.* The greed, extravagance, and capriciousness of the aristocracy were for him the real causes of the revolution, and so his opposition to it could not have been founded on a simple defense of the ancien régime. In *The Agitated*, his comedy about the revolution, there is a judicious countess whom Goethe later described to Eckermann as what an aristocrat should be: *She has persuaded herself that one can put pressure on the people but not oppress them, and that the revolutionary uprisings of the lower classes are a result of the injustices of the upper class.* In Goethe's view, when things come to a revolutionary pass, problems are not solved but made more acute. Instead

---

* Latin: among other things.

of selfishness from above, selfishness from below holds sway, even more calamitous, as it is paired with pent-up fury and envy and a barbarous lack of culture. For Goethe, the revolution was a terrible, elemental event, a sort of natural disaster in the political world, a volcanic eruption. It was likely no accident that, in the months that followed it, he was preoccupied with volcanism and Neptunism and the controversy about the relative importance of fire and water in the formation of the earth's surface. Goethe was an adherent of Neptunism, which claimed that the oceans slowly effect change in the surface. He was attracted by the gradual nature of that change and repelled by the sudden violence of volcanic change, in both nature and society. He was on the side of evolution, not revolution.

It was not just the forced aspect of revolution that dismayed Goethe. Revolution was terrible because he had also no illusions about its possible consequences for himself. He feared that in Germany, too, the social order that had protected and privileged him could be undermined and, in the end, destroyed. The possibility awakened panicky thoughts, as it had a few years earlier during the Diamond Necklace Affair in France, which had made an *unspeakable impression* on him; revealing the decadence of the aristocracy and monarchy, it foreshadowed a breakdown of the existing order. As he wrote in the *Annals* (a chronological record of his works) for 1789, he reacted in such a way that, to his friends, he *seemed almost to have lost my mind.*

Goethe resented sympathizers with the revolution who lived well under the old order but did not feel they owed loyalty to those who had granted them privileges. He wrote self-ironically and provocatively to Herder, who intermittently counted himself among the friends of the revolution, *I shall now adopt the principles of my gracious lord. He feeds me and therefore I am obliged to be of his opinion.* Even many years later, Goethe was still irritated *that people in the Fatherland amused themselves by making light of sympathies which, after all, held a similar fate in store for us.* Because the revolution threatened his own social and material existence, it was a truly serious matter for him—too serious to be an object of frivolous political discussion. That pervasive politicizing engendered by the revolution was the second aspect of the fear it instilled in him.

Politics had always been the business of the aristocracy. Whether there was war or peace, whether you were poor or passably well-off, it was all accepted as fate, like the weather. Now the masses were becoming politically mobilized, and Goethe found that sinister: *The masses have to smash things / To make themselves regarded, / Their judgment is retarded.* Political opinions that went beyond one's own experience and responsibilities were of no use to him. You shouldn't trust them even if they were your own: *Our part in public affairs is mostly just philistinism.*

The extremely well-read Goethe could make fun of the makers of public opinion who merely read a lot and were quick to pass judgment without much judgment of their own. He disapproved of idle curiosity and thought that if one seeks nothing but oneself, the search will not succeed. *Active engagement with the world* was necessary, unhurried, and thorough observation: *Man knows himself only to the extent that he knows the world. . . . Carefully examined, every new object opens up a new organ within us.* The emphasis is on *carefully examined,* indicating a relationship to reality that encompasses more of the world than mere opinion mongering.

Although Goethe could not remain entirely uninfluenced by the politicized spirit of the times (he bought a toy guillotine for his son, August, after all), he was determined to seek refuge from the pressure of current events in calm observation of natural phenomena. *Meanwhile, I become by the day more attached to these sciences* [optics and color theory] *and I can see that they will perhaps eventually become my sole activity.*

That wasn't entirely so. In addition to his studies of nature, art and literature proved a bulwark against the agitated spirit of the day. Undeterred by the restless, politicized times, Goethe kept to his goal: the individualistic cultivation of his personality. In *Wilhelm Meister,* on which he resumed work, his protagonist writes a letter to his friend Werner reflecting on whether it is possible for a bourgeois person to attain the *harmonious development* of his personality. Aside from some exceptions, he writes, that is really possible only for the aristocracy, whose self-assurance is founded not on their property or their achievements but is inherent in their very being. That self-assurance gives their lives and actions a style that never seems strained or rehearsed, but always natural and spontaneous. *Aristocratic manners* become *liberated manners,* and, as if without effort, a balanced demeanor is produced. *Ordinary matters* are treated with *ceremonious grace* and serious matters with *carefree delicacy.*

For the bourgeois individual, by contrast, everything is always external to himself. He strives for possessions, develops his talents, gets things accomplished. The aristocrat *has an effect*, the bourgeois *provides a service*. The bourgeois is never sufficient unto himself, but always out doing things and fulfilling obligations. And if he wants to count for something in and of himself, it always seems pretentious. You sense his calculation and it puts you off. It is the *way society is constituted*, however, that makes the bourgeois a bourgeois and the aristocrat an aristocrat, not just externally but from within; *whether that state of affairs will change sometime, and how it will change,* Wilhelm Meister's letter continues, *doesn't worry me much; it is enough that, as things now stand, I have to think of myself and how I will preserve myself and achieve what I feel to be an imperative requirement. I quite simply have an irresistible propensity for that harmonious formation of my nature that my birth has denied me.*

At a time when the trumpets were sounding an attack on the aristocracy, Goethe professed his esteem for aristocratic style. He knew all too well that the bourgeois awkwardness described in the novel was his as well; we have numerous contemporary reports of Goethe's stiff, formal, awkward behavior on official court occasions. It was obviously acquired rather than natural, hence officious and forced. He lacked what he found admirable in those born into the nobility.

Goethe abstracted a model aristocrat from the impression made on him by the Countess von Werthern-Beichlingen: *This small person has enlightened me. She is worldly-wise, or rather she has the world, knows how to manage the world (la manière). She is like quicksilver, at one moment dividing into a thousand fragments and in the next running back together into a single ball. Confident of her own value and rank, she acts with simultaneous delicacy and an aisance* one has to see to believe. . . . She simply lives her life among other people, and that's exactly the source of the beautiful melody that she plays by touching not every tone, but only select ones. She does it with such lightness and apparent insouciance that one might think her a child who only fools around on the piano without looking at the music, and yet she always knows what and for whom she is playing. What is genius in any art form—she has it in the art of living.* While everywhere else people are thinking passionately about changing the world, Goethe is at pains to change

---

* French: ease.

himself. He knows that in art he is a *genius*, but what he would like to learn better is *the art of living*.

In those politically turbulent years, Goethe was torn between his longing for peace and privacy—for a place *where I can lock up my house and garden*—and his curiosity and even lust for adventure: of being in attendance at, and standing his ground against, historic events. On the one hand, he was looking for a refuge from history. On the other, something drove him out into history, but not with the expectation of finding progress, like so many of his contemporaries. He was not seeking some grand meaning in history but rather to bear witness and to assert himself in it. History attracted him because he wanted to prove himself in relation to it, to wrest from it his unmistakably individual life. On the battlefields of the wars of revolution, the defiant spirit of his Sturm und Drang free-verse poem "To Chronos the Coachman" lived again:

> *Get a move on, Chronos,*
> *Rattle us off at a trot!*
> *Downhill glides our road*
> . . .
> *Briskly bumping over*
> *Sticks, roots, stones we trot*
> *Hastening into life.*
> . . .
> *Drunk on the sun's last rays*
> *Pull me—a sea of fire*
> *Foams in my eyes—*
> *Me, blinded, staggering*
> *Up to the night-dark gate of hell.*
> *Blow, coachman, thy horn*
> *Clatter the echoing hoofs*
> *So Orcus may hear: a prince is arriving.*

The first war of the Prussian-Austrian alliance against revolutionary France began in the spring of 1792. The French National Assembly must have seen danger in the overt preparations of the Prussians and Austrians and the activities of the French émigrés in German territory and decided to steal a march on them by declaring war on Austria and its ally Prussia. War was finally at hand for Duke Karl August, who had since become a major general in the Prussian army. He took the field at the head of his regiment of cuirassiers and expressed the urgent wish that his friend and minister Goethe accompany him. It was a request Goethe could not have evaded, nor did he wish to. After Italy, he felt he owed the duke a debt of gratitude, and he was also excited to venture *out into the world*, convinced as everyone that the French troops would be easily overrun: that they would be as chaotic and disorganized as their political situation. In one of his first letters from the field, Goethe wrote that he counted on being in Paris soon. He promised Christiane to bring her back one or two *notions* from the capital.

It didn't turn out that way. The French army was indeed poorly prepared, and the Prussian and Austrian troops could have seized the opportunity for a swift offensive. Instead, they took their time, partly from arrogance. When they finally did advance, the French were well positioned. The coalition troops Goethe joined up with in late August 1792 had advanced via Longwy to Verdun when heavy rains set in. *Everyone is complaining that Jupiter Pluvius has become a Jacobin too.*

In *Campaign in France, 1792*, written thirty years after the event, Goethe depicts the utter misery of this army train stuck in the mud. A column with provisions could not get through, and food became scarce. The soldiers slept in puddles. Goethe was better off; his cot was in the duke's tent. They came under heavy artillery fire outside Verdun but advanced to Valmy, where a cannonade lasting several days began. Now Goethe was no longer *the idle observer* he was still claiming to be on September 10. Despite the warnings of officers, he mounted his horse and ventured out into a hail of bullets, defying death. Later, he would describe the inner experience of this extreme situation in the calm and objective style of the optical research he was also conducting during the campaign: *Under these circumstances, however, I was soon able to notice that something unusual was happening inside me; I paid close attention to it, and yet the feeling could only be conveyed in a metaphor. It seemed as if one were in a very hot place, and simultaneously completely permeated by the same heat, so that one felt utterly united with the element in which one found oneself. The eyes lose none of their strength or clarity; however, it is as if the world had a certain brownish tint that makes one's condition even more perceptive, as well as objects more perceivable. I was not able to observe any agitation of my blood. Instead, everything seemed to be swallowed up in that blaze. This makes clear in what sense one could describe this condition as a fever. Meanwhile, it remains remarkable that the dreadful anxiety is conveyed to us only by our ears; for the thunder of the cannons, the howling, whistling, whirring of the bullets through the air is the real cause of such feelings.*

The cannonade continued throughout the night, as did the rain, and he dug himself in with only a greatcoat to cover him, a *premature burial*. In *Campaign in France, 1792*, Goethe claims that during this barrage he uttered the famous sentence *here and today a new era of world history begins, and you can say you were there.* Though there is no other witness to that, he did write a letter to Knebel directly from the field that echoes the sentiment: *I'm very happy to have seen all this with my own eyes, and that when people talk about this important epoch, I can say, et quorum pars minima fui.**

They were unable to advance farther on Valmy. The coalition troops did not even try to break through. The retreat began and turned into a disorderly rout. Supplies were disastrously short, and they slaughtered their exhausted horses. Dysentery was widespread. Goethe fell ill himself. The roads were muddy and jammed, and they came under fire from pursuing French troops. It was an inferno. *And so here I also want to add that, in my misery, I made the playful vow that if I could see us delivered and myself back home, no one would ever again hear a word of complaint from me about my neighbor's gable restricting the open view from my room; on the contrary, it's a gable I now yearn to see. Moreover, I would never again complain of being disgruntled or bored in the German theater, where one can always thank God for the roof over one's head, whatever may be happening on stage.* Via Luxembourg, Goethe reached Trier with the retreating troops, where for the time being he was in safety. He wrote to Voigt in mid-October, *This campaign, one of the most unfortunate of undertakings, will cut a sad figure in the annals of the world.*

So much for contemporary events. For Goethe, it was like death and resurrection. He felt *as if born again*. Again he was just starting *to realize that I am a human being*, he writes in mid-November. After most of his trials were over, he even permitted himself a feeling of quiet tri-

---

* Latin: and of these things I was a small part.

umph: *In these six weeks we have seen and survived more trouble, adversity, anxiety, misery, and danger than in our entire life. The duke is quite well and I too have acquitted myself well.*

His original plan was to travel home via Frankfurt. A visit he had paid his mother on the outbound trip had been too short; they hadn't seen each other for thirteen years. And there were other things to be discussed in Frankfurt. He had been honored when asked whether he would be inclined to accept a position as town councilor. In the meantime, however, Frankfurt had been occupied by the French, and it was impossible to travel there. At the moment that was convenient, for the inquiry was easier to answer by letter than in person, and once back in Weimar, he would write a letter to his mother meant to be shown to others. In it he says that as a native of the republic of Frankfurt, he feels extraordinarily honored by the offer, and that while it would actually be a pleasure to assume such a responsibility in stormy times, that desire is in conflict with another great duty: *His Highness the duke has treated me with such distinguished favor for so many years, and I am so much in his debt, that it would be the grossest ingratitude to leave my post at a moment when the state has most need of loyal servants.* It was another emphatic decision to stay in Weimar.

Rather than Frankfurt, he traveled down the Rhine to Pempelfort, near Düsseldorf, to the idyllic country estate of his friend Fritz Jacobi, there to recuperate from the *bad dream* he had just lived through in the *cozy company* of old friends and acquaintances who quickly gathered at the news of Goethe's arrival. There was a palpable sense of alienation at the gathering, however. In retrospect, it struck Goethe as so severe that, at that point in his narrative in the *Campaign in France*, he recapitulates the changes he has gone through in order to explain the present disagreement, which he reduces to the concept of *realism*. It had always made him uncomfortable, he writes, when his *realism came to the fore but didn't particularly edify his friends.*

What does he mean by *realism* in this context? His yearning of years gone by had given way to a partly sobering, partly satisfying fulfillment. *The longing within me—which I may have cultivated too much in earlier years and which I strongly strove to combat as I grew older—no longer seemed befitting and adequate for a man, and so I looked for complete and final satisfaction.* He had longed for Italy, the land of art. He had gone there; his longing had become reality. He had found art and, through it, had educated and reshaped himself. His brilliant élan had been coupled with a degree of competence and knowledge. For the Göschen edition he had brought to completion works that had remained unfinished for years. That too meant a gain in reality, for a fragment represents only the possibility of a work. He had also abandoned the enthusiast's lyrical encounter with nature and had instead begun to study and investigate it. In other words, Goethe now felt himself to be someone who had not only gained a more realistic attitude but also become more real himself.

Perhaps even too real. The hostilities he had just lived through had *hardened* his mind for the present. His friends in Pempelfort had asked him to read from *Iphigenia*, but he could not bear to do so: *I felt alienated from the sense of tenderness.*

Goethe remained there for four weeks and then paid a visit to Princess Adelheid Amalie Gallitzin, the daughter of a Prussian field marshal and wife of a Russian diplomat, and her circle of friends in Münster. In this group of aristocratic, spiritual Catholics, *the sense of tenderness* was actually the order of the day. The princess reminded him of Fräulein von Klettenberg, and the enchantment of those youthful recollections helped him to fit in now. The princess and her friends were pious and he *behaved accordingly*, which was made all the easier by the fact that these believers were *convivial, clever, and not narrow-minded.* They got along well with one another and were in agreement that *any admiration for a worthy object is always accompanied by a religious feeling.*

Goethe returned to Weimar shortly before Christmas 1792. He informed Christiane of his imminent arrival with the words *Be cheerful, my dear child. Enjoy your peace and quiet while so many thousands of people have been driven from house and home and all their possessions and wander the world without knowing where to go. Kiss the little fellow and love me. My only wish is to soon possess you once more.*

Home at last with Christiane and his son, Goethe felt like a drowning man who had made it to shore. This experience of love in a cozy nest far from the affairs of the great world played a part in Goethe's first play directly addressing the consequences of the revolution. In only three days, from April 23 to 26, 1793, he wrote the one-act comedy *The Citizen-General* as a sequel to a popular French comedy about a rascally barber by the name of Schnaps. Goethe also borrowed other characters from the French play, quickly supplying something current to the Weimar theater where the Schnaps comedy had been a hit. He called the play *a testimony to my annoyingly good mood*. He was annoyed by the popularity of the revolution in German public opinion and sought to maintain his *good mood* by making fun of the revolution through grotesque exaggeration.

Schnaps has taken the uniform, liberty cap, cockade, and saber from a French prisoner of war. Thus costumed, he declares himself to be a representative of the revolutionary government and orders the gullible peasant Märten—whose mind has been damaged by reading too many newspapers—to give him a free breakfast of sour milk and bread as a *patriotic contribution*. Märten's son-in-law Görge, smelling a rat, comes in from the fields and gives Schnaps a thrashing. The commotion brings the village judge running, and the entire house is suspected of being a nest of Jacobins. In the end, the prudent estate owner restores order and contentment. Schnaps is just sent about his business, not even punished, which would only excite *alarm and distrust in a peaceful country*. The play ends with the wise estate owner's summation, *where all classes treat each other fairly, where no one is prevented from working at his own job, where useful insights and skills are generally disseminated . . . but rebellious attitudes of entire nations will have no influence. We will give quiet thanks that we see a sunny sky above us, while elsewhere storms of misfortune hail down over vast tracts of land.*

Despite this sententious ending, the play's witty, succinct dialogue makes for a brisk tempo. In the background, the revolution threatens to be a calamity, but in the foreground, it is a farce. In the end, other things count for more here, for example, that Görge and his bride Röse have already been married for twelve weeks and are still in love. He tells her, *People say that as husband and wife, you don't love each other as much as you used to. It's not true, Röse. How long have we had each other already?* Here Goethe was speaking from the heart. He'd been living with Christiane for almost three years now, and they still loved each other.

In its day, *The Citizen-General* was one of Goethe's most successful plays, a fact he later sought to suppress. He claimed it had had an *unpleasant* reception. In fact, the lightweight farce was performed more often than *Iphigenia* or *Tasso*—fifteen times in the first few years. Goethe did not care to acknowledge the play, and it was not included in the occasional series entitled *New Works*, issued by the Berlin publisher Unger.

Encouraged by its popularity, however, Goethe immediately began work on a new play that would also treat the consequences of the revolution in Germany. He had apparently become convinced that it would occur twice: in France as tragedy, then in Germany as farce. He never finished he work, entitled *The Agitated*, but thirty years later he told Eckermann that one could *to a certain extent regard it as my political creed at that time.*

The play is considerably more serious than *The Citizen-General*. A protest movement arises out of the oppressive conditions of peasant life which are the backdrop of the play. Only the spokespersons of that protest appear onstage. They are the supposedly educated peasants, that is, those who can read the newspaper and think they know what's going on in France. They are eager to replay the great scenes of the revolution and to bask in its reflected glory. Breme von Bremsfeld, the ringleader of this agitated group, declares, *How often these valiant heroes have been painted and etched in copper! And we will enjoy that honor as well. We will go down in posterity in that pose.*

The imposter citizen-general Schnaps wore a disguise. The disguise of the agitated peasants is ideological and rhetorical, but the fraudulent effect is the same. As in *The Citizen-General*, it is the sensible aristocrats who reassert order and justice. The spunky young countess holds a rifle on a treacherous bailiff while demanding a document that justifies the actions of the peasants. The young countess's mother embodies wisdom and virtue, and Goethe puts his *political creed* into her mouth: *Ever since I perceived how easily unfairness builds up from generation to generation, and how most generous acts are merely personal gestures and apparently, only self-interest is hereditary; ever since I have seen with my own eyes that human nature can be beaten down and humiliated but not crushed or destroyed, I have made a solemn resolution to strictly avoid every single action that seems unfair to me and to express my opinion about such actions to my family, in company, at court, and in town. I will no longer keep silent about any injustice, nor accept any petty tyranny for the sake of some apparent greater good, even if I should be labeled with the hated name of democrat.*

The response of a bourgeois privy councilor in the play can be considered part of Goethe's *political creed* as well. He declares that what the countess has said is right, and upholds the principle that *Each of us is able to judge and reprove only his own class.* Any critique of one's superiors or inferiors is always contaminated by *peripheral concepts*, for example, envy of the former or contempt for the latter. Everyone should keep his own house in order—and that should go for contact between social classes as well. What remains unsaid is that pressure from below was necessary to produce the countess's laudable sentiments, something she indirectly admits: *I used to take it too lightly when some property owner was unjust.*

Goethe soon put the play aside without finishing it. Even though it was important to him to articulate some of his political convictions, he realized that a farcical chamber drama was incommensurate with the enormous events in France: the September massacres, the arrest and execution of the royal family, the bloody insurrections in the provinces, the carnage, and finally the beginning of Jacobin terror. The play was more suited to the tone of the student unrest in Jena, which featured fistfights on the market square, wrangles with the police, stone throwing, nocturnal caterwauling, and a protest march out of the town. Since students were an important source of income for Jena, this unrest was enough to keep the privy council busy for days. Even Goethe took his council seat for the deliberations.

Then the duke called upon him to be his battlefield companion one more time. From May to August 1793, Goethe took part in the allies' siege and capture of Mainz. Under the protection of French troops, friends of the revolution in Mainz—among them Georg Forster, whom Goethe had visited only the year before—had proclaimed a republic. An end was to be put to that and the insubordination punished. Atrocities were committed on both sides. The French drove noncombatants out of the city, including old people, women, and children. The besiegers—with *equal cruelty*, as Goethe noted—left the helpless civilians to their fate, without supplies or shelter. For three weeks, the town was attacked with explosives and incendiary bombs, mostly at night. There were fires everywhere, and during the beautiful summer days heavy smoke lay over the city. People from the surrounding countryside gathered to watch the bombardment. On one lovely Sunday morning, the thunder of cannon was mixed with more delicate tones as oboists played for a party of officers. The duke and Goethe were present, and the latter wrote to Jacobi, *On the one hand, we're hav-*

ing a jolly time, and on the other, it's sad. We're actors in a real historical drama (cf. Shakesp. As You Like It or The Friends), in which I represent Jaques in my own way. In the foreground, pretty women and wine jugs, in the background flames, just like a depiction of Lot and his daughters.

The city endured terrible things, and it was not even the victorious troops who acted with particular cruelty. Worse were the inhabitants who were in a mood to take revenge on the revolutionaries. At first, Goethe found it to be in order that the French soldiers were granted free passage but not the "clubbists," Mainz's home-grown revolutionaries. They should have to answer to those who had suffered under their administration. *The misery these people have caused is great*, he wrote to Jacobi. As the mood of the furious crowd grew more ugly, however, Goethe (as he later claimed) tried to intervene and calm things down. But perhaps he was not as calm and commanding after all. His letters of the time, at least, speak a different language. What he was forced to witness in Mainz affected him so deeply that he was almost paralyzed: *In my present situation I am befallen by a sort of stupor and I find that the trivial expression "my brain is numb" exactly describes the situation of my spirit.*

Work on the epic poem *Reynard the Fox*, a translation and reworking of the medieval fable that mirrors in the animal world the cruel acts of humans, helped him overcome his *stupor*. While the real world became more and more *bloody and bloodthirsty*, he found it helpful to devote himself, *half despairingly*, to the *inevitable reality* of savagery, deceit, and malice he found so vividly portrayed in *Reynard the Fox*.

In the *Campaign*, he wrote of his prevailing mood of those days, *But I sought to save myself even from this dreadful misery by declaring the whole world to be base.*

CHAPTER 21

Goethe Gathers His Circle around Him.

Love, Friendship, Science, and Art Keep Life Going.

Fichte in Jena. Goethe's New Interest in Philosophy.

The Friendship with Schiller Begins with a *happy event*.

The First Exchange of Ideas.

. . . .

SHORTLY BEFORE RETURNING TO WEIMAR, GOETHE WROTE to Jacobi, *My vagabond life and the political mood everyone is in are driving me home, where I can gather around me a circle that nothing can enter except love and friendship, art and science.* His domestic arrangement with Christiane made him happy. In "To a Woman," a series of aphorisms in distichs (couplets of one hexameter and one pentameter line), he writes, *Knowst thou the marvelous poison of love unsatisfied? / It can enliven and scorch, suck and restore thy marrow. / Knowst thou the wondrous effect of love at last fulfilled? / Loving bodies it joins when it frees their spirits.* Goethe felt looked after but not tied down by Christiane. He was proud of his little family, but could continue to live like a bachelor, connected to his home but intellectually independent. The love affair had become a loving routine: *Difficult to tame is already the mere inclination. / If thou add habit thereto it is invincible.* Nor was it necessary to keep his little family hidden anymore. They had moved out of the hunting lodge outside the town wall and back into his imposing, newly renovated house on the Frauenplan in the center of town. In the summer of 1794, the duke had made Goethe a present of the house in gratitude for his company on the military campaigns. After a stillbirth in 1791, Christiane gave birth to a daughter, Karoline, on November 21, 1793. "Since a few days ago, Goethe has a little daughter as well," Charlotte von Stein informed her son Fritz. "He is terribly happy about it, for he's as amiable as a little earwig." But the child died two weeks later. Goethe could not bear the pain, falling to the floor and thrashing about in grief.

His return from the war saw him cultivating friendships more deliberately. He wrote more frequently to Knebel and Jacobi and paid more heed to social occasions, especially with Herder and Wieland. When it's storming outside you have to stick closer together, he said. Johann Heinrich Voss, the translator of Homer, visited Weimar in the early summer of 1794 and was positively enchanted by Goethe's conviviality. "Goethe turned to me," he wrote to his wife, "and asked why I had to leave so soon; he asked me to give him another day. . . . I went with Herder to smoke a pipe together in his study. . . . We were called to tea and found the Wielands, Goethe, Böttiger, and von Knebel. They gathered around me and wanted to hear this and that about my studies of Homer, . . . Goethe came, pressed my hand, and thanked me for such a Homer. Wieland did the same. . . . At table the conversation about Homer's poems and his era continued. . . . I had to describe the Homeric house. Everything seemed new and gratifying. We became boisterous and jolly. The biblical patriarchs were critiqued with irrepressible laughter, while Herder undertook a comical defense of them. We did some serious quaffing: Würzburg wine and punch. Goethe sat next to me; he was much more jovial than people say. We parted after midnight. Wieland embraced and kissed me on my way."

The science in which Goethe was absorbed never failed to give him pleasure. When people spoke to him of the latest political news or their opinions, he would change the subject, telling them about a frog's intestines, a snail's anatomy, or the muscles of a goat's head. He drafted plans for a large-scale treatise on the morphology of plants and animals, studied the characteristics of monocotyledons, carefully dissected the seed membranes of flowers, and pressed the duke to approve the creation of a botanical garden and institute in Jena. The biologist Karl Batsch was appointed director, and Goethe oversaw the garden, at times seeming more enthusiastic about it than about the theater he directed.

He had also developed a new interest in optics and color theory. He had already formulated what would be the guiding principle of his *Theory of Color* during the siege of Mainz, and it remained unchanged in the published version of that great work: *1. Light is the simplest, most indivisible, most homogeneous entity that we know. It is not composite. 2. In particular, it is not composed of colored lights. Every light that has taken on a color is darker than colorless light. Brightness cannot be composed of darkness.* Thus it could not contain the spectrum within itself, as Newton had taught. For Goethe, light was an ur-phenomenon: colors do not develop *out of* it but rather *in contact with* it, wherever it encounters another medium.

But most academics to whom Goethe sent his essays did not agree with him, including the Göttingen physicist Georg Christoph Lichtenberg, to whom he sent a paper on "Colored Shadows." Lichtenberg sent him a deferential and witty reply insinuating that he considered Goethe a naïve empiricist. "We always believe," Lichtenberg wrote, "we *perceive* something that we actually *only infer.*" Lichtenberg praised Goethe's observations but went on to describe other observations that led to different conclusions, and mentioned some titles Goethe should consult. Goethe thought a great deal of Lichtenberg and at first forgave him his reservations about the theory of color: *I wish very much that this man will remain a friend of my undertaking, even if he was not able to persuade himself of the truth of my opinion.* When Lichtenberg later made no mention of Goethe's research in his textbook on optics, Goethe had no more time for him.

In his investigations of the natural world, Goethe had to rely on his own instincts. Outwardly, the scientific community paid him respect, but they didn't really take him seriously. As with love and friendship, here too he drew that dubious *circle* around himself to spare himself vexation. The experts could not spoil the *phenomena* he thought he could see with his own eyes.

And as for art—that fourth pillar of his existence—Goethe resumed work on *Wilhelm Meister.* On December 7, 1793, he wrote to Knebel, *Now my thoughts are bent upon deciding what I want to begin in the coming year. One must force oneself to be attached to something. I think it will be my old novel,* a project that had been in the works for almost two decades.

To press himself, he signed a very lucrative contract with the publisher Johann Friedrich Gottlieb Unger in early 1794, agreeing to deliver four volumes, each containing two of the novel's eight books, for 600 taler per volume. That Goethe could command such an exorbitant fee for a novel was a vote of confidence in his market value, and put the complaints in some of his letters that he was as good as forgotten in perspective. He either didn't believe it himself, or counted on winning readers back with this great novel. And a great, or at least long, novel was what he had in mind. Much remained to be done. When he signed the contract with Unger, only four and a half of the planned eight books were finished, and those were of the original draft, entitled *Wilhelm Meister's Theatrical Mission*. With the year 1794 to be devoted to the novel, he became more attached to the university town of Jena, where he could work in peace, without the distractions of family and court. He set up a snug study in Jena's Old Palace.

The town had become more important to him for other reasons as well. There were new friends, especially Wilhelm von Humboldt, who had moved to Jena early in 1794, drawn by Schiller. Humboldt did everything possible to persuade Goethe to look favorably on Schiller, then in Swabia. Wilhelm's younger brother, Alexander, a natural scientist and mining official, was visiting Jena, and Goethe was deeply impressed by the young man's comprehensive knowledge. He said that a single hour of conversation with Alexander gave him food for thought for a whole week. Goethe would have happily appointed him professor on the spot, but Alexander had other plans. Goethe now took a lively interest in university affairs. In addition to establishing the botanical institute, he worked on expanding and recataloging the library's holdings, and kept an eye out for ambitious young academics like the historian Karl Ludwig Woltmann, whom he recruited for the university.

After the departure of the Kantian philosopher Karl Leonhard Reinhold, he was particularly proud of bringing to Jena Johann Gottlieb Fichte, a rising star in the philosophical firmament. Within weeks after a visit to Kant, Fichte had written *Attempt at a Critique of All Revelation*, which drew the consequences of Kant's thought for the philosophy of religion more clearly than the master himself had done. Morality, he wrote, is not based on religion but rather creates religion: there are no revelations except those of the conscience. Kant was impressed by this work, and not only invited Fichte to lunch but found a publisher for him. The book by the thirty-year-old appeared anonymously in the spring of 1792.

The publisher hoped it would be attributed to Kant because it was so much in his spirit, which is what happened; the *Attempt* was regarded as Kant's long-awaited final word on the subject of religion. Kant felt obliged to correct the mistaken attribution, and in the *Allgemeine Literatur-Zeitung*, published in Jena, informed readers that the honor of being the author of this work did not belong to him but rather to the previously unknown Fichte. It made Fichte instantly famous, and there was no stopping him now: he dared to revolutionize all previous philosophy, radicalizing Kant's concept of freedom in his *Foundations of the Entire Science of Knowledge*, lectures given in the summer of 1794 in Jena. He abstracts from Kant's statement "The 'I think' must be able to accompany all my representations,"* the concept of an all-powerful self that experiences the world either as sluggish resistance or as possible material for its actions. At first blush, this might seem an extravagant and quite abstract claim, but Fichte's talents as a captivating lecturer thrilled and inspired his listeners, even if they didn't understand everything he said. Fichte didn't just talk about thoughts; he wanted to force his listeners to think. Thinking should be taking place in their heads—right now, this minute—the thinking self grasping itself. Fichte was famous for using a wall in his demonstration: listeners should first think of the wall and then think of themselves as that which is different from the wall. That was his way of shaking listeners loose from customary, fossilized thought processes. The most comfortable path—especially for scientists—is to treat yourself as a thing. Reification of the self is the secret principle of materialism. But Fichte wanted to make the living self tangible. He often said that it was easier to make people think they were a piece of lava from the moon than living selves.

Fichte's powerful performances were like bolts of lightning. It was a matter of course that the French Revolution (he published two essays in its defense) was part of the intellectual background to his radical philosophy of freedom. Thanks to Fichte, the word *Ich* (the subject pronoun "I" as well as "the self") gained enormous significance, comparable only to that later given the *Es* (the neuter pronoun "it" as well as "the id" in Freudian psychology) by Nietzsche and Freud.

It is remarkable that Fichte found such favor with Goethe, for

---

* Immanuel Kant, *Critique of Pure Reason*, trans. Paul Guyer and Allen W. Wood (New York: Cambridge University Press, 1998), 246, single quotation marks added.

the young philosopher's revolutionary sympathies could hardly have appealed to him. But Goethe simply ignored them, for which the duke would later reproach him when Fichte had to be dismissed under the charge of being an atheist. What Goethe liked about Fichte's philosophy was its energetic emphasis on activity and aspiration, the strength of the will and the impulse to create form. What was most effective were not subtle and abstract deductions, but a daring enthronement of the creative self. Goethe was prepared to integrate into his thought the idea that perception may be qualified. The first traces of that appear in his color theory, where he paid more attention to the physiology of color perception and declared his adherence to the principle that one always had to ask, *Is it the object that is expressing itself here, or is it you?* He had the printing office send him the first signature of the *Foundations of the Entire Science of Knowledge*, read it immediately, and wrote to Fichte that it contained nothing *that I did not understand or at least thought I understood, nothing that does not easily connect to my usual way of thinking. . . . As far as I am concerned, I shall owe you a great debt of thanks if you can finally reconcile me to the philosophers, whom I could never do without, but with whom I could never be at one.* Fichte did not take it as a polite compliment. He truly felt that Goethe understood him. He wrote to his wife, "Recently he described my system to me so clearly and concisely, that I couldn't have done it more clearly myself."

Goethe's new interest in philosophy also laid a path to the epoch-making event of that summer, the beginning of his friendship with Schiller. Thanks to Fichte, it was Schiller's philosophical bent that now attracted Goethe.

Since their first, unsuccessful encounter in the fall of 1788, the two writers had had only infrequent contact. Although Goethe had promoted an appointment for Schiller in Jena, Schiller could not be especially grateful, since the remuneration was humiliatingly modest. Nevertheless, Schiller made the most of his professorship in Jena. His inaugural lecture in the summer of 1789 became legendary. No other professor had ever attracted so many listeners. The rise of the University of Jena really began with Schiller. By the end of the eighteenth century, it was briefly the capital of German Idealism and Romanticism. (A few years later, Napoleon would consider raising Jena to the status of the major university of the Confederation of the Rhine.) Schiller's self-confidence was strengthened, and he no longer felt it necessary to awkwardly court Goethe. Though he remained interested in making fruitful contact after his initial failure, he waited for it to happen in an unforced way, on some specific occasion, and without any pretentiousness. As he wrote his sister-in-law Karoline, he had been determined to stop looking at Goethe in sidelong envy, which only hindered his own development. "If someone puts his entire strength into his work, he will not go unnoticed by another. That is my plan."

It worked. Goethe had kept track of Schiller and came to appreciate him, no longer regarding him merely as the author of *The Robbers*. In his capacity as artistic director of the theater, Goethe could not help wanting to win over such a talented playwright for the Weimar stage. In the meantime, he had also discovered Schiller's philosophical poetry, which attracted him precisely because it was so far removed from his own lyric style. He also considered Schiller's historical writings masterpieces in both content and style. He was still ambivalent, however, about Schiller's aesthetic theories. While Fichte had given him a better approach to the philosophical element in Schiller's works, there were nonetheless *certain harsh passages*—in Schiller's essay "On Grace and Dignity," for example—which he took personally. He must have been thinking of the passage where Schiller criticizes so-called natural geniuses. Which is more admirable, asks Schiller, the power of a free mind that triumphs over its own resistant nature, or a born genius who has no need to wrestle his works into existence? Schiller favors the mind that builds its body. In intellectual matters, too, he thought that merit should count more than innate privilege. Goethe, who was often called a favorite child of nature and thought of himself as such, could easily infer that Schiller's remark applied to himself. Perhaps he also took umbrage at Schiller's assessment of poetic geniuses, whose entire talent, he said, lies in their youth. "But when that short spring is over and one asks after its promised fruits, they prove to be spongy and often stunted things engendered by a blind, misled impulse to create." While we don't know the exact passages that offended Goethe, it is certain that the essay "On Grace and Dignity," which Goethe in other respects admired and made use of, at first stood in the way of a rapprochement.

But then in June 1794, he received an invitation, signed by Schiller, to join the editorial board of the newly founded periodical *Die Horen*.

Schiller had already assembled a group of editors that included Wilhelm von Humboldt, Fichte, and Woltmann. They hoped to win over Goethe as well. On his trip to Swabia in 1793, Schiller had planned the journal with the publisher Johann Friedrich Cotta. It was an ambitious undertaking, meant to become the voice of Germany as a cultural nation in response to the political nation of revolutionary France, an idea articulated in the letter inviting Goethe to join: "The culture of the Germans has not yet reached the point that what is pleasing to the best among us finds its way into everyone's hands. If the nation's most outstanding writers now enter into a literary association, they will thereby unite the public that has been previously divided." This invitation to share a prestigious platform was the exact unforced approach to Goethe that Schiller had hoped for.

Schiller's intention was that the journal might bring his ideal of grace and dignity to fruition; its literary offerings were to be entertaining and tasteful, its learned articles brilliant. Mere diversion or stuffy academic essays would be excluded. It must have been especially appealing to Goethe that Schiller, as tired of politicizing as Goethe, intended to open *Die Horen* to all topics except politics. Although Goethe's own contributions to *Die Horen* would not always adhere to that principle, and Schiller's *On the Aesthetic Education of Man*, first published there, also had a political orientation, at the moment both thought that abstention from politics would benefit intellectual life.

Goethe did not respond immediately, although he instantly recognized the opportunity to give new impetus not only to literary life in general but to his own output. He could see the advantage for himself if a man like Schiller, a professional writer with widespread connections and influence, was willing to pilot him out of the quiet harbor of the fairly unsuccessful Göschen edition of his works and back into the open seas of popular literary life. It was a publicity campaign that would perhaps benefit the soon-to-be-published *Wilhelm Meister* even if, by contract, an excerpt in *Die Horen* would not be possible. Yet Goethe held off on his answer for a little while, perhaps because he sensed that this was the beginning of what he would call a *new epoch* in his life. With great care—several drafts of the letter survive—he formulated his answer with a mixture of diplomacy and confession: *I shall be heartily delighted to become one of the company. Should there be anything*

*among my unpublished works that would be suitable for such a collection, I shall
be happy to let you have it; what is certain, however, is that a closer association
with men as stouthearted as the participants will put new life into the course of
works of my own that have become bogged down.*

This was Goethe's first letter to Schiller. The younger man was
happy to have secured such a prominent colleague for his project, but
he didn't yet dream he was about to make an incomparable friend as
well. Schiller wrote to Körner about Goethe's acceptance, "It is turning out to be a very select society, the likes of which has never come
together in Germany before." At the same time, Goethe commented
on the new connection with pleasure, but still with some reserve, *I must
add that since this new epoch, Schiller too is becoming more friendly and trusting.*

Then came an encounter that Goethe would later call a *happy event.*
His later depiction of it, in the *Morphological Notebooks*, comes in the
context of his theory of the *Urpflanze.* The primal scene of the friendship with Schiller, amid discussion of the primordial plant—what a
perfect conjunction! A passage from the *Annals* lays particular emphasis on this organic-metaphoric correlation: *for me it was a new spring in
which everything was sprouting happily together, emerging from opened seeds and
branches.*

It happened on July 20, 1794, a Sunday. Goethe had come to Jena to
consult with the editors of *Die Horen*—Schiller above all, of course—
during the coming week. He had not counted on meeting Schiller
beforehand on this hot afternoon, however, at a lecture for the Society
of Naturalists in the cool rooms of the palace. Schiller did not often
attend such events, and the surprise added to the effect. After the lecture, as groups of people left the hall chatting with one another, *by
chance*—according to Goethe's description—he suddenly found himself standing next to Schiller and they fell into conversation. Schiller was critical of what they had just heard. The lecturer had treated
the world of plants in a fragmentary way, with no inner coherence or
life. It was no way to inspire public interest in natural science. Goethe
agreed, but pointed out that there had certainly been other attempts
to explore and portray the interconnectedness of natural phenomena.
Schiller conceded the point but stressed that it was possible only with
the aid of the ideas one brought to observation. In and of themselves,
observations were always isolated and yielded no context.

They had stumbled unwittingly into contested territory, as that was exactly what Goethe was then slaving away at: a synopsis of phenomena that yield a direct, unforced, natural experience of interconnection, the metamorphosis of plants being a prime example. He was convinced that one needed only to observe in order for it to become obvious that the leaf was what recurred in all the various plant forms and thus constituted both their variability and their constancy. *For I had realized that in the organ of a plant we usually call its leaf, the real Proteus lies hidden, which can conceal and reveal itself in all configurations. Forward and backward, a plant is always only a leaf.* He formulates it that way in the *Italian Journey*, and he must have depicted the leaf as the ur-phenomenon of plant life to Schiller in similar terms. What was ineluctable about this ur-phenomenon, however, was that one could see it. The leaf as a prodigious *Proteus* was something utterly ostensive and not a mere idea. From that conviction, Goethe went on to ask, could it not be that there was a sort of exemplary incarnation of a plant that had developed from a leaf, some *Urpflanze*? In the *Italian Journey* he remarks, *There must be such a thing! Otherwise how would I know that this or that object was a plant if they weren't all formed according to a single pattern?*

Spurred on by Schiller's questions, this is the line of thought Goethe must have developed. In his depiction of the *happy event*, he says merely, *I propounded the metamorphosis of plants in a lively manner.* So *lively*, in fact, that he lost track of everything and suddenly found himself in Schiller's house. Schiller himself had remained conscious enough of their surroundings to steer his enthusiastic interlocutor in that direction. And there they sat, side by side. Perhaps Schiller's wife, Charlotte, brought them something cool to drink, to slake their thirst and because the discussion was heated. Goethe got up a head of steam, grabbed pen and paper, *and with some characteristic strokes, I made a symbolic plant emerge before his very eyes.* Schiller, however, returned to their point of departure, namely, the question of whether it is an idea or a concrete, intuitively accessible object that vouches for inner cohesion. For Schiller, it could only be an idea, and pointing to Goethe's drawing of the symbolic plant, he said, *That is not an experience, it's an idea.* With that, writes Goethe, *the point that divided us was most precisely identified.* And although Goethe had the presence of mind to retreat with the witty remark *I find it so nice that I have ideas without knowing it, and even see them with my eyes,* their difference remained: *neither of us could consider himself the victor. We both thought we were unassailable.*

How could this encounter, largely the passionate articulation of a difference of opinion, become the primordial event of their friendship? Perhaps it was for that very reason, as it was a difference in which the two poles had powerful attraction for each other, as though each could find in the other the complement needed for its own completeness. That is certainly how Goethe later interpreted his relationship with Schiller. *It is, however, rare that two people constitute, as it were, half of each other, do not repel but attract and complete each other.* If everything seemed to push the one toward ideas and the other toward intuitive accessibility, each would be able to give the other something of what he had. The ideal becomes more sensuous and the observable more cerebral.

On that warm summer afternoon in 1794, their latent mutual attraction was finally able to blossom freely. It was hastened by other favorable circumstances, which Goethe does not fail to mention: his long acquaintance with Schiller's Charlotte, née Lengefeld, and Frau von Stein's goddaughter; their mutual interest in *Die Horen*; and the encouragement of other friends. Here Goethe means above all Wilhelm von Humboldt, who had pleaded Schiller's case to him.

Their second meeting two days later was in fact at the Humboldts'. For Schiller, it was the more important encounter. He dated their friendship from that day. On Sunday, they had discussed nature. On Tuesday at the Humboldts', it was culture. If their differences dominated the first meeting, there was more agreement about culture, even if they approached it from different directions. Schiller wrote to his friend Körner about it a few weeks later: "We had . . . spoken at length and breadth about art and art theory and told each other our main ideas, at which we had arrived by different paths. . . . Each had something to give that the other was missing, and each got something in return. Since then, the ideas sown on that day have put down roots in Goethe, and now he feels a need to join me and in my company follow the path he had been treading alone and with no encouragement. I very much look forward to an exchange of ideas that will be so fruitful for me."

That exchange got off to a powerful start with Schiller's famous first, long letter to Goethe. It came over a month later, on August 23.

Schiller had held back at first because he knew Goethe would be spending the next few weeks on a diplomatic mission with the duke. In his moving reply, Goethe wrote that he could not imagine a more beautiful birthday present than this letter, *in which with a friendly hand you draw up the sum of my existence and through your interest, encourage me to make more active and lively use of my abilities.*

The *sum of my existence*—the phrase indicates emphatic agreement and is a flattering compliment for Schiller's skill as a portraitist. Goethe found Schiller's image of him to be accurate. He portrayed him as someone who can trust his powers of observation, who thinks with his eyes and is guided by a strong "anticipation" of possible connections between things; he is not led astray into idle speculation, however, because he always keeps in contact with genuine experience, beginning with the simplest facts and elements of life and then mounting step by step to the complex forms of human experience, thus undertaking to develop spirit from elemental nature. The end point could be a perfected image of spiritual nature, but an individual life is too short to reach that goal. "But even to have set out on such a path is worth more than to complete any other."

These remarks apply more to the scientist. Goethe the poet had a unique formative power that, according to Schiller, drew its best from unconscious sources. "In your authentic intuition, everything that analysis tediously searches for is present, and much more completely so, and your own riches remain hidden from you only because they reside complete within you." In short, unconscious genius is at work in Goethe.

At this point, Schiller brings himself into play. He presents himself as a complementary figure, but also as someone of genius. If Goethe proceeds from the particular and concrete to the general and conceptual, Schiller seeks a concrete embodiment of the conceptual idea. One operates inductively, the other deductively. And both run into problems. A thought can fail to achieve concrete experience and evaporate into abstraction; experience and intuition, conversely, do not always achieve the necessary clarity and transparency. But if such different minds listen to and help each other, they can achieve happy moments of complementary enrichment. Schiller's letter is propelled by euphoric confidence in the success of this friendship: Goethe will use Schiller as a mirror of his consciousness, and Schiller will learn from Goethe how to trust in the powers of the unconscious and intuition. Then they would be in fact the *two halves* of a circle, as Goethe would later regard the friendship.

Goethe accepted this interpretation. In the letter he sent in answer there is a remark, however, that is not without irony: *You will soon see for yourself what a great advantage your participation will be for me, when you know me better and discover a sort of darkness and wavering in me that I cannot control, although I am very well aware of it.* Thus Goethe already hints that he will make use of Schiller's penetrating intellect with a proviso. Too much transparence and consciousness can also prove harmful. He will know how to safeguard his *darkness*, for he needs it, as a plant sinks its roots into the dark earth.

This first exchange of ideas put Goethe into a state of eager antic-ipation, and on September 4 he invited Schiller to Weimar for a lon-ger visit. The court was removing to Eisenach for a while, and they would have quiet and time for each other. After some hesitation, Schil-ler accepted the invitation, but with the warning that he would not be able to follow the ordinary schedule of the house, "since unfortunately my cramps usually compel me to devote the entire morning to sleep, because they leave me no peace at night . . . . I ask only for the tedious freedom to be sick at your house."

Schiller stayed in Weimar from the fourteenth to the twenty-seventh, two densely packed, unforgettable weeks. They told each other their life stories, described the various intellectual paths they had taken, and spoke of plans for the future: Schiller's Wallenstein project and a new philosophy of aesthetics on which he was then at work, later entitled *On the Aesthetic Education of Man in a Series of Let-ters*. Goethe expounded on some of his nature studies, including optics, anatomy, and color theory. They also discussed possible topics for *Die Horen*. After a few days, they had become quite intimate, and Goethe read aloud from the not yet published "Roman Elegies." As mentioned before, Schiller found them "although lubricious and not very decent," nevertheless among the "best things" Goethe had done. Goethe declared himself willing to publish them first in *Die Horen*. They also talked about how best to promote the Weimar theater. Goethe asks Schiller to edit *Egmont* and tried to convince him that it was high time to put on a new production of *Fiesco* or *Cabal and Love*.

With each passing day, as if their attachment had been of long duration, their conversations became friendlier and it seemed they would never end. "A few days ago," Schiller wrote his wife, "we were uninterruptedly together from 11:30, when I got dressed, until 11:00 o'clock at night." When the weather was fair, Goethe persuaded his guest to go for walks, and the two of them were seen in the park and on the paths along the Ilm River. They walked to Goethe's garden house or to the construction site of the new palace. Goethe always had something to show Schiller, and his tall friend eagerly stepped forward to take a closer look. One gestured animatedly and the other walked with a slight forward lean, his hands clasped behind his back.

The two together were the talk of Weimar. It was considered an important event. They were delighted themselves to have laid the groundwork for a promising future during these golden days of September 1794.

CHAPTER 22

Writing for *Die Horen*. Two Ideas against
the Evils of the Times: Schiller's *Aesthetic Education*
and Goethe's *sociable education*. The *centaur*.
The "Xenia": Joint Attacks on the Literary Establishment.
Schiller as Midwife to *Wilhelm Meister*.
An Anti-Romantic Work? The Peaceful End of *Die Horen*.

. . . .

GOETHE HAD PUBLISHED ONLY SPORADICALLY IN MAGAZINES,
supplying a few poems to short-lived journals in his Sturm und Drang
days and later publishing some work in progress in Wieland's monthly
Der Teutsche Merkur. It was new to be an active contributor to a journal
like *Die Horen*. Owing mainly to his friendship with Schiller, it also
evinced a willingness to adjust to the growing importance of the literary establishment and the reading public. Goethe had learned how to
sell himself, as proved by his contract for *Wilhelm Meister*, and now he
began to study literary periodicals he had previously ignored. While
he did not see himself as a professional writer like Schiller, he acted
like one at times.

Goethe was reacting to what Schiller dubbed the "ink-stained
epoch," an age of social transformations produced by prolific writers
and readers eager for more. Literature had gained public influence. The
number of literate people had doubled between 1750 and 1800, to about
a fourth of the population by century's end. Reading behavior had also
changed. People no longer repeatedly read a single book—usually the
Bible—but many books only once, often into the wee hours. The market was soon flooded with books intended to be not so much read as
devoured. That raised a moral concern: was an abyss of decay opening

beneath the cloak of a supposedly educational medium? Even young-sters barely out of school could now experience thrills and take part in fantasies unimagined by their parents and teachers. With *Werther*, Goethe had gotten a taste of the power both of literature and its mor-alizing opponents. He had sown the wind and reaped a whirlwind. Despite all supervision and admonition, the joy of reading spread like an epidemic.

The German fever for books ran an even higher temperature than in other countries. The German lands lacked a metropolis, a great social center like Paris or London. With no real high society, peo-ple in small, out-of-the-way places sought imaginary sociability in books. The English could hear true stories of adventure on the high seas, the French had the accounts of witnesses to great historical events, but Germans could experience such things only in the ersatz form of literature. Already in 1780, Goethe had remarked succinctly that *the honorable public is familiar with the extraordinary only through novels.* He has Wilhelm Meister sigh about the mania for writing, *One can't even imag-ine how much people write.* And it didn't have to be genuine novels: mere letters and diaries could be turned into novels of sorts. People wanted to get into print. It was the most impressive proof of their existence. *In the sphere I inhabit at the moment,* Wilhelm continues, *people spend almost as much time writing to their relatives and friends about what they are doing as they spend doing it.*

The increase in reading and writing was bringing life and literature closer together. The sentimentalism of the 1770s had already begun to transform into literature what touched the heart in life. Conversely, readers searched literature for traces of the author's life. The cult of celebrity began in the Age of Genius. Authors acted a role, their life was now part of their work and was itself a work of art. People acclaimed Goethe as a real-life Werther and were a bit disappointed that Schil-ler had so little of the robber about him. Readers imitated the feelings they had read about in books. They fell in love, were jealous, struck up friendships, and got involved in politics according to the book. Liter-ature had become a medium of existential guidance. Life gained value in the mirror of literature, became more concentrated, had more drama and atmosphere. The second generation of Romantics was particularly aware of this and already bemoaned the fact. Ludwig Tieck sighed that they were completely made of literature, and Clemens Brentano was convinced that reading novels determined one's behavior. The living power of literature and the theater is also the great theme of *Wilhelm Meister*, which for that very reason would soon be regarded as the representative novel of its age.

At a time when literature was becoming a leading medium, the editors of *Die Horen* wanted to improve literary taste and raise the intellectual level of the public rather than conform to it. Great things were expected from its contributors: Schiller, Wilhelm von Humboldt, Fichte, Woltmann, and now Goethe as well. Two thousand subscribers had already been enrolled, an impressive number for the time. Cotta, the publisher, paid the highest fees, which encouraged other well-known authors to contribute. It promised to be a successful undertaking that would add to the prestige of its writers.

Goethe opened the first number of *Die Horen* with a kind of poem of welcome, two "Epistles" in dactylic hexameter. Schiller had asked him to write it, but was not completely satisfied with the result, which was somewhat ironic about the lofty standards of the project, pointing out that the ink-stained epoch included its critics as well:

> *Now that everyone reads and so many readers only*
> *Leaf through the book with impatience . . .*
> *You're asking me, my friend, to write for you something on writing and*
> *Thus, by writing, to add to the mass and make known my opinion,*
> *So that others can form an opinion about what I've written and*
> *Thus the tottering wave rolls on into all eternity.*

The same number contained the first of Schiller's letters *On the Aesthetic Education of Man* in which he develops the idea that the free play of art leads to human improvement. Goethe's introductory poem makes reference to that as well: *Noble friend, you who wish the welfare of human kind . . . / Shall I tell you what I think about it? I think that / What forms the man is only his life and words mean but little.*

It wasn't what Schiller wanted to hear, for he put great faith in the power of the literary word. "Humanity has lost its dignity," he writes in *Aesthetic Education,* "but art has rescued it. . . . Even before truth has beamed its triumphant light into the depths of the heart, the power of poetry has captured its rays and the peaks of humanity will glisten when damp night still covers the valleys." Goethe was moved by Schiller's sublime emotionalism. *I read the manuscript you sent me at once and with great pleasure, quaffed it down in a single gulp.* But upon reflection, he was not able to share Schiller's belief in the possibility of art's extravagant social effects. His point of view was that Schiller expected too much from art, nothing less than the inner transformation of man, who could thereby achieve the ability to be free. According to Schiller, art should initiate a revolution of thought and feeling and thereby improve what the political revolution had failed to achieve. The latter had revealed only man's barbarity when all restraints were cast off.

Goethe and Schiller were in agreement in their diagnosis of the negative results of the revolution, but not about the necessary therapy. In his first "Epistle," Goethe implies their difference of opinion, and in the *Conversations of German Émigrés,* his first prose contribution to *Die Horen,* he makes it even clearer, but still indirectly.

Schiller had hoped to start the journal's first number with a bang, but Goethe supplied only the beginning of the frame narrative for a series of stories yet to be delivered. The frame depicts a party of aristocratic refugees who have fled over to the right bank of the Rhine to escape the advancing troops of the revolution. They are engaged in a lively debate about its merits and drawbacks, although all are suffering its effects. They fall into vehement argument, showing that among those agitated by politics, good manners and a polite tone are soon abandoned. People surrender *to the irresistible temptation to wound one another* because they all believe their personal views represent the best interests of humanity in general. A privy councilor, the spokesman for the old order, gets so worked up he declares that he would like to see all the Jacobins of Mainz hanged, whereupon his adversary, the young Karl, replies that he hopes *the guillotine would be blessed with a good harvest in Germany, too, and not miss a single guilty head.* This blowup almost fractures the little group of aristocrats, but with some difficulty a fragile peace is restored. Telling stories is supposed to help heal the breach, but first they are admonished by a baroness: while they are together, they must keep their passionate convictions to themselves. She calls for consideration and *sparing one another's feelings*. Self-righteous anger is out of place when people with different points of view must exist in close proximity, and so the baroness urges moderation, not *in the name of virtue*, which would be too lofty, *but in the name of the most common courtesy*.

Here Goethe shows that what is called for in situations of political unrest is not Schiller's "aesthetic education" but elementary *sociable education* that has no need for highbrow theory. It simply reminds us of the healing power of courtesy and consideration. Goethe agrees with Schiller, however, that it depends on the culture of "play" that Schiller formulates so concisely in the fifteenth letter: "For—to say it once and for all—a human plays only when he is human in the full sense of the word, and he is fully human only when he plays." Goethe's model of *sociable education* is also play, a party game if one will, in which people act "as if." Civilized manners are called for, not uncompromising authenticity, not the tyranny of intimacy or the blunt protestant candor of Luther's "Here I stand, I can do no other." In society you have to be able to "do other." What is needed are measured doses of the words and actions that allow us to slide past one another and float over chasms of difference. We *who depend on society must educate and adjust ourselves to society's example*. The sociable person brings along his shell of good form as a guard against chaos, anarchy, and disintegration.

Perhaps Goethe made all too many concessions to *sociable education* in the stories that are told by the little circle of refugees: *You will at least want to recite your stories with some delicacy, won't you?* asks one of their number. His stories of harmlessly thumping poltergeists and creaking furniture, or of beautiful but all-too-loyal women, turned out to have too much *delicacy*. Readers thought they could have been a bit more exciting. Not even the final story, entitled simply *The Fairy Tale* and later celebrated by philologists as the model for all such literary tales, could salvage this—on the whole—rather dull collection. *The Fairy Tale* is an excessively calculated construction of symbols and allegories, a kind of higher crossword puzzle. If you weren't a puzzle fan, you found it boring, as Humboldt reported sardonically from Berlin. Others made a sport of trying to interpret the story, turning it into a kind of treasure hunt. Like a parlor game, it passed the time and at least kept readers occupied. Goethe was pleased as Punch by all this, and when

Prince August of Gotha asked for a definitive interpretation, Goethe replied that he would not provide one *until I see 99 predecessors in front of me* giving their interpretations.

Die Horen was not off to a good start, because its first features were not hits. Readers found Schiller's *On the Aesthetic Education of Man* difficult and Goethe's *Conversations of German Émigrés* boring. The journal needed something more exciting; the time had come for the "Roman Elegies." Goethe had long since promised them to *Die Horen*. He weeded out the explicitly priapic ones, to Schiller's regret, although he agreed that they *had to be sacrificed.* All the others were to be published, however. But since Goethe still hesitated, Schiller proposed making some cuts, likely the undressing scene in the second elegy, and the verses about the marriage bed as a source of venereal diseases in the sixteenth. Goethe was opposed to deletions and preferred to simply leave out the two offending elegies altogether, which they agreed to do. In the fall of 1795, the most commercially successful number of *Die Horen* appeared, and Goethe called it a *centaur*: Schiller's theory in the *Aesthetic Education* constituted the head and Goethe's elegies the body of the beast. Herder joked, "*Die Horen* will have to be printed with a *u* from now on": *Die Huren* (the whores). We have already seen that the duke did not approve of the publication of the "Elegies" and found "a few thoughts that were too lusty." Frau von Stein's reaction was no surprise: "I have no appreciation for this kind of poem." Humboldt wrote a letter to Schiller about a rumor circulating in Berlin: Goethe was said to have been consorting in Carlsbad with "two baptized Jewesses" and telling them in minute detail about the individual incidents that had inspired the elegies, especially the verse *And the barbarian rules Romans, body and soul.*

Die Horen was more talked about than actually read, except for the scandalous "centaur" number. The big names, the money, and the self-important manner of the editors (who gave the impression that they were intending to educate the entire literary establishment) provoked resentment and then schadenfreude when the journal's demise loomed after only a few issues. Goethe and Schiller were vexed by the difficulty of elevating public taste and by the malicious criticism of competing periodicals. It was Goethe who had the idea of composing "xenia," satirical jibes at the literary scene written in distichs modeled on Martial's epigrams. On December 23, 1795, he sent Schiller the first of these couplets, asking his opinion, and Schiller was immediately and enthusiastically on board. The two could swear like troopers when it came to the public and the critics. Why not set off some literary fireworks against the rise of mediocrity? They found the work greatly amusing. As they composed their couplets in Schiller's lodgings in 1796, they sometimes laughed so loud that Schiller's Charlotte closed the windows as a precaution.

Both men were inspired by a boisterous feeling of success. In Schiller's case, there was an additional kick; back when his love for Goethe still had a blatant admixture of hate, he had fantasized about treating him like a "proud, prudish woman" you had to "get with child to humble . . . in the eyes of the world." Now he could write in triumph to his friend Körner about himself and Goethe making babies together: "The child whom Goethe and I have begotten together is becoming a bit naughty." Goethe was also having fun; later he would declare that Schiller helped him enjoy a second youth as a poet.

They had a collection of several hundred couplets by early summer 1796. The arrangement they had first agreed on, in which polemical and aphoristic ones would be mixed together, pleased Goethe but not Schiller, who thought it made the whole endeavor look too harmless. He suggested separating out the critical distichs and collecting the others under the title "Innocent Xenia." He didn't want to dilute the strength of the polemical tribunal with sweeter notes. Goethe, who had begun with disputatious glee, now wanted to show some mercy, but his objections came too late. The *Muses' Almanac for the Year 1797*, edited by Schiller and containing the polemical "Xenia," was already in print. It sold out quickly, making a second printing necessary. The publisher Cotta would have liked the "Xenia" to appear in *Die Horen*, but for Schiller it was a matter of genre. He did not want to burden his proud flagship with material that was too satirical and topical.

Die Horen, however, was barely limping along. Schiller had great hopes for prepublication installments of *Wilhelm Meister*, but that did not come to pass. Nevertheless, the completion of the novel in 1795–96 was an auspicious event and a high point in the friendship between the two writers. Goethe, who usually played his compositional cards close to his chest, had done something extraordinary. With great confidence in Schiller's literary judgment, he'd asked his friend's help in completing the novel. The first two books had already gone to the printer in early 1795, but he decided to send Schiller the manuscript of the books that followed, urging him not to spare criticism and suggestions for improvement. Goethe also wanted to discuss the further structure of the novel with an eye to possible changes. He hoped for extensive input from his friend, and he was not disappointed. Schiller put his heart and soul into the novel in progress and promised to devote months to the project. "It is one of the greatest joys of my life," he wrote, "that I experienced the completion of this product, that it occurs in the period when my ambitions are still powerful, that I can still draw from this pure source; and the beautiful relationship between us makes it a sort of religion for me to make your affairs my own, to develop every reality within me into the purest play of the spirit."

Schiller had high praise for the first packets of manuscript, and by late June 1796 Goethe sent him the final pages and Schiller read the entire novel once more straight through. The series of long and detailed letters that analyze and comment on the novel opens with the famous sentence "How vividly this opportunity makes me realize that, confronted with excellence, there is no freedom except love." Seven years earlier, Schiller had told Körner he hated Goethe. Now he was bound to him in friendship. But how does one fend off incipient envy in the face of excellence? The answer Schiller could now give was: by loving that excellence.

Schiller's pithy sentence was so precious to Goethe that ten years later he adopted it in slightly altered form for Ottilie's diary in the novel *Elective Affinities*: *There is no escape from the excellence of another person except love.* At first glance, there's not much difference in meaning. But it is characteristic that where Schiller writes "no freedom" Goethe writes *no escape*. For Schiller, everything revolved around freedom. Thus, he struggled for freedom from envy and resentment, which in the end are nothing but self-poisons. Love frees him from them, and freedom chooses love. For someone like Schiller, it's almost a strategy. Love as an *escape* in the face of excellence, as Goethe would have it, is more about not having a negative effect on one's own nature. Thus Schiller defended his freedom with love, while Goethe defended his better nature via love, returning to congruence with himself. It is a difference that Goethe later summed up in the formulation: Schiller *preached the gospel of freedom; I wanted to make sure the rights of nature didn't come up short.*

When Goethe began working on *Wilhelm Meister* again in 1793, he hadn't known how it would continue or end. This uncertainty persisted even when he was already deeply immersed in the work and ought to have been able to foresee the end of the novel. As late as June 1796, just four weeks before its completion, he wrote to Schiller, *The novel goes along quite well. I find myself in a truly poetical mood, for in more than one sense I don't really know what I want or should do.*

Schiller couldn't believe it, since his own working method was so very different: unable to simply entrust himself to a *poetical mood* like Goethe, he needed to have a work precisely mapped out before he began to write. While Schiller had to have command over poetry, Goethe allowed it to seduce him. *Like my other things*, he would admit two decades later, he had *written this little work as a sleepwalker.*

At this point, all he had decided was that, contrary to what the *Theatrical Mission* of the original title suggested, it would not end with Meister's success in the theater. The more Goethe became enmeshed as director of the day-to-day operations of the Weimar theater, the less attractive a theatrical career seemed for his protagonist. So what sort of mastery were Wilhelm's years of apprenticeship leading to? Schiller asked this when the first two books of the novel appeared at the beginning of 1795, and Goethe wasn't able to answer. Hadn't Schiller emphasized the playful character of art in his letters on aesthetic education? Goethe found the idea persuasive, and he took it as permission to try out various plot lines with poetic nonchalance. He even has Wilhelm expressly declare to his son, Felix, that he is devoted to play as a maxim for life: *"You are a true man!" Wilhelm exclaimed. "Come, my son! Come my brother! Let us play in the world without purpose, as well as we can."*

This declaration occurs in the final book of the novel, at a point when Wilhelm has overcome his inclination to be an actor but obviously not the playfulness in his character. Looking back from the end of the novel, it becomes obvious that he has actually never done anything but play. The novel's plot begins with Wilhelm as a young boy, playing with a set of wooden puppets that to him represent the world. Later, his lover Mariane introduces him to the world of the theater, which he remains connected to even after they separate. Instead of collecting receivables for his father's business, he collects a troupe of unemployed actors and intends to become an actor himself. Through acting, he hopes to become *acquainted with himself in the gentlest* way, and better than in real life. What was there to object to about playing in order to discover oneself? Nothing, except that it's no way to become a good actor, for if you only play yourself, you're a bad one. That, however, is Wilhelm's case exactly, and the reason he takes his leave from the theater, but not from play. It continues, since he discovers that others are playing with him while he believes he is playing himself. In the realm of Baron Lothario, Wilhelm is introduced to the Society of the Tower, which has obviously been supervising and steering him from afar. He meets the abbé, the mastermind of the society who *likes to play destiny a bit.* With its network of connections, the Freemason-like Society of the Tower constitutes a world of play in which Wilhelm has unwittingly had a role. Even if they have by no means played him a dirty trick, his initiation into the secret society is a disappointment. Had all the fateful events of his life been simply concocted, manipulated, and steered? *So you are merely playing with these worthy symbols and words?* Wilhelm asks one of its leaders. One could ask the author the same question. Why all this machinery in the background?

It was a question Schiller asked, if reticently at first. After all, his *The Apparitionist* was a novel about a secret society, and he knew that such "machinery" was a hit with the public, and that authors bet on that fascination. "I think I see," he writes to Goethe, "that you were led astray by a certain condescension to the public's weakness."

The matter is so important to Schiller because it touches on the problem of freedom. If Wilhelm has found his way out of the theatrical world and into the active world of Lothario, how does he do it? Has Wilhelm Meister made something of himself, or has he been made into something? From without (by the Society of the Tower) or from within (through his own good nature)? Schiller didn't beat around the bush, but openly declared that he would like it best if Wilhelm Meister were a protagonist of freedom, if his destiny was due to his own plan and determination. He concedes that there is such a thing as a "healthy and beautiful nature" that does not need to force itself to be moral, but takes the right path from its own inclination. But Wilhelm cannot be considered to have such a nature as long as he is being pushed and pulled by the Society of the Tower. Its background machinations, according to Schiller, deprive Goethe's hero of both the freedom to steer his own course and the beautiful nature that does not need to be steered. What remains is a fairly pitiful figure who has had the good fortune to be coddled by fate in the form of the Society.

We see a flash of the old resentment of Goethe in Schiller's critique of the figure of Wilhelm Meister. "How easily *his* genius was supported by his destiny," he had once written to Körner, "and how I must struggle right down to the present moment!" Isn't Wilhelm Meister but a darling of fate who has no need to struggle and so doesn't know what freedom is? Once, this resentment was aimed at Goethe, but Schiller had learned to love the excellence in the man; Wilhelm Meister gets the rod his creator is spared.

What Schiller has trouble accepting is that Goethe wields the background machinery—the Society of the Tower—so casually. He doesn't really take it seriously. As Jarno tells Wilhelm, *Everything you have seen in the tower is actually merely the relics of a youthful enterprise that most of the initiated took very seriously at first, but about which now they all just smile from time to time.* It is explicitly *not* the Society of the Tower that bestows the necessary powers when apprenticeship is completed; nor are they bestowed by the apprentice's freedom. Rather, it is by benevolent nature. It is solely because Wilhelm Meister has become a father in the meantime and consciously accepts and resolves to fulfill that role that his *apprenticeship is completed.*

The result of this inner growth is a certain rootedness: *He no longer regarded the world like a bird of passage, no longer thought of a building as a hastily knocked-together bower that dries out even before one is done with it. Everything he intended to lay out would develop along with the growing boy and everything he produced would last for several generations . . . with the feeling of being a father he had also acquired all the virtues of a citizen.*

Sometimes Goethe wondered whether the novel had to end at all, or whether he shouldn't simply continuing spinning it out without a real conclusion. Wilhelm settling down with a wife and son—that could have been a real ending. Since a marriage to the dry and diligent Therese does not come to pass, fortunately for Wilhelm, and Natalie still seems unattainable, Goethe kept prolonging the story *like a sleep-*

walker, as was his custom. As soon as Wilhelm Meister's apprenticeship is over, he decides to escape into an unfinished and provisional future. *The decision to leave, take the child with him, and divert himself with the things of the world was now his firm intention.* Events then take a new turn. Wilhelm is given hope that he can marry Natalie after all. Yet a wedding is still postponed, and Wilhelm again intends to head south across the Alps. At the same time, with Mignon's failing health, *the land where lemons are in bloom* has lost some of its magic. Schiller had criticized the way Goethe removed this envoy of the South and symbol of Romantic mystery at the end of the novel. Mignon dies, and Wilhelm is in a great hurry to prepare her body, with the physician's help, for embalming— as if the symbol of longing were now going to be stuffed. Schiller was offended by the irreverent haste of it all; the sentimental demands of the readers had to be taken into account, and Mignon should be mourned a little. Goethe was quick to agree, and Wilhelm is permitted to weep out his pain on Therese's breast.

It was enough to satisfy Schiller, but not the Romantic critics, who refused to accept that he would demote a miraculous being to a mere oddity. It's true that at the end, the stage is swept clean, riddles are solved, and secrets revealed. Mignon and the harpist become pathological cases with obscure pasts involving superstition, incest, and everyday madness. For the arch-Romantic Friedrich von Hardenberg, who wrote under the pen name Novalis, the end of the novel is proof that here poetry has been betrayed: "Aesthetic atheism is the spirit of the book." The theme of the novel was not an apprenticeship but "a pilgrimage toward a patent of nobility."

Seen in that light, Wilhelm Meister's history of apparent success would also have to be read as a story of curtailment and loss, and not only from the author's perspective. Wilhelm himself cannot help but feel a loss in the encounter with Therese: *when I led an easy and even frivolous life—without purpose or plan—friendship, love, inclination, and confidence came to me with open arms and even forced themselves upon me; now that things are serious, fate seems to be taking another course with me.* There are numerous indications that Wilhelm's story can also be regarded as a rise to true fulfillment, because prosaic, ordinary life is simply closer to common understanding than is poetry.

Be that as it may, the work remains bathed in a kind of odd twilight.

Goethe had his reasons for writing to Schiller, who urged more clarity, *There is no question that the apparent results—results I explicitly state—are much narrower than the content of the novel.* This more comprehensive *content of the novel* would then be the poetic medium in which Wilhelm Meister's prosaic descent should be seen as the *narrower* result. Looked at in this way, the spirit of the novel is more than Novalis's infamous "pilgrimage toward a patent of nobility" after all.

It likely would not have helped *Die Horen* much if *Wilhelm Meister* had appeared in installments in advance of publication, as Schiller had hoped. The novel would later be regarded as a milestone, but its immediate reception was negligible. The reading public had expected something with the passion of *Werther* and was disappointed and bored by the new novel. The philosopher Christian Garve joked that if Wilhelm's lover Mariane falls asleep when he tells her stories, what made the author think that readers who were not in love with Wilhelm would react any better? Though Goethe had written Schiller that he had refrained from pouring *more water of reason* into the novel, there was still too much for his readers. All those endless discussions of God and the world and the theater! If people weren't bored, they were offended by the immorality of the theatrical world, whose depiction makes up most of the novel. "Moreover, the women in it all behave indecently," Charlotte von Stein wrote to her son, "and when he now and then introduces noble feelings in human nature, he smears them all with a bit of excrement, so as to leave nothing heavenly in human nature." Nor was Charlotte mollified by the "Confessions of a Beautiful Soul" in book 6, where heaven certainly gets its due. She simply didn't buy that much religious edification coming from her former beloved and suspected that he inserted those chapters "because those sheets also earn him money."

There were others, however, who read only about the Beautiful Soul in book 6 and were so shocked by the indecency of the rest of the novel that they actually burned it, as Schiller reported to Goethe in a letter of July 25, 1796. Goethe's brother-in-law Schlosser didn't go that far, but in a letter to his son-in-law he remarked, "I cannot yet stifle my displeasure that Goethe assigned this pure soul a seat in his bordello, which should serve only as an accommodation for vagabonds and riffraff."

Die Horen was able to struggle along, without *Wilhelm Meister*, for a little while longer. After Schiller's falling-out with the brothers August Wilhelm and Friedrich Schlegel—August Wilhelm had been an especially frequent contributor—the enterprise lost an important pillar of support. Fichte, Herder, Humboldt, Garve, Bürger, and even Kant had promised articles but either failed to deliver or sent in only slight pieces. Goethe, meanwhile, continued to be a prolific contributor. Following the *Conversations of German Émigrés* and the "Roman Elegies," his translation of Benvenuto Cellini's autobiography appeared serially until early 1797. It would be his last piece for the journal. *Die Horen* limped along for another year and a half, its promise having evaporated. Schiller's sister-in-law Karoline von Wolzogen, Louise Brachmann, Friederike Brun, Amalie von Imhoff, Sophie Mereau, and Elsa von Recke all published in the dying publication; Goethe spoke mockingly of its *feminine epoch*. On January 26, 1798, Schiller told Goethe that the periodical under whose banner their friendship had begun was about to fold. "It is understood that we will not let its end become a scandal," he writes. Half ironically and half in earnest, the playwright so versed in theatrical fireworks continues, "Otherwise, in this twelfth issue we could have printed a mad politico-religious essay that would have provoked a ban of *Die Horen*, and if you know of such a thing, we still have room for it."

Apparently nothing of the kind occurred to Goethe. Schiller didn't mention it again, and in the end *Die Horen* died a peaceful death.

—

CHAPTER 23

Herrmann and Dorothea. Living Despite History.
Looking for Real Estate. The Treasure Hunter.
The Summer of Ballads.
Return to the *path of mist and fog.* At Work on *Faust.*
Travel Preparations. An Auto-da-fé.
An Encounter with Hölderlin. The Third Trip to Switzerland.
Overcoming Terror at the *immensity of the world.*

· · · ·

A LITERARY QUARREL CAN BE LIKE A REFRESHING SUM-
mer thunderstorm, and may even be the occasion for beginning a new
work. Just as often, however, the squabblers cling to their positions and
need a chance to get everything off their chest, or they'll never stop.
Whoever *has some claim to posthumous fame* must force his contemporaries
*to come out with whatever they silently hold against him, and he will always
erase that impression by his presence, life, and influence.* Goethe wrote this to
Schiller after he had finished three cantos of the verse epic *Herrmann
and Dorothea,* a work that, second only to *Werther* in popularity, might
once and for all *erase* the *impression* made by hostile criticism.

Goethe had discovered the material for his epic three years earlier
in a chronicle of the expulsion of Protestants from Salzburg in 1731:
the story of a young man who comes to the aid of a girl, one of the
refugees, and then takes her as his bride after having overcome his shyness and the opposition of his father. Goethe transposed this story of an
unusual courtship into the contemporary situation of refugees fleeing
the wars of revolution. He made use of several details from the chronicle, for example, the girl's misapprehension that she is only being
employed as a maidservant. As in the *Conversations of German Émigrés,*

these refugees are fleeing their homes on the right bank of the Rhine before the advancing French army. They pass a rural town fortunately still untouched by the war. Curious and ready to give aid, its inhabitants come streaming out, among them Herrmann, the industrious but bashful son of the proprietor of the Golden Lion Inn. The lovely young Dorothea catches his eye.

In distress herself, her only concern is to help her fellow sufferers, and Herrmann is so moved he falls in love. In his father's eyes, Herrmann is too modest. He lacks any *sense of honor* and simply has *no ambition*. Herrmann is insulted and goes off to sulk. His mother goes after him and finds him weeping beneath a tree at the far end of the garden. He is resolved to volunteer as a soldier, but his mother dissuades him and encourages him instead to be more energetic in wooing the girl he has chosen. Mother and son return to join their neighbors, who are still sitting together.

It is Herrmann's mother who begins to talk about the girl he has fallen for, thereby again angering his father, who wants no refugee as a daughter-in-law. But the mother is practiced in such matters and breaks down her husband's resistance. The apothecary and the doctor are sent out to learn what they can about the young woman's reputation. They hear nothing but good of Dorothea. With a pistol in her hand, for instance, she has defended the children entrusted to her from plundering soldiers. Herrmann can now propose to her, but shy as he is, he leaves her with the impression that she is only being offered work as a maidservant. When she finds herself treated like Herrmann's betrothed, Dorothea thinks they are making fun of her. In the end, all misunderstanding is transformed into delight. The couple confess their love for each other, and Herrmann's father agrees to the match. Dorothea, who has lost her first fiancé, a revolutionary, to the Parisian guillotine, still feels the tremors of history in Herrmann's arms: *Thus to the sailor, landed at last, / The solidest ground, the safe terra firma still seems to be swaying.* Herrmann, matured to manhood in just a few hours through *genuine inclination*, utters the emotional closing words: *Let then our union, Dorothea, be all the stronger! / In the general convulsion we shall hold firm and survive, / Stand by each other and cling to the beautiful things that are ours.*

The idyllic story of a courtship in evil times—could one make an epic poem modeled on Homer out of such material? Goethe accepted the challenge. He said he wanted to prove that you didn't need a large theme to produce a great work. Schiller's elegy "The Walk," published the preceding year, ends with the line "And Homer's sun—behold!—it smiles upon us as well."

It was a coincidence that the philologist Friedrich August Wolf had just published the results of research purporting to show that the Homeric epics were not the work of a single author, but rather represented a collection of numerous epic songs by various authors. So there was no Homer, only Homeridae. Goethe otherwise had great respect for Wolf, but felt, once again, that the assiduous philologists were not content until they had broken everything down into its smallest components. He sensed that they did it out of resentment of works that were sublimely great, and for him, this belittling, tearing down, making everything equal and collective, fit with the rising spirit of democracy. That said, the new theory also offered an advantage—though one couldn't hope to compete with Homer, one could with the Homeridae—and he exploited the belittling business by setting to work as one of them. With *Luise* of 1795, Voss had attempted a bourgeois-idyllic verse epic in the spirit of Homer, and Goethe now hoped to outdo him. In mid-1796, he wrote Schiller that he had begun the project *because I need to have done something of this sort too.* The remark may have struck him as too offhanded; he deleted it in a later edition of their correspondence.

Reading *Herrmann and Dorothea*, one can sense Goethe's pleasure in dressing up bourgeois situations and characters in Homeric language. The Muses are invoked even though he was writing about farmers and apothecaries rather than Hector and Achilles. His revelers sit in the hot afternoon sun before the inn on the market square as if on Olympus. From a distance, the somewhat choleric father resembles the easily irritated Zeus, and the pastor is like a jovial Tiresias. Herrmann whips up the rearing, foaming pair that pull his curricle like some Achilles, and at the end supports with an increased *feeling of manhood the heroic greatness of this woman*—Dorothea, who has twisted her ankle. The charming young woman is like a rural Helen. The reader is to recall Homer at every step in the familiar world of a German country town. Nearby things are illuminated by a distant light and the faraway, ancient world is brought close. Goethe indulges in ironic play with the classical antiquity he so revered.

The writing flowed easily, and he was never less than cheerful at the work, to Schiller's amazement. The latter wrote to the Swiss painter Johann Heinrich Meyer, "While the rest of us must laboriously collect and examine in order to slowly produce some tolerable thing, he only has to gently shake the tree and the loveliest fruits fall down, ripe and heavy. The ease with which he now reaps the fruits of a well-spent life and continual learning is unbelievable."

He was fairly certain that this work would please the public. Convinced of success, he delivered to his publisher, Johann Friedrich Vieweg, a sealed envelope in which, on a slip of paper, he had written the fee he expected. If Vieweg offered less, Goethe would break off negotiations. If he offered more, he would have to pay only what Goethe was asking. He wanted to find out how much he was worth to the publisher and whether Vieweg's judgment matched Goethe's own estimate of his value, which was hardly modest. He was asking a thousand taler in gold, twenty times what Friedrich Hölderlin had recently received from Cotta for his novel *Hyperion*. Vieweg, annoyed, nonetheless offered exactly the amount Goethe had requested in his sealed bid, got the work, and made a handsome profit from numerous special and deluxe editions. The book became a favorite wedding present among the educated bourgeoisie. In *Herrmann and Dorothea*, Goethe wrote to Schiller in early 1798, *for once I gave the Germans what they wanted and now they're extremely satisfied.* The work pleased not only his *dear Germans*; he was extremely pleased himself. For many years to come, he never read it in private or public without being *greatly moved*.

In the last canto, Dorothea recalls her former betrothed, who has lost his life fighting for freedom in revolutionary Paris. She repeats the impassioned legacy he left her. These verses, which Goethe composed in the spring of 1797, show how far he had by then distanced himself from a merely polemical attitude toward revolution. He had begun to see something else in it: an elementary fate, an all-leveling earthquake, a human and superhuman force of nature that dismantles everything and reassembles it anew.

> *. . . for now all the world is in*
> *Motion and now, everything once conjoined is detached,*
> *Basic laws of the mightiest states are coming undone.*

Those who once possessed are detached from their possessions,
Friend separated from friend, and love cut off from love.
. . .
True is the saying that man is but a stranger on earth.
Now more than ever, everyone has become a stranger.
We no longer possess the land. Its treasures are mobile;
Gold and silver are melted down from their ancient forms.
Everything's moving, as if our structured world were sliding
Back into night and chaos, to shape itself anew.

As Goethe wrote these lines, he was keeping an eye out for real estate. He expected inflation to follow the wars of revolution, and going into debt to purchase a country estate seemed a rational bet: inflation would reduce his indebtedness, and at a time when revolution was making *the solidest ground, the safe terra firma* tremble. He was interested in the estate of Oberrossla, eleven miles northeast of Weimar and not far from Ossmannstedt, where Wieland had already purchased land. The estate had been up for auction since 1796, and for a short time in the spring of 1797 it looked as if Goethe's bid would be accepted, but the matter dragged on for another year. In March 1798 he was at last able to acquire the estate for 13,125 imperial taler, and he immediately leased it out to a tenant. Five years later, after much aggravation, he was glad to be able to get rid of it at a loss.

While still negotiating the purchase of Oberrossla, Goethe bought a hundred-taler ticket for the Hamburg lottery in May 1797. First prize was a country estate in Silesia. It was another way to acquire real estate, he thought. But he came up empty-handed, despite having spent some time thinking about what lottery number to choose. He had calculated it using his own and Schiller's birthdates. Three days later, on May 23, 1797, he sent his first ballad, "The Treasure Hunter," for a cycle of ballads he and Schiller had agreed to compose for the *Muses' Almanac* that would appear the following year. Schiller, who knew about Goethe's flyer in the lottery, made an amicable reference: "By the way, I was amused to notice in this little poem an allusion to the intellectual atmosphere in which you may be living now." The ballad's opening lines are *Penniless and sick at heart, / I was dragging out my time. / Poverty's the greatest crime, / Wealth the only goal to strive for.* The treasure hunter then deploys tried and true magic practices—circles of fire, selling his blood and his soul, offerings of herbs and bones. But no treasure chest opens, no vein of gold is discovered. Instead, a beautiful boy appears with a message meant for both the treasure hunter and the lottery player: *Dig no more, it's all in vain. / Workdays—friends as compensation, / Bitter weeks, then cele-bration: / Let them be your magic spell.*

"The Treasure Hunter" was the first salvo in a ballad competition between the two friends. Schiller found it easy to write ballads. In quick succession he turned out a series of them, including "The Diver" and "The Pledge," which would later gain great popularity, as well as "The Cranes of Ibykus," perhaps the most beautiful of all his ballads. Goethe had given his friend the idea for the subject, the fantastical story of the young singer murdered while on his way to the great sing-ing competition in Corinth. The only witnesses are some cranes flying by. During the competition they reappear, and one of the murderers takes fright and inadvertently reveals himself. Goethe, who wanted to see everything *play out naturally*, would have preferred a more gradual unmasking, but Schiller always aimed for the dramatic surprise. The result met with Goethe's approval.

Schiller's ballads seemed to him the perfect realization of the ideal narrative poem. Goethe thought his own contributions—especially "The Bride of Corinth" and "The God and the Bayadère"—didn't truly fit into the genre. They were too mysterious and also too morally ambiguous. "The Bride of Corinth" tells of a young man from Athens on a visit to family friends in Corinth. The daughter of the house had been promised to him as a bride. The youth enters a world foreign to him, for in the meantime, this family has converted to Christianity, an ominous sign: *When new faith germinates, / It often extirpates / Love and loyalty like some noxious weed.* The daughter has been sent to a cloister and has died there, but the youth does not know it. The girl appears to him in a dark room, and they spend a night of love together. When her mother bursts into the room at dawn, it all becomes clear: the girl is undead and will carry the young man off with her in a liebestod. She wants to be cremated with him: *When the sparks are blowing / With the ash still glowing / We shall hurry toward the gods of old.* It is a moving lament for the fall of the ancient gods, who were better disposed toward Eros, a complaint against the monotheistic demystifying of the world: *And of the ancient gods, that lively swarm, / The quiet house was in an instant cleared. / Now only one, invisible, was the norm, / As savior, hanging on a cross, revered.* It is reminiscent of verses from Schiller's elegy "The Gods of Greece": "Fallen now are all those lovely flowers, / Brought down by the north wind's wintry blast. / In order to increase the one god's powers, / The others had to die, they could not last."

Goethe ironically called "The Bride of Corinth" his *vampire poem.* When the ballads of that summer appeared in the *Muses' Almanac for the Year 1798,* almost all were praised, especially those by Schiller, while "The Bride of Corinth" provoked heated debate. "Nothing occasions more difference of opinion," reported Böttiger, "than Goethe's 'Bride of Corinth.' While one party calls it the most disgusting of all bordello scenes and regards it as a desecration of Christianity, others call it the most perfect of all Goethe's shorter works."

The critics also claimed they had already discovered "bordello scenes" in *Wilhelm Meister* and the "Roman Elegies," but it was not enough to particularly annoy Goethe. The benefit of the summer of ballads was also that it provided an opportunity to once again unpack his prodigious packet of notes and drafts for *Faust.* He wrote to Schiller, *Our study of ballads has brought me back to this path of mist and fog.*

The unfinished play, begun in the early 1770s, constantly preoccupied him. He took it up to salve his artistic conscience, and when important life events were in the offing: in 1775, before he moved to Weimar; in 1786, before the Italy trip; now again in the early summer of 1797, when he thought he might be able to leave for a long-planned third journey to Italy. Everything was to be thoroughly planned and organized this trip; there was to be no question of dashing off into the unknown. Goethe had even sent the painter Johann Heinrich Meyer in advance to scout out places and sights to be visited, and the two were going to coauthor a great work on the cultural history of Italy from the material gathered.

Even if existential renewal was not the foremost goal as it had been on the first Italian journey, the feeling of a turning point in his life was strong enough to prompt Goethe to write a will and choose Schiller and his colleague Voigt as editors for his posthumous works. Continued hostilities in southern Germany and Italy were causing unrest, making travel there perilous, and it therefore seemed prudent to put his house in order. Goethe was now a family man who had to provide for a wife and child. A recent survey of his personal finances also troubled Goethe, who found he had run up considerable debt.

An auto-da-fé also marked this as a turning point: on the first two Sundays of July 1797, Goethe burned most of the letters he had received up to 1792. He did not mention it to Schiller, whom he had just appointed as one of his executors. Apparently, there were very personal matters as well as some official business he wanted to keep secret, even from the eyes of his friend.

While it was another instance of *molting*—a mood of leave-taking, of stocktaking, of housecleaning—that induced Goethe to take out the *Faust* manuscript again, this was not another impatient attempt to finally finish the unwieldy work. Instead, in an elegiac mood, he was seeking contact with his past life and with the story of his obsessions. That mood emerges clearly enough in the stanzas preceding the drama, entitled "Dedication," stanzas composed during these weeks of sweeping up and the search for lost time:

> *Once more, you wavering figures, you draw near me,*
> *I glimpsed so long ago through murky haze!*
> *Shall I hold you fast this time, and will you hear me?*
> *Will my heart still follow you on tangled ways?*
> *You throng about! Well then, I'll let you steer me.*
> *You rise from mist and fog to meet my gaze.*
> *I feel a youthful stirring in my breast*
> *And by your magic breeze I am caressed.*

To whom are these verses "dedicated"? To some future, sympathetic audience? He doesn't say so. It is the entire imaginary world of figures populating the play that is directly addressed: *Once more, you wavering figures, you draw near me!* But they do not merely entice him back into that magic realm, the lost world of his early productivity when he wrote the first scenes of *Faust*. This created world also brings with it the real world of those times, *the scenes of happy days* when he read those early drafts of *Faust* aloud and discussed them with friends and lovers.

That circle of listeners had been long dispersed. Some, like his sister

Cornelia and his friend Merz, have died. Others, like Herder, are still nearby but have become less intimate. And still others, like Lenz, have dropped completely out of sight. *No longer will they hear the songs to come, / Those souls for whom I sang in long years past, / That friendly crowd, now scattered, deaf, and dumb, / Their fading echoes dying out at last.* Once the work in progress belonged to his circle of friends, where it originated. They have been replaced by an anonymous reading public: *Nameless now the hearers of my woe.* Thus we get the impression that the "Dedication" is addressed to that scattered or deceased circle of former boon companions whom this work will remind of their own youthful years, as if in the play's orbit their fellowship could be brought back to life. In the meantime, however, that fellowship is just as imaginary as the play itself.

The last strophe of the poem takes a surprising turn. Even if the earlier reality in which *Faust* originated and made an impression has disappeared and thereby become imaginary, the opposite is true of the work itself. In it, everything is at first imaginary, but if you give it your attention, it draws you into its spell and becomes more and more real. Past reality becomes a shadow of itself, and the shades in the play become real: *A shudder grips me, I begin to weep. / My heart, so often stern, grows mild and soft. / The things I have seem far away, asleep. / Awake and real is what I thought I lost.* The poem is likely a double dedication—to the friends of old who have disappeared and to those *wavering figures* from the work who are forcing their way into reality.

As distant things drew near in these early summer weeks of 1797, Goethe was working on the portals that lead into *Faust*. After the "Dedication" comes a "Prelude at the Theater" and then a "Prologue in Heaven," three gates opening into three different intellectual spaces. The "Dedication" is the mostly intimate chamber drama between memories and the shadowy figures of the work. The "Prelude at the Theater" is concerned with a work for the "boards that signify the world," as Schiller would later call the stage, a place where profit and loss are also at play; here, it is Goethe the theater director speaking. And finally, the "Prologue in Heaven" gazes down from on high at the *theatrum mundi* and at a Faust who is, as in Spanish baroque drama, a piece in a game between God and the devil.

In those momentous weeks before his departure for Italy, the various dimensions of the play opened up for Goethe; it struck him as even more roomy than he had thought, but also more labyrinthine. That brought a state of creative restlessness, Goethe sensing that without his being fully aware of it, the play had grown into a monstrous hybrid of stage play, closet drama, folk play, and mystery play, slapstick and metaphysics—a divine comedy. It made his head spin, and he appealed for help to Schiller's cooler judgment: *Now, however, I wish that you would have the goodness to spend a sleepless night thinking through the matter and presenting me with the demands you would make on the entire business, thus recounting to me my own dreams and interpreting them like a true prophet*— Goethe as Pharaoh, dreaming an entire world, and Schiller as his Joseph, interpreting his dreams. Schiller knew he had nothing to lose; he slept little, in any case, and quickly helped his friend by providing insightful remarks: Faust, an accident of nature, embodied the "duplicity of human nature," between God and beast; he was an expression of the "unsuccessful attempt to unite the divine and the physical in man." One consequence, for Schiller, was that the work could get out of hand, turning into either slapstick comedy or solemn abstraction. Both extremes had to be avoided. Of course, life should be presented as bursting with powerful sensuality, but it must also submit "to the service of a rational idea." Schiller's momentous suggestion was that Faust should not just appear as a learned man and seducer but also be "led to a life of activity." Famously, Goethe would seize on this and make Faust into an industrious globetrotter in the second part of the play.

This flood of ideas in the weeks before Goethe's planned departure took him by surprise. *It would now only be a matter of a month of quiet and the work would spring from the earth like a huge family of mushrooms, to general astonishment and horror. If my trip comes to nothing, I have placed my entire trust in these capers.*

He calls his Faust stories *capers*—we will need to keep that in mind. In any case, Faust again disappears among the shades: after the tense political and military situation postponed the departure for Italy several times, a definite date was scheduled. On July 5, 1797, Goethe writes to Schiller, *Faust has been postponed for the time being; the northern phantoms have been pushed back for a while by southern reminiscences.*

In the midst of travel preparations, Goethe received two poems from Schiller, who asked for his opinion without telling him the name of the poet. They were the hymn "To the Ether" and the elegy

"The Wanderer" by Friedrich Hölderlin, who had submitted them to Schiller for the *Muses' Almanac*. Hölderlin venerated Schiller, and Schiller had a high regard for his younger colleague and fellow Swabian. Goethe, however, had barely taken notice of Hölderlin, although the remarkably handsome young man had spent several months in Jena. In fact, they had even encountered each other in the winter of 1794–95, in Schiller's house, where Hölderlin had committed a faux pas. In the excitement of waiting for Schiller, he had ignored a stranger in the same room who turned out to be Goethe. "May heaven help me," Hölderlin wrote to a friend, "to make up for . . . my misfortune when I get to Weimar." He was tormented by the feeling that he could not do so, for Goethe remained reserved toward him.

Now Goethe had the two poems in front of him and was asked to render an opinion; he gave them some muted praise: *has the makings of a poet, which by themselves, however, don't make a poet*. Nevertheless, he recommended printing them and gave the unknown poet some advice, *Perhaps it would be best if he once chose a very simple idyllic event and presented it. Then it would be easier to see how well he succeeded at depicting people, which is what everything comes down to in the end*. Schiller did not pass this critique on to Hölderlin, for he knew that to recommend a smaller form and the idyllic depiction of people would be an insult to this author of highly emotional hymns. That was exactly how Hölderlin reacted, several weeks after Goethe's departure from Weimar for Italy, when the young poet paid him a visit in Frankfurt and heard from Goethe's own lips the advice that Schiller had wisely suppressed: he should restrict himself to a *simple idyllic event*. It was a heavy blow to Hölderlin's poetic self-confidence, and it took him a long time to recover.

On the night before leaving for Italy, Goethe—who had been wrapping up work for weeks and making thorough travel preparations—was suddenly seized by a reluctance he was at a loss to comprehend. *I'm already dreading the empirical immensity of the world*, he wrote to Schiller on July 29. He was afraid of being swallowed by the *million-headed Hydra of empiricism*. He had never felt anything like this before. He had always had an unlimited curiosity and the conviction that he could assimilate anything that seemed to him worthwhile. Whatever failed to make an impression on him was casually or summarily brushed aside; it didn't concern him, and he couldn't be persuaded otherwise. He would decide for himself what was important and meaningful. But now he came to feel it possible to be overwhelmed by the *wide world*. The unconcern of earlier years had disappeared, and he came up with a new strategy. He would not flee the crush of reality by retreating like a bad poet to the *phantoms* of his inner life. He wouldn't allow himself that luxury. He wanted to remain open, but it had to be a controlled openness. If social reality distracted and beleaguered him, it was important to behave just as he did when botanizing: keep a cool head and devote himself to observation even in the middle of the jungle.

Goethe proceeded systematically, with nothing left to chance: *Therefore, I have made myself folders in which I file all sorts of public documents I encounter at present—newspapers, weeklies, excerpts from sermons, regulations, comedy programs, price lists—and then I also record both what I see and notice as well as my immediate evaluation of it. Whereupon I talk about these things when in company and advance my opinion, and then soon see to what extent I am well informed and to what extent my judgment coincides with the judgment of well-informed people. Whereupon I again record and file my new experience and what I've learned, and so I have material that will remain of sufficient interest to me as a history of things external and internal.* His initial dread at the immensity of the world is transformed into this oddly pedantic processing of the world. For example, while gazing at the lofty mountains surrounding Lake Lucerne, he notes, *these enormous rocks must not fail to be a rubric in the chapters about my journey. I have already accumulated some hefty bundles of papers. . . . In the end, one enjoys something when one feels one can absorb much of it.* By way of such pedantry, Goethe had rediscovered his lust for the world and was now enjoying his reconstituted *lightness*.

Frankfurt was his first lengthy way station. He had brought Christiane and August along that far to introduce them to his mother, who welcomed and doted upon her grandson and her son's "bedmate." In Frankfurt he was less interested in seeing old acquaintances than in inspecting the traces of recent history. He stood before the ruins of his grandfather's house, which had been destroyed in the last French bombardment. The French had cut a wide swath of destruction through the city and its bourgeois culture. That too was an effect of the revolution. Rubble and ruins were everywhere to be seen, and yet he knew *that it all would be purchased and restored by some new entrepreneur.* The speculators were already lying in wait. Frankfurt would rise again, but in a way that would make it unrecognizable. For the time being, everything was still full of reminiscences: here was where he played as a child and the emperor had passed in grand procession on his way to be crowned.

He had mixed feelings. On the one hand, he was attracted to the enchantment of a vanishing world that still preserved the atmosphere of his youth. There were moments of great emotional intensity that awakened his creative energy. In the ruins of the city of his childhood, Goethe thinks of *Faust*. Poetically inspired by the town, he could resume work on it at once. Yet Frankfurt is also a place of fatal distraction. People here lived *in a constant whirl of buying and consuming . . . I even think I have noticed a kind of dread of poetic productions—or at least, to the extent that they are poetic—which strikes me as quite natural for exactly the same reason. Poetry needs, nay demands, composure. It isolates someone against his will, obtruding itself repeatedly, and in the wider world it is . . . as uncomfortable as a loyal lover.* The city as a place of temptation, then. In the world of business sense and *distraction*, it wasn't easy to remain true to poetry.

From Frankfurt, Christiane and August returned to Weimar while Goethe continued south. First he had to reassure Christiane, who had a thousand fears that she might lose him to Italy. *You surely know*, he wrote to her on August 24, *and you saw on the last trip, that I am careful and cautious in such undertakings, . . . and I can certainly reassure you that this time, I'm not going to Italy.* Forgoing Italy was a result of the military and political state of affairs, for late in the summer of 1797, hostilities had broken out again in northern Italy. It was simply too dangerous to go.

In Stuttgart, his next way station, Goethe made contact with Schiller's Swabian friends and acquaintances. *They remember you with much love and joy, indeed, I can say with enthusiasm*, Goethe wrote his friend. Schiller was touched and fell to daydreaming: "What would I have given 16 years ago to encounter you in that place, and how wondrous it seems to me when I think about the circumstances and moods that place recalls to me and put them together with our present relationship." But Goethe had other feelings. He was meeting people who enthusiastically recalled the Schiller of *The Robbers*, and so he writes his friend, *I think it was an advantage for both of us that we met later and at a stage when we were more mature.*

Goethe continued on via Tübingen and Schaffhausen to Zurich, where he met the painter Meyer, who was returning from Italy. In contrast to his previous visits, this time he took no pleasure in Zurich, where the encounter with a haggard, stooped Lavater occurred in a narrow street. At one time, Goethe had traveled to Zurich just to see him, but now he avoided a meeting. Fortunately, Goethe had put on weight and Lavater failed to recognize him; he slipped past. It was the end of their story.

There was bad news from Italy. Goethe and Meyer learned that General Bonaparte was shipping off to Paris works of art that they had intended to study. If Goethe had not already canceled his Italian plans, he would have done so now. He still wanted to retrace his steps up to the Gotthard Pass, however. It was the best place to bid farewell to the South he would not reach again. He recalled his first journey to Switzerland in 1775, and it seemed to him now it had marked the end of his youth. *I felt*, he writes to Schiller, *a strange longing to repeat and rectify those experiences.* Of course, he had become a different person, but he was proud that at his age he could still climb to the top of the pass. At the foot of the Gotthard, in Uri, he wrote a poem in distichs that he enclosed in a letter to Schiller on October 17:

> *Yesterday your head was still brown as the locks of your lover,*
> > *She whose lovely face beckons from far away.*
> *Silvery gray now, the early snow covers the summit,*
> > *Snow that in stormy nights powdered your aging head.*
> *Ah, so near to age is one's youth; linked together by life,*
> > *Just as a lively dream mixes present and past.*

The proprietor of the inn at the summit of the pass was the same person who had been there twenty years earlier. After descending, they reached their starting point, Stäfa on Lake Zurich. It was Wilhelm Tell country they were walking through. They had passed the Rütli meadow, where the legendary oath against tyranny is supposed to have been sworn, the beginning of the Swiss Confederacy. They stopped at the chapel commemorating Wilhelm Tell's leap to freedom and visited Uri, his reputed birthplace. Here Goethe had an idea for a work about Tell—not a drama but an epic poem. He wrote to Schiller that it was a poetic theme that *instilled much confidence* in him. Goethe's idea caught fire in Schiller. "How much I wish," he wrote to Goethe, "to be reunited with you soon, also because of this poem." Goethe would hold on to the idea for four more years before finally surrendering it to Schiller.

On a rainy, windy November 20, 1797, Goethe returned to Weimar. Christiane was relieved and celebrated his return with champagne. Two days later, after distributing gifts and stowing away his acquisitions, paintings, and rock specimens, he was already attending the theater again. The trip had not been the turning point he had hoped for, as always when the goal was Italy. Not much had changed in his absence. But it was also very good to keep hold of what he had.

CHAPTER 24

The Clogged Springs of Poetry. Thinking about Genres:
Drama and Epic. *Propyläen* Classicism. *The Collector and
His Circle*. Contra Dilettantism and False Proximity to Reality.
Theatrical Reform. Weimar Dramaturgy. Translating Voltaire's
Mahomet: A Reparation. Fichte and the
Atheism Scandal. Back to *Faust*.

....

H AVING SET *FAUST* ASIDE BEFORE LEAVING FOR SWITZERLAND,
Goethe had other plans in mind upon his return to Weimar: an old
idea for an epic continuation of the *Iliad* relating the death of Achilles,
and another epic about Wilhelm Tell. He had not yet written a word of
the latter but had talked about it.

In his letters to Schiller, who was then in the midst of an burst of
inspired work on his Wallenstein trilogy, Goethe complained that in
Weimar his *productive self is constrained in so many pleasant and unpleasant
ways*. He would come over to Jena as soon as he could. He would even
leave behind his artistic adviser Johann Heinrich Meyer, who had taken
up residence in Goethe's house: *I can work only in absolute solitude . . . , it
is not just the conversation, but even the very presence, of loved and esteemed
persons in the house* [that] *completely diverts my poetic springs*. Goethe was
unable to escape Weimar in the coming months, however, and his *poetic
springs* clearly were not flowing. He began to ponder the idiosyncrasies
of his productivity.

In an *exchange of ideas* with Schiller, he hoped to gain clarity. Schiller had told him how mentally exhausting the work on *Wallenstein*
was and how for him, working on a tragedy always had something
"aggressive" about it, despite aesthetic distance. In his reply, Goethe
reflected on his own relationship to tragedy: *I don't know myself well*

enough to know whether I could write a true tragedy, but I am terrified to even undertake one and am almost convinced that I could destroy myself by the mere attempt. At this time, Goethe was brooding over how he could help his protagonist Faust get beyond the tragedy of Gretchen, for everything within him resisted ending the play with the prison scene. Schiller was skeptical that his friend was really so averse to tragedy "because of its emotional violence." Might it not be external and more technical demands that put him off instead? For instance, Schiller said that tragedy demands a strict structural consistency, a logic that Goethe found abhorrent since his poetic talent "wants to express itself with relaxed freedom." Goethe's talent was more narrative than dramatic. Moreover, the writer of tragedies must also keep in mind the effect or impression he's making on the audience and that, according to Schiller, "embarrasses you." So Goethe's aversion was not to tragedy itself but to the genre's dramaturgic demands.

Goethe's comments on his relation to tragedy had spoken to its existential aspects, and it was Schiller who shifted the problem to the practical level. That was fine with Goethe, who did not wish to continue exploring his feelings about tragedy—apparently a subject he preferred to hint at but not pursue in depth. As he had warned in one of his first letters to Schiller, one had to expect *a sort of darkness and wavering* in him. Goethe suggested that they continue the conversation about literary genres they had begun before his trip to Switzerland. It was less sensitive and yet of great interest to him. He was especially attracted by the distinction between epic and dramatic modes. It was a question raised by his *Achilleid* project; he had begun to feel that the death of Achilles might be better suited to a drama than his planned epic poem. To get the conversation about genre going, Goethe sent his friend a summary of the ideas they had already discussed. A quarter century later, he would publish the revised text under his and Schiller's names as "On Epic and Dramatic Poetry." He had always felt that the ideas developed there were their mutual work.

They agreed on the precept that *the epic poet recites an event as completely past and the playwright depicts it as completely present.* In their correspondence, they draw consequences from this precept that go beyond what was contained in the later essay.

The past-time character of an epic creates distance. One can, as it were, stroll around the narrated events and view them from different angles. By keeping his distance, the epic poet allows his hearers to maintain distance in their turn. With control of the event and of time, the epic poet can go forward or backward, digress or make temporal leaps. Epic distance also provides opportunity for reflection. One can shift to a higher plane. The narrator enjoys a triple sovereignty: he stands above the action, is the master of time, and rises intellectually above his protagonists.

Schiller saw this triple sovereignty as increased "freedom." The narrator is free vis-à-vis the world he presents, and the recipient—who is able to move to the proffered plane—is equally freed. He is given space in which to play. However, he has a demand placed on him, namely, he must first imagine the narrative played out on his inner stage. Theater is different: the action comes to the audience from without, already complete. According to Goethe, the theater or the sets make it easy and comfortable for the recipient. Instead of putting in the effort to read an entire novel, people want the story presented on the stage, short and exciting. The theatrical performance saves them the trouble of imagining something for themselves. It boils down to this distinction: epic demands more individual participation from its recipients, while drama spares them the effort. As Schiller formulated it: "The dramatic action moves before me. I myself move around the epic action."

With regard to freedom and individual participation, then, the epic would rank higher. And Goethe, whose plays show a tendency toward the epic in any case, seems to accept this evaluation when he writes to Schiller, *Why are our epic works so seldom successful? Because there is no one to listen to them.* Schiller replies, "If drama really needs to be defended on account of the negative propensity of the times (of which I have no doubt), then you'd have to begin by reforming the drama, and suppress the common imitation of nature to provide more light and air for art."

Refining theatrical art by suppressing the "common imitation of nature"—thus Schiller formulates the goal of a theater reform that the friends saw from then on as their mutual task. Schiller thought that it was precisely because of its immediacy and lack of distance that the theater was inclined to "naturalism," which both men liked to call the "common imitation of nature." For both, it was crucial to transform mere natural truth into aesthetic truth, which involved both alienation and intensification. These were the same ideas that Goethe had made the programmatic underpinnings of *Propyläen* (*Propylaea*), the journal he had just founded with Meyer. At stake here, as in the planned theater reform, was a deeper understanding of artistic truth as opposed to naturalistic tendencies.

In the fall of 1797, with the end of *Die Horen* clearly in sight, Goethe had made a plan to bring out a new periodical that would be more monograph series than journal. It was Meyer who suggested the title *Propyläen*, after the entrance gate to the Acropolis. Here the reading public was to be instructed in the spirit of Winckelmann's classicism about what *aesthetic truth* was and how it was founded upon but transcended *natural truth*.

As for *natural truth*, it provided Goethe with the opportunity to publish his essays on anatomy and optics in *Propyläen*. They were meant to be an aid to painters and sculptors, who were expected to school themselves first in natural objects according to the principle that one needs to know reality before one can cross its boundaries into idealism. If the world of natural scientists barely took notice of Goethe's scientific publications, at least they could be useful to artists and those interested in art.

Goethe based *aesthetic truth* on the model of classical antiquity. In antiquity, he wrote in an essay on Winckelmann, people understood that man as a natural being is placed at the peak of nature, and that he has an obligation, *to produce another peak in his turn. . . . He can raise himself up to that point by saturating himself with all perfections and virtues, invoking selection, order, harmony, and significance, and finally uplifting himself to the production of a work of art that will assume its radiant place alongside his other deeds and works.* Aesthetic truth is thus not simply an imitation but an enhancement of nature. Ancient works of art that Goethe had become familiar with in Italy, works that corresponded to this idea of an enhanced nature, were to be made known through descriptions, illustrations, and explications. *Propyläen* promulgated an ideal art, but at the same time intoned an elegy for what had been lost. Although Napoleon was plundering Italy's artistic treasures before their eyes, people still had not realized *what the world is losing in this moment, since so many parts of this great and ancient whole have been torn down.*

The first issue of *Propyläen* appeared in October 1798, followed by four more in January, April, June, and December of the following year. Owing to poor sales, the last issue did not appear until a year later. As compensation for the publisher Cotta's financial losses, Goethe offered him options on his next longer works, and so Cotta uncomplainingly printed the last and all but unsellable issue in the fall of 1800.

From his conversations with Schiller about natural and aesthetic truth, Goethe developed the novel-like text *The Collector and His Circle*, a lengthy contribution to *Propyläen* that he called a *little family portrait in letters*. Its theme was *the various directions that artists and connoisseurs can take*, from an objectivity totally lacking in imagination to a fantastical imagination lacking any concrete object. His publisher was pleased— at long last, not another didactic monograph but an entertaining epistolary novella full of wit and charm! Its premise is that an art collector writes letters to the editors of the *Propyläen* about how his father, his uncle, and he have acquired their paintings.

It is a hodgepodge of very divergent tastes. Some painters strive for realistic imitation of nature. For others, nothing is too fantastical. And in between are the composite characters: the *sketchers* who only ever do studies but never finish a painting; the *dotters* who are obsessed with detail and lose sight of the whole; the *drifters* and *foggers*, *wrigglers* and *undulators* who prefer decoration, playfulness, and portentousness. On the other hand, there are the *skeletists* and *rigorists* who seek the essence in emaciated abstraction. Schiller had helped put together this typology. At the time, he was particularly annoyed at the circle of young Romantics around Friedrich Schlegel and Ludwig Tieck, so he made sure they got what was coming to them as well. They were the *imaginators* who *try to appeal to the imagination without worrying about giving it something vivid to imagine*.

This epistolary story had grown out of Goethe's and Schiller's schematizing, one of their favorite occupations. The text was barely completed before they were at it again. The two friends were collecting and ordering the reasons why artistic *dilettantism* represented a great danger for art. Both were convinced, where art is concerned, that the antonym of "good" is "well-meaning," which there was far too much of for their taste. It is true that, at the end of the eighteenth century, there was a great increase in artistic activity by aristocratic and bourgeois amateurs. In Weimar, it was the court circles, in Jena, the middle class. Everywhere people were painting watercolors, cutting silhouettes, writing stories and poems, singing, and playing instruments. Acting was especially popular. People wanted to appear onstage and play themselves. When Goethe's *Iphigenia* premiered at the Weimar amateur theater, even the young duke participated. Taking the directorship of the theater in the early 1790s, Goethe became intent on professionalizing the performances. He knew that dilettantism can bring one closer to art—as with his experience with painting, at which he remained an amateur—but was useful only when not confused with genuine art. Goethe liked to compare himself to a gardener who prunes and waters and weeds. Schiller, on the other hand, defended his honor as a professional writer. Goethe preferred to teach the dilettantes; Schiller wanted to repudiate them, especially when they had the gall to assume they were his colleagues. In that sense, Schiller considered many of the Romantics nothing but dilettantes. Lacking a pulpit from which to rebuke them after the demise of *Die Horen* and *Propyläen*, however, Goethe and Schiller never got beyond a "General Schema" on the topic of dilettantism.

Their next projects were theater reform and a new dramatic theory, which they had been discussing for some time. Schiller had moved to Weimar, and they intended to apply the principles of *natural truth* and *aesthetic truth* to practical work in the theater, drawing both on their discussions and actual plays, especially those by Schiller. Their first principle was that theatrical art *should stick to nature, study it, imitate it, and produce something that was similar to natural phenomena*, as Goethe had written in his introduction to *Propyläen*. Theater should orient itself to nature.

Secondly, this orientation should follow the formal laws of art, which shapes its own particular context of meaning, a realm of its own order. Thus *natural truth* becomes *aesthetic truth*. Goethe had formulated the principle in the introduction to *Propyläen: Once the artist has taken up some natural object, it already no longer belongs to nature. In fact, one can say that the artist creates it at that moment by extracting from it what is significant, characteristic, interesting. Or rather, the artist first introduces a higher value into it.* By way of the free play of *imagination*, aesthetic truth becomes playfully heightened *natural truth*.

The third principle, pertaining to artistic technique, is that the work of art must not deny its aesthetic character. Ideal art is not achieved when birds peck at trompe l'oeil grapes. The true stage, writes Schiller, is like

> . . . the barge of Acheron
> Which transports but the shadows of the dead,
> And if raw life would book a seat thereon,
> The craft would cease to float, capsize instead.
> The riders are spirits, ephemeral, soon gone.
> Illusion must not turn real in a play.
> If nature triumphs, art must fade away.

To prevent a false victory of nature, Goethe bets on the alienating effect of explicit artificiality, already present in poetic meter. Schiller adds that the work of art lays claim to "nothing but a story, / Confident that its deeper truth will move us. / The false Muse pretends she's real to bemuse us." The most urgent task for the reform of the art of theater was a battle against *naturalism*.

Their attempt to establish verse on the stage encountered a naturalistic critique in its most straightforward form: the objection was that people don't talk in such an artificial way. Why not let them speak as they do in real life? But Goethe and Schiller insisted on language enhanced by rhythm and rhyme precisely because of its artificiality, for it thereby breaks the illusion of realism. Figures on stage should not talk as people do in life. The unaccustomed language of verse imposes the discipline needed to bring out a work's significance. When Schiller was in the process of drafting *Wallenstein* in blank verse, he wrote to Goethe, "One should really conceive everything that needs to rise above the common level in verse, . . . for vacuity is never as obvious as when it is spoken in verses." In his reply, Goethe makes Schiller's remark into a principle. He declares that the public wants to have it easy and therefore demands prose, while a truly *independent work* requires verse. *In any event, we are obliged to forget our century if we want to work according to our convictions.*

Measured against ordinary life, verse is as artificial as everything else about the theater, from sets to lighting, from makeup to action compressed in time. One should learn from opera, Schiller thought. It was popular though entirely antinaturalistic. Its audiences accepted the lofty, bizarre, or magical without trying to measure them against reality. Only a died-in-the-wool philistine would be surprised that the actors go to the trouble of singing instead of just talking to each other. "In the opera people really waive such servile imitation of nature," Schiller wrote. That was exactly the opinion held by Goethe, then working on a libretto for a sequel to Mozart's *Zauberflöte*. Schiller also used operatic elements in his tragedy *The Bride of Messina* with great artistry, if less public success.

Naturalism was one potential danger for art; the other was *affectation*. The former had too little form, the latter too much. A cautionary example was the classic French tragedy Lessing had once fought against. Schiller was deeply surprised when, shortly before he moved to Weimar, his friend Goethe began to translate Voltaire's *Mahomet*, one of the prime examples of the genre. The premiere of Goethe's translation was performed on January 30, 1800, in honor of the duchess's birthday. Goethe asked Schiller to help with the preparations. It was the first work Schiller had done in Weimar, a favor for his friend that brought him little satisfaction.

Goethe himself had not undertaken the Voltaire translation entirely voluntarily, but at the request of the duke. Until then, Goethe had been his own master at the court theater, but the duke was intent on having something after his own taste for once. As a favor to Goethe, he had agreed to the latter's cultural innovations—the newest philosophy of Fichte, for instance, who would soon cause him trouble; the new art of the theater; and Schiller's *Wallenstein*, which he was not wholly satisfied with. As he wrote to Goethe, "The character of the hero, who in my opinion also needs improvement, could certainly . . . be made more steady." In fact, all the new activity was hardly to his taste. Class conscious as he was, he preferred the great court theater of France with its awe-inspiring sublimity, clear contours, and sharp contrasts between high and low, good and evil, not the vacillating, mysterious, brooding, complicated characters modeled on Shakespeare. The duke had also chosen Voltaire's *Mahomet* because the play seemed to fit well into the present political landscape.

Voltaire's Muhammad is a fraud who inspires terrible fanaticism in his followers. This motif could be read as a parallel to the Jacobin ideologues and rabble-rousers, and even to Napoleon, risen like a comet into the skies of European politics and rushing from one victory to the next, dragging an entire nation into irrational passions. It was the duke's idea that this project would set the classic theater of the French against the newer French troublemakers, and Goethe had no desire to beg off. He stated frankly that it was gratitude to the duke that had persuaded him to take on the assignment. Goethe felt particularly in the duke's debt at the time, because he had to make amends for a scandal that the duke partly blamed Goethe for, which had caused an aggravating ruckus and ended with Fichte's dismissal.

In December 1798, the philosopher Friedrich Karl Forberg's essay "Development of the Concept of Religion" appeared in the *Philosophical Journal*, which Fichte edited. Forberg explicitly rejects the God of revelation and declares that religion is founded solely on ethics. His argument was no different from that of his teacher Kant, but, fearing the worst, Fichte had prefaced Forberg's essay with a brief one of his own, "On the Basis of Our Belief in a Divine World Order," intended to ward off any accusations of atheism. In it, he denounces the orthodox belief in a God of rewards and punishments as deeply irreligious. One cannot calculate God's intentions, Fichte explained, as God exists only in our absolute moral decisions. This explanation, however, only made things worse. In Electoral Saxony there appeared an anonymous brochure accusing Fichte and Forberg of atheism. On the strength of this denunciation, Saxony forbade the dissemination of Fichte's journal and demanded that the "conservators" of the University of Jena—including Duke Karl August—confiscate the essays and punish their authors, or else Saxon students would be prohibited from attending the institution.

This came at an extremely inopportune moment for Karl August. Intending to marry his son and heir to a daughter of the tsar, he had to keep his reputation as an opponent of the revolution unsullied. He wanted to avoid unwelcome attention and dispose of the affair as quietly as possible—with a reprimand and an injunction to be cautious in the future about discussing religious questions. The duke, hardly devout himself, was most concerned with caution. He thought religion useful for the lower classes, while educated men could talk to one another about whatever they liked as long as they didn't put it all in print. Fichte, however, was not about to agree to the duke's distinction between an esoteric critique of religion and exoteric conformity. He replied with the passion of a Luther: here I stand, I can do no other—writing a letter to the duke's minister Voigt threatening to request dismissal if he were reprimanded, adding that other colleagues would follow him. It was decided that Goethe would announce the reprimand and accept Fichte's proffered resignation.

The affair had an embarrassing denouement when Fichte withdrew his threatened resignation and requested reinstatement. In the eyes of the duke, he had thereby unmasked himself as a blowhard and coward. The duke wrote that Fichte was one of those people who "with all their talk of eternity" were "a very limited race clinging to their post and income."

Goethe himself found Fichte's blustering out of place and, while regretting the whole affair, agreed to his dismissal. *As for Fichte,* he writes Schlosser on August 30, 1799, *I'm still sorry that we had to lose him and that his foolish arrogance cast him out of a life that he will not find again . . . in the whole wide world. . . . He is certainly one of the most outstanding intellects, but as I myself fear, lost to himself and the world.* Goethe later destroyed the written records of this incident in his possession.

Goethe knew that the duke was indeed dissatisfied with him this time. Karl August had made it clear that the entire direction things had taken in Jena did not suit him. He already considered Fichte an out-and-out Jacobin and blamed Goethe for recommending his appointment. He went on to criticize Goethe in general for consorting too frequently with questionable people at the university. The duke wrote to Voigt and wanted the scolding passed on to Goethe: "I must have been vexed ten times nearly out of my mind by Goethe. He's positively childish about that foolish critical philosophy, and has such a taste for it that he's almost spoiled his own taste thereby. He views the thing, and the whole academic business, so carelessly that he neglects all the good he could do by being in Jena so often; it would be easier for him than for anyone else to know what those rogues are teaching, advise us of it, and have a word with them himself from time to time and keep them in line with reproofs. . . . Instead, he finds the dirty fellows charming, and the people then think that we approve of them when they throw anything so-called positive . . . out the window. . . . I can't talk to Goethe about these things at all anymore, for he immediately loses himself in such a verbose and sophistical discussion that I have no patience with it." Goethe, he continues, has allowed himself to be flattered by those people and therefore does their bidding. It was time to put a stop to it.

Goethe's reaction to this dressing-down, delivered to him in writing by Voigt, was outwardly calm—*Serenissimi philippic** . . . *is well thought-out and well written*—but he clearly felt it his duty to further oblige the duke. The translation of Voltaire's *Mahomet* came at a time when he was bemoaning his *lack of feeling for my own production*. It was not easy going, for his image of Muhammad was very different from Voltaire's.

For Goethe, Muhammad was not the fraud Voltaire makes him out to be but a great man, an example of powerfully infectious inspiration and worth studying. His admiration stood in stark contrast to the polemical tradition of Voltaire's play: the mostly hostile eighteenth-century European literature on the founder of Islam. It took Enlightenment figures like Leibniz, Lessing, and later Herder to promote a fairer appreciation of non-Christian religions, but their voices remained in the minority. As we have seen, in his youth Goethe composed "Mahomet's Song," a poem celebrating Muhammad's spiritual leadership as a river swelling from tiny sources into a gigantic stream and finally emptying into the ocean, the symbol of all-encompassing divinity: Muhammad as a divinely inspired genius of humanity. At seventy, in the *West-Eastern Divan*, Goethe would confess provocatively that he was thinking of celebrating *that sacred night when the entire Koran was brought to the Prophet from above*. All his life, Goethe found it tempting to think of himself in the role of a prophet; he perhaps at times even thought he truly was one, in the sense expressed in the paralipomena to the *West-Eastern Divan*: *Miracles I cannot do, thus says the Prophet, / The greatest miracle is that I am*. That's pretty close to his own self-assessment. Naturally, there were also critical differences. Goethe's gentle devotion to nature was far removed from Muhammad's rigid devotion to the law. Goethe was repulsed by Islamic *religious patriotism*

---

* Latin: the philippic of His most serene Highness.

as he was by all narrow patriotism. He hated fanaticism as much as Voltaire did.

In his translation and adaptation, Goethe was not able to soften Voltaire's Muhammad as he would have liked. The Prophet remains a dark and dubious figure. Although no longer the fraud and criminal of the French original, he is still a demonic presence. It is his passionate love that ignites the demonic fury within him. To win the young Palmire, he plunges whole nations into ruin: *My consolation is her love and it alone / Is my reward, my effort's only goal.* Goethe's Muhammad stops at nothing for the sake of passionate love, not because of lust for power, as in Voltaire's original. The translator lent his characters a certain warmth and suppleness of speech, replacing most of the French alexandrines with more flexible German iambic pentameter. In the end, he was satisfied with the work, finding it particularly useful for the new Weimar dramaturgy. In *Propyläen* he wrote, *The necessity for our tragic theater to distance itself from comedy and drama through versification will become more and more evident.*

The court was delighted with Goethe's translation and celebrated it as it had no other dramatic work of his. Goethe read aloud from the work at several important soirees. That was how the aristocracy commemorated the revival of classical French cultural supremacy. Like Fichte's recent dismissal or the prohibition of the bourgeois amateur theater in Jena, which also occurred at this time, the *Mahomet* readings had the ostentatious character of a restoration of princely authority.

Onstage, the play was not a brilliant success. The bourgeois audience, keen on verisimilitude, grumbled as much as the patriots who hated anything French and the Romantics who had little patience for what the novelist Jean Paul called the "unpoetical ceremonial stage." When Goethe began another translation in the summer of 1800, of Voltaire's *Tancred*, again with a *lack of feeling for my own production*, Schiller badgered him with his oft-repeated exhortations to get back to work on *Faust*. This time, Schiller deployed the publisher Cotta as his vanguard, recommending that he lure the author back to his manuscript by offering the absurdly large fee of four thousand taler for *Faust*. The maneuver worked. Goethe, who felt indebted to Cotta for the failure of *Propyläen*, set to work on *Faust* again. He expressed his thanks to Schiller for having orchestrated the whole thing.

In the summer of 1800, Goethe wrapped up some scenes from the Walpurgis Night episode and then turned to the act about Helen of Troy, befitting his preoccupation with *Propyläen*. He reported triumphantly to Schiller, *My Helen has really appeared*, referring to the scene from the second part of *Faust* set in ancient Sparta. Helen, whom Paris had abducted to Troy, has been liberated and returns home. Her husband, Menelaos, has sent her ahead to take possession of the palace once again. But instead of her servant girls and assistants, she finds within its deserted walls Phorkyas, a hideous creature with the head of a Gorgon. On his search for absolute beauty, Faust is meant to encounter an absolute monstrosity. And here Goethe hesitates. *Now I am so much drawn to beauty in the situation of my heroine that I am saddened to have to transform it first into a hideous face.* This refers not only to Phorkyas, behind whose mask Mephistopheles lurks, but more generally to the problematic connection between antique classicism and the demonic Faust, between formal perfection and formlessness along the *path of mist and fog*.

Alarmed by Goethe's hesitation, Schiller writes a letter of encouragement containing the first known mention of a plan to divide *Faust* into two parts: "Don't be unsettled by the thought that when the beautiful figures and situations come, it's a shame to barbarize them. This could occur often in the 2nd part of *Faust*, and it would be good to silence your poetic conscience about it once and for all. . . . It is a very significant advantage to consciously move from the pure to the more impure instead of seeking an uplift from the impure to the pure, which is, by the way, the case with us barbarians. So everywhere in your *Faust*, you have to assert your *Faustrecht*."*

Goethe was delighted by his friend's pun. He would make use of his *Faustrecht* several times, especially when people pestered him with the plea to finally finish his play. Before breaking off work on it again in the spring of 1801, he drafted an "announcement of discontinuation" in which he strongly asserted a *Faustrecht* to be fragmentary: *To connoisseurs this play is recommended! / . . . / Resembling the life of man's this poem's lot: / It has a beginning and an end, / But a completed whole it's not.*

---

* See page 81 above.

CHAPTER 25

Among the Romantics. Schelling. Gravely Ill.
Return to Life. Drawing the Balance of
the Revolutionary Epoch: *The Natural Daughter*.
Partisan Quarrels. Trouble with Kotzebue.
Alienation from Schiller and Friendship Restored.
Schiller's Death.

. . . .

A NEW RELATIONSHIP WITH THE CIRCLE OF YOUNG ROMANTICS around the Schlegel brothers developed after Goethe's return from Switzerland. The two Schlegels had a considerable reputation as sensitive and sharp-tongued literary critics. Schiller recruited August Wilhelm, the older brother, for *Die Horen*, introducing him to Goethe. But then he broke with him in the summer of 1797 when August Wilhelm's brother Friedrich published a mordant review of *Die Horen*. With their connection to Schiller severed, the brothers intensified their courtship of Goethe, who was very flattered by the attention. Friedrich declared that the French Revolution, Fichte's *Foundations of the Entire Science of Knowledge*, and Goethe's *Wilhelm Meister* represented the greatest trends of the century. Despite such encomiums, Goethe didn't care much for the restless, feisty Friedrich, once calling him a *stinging nettle*. He had less personal contact with him than with August Wilhelm, who spent several years in Jena, where his wife, Karoline, presided over a lively salon that became the center of the first circle of German Romantics. Tieck, Fichte, Schelling, and Novalis were frequent guests. Friedrich Schlegel was a hothead, while August Wilhelm played the part of judicious scholar and accomplished man of letters with a reputation as a virtuoso of rhyme and prosody. Goethe sought his counsel on metrical questions and praised his translations of Shakespeare. In the *Annals* for 1799, he wrote about his contact with August Wilhelm, *Not a moment was idly spent, and one could foresee common intellectual interests for years to come.*

Goethe did not tell his friend Schiller that he was acting as an adviser to *Athenäum*, a periodical the Schlegels had founded in 1798 and which Schiller denounced as "cheeky" and "one-sided." Goethe attempted to mollify his friend. *What would remain to be said in favor of the Schlegels we shall leave for a face-to-face negotiation.* Goethe also met the young Ludwig Tieck, who read his tragedy *Life and Death of Saint Genevieve* aloud to him in the winter of 1799, an unforgettable experience, as Goethe would later write: *When he began it was striking eight, when he ended, eleven. I didn't even hear it strike nine or ten.*

In the fall of 1799, the Romantic circle had to decide whether *Athenäum* should publish Novalis's essay "Christianity or Europe"— provocative because of its sympathy for Roman Catholicism and idealization of the Middle Ages. Unable to resolve a difference of opinion among themselves, they appealed to Goethe, who advised against printing it: he did not wish to see the journal provide a pretext for defamatory attacks. The brouhaha around Fichte's atheism still fresh, it was preferable, he said, for them not to expose themselves to possible charges of obscurantism. Goethe dreaded that specter as much as he dreaded the specter of revolutionaries. Novalis's essay did not appear in *Athenäum*.

Friendships among the Romantics began to fray after this debate. Karoline Schlegel, who played such an essential part in keeping the group together, fell in love with Schelling, twelve years her junior, and powerful tensions ensued. On one side were Friedrich Schlegel and his companion Dorothea Veit, who resented her sister-in-law Karoline's dominant role. They attracted Novalis, Tieck, and Friedrich Schleiermacher to their party. On the other side were Schelling, Karoline, and her highly gifted daughter from her first marriage, the sixteen-year-old Auguste, who was a little in love with Schelling herself. In the middle was August Wilhelm Schlegel, who was not passionate enough to be jealous and more inclined to be an intermediary. There was much gossip in Jena about these tangled relationships, confirming suspicion of crazy goings-on in the Schlegel household. The affair turned into a full-blown scandal when Karoline, having recovered from a grave illness, went to the spa in Bad Bocklet, near Kissingen, with Schelling and her daughter in May 1800. Auguste suddenly fell ill and died in just a few days. The rumor circulated in Jena that Schelling had caused Auguste's death with dilettantish attempts at a naturopathic cure and that Karoline had intended to pair her daughter off with Schelling to keep him nearby. That was too much for Karoline. She suffered a breakdown and did not dare to return immediately to Jena. At first, she withdrew from Schelling, who became depressed and considered suicide. Karoline recommended that he seek Goethe's help: "He loves you like a father, I love you like a mother—what marvelous parents you have!"

Goethe and Schelling had become increasingly intimate since Schiller had introduced them in 1796. Goethe was impressed by the powerful, self-confident young man, whom he recommended to his colleague Voigt for an unpaid professorship with the words, *He has a very lucid and energetic mind, organized according to the newest fashion; nor have I been able to discern the slightest hint of a sansculotte turn of mind in him. On the contrary, he seems moderate and educated in every sense. I am convinced that he would do us honor and be useful to the academy.* When Goethe called his mind *organized according to the newest fashion*, he meant to characterize him as a philosopher of Fichte's school, a so-called transcendentalist who was investigating the subjective prerequisites for the possibility of perception. While that would not have particularly attracted him, Schelling showed definitive signs of moving toward natural philosophy: he was searching for a transition from the principle of the ego to the creative powers of nature, which pleased Goethe, who was eager to get involved in discussions with him. Mind is unconscious nature, and nature unconscious mind: this was a key statement of Schelling's that Goethe found very sympathetic. He secured Schelling's latest writings on natural philosophy and not only cut the pages but read them too. At first, however, he kept his distance. He summarized his feelings about what he had read in a letter to Schiller. He found both the natural philosophers, who wanted to *direct us from above to below,* and the ordinary natural scientists, who wanted to *direct us from below to above,* unsatisfactory. He discovered his own salvation *in observation alone, which stands in the middle.*

His reserve vanished as he felt his proximity to Schelling's thought more clearly: clarity of perception, the overcoming of mechanistic thinking, a sense and feeling for the creative power in nature. For Goethe, Schelling was the triumphant culmination of a train of thought that led from Kant to Fichte. He wrote to Schiller, *We intend to do our utmost to enter the new century with this third wonder.* To Schelling himself, he wrote, *Ever since I tore myself free of the traditional kind of nature study and, like a monad thrown back on myself, had to float around in the cerebral regions of science, I have seldom felt a pull in one direction or another; the pull toward your teaching is decisive. I wish for a complete confluence, which I hope to effect by studying your writing or, even better, by personal contact with you.*

Karoline Schlegel's advice to the despondent Schelling to pay Goethe a visit—and the remark, he "loves you"—was exactly the right thing. If not exactly love, it was certainly great admiration and personal sympathy for the young philosopher who found himself in such a difficult spot. On December 26, 1800, Goethe picked him up in Jena in his equipage and took him to Weimar, where he remained as a guest in the house on the Frauenplan until January 4. They spent New Year's Eve in lively conversation with Schiller.

Three days later, Goethe came down with a serious case of shingles. His face, eyes, neck, and other parts of his body badly inflamed, he went temporarily blind and suffered choking fits. His brain was affected; he was disoriented, delirious, and drifted in and out of a coma, battling for his life. Later he said he felt as if he was dissolved into a landscape: completely awake and perceptive but without consciousness of himself. Schiller was with him every day, and the duke was a frequent visitor to his bedside. The entire court and citizenry of Weimar was deeply concerned, and while unaware of everything that was happening, Goethe was moved to hear of it later. *At least I can flatter myself that people have some fondness for me and attribute some significance to my existence,* he wrote his mother after the crisis had passed.

Within two weeks, he began a translation of Theophrastus's color theory and was able to receive visitors and dictate letters. He called it his *reentrance into life.* With Schiller, Schelling was among those who first received word of Goethe's recovery. The young philosopher had been present when Goethe fell ill. Goethe wrote him on February 1, 1801, *Unfortunately, when we parted, the illness had already set in quite forcefully and soon thereafter I lost consciousness of my condition. Even while you were still here, I felt that I was no longer in complete command of my mind.*

Goethe regained strength with astonishing speed, but the recollection of his brush with death was not quickly forgotten. Conscious of a turning point, he put his affairs in order. He wanted to free himself of liabilities and so looked for someone who might want the estate in Oberrossla, which had brought him nothing but trouble and worry. He pursued the legitimation of his son, August, so that he would be recognized as his heir. He showed his gratitude to those who took part in his care during his illness by founding a "Wednesday Circle," a *cour d'amour* where one could take pleasure in relaxed conversation, brief performances and readings, light refreshment, and simply the fact that one was alive. He spent almost three months at the spa in Bad Pyrmont and the nearby university town of Göttingen, where he spoke with professors of natural science and students—the poet Clemens Brentano among them—gave him a cheer and wished him long life. Everywhere he was received like a man risen from the dead.

His poetic work was at a standstill, particularly difficult to bear with Schiller then enjoying an extraordinarily productive phase. Following the *Wallenstein* trilogy, *Mary Stuart* and *The Maid of Orléans* were completed in rapid succession and performed to great acclaim on stages all over Germany. When Schiller visited Leipzig, there was a mob scene with fathers lifting their children in the air to catch sight of the poetic miracle worker. Goethe did not begrudge his friend his productivity and fame, but it did make him dissatisfied with himself.

After the existential crisis of his grave illness, Goethe felt a strong urge to gain a true understanding of the social and political turning point that ten years of revolution had wrought, which seemed to have culminated with the rise of Napoleon. Since 1795, peace had reigned north of the border represented by the Main River. Though Prussia and a few other states, including the duchy of Weimar, remained neutral and enjoyed a measure of quiet in a Europe torn by conflict, the war continued further south, and the great commander was keeping Europe in suspense. *We shall wait and see,* Goethe writes to Schiller on March 9, 1802, *whether Bonaparte's personality continues to please us with that marvelous and dominant appearance.* The *marvelous appearance* Napoleon could present was as the man who had prevailed over the revolutionary epoch. In the same letter, Goethe summed up the revolution in the grandiose image of a natural disaster: *As a whole, it is the prodigious sight of brooks and streams tumbling together according to natural law from many heights and valleys and finally causing a great river to rise and flood its banks. Those who saw it coming perish therein as well as those who had no idea. In this monstrous empiricism, one sees nothing but nature and nothing that we philosophers are so pleased to call freedom.* Only Napoleon would be able to give shape to and breathe his own spirit into this *monstrous empiricism.*

Goethe wrote this while at work on *The Natural Daughter*, a play that, as he said in his *Annals*, became the *vessel* for everything he had thought and written about the French Revolution. The idea had come to him at the end of 1799, but Goethe began serious work on it only after his illness, at first with great effort and under a blanket of secrecy, even Schiller learning nothing of it. It was his old *superstition* that he *must not reveal a project if it was to succeed.* He planned to write a trilogy, but never got beyond the first play, completed in March 1803 and performed on the Weimar stage on April 2—still under the title *Eugenie* and with very modest success.

Goethe had been inspired by a work billed as the memoirs of Stephanie de Bourbon-Conti, natural daughter of the Prince de Bourbon-Conti. The tale of a noblewoman brought low by a court cabal and of the difficulties of maintaining her nobility of heart in hard times, it was already known to be a forgery. Goethe liked it and used this "fairy tale," as Schiller called it, as the basis for his play.

Eugenie, the illegitimate daughter of a duke, is robbed of her claims and social rank and learns self-denial. She is given the choice of spending her life in fruitless isolation and the bitter but proud consciousness of her lofty birth, or accepting the hand of a bourgeois man and leading a productive if obscure life. She chooses bourgeois obscurity and preserves the nobility of her heart, at first only inwardly, but with the prospect that a new external order might one day emerge. She must endure and persevere until then: *For if a miracle occurs on earth, / It's through the loyalty of a loving heart.* As in *Iphigenia*, humaneness is preserved in secret, shielded by the form of her elevated nature. And as in *Iphigenia*, the solemn rhythms of highly stylized pentameter—and a thoroughly worked-out web of motifs and symbols, which lend it a sedate quality—make the play a formal alternative to the chaos of revolution and corruption.

The Natural Daughter is written completely in the spirit of the Weimar dramaturgy that Goethe and Schiller had developed in the preceding years. Much as Eugenie preserves her morale amid the fall of the old order, the strict formalism of the drama opposes the classicist ideal of art to the *muddy tide* of banality (the party of the playwright August von Kotzebue, whom we shall soon encounter) and wild eccentricity (the party of the Romantics). The most important thing for Goethe was to remain above *partisan endeavor*:

> At home, securely ruled by a husband,
> Is where peace reigns, a peace that you will seek
> In vain out in the world far and wide.
> Not restless envy, not malicious slander,
> Nor echoes of some partisan endeavor
> Have any impact in that sacred sphere!

As with *Iphigenia*, the play itself is rounded into a *sacred sphere*. Goethe refused to adapt *The Natural Daughter* for actual performance. It's a play like a closed oyster, a *talisman* whose magical powers one uses but doesn't actually display. No wonder the play had little success on the stage. The public marveled at its craftsmanship and stayed away. Madame de Staël, then visiting Weimar, attended a performance and felt nothing but "noble ennui."

For Goethe, *The Natural Daughter* was a refuge from the upheavals of history and from *partisan* strivings of all kinds. Partisan squabbles in the duchy were at their height. August von Kotzebue, who had started it all, was the most successful playwright in Germany at the time. Goethe staged his plays often for a public that wanted to see them, though they seemed to him the epitome of the banal naturalism he and Schiller were campaigning against.

Kotzebue had just returned to Weimar from an eventful trip to Russia. At the border he had been arrested as a spy and deported to western Siberia. The author had a substantial following in Russia and was released a short time later at the intervention of the tsar, brought to St. Petersburg, and, for the injustice he had suffered, given an honorary pension and a country estate with six hundred serfs. Returning to Weimar a rich man and the talk of the town, Kotzebue purchased a house, where, since he wasn't invited to Goethe's Wednesday Circle, he founded a circle of his own. The atmosphere was more relaxed and entertaining than at Goethe's and the food was better. Goethe was annoyed at Kotzebue's social success and very susceptible to his needling. Although he produced Kotzebue's play *Small Town Germany*, he deleted passages he considered a slur against his protégés the Schlegels, whereupon Kotzebue withdrew all his plays from the Weimar theater. Goethe brought August Wilhelm Schlegel's *Ion* to the stage in January 1802 and Friedrich Schlegel's *Alarcos* in May 1802; both were unsuccessful, and it was generally surmised he did it only to antagonize the Kotzebue faction. There was a scandal during a performance of *Alarcos*, when laughter drowned out the dialogue of the ambitious tragedy. Goethe turned around in his raised seat in the orchestra and commanded, "No laughing!" He considered it a plot by Kotzebue.

In 1802, Kotzebue attempted to drive a wedge between Goethe and Schiller. People were already beginning to compare the two "Dioscuri" and discuss who was the greater. Factions formed for one or the other, and Kotzebue looked to exploit the squabbling. He planned an ostentatious celebration of Schiller's name day, March 5. Scenes from Schiller's plays were to be presented and his poem "The Song of the Bell" recited in the festively decorated council chamber of the town hall. At the end, Kotzebue was to appear as the master bell caster and smash a papier-mâché bell revealing a bust of Schiller, which a circle of virgins in flowing white robes would dance around and then crown with a laurel wreath. All Weimar talked about the event before it took place, and far more did so when it didn't come off. Everything had been carefully rehearsed, but on the night of March 4, the library custodian refused to lend the bust of Schiller, claiming he had never gotten a plaster bust back from a celebration undamaged. Worse was to come. When workmen went to erect the stage in the council chamber, they found the town hall locked. People suspected Goethe's machinations. It may simply have been the mayor's preemptive solicitude. Whatever the truth, a group of young women who had intended to make a splash at the celebration stopped attending Goethe's Wednesday Circles. The affair was an embarrassment for Schiller, who later indicated that he had wanted to plead sickness and fail to report. Goethe had made a timely withdrawal to Jena, and from there obtained eyewitness reports of the proceedings as they unfolded.

When it was all over, Schiller wrote him, "March fifth passed more happily for me than the fifteenth did for Caesar. . . . I hope you will find tempers cooled upon your return."

They were not. Pockets of insult, envy, enmity, and schadenfreude remained, and the affair had even done some damage to their friendship. There was tension between them. By summer, Goethe was worrying about the financial stability of the theater and a dearth of plays appealing to his audience; he tried to spur Schiller on with the fairly brusque remark that he shouldn't spend so much time conceptualizing but should work more rapidly and *with more concentration, so you can supply more—and, if I may say so, more theatrically effective—productions.*

Schiller took umbrage at being accused of lack of effectiveness at a time when *The Maid of Orléans* was conquering stages all over Germany. He replied on the very next day, "If I ever succeed in writing a good play, it can only be via the path of poetry, for I can never make my goal an effect ad extra,* which occasionally succeeds for someone with a common talent and mere cleverness. Nor, even if I wanted to, could I achieve it. Here I am talking only about the highest endeavor, and only a fulfilled art will be able to overcome my individual tendency ad intra,† if it is to be overcome at all." Schiller declared that in no case would he lower his high artistic standards, and he accused Goethe of recommending precisely that for the sake of audience appeal. It amounted to inciting him to betray his art.

During this nerve-racking time, Schiller turned down a lucrative offer from Berlin, for which Goethe gave him great credit. After their temporary altercation, productive, amicable intimacy was soon reestablished, one expression of it being that Goethe relinquished the material for a work about Wilhelm Tell to Schiller, who turned it into his most popular play. Goethe had the satisfaction that it premiered not in Berlin, which had lobbied intensely for it, but in Weimar, and he devoted a great deal of time and effort to its staging and took almost childish delight in the brilliant success of what they had concocted together. Their collaboration was again as close as in the first three years of their friendship.

---

* Latin: on the outside, externally.
† Latin: on the inside, internally.

Schiller had received a manuscript of Diderot's as yet unpublished dialogue *Rameau's Nephew*. He asked Goethe to translate it, and Goethe enthusiastically threw himself into the task. They discussed Schiller's plans for new plays. Goethe thought that *Demetrius* was especially promising, and occasionally remarked that it would probably become his friend's best play. After Schiller's death, he would try to complete it, but never did. Goethe worked for Schiller and snowed Schiller under with work, too, even when his friend fell seriously ill in early 1805. He gave him the Diderot translation complete with annotations and asked him to edit it. He also gave him the manuscript of the *Theory of Color* to study. He didn't want to publish it before he heard what Schiller thought of it. He expected a lot of his friend, but was only treating him the way he was used to treating himself when he was weak or sick, encouraging him to keep busy. One should not grant death any power over one's life as long as it lasted. Yet Goethe sensed that he would soon lose his friend. He wrote him a New Year's greeting at the beginning of 1805 with the words *On our last New Year's Day*. Shocked, he tore up the page and began a new one, again writing *On our last New Year's Day*. He visited Frau von Stein that same day, told her what had happened, and said he had "a premonition that either he or Schiller would pass away this year."

On February 8, 1805, Goethe was tortured by shingles, as in 1801. This time, it affected his eyes but was not life-threatening. Schiller, himself plagued by illness, was worried. He wept. Goethe began to recover and wrote his friend, *By the way, I feel well as long as I go out riding every day*. Schiller thereupon acquired a horse for himself, but never got to ride it.

The friends met for the last time on May 1 on their way to the theater. They exchanged only a few words. Feeling unwell, Goethe turned around and went home again. The early resumption of theater attendance was also not good for Schiller, who suffered another breakdown. Goethe had sent him a letter on April 27, 1805, with a schematic overview of the *Theory of Color* and commentary on *Rameau's Nephew*, and Schiller read some of it. He suffered through a few more days and died on the evening of May 9.

The news reached the house on the Frauenplan within an hour. Meyer, first to hear it, couldn't muster the courage to tell Goethe and left the house without saying goodbye. Goethe was restless, noticed that something was being kept from him, and perhaps wanted it that way. Christiane had been informed and pretended to be asleep so as not to make Goethe suspicious. She told him the following morning. He covered his eyes with his hands and withdrew. When they asked whether he wanted to see the dead man once more, he cried, *Oh no! Destruction!*

Pleading illness, Goethe did not attend Schiller's funeral on May 11. He could not stand death. *Unannounced and without fanfare he came to Weimar,* Goethe said later, *and without fanfare he departed from here. I have no love for the parades of death.*

Three weeks later he wrote Karl Friedrich Zelter, *I thought I would lose myself, and now I lose a friend and, in him, half my existence.* At the death of his beloved friend, fortunately another friend stood ready to take his place: Zelter, the composer and master mason from Berlin. He would become Goethe's most important confidant in his last years.

INTERMEDIATE REFLECTION

———

Red Tape and Pegasus

GOETHE, THE BRILLIANT HIGHFLIER, GOES TO WEIMAR as if he needed to take a chance on finally settling down on solid ground. You learn by teaching, he used to say later on. But what can he teach Karl August, the young duke? Goethe doesn't know how official business is conducted. He doesn't know how to administer a state. All he had done was read Justus Möser and embrace his liberal-conservative recommendations: preserve tradition and develop and preserve what is characteristic of a particular country, its so-called local wisdom. Those were the few principles he hoped would help him find his way in this new situation. He had actually intended to try leading a realistic and industrious life, but at first he was drawn into a wild and boisterous one. The early years in the duke's orbit were full of tempestuous, youthful high spirits, what with hunting, camping in the woods, skirt chasing, drinking bouts, and nights spent in hunting lodges. Goethe was always in attendance as a friend and master of ceremonies, but also as an older brother, ensuring a modicum of common sense and propriety. It was what the court expected of him, but there were those who didn't think he could do it. The teacher needed teaching himself, they said; with his ingenious pranks, the genius was only infecting the duke. Goethe encountered suspicion, and he himself was still not clear about what role he should play—or, more importantly, wanted to play.

He no longer wanted to be just a writer. Friends like Lenz and

Klinger who visited Weimar were reminders of his former life, and he kept his distance from them. Literary life with its insouciant bombast he now found suspect. Poetry was all well and good, but not for leading one's life. People who knew only about literature knew too little about life. He couldn't stand the agitated enthusiasts of the Sturm und Drang, but also refused to accept moral admonishment from an unctuous, sententious poet like Klopstock.

Goethe put literature aside for the time being, although he did continue to lard his letters—especially those to Charlotte von Stein—with poems, poems of the moment and for the moment. Mainly, however, he wanted to learn the business of *governing*. He had pledged himself to the task during the Harz journey in winter, on the snow-covered summit of the Brocken. He threw himself into official business, and little by little, he gained experience in almost all departments, from road building, school administration, and finances to the military. He also tried out foreign affairs, pondering how Weimar might maneuver between its two large and powerful neighbors, Prussia and the Habsburg Empire. On his first and only visit to Berlin, he wore the mask of the cool diplomat. But his favorite hobbyhorse was mining, which he pursued during the early years with passion, if no economic success.

It was mining that first awakened his interest in natural science. Attracted by the history of the earth, he collected earth's mineral and fossilized remains. He studied anatomy and collected bones and skeletons.

For a while he quite enjoyed being both a bureaucratic draft horse and a poetic Pegasus, so long as the two didn't get entangled in each other's traces, as happened when he tried to work on *Iphigenia* while traveling through the duchy recruiting troops. He had been captivated by the idea of purity, and the different spheres were to be purely, cleanly separated: art here and the active life over there. Each sphere had its own logic and required its own skills and commitments. The idea of purity applies to the conscientious fulfillment of assignments—to the proper way of doing things. In his personal life, it has an ascetic aspect: discipline, self-control, self-denial, being honest or keeping silent.

After eight or nine years in Weimar, Goethe saw that while he had learned to meet the daily demands of his position, his poetic vein was in danger of petering out. He sought a decisive answer: did he still have a future as an author, or only a past? Did he still have it in him to complete something, or could he only collect his fragments? In escaping to Italy, he wanted not only to visit the land of art but also to discover whether he was still an artist. To his delight, he rediscovered the artist in himself: a poet, not a painter, which would also have pleased him. But the poet not as a Man of Sorrows, a victim in despair among the worldly, like Tasso—but one who rises above the dichotomy between the artist Tasso and the man of the world Antonio, who understands the differences but does not allow them to tear him apart. Goethe returns from Italy with the idea of being a sovereign human being.

Whether in his official duties, his scientific endeavors, or his art, he was intent upon achieving the best possible results and combining his various activities so that they were mutually beneficial. He had lost this inner balance shortly before his Italian journey, when it was no longer clear where his primary focus should be. He rediscovered it in Italy: he was an artist. He stuck by that decision after his return, but was still faced with the task of keeping it in balance with other activities. Crucial help was provided by his friendship with Schiller, who not only energetically steered him toward art but gave him a certain consciousness of self that he hadn't yet achieved. Until then, poetry had been almost a hobby. Spurred on by Schiller's profound aesthetic judgment, he wrote with professional seriousness and hard-nosed technical skill. Questions of form and technique were now matters of reflection. The two friends each developed a self-confidence that in the end allowed them to play the role of preceptors to German literature. Schiller's contribution was the concept of powerful mastery of their material, Goethe's the concept of natural purity.

The epochal phenomenon of the French Revolution was the background for their determination to make art at the highest level. At a time when everything is in turmoil, art must provide orientation and cohesion. Schiller emphasized cultivated freedom; Goethe, refined naturalness. Both set great store on the play of art, with Schiller thinking of humanity at large and Goethe of a small circle of connoisseurs. His expectations and hopes with regard to the social effectiveness of art were more modest than Schiller's. Against the course of the world, he thought there was little the *delicate empiricism* of art could do.

Schiller's death marked a turning point. For Goethe, it meant bidding farewell to a period of artistic endeavor, a golden age of short duration in which art belonged not just to the most beautiful but also to the most important things of life.

CHAPTER 26

Mourning Schiller. Flirtation. *Faust* Again.

A Long Conversation about *Faust* with Heinrich Luden.

The Disaster of October 14, 1806: Weimar Plundered

and Occupied. Goethe in Fear and Happiness.

Life Changes. Meeting Napoleon in 1808.

....

GOETHE WAS NUMB IN THE DAYS FOLLOWING SCHILLER'S death on May 9, 1805. He was again tortured by a case of shingles, and mostly kept to his study. *In defiance of death*, he got himself through the crisis by improvising his own personal dialogue with the dead: he resolved to complete Schiller's last, unfinished play, *Demetrius*, intending to make it a posthumous joint project. Goethe wanted to preserve the atmosphere of collegiality, to feel as if his friend were still alive. *His loss seemed compensated for by my continuing his existence.* Goethe imagined a production of *Demetrius* at the Deutsches Theater in Berlin that could be the *most marvelous funeral.* He saved himself from *despair* in the *enthusiasm* of feverish planning and was for a moment able to dream away his friend's death. This mood, however, was not conducive to the artistic *levelheadedness* necessary to bring Schiller's monumental plan into *narrower focus.* In *Demetrius*, the fascinating story of a false tsar in the sixteenth century, Schiller completely shattered the unities of place and action. The gigantic spaces of Eurasia were the setting for a bewildering plot, which, in its unfinished state, remained incalculable. Individual scenes that Schiller had finished emerged as if from under a gigantic blanket of snow—or perhaps a shroud. Schiller had sometimes felt the same way about the play.

Lovely early summer weather set in after Schiller's death, but Goethe stayed in his back room, immersed in a work full of the wintry crunch of ice and snow. He didn't keep at it very long, however, before abandoning the attempt. In his diary from that time there is nothing but empty white pages. Later he would say that they indicate the *hollowed-out mood* he was in.

With the failure of the *Demetrius* project, the atmosphere of continued collaboration that enveloped him evaporated, and his friend's death sank in in all its irrevocability. *Only now did he begin to decompose for me.* Seized by a pain greater than any he had known before, he also felt guilty, as if he had at last *unceremoniously locked up* Schiller in his tomb. He suffered another twinge of regret when the manuscript of the *Theory of Color*, which Schiller had studied in his final days, was returned to him. His friend's underlinings gave him the impression that Schiller's *friendship still continued from beyond the grave*, while Goethe himself had not been able to remain awhile with his friend after his death.

His next plan to commemorate Schiller, a memorial celebration including performances of scenes Goethe would write, also fell flat. Zelter had promised to compose accompanying music, but could not begin since Goethe never got beyond a few sketches. He felt paralyzed. The only thing he completed was the "Epilogue to Schiller's 'Bell'" for a memorial celebration in Lauchstädt on August 10, 1805. Some scenes from *Maria Stuart* were played, followed by a scenic reading of "The Song of the Bell." Goethe's "Epilogue" combines the lofty tone of official mourning with the language of personal emotion, intensely present in lines like *His mind forged on at its accustomed pace / Toward beauty, truth, and never-ending good, / Leaving behind the vulgar, commonplace / That hinders us from being what we could.* Verses about Schiller's infectious enthusiasm are themselves enthusiastic and affectionate: *Now his cheeks were glowing, red and redder, / Bright with youth, a deathless flag unfurled, / Aglow with the courage which, sooner or later, / Conquers the dull resistance of the world.* The actress Amalia Wolff, who recited the "Epilogue," later recounted that while she was rehearsing some striking passage, Goethe had interrupted her, taken her arm, covered his eyes, and exclaimed, *I cannot . . . cannot forget the man!*

Schiller's death marked a turning point in Goethe's life. He *really ought to begin a new way of life*, as he wrote to Zelter, but he was probably too old to do so. What great plans he had made with Schiller! What would they not have tackled: reforming the theater, criticizing and improving the literati, instructing the artists, and, in general, elevating and refining the culture! Suddenly, all that seemed very far away. *So now I only see each day directly ahead of me and do the next thing without thinking about its consequences.*

Even more than before, Schiller now became for him a touchstone in his dealings with others. That was already evident in the case of his first visitor after Schiller's death. The classical philologist Friedrich August Wolf, a man Goethe regarded highly, and his daughter stayed in the house on the Frauenplan for two weeks in early June. There were lively conversations, jolly entertainments, and new things to be learned. However, when differences of opinion arose—for example, about the inner unity of ancient texts, which Wolf's philological erudition regularly picked apart—they soon proved oppressive conversation stoppers. Wolf would not stand for any contradictions to his professional opinion, especially not from so-called dilettantes. Schiller had been another story entirely. Disagreements with him were always stimulating. *Schiller's idealistic tendency,* Goethe wrote in his *Annals, was able to nourish my realistic one very well, and since neither tendency reached its goal by itself, in the end the two coalesced in a vivid sense.* Wolf was an especially difficult case and notoriously argumentative. If one accepted his opinion and then repeated it to him a few days later, it could happen that he treated it *like the greatest absurdity.* Goethe joked that once he had prompted Wolf to depart on the day before his birthday, *because I was afraid that on my birthday he would deny that I had been born.* Although Wolf was such a difficult person, the visit at least distracted Goethe from his grief.

The aftereffects of Schiller's death lasted a long time. In the winter of 1807–08, for instance, Goethe would connect a little crush he had on Minna Herzlieb, the ward of the Jena publisher Friedrich Johannes Frommann, with the death of his friend two years earlier. In an unpublished note for the *Annals,* he writes of his *longing for the deceased* and that the recurringly painful *loss* of Schiller required *compensation.* Thus he explained his suddenly ignited *passion* for Minna Herzlieb. He added that the only reason it did not have a *pernicious* effect was that he was able to redirect his excitement into sonnets composed in competition with Zacharias Werner, famous as the author of religio-Romantic dramas and infamous as a lothario: *In order not to bore us, poets tend / To stir up all their deepest wells of feeling; / However, their own wounds they treat with healing / Powers from the magic words they've penned.*

Minna Herzlieb was a pretty eighteen-year-old. Goethe had watched her grow up, and, as he aged and she came of age, he succumbed to her charm. It was said of Minna that she was refreshingly free of coquettishness but a little slow on the uptake. She was the epitome of a naïve beauty and everyone liked her. They called her the "loveliest of all the virgin roses." She was talkative but elusive, which only increased her attractiveness. There was something mysterious about her. Goethe had fallen in love with her, and Zacharias Werner was courting her too. The dalliance lasted only one winter but left enough of an impression to have influenced the figure of Ottilie in *Elective Affinities*, Goethe's third novel. Minna's end was as sad as Ottilie's. She languished in an unhappy marriage and succumbed to mental illness.

The immediate consequence of Schiller's death was that Goethe took up work on *Faust* again. Schiller had always urged him to do so, and Goethe now felt duty-bound to finally finish the work, if only for the sake of his deceased friend. To be sure, there was external pressure as well. The eighth volume of Cotta's edition of Goethe works was supposed to contain the complete *Faust*. Hoping for a financial success, Cotta had specified as much in the contract. The publication date for this volume was now approaching, and with the help of his secretary Riemer, at the end of March 1806 Goethe began once again to go through the scenes of the fragmentary version of 1790. He was under significant time pressure since Cotta was to be given the completed manuscript, ready for printing, on his way back from the Frankfurt book fair. A few things needed to be supplemented from the supply of unpublished scenes so that the play would at last have some sort of ending, for the version in the Göschen edition of 1790 was really only a fragment that broke off before the Walpurgis Night and the scene of Gretchen in the dungeon. Even the 1808 version, however, would be unfinished. He called the play "Part One of the Tragedy," thereby lending special weight to the "Prelude at the Theater," the "Prologue in Heaven," and also the "Dedication," for they apply to the entire drama. At this point, it was still uncertain whether Part Two would ever be completed. In any event, *Faust* would continue to be the author's constant companion.

As he was completing *Faust I*, Goethe embarked on a long and memorable conversation about the play with a young historian named Heinrich Luden, who had just received an appointment in Jena. Luden immediately wrote down what had been said and later published it. He had given his notes to friends and acquaintances to read, and they were preserved only because he had lent them out; all the other manuscripts in his house were destroyed during the plundering that went on after the battles of Jena and Auerstedt in the fall of 1806.

Luden's published account begins with a summary of the interpretations—still largely accepted today—that were circulating after the publication of the *Faust* fragment in 1790. As Luden describes people's expectations, "When a complete version of this tragedy appears, the spirit of world history as a whole will be presented; it will be a true picture of the life of mankind, comprising the past, the present, and the future. In Faust, mankind is idealized; he is the representative of mankind." Luden continues that Faust strives for the absolute but finds his connection to it painfully severed. Ever since, Faust has been filled with a yearning for reintegration, which he seeks first with his intellect and insight, but then with his body, his life, and his love. In so doing, he loses his way on false paths that lead only to crime and guilt. Yet the fragment is not without hints that Faust will eventually be purified and united with the spirit of the absolute.

In Luden's telling, Goethe interrupted after a while: that was all very well and good, but what did Luden himself think? The young man squirmed at first, but then got to the point: there was no basic idea in the play, he replied, nor was anybody the representative of humanity. Either everybody was a representative, or nobody. There were only individuals and particulars, and Goethe's play was rich in impressive individuals and particulars worth thinking about. He had only begun to enjoy Goethe's play, he wrote, "[o]nce I decided to enjoy particular things and completely gave up the search for a basic idea or central point, which had destroyed my pleasure."

This was very much what Goethe himself sometimes said when readers who discerned a higher significance in the play would get on his nerves. But he was not so pleased to hear these remarks from the mouth of a brash young man. His brow darkened even more when Luden trotted out his conjectures about how the play came to be in the first place, namely, not as a single conception but rather "haphazardly." Scenes were "written like a shot in the dark," and then these "separate pearls" had been threaded onto a string to keep them "from being scattered." The scene in Auerbach's cellar was probably written first, during Goethe's student years in Leipzig, for it was fresh and youthful, free and lively; then the scene with Mephisto and the pupil, which was also something like a rarefied sophomoric prank. But then the Faust from Auerbach's cellar had to be brought together with the Mephisto from the scene with the pupil, and that resulted in the scene between Faust and Mephisto. And out of that meeting developed the dynamic that turns the learned scholar into a seducer. And so Faust grows and develops and only at the end is the opening monologue, so pregnant with meaning, written. At this point, Goethe declares the conversation at an end. *Meanwhile*, he says, *we will break off for now and not take up the topic again until the whole tragedy is finished.* And we will follow the same advice, adding only that in his diary, Goethe does note down Luden's visit, but not the topic of their conversation. Was he put out? In any event, he is very precise about the topic of another conversation on the same day, in which the *harmful effects of potatoes* were discussed.

Another lasting effect of Schiller's death was Goethe's increased readiness to view his own life historically. *Since the great breach that was opened in my existence by Schiller's death*, he wrote in April 1806 to the painter Philipp Hackert, a friend from his Italian journey, *I am more vividly aware of the need to remember the past, and I feel quite passionately the duty to preserve in memory what seems to have disappeared forever.* This is an early hint of the beginning of an autobiographical period in Goethe's work. Shortly thereafter it would be powerfully manifest as he started work on *Poetry and Truth*.

But other things had to occur first, significant events perhaps even more decisive to Goethe than Schiller's death: Prussia's disastrous defeat by Napoleon at the battles of Jena and Auerstedt on October 14, 1806, and the occupation and plunder of Weimar by the French. Goethe was in danger of losing everything in those days: his property, his office, his duke, and even his life.

Since the beginning of the new century, Weimar—under the wing of its powerful neighbor Prussia—had enjoyed peace in neutralized northern Germany. Karl August, related through his mother, Anna Amalia, to Frederick the Great, held the rank of major general and had commanded a Prussian contingent in the War of the First Coalition against revolutionary France. He knew that he could preserve his little duchy's independence only by exploiting the differences between his big neighbors. He cleverly arranged a match between his heir, Karl Friedrich, and the tsar's sister Maria Paulovna in 1804, which made Russia his backup against Prussian presumption and Napoleonic aggression. Goethe supported Karl August's cautious policy of maintaining a fragile neutrality, but differences also emerged. Goethe was not as enthusiastic about Prussia and bet more on the good will of France, but during the period of neutrality that made hardly any difference. For both of them, the old Holy Roman Empire had by then lost any significance as a guarantor of stability. Goethe had no illusions about that. After the Reichsdeputationshauptschluss (Principal Decree of the Imperial Deputation) of 1806, the empire lay in ruins and there was no point in having any political hopes to the contrary.

The news that Francis II had solemnly abdicated the throne of emperor of the Holy Roman Empire of the German Nation on August 6, 1806, accepted the title of emperor of Austria, and thereby officially sealed the end of the old empire, reached Goethe en route back to Weimar from Carlsbad, where he had spent the summer. The fall of the empire could no longer stir up any passion, because its fate had long since been sealed, as Goethe noted in his diary: *Dispute between the servant and the coachman on the box that excited more passion in us than the split-up of the Holy Roman Empire.* Nevertheless, Goethe took an active interest in political developments. As a court official, he could hardly help but do so. His diary from Carlsbad and on the return trip records frequent political conversations, which is not surprising given the tense atmosphere of those weeks. At stake was whether Prussia (and thus Weimar too) could maintain its neutrality or would be provoked into a war. Rumor had it that Napoleon intended to give Hanover, which he had promised to Prussia, back to the English. Would Prussia answer this affront by declaring war on France? *Reflections and discussions,* Goethe writes, noting down the departure of Prussian troops in the direction of Hanover.

For the moment, however, the argument on the coach box really did force itself into the foreground: on the return from Carlsbad, Goethe's manservant Johannes Gensler had a fistfight with the coachman that left the vehicle driverless, swerving and almost tipping over. Goethe turned Gensler over to the police in Jena the next day. His manservant had been *extremely rough, obstinate, coarse, and irritable. Since I now saw myself in the position of losing the entire benefit of my completed spa treatment from anger and annoyance and was also on the point of being forced into an unseemly and wanton act of taking the law into my own hands, there was nothing left to do but to have the fellow put into military detention.* His tone suggests that he himself had almost gotten into a fistfight with his man.

This aggravation distracted him only briefly from grave political concerns. What Goethe feared had now come to pass. Since Austria and Russia remained passive for the time being, Prussia abandoned its neutrality and declared war on France on its own. Goethe thought it too risky a step. The duke, appalled by Prussia's rash act, would have preferred to forge an anti-Napoleonic alliance. Family loyalty requiring him to remain on Prussia's side, he took leave on September 17, 1806, to fight with the Prussian army against France. Goethe's colleague Voigt ran the administration of the duchy and was best informed about developments. Goethe turned to him with the words *I am most obliged to you for being willing to give me a hint of external conditions, since in the midst of such volatile tempers it is very difficult to keep one's balance.* He would later write about the levelheaded Voigt, who bore the primary political responsibility during those weeks, *It would be difficult to describe what anxious conferences I had at the time with my loyal and unforgettable colleague, State Minister von Voigt.* Voigt's political ideas were similar to Goethe's: to maintain neutrality as long as possible and at all costs avoid making enemies of France and Napoleon. But now it had happened. It was war.

As often when in the midst of external tension and extreme danger, Goethe immersed himself in the study of nature. He worked on the *Theory of Color,* and in the evenings there were concerts at the residence of the duchess's mother in Tiefurt. *Kapellmeister Hummel was present and people made music with heavy hearts.* From the middle of September, Prussian soldiers were billeted in Jena, and Goethe vacated his room in the Old Palace for Prince Hohenlohe-Ingelfingen, commander of a Prussian infantry corps. Undeterred, Goethe cataloged the collection of granite he had brought from Carlsbad and sent selected stones to Professor Johann Friedrich Blumenbach in Göttingen, who was surprised that Goethe apparently had nothing better to do in the situation.

Goethe met with Hegel, who was working on the final chapter of *Phenomenology of Spirit*, for a philosophical discussion *despite the gloomy outlook*. A Prussian colonel named Christian von Massenbach had had a patriotic pamphlet printed whose first words were "Napoleon, I loved you!" and whose last words were "I hate you!" The pamphleteer confided in Goethe, who was horrified. He believed that such a provocation would *necessarily bring down ruin on the city when the French army entered it.* They must prevent publication at all costs. Goethe discovered he was dealing with a *tenacious author. But I remained just as tenacious a citizen, . . . so that he finally gave in.* Some professors and students departed Jena as a precaution. People hid their money and other valuables. Courage was ginned up at patriotic events. At one such gathering, Goethe recited the completely inappropriate poem "Vanitas! Vanitatum Vanitas!" whose first line is *I put my trust in nothing!* Even Wieland was outraged at such a lack of patriotism. The Austrian writer and statesman Friedrich Gentz, in Weimar on a visit, was also irked by Goethe's attitude. "He is shamefully egotistical and indifferent," Gentz wrote later. "I will never forget the moral situation I found him in 2 days before the Battle of Jena in the year 1806." Even on the eve of the battle, Goethe had his theater perform. *Fanchon the Hurdy-Gurdy Girl* was on the playbill, and in her fury at Goethe the female lead—the singer Marianne Ambrosch—is supposed to have said, "It's really horrible how much we're tortured by this man Göthe. We should be holding prayer vigils and we have to play comedy."

The battle on October 14 ended with the devastating defeat of the Prussian army, its final skirmishes reaching the eastern edge of Weimar. People heard the thunder of cannon all day long. In the house on the Frauenplan, they nevertheless sat down to the midday meal as usual, but were frightened by louder cannon fire and cries of "The French are coming!" Friedrich Wilhelm Riemer, Goethe's secretary and his son's tutor, wrote down the following events in great detail. Goethe himself merely noted in his diary, *At five o'clock in the evening, cannonballs fell through the roofs and at five-thirty, arrival of the chasseurs. At seven o'clock fire, plundering, terrible night. Our house preserved by steadfastness and luck.*

These few words conceal perhaps the worst ordeal Goethe had ever gone through. For the first time, the foundations of his existence had been shaken. Aside from his taste of war in the campaign of 1792–93, he had always managed to create a homogeneous space around himself, a world that was his or soon would be, thanks to his personal charisma. He was able to keep foreign or disturbing influences at bay or to somehow incorporate them into his world. But the Battle of Jena, the plundering, the catastrophe for the duchy—these were disruptions against which it was impossible to defend himself.

Goethe had also been lucky. For one thing, it was fortunate that one of the French hussar officers he encountered on the market square—a Baron von Türckheim—was the son of his former beloved Lili Schönemann. The man made sure that the best possible soldiers were billeted in Goethe's house: Marshal Ney and his entourage. But the marshal kept them waiting, and in the evening the "spoon guards," as the simple foot soldiers were called, forced their way in, demanded wine and food, ran riot, made a racket, and insisted on seeing the head of the household. Riemer records the following scene: "Although already undressed and wearing only his voluminous nightshirt—which he used to call in jest his prophet's mantle—he descended the stairs, approached them, and asked what they wanted from him. . . . His dignified appearance commanded respect and his spirited countenance also seemed to infuse them with respect." But it didn't last long. Late at night—the marshal had still not arrived—they burst into Goethe's bedroom with drawn bayonets. Riemer learned only the following morning that Goethe had been in mortal danger. Goethe himself said nothing about it, as if ashamed. Even later, he would only allude to the incident, as in a letter of mid-December to the duke: *But I suffered something . . . also something physical, that still touches me too closely to be able to express it.*

In this situation, with marauding soldiers threatening Goethe's life, Christiane proved especially brave and quick-witted. She began to scream, and that persuaded several stalwart citizens who had taken refuge in Goethe's house to push the armed and drunken fellows out of Goethe's bedroom. As long as the threat lasted, Christiane possessed the oversight necessary to maintain at least some order in the house. The man of the house, however, was for the time being a nervous wreck. As Heinrich Voss reported, "In those sad days, Göthe was the object of my heartfelt pity; I saw him shed tears and exclaim, 'Who will take my house and home so that I can go far away?'" His entire way of life was indeed at risk, and the fate of the duchy also hung by a thread as Napoleon considered destroying the town entirely. Goethe had already been preparing himself to be dependent in the future on author's fees and advances. At the *worst moments*, he wrote to Cotta, he had been hoping for the publisher's *willingness* to help.

How lucky Goethe was in the end became apparent the next day, when they learned how others had fared. Some houses had been burned to the ground, and their inhabitants had fled into the woods. A wagon full of gunpowder was parked in front of the painter Meyer's house, and the sensitive fellow was atremble all night long for fear it would explode. Because the soldiers had found nothing worth stealing in the house of Herder's widow, they had rampaged through his manuscripts. All the Ridels' furnishings had been destroyed except for one dresser and a silver tea urn. The aged municipal treasurer had been watching over the cash box. Johanna Schopenhauer, the mother of the philosopher, had recently moved to Weimar, and Goethe told her that he had *never seen a greater image of misery than this man in an empty room, all around him torn and scattered papers. He sat on the ground, cold and as if petrified . . . he looked like King Lear except that Lear was mad, and here it was the world that had gone mad.* The painter Georg Melchior Kraus, a friend from Goethe's youth, had his entire house burned down with all the precious paintings it contained. The old man died in despair soon afterward as a result of the roughing up he had suffered at the hands of the soldiers.

What a turning point in Goethe's life these events represented can also be gathered from the fact that, following the catastrophe of autumn 1806, he implemented the "legal and social modernization of his personal life" in three respects, as Gustav Seibt has shown.* First, the status of his property: although the duke had given him the house

---

* Gustav Seibt, *Goethe und Napoleon: Eine historische Begegnung* (Munich: C. H. Beck, 2008), 36 ff.

on the Frauenplan, the property was not entirely his. Remnants of feudal dependency remained: the duke paid the property taxes and, in exchange, claimed the building rights associated with the property. Now Goethe wrote a letter to the absent duke asking that those old obligations be dissolved so that he might own the house free and clear. *It will be cause for celebration by me and my family when this particular property becomes, in its foundation, firm beneath our feet after many a day when it has trembled above our heads and threatened to collapse.*

Not until his next letter did Goethe reveal the other piece of news, which also pertained to the bourgeois normalization of his circumstances: he had married Christiane Vulpius. He actually ought to have included the duke in this decision, not only because it would affect Christiane's status at court and in the upper echelon of society but also because the duke was his friend. He was very well aware of this, as one can see in the clever way he informs the duke of the marriage in a letter of December 25, 1806. He congratulates the duke on the recent birth of a son to his mistress, the actress Karoline Jagemann. Then he turns to the subject of August, his own illegitimate son, thereby allowing the transition to the real news: *He is still making good progress and I could promise myself Your Highness's consent from afar as, at these most insecure moments, I gave him father and mother by means of a legal bond that he has long deserved. When old bonds are dissolved, one is thrown back on domestic ones, and in general, one now feels only too well the need to look inward.*

The marriage was decided upon and performed fairly precipitately. Three days after the battle, on October 17, Goethe wrote to the court chaplain Günther, *In the last few days and nights, an old intention of mine has matured; I want to fully and officially acknowledge my little friend—who has done so much for me and also lived through these hours of trial with me—as my wife.* He wanted the wedding to take place as quickly and quietly as possible and, with his faithful colleague Voigt speeding up the bureaucratic formalities, it happened two days later, with their son and Riemer as witnesses, and no wedding feast. Later the same day, Goethe went to court—without Christiane, it goes without saying—and spent his time there largely with French officers, Weimar being now officially under French military administration. He took Christiane into polite society only once, to tea at the house of the newly arrived Johanna Schopenhauer. She wrote her son Arthur that he "introduced his wife to me. I received her as if I didn't know who she had previously been. If Göthe gives her his name, I think we ought to be able to give her a cup of tea." Such liberality would benefit the salon she had just founded: if Goethe was pleased to be seen there, others would be as well. As a rule, his behavior was especially free and easy in her house. He sat in a corner, sketching, reading from his works, declaiming, and sometimes inducing the ladies to sing together. Johanna proudly reported all this to her son, Arthur, whom it made very envious—probably less of the choral singing than of Goethe's conversation, which he would have liked to hear.

Goethe was now a married man. In the letters he wrote to friends and acquaintances summing up the dark days he had lived through, he says not a word about his marriage. The newspapers, however, were quick to pick up the story, sometimes in a quite suggestive and malicious way. One could read in the widely circulated *Allgemeine Zeitung* (*General Newspaper*) on November 24, 1806, "Amid the thunder of cannon from the battle, Göthe got married to his longtime housekeeper Demoiselle Vulpius, and so she alone drew a winner, while many thousand others drew a blank." Goethe was furious. He wrote Cotta, who published the paper, a long, sharply worded letter that he ended up not sending—sending instead only a note that he had felt *treated very inappropriately and indecently*. Not looking to break with Cotta, with whom he had agreed to a new and very well-remunerated edition of his works, he ends the note very engagingly: *If you feel the beauty of our relationship in its entire extent, then put an end to this unworthy gossip that must very soon destroy our mutual trust.*

In addition to clearing up the ownership of his house and domestic arrangement, the collapse of the old order—the *about-face of things*—also engendered a new conception of his role as an author. Even more strongly than before, Goethe now began to act with determined professionalism. *In the worst hours, when we were worried about everything, the fear of losing my papers was the most painful, and from then on, I have been sending everything I can to the printer.* Indeed, from then on he was less hesitant to turn his manuscripts over to publishers. He first sent the *Theory of Color* to the printer, though it was still unfinished. Later he would separate the text of *Elective Affinities* from the manuscript of *Wilhelm Meister's Journeyman Years*, where it had first been conceived as a novella, and have it rather speedily published as a novel, something he would hardly have considered before.

Contemporaries were quite surprised at how quickly Goethe made his peace with the new political situation. For German patriots and opponents of Napoleon, it was altogether too quick. Goethe vexed them by remarking in conversation that the Germans had simply succumbed to a greater power and that only a *childishly egotistical spirit of contradiction* would deny it. *In most people, the spirit of freedom and love for the fatherland that are thought to derive from the ancients becomes a caricature,* he told Riemer, who wrote it neatly down, as he did an offhand remark about the *pride of the professors,* which was utterly laughable because they had it all out of books. Instead of using up one's energy in a pointless spirit of opposition, it would be better *to most jealously preserve the still untouched palladium of our literature.* There one could accomplish something and prevent *the person in whose hand Germany's fate now lies from losing the esteem we command from him by our intellectual preponderance.*

They were indeed dependent on Napoleon's esteem, for Weimar's fate hung in the balance. Napoleon had taken angry note of the duke's having fought on the Prussian side, and intended to punish him for it. In the end, however, he decided not to divide the territory and terminate the duchy, perhaps primarily because of the ducal family's connection to the tsar. His sister was now Karl August's daughter-in-law. Napoleon wanted no trouble as yet with Russia.

Thus the duke was able to return to Weimar in February 1807 and take up the reins of a Weimar that was now one of the states in the Confederation of the Rhine and subject to French oversight. France demanded contributions that totaled more than two million francs. Voigt filed an appeal, pointing to the duchy's meager annual income of 150,000 francs. At first, there was almost no cooperation from the French. Nor did it help when Weimar's ambassador (and later chancellor) Johannes Müller adduced the scientific and literary accomplishments of the duchy as reasons to treat it less harshly. Goethe had hoped that Weimar's culture and *intellectual preponderance* would command the victor's *esteem.* But while Wieland and Goethe enjoyed renown among French officers, and even with Napoleon himself, it didn't lessen Weimar's required contributions and obligations.

The duke accepted the situation with inner reservations and regularly alarmed his privy councilors by telling dirty jokes about Napoleon in the relaxed atmosphere of Carlsbad or Marienbad. Goethe, however, was thoroughly satisfied with the new situation. He was ready to acknowledge Napoleonic hegemony for the sake of peace. In a conversation with Riemer, he declared, *When Paul says to obey the authorities because they are God's order, it's an expression of enormous culture . . . a rule which, if all the conquered would obey it, would deter them from all arbitrary and unreasonable actions that only result in their own undoing.*

One should accept the given and not waste time in futile opposition. This was especially important for the development of culture. In a letter to Zelter of July 27, 1807, he directed harsh sentences against the patriots whose numbers were on the rise among educated Germans during the Napoleonic hegemony: *When someone complains about what he and his surroundings have suffered, what he has lost or fears to lose, I listen in sympathy. . . . But when people bewail an entity that has supposedly been lost, an entity that not a soul in Germany has ever seen in his life, much less bothered about, then I have to conceal my impatience so as not . . . to be thought an egotist.* A few sentences later, he explains his understanding of the individual's relationship to the whole. For him, what is important is one's ability to develop in a unique way. To identify too much with a political entity is to run the risk of collectivism. In his view, that applied to the newly awakened nationalistic movement, as he considered Germany's traditional lack of political unity a strength. It had been an advantage *that Germany . . . in its old form allowed the individual to develop as far as possible and left everyone to do whatever they considered right, but without society as a whole ever evincing any particular sympathy for it.*

This lofty indifference of the whole toward the individual can thus be understood as an opportunity. As long as people exist in the shadow of this indifference, everything depends on what they make of themselves for their own sake. That was Goethe's conservative liberality. As a cultured citizen, he wants to be left in peace by that dubious entity the patriots were so enthusiastic about. He kept his distance from it, for art and science constitute an entity separate from politics. As the citizen of a state and even a servant of that state, he was of course willing to render unto the state what was the state's. But no more than that.

The new entity Goethe now had to deal with in the overpowering person of Napoleon was, however, something that began to fascinate him beyond purely political considerations. In a letter to Knebel in early 1807, he calls Napoleon *the highest phenomenon possible in history, at the summit of this so highly—even too highly—cultivated nation.*

Europe had breathlessly watched Napoleon's meteoric rise. It was almost incredible how this powerful ego had come to dominate world history. That the philosophy of German idealism, especially in Fichte's work, was capable of assigning such a key role to the ego is unthinkable without this monumental Napoleonic ego, now both so far away and so near. For Napoleon's European campaigns of conquest and plunder invaded the everyday life of many Germans. Napoleon was more than a political reality; already in his lifetime he was a mythic figure, for both those who adulated and those who loathed him. Some saw him as the embodiment of the world spirit, others as an anti-spirit, a monster from hell. Everyone, however, had the lively perception of a power not sanctified by tradition or convention but rather created by a charismatic personality. Napoleon's career was the exemplar of a political rise from nothing. The representatives of the old powers regarded him as a swindler even as he defeated them. It was no accident that parallel to Napoleon's rise, intellectual Europe was bewitched by fads of animal magnetism, somnambulism, and hypnosis. Napoleon seemed a great mesmerizer who, holding sway over the unconscious, turned things upside down and inside out. In that sense Goethe called him a *Prometheus* who had ignited a *light* for mankind, a light that made things visible that otherwise would have remained hidden. He had *drawn everyone's attention to himself.*

Then came the moment when Napoleon's own attention turned to Goethe. On October 16, 1806, the Weimar privy councilors were required to appear before Napoleon, but Goethe had excused himself on account of illness. However, when Napoleon convened a congress of European princes in Erfurt two years later—from September 27 to October 14, 1808—the duke brought Goethe along in order to impress the assembly. Napoleon then summoned Goethe to a private audience. Goethe probably saw Napoleon for the first time on September 30 during a gala performance of Racine's tragedy *Britannicus* by the Comédie française, performed before the crowned heads of Europe at Napoleon's command. The famous actor François-Joseph Talma played Nero. Was this play about usurpation of power supposed to be suggestive? At any rate, Napoleon himself had chosen the plays to be performed. The entire congress was calculated to make an impressive show of his power—then at its height—especially for Tsar Alexander, who was meant to be courted or intimidated. Two days after the performance of *Britannicus*, on Sunday, October 2, Goethe was summoned to an audience.

Goethe himself never published a report of the meeting. In the *Annals* he notes only that the *congress in Erfurt is of such enormous significance, and also the influence of this epoch on my situation so important, that a separate depiction of these few days should probably be undertaken.* Such a depiction never came to pass, and only two drafts survived, later cobbled together by Eckermann. Even in conversation, Goethe revealed little about it, although some pointed hints of his were immediately circulated. They also reached Karl Friedrich von Reinhard, a French diplomat of Swabian extraction who had made Goethe's acquaintance a year earlier. He wrote Goethe on November 24, "The emperor is supposed to have said about you: Voilà un homme! I believe it, for he is capable of feeling it and saying it." Whereupon Goethe replied, *Well, so the wonderful words with which the emperor greeted me have also reached your ears! You can see from that what a real, outright heathen I am, since the Ecce homo was applied to me in the opposite sense.*

It's not clear whether this remark of Napoleon's was intended to be emphatic or was merely offhanded. The version that Goethe recounted in an unpublished note speaks for the latter. There, as the emperor gestures for Goethe to approach, he says *"vous êtes un homme,"* which could be understood as much less emphatic. In fact, several people had been summoned to an audience at the same time, and there was a lot of coming and going. Napoleon was eating breakfast and very busy, but also probably making a show of governing. Daru and Talleyrand were present as well. According to Goethe's notes, the conversation began with Voltaire's play *Mahomet*, which Goethe had translated. The emperor said it wasn't a good play because Voltaire had put a *world conqueror* on the stage who *gave such an unfavorable depiction of himself.* Then Napoleon brought the talk around to *Werther*, which Goethe describes Napoleon as *having studied very thoroughly.* He immediately gave proof by referring in detail to a passage he thought worthy of criticism, then asked, *Why did you do that? It's not natural.* Goethe, quite at ease, gave a *cheerful smile* and replied that the emperor was right, but that a poet should of course be forgiven for *making use of a device that was difficult to detect*.

When Goethe later revealed a bit about this part of their conversation, people wanted to know exactly what Napoleon had criticized. Goethe never said. He let Eckermann try to guess, but his efforts were in vain. Wilhelm von Humboldt, to whom Goethe presumably gave a hint, wrote to his wife that it must have been that the true story and the fiction had been sewn together in an inconsistent way. That fits Goethe's word *device* better than Chancellor Müller's conjecture that Napoleon had criticized the combination of erotic passion and frustrated professional ambition. *Device* refers to something technical, a narrator or editor revealing something about his protagonist he could not possibly know, for example, and such passages are in fact present in *Werther*.

After *Werther*, the conversation returned to the theater. Napoleon objected to the popularity of *dramas of fate*. It must have been in this context that Napoleon made the famous remark *What . . . has fate got to do with it? Politics is fate*. Then Napoleon began talking to other people for a while, giving Goethe an opportunity, here in the center of power, to gather his thoughts and *recall the past*. The audience was being held in the Erfurt governor's office, where he had passed happy hours with Schiller and Bishop Dalberg. Then Napoleon returned to Goethe and inquired about his personal circumstances. He also wanted to hear something of the duke and his family, which may well have been what Napoleon really hoped to get out of the encounter. Goethe's notes, however, deal with this point very briefly. He summarizes by saying that Napoleon's *manifold expressions of approbation* were *admirable*.

Goethe could thus return to Weimar confident he had received the highest possible recognition from Napoleon. He had two more opportunities to speak there to Napoleon, who visited the duchy after the close of the congress of princes, though it was noted that Napoleon spoke to Wieland longer than to Goethe this time. On October 14, 1808, both were awarded the order of the Légion d'honneur.

At the beginning of December, Goethe wrote to Cotta, *I'm happy to admit that nothing higher and more gratifying could happen to me in my whole life than to stand before the French emperor in such a way. Without going into detail about our conversation, I can say that no superior has ever received me in that way, by allowing me with special confidence to be—if I may use the expression—myself, and clearly stating that my character was in accord with his . . . so that in these strange times, I at least have the personal assurance that wherever I may encounter him again, I will find him to be my friendly and gracious lord.*

Cotta had hoped to hear about the progress of Goethe's literary work. Instead he was informed, *it is unfortunately probable that all my literary work as well as all other business has been disrupted by these events. I'm attempting to get back to work on this and that, but as yet, nothing seems to be flowing.*

CHAPTER 27

Pandora or Goethe's Double Mask: Diligent Prometheus
and Dreaming Epimetheus. *Theory of Color* Completed.
On the Deeds and Sufferings of Light. Contra Newton.
In Praise of the Observable. Nature as a Sense
of Life and Object of Research. Encounter with
Schopenhauer: The Pupil Who Would Be Master.

. . . .

ONE WORK THAT DID NOT CONTINUE TO FLOW AFTER THE
encounter with Napoleon was the drama *Pandora*. Goethe had begun
drafting it in November and December 1807, continued until June 1808
in Carlsbad, and then abandoned it. Calling it a *somewhat abstruse little
work*, he nevertheless had it printed in its unfinished state, saying that
he believed it would only be effective if read out loud. The Viennese
periodical *Prometheus* had persuaded him to write a play in which the
Prometheus motif would play a role, a motif that had already attracted
him on two previous occasions. This time, however, Prometheus is not
the daring, defiant creator of men who tangles with Zeus, but a paragon of solid industriousness, a spur for the *plucky, loyal, hardworking people*. This Prometheus requires *commitment* to useful enterprises, unlike
his brother Epimetheus, a dreamy, meditative soul who dwells on
melancholy memories of his vanished lover Pandora and hopes for her
return. Goethe departs from the Pandora of myth and makes her something of his own invention. The box his Pandora opens contains not
calamity but mirages of beguiling beauty, and it is Epimetheus who
allows himself to be enchanted by them. He becomes an otherworldly
figure, pining away over ecstatic memories, becoming thereby the
patron saint of poets. By contrast, Prometheus appears as the tough-
as-nails representative of reality, under whose aegis tools are produced

for peasants and shepherds, as are weapons of war. His followers sing a song into which Goethe wove his recent impressions during the plundering of Weimar:

We set off boldly
On a march,
And what we find
Belongs to us,
And you won't get
It back again.
But what is yours
We'll gobble up.
If someone's rich
And still wants more,
Our rowdy troop
Will rob the store.
We fill our sacks
And torch the house
And grab the spoils
And get out fast.

Prometheus and Epimetheus remain lofty background presences; the foreground is occupied by a complicated plot. Epimeleia, a daughter of Epimetheus, is in love with Phileros, Prometheus's son, who has inherited his father's love of action but not his levelheadedness. He thinks he has grounds for jealousy and almost kills his presumed rival and with him his beloved. His father, Prometheus, angrily commands his son to throw himself off a cliff into the sea. The goddess Eos, however, rises from the sea and saves Phileros and his lover.

This final reconciliation comes quickly and unexpectedly, before the play has had any real development. Goethe had obviously lost patience with it and wanted to get the project off his desk. A few notes for a sequel, *Pandora's Return*, have survived. Apparently the contrast between the spirit of poetry—the gift of transforming the past into an image—and the ethos of useful work was to be made even more drastic.

In this mythical setting, one senses the image of Napoleon behind the ominous and yet fascinating Promethean age that is beginning. The dominant spirit of the present is political, practical, and useful; poetry is suspect: endearing to be sure, but also likely to have a weakening effect and perhaps even superfluous. For the time being, Pandora and her blithe phantasmagoria will not return. Goethe broke off work on the play. In June 1811 he wrote to Zelter, *Alas, I seem to myself a double herm, one of whose masks resembles Prometheus, the other Epimetheus, and neither of them . . . able to smile.* The struggle between Prometheus and Epimetheus remained unresolved. Another work, the *Theory of Color,* overshadowed them and demanded completion.

Goethe had begun to note down observations and conduct modest experiments with color almost twenty years earlier. Though his notebooks bulged with manuscripts, color charts, and sketches related to the topic, and he'd had a large paper sack made in which to store everything, he'd published only two small essays in the early 1790s. He had discussed some of it with Schiller, who helped him sort through all the material and put it in order and in early 1798 had written Goethe that it was still not clear whether he was talking about light and its effects or about the operation of the eye. He prompted Goethe to make a distinction between subjective and objective color, between the independent, physiological operations of the eye and the physical and chemical properties of colors themselves.

Goethe often took refuge in his studies of color at moments of external turbulence or inner turmoil. On the battlefields of France and during the siege of Mainz in 1793, he recorded his observations of color phenomena. He often said that there was something calming about nature's wonderful consistency. Over the years, so much material had accumulated that he finally began a general revision in 1803, destroying things that were outdated or otherwise of no use. *You must have no mercy with the dross if you want to finally extract the metal,* he wrote to Schiller, who had encouraged him to at last subject his *Theory of Color* to the light of public opinion. After Schiller's death, Goethe began to publish sections even though he had not yet completed the entire work. He wanted to force himself to finish. Now it was the thankless duty of the Jena publisher Frommann to put pressure on the tardy author. Goethe had written Schiller that he *had no other wish than to be delivered from chromaticism.* When the work finally appeared in two octavo volumes of text and a quarto volume of illustrations on May 16, 1810, it was a *day of liberation*, as he would later write in the *Annals*—with an ironic undertone, since the subsequent victory over Napoleon, officially described as a "liberation," was no such thing for him. While all around him patriotic fervor reached fever pitch, Goethe devoted himself to his peaceful reflections on the ur-phenomena of light, darkness, and the mixture of the two: the opacity that appears to our eyes as color.

In sharp contradiction to Newton's color theory, the central idea of the *Theory of Color* is that colors are not—as Newton maintained—contained within light and capable of being made visible as spectral colors through refraction. Light, Goethe says, cannot contain something darker than itself. Instead, color arises when light collides and mixes with darkness, or when light penetrates a darker medium. Closest to light, the color yellow is created; it is shadowed light. Closest to darkness, the color blue is created; it is illuminated darkness. The combination of the two primary colors blue and yellow produces green. And so one begins with an inverted color triangle, with blue and yellow at the top and green at the bottom point. The array is rounded out to a color wheel only when the two primary colors blue and yellow are transformed—*enhanced*, Goethe calls it—by further admixtures of darkness. Blue thus becomes purple and yellow becomes orange. Enhancements of purple and orange yield red. Thus one has the *polarity* of the primary colors yellow and blue, then their *enhancement* leading to red and their *mixture* leading to green. The circle of colors is closed via polarity and enhancement—blue on the left, yellow on the right, red on top, green on the bottom—and the transitions in between: greenish yellow, brown, bright red, etc. Always at play are shadings or brightenings, superimpositions and admixtures of the primary colors. In all cases, the basic principle is unchanged: light is an *ur-phenomenon* that cannot be dissected or traced back to something else.

But what is light itself? The question of its essence, its substance, doesn't really concern Goethe, who, in an almost scientific sense, isn't exploring the essence of a thing but its effects. And why is that? Because in principle, we cannot know anything about a thing's essence, but only its effect, which in the final analysis means its effect on us. The location of these effects is the totality of our sensory and intellectual impressions, and not merely in isolated individuals, but in the exchange and correlation of multiple perspectives and experiences. If the individual is an organism apprehending the nature he encounters, mankind at large is also—at least potentially—a superorganism for the comprehension of both human and nonhuman nature. Goethe once wrote in a letter to Schiller that nature cleverly conceals itself by not allowing men to work together at perception. If it were possible, humanity would really unite as a perceiving subject. Then all veils would fall, and nature would be for us the open book it is not at present.

Even if we cannot survey and understand the entire text, perhaps we can at least read from it. To read from the book of nature, however, means registering its effects on us, refining our appreciation, sharpening our judgments, relating effects to one another, and so on. These effects on us constitute our reality as a whole. One cannot transcend their perimeter. In the foreword to the *Theory of Color*, Goethe emphasizes this: *For in truth, it is a vain undertaking to express the essence of a thing. We are aware of effects, and a complete account of those effects would in any case encompass the essence of that thing.*

That is why Goethe's *Theory of Color* does not address the so-called essence of light, but rather its effects when it interacts with impeding, refracting, and darkening elements. Colors arise from these interactions. The subject of Goethe's work is not the essence of light but its effects, or as he puts it pointedly in his foreword, *the deeds of light, its deeds and its sufferings.* Rejecting the question of essence and restricting himself to effects, he forgoes metaphysical speculation. *What spectacle! but alas! the merest show! . . . Thou, spirit of the earth, art closer to me,* Faust declares when taking leave of the realm of Neoplatonic ideas in his great opening monologue. The *spirit of the earth* to whom he then turns, however, is too all-powerful, although Faust is on the right track—the track of earthbound effects—and is also liberated to new effectiveness. The question of why he needs Mephisto's help will concern us later.

While restricting himself to the world of effects, and rejecting metaphysical speculation, Goethe also rejects the temptation to step outside the circle of the directly observable. Objecting to the mathematical attenuation of reality as well as to the metaphysical, he thus contradicts both venerable Platonic tradition and the spirit of modern science to which Newton gave impetus, a spirit that strays into realms not accessible to direct observation. Goethe could have had no idea of the enormous consequences of modern science making its way into phenomena that are not directly observable. He was, however, well aware that operating in the realm of the unobservable and acting on the basis of what one discovers there can become untenable, incalculable, and ruthless and can lead to demoralization and a loss of orientation. He sensed the Promethean shame at one's own fabrications and machinations, the shame that one is no longer able to imagine all the things one is capable of.

At first, Goethe had no intention of picking a quarrel with Newton. The turning point came in a sort of primal scene that he describes in the "Historical Section" of the *Theory of Color*. The year was 1790. The scientist and privy councilor Christian Wilhelm Büttner had lent him some prisms. Goethe had not made use of them, and the time came to return them. At the last moment, he finally unpacked one and peered through the glass onto a whitewashed wall. It was a revelation, like Saint Augustine's depiction of his conversion when he follows the commandment "Take up and read!" [*A*]*s I placed the prism in front of my eyes, with Newton's theory in mind, I expected the entire white wall to be colored in various stages and the light returning from there to my eyes to be split into as many colored lights. But how amazed I was that the white wall, seen through the prism, remained white as before, and that only where a darker area touched it did a more or less definite color appear. . . . It required no long consideration to realize that a boundary was necessary to produce colors, and as if instinctively I told myself out loud that Newton's theory was false.*

Goethe never allowed himself to be persuaded otherwise about what his eyes had seen. He remarks derisively in the "Polemical Section" of the *Theory of Color* that no one had succeeded either in reuniting colored rays into white or in mixing something white out of colored particles. When Newton tried it, the result was something *that looked mouse-colored, ashy, stone-colored perhaps, or like mortar, dust, or horse droppings and such.* One wishes, he continues, *that all Newtonians had to wear similar undergarments so that one could thereby tell them apart from other, sensible people.*

So white is not a synthesis, but the beginning of all syntheses. White is the fountainhead along with darkness, the other original power.

From their polarity derive the blurrings, mixtures, enhancements—the whole world of color. And that's why our lives are so colorful.

Colors open a way for Goethe to understand basic human states. In the text of the *Theory of Color* itself, he is reticent about this; in paragraph 920, for example, he writes, *But it is better here at the end not to allow ourselves to be accused of rhapsodizing.* In the reflections that followed the *Theory of Color*, Goethe expressed this idea more directly, as in a diary entry of May 26, 1807: *Love and hate, hope and fear are also only different conditions of our murky inner life through which our spirit looks either toward the light or toward the shadows. If we look through these murky organic surroundings toward the light, then we love and hope; if we look toward the darkness, then we hate and fear.*

Since the *Theory of Color* aspires to be an important, fundamental work, its author, who had just had his encounter with Napoleon, liked to compare himself to the great emperor. Just as Napoleon had to accept and clarify the dark inheritance of the French Revolution, Goethe had inherited an equally dark legacy, namely, the *error of the Newtonian theory*, which he had to clarify—as he expressed it to Eckermann. And, like Napoleon, he had had to knock some heads together, as he later said, apologizing for the combative attitude with which he had set to work. This bellicose tone is audible in the foreword to the *Theory of Color*: *Thus we are not talking about a wearisome siege or a questionable feud. Instead, we find that eighth wonder of the world* [i.e., Newton's *Opticks*] *already an abandoned antiquity threatening to collapse, and without further ado, we immediately begin to dismantle it from the roof and gables down, so that the sun can shine into the old rats' and owls' nest at last.*

Goethe sees and dramatizes himself as the defender of light against the obscurantists of modern science. *I perceived light in its purity and truth,* he told Eckermann, *and I considered it my duty to fight for it. That party sought in earnest to obfuscate light, for they claimed that shadows were a part of light.*

Modern science recognizes the legitimacy of most of Goethe's observations of physiological colors, particularly the discovery of so-called afterimages. When presented with a certain color, the eye's own physiology elicits its complementary color according to the color wheel: yellow elicits purple, orange elicits blue, and crimson elicits green. This can be proved with a simple experiment. If one looks for a long time at some color and then turns one's gaze onto a white surface, the complementary color appears for a moment. *These phenomena are of supreme importance because they point us to the laws of seeing. . . . The eye actually demands totality and completes within itself the circle of colors.*

From the subjective aspect of seeing color to the description of the emotional effect of the colors, all this is explained with a wealth of subtle observations that refer to the phenomenon in the literal sense—the "thing appearing to view," the apparent reality of the colors. Goethe wanted the science of nature in general understood as phenomenology—how he practiced it himself. *Let no one search behind the phenomena; they are themselves the science,* as one of his maxims declares. Theoretical constructs that distort observation were to be avoided. One should open one's senses to the phenomena and let them have their effect. *Theories are mostly the hasty result of an impatient intellect that wants to be done with the phenomena.* To be sure, man—himself a natural creature—must be in top form to function as an organ for the perception of nature. Thus the perception of nature is nature's perception of itself. It opens its eyes within the human being and perceives what it is. For Goethe, the requisite top condition that man has to achieve does not mean the assistance of artificial apparatus (although he also enjoyed using prisms and telescopes), but rather careful observation, trained senses, precise memory (to enable comparisons), judgment, exchange of experiences, and, last but not least, reverence for the mysterious. Another maxim says, *The greatest happiness of the thinking man is to have explored the explorable and to calmly revere the unexplorable.*

Goethe's nature study restricted itself to what could be observed. He preferred to look at the morphology and typology of things. Morphology inquires into interconnections in a series of forms, their transitions and developmental stages; it asks how one thing develops from another. Typology inquires into the order and comparison of types, their similarities and differences, as well as the forms of their linking and blending.

With phenomenological apprehension and description, the work of perception is basically done as far as Goethe is concerned, if only provisionally: the circle that we pace out by living and perceiving remains forever limited and—measured against the whole of nature— provisional. Yet within that circle, what our senses have taken in can claim the value of truth. In other words, Goethe adheres to a science in which we *can* trust and believe our eyes and ears. His model is an individualized whole, a whole that is not understood as a theoretical construct behind natural phenomena, but within them. Just as each of us is a whole within ourselves—as, for example, the eye seeing colors and completing the totality of the entire color wheel on its own—everything strives toward and responds to such completeness. Each individual thus appears as something that is a whole within itself. At the sight of a rare sea creature on the beach of the Lido, Goethe exclaimed, *What a precious, marvelous thing is a living creature! How well fitted to its condition, how true, how alive!* The way Goethe devoted himself to nature and pursued his studies of it was central to his understanding of himself and the world.

Let us take a brief look back over his life. For the Goethe of Sturm und Drang, nature was the epitome of subjective, highly emotional, and self-granted authority—what was, in Rousseau's sense, alive in contrast to social conventions and rules. At stake was this subjective nature's unimpeded outpouring, which could engender conflict. The waves of natural spontaneity could break on social reality. Thus nature was primarily creative natural power in man himself, making free verse therefore pure nature and not mere clumsy workmanship. As for external nature, he regarded it much as he experienced his own nature: as creative, wild, rich.

As he grew into the duties of office in Weimar and took on social responsibilities, his life became more objectified and nature as an objective power came more clearly into view. The brilliant poet, so happy to follow his own nature, became schooled in reality and his interest in nature changed. Although Goethe's journey to the Harz in the winter of 1777 was a path to his inner self, he was also on an inspection tour of the mines. Both were now at stake: reencountering his own creative nature and useful work on external nature. It is striking that the mineral realm—petrified nature, if one will—attracted him more and more in the years just before he set off for Italy. This was a troubling symptom of his growing sense of paralysis and lifelessness in everything, from which he had to escape before the possible conflicts came to a head. Through the pleasures of Italian life and art, he recovered the balance between his sense of reality and his poetry, a balance in which his interior life did not damage his exterior life or vice versa.

This struggle for harmony can be read in *Torquato Tasso* as well. Goethe had conceived the drama at a time when he had not yet found the *middle voice* between the world and poetry; only after he returned from Italy was he able to finish the play. Although Tasso is still a poet who suffers in his surroundings, the real world in the person of Antonio is also given its due. Goethe the author thereby rose above his figures; on the one hand he is Tasso the poet, but he is also Antonio, the man of the world. He intended to embrace both the poetic and the realistic in his relationship to the world.

Goethe wanted to hold together what powerful tendencies of the age were tearing apart: analytical intelligence and creative imagination, abstract concepts and sensuous observation, artificial experiment and lived experience, mathematical calculation and intuition. In the tension between poetry and natural history, he wanted to preserve poetry's right to exist in the realm of truth. *Delicate empiricism* was not to be ousted by the robust, heartless, pragmatically successful methods of modern science. In that defensive war he felt obliged to wage, however, he did not want to become a Tasso, making what was bound to be a last stand against the men of the world. He had no wish to defend his borders against science but rather to transport the poetic spirit into science. He wanted to contest science's claims to dominance on its own terrain—claims made on the basis of its epoch-making modernization. He did not want to defend anything, but with his own phenomenology, to carry the fight into the heart of his opponent. He was guided by his own ideal of personality. Perception should be integrated into a unity of man's multifarious endeavors and abilities; sensuality and reason, imagination and intellect should work together. These abilities are originally in balance. Although discoveries can be made by the use of perceptual prostheses—a telescope or a microscope—the person who does so runs the risk that *in the process his outward sense is put out of balance with his inner judgment.*

Goethe here anticipates something that would fully emerge only in the age of modern media, namely, the disproportionate reactions when artificial means confuse what is near and far, for example, when a distant danger reported is experienced as an imminent threat. In order to ensure that distant events kept their distance, Goethe would leave newspapers lying around for a while before he read them. For him, it was still obvious that lives lived at a spatial distance from one another are simultaneous only in an abstract sense. People lived in different times when they lived in different places, and what one learned about distant places was always already past by the time one got news of it. Goethe was already warning of the dissolution of personal boundaries that we are experiencing today.

A physicist gave Goethe an expensive, modern polarimeter that was capable of confirming Newton's theory about the origin of colors, for it polarized light into the colors of the spectrum. Goethe stubbornly refused to use the apparatus, just as the Inquisition had spurned Galileo's telescope two hundred years earlier. As a rule, Goethe rejected information about nature that was arrived at by the use of perceptual aids rather than by the five senses we were born with. Equipped with his normal senses, he declared, man was *the greatest and most precise physical apparatus there can be.* As we have seen, however, when he felt like it he would not hesitate to use instruments in order to investigate micro- or macrocosmic relationships, and would surely have made wise use of modern means of communication in the service of life.

His great work on color appeared in May 1810. Weeks and months went by, and, aside from dutiful praise from friends and acquaintances, there was no reaction to speak of. Goethe looked on with growing ire. He had labored on the huge work for twenty years, and the public acted as if a mouse had been born. A few painters, especially Philipp Otto Runge, felt inspired by it, but the scientific world dismissed it. "Experts will find nothing new," wrote the *Gothaische Gelehrte Zeitung* (*Gotha Learned Journal*). The reading public regretted what were considered unnecessary digressions, and the political world had other things to worry about. People asked reproachfully why Goethe was not addressing the burning questions of the day. Goethe took it all as a conspiracy of silence.

In fact, his publisher had been extremely cooperative, although he had feared he would lose money on the opulently produced and expensive volumes. That didn't happen, however, since it was at least an elegant ornament to one's library. Success in the scientific world, however—Goethe's main ambition—eluded him. At best, as mentioned above, the chapters on the physiological colors received some recognition, but in a way that was bound to displease him. He had wanted to inject poetic spirit into natural science, but the *Theory of Color* was seen as a document of aesthetic, not scientific, experience. The book might be intellectually stimulating, well written, profound, and heartfelt, but unfortunately it disregarded reality—at least in a scientific sense. That was how it was judged. Contemporaries were not as harsh as was Professor Emil du Bois-Reymond a few decades later, when he called Goethe's *Theory of Color* the "stillborn bagatelle of a dilettantish autodidact," but that's how it was regarded in scientific circles. Goethe was so angry he defiantly downplayed his poetic accomplishments to extol his scientific ones: *I take no pride . . . in anything I have accomplished as a poet. Excellent poets have lived at the same time as I, even more excellent ones lived before me, and there will be more of them after me. However, I am very proud of the fact that in my century I am the only one to know the truth in the difficult science of color theory, and that is why I am conscious of my superiority over many others.*

Let us jump ahead a bit to the winter of 1813–14. Polite silence continued to surround Goethe's work on colors, and he had adopted the role of the keeper of an open secret. He once said that he had to *make proselytes.* And then just such a proselyte showed up on his doorstep: the young Arthur Schopenhauer.

Schopenhauer had just finished his dissertation *On the Fourfold Root of the Principle of Sufficient Reason* and was living for a while with his mother, whose Weimar salon was enjoying great success. They were at loggerheads because she would not allow him to play the ersatz paterfamilias since his father's death. Their power struggle ended with a falling-out; Arthur left her house in a fury in the spring of 1814, and, appropriately enough, Goethe wrote in Schopenhauer's album, *To rejoice in your own worth / You must grant worth to life on earth.*

Before that happened, while Arthur was still living with his mother, a lively discussion about the *Theory of Color* had sprung up between him and Goethe. Schopenhauer would later count these weeks among the most important of his life. They also thrashed out their differences, which had no negative effect on Schopenhauer's admiration for Goethe. The privy councilor had drawn the young philosopher into a discussion for the first time in Johanna Schopenhauer's salon in November 1813. *Young Schopenhauer presented himself to me as a remarkable and interesting young man,* was his low-key commentary to Knebel. Schopenhauer, on the other hand, could hardly contain his enthusiasm, "Praised be his name in all eternity!" he wrote in a letter after their first meeting.

Goethe had no interest in an easy, conventional relationship with Schopenhauer, which would hardly have been possible in any case. According to Schopenhauer, Goethe once told him that with others, he conversed; with him, the young Dr. Arthur, he philosophized. The philosophizing referred to the *Theory of Color.* Goethe went through some passages with the young man and elucidated a few things, Schopenhauer commenting and contributing epistemological insights. They organized some experiments, consulted plates from the *Theory of Color,* and got out a prism.

After a few weeks of working together, Goethe wrote down a couplet he later included in the *Tame Xenias: Teaching's a chore, but could be a downright boon / If pupils didn't turn teacher so soon.* But so it was: Schopenhauer didn't have a modest bone in his body, and soon set himself up as a know-it-all. Agreeing with Goethe's physiology of color, but not convinced that his illuminating observations were a comprehensive theory yet, he set out to develop a complete theory of the origin of color in the eye. A few weeks after leaving Weimar, he worked up his theory and considered it a success. While Goethe's work is about the *deeds and sufferings of light,* one could say that Schopenhauer's is about the deeds and sufferings of the eye. He concentrates completely on the subjective, physiological aspect, the question of how color originates in the eye, not what it is in and of itself. For Schopenhauer, the phenomena of light are the result of different activities of the retina occasioned by modifications of the incidence of the light. It is in this context that he adopts Goethe's notion of a complete whole. Since in each case the incident light only partially activates the potential of the retina, the retina strives to optimize its potential, engendering the seeing of complementary colors and the accompanying feeling of harmony. Here Schopenhauer followed Goethe closely, but he preferred not to treat other aspects, or left them to the physicists and chemists. And he got involved in color theory in the first place only in order to be close to his revered master. It is certain he was wooing Goethe, but he was unwilling to tell him merely what he wanted to hear. In fact, a covert struggle between them began.

The story of that struggle began when Schopenhauer, in Dresden in July 1815, sent Goethe the manuscript of his completed treatise "On Vision and Colors" and asked him to be its editor and make it available to the public. Goethe was traveling at the time and did not respond immediately. Schopenhauer became impatient and wrote him a reminder, saying that he realized that, for Goethe, literary business was of secondary importance compared with his other activities. In his case, however, the opposite was true. "What I think, what I write, is of value and importance to me; my personal experiences and what happens to me is of secondary importance." After a few weeks in which Schopenhauer almost lost hope, he received a cordial but brief reply that held out the prospect of a more complete letter that would address the manuscript. But another good month went by until Goethe wrote on October 23, 1815, that at the moment, he was too far removed from the *Theory of Color* to want to thrash out differences—which, after all, were what was at stake. In the meantime, he said, Schopenhauer should get in touch with Professor Seebeck, who was an ally in their investigation of colors and to whom he was turning over the manuscript.

Schopenhauer felt he was being pawned off on one of Goethe's domestics. His wounded pride set the tone of an enormous letter to Goethe on November 11, 1815. In terms of his image of himself, it is probably the most important letter Schopenhauer ever wrote. With a self-confidence bordering on brashness—and yet with great respect— he squares off against the man he had chosen as a substitute father. He pays Goethe obeisance but also openly and massively denigrates the *Theory of Color*. Goethe, who understood his work as a new type of theorizing, is given to understand by Schopenhauer that all he had done was collect excellent observations, but not develop a real theory. "If I compare your Theory of Color to a pyramid, my theory represents its peak, the indivisible mathematical point from which the entire great edifice extends, and which is so essential that without it, there is no more pyramid, while from below, one can always cut something off without its ceasing to be a pyramid." Schopenhauer could assume that Goethe knew his Aristotle and that the essence (idea) of a thing (material) lay in the entelechy of its form. The image of the pyramid was basically a suggestion that Goethe regard his work as material that gets brought to life only by Schopenhauer's theory. Schopenhauer's self-confidence was just getting warmed up, with sentences like the following flowing from the pen of the young philosopher: "I know with absolute certainty that I have provided the first true theory of color, the first in the entire history of science."

Recall that Goethe thought the *Theory of Color* was the work with which he had gained *superiority over many others*, that made him feel like a Napoleon of the intellectual empire. And now an unknown philosopher still in his twenties claims to be the one who first elevates this work to the level of a theory and also—the height of impertinence!—claims that to do so was a minor matter. Goethe had been working on the *Theory of Color* for half his life and this young philosopher had the gall to write, "Except for a few weeks, I too always treated it as a minor matter, and carry around in my head theories entirely different from that of color."

Goethe's reply is remarkable in its amiable equanimity and sovereign irony. Alluding to Schopenhauer's philosophical subjectivism, he writes, *Whoever is himself inclined to construct the world out of the subject will not dismiss the observation that the subject, in its appearance, is always only an individual, and therefore needs a certain amount of truth and error to maintain its singularity. There is nothing, however, that divides humans more than the fact that the portions of those two ingredients are mixed according to various proportions.*

Schopenhauer was unwilling to accept that, with this sentence, Goethe's judgment of the entire matter had been pronounced and nothing more was to be said. But what did Schopenhauer expect? Did he think Goethe would write him and say, Yes, you have elevated my scattered observations into a genuine theory. It is astonishing, young man, the way you've managed to crown my life's work in just a few weeks. I shall hasten to make your work—which for the first time allows the full sun to shine upon my work—available to the public?

Perhaps Schopenhauer really did hope for some such reply. At least, he hoped that his treatise on colors would receive the blessing of his ersatz father. Goethe did not accept the proffered role. But he respected this pupil even though he was too eager to appear as the teacher. And so he sent the manuscript back with a request that Schopenhauer summarize the views expressed there *briefly* so that Goethe could quote them when occasion arose. He had responded with benevolent nonchalance to this young man whose head was teeming with such enormous thoughts, and Schopenhauer's treatise on colors appeared without Goethe's blessing.

In the *Annals*, Goethe recalled that *Dr. Schopenhauer sided with me as a sympathetic friend. We debated and agreed about many things, but in the end, a certain parting could not be avoided, as when two friends who have been walking together shake hands: One intends to go north, the other south, and then they very quickly lose sight of each other.*

CHAPTER 28

Theater Squabble: A First Clash with Karoline Jagemann.
Work on *Elective Affinities*. The Novel as the *second part of
the Theory of Color*. The Chemistry of Human Relations.
How Free Is Love? *Consciousness is not
an adequate weapon*. Inner Nature as Fate. A Split with
the Romantics. The Physics and Metaphysics of Sexual Love.
Nature as an Abyss. Renunciation.

....

EVEN WHILE HE WAS STILL SENDING THE *THEORY OF COLOR*
chapter by chapter to the printer, Goethe allowed himself a small
digression that he once called the *second part of the Theory of Color*. On
April 11, 1808, he began to write what he planned as a relatively short
novella to be interpolated into *Wilhelm Meister's Journeyman Years*. It
would eventually grow into the novel *Elective Affinities*, which Goethe
sometimes described as the best thing he had ever written. His letters
tell how proud of it he was. He made a special point of telling Zelter
that this work was really only meant to allow him *to once again converse
at length with distant friends*. It was a novel for riddle solvers that needed
to be read at least three times to be properly understood. *I put a lot into
it*, he tells Zelter, *and hid some things. May this open secret give you joy*.

He dictated the first part of the novel and worked out its entire plot
at the spa in Carlsbad in the summer of 1808. The events surrounding
his meeting with Napoleon caused a first interruption, and, at the end
of 1808, a crisis at the Weimar theater led to a second. Both the *Theory
of Color* and *Elective Affinities* had to be laid aside, for something had
happened that demanded Goethe's full attention and entire energy.

The actress Karoline Jagemann, who had become the duke's mistress, ventured to start a power struggle in November 1808 with the director Goethe. An elaborate production of an opera by Ferdinando Paer was scheduled for a repeat performance on the Weimar stage. The tenor Otto Morhardt submitted a doctor's note certifying that he was suffering hoarseness that would prevent his appearing in the production. For Jagemann, a talented and thoroughly professional actress and singer, it was one more example of the sloppiness that had invaded the theater owing to what she considered the unfortunate directorship of Goethe, whom she considered a dilettante. Jagemann persuaded the duke to make an example of Morhardt. He punished the singer with house arrest and then required Goethe to fire him on the spot and expel him from the duchy without paying him the fee he was still owed. Goethe refused to obey. He had no intention of being ordered around behind his back by an actress, no matter how talented. On November 10, 1808, he asked the duke to release him *from a business . . . that will turn my otherwise so desirable and gratifying position into a hell.* Karl August, however, would not relent.

The duke had other reasons for dissatisfaction with Goethe: his old friend was decidedly too fond of Napoleon. Karl August joined the Confederation of the Rhine and placed the duchy under Napoleon's dominion only with inner reservations, and he was waiting for the first opportunity to switch sides again. He placed great hopes in the tsar, to whom he had familial attachments, and he was confident that the Russian monarch would someday put an end to Napoleon's hegemony in Europe. Goethe, who was quite content with the peace Napoleon's power had imposed, wore the cross of the Légion d'honneur at every appropriate and inappropriate moment and called the man who had awarded it *my emperor.* The political disagreement between Goethe and the duke played into the dustup about the theater.

It was Duchess Luise who intervened and calmed the angry waves. Goethe remained in his post, his prerogatives and responsibilities precisely laid out to exclude future infringements of his authority, but his relation to the duke remained troubled. It was no accident that in these weeks of acute conflict, Goethe was particularly emphatic in his praise of the emperor; one can hear the undertone directed against the duke. Goethe still felt he owed allegiance to the duke, but it was good to know that he had a sort of kindred spirit in the emperor, who had given him an open invitation to come to Paris. While working on *Elective Affinities*, it was easy to toy with the notion of giving up the old obligation in favor of a new one. At any rate, in these weeks he did procure a practical grammar book to brush up on his French.

At the beginning of 1809, once the theater matter had been settled, Goethe resumed work on the *Theory of Color* and *Elective Affinities*. Over long stretches, both works advanced in parallel, one reason why the novel seemed to him the *second part of the Theory of Color*. However, there was a deeper connection between the two works. Goethe was at work on the chapter entitled "History of the Theory of Color" and writing about the theme of *natural magic* when he got his first inspiration for *Elective Affinities*. A passage about the sixteenth-century naturalist Johann Baptist Porta, written shortly before he began work on the novel, declares, *There are so many connections between the specified entities that are real and yet miraculous enough, as for example, between the metals in galvanism. . . . Let us recall, in a cruder sense, effluvia, odor; in a more delicate sense, connections between bodily form, gaze, and voice. Recall the power of the will, of intentions, wishes, prayers. What never-ending and unfathomable sympathies, antipathies, and idiosyncrasies intersecting one another!*

People at the time imagined such *connections* to be modeled on magnetism or the chemical attraction of elements that separate from old bonds and join in new ones. Since about 1780, these chemical processes were called "elective affinities," and Goethe adopted the phrase for the first time in 1796 in a lecture on comparative anatomy. He explained that such processes of de- and recomposition looked *like a kind of inclination . . . which is why the chemists attribute to them the honor of choosing to enter into these relations*. In reality, however, it was not a question of choice but of *determination*, he continued, with the pointed addition *although we by no means wish to deny them the tender part they play in the general breath of life*.

If organic nature can thus have a part in the *breath of life*, then we can sometimes conversely see the *breath of life* between people from an organic-chemical perspective. In chemistry, the expression "elective affinity" is a metaphor that anthropomorphizes nature, whereas the novel *Elective Affinities* attempts to do the opposite, to connect what is human to natural processes. In the first case, one attributes freedom—at least metaphorically—to the elements. In the second case, human freedom appears as unconscious necessity.

How free is love? How much natural compulsion does it involve? These are the challenging questions the novel sets out to answer. Goethe explained his title in the advertisement released by the publisher: *It seems that the author's continued exploration of physical nature caused him to choose this strange title. He would like it noted that in natural history one often makes use of ethical similes in order to bring closer something far removed from the circle of human knowledge; and so, in this story of a moral crisis, he was pleased to restore a chemical simile to its spiritual origin.*

What does it mean in this case when a *chemical simile* is restored to its *spiritual origin*? The chemical elements that form new bonds have no choice in the matter. And yet it looks as if they do. When humans form new bonds, they choose to do so. But does it only look that way in their case too? That would then be the origin of the simile. Both times—in the chemistry of the elements and in the chemistry of human interactions—there is necessity and what at most appears to be freedom, freedom as a simile, not as reality.

The novel's figures themselves discuss this problem. Charlotte protests against absorbing the human world into the natural realm. *But after all, man is so many levels above those elements, and if in this case he was somewhat generous with the lovely words "choice" and "elective affinities," he would do well to look inside himself and reflect on the value of such expressions on this occasion.* For Charlotte, to reflect on their value means to reserve the expression "choice" for the human sphere and remove it from the realm of nature. But that is not what Goethe thinks. He says in a letter that he wants to show how *traces of murky, passionate necessity are constantly infiltrating the realm of cheerful freedom and rationality and can be completely extinguished only by a higher hand, and in this life perhaps not at all.*

The novel is set up as an experiment to examine the relative power of freedom and necessity in erotic interaction. It begins with a mature couple, bound together by a gentle love and living a withdrawn and protected life in their manor house and garden, free of all obligations and in a situation that allows—but also constrains—them to find satisfaction in themselves and each other. The story begins at the moment that this previously idyllic, closed world is opened up.

Eduard, the husband, wants to invite an old friend for a visit, a captain who has resigned his commission. Charlotte, the wife, hesitates and warns of unwelcome and unforeseen changes. Eduard seeks to dispel her concerns: *That could well happen . . . to people who live gloomy, introverted lives, but not to those who have been enlightened by experience and are more conscious.* Charlotte responds with an ominous sentence whose significance will be revealed in the course of the story: *Consciousness,* she says, *is not an adequate weapon, and is sometimes even a dangerous one for the person wielding it.* The sentence points early on to the ambiguity of the action. What unconscious desire is hidden behind the rational decision to invite the captain? People exchange ideas and talk reasonably with one another. It all seems to be directed by consciousness, but, in reality, there are unexpressed feelings and desires. In any event, Eduard stubbornly insists on his plan, and they finally agree that they will invite both the captain and Ottilie, Charlotte's foster daughter. And so the elective affinities—at first felicitous, then disastrous—can begin.

What sort of powers are these that apparently assert themselves behind and against the conscious will of the participants? They are the divine or demonic powers of a fate that operates not from without but within and between people. For Goethe, they are natural powers that leave their *murky* trace in the realm of *cheerful freedom and rationality,* where people think that they are falling in love of their own free will, and that love in general proceeds from freedom.

Politics is fate. That's what Napoleon told Goethe in October 1808 when he was already at work on the novel. One's inner nature is also fate. That's what it comes down to in *Elective Affinities.* Politics plays no role in Eduard and Charlotte's garden landscape. It's true that Eduard rushes off to war at the end of the first book, but he does it to be able to bear the separation from Ottilie and not for the sake of politics. *Eduard yearned for external danger to keep his internal danger in balance.*

It is not just the fateful power of politics that is excluded but also the transcendent power of divine providence beloved by the Romantics as it appears, for instance, in the tragedies of Zacharias Werner. It is no accident that at the same time Goethe was working on the novel, he was voicing especially strong criticism of Romantics like Tieck, Schlegel, and Joseph Görres, whom he regarded as fishing in troubled waters by giving free rein to their sympathies for Roman Catholicism. Although he had once been flattered when the Schlegel brothers praised him to the skies, he had since soured on the whole movement. One annoyance was an article that appeared in the *Zeitschrift für Wissenschaft und Kunst* (*Magazine for Science and Art*) in early 1808, ranking the Romantics, especially Novalis and Friedrich Schlegel, above Goethe as poets. It said that only Romantic poetry was "idealistic, i.e., like Christianity, it transfigures the dualism of heaven and earth into a spiritual unity in the idea of the divine and holy; on the other hand, Göthe's poetry, like pagan poetry, is realistic."

With angry defiance, Goethe took what was meant as criticism for praise. In March 1808 he wrote to Jacobi, *What's more, I am only too honored by what those gentlemen say about me. I had wished but not hoped to receive such praise, and it shall now be extremely pleasant to live and die as the last pagan.* Not long thereafter, Goethe stormed against the Romantics at a gathering in Johanna Schopenhauer's salon. Each season, he said, a new literary emperor was declared. Now it was the Romantics' turn. It reminded him of the end of the Roman Empire when any canteen cook or foot soldier could become a Caesar. Today Friedrich Schlegel was the crowned head, and it could just as well have been Novalis if he were still alive. The poor fellow was in too much of a hurry to die. *As demanded by the speedy progress of our newest literature, you should clothe yourself with fame as quickly as possible and with earth as slowly as possible.* Goethe harbored a particular grudge, having discovered a disparaging remark about *Wilhelm Meister's Apprenticeship* in Novalis's literary remains, which Tieck had edited and published.

Goethe's witty *diatribe against the new poetasters* soon made the rounds in Weimar. He also said that the literary emperor lived in complete safety, thank God. *Each one dies peacefully in his bed instead of being strangled like most of the Roman Caesars.* And at least he was glad to wake up in the morning with his head still on his shoulders, even though he wasn't emperor anymore. All this wouldn't bother the Romantics very much, he continued, since they had one foot in the hereafter anyway. Romantic piety? He couldn't take it seriously. It was nothing more than a search for interesting material. *The common topics writers usually chose to treat had been exhausted and made contemptible. Schiller had still hewed to what was noble; to surpass him, they had to reach for what was holy.*

In the summer of 1808 came news that Friedrich Schlegel had converted to Catholicism. To Reinhard, who had told him about it, Goethe replied, *Schlegel's conversion, however, is very much worth the trouble of following step by step, both because it is a sign of the times and also because at no time has such a remarkable case ever occurred: that such an outstanding and highly educated talent, in the brightest light of reason, intellect, and broad outlook, gets misled into veiling itself, playing the bogeyman—or if you prefer another metaphor—with shutters and curtains closing as much light as possible out of our common house, producing quite a dark room, in order to later allow in through a foramen minimum* only as much light as is necessary for hocus pocus.*

All of these comments occurred while he was working on the novel. They clearly reveal that although Goethe was fascinated by the unconscious chemistry of human relationships—the monstrous aspect of nature—what he calls the *hocus pocus* of supposedly extraterrestrial powers did not interest him. All the more surprising, then, is his occasional intimacy with Zacharias Werner during this year of the *Elective Affinities*. Werner was a genuinely sanctimonious author, but at the same time very sensual. For Goethe, he was an example of a suspect salaciousness in which pining after holiness is connected to sexuality rather than morality. He called Werner's life and activities *a lascivious masquerade ball and quasi-bordello*. Yet, he called Werner *an outstanding talent* as a dramatist who had an especially powerful effect on the ladies. As theater director, Goethe needed attractions and Zacharias Werner was one.

The son of a professor of elocution, Werner had grown up in Königsberg in the same building as E. T. A. Hoffmann, who was a few years younger. After his father's early death, he had fallen into the hands of his half-mad mother who believed she would be giving the world a second Christ in her highly educated son. Hoffmann later told of the piercing shrieks from the woman on the top floor who thought she was the Virgin Mary. Werner was already a successful dramatist by the time his restless life brought him to Weimar in 1808. He had scored a huge hit in Berlin with his play *Martin Luther, or The Consecration of Power*, under the direction of August Wilhelm Iffland. It ran for weeks. The Protestant Berliners couldn't get enough of a Luther

---

* Latin: small hole.

who was simultaneously saintly, berserk, and a ladies' man. "The general impression is repugnantly religious," Zelter reported. The success went to Werner's head and when Schiller died, he immediately felt called upon to take his place. As a celebrated dramatist, Werner could now pursue chambermaids and countesses with even more success. He fobbed off his third wife—a Polish beauty—on a Berlin privy councilor in exchange for a post in the ministry in Potsdam from which he had already resigned by the time he got to Weimar, where he was now a frequent guest in Goethe's house. For the duchess's birthday on January 30, 1808, Werner's play *Wanda, Queen of the Sarmatians*—the bizarre story of an Amazon who wages war on an enemy prince whom she loves but kills in the end—was performed.

Goethe must have felt besieged by raging Amazons. Not long before, he had received several acts of a play called *Penthesilea*, sent to him by a certain Heinrich von Kleist "on the knees of my heart," as he wrote in his cover letter. Penthesilea was another of those hysterical women Goethe couldn't stand. On February 1, two days after the performance of Werner's play, Goethe wrote to Kleist, *I cannot warm up to Penthesilea yet. She is from such a prodigious race and moves in such a strange region that I need time to familiarize myself with both.* He was repelled by the emotional extremism and absolutism in *Penthesilea*. He did produce Kleist's comedy *The Broken Jug*, but deprived the more moderate play of any success by an incorrect division of the acts and lukewarm directing. It remains a mystery why he rejected *Penthesilea* on the one hand but esteemed the no less murderous virago Wanda on the other. Perhaps it was Werner's gesture of enlightenment after Wanda kills her beloved ("You poor souls whom love now blinds, / Calm yourselves and clear your minds") that pleased him more than Penthesilea's frenzied rage.

Whatever the case, Goethe counted Kleist among the Romantics from whom he wanted to distance himself. In his *diatribe against the new poetasters* in Johanna Schopenhauer's salon, he also went after Kleist. He called *Penthesilea* an unintended *parody* and made fun of the scene in which the Amazon declares that all her hard feelings have moved from her left breast, which she cuts off so it won't interfere with her shield, into the remaining right breast. Goethe said things like that belonged in an Italian comedy and even there would be disgusting.

Thus at the same time Goethe was writing *Elective Affinities*, there was a craze for bizarre erotic enthusiasms in contemporary literature, spurred on by the Romantic spirit. Yet Goethe tells his story, which itself has no lack of bizarre amorous complications, without any exalted Romantic feelings but rather in the observant and distanced posture of a natural scientist.

Let us examine the situation at the beginning of the novel in more detail. In their youth, Eduard and Charlotte had fallen in love with each other but were not strong and determined enough to follow their true feelings. Each entered a conventional marriage of convenience with someone else. The deaths of their respective spouses finally leave them free to marry, and they withdraw to the isolation of Eduard's country estate to enjoy their yearned-for happiness at long last.

They think that now they will be able to follow their real inclination, but here begins a first ambiguity. How strong is their inclination? Is it still love, or only the memory of love, a sort of postlude? Charlotte had an inkling of this, for she hesitated before agreeing to marry Eduard. Eduard had pressed his suit with the feeling that his wishes were to be fulfilled at last. And yet now, from time to time, a suspicion of boredom steals over him, although he won't admit it to himself. That is why he is so eager to invite the captain, his friend who is having some trouble, for a visit. Charlotte is surprised by his sudden haste. Why not take more time to think it through? But Eduard, threatened by boredom, cannot take more time. Impatience and irritability suggest that the couple no longer satisfy each other but cannot acknowledge it. They lay out paths in the park, graft slips onto young branches, make music, and read to each other, but under the calm surface of their lives, emptiness yawns.

With the arrival of the captain and Ottilie, the situation changes. New force fields are formed as Charlotte is attracted to the captain and Eduard to Ottilie. The participants react in different ways. The captain and Charlotte try to resist their growing attraction, while Eduard surrenders himself to his feelings for Ottilie, who for her part attaches herself to her lover like a sleepwalker, without really being clear about her feelings. Even her handwriting begins to look like his. A turning point, when they grow conscious of their feelings, comes in a famous scene in which the married couple commit adultery with each other. Charlotte and Eduard lie in bed together, but their minds are elsewhere: *Eduard held only Ottilie in his arms; the captain hovered, nearer or more distant in Charlotte's soul, and so wondrously enough, absence and presence were woven charmingly and blissfully together.*

The next morning, the spouses encounter the others *as if in shame and remorse* and confess their love to the recipients of their respective *elective affinities,* Charlotte to the captain and Eduard to Ottilie. Nevertheless, Charlotte is ready to abjure her love in order to uphold her marriage vows. Eduard is not willing to continue living with Charlotte or to give up Ottilie. He departs, leaving Ottilie in Charlotte's care for the time being. Nine months later, Charlotte gives birth to the child of their *double adultery,* and miraculously the little boy has the facial features of the captain and Ottilie's eyes. For Eduard, however, the child is nothing but an obstacle to his union with Ottilie. In despair, he volunteers for the army and goes off to war, hoping to die in battle.

He survives and takes it as a sign that he has earned the right to Ottilie, who in the meantime has been caring for Charlotte and Eduard's child. He returns and importunes her, and the young woman, who seems to come from some *vanished golden age* and is already half turned toward the things of heaven, agrees to marry Eduard, provided that Charlotte forgoes him, which now seems likely. The story is about to end happily when disaster strikes. Ottilie is rowing across the lake in happy anticipation when the little boy who is with her falls into the water and drowns. The death of the child seems at first like a deliverance from their problems. For Eduard, it is an *act of providence,* the removal of the last obstacle to his marriage with Ottilie, and even Charlotte agrees to a divorce because she too believes the child's death is a sign of fate: *I ought to have made the decision sooner; it was my hesitation and resistance that killed the child. There are certain things that fate adamantly undertakes to do. Reason and virtue, duty and all that is holy try to block its course in vain; fate wants something it deems right to happen, although it doesn't seem right to us; and so in the end it asserts its will no matter how we act.*

What kind of fateful power is it that overrides everything and even sacrifices a child? It is the attraction between the lovers that nothing can resist, a power of nature stronger than any culture of duty and reason, stronger even than freedom.

This power of attraction perhaps affects Ottilie most purely. For Eduard, it takes the form of desire, but in Ottilie it is almost a somnambulistic enchantment. She wants to tear herself away from Eduard but cannot do it, not even when she is tortured by feelings of guilt, because for Ottilie the child's death is not the removal of an obstacle, as it is for Eduard, but the establishment of a new obstacle. Yet toward the end, when it is clear that they will not marry, the two of them still remain caught in love's force field, whose gentle might Goethe describes as follows: *They still exerted an indescribable, almost magical power of attraction for each other. They lived under the same roof; but even at moments when they were not thinking of each other but were busy with other things, pulled hither and thither by the company of others, they drew nearer to each other. If they found themselves in the same room, it didn't take long before they were standing or sitting next to each other . . . it required no glance, no word, no gesture, no touch, only the purest proximity. Then they were not two persons, it was only a single person in unconscious, utter contentment, satisfied with itself and with the world. Even if someone had forced one to remain at the farthest end of the house, the other would have found the way there, little by little, without intending to. For them, life was a riddle whose solution they found only in each other.*

Eduard and Ottilie get headaches at the same time, she on the left side and he on the right. The power of attraction is so great because only together do they constitute *a single person*, an allusion to the Platonic image of the original complete person whose separated halves have been seeking each other ever since.

Is this the *riddle* of life, this yearning for completion in *purest proximity*, when desire finds peace in fulfillment? Is this desire, which can defy conventions, institutions, and laws, our inner nature operating as fate? Is this nature's way, this search for the great complement which, once found, makes the individual for the first time complete and whole again? It would seem so. In Goethe's *Maxims and Reflections*, assembled after his death from his literary remains, we find the sentence *Whoever makes a serious descent into his inner self will always discover that he is only a half; it is all the same whether afterwards he takes a girl or a world in order to constitute a whole.* Seen in this light, the individual would not be indivisible, but what has been divided and now seeks its proper other half. Elective affinity reveals a stronger or weaker affiliation; the divided parts can regroup and fuse, not always in a peaceful process, but sometimes with pain and weeping, for what seems to some a unifying power can appear to others as destructive violence.

Thus ambivalent powers are at play, powers Goethe also refers to as *the tremendous, importunate forces.* Ottilie seeks refuge from them by *devoting* herself to *holiness.* Yet since she lingers on in the magnetic field of *proximity,* she cannot complete an external renunciation by returning to the boardinghouse where she had previously lived. What remains is her inner renunciation, the only way she can forgive herself for the death of the child. But what does it mean to renounce but at the same time be tied to the force field of love? An inner dying is all she has left. And so she declines, refusing food, and Eduard quietly follows her in death.

The power of attraction between people is no mere metaphor. For Goethe, it is a fact. We are not talking about a metaphysics of sexual love but about its physics. A natural coercion unites Eduard and Ottilie. What Charlotte tells Eduard in the first dialogue of the novel is applicable here: *Consciousness* is simply *not an adequate weapon.* And since consciousness is connected to freedom, freedom also reaches its limits. To be sure, it is not completely overpowered everywhere. In the end, Charlotte can control her longing, as can the captain. But Eduard cannot master his passion and is destroyed. In him, almost every trace of freedom is erased. Ottilie's decline, meanwhile, is not simply natural but also the consequence of her decision to stop eating. She thereby escapes Eduard, even though the attraction continues in full force.

In the end, their deaths are elevated to the level of a saint's legend: *Peace hovers above their resting place, cheerful, familiar images of angels look down on them from the ceiling, and what a happy moment it will be when, one day, they awake together.*

Although those are the last sentences of the novel, they are surely not the narrator's actual commentary. It is to be found a few pages earlier, in reflections on Ottilie as she lies on her bier. The narrator observes that she embodied so many *quiet virtues only recently called forth by nature from its capacious depths and quickly extinguished again by its indifferent hand—rare, beautiful, lovable virtues whose peaceful influence the needy world at every moment embraced with joyful satisfaction and whose absence it longingly mourns.*

At this point the reader tends to balk. Ottilie and Eduard don't really perish from their feelings for each other but rather from the fact that the institution of marriage and the marriage vows—i.e., culture and morality—have erected barriers. Seen in this light, it is not nature's *indifferent hand* but the clash between nature and culture that brings them down.

It is necessary to see nature and culture together, as *a single nature*, as Goethe does in his preface to the novel, to grasp the conflict—which in certain circumstances can be deadly—as a tension between two aspects of nature: a first, original nature in collision with a second, cultural nature. Customs and laws, made by men, would then be what human nature requires to commit itself to this nature. Only when we assume *a single nature* that also includes culture does nature appear in all its ambivalence, an ambivalence that can lead to tensions in which man is torn apart. Then we cannot wholly embrace either desire or law and order, but rather see with a certain shudder how the two necessities collide. And only then is the meaning of the above passage clear: from its *capacious depths* nature brings forth figures and then *extinguishes* them with *its indifferent hand*. Heraclitus described nature functioning similarly, like a child who builds something in play and then knocks it down again.

It is possible to mistake the apotheosis of the lovers in the image of holiness for the author's final word. Yet his reference to nature's horrible ambivalence remains, and wise readers of the time understood it as Goethe's point. Karl Friedrich von Reinhard wrote him on February 10, 1810, after a first reading of the novel, "Of course, your characters and actions are not spiritualistic . . . however, if we ever achieve deeper knowledge of the mysteries of our nature, so that we are in a position to give an account of them, it is possible that your book will then be revealed as a wonderful anticipation of truths of which we now have only a dark inkling."

At issue is the complex nature of man, as Reinhard rightly sees. Man creates moral ways of living, but the inscrutable passions remain. At times, they may have no moral justification, yet we sense that they represent life at its most vivid.

Goethe was writing a novel neither in defense of marriage—which he was accused of by some—nor in defense of the passions. The latter might have been expected; Goethe had once stood at the center of the Sturm und Drang, and passions lend themselves to poetry. But must they be defended? The answer provided by the novel was that they need no defense, and that it was foolish to come to their aid with rationalizations. Just as foolish, however, is the stance of Mittler, a theologian and acquaintance of Eduard's and Charlotte's whose name means "mediator." He is almost a caricature of a defense of the moral principle. He comes when they don't need him and is absent when they do. He's called *mediator* but can't mediate, as all he knows is the moral realm. He ignores the passions because he fears them. Thus he cannot defend moral culture, because he understands too little of life.

Let us take a last look at Ottilie. She never stops loving Eduard, but she renounces love, and thus forgoes its actualization. This renunciation, however, will kill her in the end. To actualize her love would have meant living with guilt, which would also have ended up killing her. She becomes a tragic figure in the conflict between the nature of desire and the nature of morality.

The theme of renunciation would play a great role in Goethe's works from now on. Yet Ottilie as saint is not his final word of wisdom. Goethe would be on the lookout for more survivable forms of renunciation.

A beginning was made with the poem "The Diary," which he wrote shortly after the novel, read aloud only occasionally in all-male company, and never gave to anyone in written form. It was not published during his lifetime, not even in the last edition of his works that he supervised. It is a comic, burlesque reply to the tragedy in *Elective Affinities*. The magnetism of sexual love is the theme as well, but here in a more physical and physiological sense, and with a different course taken:

> *We've often heard, and must at last believe*
> *No one has ever fathomed the heart of man,*
> *And, however much we bob and weave,*
> *Christian or heathen, we're all prone to sin.*
> *We know the rules and follow them when we can,*
> *For if a demon tries to make us stray*
> *Virtue's safe if higher powers hold sway.*

The poem goes on to explain exactly what it is that keeps virtue *safe*. A traveler eager to return home is held up by an accident with his coach. In an inn, he is drawn into a ticklish situation, for the charms of a pretty chambermaid are all too tempting. All this is depicted with relish in broad and witty strokes. At last, the two are lying in bed together. But unlike the *adultery in the marriage bed* in *Elective Affinities*, this one finds *Master Iste** on duty only when the traveler, in order to get himself excited, thinks about his wife and the stormy passions when they first fell in love: *And then at last he's there: all of a sudden / He rises up and stands in all his glory, / Ready to do whatever he is bidden.* Now the traveler has lost his desire for the pretty servant girl. He wants to rush back into the arms of his wife as fast as he can. And so virtue is rescued by physiology.

---

* Latin: this thing.

CHAPTER 29

Leave-Takings: Anna Amalia and Goethe's Mother.
An Occasion to Look Back. Work Begins on the
Autobiography. Self-Reflection. How Much Truth Is Possible,
How Much Poetry Is Necessary? Narrated and Narrative
Time. Recollections of the Old Empire and Thoughts on the
New Power Structure. Pondering the Demonic. Another
Farewell: the Death of Wieland. Thinking about Immortality.

. . . .

WE KNOW THAT SCHILLER'S DEATH WAS ONE OF THE GREAT
leave-takings that led Goethe to look back on his life and give an autobiographical account of himself. Other farewells that awakened the
feeling of a caesura were the deaths of the duke's mother, Anna Amalia,
on April 10, 1807, and of Goethe's own mother on September 13, 1808.

There was much that bound Goethe to Anna Amalia. Back in 1775,
it was she who turned his sojourn in Weimar—at first thought of as
only a visit—into a lasting connection to the place and the ducal family. Anna Amalia's "Court of the Muses," over which Wieland initially presided as intellectual focal point, had attracted Goethe from
the first. Anna Amalia's attitudes had been shaped by French Enlightenment thought, and her aim was to connect the aristocracy to the
bourgeoisie under the banner of aesthetic and scientific education.
Her charismatic personality had long ensured that cohesive sociability
reigned, first in Tiefurt, then in the Wittum Palace and at her summer
residence in the Ettersburg castle, where *Iphigenia* and other smaller
plays by Goethe had their premieres, with amateur casts drawn from
Anna Amalia's social circle.

There, Goethe found his real audience in his early years in Weimar, whereas for the reading public at large he had basically disappeared. Some of his poems of the time first appeared not in print but in the *Tiefurt Journal*, which was distributed in manuscript copies and sometimes edited by Anna Amalia herself. She was very attached to Goethe. He inspired her with his yearning for Italy, and she traveled south in his wake. In 1790, he came to meet her in Venice and accompany her back to Weimar. He read her his "Roman Elegies"—but obviously not all of them. He dedicated a selection of his "Venetian Epigrams" to her with the distich *Who should receive this volume? The Princess who gave it to me. / Italy she still gives, even here in Germania*. This was laying it on a bit thick, but when he wrote it, he felt very much obliged to her for giving him some letters Winckelmann had written to her and permitting him to quote from them in his book on the art historian. In that volume he thanks her once more and says that she has ushered in the beginning *of a glorious epoch*.

Anna Amalia always backed up Goethe in his set-tos with arrogant, conservative aristocrats at the Weimar court. Their relationship was so close in the early Weimar years that there were even rumors of a love affair, which made Charlotte von Stein a bit jealous. In a playlet of 1800 entitled *Palaeophron and Neoterpe* and written for a belated celebration of Anna Amalia's birthday, he wrote of her, *And it was she who founded our union in this town*.

For Goethe, Anna Amalia was the benevolent genius of an entire epoch of his life. Her death compounded his elegiac mood and the feeling that times were changing. Much was in flux after the Battle of Jena in October 1806—militarily, socially, and politically. What was customary and reliable was disappearing. *The difference from earlier times*, he wrote to Charlotte von Stein a few weeks after Anna Amalia's death, *is simply too great. The old is past and the new has not yet emerged*. In Goethe's eulogy for the dowager duchess, which was read from pulpits throughout the duchy, he suggested that Anna Amalia was not able to absorb the changes in the world. Her *heart* had no longer *held out against the press of earthly powers*.

In September of the following year, Goethe's mother died at the age of seventy-seven. He learned of her death on September 17, the day he returned from taking the waters in Carlsbad. His diary does not mention it. People in his immediate entourage were surprised that he didn't want to talk about it, and his letters contain hardly a word. *My dear mother's death cast a dark shadow over my return to Weimar,* he wrote laconically to Silvie von Ziegesar, and in a letter to a Frankfurt acquaintance he said that *at her advanced age, it was natural to fear the approaching end.*

In *Poetry and Truth* Goethe always refers to his father as *der Vater* (Father or the father) but to his mother as *meine Mutter* (my mother). The autobiography presents Johann Caspar respectfully but critically, Goethe accusing him of pedantry and stubbornness. However, he almost always writes with love of his mother. Yet he seldom visited her—only four times after leaving Frankfurt in 1775: in 1779 on his way to Switzerland, in 1792 and 1793 when he accompanied the duke on the campaigns against France, and a last time in 1797 on his third trip to Switzerland. His mother gave no hint of her disappointment at his infrequent visits and did not reproach him with anything. Undaunted, she continued to write frequently, and he was so delighted with her lively and vivid letters that he showed them to his friends and on occasion even read them aloud. He once sent one of his mother's letters to Charlotte von Stein with the comment, *With a "good morning" I send my dear one a letter from my mother, to regale her with the life it contains.* He wrote to her less often, but then at length. In his letters to his mother there are detailed self-characterizations such as the one quoted earlier from 1781 about the *breadth and speed of* his *nature.* He would remain in Weimar, the letter continues. He was of good cheer since he was there *voluntarily*; he could leave whenever he wanted *to find in your company, in absolute tranquillity, the necessary and pleasant things of life.* His mother would have been happy to have him return. But neither then nor later did she trouble him with her wishes and longings. Although she didn't like to travel, she would also have been happy to visit him in Weimar. However, her son did not invite her to come except once, to offer refuge during the turmoil of war, an offer she ended up not needing to accept.

People in Weimar who read her letters regarded her very highly. Anna Amalia took the initiative to make contact with her, and Goethe was filled with pride that the two maintained a cordial correspondence.

Anna Amalia and the duke also visited his mother from time to time. Katharina Elisabeth Goethe kept a convivial house as long as she continued to live on the Hirschgraben and was a gracious hostess to all Goethe's friends and acquaintances. Yet Goethe balked at inviting her to Weimar, to say nothing of having her come to live in his house. Convinced she would lose the source of her vitality if she were to be transplanted, he was able to keep her at a distance with a clear conscience.

He did not immediately inform his mother of his marriage to Christiane or of the birth of his son. She first heard about both events from others. And yet she bore her son no grudges, and when she called Christiane his "bedmate," she by no means meant it disparagingly. She regularly sent large packages of presents to her grandson and adhered to a principle she once described to Charlotte von Stein: "I like people very much . . . never get preachy with anyone —always try to find their good side—leave their bad side to Him who created man and knows best how to file down their sharp corners."

She took an active interest in Goethe's literary works, read and commented on them, and proudly gave them as presents to her Frankfurt friends. She also kept him up to date on the Frankfurters' opinions of their celebrity son, and since she was out in society and often attended the theater, there was much to tell. In one of her last letters, she calls the first volumes of the Cotta edition of the complete works "heartwarming" and praises in particular the ballads "The Bride of Corinth" and "The God and the Bayadère." She always liked his erotic works best and was not one to take exception to the "Roman Elegies." In her last letter, shortly before she died, she put in a good word for August: they shouldn't "plague" him with demands to write letters to her. Young people had other things on their minds, so please, no "thumbscrews" for her sake!

Goethe had the exact circumstances of her death described to him. Katharina Elisabeth had proved to be as plucky and witty at the end as she had been all her life. The coffin maker had appeared at her bedside to take measurements, and she expressed her regret that everything had already been arranged and he had made the trip for nothing. She slipped away quietly soon thereafter.

During the two preceding years, the young Bettine Brentano, daughter of Maximiliane (whom Goethe was once a little in love with), had tightened the bonds between Goethe and his mother. She got Katharina Elisabeth to tell her stories about Goethe's childhood, wrote them down, and sent them to Goethe, who assiduously collected them. Bettine was infatuated with Goethe and after his death published a book entitled *Goethe's Correspondence with a Child*, which was more poetry than truth. However, Bettine's original transcripts of the stories his mother told served him well when he began to assemble material for *Poetry and Truth*. They refreshed his memories of childhood and adolescence, and he encouraged Bettine to have no qualms about continuing to ask his mother questions: *And now I'm hoping for some news soon about how my dear mother seemed to you . . . and what kind of conversations are in progress.*

According to his diary, he began the first draft of a plan for his autobiography in October 1809, a year after his mother's death. He started to dig out old notes and letters. He used his diaries mostly to simply record the day's events. The few passages of extensive self-reflection stand out, like the following entry, previously quoted but worth repeating because of its importance: *Tranquil review of my life, of the muddle, bustle, thirst for knowledge in my youth, how the young roam everywhere in search of something satisfactory. How I took special delight in secrets and dark, abstruse relationships. . . . How there was such a dearth of accomplishments and of purposeful thought and writing, how many days and hours were wasted in sentiment and shadow passion, how little of that was useful to me, and now that half my life is past, I have covered no ground along its path, but rather am just standing here like a drowning man who has pulled himself out of the water and whom the benevolent sun begins to dry off.*

He wrote that in 1779, at a time he was resigned to admitting that his life had been full of disorder, confusion, and profligacy. He had failed, and rescue had come from without. When he begins his autobiography thirty years later, he no longer sees his youth in such dark terms. He views it now more as he had in a letter to Knebel, written three years after he drew up the depressing balance quoted above. Confusion no longer reigns; he feels himself inwardly supported and guided: *At the core of my plans and resolutions and undertakings, I stay true to myself in a mysterious way and thus tie together my social, political, moral, and poetic life in a hidden knot.*

Goethe does not claim to know the details of this mysterious knot that holds his life together, but he is sure it exists and must be found if one wants to write an autobiography. In a letter to Zelter, he says that in biographies, as a rule, the good and the bad, the successes and the failures, are simply set down next to each other *in hypocritical self-righteousness.* Yet without some spiritual bond, the personality is destroyed, *which can be conceived only in the living unification of such opposite qualities.*

Goethe lived his life from a productive center, but felt a growing need to grasp more clearly the workings and sources of his productivity. He was in search of the *hidden knot.* In this way, too, he was inspired by his friendship with Schiller, who had been able to characterize him so brilliantly. He paid the debt of gratitude to his friend with the remark that Schiller had drawn his attention to himself. It was no accident that precisely in the years of their friendship, Goethe made several attempts to characterize himself, in one of which he noted, writing of himself in the third person, *The center and basis of his existence is a forever active, continuing poetic drive to develop himself inwardly and outwardly; once that has been grasped, all the other apparent contradictions are resolved.* This *drive to develop himself* was also effective in areas where he had no real gift, as in the visual arts. But he identified shortcomings in other areas as well. For official business, for instance, he didn't possess enough *flexibility* and for natural science not enough *perseverance.*

This analysis is from the year 1797, at a time when he was considering where improvements might be possible. More *flexibility* in practical affairs? He gets impatient too quickly when he meets with resistance or delay, so he must learn to accept things that don't submit to his creative will. But it is difficult for him because he can put up with his official duties only when *in one way or another, they give rise to something lasting.* That was decisive for Goethe, who was unable to let official business simply take its course; it had to result in something clearly delineated, to assume a shape. That is in fact what he wished for all his activities. Everything should shape itself into a work. But that is hardly possible in the hurly-burly of life, which is what government has to deal with. And that is why, as he writes, he so often has to *avert his eyes* so as not to despair at the amorphousness of day-to-day life. As we have seen, Goethe devoted himself energetically and consistently to his official duties in his first years in Weimar. Later, mindful of his inner and outer limitations, he had slacked off and thereby gained more flexibility.

The problem with natural science was similar. There it was a question of material that yields a complete work only with great difficulty. The stuff of science is so heterogeneous that it can disrupt and dissipate your concentration. How could one ever give coherent shape to this heterogeneity, this inexhaustible empirical evidence? Here, Goethe finally discovers a surprisingly simple answer. If the phenomena resist a unified form, then it falls to the intellect to become unified in its perception of them. He writes, *Since he learned to accept the fact that the natural sciences depend more on the development of the mind that engages in them than on the objects themselves . . . he has not abandoned this intellectual enterprise but only regulated it more and become more fond of it.*

When Goethe identifies the *poetic drive to develop himself* as the center of his existence, he uses the word *poetic* not only in a literary sense, but also in the original sense of the Greek *poiesis*, from the verb meaning "make" or "shape." He writes that he cannot help responding to what he encounters by shaping it. Everything that has an effect awakens in him the urge *to respond to it actively.*

It is this will to effective activity that constantly pushes him beyond his own limits—or better, out into the world—and thereby preserves him from brooding self-absorption. For him, self-awareness occurs only via the world. *I hereby confess*, he writes late in life, *that the great and so weighty-sounding injunction to "know thyself" always seemed suspect to me, like the ruse of a secret society of priests to distract people by demanding the unattainable and entice them away from activity in the external world and into a false, inner contemplativeness. Man knows himself only to the extent that he knows the world, and he becomes aware of the world only in himself and of himself in it.*

That means, first, that we know ourselves primarily from what we have done, not from accompanying reflections and not at all from those inner, mental worlds that never really take shape; and second, that we need the reactions and insights of others. Self-knowledge develops in the mirror of the knowledge of others. I recognize myself because I am recognized. But here Goethe makes a notable exception. It is not every person who can act as a mirror for him: *Adversaries are out of the question, for my existence is hateful to them. . . . I therefore reject them and ignore them, for they cannot benefit me, and that is what everything in life depends on.* This point of view is of the greatest importance for Goethe.

Knowledge and self-knowledge deserve their names only when they promote and serve life. The function of knowledge is to preserve and enhance life. If it undermines the powers of life, it doesn't deserve to be called knowledge, for then it is only an expression of enmity and the destruction of self and other in the guise of knowledge. The art of living consists in repelling or keeping at bay these hostile powers. For Goethe, the will to know is integrated into the art of living. That is why he could become an exemplar for Nietzsche.

When someone with as little inclination for brooding introspection as Goethe undertakes to write an autobiography, he will turn his attention to the things about himself that have been realized, not to the mere shadows of interior worlds. But what is truly real?

A reflection about the importance of what is individual comes from the time he was beginning to write *Poetry and Truth*: *Everyone is himself only an individual and can really be interested only in what is individual.* However, we never cease to move in the supra-individual reality of nature, culture, and society, where the individual can feel like a nonentity. Yet what is individual remains connected to the strongest feeling of being, and that is why we crave traces of individuality in the midst of that supra-individual world of society and history. *We love only what is individual; hence the great pleasure we take in portraits, confessions, memoirs, letters, and anecdotes of the deceased, even if they were insignificant.* And that includes biographies. *One cannot hold it against the historian*, says a preparatory note, *that he searches for results; but what is lost in that search . . . is the individual human being.* That is why people read biographies, *for we live with the living.*

Yet despite all our curiosity about individual characteristics because they are what is truly alive, our interest in biographies is not only peaceful and friendly. Biographies also are read *to learn about what is denigrating.* Goethe loathed biographies written in a spirit of resentment. He resolved not to serve such interests, and thus decided not to continue his autobiography up to the present. In his first outline from 1809, he had intended to do so. But he changed his mind out of consideration for living persons such as the duke and Frau von Stein. He did not wish to commit any indiscretions. He discussed other reservations with Riemer on May 18, 1810, on the way to Carlsbad and recorded them in his diary because of their importance: *Anyone who writes a con-*

fession is in danger of becoming lachrymose, because one is supposed to confess only weaknesses and sins and never one's virtues.

A course had to be steered between the Scylla of self-accusation and the Charybdis of self-congratulation. There are two sorts of dishonesty: you denigrate yourself or you boast. Both are to be avoided. Rousseau committed both kinds simultaneously by boasting about denigrating himself. Nobody could beat him at honesty, and he therefore indicted himself mercilessly and yet concealed what was especially embarrassing, such as the fact that he packed his children off to an orphanage. Rousseau's *Confessions* were a reminder to Goethe not to do as that genius of dishonesty had done. In general, he found Rousseau's emphasis on truth suspect. Goethe applies to the truth about human beings the requirement of *decorum*, which is his favorite word for it. Whereas with supposed truths you can offend, belittle, or wound, *decorum* urges consideration for others. And caution is also called for, as truths are always a matter of perspective. The consideration and caution required by decorum and the relativity of truth produced the attitude that Goethe in his diary called the *ironic view of life in a higher sense.*

Goethe entitled his autobiography *Dichtung und Wahrheit—Poetry and Truth.* How much truth is there in an autobiography, and how much poetry is necessary? In a letter written late in his life (sent first to the king of Bavaria and followed by an identical text to Zelter), Goethe explains the title. He writes that his *most earnest endeavor was as far as possible to present and express the actual basic truth which, as far as I could tell, had prevailed in my life.* This *basic truth* is not primarily the outward facts. Reproducing them as accurately as possible goes without saying. To help convey them, Goethe drew upon chronicles and works of history, made inquiries, used letters and diaries. But the *basic truth* is the inner logic, the inner coherence of his own life as it appeared to him at the moment he was writing it. He also calls it the *results.* It is the personality he now grasps as his own in the course of a development determined by influences and counterinfluences. The *basic truth* is the personality and what made it into what it is. But since he approaches this development not from without—like a historian—but from within, from the perspective of *recollection*, the imagination comes into play. It is nothing but his *poetic capacity.* It awakens the past to life and thereby allows one to see how much of it is truth.

To avoid misunderstandings, Goethe distinguished (in a conversation with Chancellor Johannes Müller) between the poetry (*Dichtung*) of recollection and mere *inventing* (*Erdichten*). Müller had asked if he would describe life in Tiefurt in the days of Anna Amalia, and Goethe answered, *It would not be too difficult, . . . one would only have to quite faithfully depict conditions as they presented themselves to the poetic eye at the time—poetry and truth, but without any admixture of invention.*

Invention would mean being free to make things up. *Poetry* in this context is reality reflected in recollection. What is past but continues to live in him is discerned by the *poetic eye*. Sometimes, the truth of an experience is revealed only in recollection. Some impressions and experiences need time to develop, and only in this developmental period do they attain the status of truth. What constitutes a person in experience and action, and how much of that the poetry of recollection is able to make present, is thus the *basic truth*.

How the *basic truth* of the past is linked to the present, and how its consequences sometimes become clear only in the present, is shown by *taedium vitae*, the weariness with life that Goethe presents in the third and provisionally last book of *Poetry and Truth* while discussing *Werther*. Not until dictating the relevant passages in 1812 did Goethe fully realize that this was a permanent if mostly subliminal motif of his emotional life, but also a phenomenon of that entire epoch. It came from both within and without.

Goethe introduces the depiction of that gloomy period with an encomium to poetry as a power that truly makes life easier. In chapter 8, we already quoted the wonderful passage about poetry: *Like a balloon, it lifts us and the ballast that we carry into higher regions.* It frees us for a time from *earthly burdens* and allows us *a bird's-eye view* of *earth's tangled paths.* Conversely, a crisis arises when a clear view is no longer possible. Although the burdens of life are always there, they become oppressive only when there is no inner flexibility to balance them out. However, such constrictions and burdens, for which poetry can provide a counterweight, are not the darkening of the mind that Goethe calls *taedium vitae*. Weariness of living does not result from great pressures or labyrinthian complications. The problem is not that things are complex and difficult but rather that they are empty and monotonous. It is the threat not of too much but of too little. There is no wildly flailing despair, only paralyzing boredom. In the midst of life, it is anticipated death that makes suicide seem a mere matter of form. Here at last, the weariness of living hits bottom. In *Poetry and Truth*, Goethe relates how this happened to him, and how he pulled himself together and performed grandiose, histrionic acts in order to escape the emptiness he felt, keeping a dagger beside his bed and musing on the splendid suicides of great historical heroes like Emperor Otho, who fell on his sword, and Seneca, who opened his veins in the bath. Yet he knew that they were figures who had lived active, meaningful lives and then had fallen into despair when they encountered great adversity. Their despondency was based on specific deeds. The weariness of living, on the other hand, was despair at a *lack of deeds*. Those men had too much life, whereas he had too little. Goethe tells how he pulled himself out of his depression by becoming active. He *decided* to live, but in order to do so with *good cheer*, he needed to *bring a poetic task to completion*. The way he presents this turning point suggests that any other activity could have had the same effect of dispersing his *hypochondriacal fancies*.

In November 1812, just as Goethe was developing his thoughts about *taedium vitae* as both personal experience and a phenomenon of the entire epoch, he received a letter from his friend Zelter, who was struggling desperately to maintain his composure in the face of his stepson's suicide. Past and present, narrated and narrative time, were meshing.

A similarly significant conjunction occurred with religion. Religion shows up in many passages of the autobiography, not just where it played a role in the narrated life but also when Goethe feels himself challenged in the present to ponder certain religious questions. In 1811, for example, he had long conversations about the spiritual world of the Catholic Church with a new young friend, Sulpiz Boisserée, a great collector of older German art and a believing Catholic. They inspired him to read Chateaubriand's *The Genius of Christianity*, which led to a more sympathetic view of the sacramental order of a Catholic's daily life. He placed his critique of Protestant austerity—*the Protestant has too few sacraments*—and his defense of the Catholic way of life in the chapter about his time in Leipzig, where it doesn't really belong. In any case, these reflections articulate what he had to say at this point about religion and its practice: if there had to be religion, then it should have powerful visual images, vivid rituals and sacraments that were effective aids for day-to-day living.

At the time he was writing *Poetry and Truth*, he was also involved in a dispute with his old friend Jacobi, an additional spur to come to terms with religion that also left its traces in the autobiography. Jacobi had sent Goethe a copy of his book *On Divine Things and Their Revelation*, in which he develops the thought that God cannot be comprehended from nature. "Man reveals God by raising himself above nature with his mind," writes Jacobi. It was the polar opposite of Goethe's position, and Goethe even had the impression that his friend's work was consciously directed against him. In great annoyance he wrote to Knebel, another of his oldest friends, *Whoever can't get it into his head that mind and matter, soul and body . . . were, are, and will be the necessary double ingredients of the universe, . . . whoever cannot rise to the level of this idea ought to have given up thinking long ago.* He went on to say that Jacobi had been tormenting him for years with his religious ideas, and now it served him right *if his old gray head sinks sorrowfully into the grave.*

The last time Jacobi visited Goethe had been in 1805, shortly after Schiller's death, and they hadn't seen each other since. After his initial anger about Jacobi's pious book had cooled, Goethe wrote him a friendly letter early in 1813 in which there is a succinct and effective description of his relationship to religion: *As for me, with the multifarious directions of my character, a single way of thinking cannot be enough; as a poet and artist, I'm a polytheist, as a natural scientist, however, a pantheist, and I'm the one as decisively as the other. If I have need of a god for my personality, as a moral person, that has also already been taken care of.* In the posthumous *Maxims*, that thought became the short and sweet: *Investigating nature / We are pantheists, / Writing poetry, polytheists, / Morally, monotheists.*

These are the categories in which Goethe presents an account of his relationship to religion in his autobiography. He relates how, as a boy, he developed a pantheistic feeling for nature, how the polytheistic pantheon of the ancients awakened his poetic enthusiasm, and how finally the severe, monotheistic God of the Old Testament became the epitome of moral law.

Every account of the past, Goethe wrote to Zelter, brings *with it something of the time in which it was written.* The link between present experience and the presentation of the past applies, as we have seen, to the depiction of moods like weariness with living. It also applies to the engagement with religious matters. And it applies to history and politics as well.

Goethe worked on the first three books of *Poetry and Truth* at a time of great political excitement. Part 1, with its recollections of a childhood in the Holy Roman Empire, came in 1811, when Napoleon's power in Europe was at its zenith and Goethe, after his audience with the emperor, proudly wore the cross of the Légion d'honneur, as we have seen. Part 2, covering his years in Leipzig and Strasbourg and the idyll in Sesenheim, was written as Europe held its breath during Napoleon's Russian campaign; it was published after that campaign had ended in disaster. Part 3, treating the creation of *Götz* and *Werther*, was written in 1813, as the European allies were defeating Napoleon and a nationalistic movement was being born in Germany. Napoleon had been banished to Elba when this third volume was published in the early summer of 1814.

At the peak of Napoleon's power, and after the disappearance of the Holy Roman Empire, Goethe depicted the splendid coronation of a new emperor that he had witnessed as a boy in Frankfurt. That world had vanished as completely as the world of his first boyhood love. Now it lived on only in recollection, bathed in a fairy-tale beauty. But there are also flashes of irony, for something was amiss in his attachment to the girl, the first *Gretchen*, as there was in the old empire. That becomes clear when he tells of his time at the Imperial High Court in Wetzlar. Goethe gives his readers a sense that the old order had outlived its time, describing the *monstrous condition of this thoroughly sick body, which only a miracle was keeping alive*. That is also a jab at the Romantics' historical sentimentality and at those patriots who dreamed of restoring the old empire.

While people in Weimar and elsewhere were bemoaning the burden of quartering French troops, Goethe was describing how the French were once billeted in the house on the Hirschgraben in Frankfurt, how bitter it made his father, and his boyhood delight at the opportunity it gave him to discover the world of the theater. This section of *Poetry and Truth* is a love letter to French culture, written at a moment in history when, all around him, anti-French sentiment was on the rise.

Part 3 of the autobiography, which treats the youthful Sturm und

Drang movement, contains a covert commentary on the German wars of liberation against the French. With a sidelong glance at the present, he writes of the Sturm und Drang, *The aesthetic spirit combined with youthful boldness pressed onward. From it there arose a world of effect and countereffect, half chimerical and half real, in which we later experienced the most virulent boasting and indoctrination.*

Both then and now, such a liberation movement struck him as the rhetorical, bookish, secondhand excitement of schoolmasters, literati, and journalists, not as a real-life power. His opinion of patriotism was the same; he accused it of being merely rhetorical and abstract. In July 1807, after the Prussian defeat, he wrote Zelter in a letter quoted above, *But when people bewail an entity that has supposedly been lost, an entity that not a soul in Germany has ever seen in his life, much less bothered about it, then I have to conceal my impatience so as not to become impolite.*

The reflections on the *demonic*, published only posthumously in part 4 of *Poetry and Truth*, were written in April 1813 after Napoleon's catastrophic defeat in Russia. While in the narrated time of the autobiography, the phenomenon of the demonic is linked to the figure of Egmont, in Goethe's narrative time it has to do first and foremost with Napoleon. Goethe sought to trace his fascination with the demonic—part terror and part admiration—to the figure of the Corsican.

His approach is cautious. He writes that the demonic emerges at the borderline of *what is monstrous, incomprehensible.* It is religious in a nonreligious guise. With the attraction it exerts on the masses, it reaches down into the depths of irrationality, is stronger than all reason, and can be a force for good or evil. It enters history suddenly, as if from nowhere. It looks like *pure chance*, yet we discover its necessity. It resembles *providence*, for it points to *interconnectedness.*

Those are his first attempts to adumbrate the phenomenon, and the autobiography suggests that these observations probably don't apply very well to Egmont—whom it uses as an example—and should actually be applied to someone else. *And so*, notes the author, *I want to get ahead of myself and—since I don't know whether I will get back to the topic anytime soon—will say something I became convinced of only much later*, that is, long after he had written *Egmont*. What then follows is a dense description of the phenomenon of Napoleon, but without naming him: *This demonic quality appears most terribly when it emerges predominantly* *in some person. . . . They are not always the most outstanding people, neither in intellect nor in talents, and seldom recommend themselves by the goodness of their hearts; but they exude enormous power and exercise unbelievable force on all creatures. . . . All moral strengths combined can do nothing against them; the brighter part of mankind tries in vain to make them suspect as either deceivers or deceived: the masses are drawn to them. Seldom or never is there a contemporary to equal them, and nothing can overcome them but the universe itself that they have begun to fight; and it is from such observations that the strange but prodigious saying may derive: nemo contra deum nisi deus ipse.**

That a demonic person can be overcome from time to time only by *the universe itself* is a clear reference to Napoleon, who was defeated not by his opponent but by the Russian winter and the enormous distances. Later, Goethe would explicitly reiterate to Eckermann that the demonic is not to be regarded as only negative and of the devil. Mephisto, for example, is not at all a demonic figure. The demonic individual has enormous energy—in a positive sense as well. For that very reason, Goethe included the duke among people with a demonic nature: he was *full of boundless energy and restlessness, so that his own realm was too small for him and the largest would have been too small as well.* In the conversation with Eckermann in which he said that, Goethe also speaks to whether something demonic was at work within himself. *It is not in my nature, but I am fascinated by it.* It was an old man who said that, a man who at that moment perhaps could no longer picture the bewitching magic of his younger self. As so often, it is still in the eye of the hurricane.

By late 1812, Goethe had decided to end the autobiography with his move to Weimar. It was clear to him that later autobiographical writings would be detailed descriptions of only those periods that were particularly eventful—such as the campaigns against the French on which he had accompanied the duke—or in which he had succeeded in completely *belonging to himself*, as during the Italian journey. After finishing part 3 of *Poetry and Truth* and even before completing part 4, he was already beginning work on the *Italian Journey*, which then continued the smooth progression of autobiographical works: the first three parts of *Poetry and Truth* in 1811, 1812, and 1814 and *Italian Journey*

---

* Latin: No one against God if not God himself.

in 1816 and 1817. Cotta waited to distribute the third volume of *Poetry and Truth* until the 1814 campaign in France was over; despite the political turbulence of the time, however, they met with great interest from the reading public. Perhaps it was precisely because people liked to be reminded of old times, or of the days of their own youth. In any event, that was the effect Goethe surmised they had on his readers. What more can one hope for his book than a reader moved to read his own life in its pages? Reinhard depicted some of his own youthful experiences after reading *Poetry and Truth*, and Goethe wrote him, *From the way I handle the material, it had to have the inevitable effect that anyone who reads the little book is powerfully led back to himself and his younger years.*

The deaths of Schiller, Anna Amalia, and his mother had been the impetus for retrospection and, in the end, for the autobiography. As Goethe worked on the third part, another farewell marked the end of an epoch: the death of Wieland. They had lived in close proximity for thirty-seven years, more than half a lifetime. As a cocky youth, Goethe had written a satire poking fun at Wieland—fifteen years older and already famous—as a decrepit fellow who presumes to play the schoolmaster to tough guys from antiquity. Even before the move to Weimar, he had made an abject apology, and once there, he conquered Wieland's heart in a trice. Wieland had called him a "splendid man" and confessed that he was "quite in love" with him. While the ties to Wieland were never as strong as those to Herder, there weren't the same dramatic ups and downs of closeness and alienation as with Herder. Wieland and Goethe were equally fond of each other. Wieland admired Goethe without envy, and Goethe respected Wieland and trusted him absolutely. He saw in him a man of great liberality, liveliness, and sound principles. In a long eulogy first read at an assembly of their Masonic lodge, Goethe memorialized the deceased with the famous words *This brilliant man liked to make a game of his opinions, but—I can call on all my contemporaries to bear me out—never of his convictions. And so he acquired many friends—and kept them.* This remark was directed against the prejudice that Wieland was a frivolous, unreliable, and merely witty man of the world. Wieland loved his freedom above all else and made creative use of it. Goethe especially admired the fact that he didn't envy others their success but helped and promoted them, yet also had the courage to criticize even his friends when necessary.

Goethe had had personal experience of that, for Wieland—who had the better head for politics—was unimpressed by Goethe's mediocre plays about the revolution and let him know it. In his eulogy, Goethe explicitly praises Wieland's strong grasp of politics. Full of *admiration*, he had observed *with what attention he followed the rapid events of the day, and with what wisdom he always conducted himself as a thoroughgoing German and a thinking, participating man.*

He also singled out other qualities for praise, such as Wieland's meritorious promotion of elegant, literary German; the beauty, grace, and charm of his verse epics; and his free and undoctrinaire philosophy. But what Goethe esteemed above all else was Wieland's generosity and the rare trait of being able to take genuine delight in others' accomplishments. It was something only a wise person could do, someone who regards his fellow man with cheerful benevolence. Goethe's eulogy is appropriately elegiac, but there's also something sunny about it—perhaps a bit of the earnest *cheerfulness* he praised in him.

This was another funeral Goethe did not attend, nor did he take final leave of his friend at the bier. He told Falk on the day of the funeral, *Why should I allow my lovely impressions of the faces of my friends to be destroyed by a mask? . . . Death is a very mediocre portraitist. As far as I'm concerned, I want to retain more expressive images of all my friends . . . in my memory. . . . I have no love for the parades of death.* In this long conversation with Falk, Goethe said things about eternal life not heard from him before: *Under no circumstances can there ever be talk about the extinction of such great faculties of the soul in nature; nature does not treat its capital so profligately. Wieland's soul is by nature a treasure, a true jewel.*

In a letter to Zelter, Goethe would later again allude to the idea of a great soul's indestructibility: *Let us continue to act until—one before or after the other—we are called by the world spirit to return to the ether! May the eternally living one then not refuse to give us new activities analogous to the ones in which we have already proven ourselves here below!*

Goethe was convinced that the inner goal-directedness of active natures—their entelechy—was not used up at death. If the world was as it ought to be, then an unspent entelechy should be given a further field of action. Of course, not everyone could hope for such a thing. You needed to have something within you worth continuing.

CHAPTER 30

Political Events Cast Long Shadows.
Napoleon's Downfall and a Dubious Liberation.
Guarding the *sacred fire*. Paying Tribute to the Spirit
of the Times. Hafez and *patriarchal air*. *West-Eastern Divan*.
Goethe and Marianne. The Lyric Interplay of Love.

. . . .

WHILE GOETHE WAS AT WORK ON THE SECOND AND THIRD parts of *Poetry and Truth*, he was determined to remain stoic in the face of the political events coming thick and fast. *I'm not at all affected by the burning of Moscow*, he wrote to Reinhard. *World history will now have a tale to tell in the future.* He was by no means so calm in reality, however. In a draft of the same letter he wrote, *Our imagination is incapable of conceiving and our mind of understanding it* [i.e., world history].

Goethe was inwardly shaken. After all, he had taken Napoleon's side and could not be indifferent to, much less triumph in, his catastrophic defeat. On the dark and foggy night of December 15, 1812, as Napoleon passed unrecognized through Weimar on his flight from Russia, he had the French envoy in Erfurt convey his greetings to Goethe. The duke joked that Goethe was now being ogled by both heaven and hell, since Empress Maria Ludovika of Austria had also sent him greetings for the entertainment he had provided her in Carlsbad.

After the disastrous Russian winter campaign, 1813 proved a year of decision. Napoleon cobbled together a new army. Prussia switched sides and declared war on France in the spring. For the time being, the duke was still maneuvering. French troops were again quartered in Weimar, then Russians and Cossacks, and then the French again. From east and west, misfortune washed over Weimar. The *West-Eastern Divan* became Goethe's refuge.

The war fought on German territory in 1814 had a new character. From Berlin, the call had gone out to the inhabitants of Prussia and the states of the Confederation of the Rhine to form irregular militia units. The spirit of nationalism that had begun with the French Revolution was now spreading into the countries rising against Napoleon. Patriotic mobilization and military buildups driven by nationalistic fervor were turning what were once wars between princes into wars involving entire peoples. Anticipated intellectually by the Sturm und Drang, nationalistic consciousness took on a political dimension. Nation, fatherland, and freedom were now values for which men were prepared to die. The official announcement of the Prussian defeat in 1806 called for calm as the first duty of a citizen. In contrast, an 1813 appeal was explicitly made to the new nationalistic feeling of being a Prussian and a German. It was the voice of a new politics that demanded active engagement and sought to woo people with the future possibility of a constitution. Not only nationalistic emotions were being mobilized. There was also at least a rhetorical gesture toward the demands for democracy that the Prussian reforms had awakened but not satisfied. In the months of the war of liberation against Napoleon, propaganda was used systematically for the first time to mobilize the populace. The great Fichte, who first took up the cause in his *Addresses to the German Nation*, went to the Prussian headquarters and volunteered to be a military chaplain. If his offer had been accepted, he would have become the very first political commissar, although he did plan to keep open the option of retreating back into the world of pure thought. Neither occurred, however, for in January 1814 the doughty professor died of the typhoid fever introduced into Berlin by the wounded in the war of liberation. These were weeks and months of more than mere patriotic fervor; people acted by forming volunteer militia units. The *Freikorps* of Major von Lützow, which would later gain great renown, was one such, composed of volunteers from the German states and operating as a band of partisans. Although the unit had little military significance, the black, red, and gold of its uniforms became a powerful symbol that lives on today on the flag of the Federal Republic of Germany.

In this eventful year, made especially difficult by the billeting of troops, Goethe left—practically fled—Weimar in mid-April. As in the preceding year, he traveled to the spa in Teplitz, not far from

Marienbad. For reasons of security, he had disguised himself but was still recognized by militiamen, whose weapons he was compelled to consecrate with a verse. In Dresden, he caught sight of Napoleon in the distance, inspecting the fortifications. He was a guest in the house of the Körner family and there met their son Theodor, a member of Lützow's militia and already famous for his soldiers' songs. The discussion revolved around the present uprising and the strong emotions elicited by the fight against Napoleon. Goethe remained silent at first and then finally growled, *Rattle your chains as you will, the man is too great for you. You'll never break them.* They could hear the sounds of battle in the normally quiet Teplitz, and at night saw *the fiery signs in the sky . . . where some unhappy village is burning. Since one is surrounded by refugees, the wounded, the fearful, one tries one's best to get away.*

Goethe returned to Weimar in August, not wanting to leave Christiane alone any longer. Something extraordinary happened in his study on October 16, 1813, the first day of the Battle of Leipzig, which ended with the defeat of Napoleon. A plaster bas relief of the emperor that hung beside Goethe's desk mysteriously fell to the floor but suffered only minor damage. It was rehung and continued to occupy its place of honor even after Napoleon had been driven out.

Goethe didn't trust the communal feelings of patriotism. When the victorious coalition troops invaded France toward the end of the year, Goethe wrote to Knebel that he'd never seen the Germans more closely *united than in their hatred of Napoleon. I just want to see what they'll do once he's been driven across the Rhine.* When the mass of people surrender themselves to political and military passions, one must not neglect *to call on the friends of science and art who remain at home, that they may preserve—if only under the ashes—the sacred fire that the next generation will sorely need.*

Goethe wanted his son, August, who had volunteered, to stay at home. He persuaded the duke to see to it that August received an assignment as a secretary at army headquarters in Frankfurt, far from the fighting. It was not what August wanted; he feared it would make him look like a shirker and a coward, which is exactly what happened. When he returned to Weimar from Frankfurt, he was mocked and insulted. He almost got into a duel, and again it was his father who intervened to stop it. All this deeply affected the son, who never completely got over it, feeling he had been prevented from proving his manliness. He would remain the son of an overpowering father whose shadow he could never escape. Goethe, however, was relieved that August had returned unharmed, and began to employ him as his secretary.

Even if he wasn't happy about Napoleon's defeat and deplored the entire patriotic movement, Goethe was enough of a businessman to suggest, a few days after the Battle of Leipzig, that his publisher bring out a pocket-size edition of *Herrmann and Dorothea*. He suspected that Herrmann's final words would be very appropriate for this moment:

> *. . . and if our enemies threaten,*
> *Now or tomorrow, then arm me, give me my weapons,*
> *. . .*
> *Ah, thus armed I will face our foes with calm assurance,*
> *And, if every man thinks as I do then might will rise to*
> *Counter their might and we all shall enjoy the fruits of peace.*

His speculation proved correct. The verse epic *Herrmann and Dorothea*, already a great success with readers when first published, found many buyers in this new edition and a positive response from the public. Goethe was so pleased about it that in conversation he suggested he might try his hand at a continuation. But that plan came to nothing. In the spring of 1814, the theater director Iffland wrote from Berlin to inquire whether Goethe would be willing to write a festival play for the celebration of victory over Napoleon. That same summer, the tsar, the Austrian emperor, and the Prussian king were to meet in Berlin, so speed was of the essence.

Goethe demurred at first, but did not fail to mention that he had experience composing *occasional poems*—he had for instance written something suitable for the spa administration in Halle—an inappropriate remark, as the Berliners wanted something lofty and not a comedy for a spa. A few days later, Goethe decided he was interested in the offer after all. He said it was much too *flattering* to turn down. He already had an idea he didn't want to reveal as yet. Iffland was overjoyed to have landed Goethe: "There is no celebratory act more lofty than to have the first man of the nation write about this great event." For Iffland, it was the matchup of his dreams: the greatest German poet writing for the greatest festival of the Germans.

Iffland was surely hoping for a play more closely linked to current events than the one he received from Goethe a few weeks later, *Epimenides Awakes*. It is a strange sort of play, quite unsuited to the occasion; instead of celebrating the victory, the author brings his own problems to the fore. We get private rather than official matters, and in order to present them objectively, Goethe tricked them out in ancient costumes and presented them allegorically. When the play was finally performed—after a year's delay—Berlin wits turned the title *Epimenides* into *Ja-wie-meent-er-das* ("What the deuce does he mean?"). Goethe uses an ancient fable about a favorite of the gods who is not punished although he sleeps through an entire epoch, and is instead rewarded with an increase in his prophetic power. In the next-to-last scene, Epimenides is contrite and full of self-reproach: *I'm ashamed of my hours of leisure. / To share your afflictions had brought more gain. / You are greater by any measure, / For you have suffered greater pain.* The priest responds, *Do not condemn the high gods' will / Since it has bought you many a year. / They have kept you sleeping, still, / So that your feelings can be pure.*

The performance of the play was delayed: first, the meeting between the emperor, the tsar, and the king of Prussia did not take place, and then Iffland died. It was finally performed in March 1815 on the anniversary of the allies' entry into Paris. Inaccessible, chock full of sententious statements, and with little or no action, the play was not a hit with the public. Goethe was nevertheless relieved to have done his duty and fulfilled an obligation, and could turn to things that mattered to him.

In the spring of 1814, the allies marched into Paris and banished Napoleon to the island of Elba. Goethe, who had admired Napoleon as the guarantor of order but found him sinister as the embodiment of a warlike spirit, placed his hopes for peaceful order in the new regime. Peace was what was most important to him, and he felt an initial relief. In retrospect, he realized how much outward events—the wars and billetings, the desperate public mood—had weighed upon and distracted him. Relations with the duke also improved, their difference over Napoleon now moot. Now he could write, *Here in Wei-*

mar we live peacefully enough and in tolerable contentment. He could feel a *spring ether*, he writes to Zelter, and perhaps he would again *launch* his sequel to *Die Zauberflöte*, which he had left unfinished. He got out his notes from the Italian journey and started editing his diaries and letters for publication. He felt invigorated recalling those beautiful months. Work on *Epimenides* had torn him away from this work for a while, but in the play, too, the theme is the awakening of the spirits of life. *And all of us are born anew, / Our greatest yearning has been stilled,* Epimenides declares.

It was not until a few weeks later, however, that he felt truly *born anew.* In mid-May 1814, Cotta sent him a copy of the *Divan* by the fourteenth-century Persian poet Hafez in a new translation by Joseph von Hammers. He already knew of Hafez and had read translations of individual poems. Herder had published some of them as early as 1773, and Goethe had familiarized himself with Arabic and Persian culture for the *Mahomet* drama he planned to write. For him, that world—along with the Old Testament—constituted a single cultural sphere. He read the Old Testament as poetry just as he did the Koran, which he had studied in the early 1770s. He saw no great difference between the Song of Solomon and Hafez's love songs, just as he saw no great divide between the stories of Abraham and Jacob and the *Thousand and One Nights. Patriarchal air* wafted through them all. As he refreshed his memories of all this while working on *Poetry and Truth*, he wrote to Johann Friedrich Rochlitz about the *Asian beginnings of the world*, as he called it: *The culture I have gained from there winds itself through my whole life and still sometimes emerges in unexpected guises.*

That is exactly what happened two and a half years later. In a creative euphoria elicited by his reading of Hafez, by the summer of 1814 he had already written over thirty poems, at first collected under the provisional title "Poems to Hafez." By the end of that year, as more and more poems were added, Goethe wanted to call the collection the *German Divan.* By the time he put together a catalog in the early summer of 1815, there were already more than a hundred poems, which he divided into individual "books" at the end of that year. They were the compartments into which to put additional poems, whose number continued to grow right up to publication in the summer of 1819. In the end, the *West-Eastern Divan* turned out to be Goethe's longest lyric cycle. He had prepublished some of the poems in Cotta's *Taschenbuch für Damen auf das Jahr 1817* (*Pocket Book for Ladies for the Year 1817*) to test the reaction to them. It was a disappointment, and therefore he proceeded to write the "Notes and Essays toward a Better Understanding of the West-Eastern Divan," a work that not only contains explanations of Persian and Arabian culture but also develops some fundamental thoughts on religion and its relationship to poetry.

Looking back on his reading of Hafez from the early summer of 1814, Goethe writes in the *Annals* that he had to *react productively* to his strong impressions as he otherwise *would not have been able to survive such a powerful phenomenon.* He entrusted himself and his creative urge to this newly awakened lyric mood, because he wished *to escape the real world—which was a threat to itself both outwardly and inwardly—into an ideal one.* The cycle's introductory poem takes up the motif of a world under threat:

> North and West and South are shattered,
> Thrones are toppled, empires battered.
> Flee to the pure Orient, there
> To breathe the patriarchal air.
> Love and drink and song in truth
> At Kizr's spring restore your youth.

In Arabian tradition, Kizr appears as a youth who has discovered the water of life and sits at its source in a green robe with green fuzz on his lip, wearing the color of spring growth and fertility.

As he worked on the *West-Eastern Divan* in the summer months of 1814 and 1815, Goethe experienced what he later described to Eckermann as a *recapitulation of puberty.* He depicts his creative exhilaration: *When . . . the poems of the Divan had me in their power, I was often productive enough to write two or three in one day; and it didn't matter whether I was out in the fields, in a wagon, or at an inn.*

What attracted and inspired Goethe about Hafez was a light, playful tone, palpable even in translation, in which the everyday and the lofty, the sensuous and the spiritual, thought and imagination, wisdom and wit, irony and devotion alternate and combine. Goethe writes in the "Notes and Essays" that the Near Eastern poet liked to *lift us from earth to heaven and then plunge us back down, or vice versa.* Love, song, drink, and prayer are his inexhaustibly recurring themes.

Goethe particularly emphasizes certain aspects of Hafez in the "Notes and Essays." A teacher and serious scholar concerned with theological and grammatical questions, Hafez obviously wrote poems in a way that was different from the way he thought in other areas. Playful, ironic, erotic, and sometimes frivolous, the poems are an example *that the poet must not exactly think and experience everything he expresses.* We should keep that in mind and not be tempted to separate the love story that began in the fall of 1814 at the Gerbermühle in Frankfurt and continued the following summer from the literary masquerade in which it found expression. Like Hafez, Goethe did not experience everything he said in the poems. Both Marianne Willemer and Goethe were fully aware of that. He writes to Zelter that he had discovered a *kind of poetry* that allowed him *to be as foolish in romantic matters as ever a young person was.*

On July 25, 1814, Goethe left for Wiesbaden. Rather than going to the Bohemian spas, he wanted this time to take the waters farther west, inadvisable in the preceding year with the war still in progress. Zelter had also decided to travel to the spa in Wiesbaden, and the two friends could be together. Goethe intended to visit Frankfurt for a long-planned meeting with his young friend Sulpiz Boisserée, who wanted to show him some things from his collection of older German art, which Goethe had agreed to write about. So several factors motivated the trip. He set off in especially high spirits, and that very morning in his coach he wrote a poem of anticipation and premonition. It would find its place in the first book of the *West-Eastern Divan* under the title "Phenomenon":

> *Where, with a wall of rain*
> *Phoebus is mated,*
> *There is an arc of light,*
> *Colorfully shaded.*
>
> *Second arc: from the mist*
> *I see it beckon.*
> *Though it be only white*
> *It comes from heaven.*

So you must not despair
Old man, be jolly.
For, although white your hair,
Love still is calling.

On August 4, Goethe received a visit in Wiesbaden from Johann Jakob von Willemer and his foster daughter Marianne Jung. Willemer was a Frankfurt banker, a patron of the arts and theater, and himself the author of plays and works on moral philosophy. He was a large, imposing man, considered handsome by women. As a young girl, Marianne Jung had been an extraordinarily talented dancer. Droves of men fell in love with her, including the poet Clemens Brentano, who wanted to marry her. In 1800, the newly widowed Willemer had taken the lovely, black-haired fifteen-year-old into his house, perhaps, as it was rumored in Frankfurt, having purchased her from her mother, an unsuccessful actress. Marianne was raised alongside Willemer's own daughters. When she and Willemer visited Goethe in Wiesbaden, she was twenty-nine.

The two men had known each other since their youth. Whenever Goethe came to Frankfurt, he paid Willemer a visit, and the banker occasionally lent him money. He admired Goethe, having once told Goethe's mother that he had never read anything as moving as *Wilhelm Meister.* Later, when he took Marianne into his house, Goethe's mother remarked sardonically that Willemer was apparently emulating the theater addict Wilhelm. The relationship between Willemer and his foster daughter is never mentioned in the letters he exchanged with Goethe over the years, although Willemer was otherwise quite candid. He wrote that although he had achieved success as a businessman, "the wings of my spirit are clipped." In the same letter, from 1808, is a remark that may refer to Marianne: "the future has been squandered on a foolish hope—about which 8 years of experience have taught me that it can never come to pass." Exactly eight years earlier, Marianne had come to live in his house.

Goethe visited Willemer in mid-September at the Gerbermühle, an old mill on the Main River, upstream and outside the walls of Frankfurt. He visited the Gerbermühle again in October, reporting to Christiane, *In the evening to Frau Privy Councilor Willemer, for our worthy friend is* *now in forma* married. She is as friendly and dear as before.* In a hurried ceremony, the twice-widowed man had married Marianne on September 29, 1814. Did the visits with Goethe encourage him to hazard this step? Was he inspired by Goethe's unconventionality in such things? Did the three perhaps discuss the matter together, and did Goethe advise in favor of it, causing Marianne to agree? We know only that the marriage took place in haste and shortly after Goethe's mid-September visit to the Gerbermühle.

On October 12, Goethe was alone with Marianne, the brand-new Frau von Willemer, for the first time since the wedding. The day meant so much to Marianne that she used it to date a poem written later for Goethe's album. The poem plays with one of Goethe's favorite turns of phrase, *the length and breadth*:

> Among the many I'm but one,
> And you call me your Little One.
> I'd be happy, you must know,
> Would you always call me so.
> I'd love you with all my strength's
> Length and breadth and breadth and length.
>
> You're a great man; people know you.
> No pantheon would dare forgo you.
> Your absence makes us feel bereft.
> We wish that you had never left.
> For now our sorrow knows no depth,
> No breadth or length, no length or breadth.

Marianne was known for her talent at improvising songs on the guitar. Goethe was enchanted, often referring in later letters to Marianne's playing and singing, and to unforgettable days spent at the Gerbermühle. On October 18, 1814, the anniversary of the Battle of Leipzig, bonfires blazed on hilltops far and near and wheels were set on fire and sent rolling down the hills. Marianne gave him a map the next day on which the locations of the fires were dotted in red. He wrote to

---

* Latin: formally.

Willemer, *When I look at the red dots above the mountains on the panorama, I fondly recall the dear hand that made them.*

On October 20, Goethe set off to return to Weimar. Once there, he wrote to Christian Heinrich Schlosser, a younger relative of his old friend and former brother-in-law, that *a new light of happy activity* had been lit. He had felt so much at home in Frankfurt, so inspired, that he would like to live half there and half in Weimar in order *to become rejuvenated and reborn to my earlier energy.*

The next year he set off much earlier, on May 24. He stayed a few weeks in Wiesbaden and from there took a trip down the Rhine to Cologne in the company of Baron Heinrich Friedrich Karl vom Stein. Then he paid a lengthy visit to Sulpiz Boisserée in Heidelberg. The high point of the summer, however—and perhaps even one of the high points of his life—were the weeks he spent at the Willemers' city residence in Frankfurt and at the Gerbermühle. When he returned to Weimar almost five months later, people were astonished by his lively manner and rejuvenated appearance. "Goethe is . . . happy and hearty," writes Meyer, "as I have not seen him for ten years and more."

In the preceding months, he had written numerous poems for the *West-Eastern Divan*, including the ones later collected in the "Book of Suleika." They are the results of an actual lyric dialogue, for Marianne had answered his poems with verses of her own that Goethe later included in the cycle without identifying them as hers.

As if he had foreseen what was to come, on the day of his departure for Wiesbaden and Frankfurt on May 24, 1815, he had written the lines in which the partners in the amorous dialogue are named. It was all still a lyrical game—and remained so—but was also something more. However, so-called reality is impossible to separate from the poetry. Both Marianne and Goethe must have enjoyed precisely this sense of hovering between the two. It gave them the exhilarating freedom to touch each other in love without needing to possess each other. The amorous dialogue of the "Book of Suleika" is lived literature—no more, but no less either:

> Yet that you whom I've so longed for
> Send me youthful, burning glances,
> Love me, whom your love entrances,

May my songs your praises strike up,
You're forever my Suleika.

Since Suleika has a name, then
I shall have to have one too.
If you'd sing your lover's fame, then
Hatem name him who loves you.

Once in this charming, playful lyric dialogue, the name *Hatem* is inserted where the proper rhyme word would be "Goethe": *Du beschämst wie Morgenröte / Jener Gipfel ernste Wand, / Und noch einmal fühlet Hatem / Frühlingshauch und Sommerbrand* (literally: You put to shame, like the red of dawn [*Morgenröte*], / The face of that mountain peak, / and once more Hatem [but to rhyme, it should be *Goethe*] feels / the breath of spring and the heat of summer).

The following exchange was also written that autumn at the Gerbermühle:

Opportunity makes thieves they say.
I think it is the thief itself,
The thief who stole my love away
And left my heart an empty safe.

And turned it over, all to you,
The love I'd saved up through the years.
A pauper now, I beg and sue
To have my life restored by yours.

Suleika responds,

What bliss it is to have your love!
I'll not chide opportunity;
It was what broke into your trove,
And what a happy burglary!

Why is there any need to thieve
When we can give of our own free will?

> *But it is flattering to think*
> *That it was me who robbed the till!*

Each separate link in the cycle, Goethe wrote to Zelter in May 1815, is *steeped in the sense of the whole . . . and must be introduced by a preceding poem in order to have an effect on the imagination or the emotions.* For instance, Suleika is made to proclaim the following maxim: *Greatest joy of the sons of earth / Is always personality.* This piece of wisdom, habitually quoted with approval ever since, appears in a different light when Hatem's response is taken into account:

> *That may be! Or so I've heard.*
> *By another truth I'm guided.*
> *All the happiness on earth,*
> *Is in Suleika now united.*

> *When she spoils me with her charms,*
> *Then I am a worthwhile person.*
> *If she spurned my open arms,*
> *I would lose myself for certain.*

The pleasure of having a personality is often not sufficient. For when one is in love, personality alone is not enough, because the lover is missing. It is she (or he) who gives my personality its value. If the lover rejects me, I am lost to myself. For lovers, personality is something best enjoyed together and not separately.

At several points in the cycle, there is explicit reflection on the connection between poetry and life. Suleika:

> *Could I stand to lose you? Never!*
> *Love gives love strength in extra portion.*
> *May you grace my youth forever*
> *With your overwhelming passion.*
> *Ah, how my desire is flattered*
> *When they praise my poet's merit.*
> *Life is love. That's all that matters.*
> *And intellect's the life of life.*

The feeling of being in love is one thing, another is its reflection in the mirror of poetry. Poetry makes something more of it: *how my desire is flattered.* There is no question here of a diminution or evaporation of reality in the intellectual sphere of poetry, no question of substitution or feeble sublimation. Rather, it represents an enhancement of life, in this poem expressed by the lovely formula *intellect's the life of life.* That can both signify intellect as the creative essence of life and refer to the prodigious doubling expressed in the famous poem about a ginkgo leaf:

> *By the East this tree's entrusted*
> *To my garden, and its leaf*
> *Has an edifying secret*
> *They can savor who can read it.*
>
> *Is it a single living essence*
> *That divides within itself?*
> *Is it two that choose each other,*
> *Whom we recognize as One?*
>
> *I can answer such a question.*
> *I've discovered its true sense.*
> *Can't you feel it in my poems?*
> *I am double, I am One.*

This alludes to the Platonic myth of love as being two halves that originally belonged together and now must seek each other. Not just the unity of two people is meant, however, but also the unity that is doubled within itself: the part of me that writes poetry is different from the part of me that lives in external reality. Thus the rhetorical question *Can't you feel it in my poems? / I am double, I am One* points to the fact that this love oscillates between literature and life, suspended there during a few intense weeks in the late summer and fall of 1815.

Marianne was brimming with ideas for Goethe's birthday celebration at the Gerbermühle. Boisserée described the festivities in his diary. Early in the morning, musicians awakened Goethe with a serenade from a boat on the Main River. Marianne had decorated the garden house in *Divan* style with oranges, dates, figs, and grapes. Bundled reeds between the windows represented palm trees, below which were wreaths of flowers in the order of the color wheel. The ladies wore turbans of the finest Indian muslin. They all dined at a long table. Willemer poured a 1749 Rhine wine. Marianne sang Goethe songs she had set to music, accompanying herself on the guitar. There were speeches both formal and playful. Marianne set a turban on Goethe's head, echoing the verse *Come Darling, come, and wrap my head in muslin! / The turban's only lovely from your hand.* The company remained together until evening, when the celebration culminated with Goethe reading his "Oriental poems."

Goethe and Marianne also were in the habit of exchanging slips of paper and letters with a series of numbers referring to pages and lines in Hammers's translation of Hafez. The result was an intimate conversation made up of a collage of quotes. One of Goethe's letters reads, decoded,

> *My wounded heart has a right to salt*
> *From your soft lips.*
> *But keep your rights. I'm going off,*
> *May God preserve you.*
> *For me you are an essence pure*
> *From higher spheres.*

One of Marianne's:

> I long to open my heart to you,
> And I long to hear from yours.
> . . .
> I shall make the only business of my whole life
> To care for his love.

One Divan poem explicitly refers to this game with encrypted messages:

> *My sweetest lady's cipher*
> *I hold here in my hand.*

It makes me glad already
Since she thought up the game.
Within the sweetest precinct
Is love's full measure found:
True thoughts and intentions
Between myself and her.

Willemer, who otherwise kept jealous watch over his beautiful and much younger wife, was so proud of Goethe's company that he never evinced the slightest jealously—if he felt any at all. When Goethe later held back and left numerous letters unanswered, it made Marianne ill, and Willemer earnestly implored Goethe to visit them. He wrote that he had set aside an apartment in their town residence for "whenever Goethe comes! So the eternal feelings need not fall silent and love can give all it is capable of."

After weeks in Frankfurt and at the Gerbermühle, Goethe again traveled to Heidelberg to spend a few weeks with Boisserée and his art collection, and Marianne and Willemer visited him there again from September 23 to 26. It would be their last time together. On that occasion she gave him her two most beautiful poems; their subject is the east and the west winds. She had written the first on the ride down to Heidelberg: *What's the meaning of this movement? / Does the east wind bring good news? / Fresh breeze rising from its pinions / Cools and salves my heart's deep wounds.* And the final strophe: *Ah! the truest, heartfelt message, / Whisper of love and life refreshed, / Come from his mouth, his alone, are / Given only by his breath.*

Her farewell gift on September 26 was the poem on the west wind: *West wind, ah, how much I envy / You your pinions, moist with rain: / With them you can bring him news of / How our parting causes pain.* And its final strophe: *Tell him this, but say it gently, / Tell him that his love's my life, / And I can rejoice in both when / He again is by my side.* Goethe included both poems in the published cycle, without attribution.

On October 17, 1815, Goethe returned to Weimar. Sulpiz Boisserée, who had been his almost constant companion during the previous weeks, traveled along part of the way. Boisserée noted in his diary, "He is very affected, didn't sleep well. Has to flee." That has often been interpreted to mean that Goethe fled from Marianne as he once had from Friederike. But there was probably a different reason for his sudden departure. The duke had paid Goethe a visit in Heidelberg at the end of September, and Goethe had gone with him to Mannheim, where the duke's mistress Karoline Jagemann—now Frau von Heygendorf—was staying. Then Goethe, accompanied by Boisserée, had undertaken a visit to nearby Karlsruhe, where he had paid his respects at court at the duke's behest, subsequently returning to Heidelberg. There he found letters that must have unsettled him. In his diary for October 6, he wrote only, *Letters. Decided to leave.* Boisserée's diary gives a bit more insight: "Suddenly, Goethe wants to leave; told me, I'm writing my will . . . Jagemann rushed him out of Mannheim—and the other ladies—now he's supposed to come over for tableaux and poses. He fears the duke," and then the already quoted "Has to flee." Thus he was avoiding another encounter with the duke and Karoline Jagemann, although he gave the duke no reason for his precipitous departure, writing only that his *daemon* had grabbed him by the *hair* and led him *home via Würzburg.* He asks the duke not to *be angry.* In the letters he opened in Heidelberg there must have been some unpleasant reminder of the argument with Jagemann concerning the Weimar theater; simmering since 1808, it would lead to Goethe's dismissal as director two years later.

Even now, despite the trouble on the day before his departure, he was still preoccupied with his *West-Eastern Divan*, and he sketches out its division into thirteen "books." The farewell letter he wrote on that day was addressed to Jakob von Willemer, but he especially has Marianne in mind when he writes of his *yearning* and then continues, *But that is too much for the state I'm in, in which there is an undeniable rupture that I'm not going to exacerbate, but would rather close.* With the comment that he would *rather close* the *rupture,* he explains his decision not to return via Frankfurt, which had likely been agreed upon, leaving the Willemers disappointed in their hope to see him again.

Boisserée accompanied Goethe as far as Würzburg and wrote in his diary on their first day of travel, "He is visibly calmed by the assurance that the duke and Jagemann can no longer reach him." He may have been calm in that regard, but in another his mood was melancholy. During the trip he wrote down Suleika's anxious question to Hatem: *Hardly do I once more have you, / Kiss you, comfort you with song, / When you suddenly fall silent—* / *What constricts you? What is wrong?* And Hatem answers, *Ah, Suleika, shall I tell you?* / *I lament instead of praising.*

From Weimar, Goethe sent three more Divan poems to Frankfurt—rather painful and gloomy ones. The first is entitled "Relief" and evokes the Greek god of the sun. Helios . . .

> *In splendor rides across the heavens*
> *As master of the firmament,*
> *And gazing forward, gazing downward,*
>
> *He spies the lovely goddess weeping,*
> *The daughter of the cloudy skies.*
> *For her alone he seems to shine,*
> *And blind to other, sunnier realms,*
>
> *He plunges into suffering, showers.*

The poem "Resonance" follows "Relief" in the final order of the cycle: *It sounds so splendid when the poet* / *Compares himself to sun or kaiser;* / *But he conceals his sadder visions* / *When skulking through his gloomy nights.* And finally, in the reflective poem "Primer," a certain distancing is already evident. It begins,

> *Strangest book of all the books*
> *Is the book of love;*
> *With attention I have read it:*
> *A few joyful pages,*
> *Chapters full of suffering,*
> *One whole section is for parting.*
> *Meeting again? a little chapter,*
> *Fragmentary.*

It never came to that *little chapter*. Goethe had planned another trip to the southwest in 1816, but the destination was Baden-Baden, with a stop in Heidelberg. For the time being, there was no talk of revisiting the Gerbermühle. But before the plan could be carried out, something happened that had been anticipated for months. On June 6, 1816, after days of agonizing cramps, Christiane died.

For the past few years the couple had lived next to more than with each other, and yet Goethe had kept Christiane informed of many—if not all—of his activities, as letters to her show, with their extensive descriptions of where he is and whom he is visiting. He had written about his journeys of the preceding year, but not of his feelings for Marianne. The tone of the couple's letters to each other is always loving. Christiane had taken care of him, run his household, and kept him company when he asked her to. Only after her death did he fully realize how indispensable she was. She had been a devoted caregiver and domestic manager but had also known how to live her life in her own circle of friends. She had a gregarious nature, was a good cook, enjoyed good food, and was very fond of wine. Theater was her passion, and Goethe respected her judgment about plays. He once joked that he put himself through the torture of directing the Weimar theater only for her sake. He explicitly urged her to enjoy herself.

Her final illness had begun in the early summer of 1815 with fainting spells, stomach cramps, and coughing up blood. Its last stages occurred the following spring. As with Schiller's death, Goethe took to his bed when Christiane died. *My wife in extreme danger,* he wrote in his diary on June 5, the day before her death. *My son a helper, adviser, the only thing I can cling to in this chaos.* On the next day: *Slept well and much better. My wife's end near: final, terrible struggle of her being. She passed away toward midday. Emptiness and deathly silence within and around me.*

Yet the very next evening he asked Riemer to come and help him with some experiments with color: activity was the only antidote to pain and despair. A few weeks later, on July 20, 1816, he set out on a trip west, accompanied by Meyer, now planning to visit the Willemers on the way to Baden-Baden. The journey ended two hours in, however, when their coach broke an axel and tipped over. Goethe was unhurt but Meyer's forehead was injured. Goethe took the accident as a bad omen and returned home. It would prove a turning point, as he forwent lengthy trips from then on. The only exceptions were a few years of regular visits to spas in Bohemia.

He and the Willemers exchanged a few more letters, in which he yearned for the Gerbermühle and Marianne yearned for her Hatem.

In one, she quoted a couplet she had found in his collected works: *Have you not yourself been thoroughly ruined? / Nothing has come of all your hopes!* Invitations to the Gerbermühle grew more urgent, almost pleading, but his letters contain only occasional, fleeting Near Eastern reminiscences. For now, that source seemed to have run dry. In October 1817, there was a letter from Goethe with a melancholy recollection of his first visit to the Gerbermühle in the fall of 1814. Then he fell silent for more than a year. "Dearest friend, what hostile genius (whether a daemon of indifference or disinclination) is the reason no friendly word of yours reaches us anymore?" Willemer wrote in some desperation. In the meantime, Marianne had composed melodies to twenty of Goethe's poems. She sang them to the guitar at family gatherings. She was so upset by Goethe's silence that her health began to suffer and she temporarily lost her voice. Willemer wrote to Goethe somewhat reproachfully. At last, in November 1818, Goethe responded. The recollection of the emergence of the *West-Eastern Divan* from their lyrical game of love had powerfully returned, for the work was finally being prepared for publication in the summer of 1818 and, while correcting the proofs, he once again fell deeply under its spell. That gave rise to even more *Divan* poems, and when he finally responded to the Willemers, he was able to include the first clean sheets. "How much joy for me," wrote Marianne. "Ennobled by your spirit, each event however small, each spontaneously uttered word, enters upon a more elevated existence. I am amazed at the familiar and am intensely happy that it belonged to me, nay, that I may in a certain sense dedicate it to myself."

Goethe would never see Marianne again, but from then on, they wrote each other more often. Her letters are no longer effusive but open, clear, and more elegiac in tone. She writes, "I was a riddle to myself; both humble and proud, embarrassed and entranced— everything seemed like a blissful dream in which you recognize an image of yourself that is more beautiful, indeed, more noble." Goethe sometimes answered in the manner of a lover, and with one poem after another. He included a manuscript of the first poem in this new series in a freshly printed copy of the *West-Eastern Divan*:

Dearest, ah! between stiff covers
Have been forced our freeborn songs.

In the purest fields of heaven
They flew back and forth between us.
Time's the ruin of all things,
Only they remain unscathed!
Every line shall be immortal,
Live forever, like our love.

For quite some time, they sent each other Near Eastern talismans and good-luck tokens: silk scarves, essence of roses, ginkgo leaves. She sends him a pair of slippers embroidered with the name Suleika and suspenders with a pattern of spring flowers, he thanks her with a poem, and so on. Only in later years does the tone of their correspondence become more sedate and serious. They begin to write about what is going on around them, rather than what is within. Going through his correspondence the year before he died, Goethe wrote to her, *and so certain special pages shine out at me, reminding me of the most beautiful days of my life.* He bundled them together and sent them to her with the request that they not be opened until after his death. Included in the package was this poem:

To the eyes of one I cherish,
To the fingers that composed them—
Once, with the most ardent soul I
Waited for their prompt arrival—
To the breast from which they sprang,
All these pages now shall wander,
Always loving, always ready,
Testaments to a glorious time.

CHAPTER 31

West-Eastern Divan and Poetry as a Life Force. Islam and
Religion in General. Poet or Prophet? What Is Spirit?
Belief and Experience. The Acknowledgment of the Sacred.
Indirect Divinity. Critique of Plotinus:
Spirit Beset by Reality. Wilhelm Meister's Journeyman Years
Put to the Test. Yearning vanishes in productive activity.
The Conflict between Prose and Poetry.
To What End Renunciation?

....

To be sure, there was more to the *West-Eastern Divan* than just the marvelous erotic role-play in the "Book of Suleika." In his announcement in advance of publication, Goethe wrote, *Even here* [i.e., in the "Book of Suleika"], *a spiritual significance sometimes makes itself felt, and the veil of earthly love seems to disguise more exalted relationships.*

The playful suggestion of higher significance is present not just in the theme of love but also at other points of the *journey,* as he called the cycle. *The poet regards himself as a traveler,* the advance announcement declares; a traveler seeking freedom more than journeying toward some goal: *Leave me in the saddle, I'm content! / Stay inside your cottage and your tent! / And I'll ride to foreign lands afar, / Above my head there's nothing but the stars.* He is a traveler investigating the customs and practices of the Near East with curiosity and amazement as he becomes better acquainted with them—and with himself.

The poet imagines the Near Eastern world as the land of poetry, where he presumes poetry pervades daily life. After love, poetry as a life force is the *West-Eastern Divan*'s second great theme. *Poetry's exuberance, / Let no one rebuke me! / May your blood be warm like mine; be / Glad and free as I am.* It is *exuberance* when it celebrates and praises and when it loves, but also when it hates. For you need to know your enemies—the enemies of freedom. They are the dogmatists, the apostles of morality, the small-minded who have no sense of beauty but appreciate only what is useful: *One thing more is necessary: / Some things must be loathed by poets. / Allow to live what's cheerful, lovely. / Don't permit what's grumpy, ugly.* An entire book, the "Book of Displeasure," is devoted to hating. The displeasure refers above all to envy—resentment at everything that is more beautiful, more successful, more noble, richer, happier, braver, and stronger than oneself. The poet expresses his displeasure in order to get his own bad feelings off his chest and then proceed calmly on his way. But first, it needs to be expressed, for example,

> *Anyone who's vexed that in His goodness*
> *God has kept Mahomed safe and wealthy,*
> *To the strongest rafter of his dwelling*
> *Let him tie a rough and sturdy rope,*
> *String himself right up! It will support him.*
> *Soon he'll feel his anger ebb away.*

In short, his displeasure is aimed at all feelings and attitudes that stand in the way of poetry. Envy cannot write poems; for that, one needs freedom—*candor*, as the *Divan* poet calls it. *Candor* and envy are mutually exclusive. Envy suppresses life, poetry enhances it. Poetry is the expression of powerful moments, and it refreshes our vital spirits—even when we are in pain and mourning—by giving sound and shape to both elevating and oppressive things. Poetry is like life, without goal or purpose, circling within itself: *Your song revolves, just like the starry vault, / Beginning, ending, always just the same.* Poetry is an imitation of this life that circles within itself, but an enhanced imitation because it overflows into beauty. There is something triumphant about the beauty of poetry, even when it comes from grief and despair.

But poetry is often closer to exhilaration, ecstasy, intoxication. The last also gets its own book in the *West-Eastern Divan*, the "Tavern Book," which celebrates inebriation both spiritual and profane—and contrary to the Prophet's prohibition, of course. Proof enough that for Goethe, the poet sometimes—especially when intoxicated—stands above the prophet. We touched upon this theme in chapter 8. *The drinker, however it may be, / Looks God more freshly in the eye.* Why *more freshly*? Because the poet sees in God not just the legislator of morality: *My glass of wine / Solo I'm drinking. / No one sets me limits. / For myself I do my thinking.* It's all said playfully, ironically, frivolously. All weighty subjects, even the serious theme of religion and the significance of the Koran and the Prophet, are infected by poetry in the *West-Eastern Divan*.

How seriously, then, does the poet take religion and especially Islam? The advance announcement of the cycle's publication declares that the poet *does not repudiate the suspicion that he himself is a Mussulman.* Is he just teasing? The young Goethe once wrote, *Prophets right and prophets left / The World's child in between.* In the *Divan* he's still a child of the world. The difference is that now, in both the cycle itself and the "Notes and Essays toward a Better Understanding of the West-Eastern Divan," he specifies which aspects of Western and Eastern religiosity are close to his heart. Basically, it is not the content, which must be revealed and believed, but rather what touches his own immediate experience. As mentioned in chapter 3, Goethe had formulated such immediate experience two years before beginning work on the *Divan*, when he wrote of his childhood in the fourth book of *Poetry and Truth*: *General, natural religion actually has no need of faith, for the conviction that behind nature was concealed, as it were, a great, productive, ordering, and directing being, in order to make itself concretely comprehensible—such a conviction is obvious to everyone.*

It is a basic conviction, beyond all question, and vague enough not to be touched by doubt. So-called revelation is another matter. It is not part of anyone's own experience, so your choice is only to believe in it or not. Such belief extends to specific occurrences like Jesus's death on the cross, resurrection, walking on water, and awakening the dead. Belief in such beatific happenings requires constant defense against doubts and doubters. It is necessary to have a homogeneous group of fellow believers who can support one another and are thereby immunized against doubt. Since the mere existence of nonbelievers or doubters threatens the faithful, their belief pushes them toward proselytizing and even fanaticism.

None of that is necessary in what Goethe calls *natural religion*. Its convictions are on the one hand much too vague to provoke doubt and on the other so self-evident that doubt can have no effect on them. His religion is not distinctive, but elementary. He speaks only of a *great being* that is *concealed* behind all nature and is definitely not manifest in a single person or a limited, unique event, to say nothing of a written document of revelation.

The Bible and the Koran were for Goethe poetic history books, interspersed here and there with wise sayings but also with the follies of their time. Within them there is a spirit that can give wings to poetry. But for an observant believer, that poetic spirit is suspect because it is free and takes liberties with dogma. The more strictly the faithful submit to moral regimentation, the more the free spirit of poetry is a thorn in their side. Airy poetic spirits must be dragged back down to earth; that is the demand of the faithful, who like to discipline others as compensation for what they deprive themselves of.

Islam for Goethe is really something poetic. But that is not what it intends to be. It is out to establish a moral regime, and Muhammad—a genuine poet with his spiritual tales—wants only to be a prophet. And so the prophet becomes the enemy of the poet, because he actually is one himself. *In his dislike of poetry, Mahomet also acts with great consistency in banning all fairy tales.* How could he not! The last thing his teaching needs is to be seen as a fairy tale. It must be the absolute truth, and therefore cannot be poetic. It must deny the dangerous fact that it springs from the same root as poetry. Through its mere existence as an inventive art, poetry undermines religion's claim to absolute truth; religion does not like to be reminded of its own invented character. Poetry accepts other claims; religion claims absolute authority, come hell or high water. That's what gives it its doctrinaire tone.

In other words, Goethe becomes uncomfortable with the Koran unless he is allowed to take it poetically. He's bored by *unending tautologies and repetitions* of commandments, threats of punishments, and promises of heavenly bliss. He admits that *again and again*, he finds this sacred text *disgusting*. But that is not his last word on the matter. In the same passage, he goes on to remark that in the end the Koran *commands his reverence* because Islam has proved that it can reshape mankind morally and create a social context. Here, Goethe is thinking historically. He writes that Muhammad's great accomplishment was to bring political unity, an expansive dynamic, and a unified moral code to scattered groups of desert dwellers. That could be done only by tailoring the guiding spiritual principle to the understanding and taste of the masses. That may be why the whole moral apparatus was necessary, as well as the promises of heavenly reward or punishment calculated to appeal to simple minds, promises that also are part of the repertoire of Christianity.

So far, so good, but the poet's business is different than the prophet's. The Prophet's goal was sovereignty and attention to the moral cultivation of the spirit; the poet's goal is the free upsurge of the individual spirit. Goethe viewed collectivist ideas of freedom with great skepticism: *Just as you never hear as much talk about freedom as when one party wants to subjugate another and aims at nothing less than shifting power, influence, and treasure from one hand to another.*

But for Goethe the moral, political, and military systems do not give an exhaustive account of Islam. Hafez is his guarantor that the spirit of Islam goes beyond them. What is its *spirit* or, as Goethe puts it, *what prevails as the supreme guiding idea?*

From a religious perspective, it is strict monotheism. The spirit may be multifarious in its appearances—and that's what poetry is concerned with—but its animating principle is the One and Indivisible, which corresponds to the human experience of identity and selfhood. *The belief in a single God always has the effect of raising the spirit by referring man back to the unity of his own inner self.* Goethe thinks that this principle is more consistently followed in Islam than in Christianity, where the idea of the Trinity was a concession to polytheism.

In the poem "Sweet Child, the String of Pearls," originally meant for inclusion in the "Book of Suleika," Christian polytheism and the symbol of the cross are pilloried from Hatem's perspective. It was provocative, even blasphemous, for Christian ears, and, on the advice of his Catholic friend Boisserée, Goethe put it away, and it was not published until after his death. Hatem calls the cross his beloved wears around her neck a thing of the devil—*Abraxas*—and counts the *miserable image on wood* as one of the objects of heathen polytheism that the Prophet has swept away: *with the one, the only God / he has conquered all the world.* But since he is in love, Hatem relents and is ready to tolerate the cross on his lover's bosom. And so he puts up with this *renegade burden*, a victory for the poetic spirit as well that overcomes the dogmatic confines of religion, at least in this one erotic situation.

In Goethe's understanding, spirit is not moral rigor but, as he says in the "Notes and Essays," an *overview of the world essence, irony, free use of one's talents*. In a letter to Zelter in which he comments on the *West-Eastern Divan*, he formulated his concept of spirit in the limpid prose of old age: *Unconditional acquiescence to the will of God, serene overview of the busy life of earth, circling and spiraling and always returning, inclination hovering between two worlds, everything real refined, resolving itself into a symbol. What more could a Grandpa want?*

Acquiescence doesn't imply determinism and defeatism, but a serenity in all one does. Do your best even though the result is not in your hands. *The will of God* does not mean something we can understand, but rather the incomprehensible. What seems superficially like chance is part of a context, but a context we are unable to illuminate in detail. Goethe tends to sense this context as primarily benevolent. The *life of earth, circling and spiraling and always returning*, on the one hand reminds us of the similarly returning *die and become* as the basic rhythm of life, and on the other is a warning not to overestimate the importance of progress. Man does not change in substance, even if the reach and depth of his technical and social tools increase and produce enormous external changes. What are the sources of the *serenity* and *irony* of this overview? They are the gentle effects of a spirit that makes things easier by allowing them to become transparent. Empirical reality is taken seriously, but by being related to a spiritual reality, it becomes translucent—*symbolic*, Goethe would call it.

What is revealed thereby? In the *West-Eastern Divan*, it is the spirit of love that pervades everything and appears everywhere, enchantingly presented in the final poem of the "Book of Suleika":

> *There are a thousand forms that thou canst hide in,*
> *And yet, my all-beloved, I shall find thee.*
> . . .
> *In purest youthful striving of the cypress*
> *I see the image of thy slender beauty.*

In limpid rippling life of the canal
I feel the touch of thy caressing hands.

. . .

And when the morning sun ignites the mountain,
Oh then I greet thee, always-cheerful one.
And when the sky spreads its pure arc above me,
Oh then I breathe thee, heart-expanding one.

Whate'er my senses and my heart have learned,
Thou all-instructing one, they know through thee.
And when I name the hundred names of Allah,
Each one contains an echo of thy name.

This lyric exaltation refers to a beloved person and at the same time to a cosmic principle—it is erotic pantheism in the form of poetic polytheism. All that's missing to complete the maxim we already know is moral monotheism: *Investigating nature / We are pantheists, / Writing poetry, polytheists, / Morally, monotheists.*

None of these three approaches is a matter of dogmatic belief, but rather of experience. That is what distances Goethe from religious communities in which individuals do not find godliness in themselves but must instead have faith in the truth of an external revelation. *There are only two true religions; one that recognizes and worships the sacred that dwells, quite formless, within and all around us; the other that recognizes and worships the sacred in the most beautiful form possible. Everything in between is idolatry.*

The sacred must *dwell* within us if it is to be a *true* religion. Thus its original foundation is experience and not simply belief and opinion. *Formless* and *in the most beautiful form*—that is the other significant differentiation. As for which forms count as *most beautiful*, Goethe made no secret of his preferences. He venerated sculptural representations of the ancient gods and demigods, ancient temples and ceremonial vessels, hymns and stories of the gods. Christianity couldn't hold a candle to the wealth of forms of classical antiquity, although he did admire the image of the Holy Family, which he used at the beginning of *Wilhelm Meister's Journeyman Years.* For Goethe, the spiritual content must be able to be embodied, which can sometimes be very difficult in the case of Christianity's transcendental faith. Goethe was capable of making irreverent jokes about the haloes and doves above the heads of the saints or the speech ribbons unfurling from the mouths of the central figures in medieval paintings. He positively hated the cross and the representation of martyred bodies and was annoyed by the sanctimoniousness of the Nazarene painters.

But what does *formless* recognition of the divine mean? One finds it where there is no special form for the recognition or even for the worship of the divine; instead, it is realized in the way that the duties and tasks of everyday life are carried out. It amounts to the sanctification of the work of life itself, as expressed in the *Divan* poem "The Legacy of Ancient Persian Faith": *Let this be a sacred legacy / To fraternal will, and a reminder: / Every day complete the hardest tasks and / That is revelation, there's no other.* The following strophes depict elementary activities, from burying the dead to working in the fields, from house construction to irrigation. These acts, the daily work of maintaining and enriching life, appear as indirect worship. You do your work, fulfill your duty, pursue your goals, and if you do it with devotion, something higher is revealed: the spirit of constructive living. That was Goethe's idea, and that's why he was an adherent of indirect divinity.

Indirectness—for Goethe it was a central theme in his thinking about God, the absolute, and transcendence. As a result of his encounter with Plotinus and Neoplatonism, after 1805 he formulated the basic principles of his theology and the philosophy of indirectness, which remained definitive from then on.

The philosopher Hermann Schmitz was the first to recognize the fundamental importance of Goethe's critique of Plotinus,* first formulated in 1805 and published only later. Goethe writes, *One can hardly blame ancient and modern idealists for vigorously urging the acceptance of the One from which everything flows and to which everything is to be attributed. For of course, the enlivening and organizing principle in a phenomenon is so beset with difficulties that it can barely save itself. However, we shortchange ourselves in the other direction if we force the forming power and the higher form itself back into a unity that is invisible to our external and internal senses.*

* Hermann Schmitz, *Goethes Altersdenken im problemgeschichtlichen Zusammenhang* (Bonn: H. Bouvier, 1959).

The *One* is what is usually called "God" or an all-determining "Spirit." The decisive statement is that this *One* is *beset* in empirical reality. With this formulation, Goethe hints at the whole modern drama of materialism and atheism: spirit is no longer found in nature and in the end, not in man either. It is no help to remove spirit from our *external and internal senses*, by which he means the abstractions of mathematics and metaphysical speculation, whereby spirit is forced back into unobservable abstraction rather than relocated in reality. That is what Goethe was protesting against. His belief is that spirit can be sensed, if not captured, everywhere in nature. To be sure, the precondition for that to happen is the abandonment of Plotinus's Platonic prejudice, which persists subliminally in the present, namely, that the transition from idea to reality always represents a loss, analogous to the divine creator's superior rank vis-à-vis his creation. And so Goethe continues in his critique of Plotinus, *A spiritual form, however, is by no means diminished when it emerges as a phenomenon, provided that its emergence is a genuine begetting, a true propagation. The begotten is not less than the begetter. Indeed, it is an advantage of living propagation that the begotten can be more excellent than the begetter.*

What Goethe here suggests is nothing less than the idea of a natural evolution that goes beyond the maintenance of life to follow the principle of enhancement of life. Thus spirit is not diminished in reality; on the contrary, it drives reality out of a state of dull self-absorption and into the sunlight—until at last the unnoticed but all-pervading spirit becomes aware of itself in the human mind. Nor is spirit diminished in nature; on the contrary, it is made manifest in nature as a productive principle that in the end comprehends itself in human beings. This is the living process of propagation, a progressive process. In the final analysis, it is the thought of a developing God in nature.

But what is "indirect" about this conceptual context? For Goethe, transcendence is never directly apprehended by means of some rare revelation, but rather immanent only in empirical reality, a deepening of empirical experience. The transcendent is what has an effect, and thus is only to be apprehended in its effects. It is the living principle that drives external reality and motivates us internally, a riddle better solved by pursuing the practical business of life than by theorizing.

The practical business of life, however, can have its pitfalls. It leads directly into the web of society. Whatever experiences, intentions, wishes, and hopes dwell within the individual, they never achieve pure expression. There are some natural impediments, but, above all, the problem is the social medium through which ideas are refracted, distracted, and distorted. This *besetting affliction* in the social sphere is caused by envy, competition, disapproval, indifference, hectic activity, and—especially emphasized by Goethe—gossip.

> *What I fear: the captiousness*
> *Of all repugnant gossip,*
> *Where talk is fleeting, nothing sticks,*
> *It disappears before my eyes*
> *And I am tangled in the coils*
> *Of a gray net of worry.*

As Goethe grew older he began to perceive society—not only, but primarily—as just such a *gray net of worry* in which it was all too easy to become enmeshed and cheated of the best that one had, a perception that would later be called alienation. It's necessary to wear a mask, and, what's worse, the mask is forced upon us and in the end we don't even know who we really are. Thus it can happen *that the absurd course of the world can intrude between what is best and most delightful.*

Of course, critiques of society have a long tradition, but it is striking that Goethe's unease about society was increasing at the moment when, in the wake of the French Revolution, society was being discovered as a location of ideas and truth. It was Hegel, whom Goethe had appointed professor at Jena and with whom he had a fairly close friendship, who ennobled that conception of society at the highest philosophical level. Ever since Hegel, there has been a new kind of philosophizing. Philosophy had been dominated by a clear duality: man is here, and being—whether divine or natural—is there. After Hegel, the newly discovered world of society intrudes between the two poles. Now society (together with its history) becomes the absolute in which all other dichotomies and polarities are contained. To Hegel, society is objective spirit. Until then, society had been simply real; now it became a truth. The old metaphysics of being disappears in this new metaphysics of society, and the old religious precepts—faith, love, and hope—are now related to society and its progress. The Hegelian zeitgeist declared that freedom originated through society. Goethe, however, believed he needed to defend his freedom against society. The best thoughts, he once wrote to Meyer, were *dulled, disturbed, and distracted by the moment, the century, by localities and other particulars.* As far as he was concerned, it was society that cheated him of his best.

But Goethe doesn't just complain about it. He is much too aware of the creative power of his singularity. He included these lines in his *Tame Xenias*: *Go ahead and wrap the world / In the net you've made! / In my own living sphere I know / How to gain life for myself.*

If Goethe thought he had to wrest the truth of his life from society, then for him, that restrictive, distorting, leveling society was part of the *affliction* that, according to his critique of Plotinus, was *besetting* the *enlivening* principles. This conviction is not at odds with the ready pleasure he took in being active, receiving new impulses, and intervening in social circumstances. He had many official social and political responsibilities. Much as he loved and practiced contemplation, he had a thoroughly active nature. When he had spent a few years in Weimar, he wrote to Knebel, *My nature forces me into multifarious activities, and even to live in the humblest village or on a deserted island, I would need to be just as busy.*

Thus society is definitely a field for Goethe to prove himself in, but also the realm against which he must assert himself to retain his integrity. Precisely because he was so receptive and sensitive, so open to the world, he was careful not to allow himself to be ensnared to the point of insensibility. Goethe calls the strict *egoism* of self-assertion in the face of an excess of worldly intrusion the *indispensable, sharp, selfish principle.* If the individual is not to go under in the bustle and whirl of society, he must have the inner coherence that Goethe once called, with reference to minerals, *the gravitational force toward oneself.* The selfish principle gives a person something off-putting, compact, impenetrable. The analogy to the mineral world was so obvious to Goethe that in his last novel, on which he resumed intense and uninterrupted work after completing the *West-Eastern Divan*, he depicts Montan (the former Jarno)—the protagonist and embodiment of the hard, impervious aspects of the selfish principle—as a man of the mountains and stones.

Wilhelm Meister's Journeyman Years, or The Renunciants is the great novel of Goethe's last decade. Its main theme is the *affliction* with which social reality besets the *enlivening principles* and the possibility of sustained resistance to it. The novel enacts models of how intellectual and spiritual life can assert themselves or become ossified. Utopias are also presented, but it is not clear whether they are realizations or betrayals of the spirit, whether they are meant as dreams or as nightmares. Between sequences of deep thought, numerous stories are interspersed with only loose connections to the main plot and no clear inner connections to one another. These tales take up so much room that the plot seems almost like a frame narrative, and the entire novel threatens to lose coherence. The frame includes depictions of several social utopias, reflective passages that expand into essays, and letters. Add to that a central character restricted to the role of onlooker and a love story that plays out between a novella and the frame narrative, and you have what can only be described as a hodgepodge.

Here the *organizing principles* are also beset, if they have not completely disappeared. This is even mentioned in an *interim remark* in which it remains unclear who is speaking—the real author or a fictive narrator. First, the hodgepodge is named and then the work on the novel is described: *So if we are not again to bog down in this business, as has happened so often these many years, there is nothing for it but to pass on what we possess, communicate what has been preserved.* Readers of this work of *quickly passing shape* must fill in the blanks for themselves in what has not been *completely developed,* i.e., its inner coherence. This disarmingly frank confession, however, is only in the first, significantly shorter 1821 version of the *Journeyman Years.* In the second and final version of 1829, it was dropped. It is typical of Goethe's style in old age: he simply claims the freedom to leave the heterogeneity of a work without feeling the need to justify it. The open form in which poetry, aphorisms, stories, essays, and letters succeed each other is left to speak for itself. *What has been written, like what has happened, asserts its right to be,* as he once wrote imperturbably to Reinhard.

As the *interim remark* concedes, work on the *Journeyman Years* had bogged down several times. Even while finishing *Wilhelm Meister's Apprenticeship* in 1796, Goethe was thinking about a continuation. In the first Wilhelm Meister novel, he built in some things that could serve as a bridgehead to a sequel, such as Wilhelm's assignment to set off as a journeyman. First he wrote a few stories that were meant to be included in the sequel, but he told Schiller that he was going to lock what was *idealistic* about it in a *little box*, hoping he could do something with it *when I finally become conscious of my own intentions.* In other words, he was writing and collecting things for the *Journeyman Years*, though the central idea wasn't clear to him yet. Most of the novellas and stories were completed by 1807. The chapters containing the wisdom of the elderly Makarie and some of the utopian schemes were not added until the 1820s. Between 1810 and 1819, he did almost no work at all on the novel, and only when he had finished the *West-Eastern Divan* did he take it up again, quickly completing the first draft, which he published in 1821 without feeling that the novel was really done. It received very little notice, and Goethe grimly remarked, *The second part will not be any more satisfactory than the first, but I hope to satisfy the reader who has grasped the latter well.* Be that as it may, such readers were few and far between, which didn't prevent Goethe from undertaking additions and revisions for the next edition.

The final version of the *Journeyman Years*, appearing in 1829, preserved the novel's heterogeneity of content and its open form; indeed, it reinforced them by inserting maxims and reflections collected under the titles "Reflections in the Spirit of the Journeymen" and "From Makarie's Archives." In conversation with Chancellor Müller, Goethe remarked that it was silly *to want to construct and analyze the whole thing systematically,* since it was nothing but an *aggregation.* He did not think this aggregative character was a weakness, but rather a sign that the novel was especially close to real life. *With a little book like this, however,* he wrote to Rochlitz, *it's like life itself: in the complex whole one finds some things that are necessary and others that are accidental, the central and the peripheral, sometimes successful, sometimes not, through which it achieves a kind of endlessness that cannot be completely grasped in sensible and reasonable words.*

The appropriate way to deal with such a book was to *become engaged in details as they emerge.* We shall take that advice and be content to emphasize a few details characteristic of the last period of Goethe's life.

First, as already suggested, what Goethe called the novel's aggregative character means that its form mirrors the problem it addresses. For what is depicted is how spiritual principles are *beset* in dispersive reality, as Goethe discussed in his critique of Plotinus. The novel is close to real life precisely because it is not a homogeneous work. Like life, it is disparate, contains *some things that are necessary and others that are accidental*. It is not as beautifully transparent and orderly as one might want, but that's exactly why there is a peculiar *kind of endlessness* to it. It is the endlessness of things unfinished to which new and different things can constantly be added, whose end is imposed from without, a breaking-off rather than a completion. If life cannot achieve such completion, however, then how is it possible to become what the *West-Eastern Divan* calls a *personality* in the chaos of circumstances that make up the life of society? The novel plumbs some of the possibilities—and impossibilities.

At the beginning a young man, *Saint Joseph the Second*, as the novel calls him, is taking care of a widow and her child and is determined to live a life like the one depicted in legends about Mary and Joseph. In the end, the three of them really do resemble the Holy Family familiar from old paintings—or from the paintings of the Nazarenes, whom Goethe was not very fond of, as we have seen. Saint Joseph the Second finds his way through the confusion of life in devotion to his role model. Given Goethe's antipathy for the Nazarenes, it is unclear whether the existence chosen by his character is after all only an example—albeit a charming one—of the continuing power of the superannuated: *Life belongs to the living, and the living must be prepared for change.* Joseph the Second avoids change as long as he can fit himself and the widow and her child into an image. Wilhelm Meister feels himself transferred into a *wondrously old-fashioned atmosphere*, as if he were seeing before him, in a dream, a series of moving images. He too is stirred by a longing to disappear into those images, but he is awakened from his drifting dreams by an encounter with Jarno, familiar to us as the cynic in *Wilhelm Meister's Apprenticeship* and now known as Montan.

Joseph is like the images he reveres; Montan is like the rocks he collects and studies. He prefers their mute company to the babble of humans. Stone is hard and durable, man mutable and frail. Stone is impenetrable, man permeable and vulnerable. Montan loves rocks more than people, on whom he has turned his back. *I decided to avoid people. There's no helping them, and they hinder us from helping ourselves.*

Thus the first two figures we encounter in this novel represent two extremes. Joseph the Second centers his life on imitating his namesake. Impenetrable as stone, Montan immunizes himself against all possible influences. He is the embodiment of the *selfish* principle at its most obdurate. And it is Montan who rejects the ideal of well-rounded education promulgated in *Wilhelm Meister's Apprenticeship*. One should specialize in something, he declares, and not flutter about like some dilettantish butterfly, taking a sip of this and that. What is called for is not universal receptivity but toughening up for a particular function; not education but training for what will benefit society—and yourself—because then you won't get lost in distractions. *Yes, now is the time for being one-sided*, he declares, and urges Wilhelm, with his multifarious interests, *Make yourself into an organ and wait to see what place well-intentioned humanity will grant you in our common life.*

Of all people, it is the reclusive Montan who promotes useful contributions to the mechanisms of society. However, that is not as inconsistent as it sounds. The lover of rocks proceeds from self-reification to self-petrification. No wonder Wilhelm, who once *sought true treasure in the human heart*, can hardly bear to listen to Montan's disquisitions. But like other figures in the novel, Montan does not remain static, condemned to represent a single principle. In the course of the novel, he becomes milder. His misanthropy is transformed into skepticism and caution. Nevertheless, he remains the advocate of a strict realism that rejects all romanticism and sentimentality.

The next stop on Wilhelm's journey, his uncle's country estate, is not particularly pleasant either. Tellingly, Wilhelm and his son, Felix, are first put into prison. That is his uncle's customary way to receive company, and soon it becomes clear that the rules for living on his estate are simply imprisonment by another name. The spirit of those rules is as utilitarian and antipoetical as anything Montan could wish. Above the doors of the workhouses stands the slogan *From Utility through Truth to Beauty*. Here too, the emphasis is on usefulness, and in order to stand a chance, beauty must pass through the eye of its needle. *In the entire castle, said the caretaker, you will not find a single picture that even vaguely refers to religion, tradition, mythology, legend, or fable. Our master wishes to promote the use of our imaginations only to envision truth. He likes to say that we fabulate enough as it is without using external stimuli to encourage that dangerous characteristic of our intellect.*

Wilhelm's uncle is pursuing a program of social reform. Nothing is wasted; everything is reinvested to increase production and provide people with work and wages. The uncle regards himself as a philanthropist. He has had pleasure gardens and parks removed and replaced by fruit trees and vegetable beds. He does not forgo owning property, but intends it to serve the community, *for the rich are only admired*, he declares, *insofar as others enjoy life thanks to them.* He aims at enjoyments that promote and perhaps even increase the ability to work. Sundays are spent in silence: *everyone remains solitary and they devote themselves to prescribed contemplation. Man is a limited being, and Sundays are devoted to reflecting on our limitation.* On workdays people are limited by their duties, and on Sundays they think about that limitation. And so they are not tempted to use at least that one day to kick over the traces. The clever Hersilie, with whom Wilhelm will fall in love, notices that something is wrong with this arrangement. *What kind of nice life is this*, she cries, *when I have to resign myself to it once a week?*

His uncle's estate is the first actual utopia that Wilhelm visits, and it is still relatively liberal. The ones to come will be even more restrictive. Common to all of them is the primacy of utility and usefulness. The individual is a mere organ in an organism or, better, a cog in a machine. You are nothing, your community is everything. What the novel's utopian projects have in common is the sober-sided and deeply prosaic principle that *yearning vanishes in productive activity.*

Yearning, fantasy, mystery, melancholy, high spirits, and all sorts of madcap antics are swept from the main (or frame) narrative and transferred to the novellas. In the frame story, the weak-willed Wilhelm Meister wanders as an onlooker from one utopian project to the next, and a group of *renunciants* drifts through this wasteland of orderliness. Once, Mignon's famous song from *Wilhelm Meister's Apprenticeship* is heard in fragmentary phrases from far away: *Knowst thou the land where lemons are in bloom, / Dark leafy shade.* . . . On the shores of Lago Maggiore, the *renunciants* have gathered. *The women threw themselves into each other's arms, the men embraced, and Luna witnessed the noblest, most virtuous tears.* But soon they are in a quandary again: *They slowly returned to their senses and separated, silently, with the strangest feelings and wishes, which, however, already had no hope of fulfillment.*

These are capable people, paragons of virtue, and yet to no avail;

despite the Romantic landscape, the reader is witness to the downfall of poetry: *As if under a magic spell, this paradise was now transformed for the friends into an utter wasteland.* Novalis, the arch-Romantic who had already accused *Wilhelm Meister's Apprenticeship* of betraying poetry, would have been appalled by this complete triumph of prose.

What is not clear is whether Goethe thought that the disappearance of yearning *in productive activity* was a good thing, or simply unavoidable in the dawning of an age of machines and objectivity. The novel itself gives no satisfactory indication of whether it is a critique or a symptom of the demystification of the world. The ideas of the emigrants and their plans for a settlement in America oscillate between dream and nightmare. We hear that measures will be taken against wasting time, *telegraphs* will be built to remind everyone day and night of what time it is. Everyone's usefulness will be *highly promoted by dividing up time and paying attention to each hour.* There will be police to enforce the schedule with the robust principle that *whoever proves disruptive will be removed until he understands how to behave in order to be tolerated.* Mignon and company would certainly not be tolerated. There will be a mobile government whose leaders travel from place to place, so that for some settlers the authorities will be absent while others will have them on their backs. In this way, everyone will enjoy the benefits of liberality and austerity in turn, and *equality* will be guaranteed. The question of democracy and majority rule elicits a cautious reply: *We have our own distinctive thoughts about the majority; of course we honor it in the necessary course of the world, but in a higher sense we don't put much trust in it. But I must not say anything more about that.* Other plans for disciplining the settlement are discussed at much greater length. Brandy taverns and lending libraries must disappear; consumption of alcohol and novels will be restricted. One might assume that a novel like the *Journeyman Years,* however, would meet with no objections from these apostles of sobriety.

But the world of the novel is not populated exclusively by *renunciants* and those who have nothing to renounce. There is Felix, for one, Wilhelm's son, the embodiment of fresh strength and lust for life. He lives and falls in love and suffers the usual follies that entails. And in any case, things are much livelier in the novellas. A problem close to Goethe's heart, the love of an older man for a younger woman, is treated—twice, in fact—using the fairly risqué situation of father and son competing for the same woman. Without making a great deal of it, we should mention here that in 1816 Goethe pressured his son, August, to marry Ottilie von Pogwisch, an attractive, intelligent young woman whom Goethe himself wanted to have nearby, and who wanted to be near him, although she wrote to her mother about the wedding plans, "Goethe frightens me;—and asks more than before how it will turn out." When Ottilie finally married August—without being in love with him—she did so only because she worshipped his father. The letters she exchanged with August are sober, businesslike, and prosaic; those to her father-in-law are poetry. In any event, the story of Ottilie could easily have found a place in the cycle of novellas in the *Journeyman Years*.

Then there is the figure who transcends the entire world of the novel, including the novella cycle: Makarie, a central star not yet risen in the book's first version. Goethe invented her as a counterweight, so that the novel would not be too dominated by the spirit of efficiency and so that *yearning* would not entirely *vanish in productive activity*. Makarie is the continuation of the Beautiful Soul in *Wilhelm Meister's Apprenticeship*, with more intellectual heft. Montan on the one hand and Makarie on the other: one attracted by stones and the other by stars; one drawn down *to the midpoint of the earth* and the other up and out *beyond the limits of our solar system*. Montan wants to bring things down to earth, to clip the wings of poetry and philosophical speculation, which is why he insists on utility and usefulness. He is the enemy of flights of fancy, and since he deprives himself of things, he is full of resentment toward those who indulge themselves. Makarie is his opposite. She lives in a vision of cosmic connections, but her body is already in *sickly decline*. Nevertheless, she is mysteriously cheerful and infects everyone who visits her with her cheer. People encountering her feel wondrously light and bright. With an ironic wink, the narrator takes special notice of the fairy-tale effect when the doors into her house open automatically. Her entire being is open, just as Montan's is closed. Makarie suffuses and is suffused by everything. She is entirely transparent and permeable. She possesses inner composure without being hard or rigid. In her *archives*, Goethe deposited some of his most brilliant maxims and reflections, including those we have already quoted on Plotinus and the *besetting affliction* of the enlivening principles. Makarie has surely transcended such affliction, but, for that reason, seems not quite real. She lives her life among the higher orders of being: the regular progression of the constellations, the play of attraction and repulsion, the oscillation between time and eternity, the music of the spheres. Makarie is on the verge of dissolving, melting away into those regions: *she seems to have been born only to deliver herself from the earthly and suffuse the nearest and farthest spaces of existence.*

At the high point of these heavenly digressions, the narrator turns back to the ground crew with the words *As we herewith bring to a close this ethereal poetry in the hope of forgiveness, let us return to those terrestrial fairy tales.*

Both versions of the novel bear the subtitle *The Renunciants.* What does this renunciation mean? It means forgoing the realization of something, even though you actually wish it and many factors urge you on. It can be a relationship, an action, or a possession. Renunciation is connected to sacrifice. You can renounce not only what you already possess but also the striving to possess it. You merely need to have some stake in what is renounced. Without a stake, renunciation is neither necessary nor possible.

But why should anyone renounce anything? Goethe wrote about that question in the late 1820s in the fourth book of *Poetry and Truth*, following an almost programmatic reflection on Spinoza: *Both our physical and our social life . . . everything calls upon us to renounce.* But why? In order to forestall an even greater loss. If we repeatedly become attached to what time will eventually take away, we will suffer repeated disappointment. Then it can make sense *to become resigned once and for all in order to avoid all partial resignations.* That can mean forgoing things, but sometimes an inner letting-go suffices—having something as if one didn't have it. Thus you can arm yourself against disappointment and say, with Heidegger, that renunciation gives rather than taking away.

The refusal to realize a plan, the accumulation of a surplus of incompletion, and the willpower involved in such renunciation can all enrich one's personality. The renunciant is better equipped for self-preservation in the face of loss. Those who don't decide to renounce will have to forgo things in desperation. The renunciant retains his sovereignty, but sometimes that's all, and it could be too little.

Of course, the heart of the matter is erotic renunciation. That's why Wilhelm and Natalie are the real renunciants in the *Journeyman Years*. They find their way to each other at the end of *Wilhelm Meister's Apprenticeship*, but forgo actualizing their love except in letters. Why do they do that? Is it to preserve the erotic suspense that might be quickly extinguished in sexual fulfillment? Renouncing to keep longing and yearning alive? That may apply to Wilhelm and Natalie, but not to the questionable utopian schemes of the *Journeyman Years*. There, as we have heard, even yearning is meant to *disappear* in productive activity, by fulfilling the practical *demands of everyday life*.

Wilhelm has also abandoned his youthful dreams. Once the world of art—and especially the theater—had allowed him to feel the protean nature of ever-changing life. The Society of the Tower and the Association of Emigrants, the Pedagogical Province and his uncle's country estate—these are the all too orderly counterworlds that assign everyone a useful place. That too is renunciation, and it colors the entire novel.

Why was such a drastic cure needed? It is astonishing that Goethe provides no satisfactory answer in his novel. Probably we will have to seek it in his life.

CHAPTER 32

Memory Work. *Repeated reflection*. Between Walls of Paper.
The Aged Goethe in Company.
Why Always Think the Same Thing?
Against the Spirit of the Times and for the Carlsbad Decrees.
Three Sojourns in Marienbad. Ulrike and the Elegy. Farewells.

....

N EARLY SUMMER 1816, GOETHE CLIMBED UNHURT OUT OF
the tipped-over coach that was to convey him to the Gerbermühle
and Marianne Willemer, and he took the accident as an evil omen. He
decided to forgo the visit and even stopped writing to Marianne for a
while. It was a genuine renunciation. He also let the *West-Eastern Divan*
languish unfinished for a few years, in melancholy recollection of those
happier days yet half hoping for their return. *But for us what bliss it is to
/ Dip our hand in the Euphrates, / In the fluid element to / Wander back and
forth.* But he was not inclined to do any such wandering these days,
so it was like a gift of fate when he received the page proofs for the
West-Eastern Divan in 1818 and that magical mood returned for a brief
time. Usually, he was even more vigilant than before not to betray his
inner feelings in public, but to maintain a reserved formality. That was
also the impression of the widowed Charlotte Kestner, née Buff—the
Lotte of his Wetzlar days—when she stopped in Weimar to visit her
brother-in-law Ridel in 1816 and was invited to dine at Goethe's house.
She wrote to her son, "I've made a new acquaintance: an old man. If
I didn't know it was Goethe—and even though I did—he still didn't
make a good impression on me. You know how little I expected from
this reunion—or rather from this new acquaintance. So I was quite
unself-conscious. And in his stiff way, he did everything possible to be
obliging to me." Charlotte was accompanied by her daughter, who also

found Goethe to be quite cold. She reported, "Unfortunately, however, all his conversation was so ordinary, so superficial, that it would be presumptuous of me to say I heard him talking or talked to him, for nothing that he said came from within or even from his mind."

Goethe had only recently recounted his memories of Wetzlar and Werther's love in the third part of *Poetry and Truth*. That long-vanished world had again been in his thoughts. Perhaps that was the reason he was chary of too close contact with what remained of it. If Charlotte was disappointed by him, so was he by her. Her presence seemed dull compared with her image in his memory. He could not summon up the magic of *repeated reflection*; obviously, that was something that happened only when a memory was reshaped as literature. *Repeated reflection* is what he called a process he compared to that of the so-called entoptic colors—in which colors appearing in a mirrored surface that has been heated and allowed to cool down become brighter and more intense in another mirror facing the first one. According to Goethe, the same thing happens to memory processed by literature. *When we consider that repeated . . . reflections not only keep the past alive but even raise it to a higher life, it will remind us of the entoptic phenomena.* Recollected images are enhanced by the medium of literature, but not by encountering acquaintances after many years. Goethe and Lotte sat together for a while and felt they had been left high and dry. It took a Thomas Mann to wring some literary charm from the unsuccessful encounter in his novel *Lotte in Weimar* (translated into English as *The Beloved Returns*).

After the publication of the first three parts of *Poetry and Truth*, Goethe continued to work on the autobiography with a growing feeling of alienation from the present. He wrote to Zelter, *I continue to live life in my own way, with which you are familiar, see few people and am actually living only in the past by attempting to sort through and edit old papers of every kind.* The ailing Schiller had complained that he was sitting between walls of written paper, and now Goethe sometimes felt the same way. In another letter to Zelter: *I've been spending my winter in almost complete solitude, busily dictating so that my entire existence is down on paper.* What ends up on the page is a reflection of a reflection of what he had written in years gone by, and he is retrospectively surprised at his own insouciance. *One certainly feels the earlier endeavor to be serious and diligent,* he writes to Boisserée, *one becomes acquainted with one's own merits, merits that are now lacking. . . . What's more, the century is spreading out in all directions, on paths both right and wrong, so that a naïveté like mine, moving innocently forward, step by step, seems to me to play a wondrous role.* Once he had put up with Schiller's definition of him as a "naïve" writer, and now for the first time he uses the word himself. He sees himself wandering like a sleepwalker, and he knows that it was the only way he could have acted. You need to be insouciant; he would later declare that the active person has to be without conscience. He would otherwise have been condemned to immobility. Acting and creating mean a narrowing, a closing off of yourself to produce something that has a breadth of its own. And so he was quite content to read his old published works and manuscripts. He was reading his way into himself and felt an inner expansion. But he preferred to recollect things instead of being recollected: he neglected to answer inquiries from Bettine von Arnim. He probably hadn't forgiven her for calling Christiane a "fat blood sausage" during an argument.

It had become lonelier in the big house on the Frauenplan since Christiane's death. Ottilie and August lived on the top floor, where they often argued loudly. Goethe was happy to put up with his noisy grandchildren, but not with the arguments. He was deluding himself when he wrote of the young couple, *they went well together even if they didn't love each other.* Not only weren't they in love; they weren't at all suited to each other, and there was constant discord. At times it was more than Goethe could stand, and he moved to the garden house. He also frequently escaped to Jena even though there was no longer a Schiller, a Schelling, or a Humboldt to be found there.

Once he confided to Chancellor Müller what he would have liked life in the house on the Frauenplan to be: *Wouldn't it be possible to have a standing invitation to a company that would gather in my house every day, now in greater and now in lesser number? People would come and stay as long as they liked and could bring any guests they wished. The rooms would always be open and illuminated from seven o'clock on, and tea and paraphernalia always at the ready. People would make music, play cards, give readings, chat—everything according to inclination and whim. I myself would appear and then disappear as the spirit moved me. And if I sometimes absented myself entirely, that shouldn't cause any disturbance. . . . Thus an everlasting tea would be organized, like the eternal light that burns in some chapels.*

A permanent open house, comings and goings like an inn, continuous socializing, and without even needing to be present to remain the center of attention. The only surprising thing is that it was supposed to be *an everlasting tea*. Wine would actually have been more appropriate in a house where it otherwise flowed so freely, both for the head of the house downstairs and for the youngsters on the top floor. The unfortunate reality, however, whether tea or wine was drunk, was that life was not so free and easy. The sedate formal dinners had become fairly stiff affairs. Many came to the house—in fact, there was an almost constant stream of visitors. People paid their respects and Goethe granted audiences—sometimes casual and sometimes elaborate. He would appear with the medal on his chest and hands clasped behind his back, ask a few questions, and respond with his famous *Hm hm*. Unforgettable, however, were his large, alert, observant eyes. Ordinarily, one was not invited to sit down. But sometimes something ignited his interest, and he would begin speaking in his sonorous and gently flowing voice, stringing words out like pearls on a necklace. The tension would suddenly relax, both in him and in his listener. But it didn't happen very often, and occasionally he remained quite silent. On many evenings when he didn't feel like talking but didn't want to be alone, his loyal helpers Riemer, Meyer, and Eckermann would have to keep him company, all nursing their wine in silence.

But when he was in an expansive mood, they had to be prepared for surprises. Since he didn't think much of mere opinions, he liked to play with them in order to confuse his interlocutors or even put their nose out of joint. He once told Chancellor Müller, with whom he liked to play Mephisto (with Eckermann he usually played Faust), *Eh, have I gotten to be 80 years old in order to always think the same thing? No, I strive to think something different, something <u>new</u> every day so I won't become a bore. You have to keep changing all the time, renew yourself, grow youthful again, so you don't get in a rut.*

The official role he had to play in public did not make it easy to be youthful again. As a poet he was the national soul; as an official, a *public personage* as he called himself. In 1815, the Congress of Vienna had promoted Weimar to the status of grand duchy, which brought with it a considerable increase in territory. The duke could now call himself "Royal Highness" and Goethe was elevated to the rank of "Minister of State," although he no longer belonged to the cabinet but functioned only in the background, as an adviser. He did not want to be burdened with day-to-day tasks, and the duke graciously excused him from them. His salary grew while his formal duties shrank. His official title was "Head Supervisor of the Ducal Institutions for Science and Art in Weimar and Jena." It no longer included the time-consuming supervision of the university or, since the spring of 1817, the direction of the Weimar theater. The friction with Frau von Heygendorf, the former Karoline Jagemann, had not been settled after the crisis of 1808. She continued to think Goethe was not a proper theater director, found him too negligent in day-to-day operations, and moreover wanted more concessions to popular taste. The leading role in a light French farce was supposed to be played by a trained poodle, and she succeeded in putting it on over Goethe's express opposition. He thereupon let it be known that he didn't intend to be there to watch the theater go to the dogs and would probably resign the directorship. The duke, hoping to prevent the poisoning of their friendship, relieved him of that obligation.

Despite the scaling back of official duties, Goethe continued to represent the Weimar state. There was not a crowned head or minister of state paying a visit to Weimar who did not also pay his respects to Goethe in the house on the Frauenplan, giving him the opportunity to wear the cross of the Légion d'honneur that Napoleon had awarded him. Such receptions were expensive affairs and to help defray costs, Goethe asked for and was granted some tax relief.

On an income that, supplemented by royalties from his books, sometimes amounted to ten thousand taler a year, he paid a tax of barely one hundred fifty taler. And yet he thought he had to save and was annoyed at the fees he still had to pay as a registered citizen of Frankfurt. He therefore requested permission to resign his citizenship and was duly removed from the municipal rolls, for which he paid thirty kreutzer without further ado.

Frankfurt was the seat of the German Confederation, the fairly toothless umbrella organization of German (as well as some non-German) principalities newly founded or reorganized by the Congress of Vienna. Goethe's friend Karl Friedrich von Reinhard, who spent decades in the service of various French governments, was there as France's representative and was able to keep Goethe informed about European politics. The efforts of the patriotic bourgeoisie to unite Germany were not appreciated by the German Confederation, and it was known that Goethe didn't think much of them either. In 1817, he published a sharply worded polemic against "New German Religio-Patriotic Art" in the second number of *Über Kunst und Altertum* (*On Art and Antiquity*), the journal he edited during his final decade as an organ for his views. It took aim not only at the Catholic art of the Nazarene painters but also more generally at patriotic masquerading and sentimental worship of the Middle Ages. He was vexed to see *Götz von Berlichingen* being exploited as nationalist propaganda. Sulpiz Boisserée had occasionally been able to interest him in medieval painting and sculpture and Goethe had advocated continued construction on the Cologne cathedral, but he did not want either thing linked to some patriotic political agenda. He loved old things when they had life in them, not when they were artificially revived to serve political ends. Thus, he gave a lovely depiction of medieval tradition in his "Festival of Saint Roch in Bingen," but with no intention of being a propagandist for the world of Catholicism. The church festival fascinated him as had the Roman carnival in times gone by.

The grand duchy of Weimar was especially attuned to the new political climate. The grand duke had granted his state the constitution promised by the German Federal Act of the Congress of Vienna, which gave the estates the right to approve taxes and guaranteed freedom of the press. Goethe was no friend of these renovations or of the switch to a constitutional monarchy. He did not perceive the duchy as representing any threat to human rights. He preferred patriarchal rule to democratic institutions, with a ruling elite selflessly looking after the interests of the people. He was in favor of free trade and the ownership of real property unencumbered by feudal privileges. That was the extent of his political and social principles and wishes. He didn't think much of freedom of the press; as far as he was concerned, it gave free reign to demagogues and idiots and encouraged general politicizing. Nothing had changed in his annoyance at *the agitated* since the 1790s, when he wrote plays against the revolution. But now, encouraged by the liberal press laws, several patriotic and democratic newspapers had opened offices in Weimar, of all places—Heinrich Luden's *Nemesis*, for instance, and Lorenz Oken's *Isis*. They printed heated polemics against the reactionary, authoritarian spirit and pilloried Habsburg and Russian predominance in German affairs as a national tragedy. For patriots all over Germany, Weimar became known as a bastion of progress. For Metternich and most of the other rulers, however, Weimar was a thorn in their flesh, and when the first *Burschenschaft*, or student fraternity, was founded in Jena in 1815, people called the grand duke the *Altbursche*—the Old Boy.

In October 1817, a nationalist festival was held on the Wartburg (where Martin Luther had taken refuge to work on his Bible translation) to celebrate the Reformation and the victory over Napoleon in the Battle of Leipzig. There was a bonfire of some books the students considered reactionary, including the works of Kotzebue, who was accused of being a Russian spy. When the fraternity member and student of theology Karl Ludwig Sand stabbed Kotzebue to death a year and a half later, on March 23, 1819, Metternich used the assassination as a pretext to pass the Carlsbad Decrees, a series of measures against so-called demagogic machinations. The politically volatile universities were placed in trusteeship, harsh press censorship was imposed everywhere, including Weimar, new police regulations were imposed, and investigations of dissidents began on a massive scale. The Carlsbad Decrees failed to stifle the newly awakened political activity, but subterfuge and imagination were needed to get around the more authoritarian regime. Goethe, completely in agreement with the decrees, was taking the waters in Carlsbad in the waning days of August 1819 and was pleased and flattered to encounter Metternich and other important people there. As he wrote to Karl August, *Your Royal Highness will surely soon have news of the results of these negotiations, and I only hope that their success may completely live up to my expectations.*

At Carlsbad and Teplitz, Goethe's spas of choice for a few years, he found an attractive and fashionable clientele: crowned heads, government ministers, aristocrats, beautiful women both married and single, wealthy bourgeois, and, last but not least, renowned artists and scientists. In the morning they took the waters and in the evening drank champagne and danced. They strolled and promenaded in elegant clothes. The spa orchestra played in the park. In Teplitz in 1812, between chats with two empresses, he had found some time for Beethoven as well, who made fun of Goethe's aristocratic pretensions but still deigned to play something for him on the piano. Goethe was very impressed, although he found the music a little too loud and passionate, and later remarked that he had never seen such a ruthlessly artistic character before. They subsequently exchanged a few politely superficial letters; Zelter could breathe easy.

In 1820, Goethe rode from Carlsbad over to Marienbad, the new spa whose great era was yet to come. Still under construction, the place was reputed to be a good investment, and it was besieged by people wanting to build. *I felt*, he wrote to Karl August, *as if I was in the forests of North America, where they build a whole city in three years.* The most impressive house in town belonged to the Brösigke family. The estate owner Friedrich Leberecht von Brösigke had built it with funds from a silent partner, Count Klebelsberg. The latter had long been waiting to marry Brösigke's daughter Amalie von Levetzow, whose first two marriages had been unsuccessful. At the tender age of fifteen, she had married a Levetzow, with whom she had two daughters. Her husband soon left her, and she married his cousin, who gambled away half her dowry, went to war, and died in the Battle of Waterloo in 1815, leaving Amalie in debt. Levetzow number one was still alive, and the Catholic Klebelsberg had to wait for him to die too before getting his turn with Amalie. Goethe had met Amalie, then a new mother, in Carlsbad in 1806. In his diary, he called her *Pandora*, both the title of a festival play he was planning to write and a word he used to describe an image of pleasurable delight. Now, in the summer of 1821, Amalie's first daughter, Ulrike, was about the age Amalie had been when Goethe had first encountered her. Pandora had returned.

A few years earlier, Goethe had written in a *Divan* poem,

> You say the years have taken much from you:
> The real pleasure of the play of senses,
> . . . contentment springs no longer
> From your actions. You have lost your daring boldness!
> What still remains that's special now about you?

Brooding melancholy and lowered self-confidence, however, don't get the last word in this poem: *There's still enough! There's still love and ideas!*

And so it was. Goethe was never at a loss for ideas. And now he was in love as well.

The summer after his first, brief visit in 1820, Goethe paid an extended visit to Marienbad, taking up residence in the Brösigkes' stately house, where Amalie was staying with her daughters. At first, the seventy-two-year-old Goethe was a sort of grandpa, found constantly in this family circle, chatting on the terrace or out on a stroll with Ulrike, looking for rocks to collect and belabor with his mineralogist's hammer. They amounted to a pretty collection and were displayed each night on the table before dinner. One time, Goethe placed a bar of chocolate among them, since Ulrike was not particularly fond of rocks—they all looked alike to her. Goethe also spent considerable time with Amalie, who radiated her own allure. She was only in her early thirties and was, as Goethe reported to the duke, a woman *who has done a pretty job of keeping her charm intact through a number of years and shifting fortunes.*

In his letters from that first summer in Marienbad, he at first wrote more about the rocks than about the women. There was no cause for alarm back in the house on the Frauenplan when a letter to August said, *Give my best to your wife and child, including Ulrike if she's there. By chance there's also quite a charming Ulrike here in the house, so that in one way or another I'm always reminded of her.*

The *charming Ulrike* in the Brösigke house was a tall, slim, pretty young woman who attended a girls' boarding school in Strasbourg and spent the summer in Marienbad with her mother and sisters. She had read Voltaire but had never heard of Goethe. Now, of course, she learned how famous he was. The first copies of the *Journeyman Years* had arrived at the spa fresh from the printer's. Ulrike began to read it, a bit bored, feeling that the story must have begun in another book she wasn't familiar with. She asked Goethe about it. He told her some of what happens in *Wilhelm Meister's Apprenticeship*—that it centered around an itinerant troupe of actors—but told her that it was not really appropriate reading matter for young women. *The Journeyman Years,* on the other hand, contained nothing harmful. Ulrike didn't read any further, preferring to go for walks and to balls in the evening. According to his diary, Goethe also occasionally attended the balls in the grand salon of Brösigke's house that summer. He attended them quite frequently the next year, and after that even more often.

Compared with daily life on the Frauenplan, which had grown gloomy, those summer weeks in Marienbad were filled with sunlight and cheerful conviviality—as well as the shadow of young girls in flower. For the most part, his letters to his son are silent on that score, but one can sense Goethe's feeling of well-being. *My daily life is very simple: in the morning I take my water in bed, bathe every third day, drink at the spring in the evening, take my midday meal in company, and so life goes on. The wine finally arrived, too.* There was no lack of wine at the Brösigkes', but Goethe wanted them to sample his own favorites.

Gossip spread about Goethe spending so much time with Ulrike. In the summer of 1822, a visitor to Marienbad writes, "He spends his evenings mostly in the company of the Levetzow family, appearing primarily at the side of the oldest fräulein, Ulrike von Levetzow, who entertains him either with a song or some jocular conversation, so that he can forget at least for a few moments the hurts he has to suffer on account of his unfortunate marriage to his former housekeeper, known by the name of Vulpius."

By the second summer in Marienbad, his feelings toward Ulrike were no longer those of a grandpa. He realized that he was in love. This was the summer he wrote *Could I but flee from my own self; / Enough's enough! / Ah, why always seek to go / Where you don't belong.* These lines were dashed out on the back of a written page, as were the following: *Ah! Could I only be healed! / What unbearable pain! / Like a wounded serpent / It writhes within my heart.*

Goethe's feelings for Ulrike had already become so powerful that he found it difficult to leave at the end of that second summer. *The present knows nothing of itself, / The farewell is horrible to feel.* On the way home, stopping in Eger, he wrote a poem in the composer Tomaschek's album. Its title was "Duet on the Pains of Love Directly after Parting." Later, it was changed to "Aeolian Harp," the instrument beloved of the Romantics, who hung them in pairs outdoors and tuned them to each other to produce enchanting music played by the wind.

> I thought I hadn't any pain,
> Yet just the same, my heart was sinking.
> And it was written on my face,
> While deep within my brain was empty.

Till finally tear on tear was falling
Releasing the restrained farewell.
And her farewell was cheerful, calm,
But now she's weeping, just like you.

Ulrike would later say, "It wasn't a love affair." The poem also suggests an asymmetrical relationship. The girl feels less pain at parting, as the *restrained* and the *cheerful, calm* farewell suggest: she seems carefree. The man in love has a *sinking* heart. Goethe had grown dissatisfied with himself and with the entire business. He was half looking forward to the following year, half fearing the dark winter months in the big house on the Frauenplan. *The days are full of tedium; / How boring it is when the night sky shines with stars.*

The following months were dark indeed. In mid-February, Goethe fell dangerously ill with what was probably a heart infarct. He lost and regained consciousness several times. Sharp abdominal pains kept him seated in a chair for entire nights at a time. Chancellor Müller was a regular visitor and wrote down Goethe's uncomplaining but sometimes also despairing comments. *Death lurks around me in every corner,* he said after one bout, continuing, *O you Christian God, how much suffering you heap upon your poor people, and yet we're supposed to extol and praise you for it in your temples!* Goethe was at loggerheads with God and with his doctors. *It's all well and good for you to practice your arts, but you probably won't save me.*

But his body still had enough powers of resistance to survive the crisis. When he recovered, he seemed to some friends to be even more mentally alert than before. He himself was astonished at how well he was able to give his *intellectual existence free rein to do what it could and what it wanted.* When spring came, his vital spirits awoke with it. He was moved to read through the pile of heartfelt letters of sympathy and get-well messages. Once again, they were evidence that even in illness he was a *public personage.* In some places, he had already been pronounced dead. A special production of *Tasso* celebrated Goethe's recovery; his bust was on stage, crowned with laurels.

The pious Countess Auguste zu Stolberg, his "Gustchen" of days gone by and now the widow of the Danish minister Bernstorff, wrote her beloved pen pal, concerned for his immortal soul. She saw the famous poet in danger, and advised him to cast off "everything in the world that is small, vain, material, and not good." The letter had arrived before he fell ill; it annoyed him, and he left it unanswered. Now, after his illness and recovery, he was in a mellower mood and wrote a lovely long answer: *To live a long time means outliving a lot: people you've loved, hated, didn't care about; kingdoms, capitals, even woods and trees we sowed and planted in our youth. We outlive ourselves and thankfully register it if even a few gifts of mind and body remain to us. . . . I've tried to be true to myself and others my whole life long and in all my earthly doings, have always kept an eye on the highest things. . . . And so let us remain unconcerned about the future! In our Father's realm are many provinces, and since he has prepared us such a happy place to settle on this earth, he surely will have provided for us both in the hereafter.*

In fact, however, Goethe was thinking less about the *hereafter* than about the upcoming summer. He could hardly wait to see Ulrike again. On June 26, 1823, he set out for Marienbad. This time he didn't stay in the Brösigkes' house, because the grand duke had taken up residence there. Instead, Goethe stayed in the Golden Grape, a genteel hotel across the way. It was only a few steps to the Brösigkes' terrace, where he could again while away the hours with Ulrike. In the evenings there were the usual masquerades and balls, and the days were spent collecting and examining rocks. And this summer, he added meteorology to his scientific interests. He and Ulrike observed cloud formations and took pleasure in their ever-changing shapes. These cloud shapes acquired such symbolic importance for him that he would later explicitly associate them with Ulrike in his great Marienbad "Elegy":

> *How light and dainty, clear and finely spun,*
> *A slender image, luminous and hazy,*
> *Floats up, angelic, from the clouds' stern choir,*
> *On high, in the blue ether, so like Her.*
> *You saw Her thus, the sovereign of the dance,*
> *The loveliest of all those lovely figures.*

But the summer was not over yet; there was still time for walks, suppers, and dances. Goethe organized parlor games that sometimes took on a slightly suggestive character. His idea was that they improvise a story based on the word "garter." The young women blushed, and Goethe talked innocuously about the Order of the Garter.

In mid-August, he proposed marriage, the duke acting as go-between. Much later, Ulrike wrote in her memoirs that she and her family were taken completely unawares and at first thought that the proposal was a joke. There may have been some roguishness in play, but Karl August put on a serious face and made the grandiose offer of a new house across from the palace for the "young couple." Ulrike was assured of a generous pension if she survived her husband. Her mother left the decision up to her. As Ulrike tells it, it didn't take her long to decide: she told her mother that she "was very fond of Goethe, like a father, and if he were all alone, so that I could think I could be useful to him, then I would take him; but because his son was married and lived in the house with him, he had a family that I would usurp if I took their place." She also reports that Goethe himself did not speak to her about the proposal. It was never explicitly rejected, and the matter remained unresolved till the end of the year.

By his return journey to Weimar, he had inwardly bid farewell to Ulrike, if at first only in the great "Elegy" that he scrawled into his pocket calendar during the trip, transferred to fine paper at home, bound in red leather, and treasured like a relic, shown only to a select few. Eckermann was one reader, and so were Riemer and Wilhelm von Humboldt. The latter wrote to his wife, "And so I began to read and I can truly say I was not just enchanted with the poem but so astonished that I can hardly describe it. This poem does not just achieve—it perhaps even exceeds the level of the most beautiful things he has ever done."

That was in November 1823, when Goethe had again succumbed to illness. Humboldt was concerned and kissed Goethe on the forehead in farewell, fearing he might not see him again. Goethe was despondent. He had to come to terms with the inevitable end of this love story, but there was also trouble at home. August, who feared for his inheritance, had read his father the riot act; Ottilie suffered several fainting fits, shut herself up for days in her room, and then took off without saying goodbye. Visitors could sense the icy mood that had descended on the house. Only Zelter, with his easygoing, jovial disposition, was able to counteract it. He described his visit to the Frauenplan, where he found his friend completely neglected, as it seemed to him: "[I] come to Weimar, drive up to the door. I wait a minute in the carriage, nobody comes out. I go in the door. A woman's face peers out of the kitchen, sees me, and withdraws. Stadelmann comes and hangs his head and shrugs. I ask, no answer. I'm still standing at the front door; maybe I should leave? Does Death live here? Where's the head of the house? Sad eyes. Where's Ottilie? Gone to Dessau. Where's Ulrike? In bed. . . . The chamberlain comes out: Father is—not well; sick, quite sick.—He's dead!—No, not dead, but very sick. I step closer and marble statues stand and stare at me.* So I climb the stairs. The comfortable steps seem to draw back. What will I find? What do I find? A man who looks as if he had love in his body, the whole of love with all the tortures of youth. If that's all it is, then he'll survive! No! He wants to hang on to it, glow like oyster lime; but he wants to have pain like my Hercules on Oeta. No medicine should help; only the pain should fortify and cure him. And so it was. It had happened: the loving heart had delivered a divine child, fresh and beautiful. It was a difficult birth, but the divine fruit of his labor was there and lives and will live." Zelter knows what to do. Since only the pain of beauty helps against ordinary pain, he reads the "Marienbad Elegy" to Goethe in his soothing bass voice—reads it again and again.

As we have seen, most of its strophes were written during his return trip to Weimar. Verses from *Tasso* serve as an epigraph: *And if a man's struck dumb by misery, / A god gave me power to say how much I suffer.* Humboldt remarked after visiting him that Goethe actually no longer felt an attachment to the girl, but rather "to the mood that the experience engendered in him and with the poetry he spun around it." It is a poem about being in love but also, and especially, about growing old. There is no mention of a difference in ages, but of a threshold the lover is forbidden to cross:

> *A kiss—the last one—cruelly sweet, cuts through*
> *The glorious web of intertwining loves.*
> *My feet, now keen now loath to shun that threshold,*

---

* *Marmorbilder stehn und sehn mich an*: Zelter here quotes a line from Mignon's song at the beginning of book 3 of *Wilhelm Meister's Apprenticeship*.

As if a flaming cherub drove them off,
I stare morosely down at the dark path,
And looking back, I see the gate is locked.

The elegy laments the passing of fleeting happiness—*And how the day did beat its hasty pinions / And seemed to drive the minutes rushing on!*—complains of the threshold of age and also of aging itself, and even of the sudden paralysis of feeling, for external aging and old age are one thing, but the disturbing experience of inner waning is another: *And now, locked up within itself, this heart, / As if it had never opened.* At this point, it is no longer merely about the loss of the beloved but about the loss of feeling. That is a big difference, a difference that long ago provided the melancholy theme for *Werther*; and it led Goethe now to group the elegy in a "Trilogy of Passion" with the poem "To Werther," written a year later, as well as "Reconciliation," a farewell to the Polish concert pianist Maria Szymanowska, whom we will meet below. The elegy invokes the *locked* gate and the heart *locked up within itself.* But everything rebels against that. Escape is possible, for there is still the world of nature, offering all its promise, alluring and alive: . . . *Is there not green / And open land, a meadow by the river? / Does not the sky unfold unearthly greatness, / So full of figures, shifting, disappearing?* And now, touched by nature's breath, the image of the beloved is reanimated and the heart, reflected therein, rejoices at *its own endurance.* It is the poem itself that asks the questions What is poetry? What is reality? and thus puts itself in question. The answer is positively defiant: everything is owed to the beloved herself, not to the phantom of poetic feelings: *If ever love gave lover inspiration, / Then I'm the one, and in the loveliest fashion; // It was through Her!* He is certain that he is not attached to a phantom, and his feelings rise to voluptuous adoration, loving devotion: *The peace of god that grants more bliss on earth / Than even reason can—as we have read— / For me is like the peace of love serene / In the presence of the being I love best.* The blissful repose in the image of the beloved does not last long; *as we have read* is already a cautious suggestion of a distance that will slowly grow. A stop must be put to that: *Where'er you be, be all, and always childlike, / And thus, in fact, you're all, invincible.* But after all, it cannot be. Time proves to be more powerful:

A thousand times I conjure up her image.
Sometimes it wavers, then it's snatched away.
One time it's vague, another, radiant, pure.
How could this bring the slightest consolation?
This ebb and flow, this constant fluctuation?

The last two strophes bring the dramatic turning point. Suddenly it's all nothing. Not even nature provides any consolation: *The universe I've lost, I've lost myself, / I who was once the favorite of the gods.* A final echo of the *Tasso* motif, the boon of expression. The elegy ends with the lines *They urged me toward that mouth so rich in giving, / They parted us and sent me to my ruin.*

In the last summer in Marienbad, Goethe met Maria Szymanowska. Celebrated throughout Europe, she had given a public performance but also played for him alone one evening. She was a charming, highly educated woman in her thirties, a widow. Goethe said it was hard to decide whether to watch her in rapt delight or close his eyes and listen more attentively. The last lines of the third poem in the "Trilogy of Passion," dedicated to her, are *And then one felt—could it but last forever!— / The double bliss of music and of love.*

In October 1823, Maria Szymanowska paid a visit to Weimar. Goethe put on a big reception in her honor and the next day invited her to dine in a small circle. At the end of the evening, she had already said goodbye and left the room when Goethe was overcome with a panic attack. He asked Chancellor Müller to run after the beautiful Polish woman and beg her to return. She agreed and came back with her sister. There was a great farewell to-do, with Goethe struggling to control his feelings. "But all efforts at humor were to no avail," Müller reports. "He burst into tears and unable to speak, embraced her and her sister, and his look of benediction followed them long after they had disappeared down the long, open passage of rooms."

It was the farewell of one who knew now that he really had become an old man.

CHAPTER 33

Faust: the Work of a Lifetime Finished at Last.

From heaven through the world to hell and Back.

*I shall see to it that the parts are charming and entertaining
and give food for thought.*

What Food for Thought Does *Faust* Give?

. . . .

GOETHE HAD NOT COMPLETELY ABANDONED HOPES OF marrying Ulrike. He wrote to her mother in late December 1823, *May nothing! nothing! stand in the way of fulfillment and success! . . . with longing, in hope and expectation*, but it was only a desperate last stand against resignation. He countered his dejection in the time-tested way—with new plans and activities—hoping to preserve and prove his youthful vigor even in the face of frustrated love. When he had recovered from his disappointment, he explained his method for combatting the melancholy of age to his friend Sulpiz Boisserée, who was thirty-five years younger: *Forgive me, dear fellow, if I seem overly effusive; but since God and his nature have left me to myself for so many years, I know nothing better than to express my thankful acknowledgment through youthful activity. I want to prove myself worthy . . . of the good fortune granted to me, and I spend day and night in thinking of how it is possible and acting so that it is. Day and night is no empty phrase, for I devote many a nocturnal hour (which, as is the fate of someone my age, I spend sleeplessly) not to vague and general thoughts but to considering exactly what I shall do the next day, which I then honestly set about doing in the morning . . . something one avoids at an age when one has the right to believe or to think that there will always be a tomorrow and a day after tomorrow.*

There were three main projects he now turned his energies to. In January 1824, he had copies made of Schiller's letters in preparation for the planned edition of their correspondence, and he sounded Cotta out about the possibility of a new, complete, and definitive edition of his own works. Both were urgent prompts to complete a third task: to continue working on and possibly even finish the second part of *Faust*. He became absorbed in rereading Schiller's letters and felt the obligation to heed his friend's words of encouragement and admonition regarding *Faust*. And as he began to negotiate with Cotta, the publisher made clear how much he wanted to have the continuation of *Faust* for the new complete edition, not least for economic reasons.

Faust was indeed a lifelong theme for Goethe. It had begun in childhood with the puppet theater and a dog-eared copy of the old chapbook. There he encountered Faust as the conjurer of the devil, a fairy-tale figure, both comical and sinister, a genuine bogeyman, especially when the devil comes to fetch him at the end. During his student days in Leipzig, the figure haunted him, especially the mural in Auerbach's cellar showing Faust astride a wine barrel. He may have drafted the corresponding scene at that time, and perhaps also the opening scene between the student and Mephistopheles, which he may have written after his audience with the great Gottsched. When he returned to Frankfurt from Leipzig and lay in bed, deathly ill, studying alchemical writings and then trying some experiments with Fräulein von Klettenberg, he felt especially close to the occult sphere of Faust the necromancer. At first, Faust was for him a figure from medieval German history, like Götz. Around 1772, after the execution of the infanticide Susanna Margaretha Brandt in Frankfurt, he had the idea of combining the story of the magician-scholar with the tragedy of Gretchen. After *Götz* and *Werther*, his friends in Frankfurt were eagerly awaiting what was rumored to be the imminent appearance of *Faust*. After a visit to Goethe in October 1774, Heinrich Christian Boie, coeditor of the *Göttinger Musenalmanach* (*Göttingen Muses' Almanac*), wrote, "His 'Doctor Faust' is almost finished and seems to me the greatest and most unique of all." During his first years in Weimar, Goethe often enjoyed reading aloud from his manuscript. Fifty years after his death, some scenes in a manuscript copy dating from the mid-1770s were discovered in the posthumous papers of Luise von Göchhausen, Anna Amalia's hunchback lady-in-waiting. They came to be known as the *Urfaust*. By the time these scenes were written down, there were certainly drafts of many more, including the act with Helen of Troy.

Goethe could not let go of the Faust theme, and that is exactly what made him uncertain about finishing the play. But he put pressure on himself to do so whenever a new edition of his works was in preparation. It happened with the Göschen edition, for which he completed *Egmont, Iphigenia,* and finally *Tasso* as well. He had hoped to bring *Faust* to an end, too, but in vain. In 1790 he published only *Faust: A Fragment,* to the disappointment of his public. For the first Cotta complete works, he at last succeeded in bringing it to a preliminary conclusion; in 1808, the eighth volume of that edition was published as *Faust: The Tragedy Part One.*

Several scenes for Part Two were already completed by that time, for the Helen of Troy act and for the end of the play, but mainly, there were only lists showing the sequence of scenes. Since beginning *Faust,* Goethe oscillated between intense proximity to the material and alienated distance from it. Sometimes its *northern phantoms* felt remote and foreign to him; at others, when he approached the world of Faust, scenes seemed to proliferate like a *family of mushrooms.* He was himself astonished at how quickly he could feel his way back into the material after a phase of neglecting it. Able to pick up seamlessly where he had left off, he once wrote that if he smeared a bit of soot on the new pages, no one would notice the difference in age of the manuscripts. It was *remarkable how much I resemble myself and how little my inner life has suffered through all those years and events,* he wrote in 1788, and there are similar statements from later years.

The version of Part One that was published in 1808 did indeed prove to be seamlessly unified. That is no longer the case for Part Two, on which Goethe began to work energetically in 1825. The atmosphere changes, as do the characters. Faust is no longer the medieval German scholar or the passionate lover. Now he enters the stage as a confident, worldly-wise gentleman. No longer a dubious character, he plays a clear-cut role—or rather, a succession of roles, each clearly defined in turn. An emperor courts him, and the stuffy air of the scholar's study is nowhere in evidence. In the Helen of Troy act, he is a German knight of aristocratic carriage, a Nordic imperator. Then he becomes a civilian attendant to the general staff and observer of battles, and ends up as a dike-building entrepreneur. Mephisto's character changes as well. He has long since ceased to be a genuine medieval Satan and has become a

man of the world, an elegant cynic, the go-to man for technical problems and dirty work; then he's a slippery business consultant and, at
the very end, a gay roué. For long stretches, their wager is completely
forgotten. These are the very different worlds in which the second part
of the tragedy is played out. The Helen of Troy act was even supposed
to appear as a separate work. In the end Goethe decided to include it in
the Faust tragedy, but still brought it out in 1827 as an advance publication under the title "Helen: Classic-Romantic Phantasmagoria."

The Helen act was the starting point for his work on *Faust II*. With
this third act, completed in 1826, serving as a center, Goethe developed the beginning of Part Two, the scenes at the emperor's court
and, above all, the "Classical Walpurgis Night" as the *antecedents* to the
Helen act. Earlier, he had finished some material for the final act, but
he still needed a transition, an act four. Goethe was still working on it
the year before he died. On July 22, 1831, his diary records, *Achieved the
main business. Final touches. Inserted everything in fair copy.* He told Eckermann, *What's left of my life . . . I can now regard as a pure gift, and it is now
basically all the same what more I do, if anything.* He informed his friends
that the work was now sealed and would be published only after his
death. We don't know whether it was really put under seal; no traces
of a seal have survived. Goethe did open the manuscript once more, on
January 24, 1832. *New excitement about Faust with regard to greater elabora-
tion of the main motifs, which I had handled all too laconically in order to finish.*

Friends, including Wilhelm von Humboldt, urged him to publish the work while he was still alive. In the last letter he ever wrote,
Goethe replied to Humboldt, *There is no question that it would give me
endless joy to dedicate and communicate these very sober jests while still alive
to my worthy, far-flung, and gratefully acknowledged friends and to hear their
responses. These days, however, are really so absurd and confused that I am convinced that my honest and long-pursued efforts on this curious contraption would
be poorly rewarded and driven onto the shore to lie there in ruins like a wrecked
ship and be covered by the flotsam and jetsam of time. Confused lessons on confused actions rule the world.*

If *confused lessons* rule the world, what about the lessons of this great
drama that Goethe wanted to keep from the public for now? Are they
also confused? Is there, in fact, some central lesson, some basic idea?
Goethe's answers to that question were contradictory. On the one hand,

he declared that the intellect had the most stake in the matter, by which he referred to the predominance of allegory. As a rule, our intellect is quite good at unraveling the meaning of allegories. They may be complex, but they remain rational. Their real appeal is to those who like riddles and are keen on finding a neat solution, as well as to literary scholars who can make a career of analyzing them. The masquerade scene explicitly refers to its own allegorical character and even lets us know how to interpret the figures. *Proclaim for each one, who they are,* cries the herald. The entire scene is the occasion for suggestive jokes, but not for ambiguity. It resembles the pageants in Weimar that Goethe arranged and composed verses for in his capacity as official poet. In them, events at court as well as the virtues and vices were usually presented as allegories. It was all playful and charming, but also quite unambiguous.

On the other hand, Goethe emphasizes the *incommensurability* of his Faust sequel. Each problem solved yields a new problem. Readers should follow the subtle clues, he said, and they might even discover more than he had put in. And so it was. People truly found many things—probably too many—in the play. Even with *Faust I*, Goethe had no objection to this hunt for meaning. He found it flattering, growing annoyed only when the riddle solvers became so involved in their decryption that they lost sight of the cryptic beauty of the work. Goethe advocated the aesthetic pleasure to be gained by a relaxed, playful approach. *The Germans, by the way, are such odd people!* he told Eckermann. *They make life more difficult than is proper by looking for deep thoughts and ideas everywhere and putting them into everything.—Good gracious! Have the courage for once to surrender yourselves to your impressions, allow yourselves to be captivated, moved, uplifted . . . but don't always think everything is vain that isn't some abstract thought or idea! . . . What a nice thing it would have been indeed had I decided to string the rich, motley, and highly multifarious life I brought to view in Faust on the meager string of a single, consistent idea!*

And why should we be satisfied with a *single* idea when there are so many in the play? Goethe wanted us to tease them out. To Schiller's remark "I am eagerly awaiting to see how the folktale is going to nestle up to the philosophical part of the whole work," Goethe replied, *I shall see to it that the parts are charming and entertaining and give food for thought.*

Let us therefore cast an eye on this great play, in its final form at last, in hopes that it will entertain us and also provide *food for thought.*

First, Faust and Mephisto: as for the devil, there was actually no room for him in Goethe's worldview. He often said that he would not *institute* an independent evil power, and when Kant introduced "radical evil" into his philosophy, Goethe declared that the Sage of Königsberg had now *beslobbered the mantle of philosophy.* For Goethe, the devil did not exist. If you believe in God, you have to believe in the devil as well, and Goethe believed in neither a transcendent God nor the devil. He had been a Spinozist all his life, and his watchword was *deus sive natura.* God is nature in its entire richness and creative power. And man can and should discover, preserve, and use this creative power, which also lives within him. Activity is thus the true service to God in nature, and the drive to create is absolutely never ending. That is also Goethe's vision of eternal life. *My conviction that we will continue to exist springs from the concept of activity,* he told Eckermann when he was almost eighty, *for if I am ceaselessly active to the end, then nature is obliged to assign me another form of existence when my spirit is no longer able to sustain the present one.*

Man fulfills his purpose when, as *natura naturata* (incarnate nature), he participates in *natura naturata* (creative nature). Goethe's dialectical formulation is that as a creative process, nature means polarity and enhancement. Opposites create a tension that enhances what is alive without becoming locked in rigid dualism. Light and darkness together bring the world of color into being. Good becomes better when it has passed through the ordeal of evil. How we are to imagine that is explained by the *Lord* in the "Prologue in Heaven":

> *I never have disliked the likes of you.*
> *Of all the many spirits of negation*
> *It is the rogue who gives me least vexation.*
> *It's all too easy for man to lose his steam.*
> *He soon becomes too fond of utter ease;*
> *And so I like to give him a companion*
> *Who's active, goading, and does the Devil's business.*

Mephisto prevents man from slowing down and losing *his steam* by keeping him busy. So Mephisto as a principle is an integral part of being human. And to that extent, Mephisto is an integral part of Faust too. Although Faust and Mephisto are independent figures, in the end they constitute one person—in the same sense that Goethe spoke of himself as a *collective singular* consisting of several persons with the same name. Faust frankly articulates the contradictory unity that binds him and Mephisto together:

> *There dwell two souls, alas, within my breast!*
> *The one desires a parting from the other.*
> *The one clings to the world with earthly lust,*
> *Hangs on for all it's worth, with all its senses.*
> *The other struggles mightily from the dust,*
> *And yearns to reach the realms of lofty forebears.*

The precarious unity of the individual does not prevent us, however, from investigating its separate poles in order to trace what they contribute to the enhancement of the whole.

The *Lord* says that Mephisto is meant to be a *companion* to man so that the latter does not slow down too early. And how does this stimulation occur? Through the spirit of negation—through criticism. Mephisto is a spirit who says no. What does he negate? We can see his first significant negation in the "Prologue in Heaven." The angels are praising the cosmos and the great works of the *Lord*. Everyone else is rejoicing and only Mephisto is carping. As the negating spirit, he is the critical reviewer of the cosmos. What is there to object to? Nothing less than an important flaw in the construction of man:

> *Of suns and worlds I've nothing much to say.*
> *I only see the way that humans struggle.*
> *The little god of the world remains unchanged,*
> *As flighty as the day when he was born.*
> *Could he do a little better? Well, he might,*
> *If only you'd not given him the spark of heavenly light.*
> *He calls it reason, employs it without cease* .
> *To be the beastliest of all the beasts.*

Mephisto sketches out an anthropology. Man has a bit of *heavenly light* and calls it *reason*. But he has too little of it to be truly reasonable and too much to be in harmony with his animal self. So the "animal rationale" has a flaw in his construction. The animalistic and the rational parts of him get in each other's way. Mephisto argues like the skeptical anthropologists of our day, who describe man as an "eccentric being,"* a "defective being,"† or even as a "stray bullet of evolution,"‡ since his instinct and his reason are not in balance, with predictable results: fear of death, self-destruction, destruction of the environment, and aggression. Mephisto sounds a warning: *And be fore-warned, this human beastliness / Will soon be marvelously manifest.* Man can plunge into bestiality—entire cultures can—and, again in the words of Mephisto, he can be *the beastliest of all the beasts.* That was also Friedrich Schiller's thesis, and it is quite possible that it was he who inspired the idea in Goethe.

So Mephisto promises he can bring about an improvement in the precarious and risky structure of mankind and do it by using Faust as his test case. He intends to relieve him of the burdensome contradiction between heaven and earth, spirit and material, by bringing him completely back down to earth. He wants to prove that it is better for man if his life is no longer confused by the *spark of heavenly light,* but can be unconditionally devoted to what earth has to offer. This is Mephisto's description of the illness he will cure Faust of: *From heaven he demands the brightest stars / And from earth's pleasures nothing but the best. / And whether they come from near or very far, / They cannot soothe his deeply troubled breast.*

What should we call someone whose yearning reaches out beyond the physical environment in which he lives? It would be best to call him a meta-physician.

But Faust is no metaphysician in the sense of seeking or providing the answers sought by scholastic metaphysics. In his first monologue, *Alas, I've studied philosophy . . .* , he shows himself to be someone who is dissatisfied with and even disgusted by philosophical and theological answers. But he remains a metaphysician in the sense that he is

---

* Helmuth Plessner, *Die Stufen des Organischen und der Mensch: Einleitung in die philosophische Anthropologie* (Berlin: De Gruyter, 1965).

† Arnold Gehlen, *Der Mensch: Seine Natur und seine Stellung in der Welt* (Wiesbaden: Athenaion, 1976).

‡ Arthur Koestler, *Der Mensch, Irrläufer der Evolution: Eine Anatomie der menschlichen Vernunft und Unvernunft* (Berne: Scherz, 1978).

still asking *Where shall I grasp you, never-ending nature?* and his yearning transcends mere physical pleasure. He wants to understand what holds the world together at its core, and he also wants to be moved by that understanding. This double desire—to understand and to be moved by the spirit of the whole—is what makes Faust a metaphysician. And that is the way he is spoken of in the "Prologue in Heaven," where the first of the two famous wagers is made, the bet between Mephisto and the *Lord*, to be followed by the one between Mephisto and Faust.

The wager that Mephisto offers the *Lord* can be summarized as follows: Mephisto bets that he can transform even as stubborn a metaphysician as Faust into a one-dimensional being: *Dust he shall eat.* With Faust as an example, he wants to prove that man is better served by clearing his head of metaphysical follies and making him into a sober realist. It's better to be earthbound than suspended in some problematic space between heaven and earth. But the *Lord* intends to prove that in the end, it will be impossible to alienate Faust from his spiritual *primal source* and extinguish the light of heaven within him: *A good man even in his dark compulsion / Is well aware of what the right path is.*

What we have is a revealing reversal of the Job story alluded to in the "Prologue in Heaven." In both cases, God and Satan make a bargain. In the story of Job, Satan intends to prove that he can destroy Job's faith in God by bringing him great misfortune. In the Faust story, Mephisto sets out to prove that he can lure Faust away from God by bringing him earthly happiness. Job's misfortune and Faust's earthly happiness are supposed to have the same outcome: the surrender of the spiritual dimension, the betrayal of transcendence.

In our post-metaphysical age, Mephisto seems quite familiar and also utterly remote from everything we usually think of as evil. He is quite simply the embodiment of the reality principle. What it demands is also what Mephisto uses to tempt Faust: he should give up on transcendence and concern himself with tangible pleasures. Mephisto will tell him, *I've administered a longtime cure / For the mishmash of your imagination.* He sounds like today's positivists, sociologists, and psychologists. In the area of cognition, he advocates reductionism:

> *Whoever would describe and understand*
> *A living being must first drive out its spirit.*

And when he holds its parts within his hand,
He finds it lacks, alas, the bond of spirit.

. . .

Next time will go much better, you will see,
Once you've learned to reduce it down
And classify it properly.

As in cognition, so also in the pleasures of the senses: Faust should become a reductionist. Mephisto wants to transform him into a robust satisfier of only his basest drives—for his own good, he claims. As the embodiment of the reality principle, Mephisto offers his services as a physician to humans whose relationship to the world is problematic. That becomes even clearer when we take a close look at the second wager, the one between Faust and Mephisto.

Faust is in despair. He feels as if he's locked in a *prison*; he is not able to grasp *infinite nature*, either in his thinking or in his life. He intends to kill himself, for it seems at least possible that beyond the gates of death a *divine height* will rise into view. But it is just as possible that one disintegrates *into nothingness*. On one side, metaphysical uncertainty; on the other, physical certainties. He decides to remain here. He does not swallow the poison. He is encouraged to continue living, first by the bells of the Easter celebration, and then by Mephisto, who promises to make him a citizen of the world from head to toe, to show him the plenitude of existence and the full enjoyment of reality. I'll serve you here and now, says Mephisto, and when we meet again *in the hereafter*, you will serve me. That is the usual pact with the devil to which Goethe alludes. But it never gets that far, for it turns into a wager with quite a different significance. Its formula is *If ever I should tell the moment, / I beg you, stay! You are so lovely! / Then I am yours to lay in chains.*

Let us look at this wager from Faust's point of view. In his hunger for experience, he proves also to be filled with a peculiar pride: his longing is supposed to be greater than the world. He wants to prove that the world is too small and cramped to satisfy him. But to avoid misunderstandings, we must also add that we're talking about a world seen and presented through the optics of Mephistopheles, a world reduced to an obscure object of desire. Mephisto offers Faust the world as a package deal of pleasure, and Faust wants to prove that a world reduced to an object of pleasure is not enough for him. Mephisto transforms the world into a consumable, and Faust wants to prove that he is more than a consumer; he wants to prove the insatiability of his metaphysical desire. Mephisto, however, is betting that Faust's metaphysical desire will be taken care of once he has had his fill of the worldly pleasures Mephisto provides. Faust sets out to prove that no single moment can do justice to his aspiration, while Mephisto plans to have him stretch out on a *bed of idleness*. Mephisto offers Faust the joys of ordinariness. He wants him to realize that he too is only *a man among men*, a consumer of the world.

By way of this wager Mephisto, whom we first meet as a spirit who says no, becomes a productive principle. Between Faust and Mephisto there is a tension that leads to enhancement. Faust really becomes Faustian only in contention with Mephisto.

How so? Faust strives upward and Mephisto drags him downward. The point is that neither the "pure," high-flying Faust nor the "pure" Mephisto who would bring him down triumphs. Instead, the result of these opposed forces—this up and down—is a movement outward, neither vertical transcendence nor pure immanence, but something else: an immanent transcending, if you will. Tempted by Mephisto, Faust becomes a transgressor of limits on a horizontal plane, hungry for experience. His urge is "outward," into the fullness of life. Mephisto's magical cape helps Faust immediately experience the things he hungers for. His vertical yearning is replaced by excitements on the horizontal plane, excitements that are extremely productive. The mechanics of this contest between Mephisto and Faust are as follows: Mephisto offers tangible pleasures, and Faust makes something sublime of them. Gretchen is an example. Mephisto obtains her as a sexual object, but Faust falls in love with her. Sex becomes eros, desire becomes ardor. This same pattern prevails throughout. Mephisto provides the goods—and Faust makes something more of them.

This interplay between the metaphysician Faust and the realist Mephisto is the proprietary secret of modernism. Therein we see how the vertical striving of previous ages is redirected into the horizontal and becomes thereby a historical force of unheard-of power. Modernism no longer strives upward, since it has discovered that heaven is empty and God is dead. But in modernism, the expansive passion that once led man to invent God—because only God seemed spacious enough to incorporate within himself the wealth of human life—was secularized, with the unexpected result that man can be considered small, yet still capable of great things. The passion formerly directed toward God becomes a passion for exploring and taking possession of the world. That is exactly what it means to move "outward." Instead of trying to approach God, man circles the globe. Modernism is no longer disposed to be cosmic, but to become global. With the wager between Faust and Mephisto and the resulting dynamic action, the momentous transformation of metaphysical furor into an engine for civilization's conquest of the world unfolds before our eyes. Aided by Mephisto, Faust has good fortune with women, reforms government finance, provides bread and circuses, becomes a successful military commander, and finally a colonizer on a grand scale. He has dikes built to claim more land from the sea. As Mephisto's student, Faust becomes a metaphysician of the physical world. Instead of transcending the world, he merges obsessively with it and so can demand of man: *Let him stand here firmly, take a look; / To the ambitious this world's an open book. / Why waste time maundering in eternity?*

Goethe imagines all the things that modernism could do with man—including, for example, producing him in a laboratory. The Homunculus scenes are his contribution to the discussion of anthropotechnology, to use a neologism of Peter Sloterdijk's.* It is not Faust himself but his eager student Wagner who finally succeeds in producing a monster in a test tube. *The terrifying hour has struck. / It echoes through the sooty walls.* These words open the scene in the laboratory and, at the crucial stage of his experiment, Wagner whispers, *A man is being made.* Goethe's original idea was to have Faust himself perform this experiment. Then he transferred the deed to Wagner, but still wanted to have Faust and Mephisto in attendance and, most important, make the experiment succeed: the *chemical manikin . . . instantly shatters the glowing flask and makes his entrance as an agile, well-formed dwarf* reads the stage direction. In the final version, however, Faust is still lying unconscious and only Mephisto is conscious and present—and

* Peter Sloterdijk, *A Critique of Cynical Reason* (Minneapolis: University of Minnesota Press, 1987).

not just as a witness but as a participant. The crucial change from the first draft is that Homunculus is not a complete person, and so is only half born. He remains trapped in the test tube, but is a person to the extent that love for his progenitor is awakened. Something made wants to be treated as something born; it wants to be loved. Love is a prerequisite for its being able to exist. And therefore, Homunculus speaks to its manufacturer Wagner, *Well, dear Father, how goes it? That was no jest. / Come, clasp me now—but gently—to your breast.* But that cannot be. Glass separates them, and so Homunculus must learn his first lesson: *That is the property of things: / For what's natural, the cosmos just suffices. / What's artificial needs enclosed devices.* Homunculus remains in the test tube. What is artificial can for the time being exist only in an artificial milieu, but the occupant of the test tube is permitted to accompany Faust and Mephisto on their journey to ancient Greece during the "Classical Walpurgis Night."

Goethe engages with the alchemical dream of creating human life at a time in the history of science when Friedrich Wöhler's successful synthesis of urea—the formation of an organic substance from inorganic material—gave rise to brave speculations about the possibility of artificially producing more complicated organisms and perhaps even human life itself. Thus in the Homunculus episode, written in 1828, Goethe refers not just to the alchemy of Paracelsus but also to contemporary experimentation. Wagner declares, *What once was thought mysterious in nature / We venture to explore it with our reason. / And things that nature used to organize / We now can have them crystallized.*

However, Goethe learned from the Jena chemist Johann Wolfgang Döbreiner—his informant on developments in that field—that the newest ideas about the creation of human life were nothing but idle fantasies. Goethe was relieved to hear it and so transferred the project from Faust to the scientifically informed but otherwise foolish Wagner. He is permitted to voice ideas that contemporary geeks still believe in and proclaim: *But in years to come we'll mock mere chance. / A brain like this, that's meant for first-class thought, / Can just as well be made by first-class thinkers.*

There is a flash of irony when, at the end of the "Classical Walpurgis Night," Goethe returns Homunculus to the elements. Artificial man must go back into nature's evolutionary process and work his way up from the bottom. And so the artificial thing learns to be born. The test tube shatters and Homunculus dissolves in the sea, the fecund ur-soup: *You'll move by everlasting norms / And pass through a thousand thousand forms, / Have plenty of time to become a man.*

Even though Homunculus is Wagner's fabrication, he still belongs in the sphere of the play between Faustian metaphysics and Mephistophelian physics. Another example is the invention of paper currency, one more modern idea that Faust and Mephisto concoct as part of their takeover of the world. Let us recall that alchemical and magical practices still play a big part in the first Walpurgis Night. There, Faust is dosed with *fluid gold,* a magic potion that makes him young and attractive so that he can make a conquest of Gretchen. But not until the paper money scene is the level of genuinely modern sorcery reached, namely, the creation of value from speculation on the future, i.e., from nothing. Apparently, the whole idea is quite simple; it just has to occur to you. Money has become short at the imperial court, with state indebtedness becoming immeasurably large. What's to be done? Faust's and Mephisto's idea is this: perhaps there is gold—some natural, some buried—to be found in the ground. The emperor should use the real estate that belongs to him as security against an increase in the amount of money in circulation. And so they print paper money. On each bill are the words,

> *Herewith let it be known to all and sundry:*
> *This paper's worth a thousand crowns of money,*
> *As for the pledge of what is in your hand:*
> *Vast riches lie beneath the kaiser's land.*
> *And it's been all arranged: this buried wealth*
> *Replaces the paper as soon as it's unearthed.*

This, by the way, was the very same idea behind the introduction of the so-called *Rentenmark* after the hyperinflation of 1923, for the *Rentenmark* was backed by the real property of the German empire.

It also seems the best solution to the emperor in the paper money scene in *Faust.* More money is put into circulation, secured by real property. Moreover, in this way money becomes unprecedentedly liquid. People don't have to drag around gold coins, that heavy form of cash:

A banknote's handy carried in the breast
Where it pairs nicely with a billet-doux.
The priest keeps one devoutly in his prayer book.
It lets the soldier turn around right quick
When he can lighten the belt around his hips.

Two things are needed for the whole scheme to function. One is imagination: you've got to be able to imagine the real value on which the paper money is based. The other is trust: you need to trust that the valuation is correct, which is why verification by a higher authority is required—in this case, by the emperor. The emperor himself is ecstatic:

Let's go, let's go! . . .

. . .

Now let us squander time in merriment!
For right on time, Ash Wednesday is approaching.
And in the meantime, we shall celebrate
The carnival with wild, carousing revels.

This is not exactly the way Faust had imagined it, however. Goethe, who for some periods was also in charge of the duchy's finances, had been inspired by the financial revolution put in motion by the Bank of England when it began basing the amount of money in circulation not just on gold and existing securities but on the expectation of future creation of real value to which the increased circulation was meant to contribute. That is also Faust's intention: to crank up production by putting more money into circulation. But instead, he only unleashes consumption until there is nothing left to consume. The final result is inflation, the *paper ghost of guilders*. Only the jester is not fooled by this modern magic. *Just looky here, this isn't worth a cent.* That's his comment on the pretentious banknotes, and he immediately puts his money into tangible assets. Before his money can trickle away, he buys a house and land. *Tonight I'll go to sleep in my own house!*

Faust and Mephisto conjure up other specters of modernity as well. The court is bored and wants to be entertained. Faust: *As a start we made it rich, / And now it wants to be amused.* People want to see Helen and

Paris, a magic lantern show, a theater of illusion. This story doesn't end well either.

Faust asks for Mephisto's help, and the latter recommends entering the *Realm of the Mothers*. What sort of *realm* is that? What does he mean by *mothers*? When Eckermann asked Goethe about it, he merely flashed his Jupiter's eyes at him and quoted his own verse *The Mothers!—Mothers!—it sounds so strange*. But the scene that follows does make it somewhat clearer. Linking to the paper money scene, it can be taken as a continuation of creating something from nothing, but this time with images instead of paper. When Mephisto sends Faust into the Realm of the Mothers, he's referring him to the inner workshop of the imagination. Here too, as with paper money, you can make from nothing something that others experience as real. Faust tells Mephisto, *You dispatch me to the void / So that I there increase both art and power*. Mephisto refers Faust, whose job is to entertain the court with his magic lantern show, to imagination which operates in *the void*. In what sense is this a creation of value from nothing? It sounds puzzling at first.

Let us think about what happens when imagination is active and we try to picture people or stories. We imagine them, and sometimes what we imagine becomes so real that it triumphs over reality itself. Honoré de Balzac, for example, threatened people who had annoyed him by saying, "Just you wait, we'll meet again in my next novel!" Imagination's seizure of power can even be political, and then we speak of the dominance of ideology. But it can also happen in the politics of everyday life. Here too, Goethe has Faust foresee things that have taken shape today in the age of media, where we all spend a considerable part of our lives not in the "first" reality but in an imaginary one, and even primary reality is shot through with the imaginary. The world consists almost completely of the images the media offer us.

So Faust learns from Mephisto how to exploit the enchantment of imagination. He gives the courtiers a performance: the abduction of Helen as a magic lantern show. The only problem is that he ends up enchanting himself. He can no longer tell reality from imagination. With the cry *Who's seen her once can never do without her*, he tries to embrace the imaginary Helen. On the one hand, what's happening is trivial: Faust tries to embrace Helen as if she were a movie star, which won't work. On the other hand, the scene is extremely interesting from the point of view of media theory, for it demonstrates that the ontological status of mediated reality is relatively unclear. We don't know exactly where figures like Helen—or in our day, Madonna—are located on the continuum between existence and nonexistence.

Mephisto, who wanted to cure Faust of the metaphysical *mishmash of imagination*, contributes to his entanglement in other, more modern forms of the same thing. That becomes clear in the war scene.

In the economic crisis unleashed by inflation, the empire threatens to sink into anarchy. Internal and external contradictions are exacerbated and result in war. Mephisto's comment is laconic and very cynical: *War and trade and piracy, / an indivisible trinity.* Faust and Mephisto act as advisers and helpers to the emperor, who must fend off a counter-emperor. They serve him well by specializing in the production of phantoms. They produce ghost armies—a sort of fata morgana—that so intimidate the enemy that he flees. It is quite possible to read this as an allegory of effective wartime propaganda, a media-enabled presentation of false information. Waging war with images—here too, Goethe is astute at anticipating future developments.

As we have seen, Mephisto plays the role of instigator of Faust's achievements in all these cases. Among other things, the drama is a song of praise for Faust's competence. Springing from the opposite tendencies of metaphysical need and a will to be worldly, his competence is meant to triumph in the end: *Whoever strives with all his might, / In the end we can redeem him.* Yet his prowess does not seem so unconditionally positive, especially since its prerequisite is Mephisto, who embodies not only the stimulus of negation and the unrestrained will to be worldly but also the sometimes ominous consequences of Faust's competence. In another context, Goethe famously said of this Mephistophelian aspect of competence, *The person who acts is always unscrupulous. No one has a conscience except the contemplative person.*

In the final act, Faust the entrepreneur wants to round out his real estate holdings. But there is still a little chapel and the cottage of Philemon and Baucis. *My grand estate is not yet whole,* says Faust, and Mephisto's assistants are immediately at hand to complete the relocation by force. The chapel and cottage are burned to the ground and the elderly couple perish in the flames. Is Faust justified by his active striving? In the "Prologue in Heaven" the *Lord* declares, *The striving man will always err.* Is that a pardon before the fact? No. Faust finds it objectionable that in his enormous domain there is still a minuscule blank spot over which he has no authority, an irritating remnant that defies his will to rule. And the more total his ambition is, the more irritating the resistant remnant. *Those few trees are not my own, / they spoil the world that I possess.* Faust is tired *of being just* and wants to make short work of them. He delegates Mephisto to *go and sweep them all aside!* Mephisto *whistles shrilly* and the thugs who will burn Philemon and Baucis appear. It is a grisly scene, and one the poet Paul Celan may have had in mind when he composed the great Holocaust poem "Death Fugue." Faust, who brings death, is also a "Meister aus Deutschland"—a master from Germany—who "steps from the house and the stars are flashing he whistles his hounds out / he . . . has a grave dug in the earth."

Goethe has not tidily apportioned the bright and the dark sides to Faust and Mephisto in the sense that Faust wants to do good and Mephisto turns it into evil. It's not that simple. Instead, their relationship is more like what Heinrich Heine portrays in his satirical narrative "Germany: A Winter's Tale." There the protagonist, a version of Heine himself, is followed by a shadowy figure with an executioner's ax. When confronted, the latter explains, "whatever thoughts are in your mind, / I carry out, I do them. . . . I am / the deed to your thought." In the same way, Mephisto is the deed to Faust's thoughts. Faust's competence casts a shadow, and the shadow is Mephisto. He makes it manifest that the competent, successful Faust becomes entangled in guilt, from the tragedy of Gretchen to the deaths of Philemon and Baucis. Goethe's world theater shows how, via long chains of causality, a successful life in one place sooner or later results in the destruction of life in another. The world is not fair, and the dead litter the course of Faust's worldly career. If the causal connection between an action and its evil consequences is short, we speak of guilt; if somewhat longer, we speak of tragedy. If the causal chain is very long, guilt and tragedy can be attenuated to mere unease. Knowing ourselves to be survivors because others have suffered and died, we cannot escape feeling such unease. Mephisto, who spurs Faust on to consume the world, also embodies this unfathomable, universal interconnection of action and guilt, the awful devolvement of a deed, sooner or later, into an evil deed.

Goethe once said he had no talent for tragedy and that it was his nature to balance things out. He calls his play a "tragedy" but ends it with Faust's redemption. At the beginning of Part Two, after the Gretchen tragedy, he puts Faust into a healing sleep, a sleep of forgetting that has caused many a Faust commentator sleepless nights ever since. What does forgetting mean here? Forgetting is the art of finding new beginnings where there aren't any. Goethe was a past master of such new beginnings, and Faust's awaking in Part Two of the tragedy is a prime example. While the sun rises and Faust still slumbers into the morning, Ariel's song is heard: *Remove the stinging, bitter darts of blame, / And cleanse his mind of horror he has seen.*

All well and good, but in the final act, we witness a macabre self-delusion. Faust, successful and powerful, is now beleaguered by a personified Worry:

> *Once I have got hold of someone*
> *Nothing in the world can help him.*
> *Never-ending gloom's upon him,*
> *And the sun's gone from the sky.*
> *All his outer senses function,*
> *Yet within him dwells the darkness.*

With the utmost effort, Faust thinks he has once again fended off this specter of worry, but it returns to strike him blind. Still undaunted, he declares, *I feel the night invading, deep and deeper, / Yet still within me all is brightly lit.*

Most commentators have extolled this inner light. Goethe, however, presents a drastic account of how miserable is Faust's end (before his final ascension into heaven) and that this much celebrated inner light does not save him from a serious misapprehension. Faust hears the clang of spades and thinks it is the sound of work on his humanitarian project of land reclamation—*I open land for many, many millions.* In fact, they are digging his grave.

In this sardonically ironic scene the wager—almost forgotten by this time—also comes up again. In his delusion that a project is under way that will last for centuries when it is only his own grave being dug, Faust surrenders himself to euphoric visions: *How I would love to see this busy swarm, / And stand upon free ground with a free people.* Inspired by this vision, he declares, *To this moment I could say: / You are so lovely! I beg you, stay!* Does this mean he has lost the bet, or is he saved by the subjunctive *"I could say"*? Entire libraries have been devoted to that question. Goethe himself said various things about it. Sometimes he talked about pulling a fast one on Mephisto, sometimes about Faust's being pardoned. One way or another, Faust's provisional end before the final end is a pitiful affair. He luxuriates in his projections and doesn't realize that his end approaches.

At the time Goethe was composing these scenes of the downfall of Faust the entrepreneur, he was himself both fascinated by great engineering projects and repulsed by the Saint-Simonian religion of industrialism, which sacrificed the individual to the collective and beauty to utility. As for modern technology, he procured a model of the first steam train and showed it off like a cult object. With Eckermann he discussed the possibility of constructing canals across Panama, at Suez, and another connecting the Rhine and the Danube. *I would like to see these three great things*, he said, *and it would be well worth the trouble of holding out for another fifty years or so for their sake.* They were projects he regarded as the peak of humanity's inventive spirit and entrepreneurial prowess. To the extent that these visions were shared by the Saint-Simonians, he welcomed the fact and confessed that *very intelligent people* were obviously *at the head of that sect*. But their socialist methods, subordination of all other goals to material welfare and technical progress, and their ideas for collective ownership were anathema to him. The collectivism he abhorred is voiced in Faust's highly emotional *I open land for many, many millions.* Perhaps the masses will then be free, but not the individual. Because his Faust had strayed haphazardly too far into Saint-Simonian territory, Goethe needed to lay him to rest with mordant irony. And he was relieved when he heard that the Saint-Simonians had been forced to disband in early 1832. He commented on them, *The fools imagine that they have the brains to play the role of Providence.* And isn't Faust himself a *fool* for not realizing that his end is near and, instead, wallowing in the idea that he will not perish for *eons*?

In any event, it is Mephisto who triumphs in the penultimate scene. He no longer appears as a clown who inspires and facilitates Faust's actions, but as an unfathomable figure of nihilism and destruction who opens up the terrifying prospect of the futility of all things. Mephisto is no longer a comic but a cosmic nihilist. As the lemures—the spirits of the dead—dig Faust's grave, Mephisto declares, *The elements are all in league with us, / and sheer destruction is our goal.* Although Mephisto is also a comic figure, he remains the menacing accomplice of night, the lieutenant of nothingness, or as Faust addresses him, *Chaos's fantastical son.*

Mephisto has many contradictory faces. One Mephisto promotes unconditional anti-metaphysical worldliness, another embodies the threat of nihilism, the great futility of the cosmos. Today we have other names for it, entropy, for example, which seems to foreordain the end of the universe and the futility of the entire life process. Mephisto, therefore, is quite simply a challenge to existence as meaningful order. That is what Faust learns, and Goethe must have experienced it in his darker moments as well. In the scene "Forest and Cave," Faust turns in a monologue to his genius, the *lofty spirit*, with the words

> *. . . To these delights that take me*
> *Ever closer to the gods, you gave me*
> *A companion and no longer can*
> *I do without him, though in ice-cold insolence*
> *He debases me before my very self*
> *And with one breath transforms your gifts to naught.*

Goethe's understanding of nature was deep enough for him to be able to grasp its immensity, which dissolves all meaningful order. He has Mephisto proclaim the primacy of darkness: In the beginning was darkness, which *then gave birth to light*, and thus everything will sink back into darkness. The world arose from nothing and will return to nothing. This Mephistophelian idea of the primacy of darkness is contradicted in the play, but it remains a shadowy presence thanks to Mephisto, the clown and lieutenant of nothingness. Perhaps that is why Goethe has Mephisto emerge from the mask of Phorkyas at the phantasmagoric end of the Helen act. He rises up to a gigantic height, as if he were the director of the entire scene. It could mean that it's all only a game, a beautiful sham contaminated by nothingness.

But is it really so bad if Mephistophelian stage managers are at work, transforming reality into semblance so we no longer know what's being played?

We have our life in the reflected colors, says the hymn to the sunrise in the first scene of Part Two. There man is portrayed as the inhabitant of an intermediate world. From the advent of some immensity—whether it be pure light or total darkness, complete being or absolute nothingness—we are protected by composite conditions, refractions, indirections, *reflected colors*. We need a world of appearance and even illusion and self-delusion, and Mephisto is also a magician, an illusionist, a stage manager to the extent that he helps construct the sphere we need in order to live our lives.

Faust consisted of *very sober jests*, Goethe wrote in his last letter to Wilhelm von Humboldt. One of these *sober jests* is surely the ascension into heaven at the end. It's quite a sublime business, but not entirely. Mephisto lurks in the wings, ready to snatch Faust's *immortality* from the angels. Unfortunately, it's *just too appetizing* to ogle those angels' backsides. Mephisto feels desire: *Absurd attraction, ordinary lust / Befall this seasoned, hard-boiled devil*. And so he misses the decisive moment when he should have struck. Nothing more stands in the way of Faust's ascension. It was made possible only by lechery at an inconvenient moment.

CHAPTER 34

Eckermann and Goethe's Other Assistants.
The Definitive Edition. Enforcing the Copyright.
Schiller Again. Zelter: Short History of a Long Friendship.
Leave-Takings: Frau von Stein, Karl August, Goethe's Son.
Last Outing to Ilmenau. *"Peace lies over all the peaks."*
Against time's *flotsam and jetsam*. Death.

. . . .

INISHING *FAUST* WAS ONE *MAIN BUSINESS* OF GOETHE'S FINAL years. Another was the preparation of the *Ausgabe letzter Hand*, the last personally supervised, definitive edition of his works. Cotta was the obvious choice as publisher, but in the meantime the trust between author and publisher had been compromised, and it was Cotta's fault.

During his last sojourn in Carlsbad, in the summer of 1823, Goethe had come upon a so-called original edition of his works in a bookstore. It was published in Vienna, and Goethe had never heard of it. It was not one of the usual pirated editions, however, but a reprint arranged by Cotta himself, as he later contritely admitted. He had hoped thereby to drive the piratical publishers out of business. But Cotta had neither informed Goethe of the edition nor paid him additional royalties. He apologized and provided tortuous explanations, to which Goethe did not respond for several months. On January 14, 1824, he finally wrote that the affair had reawakened *painful feelings* that *a German author is reminded of all too often in the course of his life*. Others who spent their life working hard received their reward, but not an author who had contributed to the *education . . . of the Fatherland* and now *sees himself injured in various ways and cheated of the just reward for his ceaseless work*.

Goethe had battled against pirated editions and reprints his entire working life, without success. For his final, definitive edition, he pulled out all the stops to put an end to this mischief, at least in his own case. He set to work so resolutely that one has the impression that toward the end of his career, he at last wanted to test his real significance to the public. He consulted with his influential friend Reinhard, the French diplomat. He activated his connections in the world of politics, wrote to ambassadors and ministers of state—Metternich, for one—and also directly to crowned heads, emphasizing his contributions to the intellectual life of Germany. He made clear to the high and mighty who he was and why he deserved to have his copyright protected.

The year 1825 was dominated by his efforts to persuade first the German Confederation in Frankfurt and then—since the Confederation had no authority in such matters—its thirty-nine individual states to grant him a *privilege* that would protect his definitive edition from unauthorized reprints. These efforts were successful, and he became the first author in Germany to obtain protection for his works, no general copyright law existing at the time. Arguing on his own behalf, Goethe always also pointed out that it was an *important matter for all German literature*, as he wrote to the German Confederation.

When grants of privilege from all members of the Confederation were finally assembled in January 1826, it seemed to Goethe like a final victory in a battle that had kept him *in suspense* all year long. The *privilege* itself meant as much to him as the *best medal*. It was also very attractive financially, both for the author and for some future publisher.

The news of copyright privilege for the definitive edition was the talk of the 1826 Leipzig Book Fair. The edition was auctioned over a period of months. Thirty-six publishers bid. The highest offer, 118,000 taler, came from a Hanover publisher.

Goethe was still negotiating with Cotta, but relished giving him a running account of his exorbitant market value. The mistrust engendered by the affair of the Viennese reprint was still festering. Cotta, who of course was intensely interested, was kept on tenterhooks for a while. He didn't want to cause Goethe any additional vexation, and so he refrained from exercising his option to purchase a future edition. Negotiations with the other publishers were conducted partly by Goethe's son, August, and partly by Goethe himself. August wanted to accept the highest bid. Goethe, however, still felt some loyalty to Cotta, who had otherwise always behaved very decently, and Goethe had special admiration for him as Schiller's publisher. With the participation of Sulpiz Boisserée and after some minor disagreements, Goethe and Cotta finally settled on a contract for 60,000 taler in February 1826. Cotta counted it among the "most important events" of his life, and Goethe wrote to him, *Since the composure achieved by our spirit cannot be expressed in words and signs, may I be permitted to tell Your Honor in general terms what is of central importance: that for the first time in many years I feel genuine satisfaction in these hours, when I am certain that the results of my literary activity have been laid in your hands. There could be no more valid testimony to our mutual trust. Step by step it will emerge that I have no other business than to complete these fruits of my life, to the honor and advantage of us both.*

In order to accomplish this *business*—namely, to collect, sift through, put in order, and prepare for printing the literary *fruits* of an entire life—Goethe had recruited a staff of assistants including Johannes John, who provided useful service as a scribe and copyist, and Johann Christian Schuchardt, who archived and extensively cataloged Goethe's papers. Other colleagues were the reliable standby Johann Heinrich Meyer, known as Art Meyer, who saw to the revision of Goethe's art-history writings, and Frédéric Soret, a trained theologian and tutor at the ducal court. As a practicing naturalist, Soret devoted himself to the publication of the scientific writings and was an important interlocutor in Goethe's final years. Friedrich Wilhelm Riemer, who had rejoined Goethe's staff in 1819 after discord arising from his tutoring of Goethe's son, was a high school teacher, librarian, and writer possessed of encyclopedic knowledge. He proved irreplaceable as a walking lexicon of philology and cultural history, particularly with advice during the work on Part Two of *Faust*.

From 1824 on, the leader of this staff of assistants was Johann Peter Eckermann. Born into extreme poverty, he had risen to the post of registrar in the military administration of Hanover. He had acquired his knowledge of literature, to him the most important thing, largely as an autodidact. Goethe was his great hero. He had read everything by him he could get his hands on, and knew it all inside-out. His ambition was to be a writer, and he had already composed some poems and was seeking a publisher for a monograph on Goethe's poetics. On June 10, 1823, the painfully shy young man was bold enough to approach Goethe and ask for his help, and Goethe immediately sensed that this admirer could prove useful. He sent Eckermann's monograph to Cotta the following day with a note saying that the young man inspired *great confidence* and he intended *to employ him in certain preparatory work*.

Goethe took him under wing and arranged lodging even before Eckermann expressed an intention to remain. He praised his poems and his monograph and gave him a first assignment: to collect Goethe's anonymously written reviews from the volumes of the *Frankfurter Gelehrte Anzeigen* from 1772 and 1773. From that day on and for many years to come, Eckermann devoted all his energy to Goethe, who took him into his confidence, spoiled him with recognition and praise, and paid him miserably. Eckermann had to give private lessons, live in poorly furnished rooms, and keep postponing his marriage because Goethe didn't pay him enough to start a household. Goethe kept him on a short leash but arranged to have Jena award him an honorary doctorate and also advised him on his hair, his clothing, and his comportment. He wanted Dr. Eckermann to be presentable and cut a fine figure in general. He didn't entirely succeed, however. There always remained something obsequious and frail about him, if only toward Goethe. With others he was quite self-confident. He knew that he was more important to Goethe than the other assistants. Goethe thought so highly of him that he conferred on him, along with Riemer, the task of editing his literary remains. In Goethe's last years, when he could be quite uncommunicative, Eckermann's greatest service was getting him to talk. His conscientiousness, phenomenal memory, intimate knowledge of Goethe's works, intelligent curiosity, and the style he had learned from Goethe made his *Conversations with Goethe* possible. Nietzsche, with some exaggeration, would later call it "the best German book there is."

Goethe had barely reached agreement with Cotta about the definitive edition in early 1826 when another project needed to be finalized with the publisher: an edition of Goethe's correspondence with Schiller. On December 19, 1806, a year and a half after Schiller's death, Cotta had first suggested publishing some of the two writers' letters in Cotta's house organ, the *Morgenblatt für gebildete Stände* (*Morning Paper for the Educated Classes*). Goethe did not respond, but seventeen years later, on June 11, 1823, told his publisher what extraordinary pleasure it had just given him to browse in Schiller's letters. He called the collection *perhaps the greatest treasure I possess*. The following year, he published a few of the letters in the periodical *Über Kunst und Altertum*. He did it as a sample, and now he intended to publish the entire correspondence. First he needed to win over Schiller's widow, Charlotte, for the project, as his letters to Schiller were in her possession. After complicated, drawn-out negotiations, mainly about the fee, he came to an agreement with Schiller's heirs (Charlotte having since died) to split the royalties fifty-fifty, which was what Goethe had offered in the first place. The correspondence appeared in 1828–29 in six octavo volumes.

Goethe's friend was once again very close to him as he prepared the correspondence for publication, almost more so than when he was alive. Eckermann relates how he and Goethe were sitting together in 1826, a bundle of the letters on the table. Goethe reads from some, interrupts the reading to pour glasses of wine, has supper brought in but doesn't touch a bite, instead pacing the room, luxuriating in memories. "Schiller was so alive in his memory," Eckermann writes, "that his conversation . . . was wholly devoted to him." And so Goethe goes on at length about Schiller's boldness—even his *appreciation of cruelty* (for instance, when he wanted to make Duke Alba a witness to Egmont's fear of death). About his protean nature (*Every week he was a different and more complete person*). And about his talent for greatness (*Schiller cutting his fingernails was greater than these gentlemen*). There is no end to his praise, but of course there is criticism too: Schiller burned the candle at both ends, he was brilliant at theory but perhaps too brilliant. Didn't he spend too much time thinking about poetry instead of just plunging in and writing it? Questions, questions—but thinking about Schiller made him feel uplifted and revitalized.

In these years, Schiller's image reached its apotheosis for Goethe in the image of Hercules in Part Two of *Faust*. In the "Classical Walpurgis Night," Faust asks Chiron, *Will you not tell me something of Hercules?* And Chiron responds,

> *Alas! Awaken not my yearning . . .*
> *. . .*
> *I saw before my very eyes*
> *What all men honor as divine.*
> *And so he was: a monarch born.*

This fits with Goethe's remark that *Schiller seems . . . in absolute possession of his lofty nature.* In one of his last letters to Zelter, Goethe even spoke of a *Christ-like tendency* innate in Schiller: *he never touched something common without ennobling it.*

A bizarre episode occurred involving Schiller's skull. Schiller had been dead for twenty years, and his remains were to be disinterred and moved to the ducal crypt. In the interim, his (supposed) skull was deposited in the ducal library. Without permission, Goethe removed it from there to his house and kept it in his study for a year, until the end of 1827. That in itself is astonishing, given Goethe's strong aversion to any cult of death. *The parades of death* were distasteful, he said. What's more, this particular death's head became the inspiration for a poem. While he never gave a title to the "stanzas," Eckermann later used a conversation with Goethe to justify entitling the poem "While Contemplating Schiller's Skull." It begins by depicting the jumble of bones and skulls in the *solemn charnel house.* Lying in a heap are parts that don't necessarily belong together. And then the poet's gaze falls on a particular skull. It is not named, but referred to cautiously as a *Gebilde*—an object—yet everything points toward it: *You cryptic vessel, source of oracles! / How am I worthy to hold you in my hand, / Devoutly stealing this treasure from decay?* Like someone who hears the roar of the sea in a conch shell, the meditating poet feels himself transported to another sea at the sight of this *object* or *vessel,* this particular skull. It is a sea that *at flood tide streams with lofty shapes and figures.* All of natural history with its unending metamorphoses is conjured up in the meditator. As if washed ashore by this immense history, the skull now lies before him, and he takes from it the message *What more can one expect to gain in life, / Except that God as nature be revealed, / And how it makes the solid melt in spirit, / And solidly preserves what spirit yields.* Not long before his own death, while contemplating Schiller's skull, Goethe gives expression to his belief in the lasting power of *what spirit yields.* But this spirit is still always nature: *God as nature.*

Given the intensity of his dead friend's presence in Goethe's life, it is unsurprising that he had high hopes for the publication of their correspondence. He wrote to Zelter on October 30, 1824, *It will be a great gift offered to the Germans—nay, I may say to mankind. Two friends of the sort that augment each other by responding immediately and at length. It gives me such an odd feeling to experience what I once was.*

There was little initial reaction when the correspondence finally appeared, and reviews were at first mixed. Goethe made the painful discovery that while the epoch on which he and Schiller had left their mark was really over, it was not far enough in the past to be accepted as something priceless. The reviews were full of either routine hero worship or polemical disagreement. While the biographer and diplomat Karl August Varnhagen von Ense, husband of the Berlin writer and saloniste Rahel Varnhagen, welcomed the correspondence as a gift of "the richest profit for life," the liberal journalist and satirist Ludwig Börne saw Goethe and Schiller treading the "well-worn path of self-interest."

Goethe did not allow the negative reviews to irritate him. Times had simply changed. At the moment, they were passing him by, but one shouldn't be discouraged. Better times for his influence were sure to come. That was the unassailable conviction formulated in a letter to Zelter: *Young people are much too easily excited and then swept away in the maelstrom of the times; wealth and speed are what the world admires and everyone strives for; railroads, express letters, steamships, and every possible facility of communication—that's what matters to the educated world: to outdo and outlearn one another and thereby remain stuck in mediocrity.* As so often in the late letters, this is followed by defiant self-assertion: *Let us cling as much as possible to the attitudes with which we grew up; perhaps with a few remaining others, we shall be the last of an epoch that will not soon return.*

Karl Friedrich Zelter, recipient of this famous and oft-quoted letter and, as we have seen, Goethe's best friend after Schiller's death, was a marvel of vitality. He had learned bricklaying from the ground up and led one of the most successful construction companies in Berlin. He was the head of a large family, well-to-do and influential in the city, robust and decisive in his person, and possessed of native Berlin wit and common sense. Intelligent, straightforward to the point of earthiness, a good judge of men, and not easily intimidated, he could also be tender and sensitive. He liked difficult mathematical problems and appreciated emotional subtlety in works of art. He also loved music, which, as was his habit, he learned from the ground up, studying composition with the court composer Karl Friedrich Christian Fasch, Frederick the Great's music teacher. In the summer, he set off on foot at three in the morning for his lesson with Fasch in Potsdam, so that he could be back at his construction site in Berlin by noon. By the 1790s, Zelter was known for his lieder and choral compositions, and it is not surprising that spiteful tongues (the Schlegels for instance) made jokes about the bricklaying composer. But envious jibes from starveling intellectuals slid off Zelter's broad back. In 1791, he played a substantial role in founding the Singakademie in Berlin; it soon became the leading bourgeois music organization in Germany and a model for the numerous song circles and men's choruses then springing up. Zelter did much to help make nineteenth-century Germany a nation of singers.

He was ten years younger than Goethe and at first admired the poet from afar. He set several of Goethe's poems to music, and the poet praised the results: *if my poems have given rise to your melodies, then I can certainly say that your melodies have awakened me to many a song.* Zelter's admiration grew into respectful cordiality, and the two became very close, Goethe desiring the intimacy as much as Zelter. They soon corresponded with increasing trust, sharing the joys and sorrows of their daily lives, and in the last twenty years of his life, there was no one in whom Goethe confided so unreservedly. Any trace of patronizing disappeared entirely, and frequently it was Zelter who acted as Goethe's adviser and helper. Zelter's varied experience had enriched him; he retained an innate curiosity, had a ready enthusiasm, and was always eager to learn. He was no genius, but did everything with solid workmanship—as the head of his household, as a builder, composer, organizer of musical events, and for a time as a member of city government. Zelter was a man after Goethe's own heart: multitalented, always active, yet calm and collected. While correspondence with other friends often slowed or stopped altogether, the exchange of letters with Zelter only grew more frequent, and Goethe could not get enough of it. *Farewell, and tell me something again soon, so there aren't such long pauses in between,* he once wrote him. *Otherwise without realizing it, someone will pause himself right into eternal life.*

An important date in the history of their friendship was November 1812. A despairing Zelter informed his friend of the suicide of his stepson, a young man who had given him some cause for worry but in whom he had placed great hopes. "Speak a healing word to me. I need to pull myself together, but I'm no longer what I was some years ago," he wrote. In his answer, Goethe suddenly switched to the familiar *du:*

My dear friend, your letter relating the great calamity that has befallen your house has very much depressed, indeed, bent me down with grief, for it found me in very solemn contemplation of human life, and only the thought of you has raised my spirits again. He writes of his own thoughts of suicide—as discussed in chapter 9 in the context of *Werther*—the *weariness of living* that he knew from personal experience, and how he repeatedly saved himself from complete *shipwreck* by undertaking some activity. And then he wrote these wonderful words of profound cheer: *And so it is in all the tales of sailors and fishermen. After a storm at night, one reaches shore at last. The soaking man dries himself off and the next morning, when the glorious sun reappears on the shimmering waves, the sea regains its appetite for figs.**

Here Goethe was consoling Zelter; later, Zelter had the opportunity to provide consolation in return. When Goethe's son, August, died in 1830, Zelter wrote, "Our brotherhood, my dear friend, is proving to be a sober one. Must we go through this, and remain quiet and still?—Yes! We are compelled to watch an approaching calamity with our own eyes, but it is not a part of us. That is the only consolation."

Zelter's first visit to Weimar was in 1802, and eleven more followed, always at Goethe's urgent invitation. Goethe himself, however, was not to be lured to Berlin. Zelter was his eyes and ears in that city and always had to give him detailed reports of what was happening in the theater, at court, and elsewhere in the social life of Berlin. Goethe had a willing ear for indelicate gossip. And he loved the delicacies available in Berlin. Zelter could oblige him in both, bringing Teltow turnips, pickled fish, and sometimes even caviar; he was a well-to-do man. Goethe returned the favor with game hens, wines, and his newest works, which Zelter commented on in detail, at times critically. It was a lifelong comradeship that encompassed both the everyday and the exceptional. Zelter survived Goethe by only two months, his vitality sapped after the death of his friend. But he retained his mordant humor to the end. He wrote to an acquaintance after Goethe's death, "So far I've been separated from him by 36 miles.† Now I'm getting closer every day and he won't get away from me."

---

* Figs were a traditional offering for the sea and also have an erotic connotation here: the sea becomes lusty again.
† At the time, a mile (*eine Meile*) was about six or seven kilometers.

The lukewarm reactions to the correspondence with Schiller had not deterred Goethe from a plan to publish his correspondence with Zelter as well. Since the mid-1820s, the two were writing letters knowing they would be read by posterity. They maintained their familiar, intimate tone, yet one can sense, especially in Goethe's letters, that he is sometimes also addressing future readers. As, for example, in his withering critique of the Schlegels: *The Schlegel brothers, with all their rich talents, are and were their whole life long unhappy men; they wanted to be more than nature had granted them and have a greater effect than they were capable of; as a consequence, they did much mischief in art and literature.* He wrote those lines in his indignation at A. W. Schlegel's criticism of the Schiller correspondence. Zelter did not take it amiss when his friend sometimes let off steam for the reading public (of the future), but he himself retained his intimate tone and continued to write unself-consciously about his daily life and work.

Goethe had Zelter's friendship to the end. Of his other old friends, only Wilhelm von Humboldt and Knebel were still alive. Charlotte von Stein had died on January 6, 1827, at the age of eighty-four. Physically diminished and barely able to hear and see, she remained mentally alert to the end. "Unfortunately, I am like a stranger on the earth," she wrote to her favorite son, Fritz, who had spent his childhood in Goethe's house. When the weather was good, she sat on a bench in front of her house beneath the orange trees. Goethe, who visited her infrequently, once sat down beside her for a bit of a chat. Afterwards, she wrote, "How do you feel, dear Privy Councilor, after sitting on my hard bench yesterday? I reproached myself for not having a chair brought for you. . . . Don't take the trouble to answer, just hearing news that you are well will be pleasure enough."

Charlotte's only concern at the end was not to be a burden to anyone. She arranged to have her funeral procession not pass the house on the Frauenplan on its way to the cemetery. It might bother the "Privy Councilor." Goethe, who never attended funerals, stayed away this time too. There is no note of it in his diary, no mention in his letters.

Karl August died the following year, on June 14, 1828. He had just visited his Prussian relations in Berlin, and an honorary military review was held for him as general of the cavalry. It taxed him quite a bit, as did the other festivities. Zelter wrote from Berlin, "The grand duke had to put up with . . . the Grosse Oper beating their drums for him, and you can be glad if he comes back unscathed." Karl August had been feeling sick for some time and had extended his visits to the Bohemian spas in recent years. He sometimes still felt young enough, however, to jocularly call his friend Goethe "old fellow." He encouraged Goethe, by then living quite a reclusive life, to move about a bit and do some traveling again. Hoping to lure him outside, he once described the spring flowers in the park, meticulously giving the Latin name for each species: "the Acacia speciosa are like a snowfall, the Acalypha hispida are extremely beautiful, and the Glabra are just opening up. There is much to admire in the Belvedere!" Goethe answered this cheerful note at ceremonious length but also with a mischievous twinkle in his eye, *Your Royal Majesty's highly flowery admonitory communication with a wondrous flower thereon having reached me through the good offices of your spouse, it had such a happy effect on my stagnant condition that I have resolved this very day to make an attempt to discover the extent to which I might join the walkers and the strollers. This experiment will be conducted at some distance from frequented areas.*

Their tiff of 1817, when Goethe stepped down as theater director, was a distant memory, and neither made waves any longer. There had always been small irritations. The grand duke may or may not have made a sardonic joke out of conveying Goethe's proposal to Ulrike in the summer of 1823. With his Prussian sympathies, Karl August was no friend of Prince Metternich and was annoyed that Goethe made so much fuss about him. Metternich had used his influence to ensure copyright protection for Goethe's definitive edition, but when Goethe enthusiastically told the duke about the *most wonderful document* to that effect from Metternich's hand, Karl August changed the subject. He preferred to discuss barometric pressure and the new snowfall in the Thuringian Forest.

Goethe was actively involved in the celebration of the fiftieth anniversary of the grand duke's rule on September 3, 1825. He hosted a party at his own house that was not a part of the official festivities: although the grand duke belonged to the great world, he also wanted to demonstrate what the duke meant to him personally. "Many, many thanks for what was done in my honor on the night of September 3 at your house, my dear old friend," Karl August wrote by way of thanks.

Two months later, the fiftieth anniversary of Goethe's own service was celebrated, counted from the date of his arrival in Weimar rather than the date of his official appointment. The duke thanked him sincerely and in highly emotional language: "The golden anniversary of the service of my first minister of state, the friend of my youth . . . winning him permanently for the duchy I regard as one of the greatest ornaments of my administration."

Almost three years had passed since these festivities when Karl August unexpectedly died on the return journey from Berlin. Goethe reacted in the way we have become familiar with. When Chancellor Müller brought him the news, he cried, *Oh, that I had to experience this!* Then he sank into silence and made it clear he did not want to talk about it. Even his diary had only the laconic note on June 15 that the news had spoiled a celebration (probably some event at court). Nothing more until June 19: *Note to Chancellor Müller declining any participation in an obituary.* Goethe had composed a lengthy obituary after the death of Anna Amalia. But now, nothing. It remains a mystery, although there was speculation that this reluctance had to do with Goethe's unclear relationship to Karl Friedrich, the duke's hereditary successor. In any case, Goethe chose not to put himself forward, and before the official obsequies began he escaped to the palace complex in Dornburg, with its enchanting view across the valley of the Saale. He had apparently received official permission to go, since he noted in his diary under July 3, *Granted privilege of a sojourn in Dornburg.* It was a place of recollection: here he had once worked on *Iphigenia* and also spent time with the duke. There's a lovely description by Chancellor Müller of how Goethe passed his time there: "He could stand up in the midst of a conversation and say, *Allow me to hurry down to my rocks alone; for after such conversation it befits old Merlin to renew his friendship with the primeval elements.*" Müller continues, "For a long time and in good spirits, we watched him as he solemnly climbed down into the valley, wrapped in his light gray coat, halting first by this rock and then by that one or by individual plants, and testing the rocks with his mineralogist's hammer. The hills were already casting long shadows in which he was lost to sight like a ghostly presence."

On November 10, 1830, Goethe received news of the death of his son in Rome. Once again, Chancellor Müller brought the message. He also recorded Goethe's initial reaction: *non ignoravi, me mortalem genuisse.**

August had left for Italy in the spring, feeling it was the only way he could save himself. He simply couldn't stand it at home anymore. His relationship with Ottilie was in shambles. After his departure, Ottilie wrote to Adele Schopenhauer, the philosopher's sister, "August's return threatens me like an ominous cloud. . . . The thought that I might never see August again causes not the slightest feeling in me." August also felt liberated. Having to play the part of a great man's son had become a torment. He wanted to find himself at last and hoped he could succeed in Italy. After a few weeks, he wrote Ottilie with news of his initial success: "Neither prodigality nor curiosity could tear me from my family. The greatest extremity drove me to make a last attempt to save myself. Some who last saw me in Weimar may not realize it, but my behavior there was a desperate mask. I wish you could see me now! What peace has entered my mind, how strong I feel again."

He was still dogged by his father's shadow, however. Like his father, he intended to write his own *Italian Journey*, and when he wrote letters home, he was being monitored and had to prove himself. Goethe read them with a critical eye, almost like a reviewer. Where August wrote of finally being happy, his father found a forced, eccentric tone and too much calculation. Later he wrote that he had expected the worst. And the worst had happened. August contracted meningitis and died in the space of a few days. An autopsy revealed that his liver was also enlarged. He had been a drinker.

For a week after receiving news of the death, Goethe—who regularly wrote several letters every day—wrote none. On November 25, he suffered a pulmonary hemorrhage. Those around him feared for his life, but he recovered in just a few days. He wrote to Zelter, *The individual is still in one piece and in his right mind. Good luck!* In triumph he sent around the doctor's note announcing his recovery, but also complained of new burdens to bear. To Zelter: *The really strange and significant thing about this trial is that all the burdens I . . . thought to have delegated to a younger person I*

---

* Latin: I always knew I had begotten a mortal.

now must drag along by myself, and worse, must continue to do so. The eighty-one-year-old had to see to the household himself. Now he kept the key to the woodshed under his pillow. He had to check the shopping lists and keep the household staff in line. Yet it all seemed to invigorate him. People found him stronger and more youthful. That was the case in early December 1830 when Henriette von Beaulieu-Marconnay sent him her reminiscences of her friend Lili von Türckheim, née Schönemann—Lili, his erstwhile beloved. *I was so moved I had to press your precious pages to my lips,* he wrote to Henriette. Those vital spirits still stirred within him.

August 1831 was sunny and pleasant. Goethe wanted to avoid festivities for his eighty-second birthday on the twenty-eighth. It was the usual: he simply didn't feel that old and wanted not to be reminded of his age. Early on the morning of the twenty-sixth, a Friday, he had the horses harnessed up. Morning fog still lay on the landscape, but it promised to be a sunny day. A last excursion to Ilmenau to visit once more—and perhaps for the last time—the scenes of his past. *I have no love for the parades of death,* he often said, but he had all the more for the parades of life. And so he packed his two grandsons, Wolf and Walther, into the carriage. His servant Krause came too, but not Ottilie. He didn't want her along.

Why Ilmenau? He had tried to revive the silver mine there—the most important project of his first twenty years in government. The memory was both happy and painful. And he had often gone to Ilmenau with his son.

In May 1776, he had spent some wild weeks there with the young duke. They had wandered the surrounding country, been guests at alfresco meals and boisterous drinking parties, played practical jokes, rolled an innkeeper's wine barrels down the street. Serious business had been conducted here too. They had really tried to accomplish something. There had been stockholders' meetings. The fledgling legation councilor had ventured into the mine shaft. At the first grand celebration of the opening of the mine in 1784, Goethe had broken off his speech in midsentence, a bad omen. The mine project did not pan out. There were several accidents, the worst in October 1796, when a disastrous influx of water cost lives and destroyed everything that had been done up to that point. Three years later, the entire undertaking was moribund, as far as Goethe was concerned. One gallery remained open until 1812, but Goethe was no longer involved. It had been thirty years since he was last in Ilmenau. In spite of the failure of the mine, the region remained important to him. It was here that he learned to know, fear, and love rocks, here that he became a mineralogist. Nearby, on the Schwalbenstein, he wrote the fourth act of *Iphigenia*. The area around Ilmenau was also connected to his first love in Weimar. Charlotte von Stein had once visited him there. The cave in the Hermannstein, a bluff on the northwest slope of the Kickelhahn, was for him a symbol of their covert happiness.

Goethe described his final excursion to Ilmenau in a letter to Zelter, probably with an eye to posterity. We also have a description by the local administrative official Johann Christian Mahr, Goethe's guide along the familiar, overgrown paths and also on some new ones he didn't know.

On the second day of the outing, Saturday, August 27, he left the children in the care of his servant, and he and Mahr set off on a pilgrimage up the Kickelhahn. There was a marvelous view from the turret on the top of the hill. *Ah*, Goethe cried, *I wish my dear grand duke Carl August could have seen all this beauty once more!* He asked Mahr about the *little forest house* that had to be somewhere nearby. He wanted to see it. "And in fact," Mahr writes, "he strode vigorously through the blueberry bushes that stand quite tall on the crown of the hill until he came to the well-known two-story hunting lodge built of wooden beams and clapboards. A steep staircase leads to its upper story. I offered to lead the way, but he refused with youthful vivacity . . . and the words, 'Don't suppose I can't climb those stairs; I'm still quite capable of it.' Upon entering the upstairs room, he said, 'In bygone times I lived . . . eight days in this room and back then, I wrote a little poem on the wall. I'd like to have a look at it again.'" Sure enough, there were the verses, written in pencil. They were already well-known, although they had never appeared in any of the authorized collected works: *Über allen Gipfeln ist Ruh*—Peace lies over *all the peaks* . . . Goethe was seeing them here again for the first time, "and tears streamed down his cheeks," Mahr writes.

That was the subdued high point of his last outing to Ilmenau. His birthday was passed in serene happiness. Breakfast with his grandsons, and then a brass band arrived and played the choral *Nun danket alle Gott* (Now thank we all our God). Girls in white dresses with flowers in their hair recited poems. When that was over, Goethe set out a drinking glass he had brought along expressly for the occasion. It was a gift from Amalie von Levetzow from the summer of 1823 in Marienbad, and bore the initials of her daughters. He wrote to Amalie, not to Ulrike, *Today . . . I put the glass in front of me that harkens back so many years and recalls to me those beautiful hours.*

Goethe's report to Zelter betrays his powerful feelings, but the episode is carefully framed by nature and humanity. *In a lonely wooden house on the highest peak of the fir forest, I recognized the inscription,* he writes, and then continues, *After so many years I could then survey what lasts, what has disappeared. Successes stood out and cheered me, failures were forgotten, over and done with. People all continued to live as is their custom, from the charcoal burner to the porcelain manufacturer. Iron was being smelted, brown coal dug from the crevices . . . pitch boiled . . . and so it went, like ancient granite. . . . In general, a remarkable exploitation of the manifold surfaces and depths of the earth and mountains prevails.*

He spent his last half year busily occupied and full of curiosity, as always. He got out his Hegel again and wrote to Zelter, *Nature does nothing in vain is a philistine old saw. Nature is eternally alive and active, superfluous and extravagant in order that what is eternal may be continuously present, because nothing can persist. With that, I even think I'm approaching the Hegelian philosophy.* Nature is not useful and goal-oriented. Only *philistines* would think so. And that's what they think about art as well: that it should make itself useful. Nonsense. The true artist knows it is quite the opposite, he writes to Zelter. He makes art as it wants to be made, not as he wants it, much less as the public wants it. The world cannot understand, because now only economics and utility matter. Hasty philistines rule the day, along with everything *veloziferisch* (a portmanteau word, coined in a draft letter to his grandnephew Nicolovius, that combines "velocity" with *luziferisch*—"satanical"). *Just as the steam engines are not to be stifled, neither is the new morality: the briskness of trade, the rustle of paper money, the accumulating debts to pay off other debts—those are its monstrous elements.* That was the world that was worrying him and troubling his rest. Not a good time for an inward-looking art, an art of contemplation and meditation that resisted quick consumption. An art that demanded attention. The draft continues, *I am compelled to think that the greatest curse of this era, which allows nothing to mature, is that every moment devours the one that preceded it. . . . No one is permitted to rejoice or suffer except as a pastime for others.*

In Goethe's last letter, written to Wilhelm von Humboldt on March 17, 1832, five days before he died, this anger at the present flares up once more: *The world is dominated by confusing lessons drawn from confused activity,* but he continues serenely, *and I have nothing more pressing to do than, if possible, to enhance what remains to me and to cohobate* my peculiarities, just as you do there in your castle, my worthy friend.*

Goethe's life was coming to an end. The last entry in his diary is also from March 17, 1832, a Friday: *Feeling unwell, spent all day in bed.* The day before, he had taken a ride in his carriage and probably caught a cold. He had sharp pains in his chest, a fever, and pressure in his bowels. His personal physician Vogel was alarmed: "He seemed somewhat distraught, but it was primarily his slack gaze that shocked me and the dullness of his normally bright, unusually lively eyes." There were periods of improvement when Goethe was eager to talk to visitors and make jokes. But they didn't last long. Vogel was called in on the morning of March 20. "A woeful sight awaited me! Terrible fear and unrest drove the aged man, long since accustomed to only measured movement, into bed—where he vainly sought relief by changing his position from one moment to the next—and then back to the armchair standing next to the bed. His teeth chattered from the chills he was having. The pain that was more and more concentrated in his chest, pressed now groans and now loud cries from the tortured man. His features were distorted, his face ashen, his eyes deeply sunk into their livid sockets, dull, bleary. His glance expressed the most terrible fear of death."

On the following day, March 22, Goethe was calmer. He was able to sit in his armchair and say a few words that were difficult to understand. He lifted an arm and drew something in the air. Letters. The doctor thought he recognized a *W.* Tradition has it that he said, "More light," but the doctor didn't hear it.

It was noon when he nestled comfortably into the left-hand corner of his chair.

---

* *cohobieren*: an alchemical term meaning to distill or purify.

FINAL REFLECTION

Becoming Who You Are

....

GOETHE WANTED TO FINISH THINGS. RIGHT UP TO THE end it left him no peace. He finished *Faust* not long before he died. The same with *Poetry and Truth*. He allowed the second version of *Wilhelm Meister's Journeyman Years* to be published in 1829 so that it would at least appear to be finished. The editors of the definitive edition still had some things to do after his death, but he had already done much (he thought most) of the work of getting his literary remains in order.

Although Goethe sought to finish individual works, he hated the idea that life was not complete until its end. Every moment of life was supposed to have worth and significance not vis-à-vis some final goal but in and of itself. He rejected a teleological concept of life. He had no intention of serving some large historical purpose or of forcing his own life toward some assigned objective, even though in 1780 he used a pyramid that he intended to complete to its peak as the image for his life's work. He was ready to accept that he would not succeed, but it was worth a try. He owed that to his conception of a work of art, which usually has a beginning and an end.

The results were one thing, his constant activity another: Goethe could not imagine that would ever end. He told Eckermann on February 4, 1829, that his conviction of continued existence sprang from his concept of activity. If he worked unstintingly to the end, then nature was obliged to assign him another form of existence, since the current one was no longer able to carry his creative spirit. What remained was a creative restlessness. As an eighty-two-year-old, he said that he was always striving forward and therefore forgot things he had written and had to take possession of them anew, they seemed so foreign to him. It's true that in old age, he carefully collected his writings and whenever possible, asked people to return his letters. He wanted to have his own works around him, but he preferred leaving it to others to figure out their coherence and interconnections. He doubted that there was such a thing and declared that whatever sense and significance each work had could stand by itself and be comprehended on its own terms. He bet on the creative moment and for him life was a series of such moments, reflected in individual works. Taken together, they might amount to a great *confession*. However, its meaning did not emerge only at the end of his life but in every motivating moment.

He created such moving moments and was also moved in turn. His influences were many, and he received, reworked, and responded to them. He had no fear of being influenced, as he did not strive for originality for its own sake. For him, the creative act was a connection between the individual and what transcended individuality. He thought of himself as a kind of medium for the spirit of the times. He wanted to prove himself as an individual but also—as he says in *Faust*—subsume within himself the lot of all humanity. Shortly before he died, he told the court tutor Frédéric Soret that he was a *collective singular* by the name of Goethe.

The exhilaration of the creative act, subjective as it was, also meant something objective for him, a sign that he had hit on a truth. He did not think much of poets who withdrew all too modestly into their own subjectivity. He wasn't satisfied with expressing himself. He wanted to grasp the world both poetically and scientifically and locate himself within it. Everything about him strove outward, sought objective form. Internalization was not what he was after. As he once wrote, he could understand himself only via the world. The world was enough of a riddle for him; he didn't look for riddles in the wrong place—in murky inner worlds, for instance.

He once wrote to Schiller that he took satisfaction from being able to get closest to nature when he followed his own nature. Goethe placed great trust in his instincts and intuition and in his sometimes somnambulistic self-assurance. He thought epistemology erroneous if it tried to define the subject out of the world, as if it were not intimately connected to it. For that reason, he was actually suspicious of Kantianism, although he always expressed great respect for the Königsberg philosopher. He was too impatient and hungry for experience to stop and analyze the instruments of cognition, even when Schiller sometimes gave him access to such an analysis. He didn't want to perceive perception, he wanted to perceive the world. When Hegel took aim at Kant by saying that the fear of error could itself be error, Goethe heartily agreed. He wanted to eat, not just study the menu.

It was simply impossible for him to think himself out of the world, as philosophers sometimes do for methodological reasons. And he was always out there in the world while also remaining collected. His character was objective through and through. He took his own creative intelligence as something through which nature could observe itself and poetry produce itself. He always contemplated his subjectivity from an objective standpoint. It is no accident that, in the letters of his final years, he often simply leaves out the first-person pronoun *ich*.

That didn't keep the next literary generation, young writers of the 1820s, from branding him the greatest egotist and a prince's toady who had feathered his own nest and was indifferent to the fate of those who labor and are heavy laden. Börne hurled thunderbolts at Goethe, saying that he had not used his "fiery tongue" to defend the rights of the common people. One heartless aristocrat fewer, some said at the news that Goethe was dead.

Something of that still clings to Goethe's image: the philistine who tends to his lovely garden and seeks shelter from the storms of history, selfishly concerned for his own welfare. That was Ortega y Gasset's judgment of Goethe in 1932, the year of crisis. And in 1947, Karl Jaspers would accuse Goethe—but even more, his admirers—of escapism and irresponsibility. We experienced situations in which evil reigned and heard the screams of horror, said Jaspers, and realized that "we had no more inclination to read Goethe." But others reacted differently; others read Goethe as a means of survival in great distress and despair. Especially in Goethe's works, we see the gentle provocation of art: even when it presents what is painful and terrible, it retains a peculiar serenity. Since his days, that serenity has become offensive for some who try to force art into a false kind of earnestness. Goethe insisted that art keeps us from foundering on reality. If someone deals us a nasty trick, we always still have play, in which we can *stroll quite well / from heaven through the world to hell.*

Heinrich Heine, who considered Goethe the representative of divine poetry on earth, explained why his liberal colleagues from the Young Germany movement were so furious at Goethe: he was like a mighty tree that put everyone else in the shade and left them to wither. He was too much of a heathen for the pious, too erotic for the moralists, too aristocratic for the democrats. His trunk grew so tall, Heine wrote, that you couldn't top it off with the revolution's cap of liberty.

Nothing but art!—that was the reproach of a younger generation that was fighting for freedom and national unity and demanded that literature be politically engaged. Heine, who shared such sympathies (he said that political engagement was the professional obligation of the nightingales), defended Goethe even while making fun of him. Goethe, he wrote, was like the ancient sculptor Pygmalion, who created a statue of a beautiful woman, fell in love with her, and yet had no children by her as far as anyone knew—voilà the uselessness of art for anything practical. Heine warned against making social usefulness the most important criterion and imagined the frightful consequence for the future should that opinion triumph: pages of poetry books used to wrap packets of coffee, flour, and snuff.

Goethe himself found contemporary German literature hardly worth a mention. The late Romantics were too fantastical and sentimental, others too pious or prissy, others too realistic or too politically agitated. In the German literature of his late years, he said he found a world that was either a blue haze or a field hospital. By contrast, he praised the authors whom he read with pleasure: the Frenchmen Balzac, Stendhal, and Hugo; the Englishmen Scott and Byron; the Italian Manzoni. In their works he found bustling life and great passion. This was world-class literature. Thus German authors of the younger generation had plenty of reason to feel themselves badly treated by the Old Master, and some paid him back in kind. Wolfgang Menzel in Stuttgart, one of the most influential literary critics of the day, managed the feat of completely ignoring Goethe's death in the literary journal he edited. It wasn't even worth a mention.

Goethe foresaw that the contemporary age would not be friendly to him, and he wrote as much in his last letter to Humboldt. He could sense the shifts heralded by the July Revolution of 1830: the triumph of industry, the age of the machine, increasing mobility, acceleration, the concentration of communication, the growth of the cities, the masses gaining prominence in politics and public life. It was the beginning of a new era, one in which the spirit of economics, social utility, and practical realism were in great demand. Art, literature, and philosophy were losing respect and prestige and becoming at best a beautiful irrelevancy.

Part Two of *Faust*, however, proves that the changing times didn't just frighten him. He also admired their dynamism and energy. But the darker aspects of such developments are also part of the theme of the play. Goethe allowed himself no illusions: it wasn't just Philemon and Baucis who would be beset by the spirit of the new age but also the entire *delicate empiricism* of poetry. Demand for the tangible, practical, and utilitarian would triumph. He also foresaw that a modern form of worry would be on the rise, for technology brings improvements but also new fears and new risks. While Faust builds dikes against the elements, a society of risk is also born in which worry about the future is omnipresent. As its personification says,

> *Once I've got ahold of someone*
> *Nothing in the world can help him.*
> . . .
> *Be it bliss or be it sorrow*
> *He puts it off until tomorrow.*

Goethe could look far and wide but in vain for an audience who would understand the *sober jests* in Part Two of *Faust*. And it was truly half a century before that part of the play was produced for the first time. His posthumous reputation was as he had feared: the *flotsam and jetsam of time* drifted over him. The hundredth anniversary of his birth in 1849 passed almost unnoticed, while Schiller's hundredth anniversary ten years later was a national holiday; the first great show of strength of the bourgeois movement for freedom and national unity after the failed revolution of 1848 came under the banner of the inspiring poet of freedom.

Goethe was absolutely unsuitable for such celebrations. He didn't trust his *dear Germans*—as he called them ironically—an inch. He preferred to keep them at a distance. And as for freedom, he had always cherished it but never demanded it rhetorically as a political goal. His outward circumstances had been favorable. But even inherited freedom must be re-earned if one is to really possess it. Goethe used his freedom creatively. He is the great example of how far you can go when you accept the lifelong task of becoming who you are.

———

I recall a complimentary reproach once made by a friend of my youth. He said, What you live is better than what you write, and it would please me if that were still true.

—GOETHE TO REINHARD
JANUARY 22, 1811

TRANSLATOR'S ACKNOWLEDGMENTS

I OWE A LARGE DEBT OF GRATITUDE TO RÜDIGER SAFRANSKI for his patience and promptness in answering the host of questions that arose during work on the translation. Thanks also to Robert Weil for his enthusiasm for the project and, especially, to Janet Byrne, whose splendid work as a copy editor made this a better book than it would have been without her.

CHRONOLOGY

1749

AUGUST 28: Johann Wolfgang Goethe born between noon and one o'clock in the house on the Hirschgraben in Frankfurt am Main. Father: Johann Caspar Goethe (1710–82); mother: Katharina Elisabeth Goethe, née Textor (1731–1808).

1750

DECEMBER 7: Cornelia Friederike Christiana Goethe born (died, 1777). Of Goethe's four other younger siblings—two boys and two girls—Hermann Jakob lived to be six years old; the others died in infancy.

1753

Goethe's grandmother gives him a puppet theater for Christmas.

1755

The house on the Hirschgraben is renovated after his grandmother's death.

1756–63

SEVEN YEARS' WAR. Goethe's father supports of Frederick the Great; his grandfather Textor, the emperor. Frankfurt periodically occupied by French troops. Clash between Goethe's father and Thoranc, the military governor of Frankfurt. Frankfurt painters frequent the house. Goethe's first acquaintance with French theater.

1763

Hears the seven-year-old Mozart in recital. Meets "Gretchen" and is exploited by dubious friends, with unpleasant consequences.

1764

Joseph II crowned Holy Roman Emperor in Frankfurt. High point followed by ennui. Goethe retreats into books.

1765

SEPTEMBER 30: departs for Leipzig to study law (until August 1768). Much socializing, literary experiments, letters; hardly any serious study.

1766

Affair with Anna Katharina (Kätchen) Schönkopf. Friendship with the tutor Ernst Wolfgang Behrisch.

1768

Friendship with Behrisch's successor Ernst Theodor Langer. Religious influences. Studies engraving and etching with Johann Michael Stock and drawing with Adam Friedrich Oeser. Avoids meeting Lessing.

MARCH: visits the painting gallery in Dresden.

JULY: pulmonary hemorrhage.

AUGUST 28: leaves Leipzig without saying goodbye to Kätchen.

Annette, manuscript book of poems. *The Lover's Spleen.*

1769

Recovers slowly. Experiments with religion. Dabbles in alchemy and magic. Among the Herrnhuters. Acquaintance with the "beautiful soul" Susanna Katharina von Klettenberg. Finishes *Partners in Guilt*, begun in Leipzig.

1770

Begins keeping a commonplace book, *Ephemerides.*

MARCH: arrives in Strasbourg to finish his legal studies.

Climbs the steeple of the Strasbourg cathedral.

SEPTEMBER: beginning of the friendship with Johann Gottfried Herder.

OCTOBER: in Sesenheim for the first time. Beginning of the romance with Friederike Brion.

1771

JUNE: Meets Jakob Michael Reinhold Lenz.

Goethe's dissertation is rejected.

AUGUST: defends a set of theses and graduates as a licentiate of law. Returns to Frankfurt, where he is not accorded the title doctor of law. Begins work as a lawyer. Makes plans for *Faust.*

OCTOBER: gives a speech in the house on the Hirschgraben to celebrate Shakespeare's name day.

NOVEMBER TO DECEMBER: first draft of *Götz.*

Beginning of the friendship with Johann Heinrich Merck.

1772

Merck becomes editor of the *Frankfurter Gelehrte Anzeigen.* Goethe contributes frequent reviews.

JANUARY: execution of the infanticide Susanna Margaretha Brandt.

BEGINNING IN FEBRUARY, frequent visits to the Sentimentalists in Darmstadt (Herder's fiancée Karoline Flachsland, Luise von Ziegler, Franz Michael Leuchsenring, Merck). Goethe as the "Wanderer." The flock of his admirers grows.

MAY TO SEPTEMBER: practicum at the Imperial High Court in Wetzlar. Falls in love with Charlotte Buff. Friendship with her fiancé Johann Christian Kestner.

SEPTEMBER: leaves Wetzlar without saying goodbye. Returns to Frankfurt on foot. Visits Sophie von La Roche and her daughter Maximiliane (later married to Peter Anton Brentano and mother of Clemens and Bettine Brentano). Falls in love with Maximiliane.

1773

JUNE: after a revision, *Götz von Berlichingen* is published. Goethe writes farces and hymns, fragments of a play about Prometheus, scenes for *Faust*, and poems in folk-song style ("Sah ein Knab' ein Röslein stehn"—"Saw a lad a little rose").

Cornelia Goethe marries Goethe's friend Johann Georg Schlosser. Goethe reads Spinoza for the first time. Scenes of jealousy in the Brentano household.

1774

APRIL: finishes *Werther*.

Johann Kaspar Lavater visits Goethe in Frankfurt. Beginning of their friendship.

SUMMER: travels down the Rhine with Lavater and Basedow: two prophets and "the world's child in between." Meets with Jung-Stilling. Beginning of the friendship with the philosopher Johann Georg Jacobi.

Werther an international best-seller. Streams of visitors and the merely curious to the house on the Hirschgraben, including prominent literary figures such as Klopstock.

LATE FALL: writes the hymn "Bedecke deinen Himmel, Zeus" ("Cover your heaven, Zeus").

Ice-skating, chess, and collaboration on Lavater's *Physiognomic Fragments*.

DECEMBER: Knebel's visit. Goethe is introduced to the Weimar princes Karl August and Konstantin on their way through Frankfurt.

Begins work on *Egmont*.

1775

Love affair with Anna Elisabeth ("Lili") Schönemann. At the same time, begins to correspond with his soulmate Countess Auguste ("Gustchen") zu Stolberg.

APRIL: engagement with Lili.

MAY TO JULY: travels to Switzerland with the Stolberg brothers, dressed like Werther. En route, meets with Karl August in Karlsruhe. Visits his sister in Emmendingen and meets with Lenz. With Lavater in Zurich. Climbs to the top of the Gotthard Pass.

SEPTEMBER: on his way to Karlsruhe, Karl August—now the reigning duke—invites Goethe to Weimar.

AUTUMN: engagement to Lili is dissolved. Ready to travel to Weimar, Goethe waits in vain for the promised coach to carry him there. Decides to travel to Italy instead. The coach catches up with him in Heidelberg.

NOVEMBER: arrives in Weimar.

NOVEMBER 11: meets Charlotte von Stein.

Spends Christmas in the forester's lodge in Waldeck.

1776

APRIL: Karl August gives Goethe the garden house in the park as a gift.

Madcap adventures with the young duke: hiking, riding, shooting, fencing, card-playing, drinking, dancing, flirting with girls, and cracking whips. Klopstock writes an admonitory letter; Goethe rejects his interference.

APRIL: Lenz visits Weimar (until December 1). Other Sturm und Drang visitors show up: Klinger and Kauffmann.

MAY: visits the mine in Ilmenau for the first time.

JUNE: Goethe is named legation councilor with a seat and a vote in the privy council and a salary of 1,200 taler.

Occasional poems.

1777

Begins to write *Wilhelm Meister's Theatrical Mission*.

JUNE: Goethe's sister Cornelia dies.

NOVEMBER TO DECEMBER: travels alone on horseback and incognito to the Harz region. Visits Plessing, a despairing reader of *Werther*. Inspects the Harz silver mines. Climbs the Brocken. A "divine signal." The poem "Winter Journey in the Harz."

1778

JANUARY: Christel von Lassberg drowns in the Ilm River with *The Sorrows of Young Werther* in her pocket.

The Triumph of Sentimentalism performed for Countess Luise's birthday.

MAY: first and only trip to Berlin on a diplomatic mission with the duke. War of Bavarian Succession impending.

Works on *Egmont*.

1779

Works on *Iphigenia* while recruiting troops.

AUGUST: "crucifixion" of Jacobi's *Woldemar*. Falling-out with Jacobi.

Burns old papers before setting off for Switzerland with the duke. The idea of purity.

NOVEMBER: on the Gotthard Pass for the second time.

DECEMBER: en route, visits the Hohe Karlsschule military academy in Stuttgart, where Schiller is a student.

1780

JANUARY: opening of the newly constructed theater in Weimar. Begins work on *Tasso*.

AUGUST: Countess Branconi visits Weimar. Goethe torn between her and Charlotte von Stein.

SEPTEMBER: on the Kickelhahn mountain in Ilmenau. Writes the poem "Über allen Gipfeln . . ." ("Peace lies over all the peaks . . .").

Begins to study natural history, anatomy, and mineralogy. Writes letter to Lavater about completing the pyramid of his life.

1781

Beginning of estrangement from Lavater. Dispute about religion.

Tensions with the duke because of Karl August's prodigal spending.

1782

Diplomatic mission to the Saxon and Thuringian courts to discuss a possible league of princes. Father dies on May 25. Goethe moves into the house on the Frauenplan as a renter. Granted a patent of nobility. Works on *Wilhelm Meister's Theatrical Mission*.

OCTOBER: reconciliation with Jacobi.

Becomes a master mason.

1783

Takes Fritz von Stein into his house and takes charge of his rearing and education.

Meets with Georg Forster in Cassel. Corresponds with Jacobi about Spinoza.

1784

Resident company installed at the Weimar theater. End of amateur theatricals.

APRIL: official opening of the mine in Ilmenau; Goethe pauses inexplicably during his speech.

MARCH: discovers the intermaxillary bone.

Organizes relief efforts for flood victims in Jena.

Financial crisis necessitates drastic reductions in the duchy's army.

Journey to the Harz. Secret negotiations with the Duke of Braunschweig. Works on the epic poem *Die Geheimnisse* (*The Mysteries*). Intensive study of rocks. Composes the poem "Kennst du das Land . . ." ("Knowst thou the land . . .").

1785

Continues correspondence with Jacobi about Spinoza. Annoyance at Jacobi's unauthorized publication of the Prometheus poem. Combats tax evasion in Ilmenau. Works on *Wilhelm Meister's Theatrical Mission*.

1786

Intensive study of natural history. Discontent in his official duties. While preparing a new, authorized complete edition for Göschen, dissatisfaction with the large number of fragmentary works. Self-doubt. Secret preparations for the trip to Italy; not even Charlotte von Stein is informed.

LATE JULY: travels to Carlsbad.

SEPTEMBER 3: leaves Carlsbad for Italy, traveling under the name Philipp Möller. Incomplete manuscripts in his luggage: *Egmont, Iphigenia, Tasso, Faust, Wilhelm Meister*.

LATE OCTOBER: arrives in Rome. Meets Johann Heinrich Wilhelm Tischbein, Johann Heinrich Meyer, Karl Philipp Moritz, Angelika Kauffmann.

Keeps travel diary for Frau von Stein, who resents his secret departure. Recasts *Iphigenia* in blank verse.

1787

Goethe shadowed by the Austrian secret service. First letter from Karl August to Italy: grants Goethe a leave of unspecified duration.

FEBRUARY: visits Naples. Meets the painter Philipp Hackert and the British ambassador Sir William Hamilton and his mistress (and later wife) Emma, who stages *tableaux vivants* in scanty attire. Climbs Vesuvius.

Hopes to discover the *Urpflanze* in Naples.

MARCH: by sea to Sicily. Visits the Villa Palagonia to see the prince's architectural and garden follies. Visits the parents of Cagliostro, whose real name is Balsamo. Plans a tragedy about Nausicaa.

MAY: returns to Naples by sea.

JUNE: returns to Rome. Lessons in drawing and painting. Works on *Egmont*. Love affair with the Roman woman "Faustina." Extensive descriptions of his travels and of works of art for his friends in Weimar.

1788

APRIL 24: departs Rome.

JUNE 18: arrives in Weimar. Cool reception from Frau von Stein.

JULY: begins an affair with Christiane Vulpius.

SEPTEMBER 7: first, unsatisfactory encounter with Schiller at the Lengefelds'.

Karl Philipp Moritz visits Goethe for several weeks. Schiller is jealous.

Works on *Tasso* and studies Kant's *Critique of Pure Reason*.

1789

Schiller in Jena, conflicted feelings about Goethe. Goethe's friendship with Wilhelm von Humboldt begins.

AUGUST: finishes *Tasso*.

NOVEMBER: at the request of the duke, moves into the hunting lodge on the edge of town with Christiane.

DECEMBER 25: Goethe's son, August, is born. Cozy family life.

1790

Completes Göschen edition of his works (with a *Faust* fragment and *Tasso, Iphigenia*, and *Egmont* completed).

MARCH: travels to Venice to escort Anna Amalia home.

More studies of natural history.

1791

Goethe directs the reconstruction of the burned palace. The Weimar Court Theater has its first guest engagement in Lauchstädt. Goethe present at opening ceremony.

Goethe's friend Merck commits suicide.

The Masonic comedy *Der Gross-Cophta* (*The Grand Kophta*). Gives his fee to the Balsamo (Cagliostro) family.

"Art" Meyer settles permanently in Weimar.

1792

JUNE: returns to his house on the Frauenplan.

AUGUST TO NOVEMBER: accompanies the duke in the campaign against revolutionary France. On the way, visits his mother in Frankfurt, the Jacobis in Pempelfort, Plessing in Duisburg, and the pious princess Gallitzin in Münster. Edifying days after the adventures of war. Simultaneous work on the *Theory of Color*. Has no more taste for *Iphigenia*.

1793

Resumes work on his novel, now entitled *Wilhelm Meister's Apprenticeship*. Writes the antirevolutionary play *The Citizen-General* in just a few days.

MAY TO JULY: participation in the siege of Mainz.

Verse epic *Reynard the Fox*.

1794

At Goethe's wish, Fichte is appointed professor in Jena.

JUNE: Schiller invites Goethe to collaborate on *Die Horen*.

JULY 20: the *happy event* of a successful encounter with Schiller. Their friendship begins.

SEPTEMBER: Schiller spends two weeks in the house on the Frauenplan; intense discussions, many plans. Gives Schiller newly written chapters of *Wilhelm Meister* to read.

Finishes the "Roman Elegies" for publication in *Die Horen*.

1795

Meets Alexander von Humboldt. In Carlsbad, meets Rahel Levin, who later marries Karl August Varnhagen von Ense and presides over one of Berlin's most prominent salons.

AUGUST: first tunnel collapse in the Ilmenau mine.

Prepares to travel to Italy, but the trip is scrapped because of armed conflict in the south.

Conversations of German Émigrés, including "The Fairy Tale," for *Die Horen*.

DECEMBER: has the idea of writing satirical "xenias" against the literary establishment. Schiller enthusiastic about collaborating on them.

1796

APRIL: production of Schiller's adaptation of *Egmont* in Weimar. Enjoys amusing collaboration with Schiller on the *Xenias*. Finishes *Wilhelm Meister*. High point of his correspondence with Schiller about the novel.

SEPTEMBER: begins work on *Herrmann and Dorothea*.

OCTOBER: tunnel collapse and catastrophic flooding in the Ilmenau mine. End of the project.

1797

The actress Karoline Jagemann, later mistress of the duke, begins employment at the Weimar theater. At first, Goethe holds her in high regard. Sends Schiller the first outline of the *Theory of Color*.

MAY: again plans a trip to Italy.

Goethe and Schiller encourage each other to write ballads. Return to *Faust*. In a great auto-da-fé, Goethe burns all the letters he has received since 1792 and names Schiller as his executor. Breaks off work before his trip to Switzerland (August to November). In Frankfurt, Hölderlin pays him a visit; Goethe has no appreciation for his work.

Goethe avoids an encounter with Lavater when he sees him on a street in Zurich.

After his return from Switzerland, begins the epic poem *The Death of Achilles*, but soon abandons it.

1798

The end of *Die Horen*. Purchases an estate in Oberrossla. Allows the Schlegel brothers to court his favor and tries unsuccessfully to mediate between them and Schiller. *Propyläen* is published.

OCTOBER: the renovated theater opens with a performance of Schiller's *Wallenstein's Encampment*. Goethe again working on *Faust*.

1799

MARCH: Fichte is dismissed in the wake of the atheism controversy. Goethe purchases a coach and horses and invites Schiller on frequent excursions.

AUGUST: first letter to Zelter. Finds a house for Schiller in Weimar.

DECEMBER: Schiller moves to Weimar.

1800

JANUARY: Goethe's translation of Voltaire's *Mahomet* performed in Weimar to great acclaim.

NEW YEAR'S EVE: celebrates the new year with Schiller and Schelling; lively discussion.

1801

JANUARY 3: falls seriously ill with shingles; near death. Gradual recovery after two weeks. Resumes work on *Faust*. Discusses natural philosophy with Schelling. Takes the water in Bad Pyrmont; discusses natural science with academic acquaintances in Göttingen. Hegel visits for the first time. Goethe works on *The Natural Daughter* and plans a cycle of plays.

1802

Produces plays by the Schlegel brothers, but the public rejects them and Kotzebue mocks them. Again Goethe considers resigning as theater director. The duke keeps him on. Goethe and Schiller collaborate on the principles of a purified theater: the *Weimar Dramaturgy*.

1803

APRIL: disappointing premiere of *The Natural Daughter*. Discord with Herder. Sale of the estate in Oberrossla at a loss. Founding of the *Jenaische Allgemeine Literatur-Zeitung* (*Jena General Literary Journal*). Riemer hired as tutor for August and as Goethe's secretary.

DECEMBER: Herder dies. Stressful visit of Madame de Staël.

1804

MAY: Schiller in Berlin, where he receives a tempting invitation to move there. Goethe succeeds in keeping him in Weimar. Their friendship is restored.

1805

At Schiller's suggestion, Goethe translates Diderot's *Rameau's Nephew*. Schiller sickens and dies on May 9. Goethe also falls seriously ill. Recovers slowly. Tries and fails to complete Schiller's *Demetrius*. Writes "Epilogue on Schiller's 'The Bell'" for a memorial service in Lauchstädt on August 10.

1806

AUGUST: has long conversation about *Faust* with Luden.

OCTOBER 14: Battle of Jena. Prussia defeated. Weimar occupied by French troops. Goethe in mortal danger. Christiane's courage. Goethe survives unscathed.

OCTOBER 19: hasty, unannounced marriage to Christiane. Puts his financial and testamentary affairs in order.

1807

Works on the *Theory of Color*.

MAY: writes the first chapter of *Wilhelm Meister's Journeyman Years*. Finishes *Faust, Part I* for Cotta's first complete edition.

Works on *Pandora's Return*.

1808

Faust, Part I is published. *Elective Affinities* is extracted from the stories in the *Journeyman Years* and expanded into a novel in its own right.

Goethe directs an unsuccessful production of Heinrich von Kleist's *The Broken Jug*.

OCTOBER 2: first meeting with Napoleon at the congress of European princes in Erfurt.

NOVEMBER: because of conflicts with Karoline Jagemann, Goethe tries to resign his directorship of the theater. The duke keeps him on.

1809

Works on the *Theory of Color*.

OCTOBER: *Elective Affinities* is published.

Drafts an outline for an autobiography.

1810

MAY: first letter to Sulpiz Boisserée; their friendship begins.

The *Theory of Color* is published to little critical notice.

In Carlsbad during the summer, socializes with Empress Maria Ludovika of Austria.

OCTOBER: asks Bettine Brentano to pass on to him his mother's stories of his childhood.

1811

Works on *Poetry and Truth*. Bettine, now married to Achim von Arnim, visits Weimar, quarrels with Christiane. Goethe breaks with Bettine.

OCTOBER: Part 1 of *Poetry and Truth* is published.

1812

French troops are quartered in Weimar during Napoleon's Russian campaign.

Goethe spends May to September in Carlsbad and Teplitz. More socializing with Empress Maria Ludovika. Meets Beethoven in Teplitz. Beethoven plays for him on July 21.

SEPTEMBER: news of the burning of Moscow reaches Goethe.

OCTOBER: Part 2 of *Poetry and Truth* is published.

On his retreat from Russia, Napoleon passes near Weimar and sends greetings to Goethe.

1813

JANUARY: Wieland dies. Goethe has long conversation with Falk about immortality.

APRIL: goes to Carlsbad early on account of the unsettled military situation.

OCTOBER: Napoleon suffers crushing defeat at the Battle of Leipzig.

Goethe prevents his son, August, from volunteering for combat duty.

Conducts color experiments and discusses the *Theory of Color* with Arthur Schopenhauer.

1814

MAY: Part 3 of *Poetry and Truth* is published.

Goethe prevents a duel between August and a returned volunteer who accused him of cowardice.

Writes *Epimenides Awakes* for a celebration of peace in Berlin.

JUNE: reads poems by Hafez.

JULY TO OCTOBER: travels to the Rhine, the Main, and the Neckar. Meets with Boisserée and friends from Frankfurt. Composes the first *Divan* poems.

AUGUST 4: meets with Johann Jakob Willemer and Marianne Jung.

SEPTEMBER 15: first visit to the Gerbermühle with the Willemers (Marianne having married Willemer in the meantime).

Celebrates the first anniversary of the Battle of Leipzig with the Willemers. Returns to Weimar, where he writes more *Divan* poems.

Plans a new complete edition for Cotta.

1815

Works on the *Italian Journey*.

MAY TO OCTOBER: travels to the Rhine, Main, and Neckar.

Extensive conversations with Boisserée about German art.

AUGUST 28: birthday celebration in the Gerbermühle. Romance and lyrical dialogue with Marianne.

SEPTEMBER: in Frankfurt for the last time. Bids farewell to Marianne and will never see her again.

Cloud studies. Goethe officially named Minister of State for the Grand Duchy of Weimar.

1816

JUNE 6: Christiane dies.

JULY 20: intends to take the waters in Baden-Baden and visit the Willemers. Carriage tips over shortly after leaving Weimar. Goethe, although unhurt, cancels the trip.

SEPTEMBER: Charlotte Kestner ("Lotte" from Wetzlar) visits Goethe.

DECEMBER: outline for *Faust, Part II*.

1817

APRIL 13: the conflict with Karoline Jagemann, now Frau von Heygendorf, comes to a head on account of a dog on the stage. Goethe is relieved of the theater directorship.

August von Goethe marries Ottilie von Pogwisch.

OCTOBER: writes the poem "Urworte: Orphisch" ("Primal Words: Orphic"). Nationalist celebration, including a book burning, on the Wartburg. Patriotic fraternity students irritate Goethe and cause trouble for the duke.

1818

Natural history studies in morphology and color theory. Systematic meteorological observation. Birth of his first grandson, Walther Wolfgang.

At Carlsbad in the summer, works on the *Notes and Essays toward a Better Understanding of the West-Eastern Divan*.

1819

MARCH: Jacobi dies.

AUGUST: *West-Eastern Divan* is published.

The assassination of Kotzebue by the Jena student Sand in March leads in September to the Carlsbad Decrees to suppress the democratic-patriotic movement.

A production of *Egmont* in Berlin is prohibited. Goethe refuses to cede disciplinary oversight over the University of Jena to a trustee.

Works on the *Annals* and the *Campaign in France*.

1820

Summer in Carlsbad. Resumes work on the *Journeyman Years*. Studies cloud formations.

SEPTEMBER: birth of his second grandson, Wolfgang Maximilian.

1821

MAY: first version of *Wilhelm Meister's Journeyman Years* is published.

Studies morphology.

Summer in Marienbad and Eger. Meets Amalie von Levetzow and her seventeen-year-old daughter, Ulrike.

Writes for the journal *On Art and Antiquity*.

1822

SUMMER: again in Marienbad. Socializes with the Levetzows. Falls in love with Ulrike, is with her at dances, parties, and rock collecting.

OCTOBER: the young Felix Mendelssohn-Bartholdy visits Goethe.

Student unrest in Jena.

1823

FEBRUARY: serious infection of the pericardium. Near death.

MARCH: complete recovery. Goethe seems rejuvenated, looks forward to another summer in Marienbad.

JUNE: first visit from Johann Peter Eckermann. Goethe asks him to stay in Weimar. Enthusiasm for and correspondence with Lord Byron.

JULY TO SEPTEMBER: Marienbad, Carlsbad, and Eger. Socializes with the Levetzows. Sends Karl August as messenger to ask for the hand of Ulrike. No official answer, but Ulrike turns him down. Goethe still has hope. Meets the Polish pianist Maria Szymanowska.

SEPTEMBER: on the journey home, Goethe writes down some lines of the "Marienbad Elegy."

OCTOBER: Szymanowska visits Goethe in Weimar. Emotional farewell.

1824

MARCH: writes the poem "To Werther" for the new edition of his first novels. Together with the poem of farewell to Szymanowska and the "Marienbad Elegy," it constitutes the "Trilogy of Passion."

Prepares the edition of his correspondence with Schiller.

Sorrow over Byron's death.

OCTOBER: Heinrich Heine visits Goethe.

1825

Studies plans for a canal in Panama.

MARCH: the Weimar theater burns down.

Franz Schubert sends Goethe some of his lieder but receives no answer.

NOVEMBER: the fiftieth anniversary of Goethe's service to the Weimar state.

1826

Becomes regular reader of the Saint-Simonian journal *Le Globe*. Ideas on world literature. Contemptuous remarks about contemporary German letters.

Succeeds in his efforts to get the German states to protect his copyright. Accepts
Cotta's offer of 60,000 taler for the definitive edition of his works.

Visit of Bettine von Arnim, the *tiresome gadfly*.

After the closing of an ossuary in Weimar, Goethe takes the (probable) skull of
Schiller home with him for a year, until it is interred in the ducal crypt.
Goethe keeps the key to Schiller's coffin in his house.

Reads James Fenimore Cooper's *The Last of the Mohicans*.

Drafts the chapter on the emigrants for the *Journeyman Years* and completes the
interpolated story "The Man of Fifty Years."

DECEMBER: Alexander von Humboldt visits Goethe.

1827

Reads Victor Hugo and writes to Sir Walter Scott.

Decides to compose the "Classical Walpurgis Night."

DECEMBER: writes the poem "Den Vereinigten Staaten" ("To the United
States").

1828

JULY: Karl August dies on the return trip from Berlin.

Goethe withdraws to Dornburg Castle.

DECEMBER: the correspondence with Schiller is published.

1829

August and Ottilie quarrel. Goethe tries in vain to reconcile them.

The second version of *Wilhelm Meister's Journeyman Years* is published.

JULY TO AUGUST: Goethe resides in the garden house for the last time.

AUGUST: first production of *Faust* in the Weimar theater.

Paganini plays for Goethe.

1830

Grand Duchess Luise dies.

APRIL: August von Goethe travels to Italy with Eckermann.

Goethe follows the events of the July Revolution in Paris with distress.

NOVEMBER: receives word of the death of his son on October 26.

Suffers a hemorrhage. Resumes work on *Faust, Part II*.

Contracts with Zelter to publish their correspondence posthumously.

1831

JANUARY: makes a will.

MARCH: returns Marianne von Willemer's letters along with a poem.

AUGUST: Finishes *Faust, Part II*. Probably seals it (but reopens it later).

AUGUST 26–31: last excursion to Ilmenau with his two grandsons and his servant.
Finds the poem "Über allen Gipfeln" ("Peace lies over all the peaks") still
written on the wall of the lodge on the Kickelhahn.

SEPTEMBER: finishes part 4 of *Poetry and Truth*.

1832

JANUARY: reads aloud from *Faust, Part II* for Ottilie.

FEBRUARY: letter to Boisserée with a detailed explanation of rainbows.

MARCH 14: last carriage ride.

MARCH 16: beginning of final illness.

MARCH 17: last letter (to Wilhelm von Humboldt).

MARCH 22: Goethe dies at noon.

NOTES

———

The following abbreviations are used in the notes:

GOETHE'S WORKS

WA   *Goethes Werke*, commissioned by the Grand Duchess Sophie of Saxony, 143 vols. (Weimar: H. Böhlau, 1887–1919). Known as the *Weimarer Ausgabe*.

MA   *Johann Wolfgang Goethe: Sämtliche Werke nach Epochen seines Schaffens*, ed. Karl Richter, Herbert G. Göpfert, Norbert Miller, Gerhard Sauder, and Edith Zehm, 33 vols. (Munich and Vienna: Hanser, 1985–98).

FA   Johann Wolfgang Goethe, *Sämtliche Werke: Briefe, Tagebücher und Gespräche*, 40 vols. (Frankfurt a. M.: Deutscher Klassiker Verlag, 1985–99).

HA   Johann Wolfgang von Goethe, *Werke*, ed. Erich Trunz, 12th ed., 14 vols. (Munich: Beck, 1981).

Tgb   Johann Wolfgang Goethe, *Tagebücher*, 5 vols. (Stuttgart and Weimar: Metzler, 1998–2007).

LETTERS

WA   See above: Abteilung (section) IV, 53 vols.

GBr   Johann Wolfgang von Goethe, *Briefe*, ed. Karl Robert Mandelkow and Bodo Morawe, 3rd ed., 4 vols. (Munich: Beck, 1988).

BranG   *Briefe an Goethe*, ed. Karl Robert Mandelkow, 3rd ed., 2 vols. (Munich: Beck, 1988).

BrEltern   Johann Caspar Goethe, Cornelia Goethe, and Catharina Elisabeth Goethe, *Briefe aus dem Elternhaus*, ed. Ernst Beutler (Frankfurt a. M.: Insel, 1997).

BW   *Christiane Goethes Ehe in Briefen: Der Briefwechsel zwischen Goethe und Christiane Vulpius, 1792–1816*, ed. Hans Gerhard Gräf (Frankfurt a. M.: Insel, 1989).

BW mit einem Kinde   Bettine Brentano, *Goethes Briefwechsel mit einem Kinde*, ed. Waldemar Oehlke (Frankfurt a. M.: Insel, 1985).

BW Reichardt   J. F. Reichardt–J. W. Goethe Briefwechsel, ed. Volkmar Braun-
behrens, Gabriele Busch-Salmen, and Walter Salmen (Wei-
mar: Böhlau, 2002).

BW Reinhard   Goethe und Reinhard: Briefwechsel in den Jahren 1807–1832
(Wiesbaden: Insel, 1957).

BW Schiller/Körner   Briefwechsel zwischen Schiller und Körner, ed. Ludwig Geiger,
4 vols. (Stuttgart and Berlin: J. G. Cotta, 1892).

BW Willemer   Johann Wolfgang Goethe, Briefwechsel mit Marianne und
Johann Jakob Willemer, ed. Hans-J. Weitz (Frankfurt a. M.:
Insel, 1965).

Schiller und Lotte   Schiller und Lotte: Ein Briefwechsel, ed. Alexander von
Gleichen-Russwurm, 2 vols. (Jena: Diederich, 1908).

Schopenhauer Briefe   Arthur Schopenhauer, Gesammelte Briefe, ed. Arthur Hüb-
scher (Bonn: Bouvier, 1978).

VB   Goethe in vertraulichen Briefen seiner Zeitgenossen, ed. Wilhelm
Bode, Regine Otto, and Paul-Gerhard Wenzlaff, 3 vols.
(Berlin and Weimar: Aufbau, 1979).

CONVERSATIONS AND OTHER BIOGRAPHICAL SOURCES

Gespräche   Wolfgang Herwig, ed., Goethes Gespräche, Biedermannsche
Ausgabe, 5 vols. (Zurich: Passau, 1965–87).

Unterhaltungen   Kanzler von Müller, Unterhaltungen mit Goethe, ed. Ernst
Grumach (Weimar: H. Böhlaus Nachfolger, 1956).

Bode   Wilhelm Bode, Goethes Leben, 9 vols. (Berlin: Mittler,
1920–27).

Gräf   Hans Gerhard Gräf, ed., Goethe über seine Dichtungen, 9 vols.
(Frankfurt a. M.: Rütten & Loening, 1904).

Grumach   Ernst Grumach and Renate Grumach, eds., Goethe: Begeg-
nungen und Gespräche, vols. 1–6 and 15 (Berlin: de Gruyter,
1965 ff.).

Ottilie   Ulrich Janetzki, ed., Ottilie von Goethe, Goethes Schwieger-
tochter: Ein Porträt (Berlin: Ullstein, 1982).

Steiger   Robert Steiger, ed., Goethes Leben von Tag zu Tag: Eine doku-
mentarische Chronik, 8 vols. (Zurich and Munich: Artemis,
1982–96).

OTHER SOURCES

Best   Otto F. Best, ed., Aufklärung und Rokoko (Stuttgart: Rec-
lam, 1976).

Leithold   Norbert Leithold, Graf Goertz: Der grosse Unbekannte: Eine
Entdeckungsreise in die Goethezeit (Berlin: Osburg, 2010).

Lenz   Jakob Michael Reinhold Lenz, Werke und Briefe, ed. Sigrid
Damm, 3 vols. (Munich: Hanser, 1987).

Schiller   Friedrich Schiller. Sämtliche Werke, ed. Peter-André Alt,
Albert Meier, and Wolfgang Riedel, 5 vols. (Munich and
Vienna: Hanser, 2004).

All quotations from Goethe are given in italics and without quotation marks. Quotations from all other sources are given between quotation marks.

CHAPTER I

1 *which may have benefited*: MA 16, 13.
2 *dressing gown like a cassock*: MA 16, 41 f.
2 *the feeling of inviolable peace*: MA 16, 42.
2 threw a knife at his son-in-law: See BrEltern, 152.
2 *never showed a trace of violence*: MA 16, 42
3 subaltern offices *ohne Ballotage*: MA 16, 79.
3 *Thereby . . . he had made himself the equal*: MA 16, 80.
3 "with no particular inclination . . . handsome man": BW mit einem Kinde, 438.
4 *My father considered his life*: MA 16, 34.
4 *to publicly declare himself*: MA 16, 75.
4 *I was not at all displeased; a kind of moral illness*: MA 16, 76.
4 *How true it is*: MA 16, 77.
4 *I cannot reconcile myself*: BW mit einem Kinde, 419.
4 *lovely, gaunt woman*: MA 16, 15.
5 *Add to that all the danger*: MA 1.1, 18.
6 *I wish they had sent you*: MA 16, 111.
6 *My father . . . was by nature*: MA 16, 17.
7 *I was supposed to follow*: MA 16, 34 f.
7 *slow to make; private articled; I completed*: MA 16, 736.
7 *Father gave me my physique*: MA 13.1, 228.
8 "don't plague the boy": BrEltern, 884 (July 1, 1808).
8 "Napoleon has even deklared": BrEltern, 838 (Feb. 2, 1806).
8 "The gift God gave me": BrEltern, 867 (Oct. 6, 1807).
8 "extremely eager": BW mit einem Kinde, 420.
8 "with shining eyes": BW mit einem Kinde, 421.
8 "I always thought": BrEltern, 402 f. (May 23, 1776).
9 *But whereas I felt relieved*: MA 16, 621 f.
9 "sworn a sacred oath": BrEltern, 473 (May 16, 1780).
9 "drink the less good wines": BrEltern, 477 (July 14, 1780).
9 "without a pinch of tobacco": BrEltern, 854 (May 16, 1807).
9 "I hear you've put on weight": BrEltern, 808 (Sept. 24, 1803).
9 "bare bottoms": BrEltern, 257.
9 "But since God has so favored me": BrEltern, 476 (May 19, 1780).
10 "He was accompanying his mother": Gespräche 1, 676.
11 "that he had done all this": BW mit einem Kinde, 420.
11 *the siblings shared and mastered*: MA 16, 14.
11 *The disaster had happened*: MA 16, 15.
12 *directly into contact; One felt free*: MA 16, 14.
12 *chance and caprice; The lad developed*: MA 16, 21.
13 *to a lovely, fruitful plain*: MA 16, 16.
13 *even when what was happening*: MA 16, 152.
14 *process, repeat, reproduce*: MA 16, 38.
14 *The lightning blazes*: MA 1.1, 81.

14 *God forbid; There'd be no honor:* MA 1.1, 23.
15 *who produced; deeply troubled me:* MA 16, 37.
15 *well-turned love letter:* MA 16, 184.
15 *And so I fooled myself:* MA 16, 187.
16 *I cannot deny:* MA 16, 240 f.
16 *weeping and raving; that I had sacrificed:* MA 16, 242.
16 *capable of penetrating:* MA 16, 243.
16 *greatest crowd:* MA 16, 244.
17 *choleric temperament; but where I have nothing:* WA IV, 1, 2 (May 23, 1764).
17 *for a hundred years:* WA IV, 1, 2 (May 23, 1764).
17 "For heaven's sake": VB 1, 6 (May 29, 1764).
17 "I learned that he is very devoted": VB 1, 6 (July 16, 1764).
17 "For the rest": VB 1, 7 (July 18, 1764).
17 "We were always the lackeys": Quoted from *Bode*, 1, 174.
17 "no matter which side he takes": VB 1, 12 (Oct. 3, 1766).
18 *taking pleasure:* MA 16, 261.

CHAPTER 2

19 *rambles through:* MA 16, 263.
19 *And in the end:* MA 16, 264.
19 *no scruples; impious:* MA 16, 265.
20 "It's off to jolly Saxony": Quoted from *Bode* 1, 180 f.
20 *I did not fail:* MA 16, 267.
21 "If you're to live in Leipzig": Quoted from Albert Bielschowsky, *Goethe: Sein Leben und seine Werke*, 2 vols. (Munich: Beck, 1905–06), 1:43.
21 *chickens, geese:* WA, IV, 1, 15 (Oct. 21, 1765).
22 "If you could only see him": VB 1, 9 (Aug. 12, 1766).
22 *I'm cutting a great figure:* WA IV, 1, 14 (Oct. 20, 1765).
22 *I have a bit more taste:* WA IV, 1, 81 f. (Oct. 18, 1766).
22 *Roman civil law:* WA IV, 1, 117 (Oct. 14, 1767).
23 *I'm going to hang myself:* WA IV, 1, 117 (Oct. 14, 1767).
23 *Just like a bird:* WA IV, 1, 13 (Aug. 21, 1765).
23 *Alone, alone:* WA IV, 1, 44 (April 28, 1766).
23 *You know how great my love:* WA IV, 1, 45 (April 28, 1766).
24 *The dust settles down:* WA IV, 1, 46 (April 28, 1766).
24 "Who opens up the womb of Earth": Quoted from *Best*, 157.
24 "Your wit would fain delight the world": Quoted from *Best*, 164 f.
25 "two valiant peoples": Quoted from *Best*, 73 f.
26 *whereupon the sizable old patriarch:* MA 16, 292.
26 *And so little by little:* MA 16, 319.
26 *Self-development through the transformation:* MA 16, 843.
26 *according to nature:* WA IV, 1, 113 (Oct. 2, 1767).
26 *Let them leave me be:* WA IV, 1, 89 (May 11, 1767).
26 *I open my eyes:* WA IV, 1, 8 (Oct. 12, 1765).
27 "If Goethe weren't my friend"; "very tenderly": VB 1, 11 (Oct. 3, 1766).
27 *I have gained her:* WA IV, 1, 60 f. (Oct. 1, 1766).
27 The little Schönkopf girl: *La petite Schoenkopf merite ne pas etre oubliée entre mes connoissances. . . . Elle est mon oeconome, quand il s'agit, de mon linge, de mes hardes,*

car elle entend tres bien cela, et elle sent du plaisir de m'aider de son savoir, et je l'aime bien pour cela: WA IV, 1, 86 (May 11, 1767).

29   *Honest man:* MA 1.1, 123.

29   He says what a pleasure it is: *C'est une chose tres agreable a voir, digne de l'observation d'un connoisseur, un homme s'efforcant a plaire . . . et de voir apres cela moi immobile dans un coin, sans lui faisant quelque galanteries, sans dire une seule fleurette, regardé de l'autre comme un stupide qui ne sait pas vivre, et de voir a la fin apportés a ce stupide des dons pour les quels l'autre feroit un vojage a Rome:* WA IV, 1, 62 (Oct. 8, 1766).

29   *With the most ardent caresses:* WA IV, 1, 101 (early Oct. 1767).

30   *Enamored eyes:* WA IV, 1, 102 (early Oct. 1767).

30   *In the bedroom:* WA IV, 1, 102 (Oct. 7 or 9, 1767).

30   *Love is misery:* WA IV, 1, 127 (Nov. 2, 1767).

30   *I can't help it:* WA IV, 1, 130 f. (Nov. 3, 1767).

31   *This hand:* WA IV, 1, 132 (Nov. 7, 1767).

31   *Ah Behrisch:* WA IV, 1, 134 (Nov. 10, 1767).

31   *My blood runs:* WA IV, 1, 134 (Nov. 10, 1767).

31   *I've cut myself a new quill:* WA IV, 1, 135 (Nov. 10, 1767).

31   *I found her box:* WA IV, 1, 137 f. (Nov. 10, 1767).

31   *I saw how coldly:* WA IV, 1, 138 (Nov. 10, 1767).

32   *Yet another quill; But I must fill up:* WA IV, 1, 139 (Nov. 10, 1767).

32   *It pleases the imagination:* WA IV, 1, 128 (Nov. 2, 1767).

32   *What shall I do tomorrow?:* WA IV, 1, 139 f. (Nov. 10, 1767).

32   *By this impetuous; What made the world:* WA IV, 1, 141 (Nov. 11, 1767).

32   *My letter has:* WA IV, 1, 143 (Nov. 13, 1767).

32   *the violence of love:* WA IV, 1, 145 (Nov. 20, 1767).

33   *It pleases her:* WA IV, 1, 146 (Nov. 20, 1767).

33   *We began with love:* WA IV, 1, 159 (April 26, 1768).

33   *good little piece:* WA IV, 1, 113 (Oct. 12, 1767).

33   *Can there be any harm:* MA 1.1, 289 f.

33   *No wonder; His jealousy's; Dear child:* MA 1.1, 291.

34   *If he tortures me:* MA 1.1, 292.

34   *Without a cause; Let him think:* MA 1.1, 293.

34   *You say you love Amine:* MA 1.1, 307 f.

34   *A little pleasure:* MA 1.1, 309.

35   *insulting and humiliating:* MA 16, 309.

35   *I never tired of pondering:* MA 16, 310 f.

35   *we have parted:* WA IV, 1, 158 (April 26, 1768).

35   *But not I:* WA IV, 1, 159 (April 26, 1768).

35   *upright man:* WA IV, 1, 157 (March, 1768).

35   *infected with the obsession; bad mood; terrible scenes:* MA 16, 307.

37   *My taste for beauty:* WA IV, 1, 178 (Nov. 9, 1768).

37   *Whether complete censure:* WA IV, 1, 179.

37   *His teaching influenced:* MA 16, 334 f.

37   *It was the first time:* MA 16, 346.

37   *I had really lost her:* MA 16, 308.

38   *And I'm going ever more downhill:* WA IV, 1, 160 (May 1768).

38   *What he had to say:* MA 16, 359.

39   *She greeted me:* WA IV, 1, 191 f. (Feb. 13, 1769).

CHAPTER 3

40 *lacked the compass; For one; cheerful, free:* MA 9, 937.
41 *before Easter:* WA IV, 1, 184 (Dec. 30, 1768).
41 *Johannismännchen:* WA IV, 1, 185 (Dec. 30, 1768).
41 *how life is lived:* WA IV, 1, 184 (Dec. 30, 1768).
41 *finding, instead of a sturdy:* MA 16, 362 f.
41 *certain smug arrogance:* MA 16, 369.
41 *aping:* MA 16, 375.
41 *all too superficial:* MA 16, 376.
41 *gloomy family background:* MA 16, 309.
42 *For the time being . . . hanged:* MA 1.1, 385.
42 *expresses playfully:* MA 16, 309.
42 *heavenly:* MA 16, 359.
42 *religious heroes:* MA 16, 144.
42 *a God stood at their side:* MA 16, 145.
42 *both in the greatest solitude:* MA 16, 152.
42 *general, natural religion; behind nature; such a conviction:* MA 16, 150.
43 *form . . . works; Natural products:* MA 16, 48.
43 *One is tempted:* MA 16, 51.
43 *in direct connection:* MA 16, 48.
43 *Praying to the Creator:* MA 11.1.2, 139
43 *pious boredom:* MA 11.1.2, 140.
43 *a kind of dry morality:* MA 16, 47.
44 *I had lost; beautiful, leafy; that a poor:* MA 16, 244.
44 *to sanctify and seclude:* MA 16, 245.
44 *effulgent sense:* MA 11.1.2, 140.
45 *when it is not fortunate:* MA 16, 245.
45 *The eye was:* MA 16, 246.
45 *image hunts:* MA 16, 301 and 302.
45 *the observer encountered:* MA 16, 302.
45 *saddest case . . . forced to idolize:* MA 13.1, 378.
45 *bigoted delusions:* MA 11.2, 181.
46 *fullness:* MA 16, 312.
46 *must be accustomed:* MA 16, 313.
46 *And so through a shining round:* MA 16, 314 f.
46 *own religion:* MA 16, 376.
46 *"monastic rule":* Ludwig Wittgenstein, *Werke,* vol. 8 (Frankfurt a. M.: Suhrkamp, 1984), 568.
46 *gloomy scruples:* MA 16, 317.
46 *lighthearted hours; strange bad conscience:* MA 16, 318.
47 *I returned his affection:* MA 16, 360.
47 *to say that what I had:* MA 16, 359.
47 *the matter of clothing:* WA IV, 51, 30 (Sept. 8, 1768).
47 *going to meetings:* WA IV, 51, 34 (Nov. 24, 1768).
47 *love . . . friendship . . . veneration:* WA IV, 51, 33 f. (Nov. 24, 1768).
47 *My fiery head:* WA IV, 51, 34 (Nov. 24, 1768).
47 *still too flustered:* WA IV, 51, 33 (Nov. 24, 1768).
48 *What's the point:* WA IV, 51, 36 (Jan. 17, 1769).

48 *Offenherzigkeit; matters of; cold and calm: WA* IV, 51, 29 (Sept. 8, 1768).
48 *the history of my heart: WA* IV, 51, 37 (mid-Oct. 1769?).
48 *You see; But worries: WA* IV, 51, 36 (Jan. 17, 1769).
48 *And I hold my little heart: MA* 1.2, 200.
49 *her favorite: MA* 16, 363.
49 *I can hardly recall: MA* 5, 422.
50 *a Herrnhuter sister: MA* 5, 400.
50 *What is belief; pull . . . is led to: MA* 5, 396.
50 *injustice . . . in order to: MA* 5, 403.
50 *What shone out: MA* 5, 519 f.
50 *She took pleasure; reconciled God: MA* 16, 364.
50 *like a heathen; earlier, when: MA* 16, 675.
50 *Pelagianism; grandeur: MA* 16, 677.
51 *inexplicable man: MA* 16, 365.
51 *mystical chemical-alchemical; treasure: MA* 16, 365.
51 *nature presented in: MA* 16, 366.
51 *quite cheerfully: MA* 16, 366 f.
52 *productive . . . from which one could hope: MA* 16, 368.

CHAPTER 4

53 *his own whimsies: WA* IV, 1, 246 (Aug. 26, 1770).
53 *so sincerely boring: WA* IV, 1, 245 f. (Aug. 26, 1770).
53 *with as little feeling: WA* IV, 1, 218 (Dec. 12, 1769).
54 *I'll get 10 rooms: WA* IV, 1, 226 (Jan. 23, 1770).
54 *"Enlarge the place": See BrEltern,* 778 (Feb. 7, 1801).
54 *an abundance: WA* IV, 1, 232 (April 13, 1770).
54 *As I looked out: WA* IV, 1, 235 f. (June 27, 1770).
55 *When the dear valley: MA* 1.2, 199.
55 *What happiness; chains of; always moving: WA* IV, 1, 236 (June 27, 1770).
55 *What am I studying?: WA* IV, 51, 43 (May 11, 1770).
55 *There's nothing: WA* IV, 51, 42 (April 29, 1770).
56 *snatched away; Only now: WA* IV, 51, 42 (May 11, 1770).
56 *When we are touched: WA* IV, 51, 43 (May 11, 1770).
56 *"the most miserable German": Quoted from Bode,* 1, 354 (n. 1).
56 *All by myself: MA* 16, 404.
57 *It was given to few; ants . . . weakling . . . will always get: MA* 1.2, 415.
57 *free, convivial: MA* 16, 405.
58 *a man of much good sense: WA* IV, 1, 246 f. (Aug. 26, 1770).
58 *weather vane: WA* IV, 1, 262 (June 1771?).
58 *Write to me: WA* IV, 2, 213 (Dec. 5, 1774).
59 *always knew how: MA* 16, 403.
59 *a certain irritability; balance: MA* 16, 404.
59 *the most significant event: MA* 16, 433.
59 *gently sought; one could never expect: MA* 16, 437.
60 *to be of service: MA* 16, 436.
60 *"Goethe is really": VB* 1, 20 (March 21, 1772).
60 *for no inclination; ringing and humming: MA* 16, 445.
61 *great affection . . . discontent: MA* 16, 437.
61 *chiding and reproving; came to appreciate: MA* 16, 436.

61 "later reason": Johann Gottfried Herder, *Werke*, ed. Michael Knaupp, 3 vols. (Munich: Hanser, 1992–93), 1370.
61 *O my friends!: MA* 1.2, 206.
62 *all noble souls: MA* 1.2, 414.
62 *I sit here: MA* 1.1, 231.
63 *happy position: MA* 16, 440 f.

CHAPTER 5

64 *who sought their salvation: MA* 16, 401.
65 *The elemental part: MA* 16, 400.
65 *sleepwalker . . . whom: MA* 16, 401.
65 "free existence . . . except that Goethe . . . reign over": Johann Heinrich Jung-Stilling, *Lebensgeschichte* (Frankfurt a. M.: Insel, 1983), 255 f.
65 *divine pedagogy. . . presumptuous; neither pleasant: MA* 16, 726.
65 *to become aware: MA* 16, 725.
66 *Such an aperçu: MA* 16, 726.
66 *In science: MA* 10, 639.
67 *operation of cognitive genius: MA* 16, 725.
67 "grew fond of him . . . It is a shame": Jung-Stilling, *Lebensgeschichte*, 258.
67 "Stilling's enthusiasm": Jung-Stilling, *Lebensgeschichte*, 276.
68 *You left, and I stood: FA* I, 1, 129 (version of 1775).
68 *I left, and you stood: MA* 3.2, 16 (version of 1789).
68 *Those were painful days: MA* 16, 532.
69 *continue along: MA* 16, 498.
69 *At that moment: MA* 16, 466.
69 *Her nature, her form: MA* 16, 489.
69 *Such a youthful inclination: MA* 16, 530.
69 *The reasons a young woman: MA* 16, 531.
69 *premature inclinations: MA* 16, 496.
69 *The virtuous heart: WA* IV, 1, 61 (Oct. 1, 1766).
70 *weather vane: WA* IV, 1, 262 (June 1771?).
70 *more beautiful; that one is not a whit: WA* IV, 1, 259 (June 1771?).
70 *the dear child continues; Not even taking: WA* IV, 1, 261 (June 1771?).
70 *double role: MA* 16, 496.
70 *the youthful urge . . . most venial attempts: MA* 16, 497.
70 *transported from this fictitious: MA* 16, 461.
71 *How brightly nature: MA* 1.1, 162.
72 *I love the angel: MA* 1.1, 158.
72 *You golden children: MA* 1.1, 159.
72 *Little leaves and little blossoms: MA* 1.1, 159.
72 *My heart was beating: FA* I, 1, 128 f. (version of 1775).
74 *can return in thought: WA* IV, 4, 67 (Sept. 25, 1779, to Charlotte von Stein).
74 *much more motley: MA* 16, 512.
74 *humiliated: MA* 16, 512.
74 *never be accepted: MA* 16, 513.
74 *We thus found ourselves: MA* 16, 524 f.
75 *Until now, however: WA* IV, 2, 2 (Fall 1771).
75 *We have within ourselves: MA* 1.2, 411.
75 *gigantic strides . . . great wayfarer: MA* 1.2, 411.

75   *I vividly felt: MA* 1.2, 412.

76   *What are you doing: MA* 1.2, 412.

76   *And I cry nature!: MA* 1.2, 413.

76   *vied with Prometheus: MA* 1.2, 414.

76   *Shakespeare's theater: MA* 1.2, 413.

76   *I lacked real knowledge: MA* 16, 505.

76   *what each individual; domestic, heartfelt: MA* 16, 506.

77   *"Herr Goethe has played": VB* 1, 29 (July 4–5, 1772).

77   *"some of Herr von Voltaire's": VB* 1, 17 (Aug. 7, 1771).

CHAPTER 6

78   *Thus for me at present: WA* IV, 51, 44 (Aug. 28, 1771).

79   *The rabble almost: MA* 1.1, 408 (from the first draft of the play).

79   *"indecent style": MA* 1.2, 919.

79   *"In this case":* Quoted from *Bode* 2, 36.

79   *a furious termagant: MA* 1.2, 558.

79   *After his deeply concealed: MA* 1.2, 564.

79   *The same register of insults: MA* 1.2, 568 f.

80   *of a rough-hewn: MA* 16, 445.

81   *subject to no one: MA* 1.1, 404.

81   *colossal stature: MA* 1.2, 414.

81   *hidden point: MA* 1.2, 413.

81   *We have within us: MA* 1.2, 411.

81   *I feel with incredible: MA* 1.2, 412.

81   *fallen in love: MA* 16, 605.

82   *cabinet of curiosities: MA* 1.2, 413.

82   *have to hum . . . all the power . . . distracted life: WA* IV, 2, 7 (Nov. 28, 1771).

82   *not to always just indulge: MA* 16, 604.

82   *And so I kept: MA* 16, 604.

83   *imagination: MA* 16, 605.

83   *You always were one: MA* 1.1, 494 f.

83   *An error that made me: MA* 1.1, 493.

83   *God, you made her: MA* 1.1, 508.

84   *that her skin . . . made an unpleasant . . . not the least: MA* 16, 769.

84   *"But how can I aspire":* Quoted from *Bode* 1, 330.

84   *by a magnet: MA* 16, 249.

84   *physical and moral powers; The inquisitiveness of youth: MA* 16, 250.

84   *I must honestly admit: MA* 16, 770.

85   *They say it: WA* IV 1, 236 (June 17, 1770).

85   *bullies; When we try; Whoever mistreats: MA* 1.1, 398.

86   *any harm: MA* 1.1, 441.

86   *noblest Germans: WA* IV, 2, 7 (Nov. 28, 1771).

86   *Charity is a noble virtue: MA* 1.1, 397.

86   *coward whose bile: MA* 1.1, 492.

86   *God reflects: MA* 1.1, 431.

86   *poverty, chastity, and obedience: MA* 1.1, 393.

86   *It's a pleasure: MA* 1.1, 395.

86   *You alone are free: MA* 1.1, 416.

86   *to see a powerful rival: MA* 1.1, 435.

86   *all feeling of greatness: MA* 1.1, 403.
87   *feel boundless joy; When their well-cultivated: MA* 1.1, 462.
87   *We'll clear the mountains: MA* 1.1, 462 f.
87   *What a life: MA* 1.1, 463.
87   *Have I not known; in the open air: MA* 1.1, 618.
87   *The time of deception: MA* 1.1, 509.
88   *To all the fools: WA* IV, 2, 10 (Dec. 1771).
88   *until you have voiced: WA* IV, 2, 11 (late 1771).
89   *I belittle him; That's annoying: WA* IV, 2, 19 (mid-July 1772).
89   "There's an uncommon amount of German strength": *MA* 1.1, 958.
89   "Hang the diapers": *MA* 16, 606.
89   *a completely new play: MA* 16, 606.

CHAPTER 7

90   *strolled around . . . the essence of any mastery: WA* IV, 2, 17 (mid-July 1772).
90   *When you stand: WA* IV, 2, 16 f. (mid-July, 1772).
91   *Writing is busy idleness: MA* 1.1, 475.
91   *Although the Bible says: WA* IV, 2, 127 (late Nov. 1773).
91   *there is a forming nature: MA* 1.2, 421.
91   *One tug: WA* IV, 2, 104 (Sept. 15, 1773).
92   "If he ever finds happiness": *VB* 1, 51 (Oct. 17, 1773).
92   "Here by secret means": Quoted from *Bode* 2, 22.
93   *jealous: MA* 16, 586.
93   *For a jaunty lad: MA* 1.2, 177.
94   "amid unceasing cries": Quoted from Ernst Beutler, *Essays um Goethe* (Frankfurt a. M. and Leipzig: Insel, 1995), 98.
94   *Just listen to the townsfolk: MA* 1.1, 187.
94   *whether a woman: MA* 1.2, 916.
94   *That lovely, innocent creature: MA* 1.2, 183.
95   *God's judgment; She has been put: MA* 1.2, 188.
95   *My friends must forgive: WA* IV, 2, 8 (Nov. 28, 1771).
95   *to be a doctor: WA* IV, 2, 1 (late Aug. 1771?).
95   *singular man: MA* 16, 540.
96   *I was as pleased: WA* IV, 2, 12 f. (late 1771).
96   "He's a man . . . fall in love": *VB* 1, 23 (March 1772).
96   "enthusiasm and genius": *VB* 1, 18 (Dec. 30, 1771).
96   *by nature an upright; in a negative: MA* 16, 541.
96   *wonderful mirror: FA* 29, 176.
96   "Hang the diapers": *MA* 16, 606.
98   "Merck, Leuchsenring, and I": Quoted from *Bode* 2, 52 f.
98   "Goethe is full": *VB* 1, 24 (April 13, 1772).
99   *When for the first time: MA* 1.1, 208.
99   *I cast a hopeful glance: MA* 1.1, 210.
99   *bewildered wayfarer: MA* 1.1, 213.
100 "In more ways than one": *VB* 1, 28 (June 6, 1772).
100 *So I also want to tell you: WA* IV, 2, 18 f. (mid-July 1772).
100 "Wanderer": *MA* 16, 555.
100 *When I was met: MA* 16, 556.
100 *Genius, he whom: MA* 1.1, 197.

101   *I live in Pindar:* WA IV, 2, 15 (mid-July 1772).

101   *To be sure:* WA IV, 2, 16 (mid-July 1772).

101   *There on the hill:* MA 1.1, 200.

101   *Gale-breathing godhead:* MA 1.1, 199.

102   *Strike him dead:* MA 1.1, 224.

102   *As police officers:* MA 1.2, 309.

102   *Herr Benignus Pfeufer:* MA 1.2, 337.

102   *pathetic twaddle:* MA 1.2, 391.

102   *with any theory:* MA 1.2, 398.

103   *Are not raging storms:* MA 1.2, 399.

103   *art is precisely:* MA 1.2, 400.

103   *walls of glass; softer and softer:* MA 1.2, 400.

103   *tribute:* MA 1.2, 402.

104   *It is our firm belief:* MA 1.2, 363.

104   *O Genius of our Fatherland:* MA 1.2, 350 f.

105   *Laws and rights:* MA 6.1, 588, lines 1972–75.

106   "Frankfurt newspaper writer": VB 1, 29 (July 18, 1772).

107   "There . . . I found him"; "You know that I don't": VB 1, 36 (Fall 1772).

107   "was no longer free": VB 1, 38 (Fall 1772).

107   *entangled and enraptured:* MA 16, 577.

107   *general favor:* MA 16, 576.

107   *Mephistopheles . . . romance:* MA 16, 588 f.

107   *Thus they continued:* MA 16, 578.

107   "qualities that can make him": VB 1, 39 (Nov. 18, 1772).

107   "of making Lottchen"; "that he would have to": VB 1, 40 (Nov. 18, 1772).

108   "He, Lottchen, and I": VB 1, 32 (Sept. 10–11, 1772).

108   *If I had stayed a single:* WA IV, 2, 21 (Sept. 10, 1772).

108   *Now I am alone:* WA IV, 2, 22 (Sept. 10, 1772).

108   "But she was happy": VB 1, 33 (Sept. 10–11, 1772).

CHAPTER 8

109   "[Goethe] has what one calls genius": VB 1, 36 f. (Fall 1772).

110   *Mama:* e.g., in WA IV, 2, 163 ff. (May–June 1774).

111   *Dear God:* WA IV, 2, 35 (Nov. 10, 1772).

111   *what it means:* MA 1.2, 409.

111   *I honor such a deed:* WA IV, 2, 30 f. (Oct. 10, 1772).

111   *anxious striving:* WA IV, 2, 40 (Nov. 20, 1772).

112   *This news was terrible:* WA IV, 2, 33 (early Nov. 1772).

112   *If that damned cleric:* WA IV, 2, 33 f. (early Nov. 1772).

112   *No clergyman:* MA 1.2, 299.

112   *lying in:* WA IV, 2, 73 (April 7?, 1773).

112   *It cost me little:* WA IV, 2, 76 (April 10, 1773).

112   *And between you and me:* WA IV, 2, 81 (April 14?, 1773).

112   *And so I dream:* WA IV, 2, 91 f. (June 1773).

113   *I don't know why:* WA IV, 2, 76 (April 10, 1773).

113   *I'm wandering through the desert:* WA IV, 2, 75 (April 1773).

113   *My poor existence:* WA IV, 2, 82 (April 21, 1773).

113   *shooting:* WA IV, 2, 43 (Dec. 1772).

113   *could succeed in sinking; laughed at myself:* MA 16, 618.

113 "vile imitation": *MA* 1.1, 970.
114 "the most beautiful": *MA* 1.1, 962.
114 "We could tell": *MA* 1.1, 960.
114 *And a drama for performance: WA* IV, 2, 106 (Sept. 15, 1773).
115 *The gods have sent: WA* IV, 2, 97 (July 1773).
115 *They want to share: MA* 1.1, 671.
115 *And you are to my spirit: MA* 1.1, 671 f.
116 *Look down, Zeus: MA* 1.1, 675.
116 *Cover your heaven: MA* 1.1, 229.
116 *Here I sit: MA* 1.1, 231.
116 *I know nothing so pitiful; Who aided me: MA* 1.1, 230.
117 *Even though one can and did: MA* 16, 681.
117 *most secure foundation: MA* 16, 680.
117 *I was ready: MA* 16, 680 f.
118 "This Goethe": Werthes to Jacobi, *VB* 1, 71 f. (Oct. 18, 1774).
118 "some sitting, some standing": Quoted from Katharina Mommsen, *Goethe und der Islam* (Frankfurt a. M.: Insel, 2001), 72.
118 "writing anything comprehensible": *VB*, 1, 64 (Aug. 27, 1774).
118 *Mahomet . . . Dost thou not: MA* 1.1, 517.
118 *The fullness of the holiest: MA* 1.2, 441 f.
119 *As a temporal Gospel: MA* 16, 614.
119 *also wants to spread; coarse world: MA* 16, 671.
119 *altered the old robe: MA* 16, 681.
120 *The things of this world: MA* 16, 672.
120 *Everything that Genius: MA* 16, 673.
120 *He thinks the world: MA* 1.1, 547.
121 *Hearken how confusion: MA* 1.1, 662.
122 *There's nothing in the world: MA* 1.1, 657.
122 *burgeoning nature . . . foreign adornments . . . enjoy the earth: MA* 1.1, 661.
122 *the old robe: MA* 16, 681.

CHAPTER 9

123 *My passion to create; but in convivial company: MA* 16, 554.
123 *fruits: WA* IV, 2, 127 (late Nov. 1773).
124 *poetic use . . . recent life: MA* 16, 621.
124 *blue striped bed jacket: WA* IV, 2, 92 (June 1773).
124 *general confession: MA* 16, 621.
124 Merck made the wicked comment: A côté de cela il a la petite Madame Brentano à consoler sur l'odeur de l'huile, du fromage et des manières de son mari: *Gespräche* 1, 88 (Feb. 2, 1774).
124 *If you knew: WA* IV, 2, 140 (Jan. 21, 1774).
125 *whims concerning suicide; hypochondriacal fancies: MA* 16, 618.
125 *bird's-eye view: MA* 16, 619.
125 *impressive: MA* 16, 614.
125 *Here we have to do: MA* 16, 617.
126 *What's more: MA* 19, 491.
126 *taedium vitae; Werther will leave: MA* 20.1, 294 (Dec. 3, 1812).
126 *recurrence of external things: MA* 16, 611.
127 *take part; such lovely offerings: MA* 16, 612.

127   *What actually uplifts:* MA 16, 612.

127   *To rejoice in your own worth:* MA 9, 127.

127   *paralyzing imagination:* MA 16, 613.

128   *I intend to enjoy:* MA 1.2, 197.

128   *when she speaks of her fiancé:* MA 1.2, 226.

129   *A shudder passes through:* MA 1.2, 260.

129   *I fear, I fear:* MA 1.2, 279.

129   *cold dull consciousness:* MA 1.2, 273.

129   *I have no power:* MA 1.2, 240.

129   *sacred, animating power:* MA 1.2, 266.

129   *heart, which on its own:* MA 1.2, 259.

129   *And now I have lent:* WA IV, 2, 156 (April 26, 1774).

130   *dialogue:* MA 16, 610.

130   *can no longer pump:* MA 1.2, 267.

130   *When I look out my window:* MA 1.2, 266.

131   *creation bereft:* MA 1.2, 268.

131   *paints the walls:* MA 1.2, 203.

131   *brought back again:* MA 1.2, 273.

132   *But whereas I felt relieved:* MA 16, 621 f.

132   "One hardly gets seduced": HA 6, 531.

132   "pleasure": VB 1, 74 (Oct. 26, 1774).

132   *I turn back into myself:* MA 1.2, 203.

133   *no argument in the world:* MA 1.2, 234.

133   *You ask whether you should send:* MA 1.2, 200.

133   *O my friends!:* MA 1.2, 206.

134   *This mutual agitation:* MA 16, 554.

134   "Everything I have read of yours": BranG 1, 55 (Oct. 3, 1775).

135   *Predestined, I to stay:* MA 13.1, 134.

135   *Very soon I will send you:* WA IV, 2, 168 (June 16, 1774).

135   *patched together with passions:* WA IV, 2, 159 (May 1774).

135   *too much:* BranG 1, 36 (early Oct. 1774).

135   *The thing is done:* WA, IV, 2, 200 (Oct. 1774).

135   *If you could feel:* WA IV, 2, 207 (Nov. 21, 1774).

136   *Werther must:* WA IV, 2, 208 (Nov. 21, 1774).

CHAPTER 10

137   *that if her brother:* MA 16, 587.

137   "Although I have long rejected": Quoted from Sigrid Damm, *Cornelia Goethe* (Berlin: Aufbau, 1987), 92.

138   *new world:* MA 16, 586.

139   *[Lotte] was used to sharing:* MA 2.2, 447 f.

139   "bashfulness . . . porcupine's skin": Quoted from Damm, *Cornelia Goethe*, 115.

139   "Doctor and Privy Councilor": BrEltern, 427 (Oct. 16, 1788).

139   "Every wind, every drop of rain": BrEltern, 232.

140   "My love disgusts": BrEltern, 233.

140   *The thought of giving herself:* MA 19, 444 f. (March 28, 1831).

140   *We have an entire house:* WA IV, 1, 226 (Jan. 23, 1770).

141   *you don't need to write:* MA 16, 706.

141   *romantic, youthful power:* WA IV, 2, 187 (Aug. 21, 1774).

141 *an indeterminate: WA* IV, 2, 171 f. (June 1, 1774).

141 *it was as if: MA* 16, 706.

141 *literary garrisoning . . . loan guarantees: MA* 16, 706 f.

142 *forgiveness of sins: MA* 1.2, 384.

142 *brooding . . . conjures: MA* 1.2, 385.

143 "I know no greater genius": *VB* 1, 51 f. (Nov. 4, 1773).

143 *I am not a Christian: BranG* 1, 17 (Nov. 30, 1773).

143 "harass . . . play the partisan"; "You shall become one": *BranG* 1, 17 (Nov. 30, 1773).

143 "By means of many": *MA* 1.2, 863.

144 *This gently descending forehead: MA* 1.2, 457.

144 *It would be a wonderful: MA* 1.2, 490.

144 *feels where he should approach: MA* 1.2, 462.

144 "with the expression": Quoted from *Bode* 2, 289.

145 "I have never found": *BranG* 1, 35.

145 *In a land to which He came: MA* 1.1, 243.

145 *Scheinding . . . Scheissding: WA* IV, 2, 262 (May 1775).

146 *As if to Emmaus we bumped along: MA* 1.1, 247.

146 "Walked up and down": *BranG* I, 33 (Aug. 26, 1774).

146 "I hope that in this epoch": *BranG* 2, 132 (Dec. 28, 1812).

147 "one of the most extraordinary": *Grumach* 1, 308 (Dec. 23, 1774).

147 "This Goethe is a vulgar": Quoted from *Leithold*, 68.

148 *save me: WA* IV, 2, 249 (March 25, 1775).

148 *Yes, dearest friend: WA* IV, 2, 231 (probably Jan. 18–30, 1775).

148 *carnival Goethe; courting a dainty; being captivated; insufferable: WA* IV, 2, 233 (Feb. 13, 1775).

148 *who, always living: WA* IV, 2, 233 f. (Feb. 13, 1775).

149 *o dear friend: WA* IV, 2, 243 f. (March 10, 1775).

149 *what people will think: WA* IV, 2, 234 (Feb. 13, 1775).

149 *to float around: WA* IV, 2, 278 (Aug. 8, 1775).

149 *The disproportion: WA* IV, 5, 179 (Aug. 11, 1781).

149 *The greatest names: MA* 1.2, 124.

150 *His lessons are not quite: MA* 1.2, 122.

150 *tamed: MA* 1.1, 267.

150 *I've no use: MA* 1.1, 271.

151 "creator of her moral . . . duty and feeling": *Grumach* 1, 371 (Dec. 3, 1830).

151 *inkling of his serious: MA* 16, 770.

152 "I admire the genius": *Grumach* 1, 358 (Aug. 4, 1775).

152 "I have enjoyed": *Gespräche* 1, 153 (July 31, 1775).

152 *Whenever I'm feeling: WA* IV, 2, 270 f. (July 25, 1775).

152 *Here in the room: WA* IV, 2, 273 (Aug. 3, 1775).

153 *I'm stranded again: WA* IV, 2, 278 (Aug. 8, 1775).

153 *Unfortunately, her distance: WA* IV, 2, 289 (Sept. 10–19, 1775).

153 "her mother asked for time": *Grumach* 1, 370 (Jan. 8, 1776).

153 *Will my heart: WA* IV, 2, 293 (Sept. 18, 1775).

153 *flee from Lili: MA* 16, 823.

154 *not for the sake: WA* IV, 2, 298 (Oct. 1775).

154 *The first moments: WA* IV, 2, 302 (Oct. 18, 1775).

155 *I packed for the north: Tgb* I, 1, 13 (Oct. 30, 1775).

CHAPTER 11

162 *to regard* [his] *intrinsic: MA* 16, 716.
162 *sleepwalking: MA* 16, 717.
162 *Through field and wood: MA* 16, 616.
162 *business of the world: MA* 16, 718.
163 *his son's reflected glory: WA* IV, 3, 14 (Jan. 5, 1776).
163 *My life is going along: WA* IV, 3, 1 (Nov. 22, 1775).
164 *I'm certainly having: WA* IV, 3, 15 f. (Jan. 5, 1776).
164 *Every day I learn: WA* IV, 3, 12 (Dec. 31, 1775).
164 *I can't tell you anything: WA* IV, 3, 1 (Nov. 22, 1775).
164 "but he is coddled": Quoted from *Leithold*, 108.
165 "This Goethe is a boy": Quoted from *Leithold*, 86.
165 "satirical masterpiece": *MA* 1.1, 990.
166 *That's the damn thing: WA* IV, 2, 217 (Dec. 23, 1774).
166 "He has an intellectual need": *Grumach* 1, 308 (Dec. 23, 1774).
166 *Wieland is and will always be: WA* IV, 2, 238 f. (March 1775).
166 "Since last you made the trip": Quoted from *Bode* 3, 88.
166 *without my knowledge: WA* IV, 2, 255 (April 9, 1775).
167 "It is certain that he no longer": Quoted from *Leithold*, 119.
168 "Maman [Anna Amalia]"; "He is constantly sad": Quoted from *Leithold*, 128.
168 "comedy of state": *VB* 1, 163 (Feb. 7, 1776).
168 "The whole court": *VB* 1, 163 (Feb. 15, 1776).
168 "There is an astonishing amount": *VB* 1, 169 (March 8, 1776).
169 *And just as I can never: WA* IV, 3, 14 (early Jan. 1776?).
169 *But God only knows: WA* IV, 3, 18 (Jan. 15 or 16, 1776).
169 *Dear lady, permit me: WA* IV, 3, 24 (Jan. 28, 1776).
169 *I'm trying to make up my damn mind: WA* IV, 3, 25 (Jan. 29, 1776).
169 *Oh, if only my sister: WA* IV, 3, 34 (Feb. 23, 1776).
169 *soother: WA* IV, 3, 20 (Jan. 1776).
170 *You are right: WA* IV, 3, 54 f. (May 1, 1776).
170 *But since my love: WA* IV, 3, 55 (May 2, 1776).
170 *No more about Lili; My heart, my head: WA* IV, 3, 50 (April 10, 1776).
170 *I cannot account for: WA* IV, 3, 51 f. (April 1776?).
170 *I'd like it in your hand: WA* IV, 3, 53 (April 16, 1776).
170 *Fate, why did you grant: MA* 2.1, 20.
171 *Tell me then, What does fate; Drop by drop: MA* 2.1, 23.
171 *Whenever I want: WA* IV, 3, 74 (1776).
171 "They say that Lotte": Quoted from *Leithold*, 151.
172 *I see now: WA* IV, 3, 114 (Oct. 7, 1776).
172 *eclipse: Tgb* I, 1, 27 (Sept. 7, 1776).
172 *Marvelous night: Tgb* I, 1, 26 (Sept. 3, 1776).
172 *a feverish night: Tgb* I, 1, 35 (Jan. 2, 1777).
172 *Didn't sleep: Tgb* I, 1, 35 (Jan. 6, 1777).
172 "The duke is one of the most remarkable": *VB* 1, 223 (Jan. 9, 1778).
173 "I'll tell you honestly": *VB* 1, 220 (Nov. 3, 1777).
173 *all too great heat: WA* IV, 3, 57 (May 4, 1776).
174 *scrawls . . . They're still. . . how much . . . Behave: WA* IV, 3, 7 f. (Dec. 23–26, 1775).

174 "quite in love . . . to destroy": *VB* 1, 145 (Nov. 10, 1775).

174 "Goethe, whom we've had": *VB* 1, 146 (Nov. 16, 1775).

175 "It is a wizard": Christoph Martin Wieland, *Werke*, ed. Fritz Martini and Hans Werner Seiffert, 5 vols. (Munich: Hanser, 1964–68), 4:623 f.

176 "lively circle . . . Here, unobserved": *Gespräche* 1, 220 (Jan. 25, 1813).

176 "amicably presiding genius": *Gespräche* 1, 222 (Jan. 25, 1813).

176 "Goethe is causing": *VB* 1, 180 f. (May 10, 1776).

176 *You just shouldn't seem: WA* IV, 3, 30 (Feb. 19, 1776).

177 "state of affairs in Weimar": *VB* 1, 189 (June 19, 1776).

177 "wild fellow": *VB* 1, 191 (July 14, 1776).

177 "what will be the unfailing": *BranG* 1, 58 (May 8, 1776).

177 *You can feel yourself: WA* IV, 3, 63 f. (May 21, 1776).

177 "Your misconstruction": *BranG* 1, 59 (May 29, 1776).

178 *Then . . . the duke came: WA* IV, 4, 296 f. (Sept. 21, 1780).

178 *And thus you can never: WA* IV, 3, 46 (March 25, 1776).

178 *My situation is advantageous: WA* IV, 3, 21 (Jan. 22, 1776).

178 *Dear Brother: WA* IV, 3, 17 (Jan. 15, 1776).

179 *I shall stay here: WA* IV, 3, 81 (July 9, 1776).

CHAPTER 12

180 "trampling on convention": *Grumach* 1, 403.

180 *Of course, I'm leading: WA* IV, 3, 15 (Jan. 5, 1776).

180 *Ah! I am so tired of striving: MA* 2.1, 13.

180 *I've sampled the court: WA* IV, 3, 38 (March 8, 1776).

181 *turn* [his] *literary career: Grumach* 1, 413 (June 18, 1776).

181 *My writing has become: WA* IV, 4, 221 (April 14, 1780).

181 *idle life at home: WA* IV, 3, 28 f. (Feb. 14, 1776).

182 *subordinate . . . exaggerated . . . unsatisfied: MA,* 16, 616 f.

182 *always had an uncomfortable: WA* IV, 7, 243 (July 12, 1786).

182 *son whom I love: WA* IV, 2, 127 (late Nov. 1773).

183 *the odd little thing: WA* IV, 3, 49 (April 5, 1776).

183 "We've spoken enough": *Lenz* 3, 306.

184 "You are the first person": *Lenz* 3, 440 (late April, 1776).

185 "through excrement": *Lenz* 3, 416 (late March, 1776).

185 "What does our soldier": *Lenz* 2, 794 and 798.

185 "I am working on an essay": *Lenz* 3, 400 (March 1776).

185 *The defects of that profession: MA* 16, 634.

186 *Lenz's asinine behavior: WA* IV, 3, 54 (April 25, 1776).

186 "Here I am engulfed": *Lenz* 3, 427 (April 14, 1776).

187 "I'm going to the country": *Lenz* 3, 472 (June 27, 1776).

187 "Rothe is a traitor": *Lenz* 2, 411.

187 "As far as I have been able": *MA* 8.1, 309 (Feb. 2, 1797).

188 "expelled from heaven": *Lenz* 3, 517 (Nov. 29 or 30, 1776).

188 "Frau von Stein finds my method": *Lenz* 3, 495 (mid-Sept. 1776).

188 *We can be nothing to each other: WA* IV, 3, 103 (1776).

189 *I'm sending you Lenz: WA* IV, 3, 105 f. (Sept. 10, 1776).

189 *I hesitated: WA* IV, 3, 106 (Sept. 12, 1776).

189 "I am too happy": *Lenz* 3, 494 (mid-Sept. 1776).

190 *I got into the water: WA* IV, 3, 117 (Nov. 3, 1776).

190 "Where into my heart": *Lenz* 3, 205.

190 "Man must not desire": *Lenz* 2, 382.

190 *How much has sprung: WA* IV, 3, 119 (Nov. 8, 1776).

190 *all sorts of stuff: WA* IV, 3, 118 (Nov. 6, 1776).

190 *Lenz will leave: WA* IV, 3, 123 (late Nov. 1776).

191 "admit to a crime": *Lenz* 3, 516 (Nov. 29, 1776).

191 *The whole affair: WA* IV, 3, 124 (Dec. 1, 1776).

CHAPTER 13

192 *Klinger with his rough: WA* IV, 3, 111 (Sept. 16, 1776).

193 *He was a loyal: Unterhaltungen,* 202.

193 "genius banquet": Karl August Böttiger, *Literarische Zustände und Zeitgenossen,* ed. Klaus Gerlach and René Sternke (Berlin: Aufbau, 1998), 75.

193 *I praise the gods: WA* IV, 3, 125 (Dec. 2, 1776).

194 *But act completely: WA* IV, 3, 265 (Dec. 14, 1778).

194 *it will also be a distraction: WA* IV, 4, 38 (May 22, 1779).

194 *I would so much like: WA* IV, 4, 46 (July 13, 1779).

194 *You have neither sunk: WA* IV, 5, 50 (Feb. 11, 1781).

194 *We should do what we can: WA* IV, 4, 290 f. (Sept. 14, 1780).

195 *Every work of man: Tgb* I, 1, 82 (July 14, 1779).

195 *all arrogance . . . beautiful strength: Tgb* I, 1, 83 (July 14, 1779).

196 *I'm adapting myself: WA* IV, 5, 222 (Nov. 14, 1781).

196 "Now it's as if": *VB* 1, 214 (June 13, 1777).

196 "not cast off": *VB* 1, 223 (Jan. 9, 1778).

196 "with such dryness": *VB* 1, 253 (Jan. 2, 1780).

196 *Good effect on me: Tgb* I, 1, 81 f. (July 13, 1779).

197 *With them he was by turns: MA* 2.2, 22.

197 *pitch that limed: MA* 2.2, 31.

198 *Werner was proud: MA* 2.2, 47.

198 *thus speech often stuck: MA* 2.2, 53.

199 *The German stage: MA* 2.2, 29.

199 *Dark, disrupted day: Tgb* I, 1, 44 (June 16, 1777).

199 "I cannot tell you": Quoted from Sigrid Damm, *Cornelia Goethe* (Berlin: Aufbau, 1987), 243.

199 "I will not complain": Quoted from Damm, *Cornelia Goethe,* 244.

200 *happy . . . nature . . . which allows: WA* IV, 3, 161 (June 28, 1777).

200 *To their favorites: MA* 1.1, 34.

200 *Ever since: WA* IV, 3, 186 (Nov. 12, 1777).

200 *I am very much changed: WA* IV, 3, 188 (Nov. 16, 1777).

200 *My thoughts are in wonderfully: WA* IV, 3, 189 (Nov. 29, 1777).

200 *the most wonderful thing: MA* 14, 478.

201 *It's a curious feeling: WA* IV, 3, 192 (Dec. 4, 1777).

201 *pure peace in my soul . . . glimpses of sun: Tgb* I, 1, 52 (Nov. 29, 1777).

201 *the sun rose; Night arrived: Tgb* I, 1, 53 (Nov. 30, 1777).

201 *I saw the long and well-lit: MA* 14, 480 f.

201 *To be sure: MA* 14, 481.

201 *Like the vulture: Tgb* I, 1, 53 (Dec. 1, 1777).

202 *Like the vulture: MA* 2.1, 37 f.

203 *adventure . . . survived: WA* IV, 3, 190 (Dec. 4, 1777).

203 *He was completely like:* MA 14, 483.

203 *one would rescue:* MA 14, 485 f.

204 *gloomy phantom . . . clear reality:* MA 14, 486.

204 *released from any further:* MA 14, 487.

204 *I was already burdened:* MA 14, 479.

204 *I can assure you:* WA IV, 6, 14 (July 26, 1782).

204 *Behind him the branches:* MA 2.1, 38.

204 *And for him the snow-shrouded:* MA 2.1, 41.

205 *sign of confirmation:* WA IV, 3, 199 (Dec. 10, 1777).

205 *I want to reveal:* WA IV, 3, 200 (Dec. 10, 1777).

205 *What is man:* Tgb I, 1, 54 (Dec. 10, 1777).

205 *however, am surrounded; duke grows closer:* Tgb I, 1, 50 (Oct. 8, 1777).

205 *He whom, Genius:* MA 1.1, 197.

205 *God deals with me:* WA IV, 3, 199 (Dec. 10, 1777).

206 *I was silent:* WA IV, 3, 201 (Dec. 11, 1777).

206 *You stand, with unfathomed breast:* MA 2.1, 41.

207 *On a winter journey:* MA 10, 49.

CHAPTER 14

208 *that steel springs:* MA 2.1, 176.

209 *sentimentalisms:* MA 2.1, 201.

209 *"Tell me something":* VB 1, 224 (Feb. 12, 1778).

210 *We worked into the night:* WA IV, 3, 207 f. (Jan. 19, 1778).

210 *A few days in quiet:* Tgb I, 1, 60 (Jan. 18, 1778).

210 *This week, often out:* Tgb I, 1, 60 (Jan. 30, 1778).

211 *I didn't get comfortable:* Tgb I, 1, 61 (Feb. 23, 1778).

211 *I was a young lad:* WA IV, 3, 214 (March 17, 1778).

211 *"through the opening created":* Gespräche 1, 222 (Jan. 25, 1813).

212 *Tom foolery:* Tgb I, 1, 62 (April 14, 1778).

212 *in the clamor of the world:* WA IV, 3, 223 (May 14, 1778).

212 *hidden gears; No dirty joke:* WA IV, 3, 225 (May 19, 1778).

213 *flower of public trust:* WA IV, 3, 224 (May 17, 1778).

213 *considered too proud:* Grumach 2, 81 (Feb. 14, 1787).

213 *My soul used to be:* WA IV, 3, 224 (May 17, 1778).

213 *destined for much alienation:* Tgb I, 1, 50 (Oct. 8, 1777).

214 *settle in and put down:* MA 2.2, 673.

214 *an unpleasant, hateful; end of trouble:* MA 2.2, 674.

215 *closer bond . . . protect themselves:* MA 2.2, 675.

215 *diabolically humane:* MA 8.1, 874 (Jan. 19, 1802).

216 *"We thought we were seeing":* Grumach 2, 115.

216 *much too carelessly:* WA IV, 47 (July 21, 1779).

216 *Little by little:* WA IV, 4, 12 (Feb. 22, 1779).

216 *Here, the drama simply:* WA IV, 4, 18 (March 6, 1779).

217 *get measured and inspected:* WA IV, 4, 20 (March 8, 1779).

217 *I enter my old castle:* WA IV, 4, 21 (March 8, 1779).

217 *Now I am living:* WA IV, 4, 14 (March 2, 1779).

217 *a lovely concert:* WA IV, 4, 17 (March 5, 1779).

218 *Inadequacy is productive:* Gespräche 2, 677.

218 *What? The king would do:* MA 3.1, 166, lines 192–96.

219 *Oh hear me!: MA* 3.1, 197, lines 1190–203.

219 *and my advice is: MA* 3.1, 194, lines 1232–38.

219 *My heart is telling me: MA* 3.1, 197, lines 1358–64.

220 *Just consider that with every breath: MA* 20.2, 1321 (Feb. 15, 1830).

220 *Oh my soul, be calm: MA* 3.1, 202, lines 1526–31.

221 *I call that worry noble: MA* 3.1, 205 f., lines 1640–60.

221 *The days of man: MA* 13.1, 186.

221 *In our actions: MA* 17, 758.

221 *I am almost convinced: MA* 3.1, 206, line 1665.

222 *Look at us!: MA* 3.1, 220, lines 248–50.

222 *the voice of truth: MA* 3.1, 214, lines 1938 f.

222 *So leave!: MA* 3.1, 220, line 2151.

222 *Farewell!: MA* 3.1, 221, line 2174.

222 *selfish principle: MA* 13, 1, 357.

223 *frittering oneself: BW Reinhard*, 198.

223 *Pure intermediate effect: MA* 17, 749.

223 "lives in fear": Georg Wilhelm Friedrich Hegel, *Phänomenologie des Geistes*, ed. Johannes Hoffmeister (Hamburg: Meiner, 1952), 462 f.

223 *In silence maintain: MA* 13.1, 204.

224 *with a rich interior: MA* 19, 549.

224 *It wasn't at all to my taste: MA* 14, 465.

224 *Performed Iph.: Tgb* I, 1, 78 (April 6, 1779).

CHAPTER 15

225 *Straightened up: Tgb* I, 1, 85 ff. (Aug. 7, 1779)

226 *muddle, bustle . . . purposeful thought: Tgb* I, 1, 86 f. (Aug. 7, 1779).

226 *May he allow us: Tgb* I, 1, 87 (Aug. 7, 1779).

227 "Recently, he read to us": *Grumach* 2, 498 (Nov. 2, 1784).

227 *Whoever desires: MA* 17, 876.

227 *yearning vanishes: MA* 17, 471.

228 *according to whose will: Tgb* I, 1, 83 (July 14, 1779).

228 *Whatever touched: MA* 2.1, 68.

228 *whiff of pretension: WA* IV, 5, 122 (May 7, 1781).

229 *it is inevitable: Grumach* 1, 48 (Oct. 31, 1779).

229 *it seems miraculous: WA* IV, 4, 58 f. (Sept. 7, 1779).

230 "I am sorry": *Grumach* 2, 140 (Oct. 16, 1779).

230 *to see Lavater: WA* IV, 4, 69 (Sept. 28, 1779).

230 "There's something uniquely": *Grumach* 2, 199 (Nov. 29, 1779).

230 *taking the waters; when one sees again: WA* IV, 4, 150 (Nov. 30, 1779).

230 *I am with Lavater: WA* IV, 4, 148 (Nov. 30, 1779).

230 *Only here do I clearly: WA* IV, 4, 150 (Nov. 30, 1779).

231 "behavior that won"; "one of Göthe's": *Grumach* 2, 220 (Jan. 17, 1780).

231 *Since I am now; In former days: WA* IV, 4, 66 f. (Sept. 25, 1779).

231 *She explains to me: MA* 9, 941.

232 *that I can now think; There too I was met: WA* IV, 4, 67 (Sept. 28, 1779).

232 *good creature: WA* IV, 4, 68 (Sept. 28, 1779).

232 *impressive social . . . everything she needed; and so there is: WA* IV, 4, 68 (Sept. 28, 1779).

232 *She seems so beautiful; In the end: WA* IV, 4, 92 and 93 (Oct. 23, 1779).

233 *I cannot answer:* WA IV, 4, 298 f. (Sept. 20, 1780).
233 *The beautiful lady:* WA IV, 4, 274 (Aug. 27, 1780).
233 *Only now do I feel:* WA IV, 4, 276 (Aug. 28, 1780).
233 *to avoid longing:* WA IV, 4, 281 (Sept. 6, 1780).
233 *Your letter could not:* WA IV, 4, 321 (Oct. 16, 1780).
234 *Peace lies over:* MA 2.1, 53.
234 *The sublime gives:* WA IV, 4, 70 (Oct. 3, 1779).
234 *If I had been alone:* WA IV, 4, 78 (Oct. 14, 1779).
234 *Even now, Italy:* WA IV, 4, 120 (Nov. 13, 1779).
235 *Neither in Israel:* WA IV, 4, 148 (Nov. 30, 1779).
235 *he is the flower of mankind:* WA IV, 4, 153 (Dec. 7, 1779).
235 *My God, to whom:* WA IV, 4, 73 f. (Oct. 8, 1779).
236 *purest mutual enjoyment:* WA IV, 4, 147 (Nov. 30, 1779).
236 *the shriveling and freezing:* WA IV, 4, 150 (Nov. 30, 1779).
236 *promise of eternal life; for my taste:* WA IV, 4, 115 (Nov. 2, 1779).
237 *The daily work assigned:* WA IV, 4, 299 (ca. Sept. 20, 1780).
237 *You must leave my earth:* MA 1.1, 230.
238 *As you beautify:* WA IV, 5, 56 (Feb. 19, 1781).
238 *every day the scales:* WA IV, 5, 88 (March 18, 1781).
238 *"strength personified":* GBr 1, 698, footnote 257.
238 *And yet, a fool:* WA IV, 5, 88 (March 18, 1781).
238 *narrow limits of; silly and; What can I say:* WA IV, 5, 214 (Nov. 14, 1781).
238 *Believe me:* WA IV, 5, 149 (June 22, 1781).
239 *that an image has remained:* WA IV, 5, 147 (June 22, 1781).
239 *bird of paradise:* WA IV, 5, 148 (June 22, 1781).
239 *Exclusive intolerance!:* WA IV, 6, 37 (Aug. 9, 1782).
240 *a blasphemy against:* WA IV, 6, 36 (Aug. 9, 1782).
240 *decidedly not; So, let me hear:* WA IV, 6, 20 f. (July 29, 1782).
240 *Nature also deserves:* WA IV, 6, 65 f. (Oct. 4, 1782).
241 *What man notices:* WA IV, 6, 65 (Oct. 4, 1782).
241 *I hereby confess:* MA 12, 306.
241 *shrivels up:* WA IV, 6, 65 (Oct. 4, 1782).
241 *We exchanged not a single:* WA IV, 7, 250 (July 21, 1786).
241 *"I found Goethe older":* VB 1, 320 (Aug. 1786).
241 *His gait was:* MA 19, 287 (Feb. 17, 1829).

CHAPTER 16

242 *Thousands and thousands of thoughts:* WA IV, 4, 246 (June 30, 1780).
242 *an image of discordantly:* MA 2.2, 488.
242 *foundation:* MA 2.2, 504.
242 *And thus anyone familiar:* MA 2.2, 504 f.
243 *"made the character of this pompous":* VB 1, 245 and 248 (Nov. 10, 1779).
243 *When we get older:* WA IV, 6, 62 (Oct. 2, 1782).
243 *"I always interpreted":* BranG 1, 81 (Oct. 17, 1782).
244 *we loved each other:* MA 14, 328.
244 *homo temperatissimus . . . extremely fair:* MA 2.2, 875.
244 *very close:* WA IV, 6, 387 (Nov. 11, 1784).
244 *vile heresy:* MA 2.2, 874.
248 *We cannot think:* MA 2.2, 480.

248   *in his view:* WA IV, 7, 63 (June 9, 1785).

248   *circle . . . in defiant; more and more simple; blessing:* MA 2.2, 482.

249   *Nature's consistency:* WA IV, 7, 36 (April 2, 1785).

249   *with the greatest:* WA IV, 7, 182 (Feb. 20, 1786).

249   *as tinder for an explosion:* MA 16, 681.

249   "If I must call myself": Friedrich Heinrich Jacobi, *Über die Lehre des Spinoza in Briefen an Herrn Moses Mendelssohn,* ed. Marion Lauschke (Hamburg: Meiner, 2000), 22.

250   "a decided Spinozist"; "conceal": Jacobi, *Lehre des Spinoza,* 331.

250   *You'll have to leave my earth:* MA 1.1, 230.

251   "The poem Prometheus": MA 1.1, 870 f.

251   *Herder finds it amusing:* WA IV, 7, 93 (Sept. 11, 1785).

252   "These are the only two philosophies"; "These are the only": Quoted from M. Kronenberg, *Geschichte des Deutschen Idealismus,* vol. 2 (Munich: Beck, 1912), 276.

253   *does not prove; Forgive me that:* WA IV, 7, 62 and 63 (June 9, 1785).

253   *Forgive me for not writing:* WA IV, 7, 110 (Oct. 21, 1785).

253   *I came to Weimar: Unterhaltungen,* 107.

254   *Enfolding enfolded:* MA 1.1, 233.

254   *For nature / is unfeeling:* MA 2.1, 90.

254   *the observing concept:* WA IV, 5, 25 (Dec. 27, 1780).

254   *May neither legend; Now if one assumes:* WA IV, 5, 24 (Dec. 27, 1780).

255   *as a text:* WA IV, 5, 217 (Nov. 14, 1781).

255   *I feel such joy:* WA IV, 6, 259 (March 27, 1784).

255   *I have found:* WA IV 6, 258 (March 27, 1784).

256   *I think a scholar:* WA IV, 7, 41 (April 8, 1785).

256   *phenomena . . . once and for all:* Quoted from Erich Heller, *Enterbter Geist* (Frankfurt a. M.: Suhrkamp, 1954), 44.

256   *Man on his own:* MA 20.1, 185 (June 22, 1808).

256   *What are you up to:* WA IV, 7, 206 (April 14, 1786).

256   *However, God has also:* WA IV, 7, 213 f. (May 5, 1786).

257   "So now he is really": VB 1, 283 (July 11, 1782).

258   "Herder's new book": VB 1, 301 (May 1, 1784).

258   "Goethe visits me often": VB 1, 310 (Dec. 20, 1784).

258   *One of the most outstanding:* WA IV, 6, 232 (late Dec. 1783).

CHAPTER 17

259   *to raise up:* WA IV, 4, 299 (ca. Sept. 20, 1780).

260   "to fetch Him back here": BranG 1, 72 (June 17, 1781).

260   *an evil genius:* WA IV, 5, 169 (July 8, 1781).

260   *I ask you:* WA IV, 5, 178 f. (Aug. 11, 1781).

260   *You recall the last time:* WA IV, 5, 179 (Aug. 11, 1781).

261   *How much more fortunate:* WA IV, 5, 180 (Aug. 11, 1781).

261   *irresponsible; Believe me, however:* WA IV, 5, 180 (Aug. 11, 1781).

261   *I follow my nature:* WA IV, 5, 220 (Nov. 14, 1781).

262   *I'm adapting myself:* WA IV, 5, 222 (Nov. 14, 1781).

262   *Just as in my father's:* WA IV, 6, 97 (Nov. 21, 1782).

262   *big tea . . . duties to society:* WA IV, 6, 96 f. (Nov. 21, 1782).

262   *Only in the innermost:* WA IV, 6, 97 f. (Nov. 21, 1782).

262   *I have long known:* MA 3.1, 445, line 697.
263   *And shall I tell you:* MA 3.1, 456, lines 1109–14.
263   *He possesses:* MA 3.1, 452, lines 943–50.
263   *permitted is what pleases; permitted is what is proper:* MA 3.1, 453, lines 994 and 1006.
264   *Would you know exactly:* MA 3.1, 453 f., lines 1013–22.
264   *Ah, dear Lotte:* WA IV, 8, 206 (Feb. 21, 1787).
264   *feelings:* WA IV, 9, 124 (June 1, 1789).
264   *You've conquered me:* MA 3.1, 515, line 3282.
265   *I've felt for quite a while:* MA 3.1, 472, lines 1704–6.
265   *Today, in the bustle:* WA IV, 4, 292 (Sept. 14, 1780).
265   *I extract as much water:* WA IV, 4, 291 (Sept. 14, 1780).
265   "Amusingly enough": *Gespräche* 1, 390.
267   "It has been a long": *MA* 2.2, 958.
267   *And so let us not:* MA 2.2, 753.
267   "[Goethe] seemed to have": *MA* 19, 682.
268   *he is useful:* MA 4.2, 516.
269   One uses the word "mein": *WA* IV, 6, 160 (May 6, 1783).
269   *Haste is the enemy:* MA 2.2, 651.
269   *How mistaken you are:* MA 2.2, 75.
269   *Really, I was born:* WA IV, 6, 39 (Aug. 10, 1782).
269   *I was created to be:* WA IV, 6, 58 (Sept. 17, 1782).
269   *it is natural; Enjoy my present existence:* WA IV, 6, 222 (Dec. 7, 1783).
270   *Just now I intended to complain:* WA IV, 7, 100 (Sept. 25, 1785).
270   *that after finishing:* WA IV, 7, 231 (June 25, 1786).
270   *at last rendered me useless:* WA IV, 8, 327 (Jan. 25, 1788).
270   *When I undertook:* WA IV, 8, 83 (Dec. 12, 1783).
271   *to travel a long:* WA IV, 8, 40 (Nov. 3, 1786).
271   *this separation:* WA IV, 8, 23 (Sept. 18, 1786).
271   *when you return:* WA IV, 7, 243 (July 12, 1786).
272   *Do not deny me:* WA IV, 8, 86 (Dec. 12, 1786).
272   *At last I can open:* WA IV, 8, 39 f. (Nov. 3, 1786).
272   *The length of my present:* WA IV, 8, 40 (Nov. 3, 1786).
273   *preserve* his *love so that:* WA IV, 8, 42 (Nov. 3, 1786).
273   *It's a curious feeling:* WA IV, 3, 192 (Dec. 6, 1777).
273   *tic by which I find:* MA 8.1, 208 (July 9, 1796).
273   *In general, at the moment:* WA IV, 8, 12 (Sept. 2, 1786).
274   "Herr Privy Councilor": *Grumach* 2, 73 (Sept. 8, 1786).

CHAPTER 18

275   *What all am I not:* MA 3.1, 19 (Sept. 5, 1786).
275   *drive and restlessness:* MA 3.1, 19 (Sept. 11, 1786).
275   *I shall return:* WA IV, 8, 43 (Nov. 4, 1786).
275   *For a new life:* WA IV, 8, 37 (Nov. 1, 1786).
275   *One must be born:* WA IV, 8, 90 (Dec. 13, 1786).
276   *But what I can say:* WA IV, 8, 41 (Nov. 10, 1786).
276   *In my dress:* MA 3.1, 79 (Sept. 23, 1786).
276   *I cannot tell you:* MA 3.1, 82 (Sept. 25, 1786).
276   *I talk to the people:* MA 3.1, 12 (Sept. 3, 1786).

277 *The people walking up and down:* MA 3.1, 40 (Sept. 11, 1786).

277 *Nordic bear:* MA 3.1, 44 (Sept. 11, 1786).

277 *but we Cimmerians:* MA 15, 51 (Sept. 17, 1786).

277 *When you . . . stand up:* MA 3.1, 57 f. (Sept. 16, 1786).

277 *I simply keep walking:* MA 3.1, 75 (Sept. 21, 1786).

277 *the glory of a great:* MA 3.1, 71 (Sept. 19, 1786).

278 *Of course,* [classical architecture] *is different:* MA 15, 103 (Oct. 8, 1786).

278 *And so, thank God:* MA 3.1, 89 (Sept. 28, 1786).

278 *On this journey:* MA 3.1, 107 (Oct. 5, 1786).

278 *studying more:* WA IV, 8, 89 (Dec. 13, 1786).

278 *It is a grand, admirable:* MA 3.1, 92 (Sept. 29, 1786).

278 *Today for the first time:* MA 3.1, 99 (Oct. 1, 1786).

279 *The first phase of my journey:* MA 3.1, 127 (Oct. 12, 1786).

279 *I take no pleasure:* MA 3.1, 133 (Oct. 17, 1786).

279 *I will control myself:* MA 3.1, 137 (Oct. 19, 1786).

279 *We'll take a closer look:* MA 3.1, 144 (Oct. 25, 1786).

279 *I don't even get undressed:* MA 3.1, 153 (Oct. 27, 1786).

279 *Now good night:* MA 3.1, 157 (Oct. 28, 1786).

279 *Now I begin to live:* MA 3.1, 157 (Oct. 29, 1786).

279 *I'm counting it as:* WA IV, 8, 77 (Dec. 2, 1786).

279 *I'm living a new youth:* WA IV, 8, 173 (Feb. 6, 1787).

280 *Since I've been in Rome:* WA IV, 8, 93 (Dec. 14, 1786).

280 *that it is, namely:* WA IV, 8, 97 f. (Dec. 12–23, 1786).

280 *The longer you look:* WA IV, 8, 292 (Nov. 17, 1787).

280 *Muses and Graces:* WA IV, 8, 134 (Jan. 13, 1787).

281 *first amour in Rome:* MA 15, 183.

281 *sweet burden:* MA 15, 124 (Oct. 19, 1786).

281 "*dearest friend . . . that there are other*": MA 15, 150.

281 *The zitelle:* WA IV, 8, 314 (Dec. 29, 1787).

281 *The girls—or rather:* WA IV, 8, 170 (Feb. 3, 1787).

282 *He's a handsome fellow:* MA 15, 428 (June 27, 1787).

282 "*The day of your departure*": BranG 1, 95 (May 10, 1788).

282 *I've hardly ever seen:* WA IV, 8, 83 (Dec. 12, 1786).

282 *It was otherwise a good life:* MA 15, 639 (April 1788).

283 "*I feel ennobled*": VB 1, 321 (Nov. 23, 1786).

283 *Moritz, who is still:* WA IV, 8, 94 (Dec. 16, 1786).

283 *So, that was all you had:* WA IV, 8, 79 (Dec. 9, 1786).

283 *Your note pained me:* WA IV, 8, 93 (Dec. 13, 1786).

283 *bittersweet; will not be; faltering times:* WA IV, 8, 115; 116; 117 (Jan. 6, 1787).

283 *a good deal freer:* WA IV, 8 116 (Jan. 1, 1787).

284 *I have looked my way:* WA IV, 8, 162 (Feb. 3, 1787).

284 *Just as in Rome:* MA 15, 231 (March 5, 1787).

284 *I forgave:* MA 15, 224 ff. (Feb. 27, 1787).

284 *I am in my own way:* MA 15, 227 (Feb. 27, 1787).

285 *Naples is a Paradise:* MA 15, 254 (March 16, 1787).

285 *The doubts about whether:* MA 15, 277 (March 26, 1787).

285 *belly of a whale:* MA 15, 283 (April 2, 1787).

285 *If you have never found:* MA 15, 287 f. (April 3, 1787).

286 *The blackish waves:* MA 15, 300 (April 7, 1787).

286   *There was nothing about:* MA 15, 369 (1787).

286   *You are not one:* MA 3.1, 232.

286   *A radiant whiteness:* MA 3.1, 232.

286   *for various nefarious escapades:* MA 15, 314 (April 13–14, 1787).

286   *desolate sight:* MA 15, 383 (May 13, 1787).

286   *Then one would perhaps:* MA 15, 409 f. (May 28, 1787).

287   *Nordic lands . . . make a joke:* MA 15, 410 (May 28, 1787).

288   *beneath this sky:* MA 15, 268 (March 22, 1787).

288   *perhaps something of this:* MA 15, 268 (March 22, 1787).

288   *without disadvantage . . . become more; I already:* WA IV, 8, 225 (May 17–29, 1787).

289   *to qualify myself:* WA IV, 8, 242 (Aug. 11, 1787).

289   *Art is serious business:* WA IV, 8, 261 f. (Sept. 28, 1787).

289   *found myself again:* WA IV, 8, 357 (March 17, 1788).

289   *It was an unspeakably:* MA 15, 516 (Nov. 3, 1787).

290   *As if lashed by:* MA 3.1, 276 f.

290   *wonderful play . . . I only intend:* WA IV, 5, 285 (March 3, 1782).

290   *immeasurable love of life:* MA 16, 821.

290   *an enormous strength:* MA 16, 822.

291   *My Egmont is almost:* WA IV, 5, 239 (Dec. 12, 1781).

292   *when I banish:* WA IV, 8, 148 (Jan. 27, 1787).

292   *It is easy for a shepherd:* MA 3.1, 306.

292   *to restrain them:* MA 3.1, 307.

292   *to keep his old constitution:* MA 3.1, 306.

293   *I have lived:* MA 3.1, 326.

293   *Sweet slumber!:* MA 3.1, 327 f.

293   *freedom of mind:* MA 15, 518 (Nov. 10, 1787).

293   *Cupid, wanton and capricious:* MA 15, 566 (Jan. 1788).

293   *to tell him how much:* MA 19, 316 (April 8, 1829).

293   *and of course:* WA IV, 8, 346 (Feb. 16, 1788).

294   *of some charming strolls:* WA IV, 8, 347 (Feb. 16, 1788).

294   *pudenda:* WA IV, 9, 9 (late July or early Aug. 1788).

294   "I fear you are angry": Quoted from Roberto Zapperi, *Das Inkognito: Goethes ganz andere Existenz in Rom* (Munich: C. H. Beck, 1999), 221.

294   "like a child": Quoted from Zapperi, *Das Inkognito*, 231.

295   *I answer your friendly:* WA IV, 8, 355 (March 17, 1788).

295   *I cannot deny . . . that I was overtaken:* MA 15, 653 (April 1788).

295   *Since that night:* MA 15, 654.

CHAPTER 19

296   *Lord, here am I:* WA IV, 8, 358 (March 17, 1788).

296   *a whole mountain:* WA IV, 8, 373 (May 23, 1788).

296   *I have gone terribly to seed:* WA IV, 8, 374 (May 23, 1788).

297   *Bidding Rome farewell:* WA IV, 8, 374 (May 12, 1788).

297   *tap on the rocks:* WA IV, 8, 376 (May 24, 1788).

297   "He has gotten leaner": *Gespräche* 1, 433.

297   "He proved more talkative": *Gespräche* 1, 431.

297   *I am happy to listen:* WA IV, 9, 3 (mid-July 1788).

298   *Eroticon:* WA IV, 9, 57 (Nov. 16, 1788).

298   *recommend erotica:* WA IV, 9, 102 f. (April 6, 1789).

298   *I haven't done anything: WA* IV, 9, 114 (May 10, 1789).
298   "Now I have it from Frau von Stein": *VB* 1, 392 (March 8, 1789).
298   "What you write": *VB* 1, 395 (March 28, 1789).
299   *I hesitated: WA* IV, 9, 123 (June 1, 1789).
299   *What kind of relationship; But I freely admit: WA* IV, 9, 124 (June 1, 1789).
299   *Unfortunately, you have long scorned: WA* IV, 9, 125 (June 1, 1789).
300   *to make a plan: WA* IV, 9, 127 (June 8, 1789).
300   *There are reasons: WA* IV, 9, 49 (Nov. 6, 1788).
300   *utterly hateful . . . mix my hot: MA* 3.2, 24.
301   *eroticis: WA* IV, 9, 117 (May 12, 1789).
301   *entertainments: WA* IV, 9, 111 (May 8, 1789).
301   *I believe my elegies: WA* IV, 9, 199 (April 3, 1790).
301   *Tell me, oh stones, and speak: MA* 3.2, 39.
301   *Mother and daughter: MA* 3.2, 41.
301   *Do not, Beloved: MA* 3.2, 43.
301   *Once she appeared to me: MA* 3.2, 45.
302   *All the night long: MA* 3.2, 47.
302   "a few too lusty thoughts": *MA* 3.2, 450.
302   *We delight in the joys: MA* 3.2, 79.
302   *the desired stiffening . . . to apply a searing: MA* 3.2, 571.
302   "filling the bed chamber": Aurelius Augustinus, *Vom Gottesstaat*, ed. Wilhelm
        Timme (Zurich and Munich: Artemis, 1955), 306.
302   *to untie the girl's waistbelt: MA* 3.2, 586.
303   *I'm maneuvering: WA* IV, 9, 163 (Nov. 20, 1789).
303   *A sacred rite: WA* IV, 9, 171 (Dec. 27, 1790).
304   "gods and idolaters": *BW Schiller/Körner* 1, 85 (July 23, 1787).
304   "I have considered myself": *BW Schiller/Körner* 1, 138 (Sept. 10, 1787).
304   "Of course, the party": *BW Schiller/Körner* 1, 254 (Sept. 12, 1788).
304   *a powerful but immature: MA* 12, 86.
304   "It would make me unhappy": *BW Schiller/Körner* 2, 16 (Feb. 2, 1789).
305   "This man, this Goethe": *BW Schiller/Körner* 2, 37 (March 9, 1789).
305   "I must tell you": *BW Schiller/Körner* 1, 295 (Dec. 30, 1788).
305   *especially since this acquisition: WA* IV, 9, 65 (Dec. 9, 1788).
306   *moral part of the play: WA* IV, 9, 37 (Oct. 1, 1788).
306   "wary of making": *VB* 1, 359 (Aug. 18, 1788).
306   "It's just a shame": *VB* 1, 365 (Oct. 17, 1788).
306   "I've had really a great": *VB* 1, 390 f. (March 2, 1789).
306   *withdrawal into my inner: WA* I, 53, 386.
306   *In Italy I felt myself: MA* 14, 463.
307   *the real result: WA* I, 53, 386.
308   "Art has completely occupied": *Gespräche* 1, 452.
308   *I've known him for years: MA* 3.1, 483 f., lines 2117–34.
309   *I feel myself relieved . . . My heart drives on: MA* 3.1, 514 f., lines 3272–73, 3281.
309   *And if a man's struck: MA* 3.1, 519, lines 3432 f.
309   *And when you seem to lose: MA* 3.1, 519, lines 3419 f.
309   *You're not as miserable: MA* 3.1, 518, lines 3405 f.
309   *Just so the drowning sailor: MA* 3.1, 520, lines 3452 f.
310   *in that strange period: MA* 14, 463.
310   *confidentially, that this journey: WA* IV, 9, 197 f. (April 3, 1790).

310   *My life on the whole: WA* IV, 9, 253 (March 20, 1791).

310   "Nothing is simpler": Karl August Böttiger, *Literarische Zustände und Zeit-
       genossen,* ed. Klaus Gerlach and René Sternke (Berlin: Aufbau, 1998), 67 f.

CHAPTER 20

311   *Accept me as a guest: WA* IV, 8, 357 f. (March 17, 1788).

312   *to get a literary grip; the preoccupation: MA* 12, 308.

313   *Who could ever deny: MA* 4.1, 592.

313   *But you know: WA* IV, 5, 312 (April 17, 1782).

313   *She has persuaded herself: MA* 19, 493 (Jan. 4, 1824).

314   *seemed almost to have lost: MA* 14, 14.

314   *I shall now adopt:* Grumach 4, 52.

314   *that people in the Fatherland: MA* 14, 512.

315   *The masses have to smash things: MA* 9, 137.

315   *Our part in public affairs: MA* 17, 860.

315   *Active engagement . . . Man knows himself: MA* 12, 306.

315   *Meanwhile, I become: WA* IV, 9, 270 (June 1, 1791).

315   *harmonious development: MA* 5, 290.

315   *Aristocratic manners . . . carefree delicacy: MA* 5, 289.

316   *whether that state of affairs: MA* 5, 290.

316   *This small person: WA* IV, 5, 76 f. (March 11, 1781).

317   *where I can lock up: WA* IV, 10, 6 (Aug. 18, 1792).

317   *Get a move on, Chronos: MA* 1.1, 260 f.

318   *notions: WA* IV, 10, 13 (Sept. 2, 1792).

318   *Everyone is complaining: WA* IV, 10, 11 (Aug. 27, 1792).

318   *the idle observer: WA* IV, 10, 15 (Sept. 10, 1792).

318   *Under these circumstances: MA* 14, 384.

319   *premature burial; here and today: MA* 14, 385.

319   *I'm very happy: WA* IV 10, 25 f. (Sept. 27, 1792).

319   *And so here I also want: MA* 14, 401.

319   *This campaign: WA* IV, 10, 33 (Oct. 15, 1792).

319   *as if born again . . . to realize: WA* IV, 10, 40 (Nov. 14, 1792).

320   *In these six weeks: WA* IV, 10, 32 (Oct. 10, 1792).

320   *His Highness the duke: WA* IV, 10, 44 (Dec. 24, 1792).

320   *realism came to the fore: MA* 14, 464.

320   *The longing within me: MA* 14, 462.

321   *hardened . . . I felt alienated: MA* 14, 465.

321   *convivial, clever: MA* 14, 490.

321   *any admiration: MA* 14, 494.

321   *Be cheerful, my dear child: WA* IV, 10, 40 (Nov. 14, 1792).

322   *a testimony to my annoyingly: MA* 14, 512.

322   *patriotic contribution: MA* 4.1, 110.

322   *alarm and distrust; where all classes: MA* 4.1, 129.

322   *People say: MA* 4.1, 95.

323   *to a certain extent regard it: MA* 19, 493.

323   *How often these valiant heroes: MA* 4.1, 164.

323   *Ever since I perceived: MA* 4.1, 160 f.

324   *Each of us is able: MA* 4.1, 161.

324   *I used to take it too lightly: MA* 4.1, 160.

324 *On the one hand: WA* IV, 10, 87 (July 7, 1793).

325 *The misery these people: WA* IV, 10, 101 (July 27, 1793).

325 *In my present situation: WA* IV, 10, 84 f. (July 3, 1793).

325 *half despairingly: MA* 14, 21.

325 *But I sought to save myself: MA* 14, 513.

CHAPTER 21

326 *My vagabond life: WA* IV, 10, 104 f. (Aug. 19, 1793).

326 *Knowst thou the marvelous poison; Difficult to tame: MA* 4.1, 774.

326 "Since a few days ago": *VB* 1, 453 (Nov. 25, 1793).

327 "Goethe turned to me": *Grumach* 4, 63.

327 *1. Light is the simplest: MA* 4.2, 361 (July 15, 1793).

328 "We always believe": *BranG* 1, 137 (Oct. 7, 1793).

328 *I wish very much: WA* IV, 10, 145 f. (Feb. or March 1794).

328 *Now my thoughts are bent: WA* IV, 10, 131 (July 12, 1793).

331 *Is it the object: MA* 17, 827.

331 *that I did not understand: WA* IV, 10, 167 (June 24, 1794).

331 "Recently he described": *Grumach* 4, 88.

332 "If someone puts his entire strength": *Schiller und Lotte*, 184 (Feb. 25, 1789).

332 *certain harsh passages: MA* 12, 87.

332 "But when that short spring": *Schiller* V, 458, footnote.

333 "The culture of the Germans": *Schiller* V, 868.

333 *I shall be heartily delighted: WA* IV, 10, 166 (June 24, 1794).

334 "It is turning out to be": *BW Schiller/Körner* 3, 126 (July 4, 1794).

334 *I must add that: WA* IV, 10, 169 (June 28, 1794).

334 *for me it was a new spring: MA* 14, 34.

335 *For I had realized: MA* 12, 930.

335 *There must be such a thing!: MA* 15, 327.

335 *and with some characteristic . . . That is not an experience . . . I find it so nice: MA* 12, 88 f.

336 *neither of us: MA* 12, 89.

336 *It is, however, rare: MA* 14, 581.

336 "We had . . . spoken at length": *BW Schiller/Körner* 3, 133 (Sept. 1, 1794).

337 *in which with a friendly hand: MA* 8.1, 16 (Aug. 27, 1794).

337 "But even to have set out": *MA* 8.1, 14 (Aug. 23, 1794).

337 "In your authentic intuition": *MA* 8.1, 13 (Aug. 23, 1794).

338 *You will soon see for yourself: MA* 8.1, 17 (Aug. 27, 1794).

338 "since unfortunately my cramps": *MA* 8.1, 22 (Sept. 7, 1794).

338 "although lubricious"; "A few days ago": *Schiller und Lotte*, 556.

CHAPTER 22

341 *the honorable public: WA* IV, 4, 311 (Oct. 11, 1780).

341 *One can't even imagine; In the sphere: MA* 17, 310.

342 *Now that everyone reads; Noble friend: MA* 4.1, 660 f.

342 "Humanity has lost its dignity": *Schiller* V, 594.

343 *I read the manuscript: MA* 8.1, 33 (Oct. 26, 1794).

343 *to the irresistible temptation: MA* 4.1, 441.

343 *the guillotine would be blessed: MA* 4.1, 444.

344 *sparing one another's feelings: MA* 4.1, 449.

344 *in the name of virtue; sociable education: MA* 4.1, 448.

344 "For—to say it once and for all": *Schiller* V, 618.

344 *who depend on society: MA* 4.1, 452.

344 *You will at least want to recite: MA* 4.1, 454.

345 *until I see 99 predecessors: WA* IV, 10, 352 (Dec. 21, 1795).

345 *had to be sacrificed: MA* 8.1, 36 (Oct. 28, 1794).

345 *centaur: MA* 8.1, 93 (July 20, 1795).

345 "*Die Horen* will have to be": *VB* 2, 41 f. (July 27, 1795).

345 "a few thoughts": *MA* 3.2, 450.

345 "I have no appreciation": *MA* 3.2, 451.

345 "two baptized Jewesses": Quoted from *Der Briefwechsel zwischen Friedrich Schiller und Wilhelm von Humboldt*, ed. Siegfried Seidel (Berlin: Aufbau, 1962), 1:177.

346 "The child whom Goethe and I": *BW Schiller/Körner* 3, 229 (Feb. 1, 1796).

347 "It is one of the greatest joys": *MA* 8.1, 187.

347 "How vividly this opportunity": *MA* 8.1, 187.

347 *There is no escape: MA* 9, 439.

348 *preached the gospel: MA* 12, 97.

348 *The novel goes along: MA* 8.1, 169.

348 *Like my other things: WA* IV, 24, 202 (March 16, 1814).

348 *"You are a true man!": MA* 5, 570.

349 *acquainted with himself: MA* 5, 190.

349 *likes to play destiny: MA* 5, 555.

349 *So you are merely playing: MA* 5, 549.

349 "I think I see": *MA* 8.1, 204.

350 "How easily *his* genius": *BW Schiller/Körner* 2, 37 (March 9, 1789).

350 *Everything you have seen: MA* 5, 549.

350 *He no longer regarded: MA* 5, 504.

351 *The decision to leave: MA* 5, 570.

351 "Aesthetic atheism": Novalis, *Werke, Tagebücher und Briefe Friedrich von Hardenbergs*, ed. Mandred Frank (Frankfurt a. M.: Hanser, 1978–87), 2:801.

351 "a pilgrimage toward": Novalis, *Werke*, 2:807.

351 *when I led an easy: MA* 5, 535.

352 *There is no question: MA* 8.1, 209 (July 9, 1796).

352 *more water of reason: MA* 8.1, 181 (June 25, 1796).

352 "Moreover, the women": *VB* 2, 79 (Oct. 25, 1796).

352 "because those sheets": *VB* 2, 52 (Dec. 6, 1795).

352 "I cannot yet stifle": *VB* 2, 145 (March 10, 1799).

353 *feminine epoch: MA* 8.1, 467 (Dec. 16, 1797).

353 "It is understood": *MA* 8.1, 505 (Jan. 26, 1798).

CHAPTER 23

354 *has some claim: MA* 8.1, 283 (Dec. 7. 1796).

355 *sense of honor . . . no ambition: MA* 4.1, 568.

355 *Thus to the sailor: MA* 4.1, 629.

356 "And Homer's sun": *Schiller* I, 234.

356 *because I need to have done: MA* 8.2, 245 (July 7, 1796).

356 *feeling of manhood: MA* 4.1, 617.

357 "While the rest of us": Friedrich Schiller, *Briefe*, ed. Gerhard Fricke (Munich: Hanser, 1955), 466 f.

357   *Herrmann and Dorothea . . . for once:* MA 8.1, 485 (Jan. 3, 1798).

357   *greatly moved:* MA 8.1, 49.

357   *for now all the world:* MA 4.1, 628.

358   *the solidest ground:* MA 4.1, 629.

358   "By the way, I was amused": MA 8.1, 351 (May 23, 1797).

358   *Penniless and sick at heart:* MA 4.1, 863.

359   *Dig no more:* MA 4.1, 864.

359   *play out naturally:* MA 8.1, 398 (Aug. 22, 1797).

359   *When new faith germinates:* MA 4.1, 866.

359   *When the sparks are blowing:* MA 4.1, 871.

359   *And of the ancient gods:* MA 4.1, 867.

360   "Fallen now are all": *Schiller* I, 167 f.

360   "Nothing occasions more difference": VB 2, 116 (Oct. 18, 1797).

360   *Our study of ballads:* MA 8.1, 360 (June 22, 1797).

361   *Once more, you wavering:* MA 6.1, 535.

362   *No longer will they hear; Nameless now; A shudder:* MA 6.1, 535.

363   *Now, however, I wish:* MA 8.1, 359 (June 22, 1797).

363   "duplicity of human nature": MA 8.1, 360 (June 23, 1797).

363   "to the service": MA 8.1, 361 (June 23, 1797).

363   "led to a life of activity": MA 8.1, 363 (May 25, 1797).

363   *It would now only be a matter:* MA 8.1, 369 (July 1, 1797).

363   *Faust has been postponed:* MA 8.1, 370 (July 5, 1797).

364   "May heaven help me": Friedrich Hölderlin, *Sämtliche Werke und Briefe,* ed. Michael Knaupp (Munich: Hanser, 1992–93), 2:554 (Nov. 1794).

364   *has the makings of a poet:* MA 8.1, 365 (June 28, 1797).

364   *I'm already dreading:* MA 8.1, 381 (July 29, 1797).

364   *million-headed Hydra:* MA 8.1, 393 (Aug. 17, 1797).

365   *Therefore, I have made:* MA 8.1, 398 f. (Aug. 22, 1797).

365   *these enormous rocks:* MA 8.1, 423 (Sept. 25, 1797).

365   *that it all would be purchased:* MA 8.1, 392 (Aug. 17, 1797).

366   *in a constant whirl:* MA 8.1, 384 (Aug. 9, 1797).

366   *You surely know . . . and you saw:* WA IV, 12, 252 (Aug. 24, 1797).

366   *They remember you:* MA 8.1, 408 (Aug. 31, 1797).

366   "What would I have given 16 years ago": MA 8.1, 412 (Sept. 8, 1797).

366   *I think it was an advantage:* MA 8.1, 424 (Sept. 9, 1797).

367   *I felt . . . a strange longing:* MA 8.1, 432 f. (Oct. 14, 1797).

367   *Yesterday your head:* MA 8.1, 437 (Oct. 1, 1797, in a letter of Oct. 17).

367   *instilled much confidence:* MA 8.1, 434 (Oct. 14, 1797).

367   "How much I wish": MA 8.1, 443 (Oct. 30, 1797).

CHAPTER 24

369   *productive self:* MA 8.1, 455 (Nov. 29, 1797).

369   *I can only work:* MA 8.1, 463 (Dec. 9, 1797).

369   "aggressive": MA 8.1, 460 (Dec. 8, 1797).

369   *I don't know myself:* MA 8.1, 462 (Dec. 9, 1797).

370   "because of its emotional"; "wants to express"; "embarrasses you": MA 8.1, 464 (Dec. 12, 1797).

370   *a sort of darkness:* MA 8.1, 17 (Aug. 27, 1794).

370   *the epic poet recites:* MA 4.2, 126.

371   "The dramatic action moves": *MA* 8.1, 473 (Dec. 26, 1797).

371   *Why are our epic works: MA* 8.1, 475 (Dec. 27, 1797).

371   "If drama really needs": *MA* 8.1, 477 (Dec. 29, 1797).

372   *to produce another peak: MA* 6.2, 355.

372   *what the world is losing: MA* 6.2, 26.

373   *little family portrait: MA* 6.2, 1003.

373   *imaginators . . . try to appeal: MA* 6.2, 123.

374   *should stick to nature: MA* 6.2, 13.

374   *Once the artist has taken up: MA* 6.2, 17.

375   "the barge of Acheron": *Schiller* I, 212.

375   "nothing but a story": *Schiller* I, 212.

375   "One should really conceive": *MA* 8.1, 450 (Nov. 14, 1797).

375   *independent work . . . In any event: MA* 8.1, 452 (Nov. 25, 1797).

376   "In the opera": *MA* 8.1, 478 (Dec. 29, 1797).

376   "The character of the hero": *BranG* I, 325 (Jan. 31, 1799).

378   "with all their talk of eternity": Quoted from *MA* 6.3, 1300.

378   *As for Fichte: WA* IV, 14, 172 (Aug. 30, 1799).

378   "I must have been vexed": Quoted from *MA* 6.2, 1300.

379   *Serenissimi philippic: MA* 6.2, 923 (Dec. 26, 1798).

379   *lack of feeling: MA* 8.1, 802 (July 25, 1800).

379   *that sacred night: MA* 11.1.2, 215.

379   *Miracles I cannot do: WA* I, 6, 476.

380   *My consolation is her love: MA* 6.1, 143, lines 567 f.

380   *The necessity for our tragic theater: MA* 6.2, 692.

380   "unpoetical ceremonial stage": Quoted from *MA* 6.1, 923.

380   *lack of feeling: MA* 8.1, 802 (July 25, 1800).

381   *My Helen; Now I am so much drawn: MA* 8.1, 812 (Sept. 12, 1800).

381   *path of mist and fog: MA* 8.1, 360 (June 22, 1797).

381   "Don't be unsettled by the thought": *MA* 8.1, 812 f. (Sept. 13, 1800).

381   *To connoisseurs this play: MA* 6.1, 1050.

CHAPTER 25

383   *Not a moment was idly spent: MA* 14, 62.

383   "cheeky . . . one-sided": *MA* 8.1, 600 (July 23, 1798).

383   *What would remain to be said: MA* 8.1, 604 (July 28, 1798).

383   *When he began: Grumach* 4, 541.

384   "He loves you like a father": Eckart Klessmann, *Das Leben der Caroline Michaelis-Böhmer-Schlegel-Schelling 1763–1809* (Munich: DTV, 1979), 229.

384   *He has a very lucid: WA* IV, 13, 168 (May 29, 1798).

384   *direct us from above: MA* 8.1, 588 f. (June 30, 1798).

385   *We intend to do our utmost: MA* 8.1, 517 (Sept. 23, 1800).

385   *Ever since I tore myself free: WA* IV, 15, 117 (Sept. 27, 1800).

385   *At least I can flatter: WA* IV, 15, 173 (Feb. 1, 1801).

385   *reentrance into life: WA* IV, 15, 176 (Feb. 5, 1801).

385   *Unfortunately, when we parted: WA* IV, 15, 174 (Feb. 5, 1801).

386   *We shall wait and see: MA* 8.1, 888 (March 9, 1802).

386   *As a whole, it is the prodigious sight: MA* 8.1, 887 (March 9, 1802).

387   *vessel: MA* 14, 60.

387 *superstition: MA* 14, 66.

387 *For if a miracle: MA* 6.1, 323, lines 2854 f.

388 *At home, securely ruled: MA* 6.1, 303 f., lines 2179–84.

390 "March fifth passed more happily": *MA* 8.1, 888 (March 10, 1802).

390 *with more concentration: MA* 8.1, 909 (July 5, 1802).

390 "If I ever succeed in writing": *MA* 8.1, 912 f. (July 6, 1802).

391 "a premonition": *Grumach* 5, 539.

391 *By the way, I feel well: MA* 8.1, 1001 (April 25?, 1805).

392 *Oh no! Destruction!: Grumach* 5, 589.

392 *Unannounced and without fanfare: Grumach* 5, 565.

392 *I thought I would lose myself: MA* 20.1, 98 (June 1, 1805).

CHAPTER 26

397 *In defiance of death; His loss seemed; most marvelous: MA* 14, 130.

398 *hollowed-out; Only now; unceremoniously; friendship still: MA* 14, 131.

398 *His mind forged on: MA* 6.1, 91.

398 *I cannot . . . cannot: MA* 6.1, 904.

398 *really ought to begin; So now I only see each day: MA* 20.1, 98 (June 1, 1805).

399 *Schiller's idealistic tendency: MA* 14, 132.

399 *because I was afraid: Gespräche* 3.1, 674, footnote (April 5, 1824).

399 *longing for . . . loss . . . compensation . . . passion: MA* 14, 678.

400 *In order not to bore us: MA* 9, 20.

400 "loveliest of all the virgin roses": Wilhelm Bode, *Goethes Liebesleben* (Berlin: Mittler, 1914), 350.

401 "When a complete version": *Gräf* II, 2, 125 f.

401 "[o]nce I decided to enjoy": *Gräf* II, 2, 141.

402 "haphazardly": *Gräf* II, 2, 150.

402 *Meanwhile . . . we will break off: Gräf* II, 2, 152.

402 *harmful effects of potatoes: Tgb* III, 1, 248 (Aug. 19, 1806).

402 *Since the great breach: GBr* 3, 20 (April 4, 1806).

403 *Dispute between the servant: Tgb* III, 1, 244 (Aug. 7, 1806).

403 *Reflections and discussions: Tgb* III, 1, 243 (Aug. 6, 1806).

404 *extremely rough: WA* IV, 19, 169 (Aug. 8, 1806).

404 *I am most obliged: WA* IV, 19, 180 (Aug. 23, 1806).

404 *It would be difficult; Kapellmeister Hummel; despite the gloomy: MA* 14, 180.

405 *necessarily bring down ruin; tenacious author: MA* 14, 181.

405 *I put my trust: MA* 6.1, 93.

405 "He is shamefully egotistical": *Grumach* 6, 149 (Nov. 21, 1813).

405 "It's really horrible": *Grumach* 6, 150.

405 *At five o'clock: Tgb* III, 1, 263 (Oct. 14, 1806).

406 "Although already undressed": *Grumach* 6, 153.

406 *But I suffered something: WA* IV, 19, 248 (mid-Dec. 1806).

407 "In those sad days": *Grumach* 6, 163.

407 *worst moments: WA* IV, 19, 244 (Dec. 9, 1806).

407 *never seen a greater image: Grumach* 6, 157.

408 *It will be cause for celebration: WA* IV, 19, 248 (mid-Dec. 1806).

408 *He is still making good progress: WA* IV, 19, 251 (Dec. 25, 1806).

408 *In the last few days and nights: WA* IV, 19, 197 (Oct. 17, 1806).

408 "introduced his wife to me": *Grumach* 6, 166.

409 "Amid the thunder of cannon": Quoted from Wolfgang Frühwald, *Goethes Hochzeit* (Frankfurt a. M. and Leipzig: Insel, 2007), 47.

409 *treated very inappropriately . . . If you feel: WA* IV, 19, 253 (Dec. 25, 1806).

409 *In the worst hours: MA* 10.1, 142 (Dec. 26, 1806).

410 *childishly egotistical spirit . . . pride of the professors: Grumach* 6, 181.

410 *to most jealously preserve . . . the person in whose hand: Grumach* 6, 210.

411 *When Paul says to obey: Grumach* 6, 172.

411 *When someone complains; that Germany: MA* 20.1, 155 (July 27, 1807).

412 *the highest phenomenon: WA* IV, 19, 258 (Jan. 3, 1807).

412 *Prometheus . . . light . . . drawn everyone's: Gespräche* 3, 2, 22 (March 8, 1826).

413 *congress in Erfurt: MA* 14, 207.

413 "The emperor is supposed": *BW Reinhard*, 77.

413 *Well, so the wonderful words: BW Reinhard*, 78 f.

413 *world conqueror . . . making use of a device: MA* 14, 578.

414 *dramas of fate . . . recall the past: MA* 14, 579.

414 *manifold expressions: MA* 14, 580.

414 *I'm happy to admit: WA* IV, 20, 225 (Dec. 2, 1808).

415 *it is unfortunately probable: WA* IV, 20, 226 (Dec. 2, 1808).

CHAPTER 27

416 *somewhat abstruse little work: WA* IV, 22, 76 (April 17, 1811).

416 *plucky, loyal: MA* 9, 157, line 163.

416 *commitment: MA* 9, 158, line 218.

417 *We set off boldly: MA* 9, 180 f., lines 915–30.

418 *Alas, I seem to myself: MA* 20.1, 263 (June 26, 1811).

418 *You must have no mercy: MA* 8.1, 937 (May 22, 1803).

418 *had no other wish: MA* 8.1, 642 (Oct. 31, 1798).

419 *day of liberation: MA* 14, 215.

420 *For in truth, it is a vain; the deeds of light: MA* 10, 9.

420 *What spectacle!: MA* 6.1, 547 f., lines 454 and 461.

421 *[A]s I placed the prism: MA* 10, 909 f.

421 *that looked mouse-colored: MA* 10, 442.

422 *But it is better: MA* 10, 263.

422 *Love and hate: Tgb* III, 1, 315 (May 25, 1807).

422 *error of the Newtonian theory: MA* 19, 105 (May 2, 1824).

422 *Thus we are not talking about: MA* 10, 12.

422 *I perceived light in its purity: MA* 19, 492.

423 *These phenomena: MA* 10, 45.

423 *Let no one search: MA* 17, 824.

423 *Theories are mostly: MA* 17, 797.

423 *The greatest happiness: MA* 17, 919.

424 *What a precious, marvelous thing: MA* 15, 108 (Oct. 9, 1786).

425 *in the process his outward sense: MA* 17, 352.

426 *the greatest and most precise: MA* 17, 846.

426 "Experts will find nothing new": Quoted from *HA* 13, 619.

427 "stillborn bagatelle": *MA* 10, 996.

427 *I take no pride: MA* 19, 297 (Feb. 19, 1829).

427 *To rejoice in your own worth: MA* 9, 127.

427   *Young Schopenhauer: WA IV,* 24, 44 (Nov. 24, 1813).
428   "Praised be his name": *Schopenhauer Briefe,* 7.
428   *Teaching's a chore: MA* 9, 92.
429   "What I think, what I write": *Schopenhauer Briefe,* 16.
429   "If I compare your Theory of Color": *Schopenhauer Briefe,* 19.
430   "I know with absolute certainty": *Schopenhauer Briefe,* 20.
430   "Except for a few weeks": *Schopenhauer Briefe,* 22.
430   *Whoever is himself inclined: WA IV,* 26, 154 f. (Nov. 16, 1815).
430   *briefly: WA* IV, 26, 235 (Jan. 28, 1816).
431   *Dr. Schopenhauer sided with me: MA* 14, 252.

CHAPTER 28

432   *second part of the Theory of Color: WA* IV, 21, 195 (Feb. 21, 1810).
432   *to once again converse; I put a lot into it: MA* 20.1, 211 (June 1, 1809).
433   *from a business: WA* IV, 10, 210 (Nov. 10, 1808).
434   *There are so many connections: MA* 10, 624.
434   *like a kind of inclination: MA* 12, 206.
435   *It seems that the author's: MA* 9, 285.
435   *But after all, man is: MA* 9, 318.
435   *traces of murky, passionate necessity: MA* 9, 285.
436   *That could well happen . . . Consciousness: MA* 9, 292.
436   *Eduard yearned: MA* 9, 401.
437   "idealistic": quoted from *Tgb* III, 2, 1095.
437   *What's more, I am only too honored: WA* IV, 20, 26 (March 7, 1808).
437   *As demanded by the speedy progress: Grumach* 6, 457.
437   *diatribe against the new poetasters: Tgb* III, 1, 430 (April 17, 1808).
437   *Each one dies peacefully: Grumach* 6, 453.
437   *The common topics: WA* IV, 20, 27 (March 7, 1808).
438   *Schlegel's conversion: WA* IV, 20, 93 f. (June 22, 1808).
438   *a lascivious masquerade ball: WA* IV, 20, 27 (March 7, 1808).
439   *I cannot warm up: WA* IV, 20, 15 (Feb. 1, 1808).
439   "You poor souls": Zacharias Werner, *Wanda* (Tübingen, 1810), 85.
441   *Eduard held only Ottilie: MA* 9, 364.
441   *I ought to have made: MA* 9, 500.
442   *They still exerted an indescribable: MA* 9, 517.
442   *Whoever makes a serious descent: MA* 17, 880.
443   *the tremendous, importunate forces: MA* 9, 507.
443   *Consciousness . . . not an adequate: MA* 9, 292.
443   *Peace hovers above: MA* 9, 529.
443   *quiet virtues only recently: MA* 9, 526 f.
444   *a single nature: MA* 9, 285.
444   "Of course, your characters and actions": *BW Reinhard,* 110 f.
445   *We've often heard: MA* 9, 37.
446   *And then at last he's there: MA* 9, 42.

CHAPTER 29

448   *Who should receive: MA* 3.2, 151.
448   *of a glorious epoch: MA* 6.2, 196.
448   *And it was she: MA* 6.1, 345.

448   *The difference from earlier times: WA* IV, 19, 337 (May 24, 1807).

448   *heart . . . held out: MA* 9, 932.

449   *My dear mother's death: WA* IV, 20, 169 (Sept. 21, 1808).

449   *at her advanced age: WA* IV, 20, 166 (Sept. 19, 1808).

449   *With a "good morning": WA* IV, 5, 184 (Aug. 26, 1781).

449   *breadth and speed: WA* IV, 5, 179 (Aug. 11, 1781).

449   *to find in your company: WA* IV, 5, 180 (Aug. 11, 1781).

450   "I like people very much": *BrEltern* 549 (Nov. 14, 1785).

450   "heartwarming": *BrEltern* 882 (June 3, 1808).

450   "thumb screws": *BrEltern* 884 (July 1, 1808).

451   *And now I'm hoping for: WA* IV, 20, 4 (Jan. 9, 1808).

451   *Tranquil review of my life: Tgb* I, 1, 85 ff. (Aug. 7, 1779).

451   *At the core of my plans: WA* IV, 6, 97 (Nov. 21, 1782).

452   *which can be conceived only: MA* 20.1, 17 (May 29, 1801).

452   *The center and basis: MA* 4.2, 515.

452   *in one way or another; avert his eyes: MA* 4.2, 516.

453   *Since he learned to accept: MA* 4.2, 516.

453   *to respond to it actively: MA* 4.2, 519.

453   *I hereby confess . . . that the great: MA* 12, 306.

453   *Adversaries are out of the question: MA* 12, 307.

454   *Everyone is himself: MA* 9, 935.

454   *We love only what is individual: MA* 9, 935.

454   *One cannot hold it against the historian: HA* 9, 843.

454   *to learn about what is denigrating: MA* 9, 936.

454   *Anyone who writes a confession: Tgb* IV, 1, 146 (May 18, 1810).

455   *ironic view of life: Tgb* IV, 1, 145 (May 18, 1810).

455   *most earnest; recollection . . . poetic capacity: MA* 20.2, 1320 (Feb. 15, 1830).

456   *It would not be too difficult: Unterhaltungen,* 138.

456   *Like a balloon: MA* 16, 614.

457   *lack of deeds: MA* 16, 617.

457   *bring a poetic task: MA* 16, 618.

457   *the Protestant has too few: MA* 16, 312.

458   "Man reveals God": *GBr* 3, 588 (footnote 956).

458   *Whoever can't get it into: WA* IV, 22, 321 f. (April 4, 1812).

458   *if his old gray head: WA* IV, 22, 323 (April 4, 1812).

458   *As for me: WA* IV, 23, 226 (Jan. 6, 1813).

458   *Investigating nature: MA* 17, 863.

458   *with it something of: MA* 20.2, 1320 (Feb. 15, 1830).

459   *monstrous condition: MA* 16, 565.

460   *The aesthetic spirit: MA* 16, 569.

460   *But when people bewail: MA* 20.1, 155 (July 27, 1807).

460   *what is monstrous: MA* 16, 820.

460   *pure chance . . . providence . . . interconnectedness: MA* 16, 820.

460   *And so . . . I want: MA* 16, 821.

460   *This demonic quality: MA* 16, 822.

461   *full of boundless energy: MA* 19, 424 (March 2, 1831).

461   *It is not in my nature: MA* 19, 424 (March 2, 1831).

461   *belonging to himself: WA* IV, 23, 136 (Nov. 12, 1812).

462   *From the way I handle: BW Reinhard,* 173.

462   "splendid man": *VB* 1, 145.
462   *This brilliant man: MA* 9, 959.
463   *admiration . . . with what attention: MA* 9, 957.
463   *cheerfulness: MA* 9, 951.
463   *Why should I allow: Gespräche* 2, 768.
463   *Under no circumstances: Gespräche* 2, 770.
463   *Let us continue to act: MA* 20, 1, 981 f. (March 19, 1827).

CHAPTER 30

464   *I'm not at all affected: WA* IV, 23, 151 (Nov. 14, 1812).
464   *Our imagination is incapable: BW Reinhard,* 477.
466   *Rattle your chains: Gespräche* 2, 795.
466   *the fiery signs in the sky: WA* IV, 23, 349 (May 21, 1813).
466   *united than in their hatred: WA* IV, 24, 43 (Nov. 24, 1813).
467   *and if our enemies threaten: MA* 4.1, 629, lines 313–18.
467   *occasional poems: WA* IV, 24, 277 (May 18, 1814).
467   *flattering: WA* IV, 24, 284 (May 20, 1814).
467   "There is no celebratory act": Quoted from *MA* 9, 1162.
468   *I'm ashamed of my hours: MA* 9, 228, lines 873–80.
468   *Here in Weimar we live: WA* IV, 24, 195 (March 13, 1814).
469   *launch: WA* IV, 24, 199 (March 15, 1814).
469   *And all of us are born: MA* 9, 230, lines 942 f.
469   *Asian beginnings of the world . . . The culture: WA* IV, 22, 252 (Jan. 30, 1812).
470   *react productively . . . to escape the real world: MA* 14, 239.
470   *North and West and South: MA* 11.1.2, 9.
470   *recapitulation of puberty . . . When . . . the poems: MA* 19, 610.
470   *lift us from earth: MA* 11.1.2, 168.
471   *that the poet must not: MA* 11.1.2, 164.
471   *kind of poetry . . . to be as foolish: MA* 20.1, 403 (March 11, 1816).
471   *Where, with a wall of rain: MA* 11.1.2, 15.
472   "the wings of my spirit": *BW Willemer,* 7 (Dec. 11, 1808).
472   *In the evening to Frau Privy Councilor: WA* IV, 25, 58 (Oct. 12, 1814).
473   "Among the many I'm but one": *BW Willemer,* 11 (Dec. 12, 1814).
474   *When I look at the red dots: BW Willemer,* 15 (Dec. 28, 1814).
474   *to become rejuvenated: WA* IV, 25, 93 (Nov. 23. 1814).
474   "Goethe is . . . happy": *Gespräche* 2, 1124.
474   *Yet that you whom: MA* 11.1.2, 67 f.
475   *Du beschämst wie Morgenröte: MA* 11.1.2, 80.
475   *What bliss it is: MA* 11.1.2, 69.
476   *steeped in the sense: MA* 20.1, 383 (May 17, 1815).
476   *Greatest joy: MA* 11.1.2, 76.
476   *That may be!: MA* 11.1.2, 77.
476   *Could I stand to lose you?: MA* 11.1.2, 80.
477   *By the East this tree's entrusted: MA* 11.1.2, 71.
478   *Come Darling, come: MA* 11.1.2, 73.
478   "Oriental poems": *Gespräche* 2, 1065.
478   *My wounded heart: BW Willemer,* 339.
478   "I long to open my heart": *BW Willemer,* 346.
478   *My sweetest lady's cipher: MA* 11.1.2, 91.

479   "whenever Goethe comes!": *BW Willemer*, 63 (July 23, 1817).
479   *What's the meaning of this movement?: MA* 11.1.2, 85.
479   *West wind, ah, how much I envy: MA* 11.1.2, 87 f.
479   "He is very affected": *Gespräche*, 2, 1118 f.
480   *Letters. Decided to leave: Tgb* V, 1,304 (Oct. 6, 1815).
480   "Suddenly, Goethe wants to leave": *Gespräche* 2, 1118 f.
480   *daemon . . . hair . . . home via. . . be angry: WA* IV, 26, 97 (Oct. 8, 1815).
480   *But that is too much: BW Willemer*, 29 (Oct. 6, 1815).
480   "He is visibly calmed": *Gespräche* 2, 1120.
480   *Hardly do I once more have you: MA* 11.1.2, 83.
481   *In splendor rides across the heavens: MA* 11.1.2, 86.
481   *It sounds so splendid: MA* 11.1.2, 87.
481   *Strangest book of all the books: MA* 11.1.2, 31.
482   *My wife in extreme danger: Tgb* V, 1, 375 (June 5, 1816).
482   *Slept well and much better: Tgb* V, 1, 375 (June 6, 1816).
483   *Have you not yourself been thoroughly ruined: BW Willemer*, 43 (Aug. 20, 1816).
483   "Dearest friend, what hostile genius": *BW Willemer*, 74 (Oct. 30, 1818).
483   "How much joy for me": *BW Willemer*, 78 (Dec. 1818).
483   "I was a riddle to myself": *BW Willemer*, 92 (Oct. 1819).
483   *Dearest, ah!: MA* 11.1.2, 33.
484   *and so certain special pages: BW Willemer* (Feb. 10, 1832).
484   *To the eyes of one I cherish: BW Willemer* (Feb. 29, 1832).

CHAPTER 31

485   *Even here . . . a spiritual: MA* 11.2, 210.
485   *The poet regards himself: MA* 11.2, 208.
485   *Leave me in the saddle: MA* 11.1.2, 11.
485   *Poetry's exuberance: MA* 11.1.2, 19.
486   *One thing more is necessary: MA* 11.1.2, 14.
486   *Anyone who's vexed: MA* 11.1.2, 55
486   *Your song revolves: MA* 11.1.2, 25.
487   *The drinker, however: MA* 11.1.2, 96.
487   *My glass of wine: MA* 11.1.2, 95.
487   *does not repudiate the suspicion: MA* 11.2, 208.
487   *General, natural religion: MA* 16, 150.
488   *In his dislike of poetry: MA* 11.1.2, 150.
488   *unending tautologies . . . again and again . . . commands: MA* 11.1.2, 148.
489   *Just as you never hear: MA* 11.1.2, 181.
489   *spirit . . . what prevails: MA* 11.1.2, 170.
489   *The belief in a single God: MA* 11.1.2, 153.
489   *miserable image on wood . . . with the one: MA* 11.1.1, 103.
490   *renegade burden: MA* 11.1.1, 104.
490   *overview of the world: MA* 11.1.2, 170.
490   *Unconditional acquiescence: MA* 20.1, 601 (May 11, 1820).
490   *There are a thousand forms: MA* 11.1.2, 93 f.
491   *Investigating nature: MA* 17, 863.
491   *There are only two true religions: MA* 17, 840.
492   *Let this be a sacred legacy: MA* 11.1.2, 112.
492   *One can hardly blame ancient: MA* 17, 835.

493 *A spiritual form: MA* 17, 836.

494 *What I fear: the captiousness: MA* 18.1, 19.

494 *that the absurd course of the world: WA* IV, 29, 222 (late June 1818).

495 *dulled, disturbed, and distracted: WA* IV, 45, 249 (April 23, 1829).

495 *Go ahead and wrap the world: MA* 13.1, 14.

495 *My nature forces me: WA* IV, 5, 228 (Dec. 3, 1781).

495 *indispensable, sharp: MA* 13.1, 357.

496 *interim remark: MA* 17, 116.

496 *So if we are not; quickly passing . . . completely developed: MA* 17, 117.

496 *What has been written:* BW Reinhard, 108.

497 *idealistic . . . little box . . . when I finally: MA* 8.1, 388.

497 *The second part will not be: WA* IV, 35, 76 (Sept. 7. 1821).

497 *to want to construct: Unterhaltungen,* 183.

497 *With a little book: WA* IV, 46, 166 (Nov. 23, 1829).

497 *become engaged in details: WA* IV, 46, 167 (Nov. 23, 1829).

498 *Life belongs to the living: MA* 17, 261.

498 *I decided to avoid people: MA* 17, 266.

499 *Yes, now is the time: MA* 17, 270.

499 *sought true treasure: MA* 17, 271.

499 *From Utility through Truth: MA* 17, 298.

499 *In the entire castle: MA* 17, 297 f.

500 *for the rich are only admired: MA* 17, 301.

500 *everyone remains solitary: MA* 17, 316.

500 *What kind of nice life: MA* 17, 317.

500 *yearning vanishes: MA* 17, 471.

500 *Knowst thou the land: MA* 17, 469.

500 *The women threw themselves; As if under a magic spell: MA* 17, 470.

501 *highly promoted: MA* 17, 633.

501 *whoever proves disruptive: MA* 17, 634.

501 *equality: MA* 17, 635.

501 *We have our own distinctive: MA* 17, 635.

502 *"Goethe frightens me": Ottilie,* 184 f.

502 *to the midpoint of the earth: MA* 17, 672.

503 *she seems to have been born: MA* 17, 677.

503 *As we herewith bring to a close: MA* 17, 679.

503 *Both our physical and: MA* 16, 713.

503 *to become resigned: MA* 16, 714.

CHAPTER 32

505 *But for us what bliss it is: MA* 11.1.2, 18.

505 *"I've made a new acquaintance": VB* 2, 662.

506 *"Unfortunately, however": VB* 2, 660.

506 *When we consider: MA* 14, 569.

506 *I continue to live life: MA* 20.1, 463 (Oct. 25, 1816).

506 *I've been spending my winter: MA* 20.1, 685 (Feb. 5, 1822).

506 *One certainly feels: WA* IV, 28, 99 (May 27, 1817).

507 *they went well together: WA* IV, 29, 198 (June 8, 1818).

507 *Wouldn't it be possible: Unterhaltungen,* 80 f. (Oct. 2, 1823).

508 *Eh, have I gotten to be 80: Unterhaltungen,* 189 (April 24, 1830).

511   *Your Royal Highness will surely soon:* WA IV, 32, 5 (Sept. 3, 1819).

512   *I felt . . . as if I was in the forests:* WA IV, 33, 1 (April 28, 1820).

512   *You say the years have taken much:* MA 11.1.1, 197.

513   *who has done a pretty job:* WA IV, 35, 44 (Aug. 16, 1821).

513   *Give my best to your wife:* WA IV, 35, 54 (Aug. 22, 1821).

514   *My daily life is very simple:* WA IV, 36, 83 (June 29, 1822).

514   "He spends his evenings mostly": *VB* 3, 113 f.

514   *Could I but flee from my own self; Ah! Could I only be healed:* MA 13.1, 72.

514   *The present knows nothing; The days are full of tedium:* MA 13.1, 73.

515   *Death lurks . . . O you Christian God:* Gespräche 3, 469.

515   *It's all well and good:* Gespräche 3, 468.

515   *intellectual existence:* WA IV, 37, 7 (April 10, 1823).

516   "everything in the world": *BranG* 2, 338 (Oct. 15, 1822).

516   *To live a long time means:* WA IV, 37, 19 (April 17, 1823).

516   *How light and dainty:* MA 13.1, 136.

517   "was very fond of Goethe": *Gespräche* 3, 549.

517   "And so I began to read": *VB* 3, 170.

518   "[I] come to Weimar": MA 20.1, 780 f. (Nov. 21, 1823).

518   *And if a man's struck dumb:* MA 13.1, 135.

518   "to the mood that the experience": *Gespräche* 3, 626.

518   *A kiss—the last one; And now, locked up:* MA 13.1, 136.

519   *Is there not green:* MA 13.1, 136.

519   *its own endurance; If ever love; The peace of god:* MA 13.1, 137.

519   *Where'er you be:* MA 13.1, 138.

520   *A thousand times I conjure up:* MA 13.1, 139.

520   *The universe I've lost; They urged me:* MA 13.1, 139.

520   *And then one felt:* MA 13.1, 140.

520   "But all efforts at humor": *Gespräche* 3, 612.

CHAPTER 33

521   *May nothing! nothing!:* WA IV, 37, 299 f. (Dec. 31, 1823).

521   *Forgive me, dear fellow:* WA IV, 41, 208 f. (Oct. 22, 1826).

522   "His 'Doctor Faust' is almost finished": *VB* 1, 71.

523   *remarkable how much I resemble:* MA 15, 619.

524   *Achieved the main business:* MA 18.1, 542.

524   *What's left of my life:* MA 19, 456 f.

524   *There is no question that:* WA IV, 49, 283 (March 17, 1832).

525   *Proclaim for each one:* MA 18.1, 129, line 5406.

525   *incommensurability:* MA 19, 347 (Jan. 3, 1830).

525   *The Germans, by the way:* MA 19, 571.

525   *I shall see to it:* MA 8.1, 364 (June 27, 1797).

526   *My conviction that we will continue:* MA 19, 278 (Feb. 4, 1829).

526   *I never have disliked the likes of you:* MA 6.1, 544, lines 337–43.

527   *There dwell two souls, alas:* MA 6.1, 565, lines 1112–17.

527   *Of suns and worlds I've nothing:* MA 6.1, 543, lines 279–86.

528   *And be forewarned:* MA 6.1, 598, lines 2297 f.

528   *From heaven he demands:* MA 6.1, 543, lines 304–7.

528   *Alas, I've studied philosophy:* MA 6.1, 545, line 354.

529   *Where shall I grasp you:* MA 6.1, 547, line 455.

529   *Dust he shall eat:* MA 6.1, 544, line 334.

529   *primal source . . . A good man:* MA 6.1, 544, lines 324 and 328 f.

529   *I've administered a long-time cure:* MA 6.1, 630, lines 3268 f.

529   *Whoever would describe and understand:* MA 6.1, 587, lines 1936–45.

530   *divine height:* MA 6.1, 554, line 713.

530   *into nothingness:* MA 6.1, 554, line 719.

530   *in the hereafter:* MA 6.1, 580, line 1658.

530   *If ever I should tell the moment:* MA 6.1, 581, lines 1699–701.

532   *Let him stand here firmly:* MA 18.1, 330, lines 11,445–47.

532   *The terrifying hour has struck:* MA 18.1, 177, lines 6819 f.

532   *chemical manikin:* MA 18.1, 810.

533   *Well, dear Father:* MA 18.1, 179, verses 6879 f.

533   *That is the property of things:* MA 18.1, 179, line 6882.

533   *What once was thought mysterious:* MA 18.1, 178, lines 6857–60.

533   *But in years to come we'll mock:* MA 18.1, 178, verses 6868–70.

534   *You'll move by everlasting norms:* MA 18.1, 227, lines 8324–26.

534   *Herewith let it be known:* MA 18.1, 149, lines 6057–62.

535   *A banknote's handy:* MA 18.1, 150, lines 6104–8.

535   *Let's go, let's go!:* MA 18.1, 118, lines 5047 and 5057–60.

535   *paper ghost of guilders:* MA 18.1, 154, line 6198.

535   *Just looky here:* MA 18.1, 152, line 6165.

535   *Tonight I'll go to sleep:* MA 18.1, 153, line 6171.

535   *As a start we made it rich:* MA 18.1, 154, lines 6191 f.

536   *The Mothers!—Mothers!:* MA 18.1, 155, line 6217.

536   *You dispatch me to the void:* MA 18.1, 156, lines 6251 f.

536   *Who's seen her once:* MA 18.1, 168, line 6559.

537   *War and trade and piracy:* MA 18.1, 321, lines 11,187 f.

537   *Whoever strives with all his might:* MA 18.1, 346, lines 11,936 f.

537   *The person who acts is always:* MA 17, 758.

537   *My grand estate:* MA 18.1, 320, line 11,156.

538   *Those few trees are not my own:* MA 18.1, 323, lines 11,241 f.

538   *of being just:* MA 18.1, 323, line 11,272.

538   *go and sweep them all aside!:* MA 18.1, 324, line 11,275.

538   "whatever thoughts are in your mind": Heinrich Heine, *Sämtliche Schriften,* ed. Klaus Briegleb (Munich: Hanser, 1968–76), 4:591 f.

539   *Remove the stinging, bitter darts:* MA 18.1, 105, lines 4624 f.

539   *Once I have got hold of someone:* MA 18.1, 330, lines 11,453–58.

539   *I feel the night invading:* MA 18.1, 331, lines 11,449 f.

539   *I open land for many:* MA 18.1, 334, line 11,563.

539   *How I would love to see:* MA 18.1, 335, lines 11,579 f.

540   *To this moment I could say:* MA 18.1, 335, lines 11, 581 f.

540   *I would like to see these three:* MA 19, 539 (Feb. 21, 1827).

540   *very intelligent people:* MA 20.2, 1496 (June 28, 1831).

540   *The fools imagine:* MA 20.2, 1496 (June 28, 1831).

541   *The elements are all in league:* MA 18.1, 334, lines 11,549 f.

541   *To these delights that take me:* MA 6.1, 629, lines 3242–47.

541   *then gave birth to light:* MA 6.1, 571, line 1350.

542   *We have our life in the reflected colors:* MA 18.1, 108, line 4727.

542   *very sober jests:* WA IV, 49, 283 (March 17, 1832).

542   *just too appetizing: MA* 18.1, 342, line 11,800.

542   *Absurd attraction: MA* 18.1, 343, lines 11,838 f.

CHAPTER 34

543   *painful feelings . . . education: WA* IV, 38, 19 (Jan. 14, 1824).

544   *important matter for all German: WA* IV, 39, 85 (Jan. 11, 1825).

544   *in suspense: WA* IV, 40, 198 (Dec. 25, 1825).

544   *Since the composure achieved: WA* IV, 40, 282 (Feb. 3, 1826).

546   *great confidence: WA* IV, 37, 63 (June 11, 1823).

546   "the best German book there is": Friedrich Nietzsche, *Sämtliche Werke*, ed. Giorgio Colli and Mazzino Montinari (Munich: DTV, 1980), 2:599.

547   *perhaps the greatest treasure: WA* IV, 37, 62 (June 11, 1823).

547   "Schiller was so alive": *MA* 19, 129 f. (Jan. 18, 1825).

547   *appreciation of cruelty: MA* 19, 130 (Feb. 24, 1825).

547   *Every week he was a different: MA* 19, 131 (Feb. 24, 1825).

547   *Schiller cutting his fingernails: MA* 19, 188 (Jan. 17, 1827).

547   *Will you not tell me something: MA* 18.1, 197, lines 7381–87.

548   *Schiller seems . . . in absolute: MA* 19, 252 (Oct. 3, 1828).

548   *Christ-like tendency: MA* 20.2, 1395 (Nov. 9, 1830).

548   *solemn charnel house: MA* 13.1, 189.

548   *You cryptic vessel: MA* 13.1, 189.

548   *It will be a great gift: MA* 20.1, 818 (Oct. 30, 1824).

549   "the richest profit for life": *MA* 8.2, 72.

549   "well-worn path of self-interest": *MA* 8.2, 127.

549   *Young people; Let us cling as much as possible: MA* 20.1, 851 (June 6, 1825).

550   *if my poems have given rise: MA* 20.1, 8 (Aug. 26, 1799).

550   *Farewell, and tell me: MA* 20.1, 103 (June 16, 1805).

550   "Speak a healing word": *MA* 20.1, 289 (Nov. 15, 1812).

551   *My dear friend, your letter; And so it is in all: MA* 20.1, 294 (Dec. 3, 1812).

551   "Our brotherhood": *MA* 20.2, 1400 (Nov. 13, 1830).

551   "So far I've been separated": Quoted from Siegfried Unseld, *Goethe und seine Verleger* (Frankfurt a. M.: Insel, 1991), 611.

552   *The Schlegel brothers: MA* 20.2, 1558 (Oct. 20, 1831).

552   "Unfortunately, I am like a stranger": Quoted from Doris Maurer, *Charlotte von Stein: Eine Biographie* (Frankfurt a. M.: Insel, 1997), 287.

552   "How do you feel": *BranG* 2, 411 (July 11, 1825).

553   "The grand duke had to put up with": *MA* 20.2, 1128 (June 13–15, 1828).

553   "the Acacia speciosa": Quoted from Friedrich Sengle, *Das Genie und sein Fürst* (Stuttgart: Metzler, 1993), 491.

553   *Your Royal Majesty's highly flowery: WA* IV, 39, 220 (June 13, 1825).

553   "Many, many thanks": Quoted from Sengle, *Das Genie*, 493.

554   "The golden anniversary": *BranG* 2, 414 (Nov. 8, 1825).

554   *Oh, that I had to experience: Unterhaltungen,* 348.

554   "He could stand up": *Unterhaltungen,* 29 f.

555   *non ignoravi: Gespräche* 3.2, 680 (Nov. 15, 1830).

555   "August's return threatens me": *Ottilie,* 90.

555   "Neither prodigality nor curiosity": *Ottilie,* 89 f.

555   *The individual is still in one piece: MA* 20.2, 1407 (Dec. 1, 1830).

555   *The really strange: MA* 20.2, 1403 (Nov. 21, 1830).

556 *I was so moved: WA* IV, 38, 31 f. (Dec. 7, 1830).
557 *Ah, . . . I wish my dear: Gespräche* 3.2, 810 (Aug. 1831).
557 "And in fact . . . he strode": *Gespräche* 3.2, 810 f. (Aug. 1831).
558 *Today . . . I put the glass: WA* IV, 49, 50 (Aug. 28, 1831).
558 *In a lonely wooden house: MA* 20.2, 1530 (Sept. 4, 1831).
558 *Nature does nothing in vain: MA* 20.2, 1513 (Aug. 13, 1831).
558 *Just as the steam engines: GBr* 4, 159 (late Nov. 1825).
559 *The world is dominated: WA* IV, 49, 283 (March 17, 1832).
559 "He seemed somewhat distraught": *Gespräche* 3.2, 865 (March 16, 1832).
559 "A woeful sight": *Gespräche* 3.2, 873 f.

SELECTED BIBLIOGRAPHY
FOR FURTHER READING

––––––––––

GOETHE'S LIFE

Boyle, Nicholas. *Goethe: The Poet and the Age.* Vol. 1, *The Poetry of Desire, 1749–1790.* Oxford, UK: Oxford University Press, 1991.
–––––. *Goethe: The Poet and the Age.* Vol. 2, *Revolution and Renunciation, 1790–1803.* Oxford, UK: Clarendon Press, 2000.
Williams, John R. *The Life of Goethe: A Critical Biography.* Oxford, UK: Blackwell, 1998.

GOETHE'S WORKS IN TRANSLATION

The Collected Works. Edited by Victor Lange, Eric Blackall, and Cyrus Hamlin. Various translators. 12 vols. Princeton, NJ: Princeton University Press, 1994–95.
The Essential Goethe. Edited by Matthew Bell. Princeton, NJ: Princeton University Press, 2016 (excerpts from *The Collected Works,* which is now out of print).
Elective Affinities. Translated by R. J. Hollingdale. London: Penguin Classics, 1978.
Faust Part One. Translated by Nicholas Boyle. Cambridge, UK: Cambridge University Press, 1986.
Roman Elegies and Other Poems & Epigrams. Translated by Michael Hamburger. London: Carcanet, 2007.
Selected Poetry. Translated by David Luke. New York: Penguin Books, 2005.
Wilhelm Meister's Apprenticeship and Travels. Translated by Thomas Carlyle. North Charleston, SC: CreateSpace Independent Publishing Platform, 2016.

BACKGROUND

Beiser, Frederick C. *The Fate of Reason: German Philosophy from Kant to Fichte.* Cambridge, MA: Harvard University Press, 1987.
–––––. *German Idealism: The Struggle against Subjectivism, 1781–1801.* Cambridge, MA: Harvard University Press, 2002.
–––––. *The Romantic Imperative: The Concept of Early German Romanticism.* Cambridge, MA: Harvard University Press, 2004.
Bruford, W. H. *Culture and Society in Classical Weimar, 1775–1806.* Cambridge, UK: Cambridge University Press, 1975.
Carlson, Marvin. *Goethe and the Weimar Theatre.* Ithaca, NY: Cornell University Press, 1978.

Eliot, T. S. "Goethe as the Sage (1955)." In *On Poetry and Poets*. London: Faber & Faber, 1957.

Fairley, Barker. *A Study of Goethe*. Oxford, UK: Oxford University Press, 1947.

Heller, Erich. *The Disinherited Mind: Essays in Modern German Literature and Thought*. New York: Farrar, Straus and Cudahy, 1957.

Loram, Ian. *Goethe and His Publishers*. Lawrence: University of Kansas Press, 1963.

Lukács, Georg. *Goethe and His Age*. Translated by Robert Anchor. New York: Grosset & Dunlap, 1969.

Mommsen, Katharina. *Goethe and the Poets of Arabia*. Translated by Michael M. Metzger. Rochester, NY: Camden House, 2014.

Nisbet, H. B. *Goethe and the Scientific Tradition*. London: Humanities Press, 1972.

Pascal, Roy. *The German Sturm und Drang*. Manchester, UK: Manchester University Press, 1953.

Safranski, Rüdiger. *Romanticism: A German Affair*. Translated by Robert E. Goodwin. Evanston, IL: Northwestern University Press, 2015.

———. *Schopenhauer and the Wild Years of Philosophy*. Translated by Ewald Osers. Cambridge, MA: Harvard University Press, 1990.

Tobin, Robert. *Warm Brothers: Queer Theory and the Age of Goethe*. Philadelphia: University of Pennsylvania Press, 2000.

Trevelyan, Humphry. *Goethe and the Greeks*. Cambridge, UK: Cambridge University Press, 1981.

Wellbery, David E. *The Specular Moment: Goethe's Early Lyric and the Beginnings of Romanticism*. Stanford, CA: Stanford University Press, 1996.

Ziolkowski, Theodore. *German Romanticism and Its Institutions*. Princeton, NJ: Princeton University Press, 1990.

INDEX

ABOUT THE AUTHOR

RÜDIGER SAFRANSKI is a freelance writer and honorary professor of philosophy at the Free University of Berlin. His important biographies of E. T. A. Hoffmann, Martin Heidegger, Arthur Schopenhauer, Friedrich Nietzsche, and Friedrich Schiller have won numerous prizes and been translated into more than twenty languages. He is also the author of books on such basic problems of philosophy and human existence as truth, evil, time, and globalization. His biographies of Heidegger, Nietzsche, and Schopenhauer as well as his book on Romanticism have already appeared in English translation. Rüdiger Safranski lives in Berlin and Badenweiler.

ABOUT THE TRANSLATOR

DAVID DOLLENMAYER is a literary translator and emeritus professor of German at the Worcester Polytechnic Institute in Worcester, Massachusetts. He has translated works by Rolf Bauerdick, Andreas Bernard, Bertolt Brecht, Elias Canetti, Peter Stephan Jungk, Michael Kleeberg, Stefan Klein, Marie-Luise Knott, Michael Köhlmeier, Perikles Monioudis, Anna Mitgutsch, Mietek Pemper, Moses Rosenkranz, Willibald Sauerländer, Hansjörg Schertenleib, Daniel Schreiber, and Martin Walser and is the recipient of the 2008 Helen and Kurt Wolff Translator's Prize and the 2010 Translation Prize of the Austrian Cultural Forum in New York. He lives in Hopkinton, Massachusetts.